"Law and order do not always go together. Vigilantism as citizens attempt to enforce order outside the law is rising. Comprehensive studies about the phenomenon have been lacking. The 17 case studies and the conceptual and comparative discussion by the editors go a long way to fill the void. A must read in these times of rising populism and xenophobia."

- **Prof. em. Alex P. Schmid**, *Editor-in-Chief of 'Perspectives on Terrorism' and former Officer-in-Charge of the Terrorism Prevention Branch of UNODC.*

"Theoretically astute, empirically sound, this volume is the authoritative source on the rowing phenomena of vigilantism around the world. This study is essential reading for anyone who is interested in understanding the changing nature of coercion, and the shifting relations of social and political order in the 21st century."

- **James Sheptycki**, *York University, Canada.*

"Vigilantism poses a serious threat to democracy. It is therefore an important, yet understudied phenomenon in criminology. This edited volume raises important issues regarding the conditions under which different kinds of vigilantism emerge. Using case studies from different countries, this edited volume provides challenging new insights which are of importance to both academics and policy makers."

- **Prof. Lieven Pauwels**, *Ghent University, Belgium.*

"This book is richly researched and extremely timely. The spread of vigilantism in our increasingly fractured world should stimulate debate about the nature and significance of state power, whether 'private' vigilante actors are in fact detached from their governments, and when right-wing vigilantism becomes a necessary component of state Fascist operations."

- **Prof. Martha K. Huggins**, *Tulane University (emerita), USA.*

VIGILANTISM AGAINST MIGRANTS AND MINORITIES

This edited volume traces the rise of far right vigilante movements – some who have been involved in serious violence against minorities, migrants and other vulnerable groups in society, whereas other vigilantes are intimidating but avoid using violence.

Written by an international team of contributors, the book features case studies from Western Europe, Eastern Europe, North America and Asia. Each chapter is written to a common research template examining the national social and political context, the purpose of the vigilante group, how it is organized and operates, its communications and social media strategy and its relationship to mainstream social actors and institutions, and to similar groups in other countries. The final comparative chapter explores some of the broader research issues such as under which conditions such vigilantism emerges, flourishes or fails, policing approaches, masculinity, the role of social media, responses from the state and civil society, and the evidence of transnational co-operation or inspiration.

This is a groundbreaking volume which will be of particular interest to scholars with an interest in the extreme right, social movements, political violence, policing and criminology.

Tore Bjørgo, Dr, is Director of the Center for Research on Extremism: The Far Right, Hate Crime and Political Violence (C-REX), professor at the University of Oslo, and adjunct professor at the Norwegian Police University College (PHS). His main fields of research have been political extremism and terrorism, racist and right-wing violence, disengagement from violent groups, delinquent youth gangs, crime prevention, and policing. He is associate editor of the journal *Perspectives on Terrorism*. He has (co)authored or (co)edited 16 books, including *Racist and Right-Wing Violence in Scandinavia* (1997), *Root Causes of Terrorism* (2005), *Perspectives of Police Science in Europe* (2007), *Leaving Terrorism Behind: Individual and Collective Disengagement* (2009), *Strategies for Preventing Terrorism* (2013), *Preventing Crime: A*

Holistic Approach (2016), *The Dynamics of a Terrorist Targeting Process: Breivik and the 22 July Attacks in Norway* (2016), and a special issue on *Terrorism from the Extreme Right* (2018).

Miroslav Mareš, PhD, is a professor at the Department of Political Science, Faculty of Social Studies Masaryk University (FSS MU). He is guarantor of the study program Security and Strategic Studies and researcher at the International Institute of Political Science of the FSS MU. He focuses on research of political violence and extremism and security policy, specifically in the Central European context. He is a member of the editorial board of the Radicalisation Awareness Network (RAN) in the EU. He is a co-author (with Astrid Bötticher) of the book *Extremismus – Theorien – Konzepte – Formen* (Oldenbourg Verlag, 2012) and co-author (with Jan Holzer and Martin Laryš) of the book *Militant Right-Wing Extremism in Putin's Russia. Legacies, Forms and Threats* (Routledge, 2019) and author or co-author of more than 200 scientific academic articles, chapters and books.

ROUTLEDGE STUDIES IN FASCISM AND THE FAR RIGHT

Series editors: Nigel Copsey, *Teesside University*, and **Graham Macklin**, *Center for Research on Extremism (C-REX), University of Oslo.*

This new book series focuses upon fascist, far right and right-wing politics primarily within a historical context but also drawing on insights from other disciplinary perspectives. Its scope also includes radical-right populism, cultural manifestations of the far right and points of convergence and exchange with the mainstream and traditional right.

Titles include:

Aurel Kolnai's 'War Against the West' Reconsidered
Edited by Wolfgang Bialas

The Ku Klux Klan and Freemasonry in 1920s America
Fighting Fraternities
Miguel Hernandez

The Lives and Afterlives of Enoch Powell
The Undying Political Animal
Edited by Olivier Esteves and Stéphane Porion

Latin American Dictatorships in the Era of Fascism
The Corporatist Wave
António Costa Pinto

The Far Right and the Environment
Politics, Discourse and Communication
Edited by Bernhard Forchtner

Vigilantism against Migrant and Minorities
Edited by Tore Bjørgo and Miroslav Mareš

Trumping Democracy
From Ronald Reagan to Alt-Right
Edited by Chip Berlet

For more information about this series, please visit: https://www.routledge.com/Routledge-Studies-in-Fascism-and-the-Far-Right/book-series/FFR

VIGILANTISM AGAINST MIGRANTS AND MINORITIES

Edited by Tore Bjørgo and Miroslav Mareš

LONDON AND NEW YORK

First published 2019
by Routledge
2 Park Square, Milton Park, Abingdon, Oxon OX14 4RN

and by Routledge
52 Vanderbilt Avenue, New York, NY 10017

Routledge is an imprint of the Taylor & Francis Group, an informa business

© 2019 selection and editorial matter, Tore Bjørgo and Miroslav Mareš; individual chapters, the contributors

The right of Tore Bjørgo and Miroslav Mareš to be identified as the authors of the editorial material, and of the authors for their individual chapters, has been asserted in accordance with sections 77 and 78 of the Copyright, Designs and Patents Act 1988.

All rights reserved. No part of this book may be reprinted or reproduced or utilized in any form or by any electronic, mechanical, or other means, now known or hereafter invented, including photocopying and recording, or in any information storage or retrieval system, without permission in writing from the publishers.

Trademark notice: Product or corporate names may be trademarks or registered trademarks, and are used only for identification and explanation without intent to infringe.

British Library Cataloguing in Publication Data
A catalogue record for this book is available from the British Library

Library of Congress Cataloging-in-Publication Data
Names: Bjørgo, Tore, editor. | Mareš, Miroslav, 1974- editor.
Title: Vigilantism against migrants and minorities / edited by Tore Bjørgo and Miroslav Mareš.
Description: Abingdon, Oxon ; New York, NY : Routledge, 2019. | Series: Routledge studies in fascism and the far right | Includes bibliographical references and index. |
Identifiers: LCCN 2019025761 | ISBN 9780429485619 (hardback) | ISBN 9781138493926 (paperback) | ISBN 9780429485619 (ebook)
Subjects: LCSH: Immigrants--Violence against--Case studies. | Minorities--Violence against--Case studies. | Vigilantes--Case studies.
Classification: LCC HV6250.4.E75 V54 2019 | DDC 362.88--dc23
LC record available at https://lccn.loc.gov/2019025761

ISBN: 978-1-138-49380-3 (hbk)
ISBN: 978-1-138-49392-6 (pbk)
ISBN: 978-0-429-48561-9 (ebk)

Typeset in Bembo
by Taylor & Francis Books

 Printed in the United Kingdom by Henry Ling Limited

CONTENTS

List of figures	*xii*
List of contributors	*xiv*
Preface	*xxi*

1 Vigilantism against migrants and minorities: Concepts and goals
of current research 1
Miroslav Mareš and Tore Bjørgo

2 Ku Klux Klan: Vigilantism against blacks, immigrants and other
minorities 31
Kathleen Blee and Mehr Latif

3 Jewish vigilantism in the West Bank 43
Nir Gazit

4 Protecting holy cows: Hindu vigilantism against Muslims in India 55
Juhi Ahuja

5 Violent attacks against migrants and minorities in the Russian
Federation 69
Martin Laryš

6 Anti-immigration militias and vigilante groups in Germany: An
overview 86
Daniel Koehler

x Contents

7 Vigilante militias and activities against Roma and migrants in
Hungary 103
Szilveszter Póczik and Eszter Sárik

8 Vigilantism against migrants and minorities in Slovakia and in
the Czech Republic 129
Miroslav Mareš and Daniel Milo

9 The Minutemen: Patrolling and performativity along the U.S. /
Mexico border 151
Harel Shapira

10 Vigilantism against ethnic minorities and migrants in Bulgaria 164
Nadya Stoynova and Rositsa Dzhekova

11 Vigilantism in Greece: The case of the Golden Dawn 183
Christos Vrakopoulos and Daphne Halikiopoulou

12 Forza Nuova and the security walks: Squadrismo and extreme-
right vigilantism in Italy 199
Pietro Castelli Gattinara

13 Beyond the hand of the state: Vigilantism against migrants and
refugees in France 213
Pietro Castelli Gattinara

14 Vigilantism in the United Kingdom: Britain First and
'Operation Fightback' 228
Elizabeth Ralph-Morrow

15 The Soldiers of Odin Finland: From a local movement to an
international franchise 241
Tommi Kotonen

16 Sheep in wolf's clothing?: The taming of the Soldiers of Odin
in Norway 257
Tore Bjørgo and Ingvild Magnæs Gjelsvik

17 The Soldiers of Odin in Canada: The failure of a transnational
ideology 272
Emil Archambault and Yannick Veilleux-Lepage

18 Pop-up vigilantism and fascist patrols in Sweden 286
Mattias Gardell

19 Comparative perspectives on vigilantism against migrants and
minorities 305
Tore Bjørgo and Miroslav Mareš

Index *335*

FIGURES

1.1 The relationship between hate crime, right-wing terrorism and vigilantism against migrants and minorities. — 2
2.1 Ku Klux Klan night rally in Chicago around 1920 (from Library of Congress, unknown photographer). — 37
6.1 Number of right-wing extremists in political parties and sub-cultural groups (Germany) — 91
7.1 Hungarian Guard's memorial march in honour of Governor Horthy, 19 November 2009 — 110
7.2 Swearing in and inauguration of new members of the Hungarian Guard, October 2007 — 112
7.3 Uniformed units of the Hungarian Guard march through the Roma community of Tatárszentgyörgy — 113
7.4 László Balázs, leader of Identitesz, on the left behind him the flag of the Outlaws' Army — 119
8.1 Members of the Land Home Guard in the Czech Republic during the ceremonial pilgrimage to Říp Mountain on 22 April 2018 — 136
8.2 March to the Ceremonial Act of the Slovak Conscripts in Trnava on 5 January 2019 — 142
9.1 A Minuteman walks towards his assigned patrol location — 159
9.2 A Minuteman on patrol — 161
11.1 The Golden Dawn logo — 191
14.1 Britain First leaders Paul Golding and Jayda Fransen at a demonstration in Telford, 2017 — 236

List of illustrations   xiii

16.1 Soldiers of Odin posing for the photographer before they start
a night patrol in Drammen, Norway, 20 February 2016   261

16.2 Soldiers of Odin in Norway are helping two young girls safely
home on a late Saturday night in Tønsberg, Norway, 13
February 1916   264

19.1 Vigilante "justice": The Duluth Lynching postcard is one of
many postcards widely distributed in the aftermath of
lynchings in the USA during the first decades of the 20th
century   308

19.2 Hungarian Guard's parade in Budapest and inauguration of
new members   311

CONTRIBUTORS

Juhi Ahuja was a senior analyst at the Centre of Excellence for National Security (CENS) at the S. Rajaratnam School of International Studies (RSIS), Singapore. Her research interests include ethno-nationalism, religious violence and extremism, and narratives to counter violent extremism. She has written and presented on Hindu nationalism in India, terrorism and de-radicalization strategies in Southeast Asia, and the power of ethnic and religious narratives in political discourse. Prior to joining CENS, Juhi was a research analyst with the Studies in Inter-Religious Relations in Plural Societies (SRP) Programme at RSIS. She holds an MSc in International Relations (with distinction) from RSIS, and was awarded the SRP Study Award. Juhi is set to begin a PhD in Contemporary India Politics at King's College, London in 2019. https://orcid.org/0000-0001-6834-2283.

Emil Archambault is a PhD candidate at the School of Government and International Affairs at the University of Durham. His research concerns the evolution of conceptions of contemporary warfare, particularly with regards the use of air power and lethal drones. His research interests include theories of warfare, drone warfare, and spatializations of war, as well as the political theory of Carl Schmitt and theories of International Relations. In addition, Emil Archambault has researched the construction of transnational ideologies among right-wing extremist groups in Canada. Emil Archambault holds an MPhil in International Political Theory from the University of St Andrews and a Bachelors in Liberal Arts from Concordia University, Montreal. https://orcid.org/0000-0001-7457-1998.

Kathleen Blee is Distinguished Professor of Sociology at the University of Pittsburgh. She has published widely on US white supremacism, including the books *Understanding Racist Activism* (Routledge, 2017), *Inside Organized Racism* (University of California Press, 2002); *Women of the Klan* (University of California Press, 1991), and *Women of the Right*, coedited with Sandra Deutsch (Penn State University Press). https://orcid.org/0000-0003-2559-2949.

Tore Bjørgo, Dr, is director of the Center for Research on Extremism: The Far Right, Hate Crime and Political Violence (C-REX), professor at the University of Oslo, and adjunct professor at the Norwegian Police University College (PHS). His main fields of research have been political extremism and terrorism, racist and right-wing violence, disengagement from violent groups, delinquent youth gangs, crime prevention, and policing. He is associate editor of the journal *Perspectives on Terrorism*. He has (co)authored or (co)edited 16 books, including *Racist and Right-Wing Violence in Scandinavia* (1997), *Root Causes of Terrorism* (2005), *Perspectives of Police Science in Europe* (2007), *Leaving Terrorism Behind: Individual and Collective Disengagement* (2009), *Strategies for Preventing Terrorism* (2013), *Preventing Crime: A Holistic Approach* (2016), *The Dynamics of a Terrorist Targeting Process: Breivik and the 22 July Attacks in Norway* (2016), and a special issue on *Terrorism from the Extreme Right* (2018). https://orcid.org/0000-0003-3985-4444.

Rositsa Dzhekova is the coordinator of the Security Program of the Center for the Study of Democracy and manages its research and policy evaluation activities in the area of EU criminal justice, security and home affairs. Her work is focused on radicalization and counter-terrorism, P/CVE, organized crime, asset forfeiture, irregular migration, policing and border control. She has contributed to several studies of the pathways and drivers of radicalization that may lead to violence, on the crime–terror nexus, as well as on online campaigning against extremist narratives among youth. Rositsa has further worked on developing practitioners' tools for monitoring and assessing radicalization and extremist trends and risks and has been involved in drafting the first Bulgarian Strategy for Countering Radicalization and Terrorism 2015–2020. She holds an MA in Social Research (Distinction) from the University of Sheffield and a BA in Political Science from the Free University Berlin. https://orcid.org/0000-0002-8286-1052.

Mattias Gardell, PhD, is the Nathan Söderblom Professor in Comparative Religion, and Director of Research at the Centre for the Multidisciplinary Studies of Racism at Uppsala University, Sweden. His research has explored the intersections of religion, politics, and racism within a variety of empirical fields, including black religious nationalism, white religious racism, white power culture, occult fascism, political Islam, human bombs, torture history, Islamophobia, white racist serial killers, lone wolf terrorism, the entangled history of racism and religion, and the affective dimensions of radical nationalism. His extensive publications include nine research monographs, and more than a hundred articles, essays, and anthology chapters. For an abridged list of Gardell's publications, please see: http://www.cemfor.uu.se/Research/research/publications-gardell/https://orcid.org/0000-0003-2491-1995.

Pietro Castelli Gattinara, PhD, is assistant professor at the Centre for Research on Extremism (C-REX), University of Oslo and research fellow at the Centre on Social Movement Studies (COSMOS). He studies comparative politics and migration in Europe, with a focus on radical right actors. He is the author of the monograph *The Politics of Migration in Italy: Local, Party and Electoral perspectives* (Routledge, 2016). His works on far-right politics, populism and mobilizations in the electoral and protest arenas have appeared in several international peer-reviewed journals, including *Acta Politica, Comparative European Politics, Mobilization,* and *South European Society and Politics.* https://orcid.org/0000-0003-1464-9903.

Nir Gazit (PhD in sociology and anthropology, The Hebrew University, 2009) is a senior lecturer at the Department of Behavioral Sciences at the Ruppin Academic Center and a research fellow at the Harry S. Truman Institute for the Advancement of Peace at the Hebrew University of Jerusalem. His research interests include governance and sovereignty, political violence, civil-military relations, and border zones. He is currently conducting research on Israeli and Jewish vigilante groups. His recent publications have appeared in Sociology, International Political Sociology, International Sociology, Qualitative Sociology, Journal of Contemporary Ethnography, and Conflict and Society. https://orcid.org/0000-0002-8807-6530.

Ingvild Magnæs Gjelsvik is a research fellow in the Research Department at the Norwegian Police University College and in the Research Group on Peace, Conflict and Development at the Norwegian Institute of International Affairs (NUPI). She is also affiliated with the Center for Research on Extremism: The Extreme Right, Hate Crime and Political Violence (C-REX) at the University of Oslo. Gjelsvik is currently writing a PhD in Political Science at the University of Oslo, focusing on the role of the police in the prevention of violent extremism. Her main research areas are police, prevention of radicalization and violent extremism and disengagement, de-radicalization and reintegration of members of violent extremist groups. https://orcid.org/0000-0001-7132-6778.

Daphne Halikiopoulou, PhD, is Associate Professor in Comparative Politics at the University of Reading. Her work focuses on nationalism and the cultural and economic determinants of far right party support in Europe. She is the author of *The Golden Dawn's 'Nationalist Solution': Explaining the Rise of the Far Right in Greece* and numerous articles on European far right parties. Her work has been published in the *European Journal of Political Research*, the *Journal of Common Market Studies, Nations and Nationalism* and *Government and Opposition* among others. She has received an award from the American Political Science Association for her work on labour market institutions and far right party support (2016). She is an editor of the journal *Nations and Nationalism.* https://orcid.org/0000-0003-1815-6882.

Daniel Koehler studied religion, political sciences and economics at Princeton University and Free University Berlin. After finishing the postgraduate 'Master of

Peace and Security Studies' at the University of Hamburg he specialized on terrorism, radicalization, and deradicalization. Daniel is also the co-founder of the first peer reviewed open access *Journal on deradicalization*, which he created together with the "German Institute on Radicalization and De-Radicalization Studies" (GIRDS) in 2014. In June 2015 Daniel was named a Fellow of George Washington University's Program on Extremism at the Center for Cyber and Homeland Security. In 2016 he was appointed to be the first court expert on deradicalization in the United States of America at the District Court in Minneapolis. In July 2017 Daniel became a member of the Editorial Board of the International Centre for Counter-Terrorism in The Hague. His major publications are: *Understanding Deradicalization: Methods, Tools and Programs for Countering Violent Extremism* (Routledge, 2016) and *Right-Wing Terrorism in the 21st Century: The National Socialist Underground and the History of Terror from the Far-Right in Germany* (Routledge, 2016). http s://orcid.org/0000-0003-2940-7050.

Tommi Kotonen, PhD, is a Political Scientist at the University of Jyväskylä, Finland, and Research Coordinator of the Academy of Finland profiling area Crises Redefined: Historical Continuity and Societal Change. Kotonen's research interests include political language, politics and the arts, politics of crises, far-right networks and subculture, and white power music. His publications include work on radical nationalist symbols and fashion, political violence, Swedish-speaking Finns and right-wing extremism in Finland, and Finnish radical nationalism in the 1990s. Kotonen's latest monograph, *Politiikan juoksuhaudat* (2018), analysed the development of right-wing extremism in Finland during the Cold War. https://orcid.org/0000-0003-2348-2519.

Martin Laryš graduated in Political Science from the Faculty of Social Studies, Masaryk University, Brno, Czech Republic. He is currently a PhD student at Charles University, Prague, Czech Republic. Laryš previously worked in business development in Post-Soviet countries and also as a foreign correspondent for a Czech newspaper in post-Soviet countries. Chairman and Co-founder of the Centre for Security Analyses and Prevention, Czech Republic, since 2012. Now, he works as the private consultant, responsible for the Post-Soviet and Balkan regions. His main fields of the academic research are Political Extremism (radical Nationalism, Islamism), Organized Crime and Armed Conflicts in the Post-Soviet area (mainly Russia and Ukraine) and Balkans. Martin Laryš is the co-author of three impact-factored journals (Europe-Asia Studies, Energy Policy) and one monograph with Routledge. https://orcid.org/0000-0003-4443-5471.

Mehr Latif is a post-doctoral associate at the University of Pittsburgh. She is currently contributing to research on white supremacist groups within the United States. Her doctoral research focuses on state formation, kinship, and the public sphere in Pakistan. https://orcid.org/0000-0001-7777-7377.

Daniel Milo is a senior research fellow at GLOBSEC Policy Institute and a former advisor on countering extremism to the Slovak Minister of Justice. Milo has work experience as an adviser at the OSCE-ODIHR and the Slovak Ministry of Interior where he served as National Coordinator of Counter-extremist Policies. He is an internationally recognized expert on radicalization, extremism and propaganda issues and since 2016 he has served as an independent expert of the EU on extremism, racism and xenophobia. Milo studied law at the Comenius University in Bratislava and holds a Doctor of Law degree in criminal law. His main field of expertise is extremism, cyberhate, hate crimes and disinformation and he published or co-authored several publications on these issues. These include the country chapter on Slovakia in Cas Mudde's *Racist Extremism in Central and eastern Europe; Racist extremism in Slovakia – Neo-nazis, their aims and organisations* – the first comprehensive report on Slovak right wing extremist scene, and *Countering Radicalisation and Violent Extremism – a European Perspective*. His most recent work focused predominantly on disinformation and hybrid threats such as *The Vulnerability Index: Subversive Russian Influence in Central Europe*.https://orcid.org/0000-0003-4196-033.

Miroslav Mareš, PhD, is professor at the Department of Political Science, Faculty of Social Studies Masaryk University (FSS MU). He is guarantor of the study program Security and Strategic Studies and researcher at the International Institute of Political Science of the FSS MU. He focuses on research of political violence and extremism and security policy, specifically in the Central European context. He is a member of the editorial board of the Radicalisation Awareness Network (RAN) in the EU. He is a co-author (with Astrid Bötticher) of the book *Extremismus – Theorien – Konzepte – Formen* (Oldenbourg Verlag, 2012) and co-author (with Jan Holzer and Martin Laryš) of the book *Militant Right-Wing Extremism in Putin's Russia. Legacies, Forms and Threats* (Routledge, 2019) and author or co-author more than 200 scientific academic articles, chapters and books. https://orcid.org/0000-0002-7102-3205.

Szilveszter Póczik, PhD (born 1957) studied modern history, social sciences and linguistics at the University Debrecen (Hungary) and the Ernst-Moritz-Arndt University in Greifswald (Germany). From 1988 he worked at the Institute for Foreign Cultures of the University of Economic Sciences Budapest. As scholar of the Hungarian Academy of Sciences and of the Hanns Seidel Foundation, he was for a long time guest researcher in the Institute of Contemporary History in Munich. Since 1994, he has been a senior researcher at the National Institute of Criminology. In the field of the criminology, he is conducting empirical research on crime and victimization of social and ethnic minorities and migrant groups, as well as xenophobia, racism, political extremism, terrorism and organized crime. He has been the leader of several research projects and international scientific networks. He is the author and editor of monographic and study books and numerous studies as well as a presenter at domestic and international conferences. He was a lecturer at the European Centre for Federalism Research at the University of

Tubingen, project leader at the Hungarian Police Academy and the Central European Police Academy. He took part in several advanced trainings, study trips and won prices, tender applications and grants, and was a grantee of the International Open Society Institute and HEUNI. https://orcid.org/0000-0001-6723-3800.

Dr Elizabeth Ralph-Morrow, PhD is a Leverhulme Early Career Fellow in the Department of Political Economy at King's College London. She completed an ethnographic study of the English Defence League for her PhD. Dr Ralph-Morrow uses a variety of qualitative methods, including ethnography and interviews, in her research. She is currently researching post-Brexit political activism in the UK and is interested in the role that gender plays in political attitudes and behaviour.

Eszter Sárik, PhD (born 1976), studied law at the University of Pécs (Hungary). She has been working at the Hungarian National Institute of Criminology since 1999, specialized in juvenile delinquency and crime prevention. She has conducted research on the topic of trajectories in child and juvenile crime, taken part in ISRD-2 and executed an examination in homicide cases. She defended her PhD thesis titled Religion, Values and Youth in the Context of Criminology in 2018. From 2016, she has broadened her research topic and taken part in the international project of PoMigra, which was to gain knowledge of politically motivated crimes in light of migration. Her main research fields are juvenile delinquency, religion and crime prevention and the correlation between moral values and criminal behavior. She was a lecturer at the University of Eötvös Loránd in Budapest, the University of Pécs and the University of Győr, and taught criminology at all the universities listed. She was the national representative at the European Crime Prevention Network for a year and she has been a member of Max Planck Balkan Criminology Partner-Group since its establishment. https://orcid.org/0000-0002-8591-7197.

Harel Shapira is an Associate Professor of Sociology at the University of Texas at Austin. Shapira is an ethnographer who uses long-term participant observation in order to study political life in contemporary America, with an emphasis on right wing politics. He is the author of *Waiting for José: The Minutemen's Pursuit of America* (Princeton 2013), an ethnography of armed civilians who patrol the US / Mexico border. Shapira has also published widely on the topic of American gun culture, including most recently, co-editor (with J. Carlson and K. Goss) of *Gun Studies* (Routledge 2019). Dr Shapira earned his PhD and Master of Arts degrees in Sociology from Columbia University, and a Bachelor of Arts degree from the University of Chicago where he majored in Sociology and learned the beautiful art of fly-fishing.

Nadya Stoynova is an analyst at the Security Program of the Center for the Study of Democracy. She has worked on a number of international initiatives focusing on the issues of radicalization and terrorism, corruption, human trafficking and

xx List of contributors

smuggling and organized crime. She has contributed to studies on tools and measures to prevent, measure and counter radicalization risks, on new far-right actors in Bulgaria, on the crime-terror nexus and on online campaigning against extremist narratives among youth. Nadya has also worked on measuring radicalization risks in Bulgarian prisons and probation with a view to enhance capacity of staff to recognize and tackle the problem. Nadya holds a BA in International Relations and International Organization from the University of Groningen and MA degrees in International Security from the University of Groningen and in Global Criminology from the University of Utrecht. https://orcid.org/0000-0002-4478-9248.

Yannick Veilleux-Lepage is a senior researcher in the Transcultural Conflict and Violence Initiative at Georgia State University, where he works on Department of Defence funded projects analysing online extremist discourse and the media products produced by extremist groups in the MENA region. Dr Veilleux-Lepage's research interests include the creation of online narratives and propaganda which foster or normalize terrorism; historical antecedents to terrorism; far-right extremism and the transnational links of far-right groups; and ideological and technical diffusion of political contention and terrorism. His first book, *How Terror Evolves: The Emergence and Spread of Terrorist Techniques*, is forthcoming in 2019 with Rowman & Littlefield. Dr Veilleux-Lepage holds a doctorate in International Relations from the University of St Andrews; a Masters in International Affairs from the Norman Paterson School of International Affairs and a Bachelor's degree in Interdisciplinary Studies (Security Studies) from Carleton University. https://orcid.org/0000-0002-5236-8734.

Christos Vrakopoulos is a PhD candidate at the Department of Politics and International Relations, at the University of Reading. Christos is also a Teaching Fellow at the same institution. His work focuses on the electoral success of extreme right parties in Europe. His research interests lie in the broad topic of extremism, voting behaviour, political behaviour and comparative politics. https://orcid.org/0000-0002-4042-1817.

PREFACE

During the so-called "refugee crisis" in 2015–2016 there was a surge of vigilante activities in Europe as well as in North America, taking the form of street patrols, border patrols and militias. Vigilantes claimed they would do what the police and other authorities were either unable or unwilling to: maintaining public safety and secure streets and borders against alleged threats from illegal refugees or crime-prone minorities. These vigilante activities were usually intimidating rather than directly violent, but there were also cases of violence, and even small-scale terrorist attacks and pogrom-like events in the name of protecting the locals against alleged criminals.

This "new" vigilantism caused considerable media attention and public concerns. However, such vigilantism directed specifically against migrants and minorities is certainly not a new phenomenon, having long traditions in many countries. As scholars in the field, we realized that although there have been some studies of vigilantism as a global phenomenon, we were not aware of any systematic comparative study of vigilantism against migrants and minorities, based on collecting comparable data of vigilante activities across countries and contexts. Such a study could enable us to develop typologies of varieties of vigilantism against migrants and minorities, and explore the circumstances under which these diverse forms of vigilante activities emerge, flourish or fail.

Although some of these movements and activities had been previously studied from the perspectives of racist violence, hate crime or right-wing terrorism, seeing these phenomena through the lens of vigilantism could add new insights. Although activities carried out by some of these vigilante groups may overlap with these phenomena, many vigilante activities cannot properly be described as hate crime or terrorism and will easily be missed out unless they are studied from a different angle.

Starting out with our general ideas about vigilantism against migrants and minorities, and some notions about relevant cases and countries, we used our international

xxii Preface

networks to contact colleagues with known expertise about these cases. This was obviously a timely topic as our invitations were received with positive interest and enthusiasm.

The scholars involved in this project were invited on the basis of their previously established expertise about vigilantism in their respective countries. They were asked to produce articles with case studies that should cover a number of issues specified by us, the project coordinators and editors. In most cases, these tasks required some extra research and data collection from their side.

Although this eventually became a large international comparative research project with 17 case studies, we have not received any specific research funding for this project. However, the Center for Research on Extremism (C-REX) at the University of Oslo has covered travel and accommodation costs for two workshops. Most of the authors met in Bratislava on 27–28 September 2017 and in Oslo on 1–2 March 2018 to discuss draft chapters.

We wish to extend our thanks to Jørgen Eikvar Axelsen, who has been our editorial assistant at C-REX, doing a tremendous job with copy editing and formatting the manuscripts. Dagfinn Hagen has been most helpful with administrative tasks in connection with the workshops. We also thank Craig Fowlie and Rebecca McPhee at Routledge, and the series co-editor Graham Macklin for their help to make this project into reality. Most of all, we will thank the authors of the case studies for their contributions.

Oslo / Brno, March 2019
Tore Bjørgo
Miroslav Mares

1

VIGILANTISM AGAINST MIGRANTS AND MINORITIES

Concepts and goals of current research

Miroslav Mareš and Tore Bjørgo

This introduction chapter discuss various definitions, typologies and theories of vigilantism. It also presents the comparative research design of the present study, which contains case studies from seventeen countries across the world.

Why research vigilantism against migrants and minorities?

Vigilantism – generally understood as taking the law into your own hands without any legal authority – has long historical traditions. This phenomenon plays an important role in the modern world as well – in many different varieties.

Some forms of vigilantism target (alleged or real) criminals or deviants within the community – whether that is punishment beatings and "knee-cappings" of offenders by paramilitaries in Northern Ireland (Silke 2007), "necklacing" of criminals in black townships in South Africa (Kučera and Mareš 2015) or "Sharia patrols" in Iran or some predominantly Muslim neighbourhoods in East London (Rubin 2001; Sinclair 2013). The case studies in this volume, however, specifically address out-group vigilantism, directed against migrants and minorities considered to represent an external crime threat to the community.

Such vigilante activities target entire categories of "others" – ethnic minorities and/or migrants – often under the pretence of controlling their alleged criminality or norm-breaking. Ku Klux Klan lynchings of blacks in the United States in the recent past, contemporary street patrols against alleged criminal migrants in cities in Western Europe and Canada, self-proclaimed border guards on the borders to Mexico and Turkey, lynchings of Muslims by Hindu cow protection groups in India, lethal attacks on migrants and homosexuals in Russia, or party militias against alleged Roma criminals in Central Europe – these are examples of such vigilante activities. This modern wave of vigilantism directed against migrants and minorities in countries all over the world has triggered our interest into the recent developments of this phenomenon.

A large part of such recent vigilante activities is connected with extreme right politics and xenophobic sentiments.[1] However, to what extent and how specific cases are related to right-wing extremism is an empirical question to be investigated.

Some of the phenomena we describe in this volume might also be studied from different perspectives: e.g. as cases of hate crime, racist violence or right-wing extremist terrorism (Bjørgo and Witte 1993; Bowling 1998; Levin & McDevitt 1993; Hall 2013; Ravndal 2017). These phenomena partially overlap with vigilantism against migrants and minorities, but only partially (see Figure 1.1 on page 00).

These alternative perspectives would have covered *some* of the cases and events we focus on here, but left others out of the picture. By choosing to see the phenomena through the lens of vigilantism we can perceive some features and connections which would not appear through these alternative perspectives. In this study, we will address the following questions, making use of our comparative perspective on a broad range of cases:

- How do these vigilante activists operate, and how are they organized? Can we develop a typology of modus operandi?

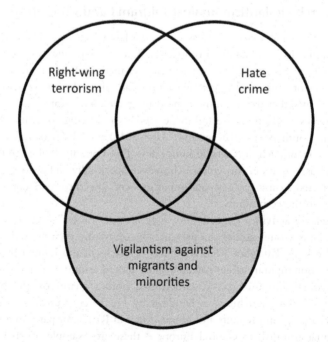

FIGURE 1.1 The relationship between hate crime, right-wing terrorism and vigilantism against migrants and minorities.

- What are the reasons, goals or purposes of this form of vigilante activism? We will explore official justifications, internal group strategies, as well as individual motivations.
- Under what kinds of circumstances do these vigilante activities emerge, flourish or fail? What are the facilitating and mitigating – or permissive and repressive – factors?
- What are the vigilante groups' relationships with the police, other authorities and political parties, and how does it influence the group and its activities?
- How can our empirical material and findings contribute to the broader academic discussion on the phenomenon of vigilantism?

One of the ambitions of this project has been to gather comparable data on a broad variety of cases of vigilantism against migrants and minorities and analyse the empirical patterns comparatively by addressing a number of relevant dimensions. This will enable us to identify and explain similarities and variation across cases. We have managed to establish a strong international team of experts who have produced case studies from different countries and contexts, collecting comparable data on the same set of issues.

Conceptualizing vigilantism

Various authors in the field are defining vigilantism rather differently, emphasising diverse aspects and criteria. The etymological root of the word "vigilantism" is in the Latin word "vigil", which means "watchful" or "alert" (Osborne 2005: 39). Vigiles ("*Cohortes Vigilum*") served as firemen patrols and also as municipal police during night hours in the ancient Rome. They belonged under the governmental structures at that time (Cartwright 2016). The current use of the terms vigilante or vigilantism has its roots in the Spanish word "vigilante". It means "watchman", "guard", "guardian" or "regulator" (Kirschner 2011: 572). The modern term "vigilantism" – in contrast to the ancient historical legacy – is dominantly connected with non-governmental actors. These actors are active in the enforcement of subjectively perceived "law and order" and they act autonomously from governmental power. Eduardo Moncanda defines vigilantism as "the collective use or threat of extra-legal violence in response to an alleged criminal act" (Moncanda 2017: 408). However, the exact concept and definition of vigilantism is still being discussed among various scholars. For example, this above-mentioned Moncanda's definition does not include the element of non-state actors (the extra-legal police violence can then be subsumed under this definition). Moncanda also understands vigilantism as a group activity (Moncanda 2017: 408). However, some individuals can do vigilante activities without engagement in an organizational structure. Although we do not have any examples of that in our volume, some lone actor terrorists do have a dimension of vigilantism behind their violent activities.[2]

4 Miroslav Mareš and Tore Bjørgo

We can sum up these approaches in the working "traditional" definition of vigilantism, which we define as "the use of extra-legal enforcement of a particular conception of justice or a threat or intention to use such enforcement, carried out by informal actors, with the purpose to protect subjectively perceived 'law and order'".

The frequently used criteria of vigilantism were elaborated by Les Johnston (1996). He identified six main elements of this phenomenon. According to Johnston:

(1) it involves planning and premeditation by those engaging in it;
(2) its participants are private citizens whose engagement is voluntary;
(3) it is a form of 'autonomous citizenship' and, as such, constitutes a social movement;
(4) it uses or threatens the use of force;
(5) it arises when an established order is under threat from the transgression, the potential transgression, or the imputed transgression of institutionalized norms;
(6) it aims to control crime or other social infractions by offering assurances (or 'guarantees') of security both to participants and to others

(Johnston 1996: 220)

The condition of using extra-legal force – or at least an explicit or implicit threat of the use of such force – is a challenge to researching extreme right vigilantism in the modern world. Due to legal conditions in democratic countries the official goals of vigilante groupings are usually declared to be within the borders of legality, despite the fact that the real intention of vigilante activists might well be to make use of extra-legal force. Many recent groups that we consider as vigilante in our volume do not act against the law of the countries in which they operate, and they avoid the actual use of violence (although they do display a capacity for violence). Some of them even declare readiness to cooperate with law enforcement agencies, rescue services or military forces. On the other hand, they were established autonomously with the intention to demonstrate their capability to act besides the present governmental agencies. Even if they sometimes declare that they want to be part of the governmental security systems, they do not want to lose their organizational independence. In fact, they understand themselves as a challenge to present security policy and they often struggle to use their capability in the security field for propagandist and other political issues (mobilization of new supporters, strengthening of recent ties in their collective, to show their capability to act for domestic or foreign allies etc.). The identification of real goals can be difficult; however, it's an important part of the current research.

Our re-conceptualization of vigilantism also requires dropping the criterion of clear extra-legal activity by vigilantes (despite the fact that in many cases also current vigilantes break the law). We substitute this condition with the element

Concepts and goals of current research **5**

of public performance of their own capabilities for violence to counter activities and groups of people that are perceived as social anomalies by vigilantes. They want to win sympathy and support from the part of the public who are inclined to share their opinions and attitudes. The fifth of Johnson's element is related to the threat from transgression is not necessary in some cases of vigilantism. The threat may not be real, but to a certain category of people it is perceived or constructed as a threat to the social order. However, how broadly the group is perceived in the community as a threat seems to be an important variable for the growth and success of vigilante groups.

Our re-conceptualization of vigilantism is also generally still based on Johnson's definition and criteria discussed above, however, with some significant changes. Our core definition of vigilantism refers to *organized civilians acting in a policing role without any legal authorization, using or displaying a capacity for violence, claiming that the police (or other homeland security agencies) are either unable or unwilling to handle a perceived crime problem.*

However, there are several border cases that may stretch or challenge the definition, such as unorganized mobs and lynchings, or individual vigilantism and lone actor terrorists. There are also some vigilante groups that are tacitly tolerated by the police or other authorities. Some organizations (in particular militias) are doing vigilante patrols or other crime-fighting activities as a minor side task. Moreover, some citizen patrol groups are declaring themselves as non-violent but may still appear rather intimidating. However, vigilantism is not a black or white phenomenon. With a core definition of vigilantism, it is to be expected that there will be a number of cases in the grey area.

Specific vigilante activities should be analysed within a time and context related framework. The use of vigilantism can be temporarily limited, real goals of some groups can be hidden (they can declare only goals without threat of the use of force, but they can intend to use it), or a mixed form of activities can be found (for example, an interconnection between vigilante groupings and private security companies in some countries). Vigilantism can also be understood as an instrument to weaken the enemies in civic and ethnic conflicts and it can serve as a training activity for paramilitary groups. Moreover, in some cases it can be supported by external actors (including hostile states) with the goal to weaken the state authorities. In this sense can it be subsumed under hybrid campaigns or hybrid warfare (Mareš 2017b).

There are several theories for explaining vigilantism. David Kowalewski identified two main theories – the "frontier" theory (represented by Richard Brown and Roger McGrath) and the "counter-movement" theory (represented by Kowalewski himself). The frontier theory is inspired by the experience of the "Wild West" and it tries to explain vigilantism as a reaction to the lack of "law and order" governmental authorities. The "counter-movement" theory explains vigilantism as a reaction to the rise of deviancy (mostly growing crime or perception of crime) in society. Vigilantes struggle to keep their life environment and life-style (Kowalewski 2002: 427–429).

6 Miroslav Mareš and Tore Bjørgo

We also want to explore the various reasons, drivers or goals behind vigilante activities – from an actor-oriented point of view. We suggest the following types:

- *External justifications* present the official mission of the group towards the public, the media and authorities: to protect the community against certain crime threats that the police and other authorities do not have the capacity (or will) to handle alone. These justifications are tailored to resonate with widely held concerns in society (e.g. on crime or migration) and issues high on the news media's agenda. Vigilante groups claim to represent the interests of society in order to control crime or other social anomies.
- *Group strategies* are the internal reasoning for why leaders believe it will serve the interests of the group to engage in vigilante activities, typically to attract media attention and public support, promote the organization and mobilize new members, to maintain group cohesion, or to undermine the legitimacy of the government. It can also serve as a training activity for paramilitary groups. These reasons are not meant for public consumption.
- *Individual motivations* are the drivers behind individual participation in vigilante activities and groups. Such motivations may have to do with a desire to improve one's personal identity and status, in particular by individuals who have a tarnished reputation as trouble-makers or criminals. Others may be attracted by the militarism or belonging to a strong group. These individual motivations are usually not fit to be publicized, as they may undermine the official justification. However, some participants may also be driven by motives that are congruent with the official mission of the group.

In the concluding chapter we will discuss to what extent these three types of reasons are matching our empirical cases.

In our volume we are dealing with vigilantism against migrants and minorities. This is a specific segment of vigilantism (besides religious vigilantism against deviants in their communities, antifascist vigilantism against fascist groups etc.). We have a broad range of cases from Western and Eastern Europe, North America, Israel/Palestine and India.

In all cases included in this book we can identify the declared goal of protecting society or the community against groups and behaviour that are – at least from the point of view of vigilantes – considered unacceptable. An anomic behaviour (mostly crime or breaking the moral norms of majority) is usually connected with specific groups of people – immigrants, ethnic or religious minorities etc. Usually vigilantes claim to protect the traditional societal order (as exemplified by the cases of Hindu vigilantes in India and anti-homosexual vigilantes in Russia, see chapters by Ahuja and Laryš, both in this volume). However, some contemporary vigilantes imagine themselves as protectors of certain liberal Western values as well (mostly in protection of women's rights against Muslims). A specific case is Jewish vigilantes on the occupied territories who defend the territory to which they claim national ownership (see Gazit in this volume).

The protected community is usually the traditional major nation state (see Koehler's chapter on Germany in this volume), however, it can also be only a local community or a region. The protected object is often used in the name of some groups, as in the case of Britain First! (see Ralph-Morrow in this volume). The pan-national and "civilization" arguments are also used, as an example of the "Defend Europe" by a multinational crew of European Identitarian shows.

Even if vigilantes do not consider the whole target group as "criminal" or "problematic", they use racial, ethnic or religious profiling in their activities. In many cases they want to protect their "own" community not only against "extraneous" entities, but also against their supporters, for example, Russian vigilante terrorists targeted also officials who helped migrants from Caucasus and Central Asia (see chapter by Martin Laryš). These "extraneous entities" are mostly accused of criminal behaviour (for example, the frequently used term "Gypsy crime" in Central Europe by local vigilantes), which is sometimes specified ("against the rape culture"), or of non-respect to other norms of the majority society (rejection of handshake etc.).

They justify their engagement with the argument that the government is not able to solve pressing problems by its own means and institutions. We can find various relations to governmental institutions – from cooperative approach (attempts of cooperation of some chapters of the Soldiers of Odin with local police) to hostility against the state (as in the case of some US militias). Some vigilantes want to fully substitute the police – as members of one Slovak group claimed, for example – while others want to improve the security situation alongside with the regular law enforcement agencies (which are to be informed in case the vigilantes observe criminal behaviour), as Nordic chapters of the Soldiers of Odin (see chapters in this volume).

Vigilantism is in many countries an important part of the national history – as is the case with the Ku Klux Klan in the United States or Hindu vigilantism in India. Current vigilantes in such countries continuously follow their predecessors. In some regions – as in East and Central Europe – the historical legacies of vigilantes from the interwar and war period (used mostly against political opponents and Jews at that time) were transferred into new forms of traditional style party militias vigilantism, aimed mostly against Roma and migrants (the Protection Corps of the Workers' Party in the Czech Republic, for example). The wave of military trained paramilitaries in Central and Eastern Europe and street patrols in Western Europe seems to be a new phenomenon, mainly emerging as a reaction to the migration crisis.

Formations without deeper ideological backgrounds were established during this crisis. They did not use (or avoided) national legacies of right-wing extremism. This is the case with some of the street patrols (e.g. the Soldiers of Odin in some countries) and parts of the Identitarian movement. Rejection of perceived Islamization (specifically counter-Jihadism) and migration are the most important ideas of their

8 Miroslav Mareš and Tore Bjørgo

program. On the other hand, at least some vigilantes used the traditions of national fascism (as CasaPound in Italy) or they used ideologies which were not dominant in the national history (as vigilante neo-Nazi terrorists in Russia). Many national right-wing ideologies are in the background of various vigilante groups (as Kahanism in Israel, Hungarism in Hungary, German National Socialism etc.). A mixture of right-wing nationalist and religious beliefs is typical of Israeli or Hindu vigilantes. Traditional "white supremacism" is propagated by the Ku Klux Klan.

Vigilantism and interconnected phenomena

Vigilantism is or can be interconnected with various other forms of activities. In the tradition of US history, lynching is a specific phenomenon which frequently accompanied vigilantism. It is named after Charles Lynch, who was the head of an irregular court in Virginia in the second half of the eighteenth century (Page 1901). However, lynching as an act is typical of many historical and contemporary societies in the world. Manfred Berg and Simon Wendt define in their study about the international dimension of this phenomenon lynching as "extralegal punishment, usually entailing death or severe physical harm, perpetrated by groups claiming to represent the will of the larger community" (Berg and Wendt 2011: 5).

From a different perspective, vigilantism can be seen as a form of "informal policing" where they claim a role in maintaining law and the social order. Research on policing emphasizes the distinction between the police as an institution and policing as an activity or process (del Barrio Romero et al. 2009). Policing in this broad sense can be carried out by organizations other than the public police, such as private security companies and various forms of voluntary policing, some of which may be sanctioned by the police. Vigilantism may then be seen as civilians acting in a police role *without* any legal authority or any sanctioning by the state (Button 2002). In this perspective, such vigilantism may challenge one of the fundamental characteristics of statehood – that the state is able to maintain a monopoly of the legitimate use of physical force (Weber 1922). One example of this is the Danish "DanerVærn" (literally, "Protect Danes") which emerged in 2014. In its manifest, it provides an archetypal justification for vigilantism:

> DanerVærn is a civil rights and vigilante group established in the recognition that the Danish state is no longer living up to its first and primary duty: to protect its citizens. According to "the social contract", we renounce our right to weapons and self-defense, in exchange of the state protecting us. The state has broken that contract. [...] We are free people; it is any free people's right to defend ourselves. The state has the necessary means to do so. If the state does not defend us, we will defend ourselves, with all necessary means … If the state withdraws, we step forward; if the state steps forward, we will withdraw.
>
> *(DanerVærn manifest, 2014)*[3]

DanerVærn also argues in its bylaws that they are not political group – a rather paradoxical claim given that their statement above represents a fundamental challenge to the defining character of the state: the monopoly on the legitimate use of physical force. Apart from its grandiose rhetoric, DanerVærn did not do much in terms of actual vigilante activities, and therefore did not justify a separate case study in this volume.[4]

However, the degree to which vigilante groups are challenging the state's monopoly of violence may vary considerably. Whereas some vigilante groups operate more or less in defiance of the police and state institutions (e.g. some fascist and Nazi vigilantes), most groups seek some kind of tacit or explicit acceptance by the police or other state agencies or from politicians (Kučera 2017: 18–19; Button 2002). In fact, many of the current extreme right vigilante groupings try to cooperate with governmental authorities, although they also want to keep their autonomy.

Another overlap can be found between vigilantes and militias. The term militia is used in various meanings. For example, it was used as the name of regular police forces in some former Eastern bloc countries (including the Soviet Union), or it was used to label paramilitary units of political parties (Capoccia 2005: 60). Recently the term "militia" is frequently used in conflict research. Sabine C. Carey and Neil J. Mitchell define militias within the context of counterinsurgency campaigns and civil wars as "armed groups linked to the government and separate from the regular forces" (Carey and Mitchell 2016). In specific situations, militias in this sense can be involved also in policing activities. In cases where they claim they are in an autonomous position towards the government, they can be labelled as vigilante militia units. Some militia movements are in direct opposition to the government, such as parts of the modern militia movement in the USA, claiming that the federal government has been taken over by "the New World Order" or the "Zionist Occupation Government" (Barkun 1998: 58–61).

The term "paramilitarism" is in many cases used for designation of the same actors as the term "vigilantism", for example, in case of the Hungarian Guard (Stojarová 2012: 265, 277). However, the term covers a very broad spectrum of cases. Governmental, semi-governmental as well as non-governmental actors are labelled as paramilitaries. Scobell and Hammitt categorize paramilitary groups according to their dependent, semi-autonomous and autonomous position towards the state as well as according to their loyalty, semi-loyalty and disloyalty to the regime (Scobell and Hammitt 1998: 222). In our concept, paramilitary units are focused on armed conflicts (as auxiliary forces in regular wars, as insurgency or counterinsurgency units or as symmetric armed forces in civil wars) (Mareš 2012a: 9–54). We define paramilitarism as a collective activity, organized in a hierarchic structure, which aims at participation in internal or international armed conflicts (including preparedness in such conflicts), where the strength and firepower of the paramilitary forces is significantly lower than the strength and firepower of the main armed forces. Paramilitary units are uniformed or they have clear insignia. They are established on non-commercial bases. Paramilitary units can be used (but not necessarily!) also for policing purposes. If they have an independent, non-governmental character, their activity can be labelled as vigilantism.

Vigilante and paramilitary activities can be used in militarist propaganda. In the contemporary era, militarism serves in propaganda of the extreme right as a contra-factor to the alleged "decadency" and weakness of liberal democracies. Modern armies are rejected as being instruments of globalized power structures without real impact on national interests (professional soldiers are often criticized as puppets, mercenaries etc.). For example, in Central and Eastern Europe, rejection of the NATO policy has a specific dimension in many countries. Several pro-Kremlin paramilitary and vigilante groupings were established during the Ukrainian crisis. Non-state paramilitary formations, organized mostly by extreme right structures, are propagated as an alternative to regular armies (Potočňák and Vicenová 2015). They also try to appeal to and recruit military veterans and even recent professional soldiers as members (Nečej and Stojar and 2013: 30–32). In some modern conflicts (former Yugoslavia, Caucasus, Ukraine etc.) non-state or quasi-state paramilitary formations played an important role. This fact served as a model for other paramilitary and militia groupings, and such formations can later be involved in vigilante struggle.

An interconnection with the military re-enactment scene and with the so-called survivalist or military prepper scene is typical of some of their activists (Mareš 2016). They organize military trainings (also with military equipment) and try to be ready for future military conflicts. In some Central European countries (the Czech Republic, Slovakia, Hungary, Bulgaria) paramilitary units have been involved in ethnic riots (mostly anti-Romani) (Mareš 2012b).

Vigilantism can be interconnected with terrorism as well. A widely used definition of terrorism is that it refers to violence – or the threat of violence – used and directed in the pursuit of – or in the service of – a political aim (Hoffman 2006). Terrorism can be divided into state and non-state forms. In case of non-state forms we can distinguish between insurgent and vigilante terrorism (Schmid 2011). In contrast to insurgent terrorism, vigilante terrorism makes use of terrorist methods to uphold a certain social or political order. Vigilante terrorism protects the identity of the "own threatened group" against "the others". These "others" are perceived as a deviant and/or criminal threat (Waldmann 1998: 92–94). It is important to mention that only some varieties of vigilante activities can be subsumed under terrorism, however, most of the various patrols, crime control activities at local level etc. do not qualify as terrorist (Schmid, Jongman, Stohl and Fleming 1988: 46).

Vigilante violence against migrants and minorities is also partially overlapping with hate crime. The overlap is only partial, as vigilantism includes a dimension of informal policing or street justice against groups of people accused of involvement in crime – a dimension that is not present in most incidents of hate crime. There are also many vigilante activities that cannot be labelled as hate crimes, simply because no crimes are necessarily committed. Most of the vigilante militias, border patrols or street patrols described in this volume did not commit violent or other criminal acts as part of their vigilante activities, even if there was often a lot of hatred and prejudices behind their vigilante activities.

Hate crime is commonly defined as "criminal acts committed with a bias motive" (OSCE 2009: 16) or as "a criminal act that is motivated, at least in part, by the group affiliation of the victim" (Gerstenfeld 2011: 11). Other definitions emphasize that it is crimes motivated by hatred towards specific groups (Hall 2013). Thus, violence against certain categories of people just because they allegedly take our jobs or belong to an inferior race is definitely hate crime or bias crime, but it is not vigilante violence unless the justification for violence is a claim that the victim category is connected to crime. However, vigilante violence may also be justified by claims that the targeted group is threatening the established social or moral order, which for example was a justification for the widespread violence against homosexuals in Russia (see Laryš in this volume). This is a dimension Barbara Perry (2001) brings into her conceptualization of hate crime:

> Hate crime involves acts of violence and intimidation, usually directed towards already stigmatised and marginalised groups. As such it is a mechanism of power and oppression, intended to reaffirm the precarious hierarchies that characterise a given social order. It attempts to re-create simultaneously the threatened (real or imagined) hegemony of the perpetrator's group and the "appropriate" subordinate identity of the victim's group.
>
> *(Perry 2001: 10)*

As we will come back to in the following empirical chapter and the comparative analysis at the end, some of the vigilante violence described in this volume has this dimension of keeping minorities down in their subordinate place or frighten them from challenging the social or moral order.

A typology of vigilantism

Vigilantism can be categorized according to various criteria. In their classical typology, Jon Rosenbaum and Peter Sederberg divided vigilantism in relation to the intended purposes of vigilante actions. They identified:

1. *Crime control vigilantism* "directed against people believed to be committing acts proscribed by the formal legal system";
2. *Social group control vigilantism* as "establishment violence directed against groups that are competing for, or advocating a redistribution of, values within the system can be considered social group control vigilantism";
3. *Regime control vigilantism* as "the use of violence by established groups to preserve the status quo at times when the formal system of rule enforcement is viewed as ineffective or irrelevant" (Rosenbaum and Sederberg 1974: 548–556).

The first two categories are the most relevant here. The intensity and brutality of used violence (or the potential to such violence) can be another criterion of typology (Kowalewski 2002: 434). The armed or non-armed character of vigilantes can be interconnected with this issue.

Vigilantism can be divided according to the dominancy of violent activity in comparison with other forms of activities (for example, military training or patrolling). In this sense we can identify "single-issue" vigilante groups, dominancy of vigilantism in the activities of some groups or subsidiarity or even random vigilantism in comparison with other activities. "Single issue" vigilantism means that the group provides vigilante activities only (as the Minutemen Project in the USA). Dominancy of vigilantism is characterized by a majority of vigilante activities in comparison with other activities. The Hungarian Guard provides a contrasting example, as it was active besides vigilantism also in the cultural and in the military sphere. Subsidiary or random vigilantism is yet an opposite case; for example, the rare vigilante activities of Slovak Conscripts as they are dominantly focused on military combat. For the Nordic Resistance Movement in Sweden, vigilante patrols are also a minor part of their activities (Gardell, this volume).

Categories of high primacy ("vigilantism is both necessary and sufficient for sustaining the organization that carries"), medium primacy ("vigilantism may be a necessary condition but is not sufficient for an organization's survival") and low primacy of vigilantism ("vigilantism can be one among a plurality of organizational activities") were presented by Moncanda. These categories are related to the level of importance of vigilantism for survival of certain groups as organized structures (Moncanda 2017: 414–115). With respect to the duration of vigilante activities or organizations we can identify long-term (years), mid-term (months) and short-term (weeks, days, or even single-case vigilantism).

The political background of vigilante activists must be taken into account, which is a main theme of our book. Some vigilantes maintain that they are not motivated politically; their main goal is to eliminate crime (Schmid, Jongman, Stohl and Flemming 1988: 46). However, claiming that the authorities are not fulfilling their duty to protect the citizens is nevertheless challenging the monopoly of the state on crime prevention, and holds an implicit political agenda. Moreover, a large part of vigilantes operate with some form of explicit political goals. These "political vigilantes" can be divided according to their specific ideological (for example, extreme right vigilantism or anti-fascist vigilantism) or religious (for, example, Islamist vigilantism) background.

The typology elaborated by Marx and Archer can be used for understanding the relations between vigilantes and the police or other governmental security forces. Their main criteria are encouragement or non-interference on the one hand, and opposition or suppression on the other hand. This typology is based on research of the US self-defence groups at the turn 1960s/1970s. Marx and Archer stated that these groups were different from traditional vigilantism, because "they have not killed or taken the law into their own hands" (Marx and Archer 1971: 53). Our view of vigilantism is wider in this book. However, a potential collaboration of vigilantes with the police and or other security forces is based on the informal or unofficial base in this concept, because in case of formalization and official recognition of such collaboration these groups lose their vigilante character (they can be labelled as voluntary auxiliary forces etc.). Some "real" vigilante groups can hide their real goals (see above) and can declare their willingness to cooperate with the police for tactical reasons. In contrast, in some societies traditional violent vigilantism can be supported or tolerated by official security forces. Police officers may turn a blind eye or even take an active part in vigilante activities in their free-time.[5] With respect to these facts we can take over Marx's and Archers's scheme for the purpose of this book and we can divide vigilante groups into:

1. Vigilante groups supplemented and encouraged by the police and/or other governmental security forces (these groups try to cooperate with the police or other governmental security forces and they are from their side unofficially respected as partners);
2. Vigilante groups supplemental and opposed by the police and/or other governmental security forces (these groups try to cooperate with the police or other governmental security forces, however, they are rejected by them);
3. Vigilante groups that are adversarial and encouraged by the police and/or other governmental security forces (they do not want to cooperate with the police or with other security forces, but they are tolerated or even encouraged by them);
4. Vigilante groups that are adversarial and opposed by police and/or other governmental security forces (they do not want to cooperate with the police or with other security forces, they are not respected and are rejected by them) (Marx and Archer 1971: 59–61). In specific cases vigilantes can use violence against the police, mostly if the police are understood as an ally of groups which are targeted by vigilantes (for example, if the police protect targeted ethnic minorities).

Regarding the typology above it is important to mention that the police staff can be divided in opinion over whether and how intensively to cooperate with vigilantes. In specific cases some police forces (for example, the municipal police) can be more open to such cooperation than other forces (for example, the state police). For the purposes of this categorization, the police staff is defined as officers acting as representatives of their own institution. Policemen acting in their free-time for vigilante purposes are not considered as governmental representatives.

Vigilantism can be categorized with respect to the environment and the regime in which vigilante activities are carried out. In relation to the conflict situation we can see vigilantism in pre-conflict, conflict and post-conflict situations (Häggqvist 2017). From the point of view of regime stability vigilantism can be carried out in stabile or unstable regimes. According to the character of the regime we can identify vigilantism in non-democratic regimes (authoritarian or totalitarian), transitional regimes and democratic regimes (Kučera and Mareš 2015).

The division into local, regional, national and transnational vigilantism can be used for understanding the geographical scope of vigilante activities. This scope can be related to the organization and the structures of vigilante groups (including the use of specific names as a franchise – as the spread of "Soldiers of Odin") or to the spread of inspiration on tactical/operational level (for example, patrolling in Roma settlements).

With regard to the general dimension of vigilante activities we can identify conventional or traditional vigilantism, carried out in rural or urban milieus, usually in public areas (patrolling, "hunting" enemies etc.). Recently, "cyber-vigilantism" (or internet-vigilantism) is on the rise, carried out in cyber space (Smallridge, Wagner and Crowl 2016; Trottier 2017), such as hacking of Jihadist accounts and websites by the Anonymous and various anti-Islamist hackers (Drmola 2017). In this volume we are dealing only with conventional vigilantism, despite the fact that extreme right cyber-vigilantism (mostly anti-Islamic) can also be found. The most unconventional case is the maritime border patrol organized by an Identitarian group that crowd-funded and rented a ship to patrol the Mediterranean Sea against migrant boats (see Gattinara's chapter on France in this volume).

The spectrum of vigilantism in contemporary world

A broad spectrum of varieties of vigilantism can be found in the contemporary world (Abrahams 1998). In some countries and regions deep traditions of vigilantism and several historical waves can be found, for example, in the United States where vigilantism is a dominant theme in many (if not most) Hollywood movies as well as in the gun culture. In other regions current vigilantism is caused by recent development without historical legacies. If we take into account the geopolitical character and ideological background, we can identify several most important categories of current vigilantism. It is important to mention that in this chapter we present only a basic overview of this phenomenon.

In the recent era of powerful drug cartels, vigilante groups fighting these cartels are popular in many countries of Latin America and in the Caribbean (Layton, Rodríguez, Moseley and Zizumbo-Colunga 2014: 99–101). Vigilante activities are very strong also in a large part of the so called Third world, especially in sub-Saharan Africa. According to Thomas G. Kirsch and Tilo Grätz, vigilante actions here often have a "breathtakingly blunt, brutal message" (Kirsch and Grätz 2010: 2). Vigilantism is here sometimes carried out by long-lasting, formalized groups. Probably the most famous are the Nigerian Bakassi boys in Nigeria (Smith 2004). Various vigilantes are active also in Southeast Asia and on the Indian subcontinent.

Recently, religious background has played an important role in vigilante activities. In India it is connected mostly with Hindu dogmatic religious extreme rightist ideology (Ajuha and Prakash 2017, Ajuha in this volume). In Southeast Asia, vigilante Buddhism is on the march (Lehr 2017). In many Muslim countries, Islamic vigilantism has been on the rise in the last decades, for example in Iran (Rubin 2001), in Indonesia (Tyson 2013) or in South Africa, where the famous group

People Against Gangsterism and Drugs (PAGAD), founded in 1996, is operating (Monaghan 2004).

Several cases of Islamic vigilantism in Western countries attracted public and media attention, such as the case of Sharia patrols in London in 2013–2014 (Sinclair 2013) or the so called Sharia police in Germany in 2014 (Mareš and Veselý 2015). This form of Islamic vigilantism is probably inspired by the governmental or semi-governmental "religious police" or by religious militias in Islamic states or terrorist proto-states (such as the Islamic State in Iraq and Levant).

Extreme right politics is interconnected with vigilantism aimed mostly at ethnic and religious minorities (however, also at the LGBT community or homeless people) in numerous European and North American countries. Recently, vigilante activities are justified mostly as a reaction to the migration crisis. In some countries, extreme right vigilantism is caused by a specific domestic situation, as exemplified by the loyalist vigilantism in Northern Ireland (Silke 2007) or the Jewish extreme right vigilantism in the Israeli-occupied West Bank (Gazit 2015, this volume).

Extreme right violence aimed at ethnic and religious minorities led to the creation of vigilante formations consisting of members of these minority communities. In the 1990s, Jewish self-defence groups were organized, in several East and Central European countries Romani home guards protected their communities during anti-Gypsy riots (Mareš 2012b: 294–295). According to some scholars, the anti-fascist activities of the Antifa and similar groups have a vigilante character, because they chase Nazi groups off the streets, punish them by using (sometimes) brutal violence, and in some cases enforce anti-racist and anti-Fascist law when the state authorities are allegedly non-active against right-wing extremist violence and propaganda (Kučera 2010).

Vigilantism and the extreme right

Our book deals with vigilantism against migrants and minorities, which in most cases is connected with the extreme right. Conceptualizing extreme right politics poses a difficult challenge (Rydgren 2018). Several key terms (such as the extreme right, far right, right-wing extremism, right wing radicalism, and right-wing populism) are given different meanings by different scholars. Moreover, these terms are also often used synonymously. Various scholars use diverse terms in various meanings or – on the contrary – they use various terms synonymously (as the extreme right, far right, right-wing extremism, right wing radicalism and right-wing populism). This situation causes definitional confusion. Attempts to define the extreme right are often connected only with specific actors, for example with political parties (Mudde 2000) or with violent and terrorist groups (Holbrook and Taylor 2013).

In this book we were inspired by some of the above mentioned authors (mostly by Cas Mudde) and we define the far right as a part of the political spectrum where the ideological core is based on intolerant nationalism, nativism and demands for strict "law and order" policy in the fields which are important for maintaining the preferred governmental order (usually on a separate territory, in a national state or in a pan-national entity). Under the broad label of the far right, a distinction is commonly made between the extreme right and the radical right. Right-wing extremist groups usually accept or even condone violence. They also reject the values of a democratic constitutional state. Between the extreme right and the traditional right is a field which can be labelled as radical right, and which is populated mainly by right-wing populist parties and some anti-immigration organizations. These parties and groups operate within the framework of democracy but they also share some of the outlook of the extreme right in terms of nationalism, nativism and demands for strict "law and order" policy. Vigilante movements tend to emerge within or in the vicinity of right-wing extremist movements but depending on their views on violence and democracy, they may also be closer to the radical right, seeking – and sometimes receiving – political support from these right-wing populist parties.

We can identify several ideological sub-categories of the extreme-right. In a simplified way it can be:

1. Authoritarian conservatism (based on traditional anti-egalitarian societal concepts, it can be interconnected with religious dogmas);
2. Fascism/neo-fascism + Nazism/neo-Nazism (based in extreme right politics from the first half of the 20st century and its ideological innovation);
3. "New right", "Identitarianism" or "Alt-right" (its part, based on ideologically adrift politics rooted in post-material conflicts in modern societies) (Bötticher and Mareš 2012)
4. White supremacy, claiming that the white race has a natural right to dominate other races, represented by e.g. the Ku Klux Klan and similar openly racist movements.

Vigilantism is historically and ideologically an expression and instrument of a part of extreme right politics. The struggle for "law and order" and the proclaimed protection of the own nation or a pan-national group or race is a common justification for the use of vigilantism. Vigilantism is typically connected more to the first two above mentioned categories (including vigilantes in South Africa in late era of the apartheid, see Haysom 1986). However, recently also groupings belonging modern extreme "New Right" or "Identitarian" movements are sometimes involved in vigilante activities as well (e.g. the maritime patrols against migrants on the Mediterranean, organized by identitarians, see Gattinara in this volume). White supremacy groups like the Klan have also been behind highly violent vigilante activities (see Blee and Latif, this volume).

Vigilantism is used by various extreme right actors. It can be connected with political parties, mostly with party militias (such as the Hungarian Guard and Jobbik). Paramilitary groups with military training can be used for vigilante purposes (as the Slovak recruits). Organizations from the milieu of social movements or subcultures can organize vigilante activities (for example, the National Radical

Camp in Poland). There exist various forms of "single-issue" vigilante groups (for example, some chapters of the Soldiers of Odin and the *Les Calaisiens en Colère*) with no or limited links to the far right (Bjørgo and Gjelsvik; and Castelli Gattinara on France, both in this volume). Right-wing extremist individuals or groups can also be involved in vigilante terrorist activities (as the Ku Klux Klan).

Regarding the last point, vigilante terrorism is one of the categories of right-wing extremist terrorism from the typology by Ehud Sprinzak (besides revolutionary terrorism, reactive terrorism, racist terrorism, millenarian terrorism and youth counterculture terrorism). Sprinzak stated: "Vigilante terror is used by individuals and groups who believe that the government does not adequately protect them from violent groups or individuals and that they must protect themselves" (Sprinzak 1995: 29).

Several significant waves of extreme right vigilantism can be found in modern history. The rise of Ku Klux Klan in the late 1860s was repeated in several later eras of the Klan's development (Blee and Latif in this volume). Paramilitaries and party militias operated after the First World War in Europe (Gerwarth, Horne 2013) and in the 1920s and the 1930s they were involved in political fights during the era of the rise of fascism. Latin American extreme right "death squads" and other groupings were used against leftist activists and criminals in the second half of the twentieth century (Huggins 1991: 2–5). In the 1990s a part of racist subcultures (mostly racist skinheads) created vigilante structures in Western democracies and in the post-communist area (Mareš 2012b: 287). In Central and Eastern Europe a new generation of extreme right vigilantes was inspired by the Hungarian Guard in the late 2000s and early 2010s. At the same time vigilantism was connected with the reaction to growing migration in Western democracies (some militias in the US, neo-fascist patrols in Italy etc.). A recent wave of vigilantism in Europe and in the USA is closely linked to the migration crisis in the mid of the second decade of the twenty first century. Of course, also many specific national variants of vigilantism arose in the past decades. The recent state of vigilantism – most of which is connected with the extreme right – is the object of our research in this monography.

A research guide for collecting comparable data on vigilantism

In order to systematically and comparatively study the phenomenon of vigilantism against migrants and minorities and address the research questions listed in the opening section, it is necessary to collect comparable data from a wide range of cases from a number of different national contexts. In order to achieve this, we have brought together a strong group of scholars who have in-depth knowledge about such vigilante groups, movements and activities in their countries of expertise. We have found a combination of cases that represent a large variation within this broad phenomenon. This means that the units of analysis may range from broad social movements like the Ku Klux Klan to small informal groups, or to tightly organized militias. Some of the chapters focus on one specific group or organization, whereas other chapters describe several groups within the same

18 Miroslav Mareš and Tore Bjørgo

country, because they are variations over the same theme, or represent important differences. We have also been interested in following the transnational diffusion of movements and styles, for example how the Hungarian Guard inspired similar paramilitary group in other parts of Central and Eastern Europe, or how the Soldiers of Odin street patrols spread rapidly from Finland to many other countries within weeks, but developed in very different directions in different settings.

Although we asked our chapter authors to collect data about the same set of questions (see below), it would not be realistic to request that they should make use of identical methods for data collection. Collecting such data is complicated and access to the groups vary a lot. Some researchers were able to interview leaders and do participant observation of patrols or other group activities, whereas this methodology would be impossible or too dangerous in other cases. However, in most cases other forms of primary data were available, such as online discussion forums, video footage, police or court documents, or secondary data like media reports or historical accounts. Most authors used a combination of data sources, primary as well as secondary.

In order to provide data that are as comparable as possible, we have asked our authors to collect information about the same set of questions for all the case studies:

- What is the political, social and economic context (who is in government, level of trust in society or to government institutions, situation regarding minorities, migrants, unemployment, etc.)?
- What is the stated purpose and justification for the vigilante group? Why do they claim they are needed? Which values or interests do they claim to defend? Who or what is the threat? Is this a new or an old movement or mode of operation in this country? Do they have an explicit or implicit ideology (e.g. nationalism, fascism, National Socialism, white supremacy, counter-Jihadism, or identitarianism)?
- How are they organized? Are vigilante activities organized top-down (e.g. by political parties) or bottom-up? Who are the participants? Numbers of active participants and supporters? What characterize them in terms of demographics, political/extremist background, criminal record, etc.
- What are they actually doing? How do they operate? Do they patrol or guard certain areas or facilities? Are they armed? Do they operate openly or covertly? Do they wear any kind of uniforms? If so, how does the police and other authorities respond to that? Do they make use of violence, force or intimidation? If so, who is targeted? Do they carry out any good-will activities to improve their image?
- What do they communicate verbally and visually (e.g. through symbols, uniforms, processions, etc.)? Is what they say verbally in accordance with what they communicate visually or do physically?
- What is their relationship to political parties, the police, other public agencies (e.g. municipalities, military, border guards, etc.), the news media, political

Concepts and goals of current research   19

opponents, and different segments of the population (including targeted minorities)? How much support and resistance do they meet, and how much leeway do they have in their operation? Is group participation stigmatized? How does this influence who becomes active participants? Is the environment permissive or repressive of vigilante groups and activities?

- Are the vigilante group's activities mainly online or offline? Which role does social media play for the activities of the group?
- Are they modelled on similar or like-minded groups abroad? Do they have actual links with these groups?

Providing that the case studies will cover all these aspects, it will enable us to carry out comparative analysis along several dimensions. This will be the task of the final, comparative chapters of this volume.

Introducing the case studies

The following section will present briefly the 17 case studies in this volume. They are ordered roughly according to a typology we develop in the concluding chapter, starting with the more violent cases of vigilante movements (terrorism, lynchings and pogroms), then describing paramilitary groups, border patrols and street patrols. However, some of the country chapters include groups of different types, for example Hungary, which has harboured terrorist groups as well as militias and street patrols.

The classic case of vigilantism in general and vigilante terrorism in particular is the American Ku Klux Klan movement, which for more than a century spread fear among blacks, Jews and other minorities, as well as among some of those who stood up against them. Kathleen Blee and Mehr Latif's chapter, "Ku Klux Klan: Vigilantism against blacks, immigrants and other minorities" describe the four major distinct eras of the Ku Klux Klan. The first Klan originated in the aftermath of the Civil War in the 1870s when the blacks' emancipation from slavery was the main issue. The second era occurred in inter-war period in the 1920s, when high rates of immigrants from Europa was on the agenda. The third era was in the 1950s–1960s, where the KKK used violence and threats to fight the civil rights movement and other challenges against racial segregation and white supremacy, and the fourth was during the 1970s until the 2000s when the Klan allied with other far-right groups in an attempt to maintain white dominance in America. The support for the Klan and the methods they used varied considerably through these four eras, as the context changed significantly. One of the main findings is that the Klan could only continue their campaigns of terror for as long as they could operate relatively freely without interference (or even with the blessing) of the local sheriff, judge, pastor and mayor. When the general social and political environment was no longer as permissive with their racism and violence, and repressive forces from law enforcement and NGOs put heavy pressure on them, and Ku Klux Klan fell apart or became severely restricted in what they could do.

Nir Gazit's chapter, "Jewish vigilantism in the West Bank", points to a similar theme. He describes how Jewish settlers in the occupied territories could continue to harass and terrorize Palestinian inhabitants for as long as the Israeli military and government did not strike down on their vigilante activities. There were different types of vigilante groups in the occupied territories, varying both on their level of organization and their relationship with the Israeli authorities. The most organized and institutionalized are the settlements' defence squads, which are organized, trained and armed by the Israeli Defense Forces (IDF) as emergency response teams in case of Palestinian attacks, and usually commanded by former IDF officers. While these groups are the most passive in their interaction with the Palestinians they often initiate violent friction by creating informal roadblocks and direct clashes with Palestinian shepherds and peasants. The second type of vigilantes is of those who belong to radical right groups or remaining factions of right-wing groups that were banned in the past. These groups are founded on Jewish supremacy ideas, radical anti-Arab sentiments, and racism. The less organized groups of Jewish vigilantes are religious-nationalist teenagers and young adults who establish outposts without a formal authorization from the Israeli government. They claim the Palestinians are "raping the Holy Land", and thus must be expelled. These groups are mostly made up of marginal young people, some of them teenagers. They are the most active in initiating anti-Palestinian violent attacks and in violent clashes with the Israeli security forces in the occupied territories. Gazit argues that the ambiguity surrounding the formal status of the Israeli state in the occupied territories creates a governmental void. This void is filled by greater freedom of action of the settlers, who, in effect, act as informal agents of the state, behaving as vigilantes and taking the law into their own hands (Gazit, this volume).

Juhi Ahuja's chapter "Protecting holy cows: Hindu vigilantism against Muslims in India" describes a series of violent attacks and lynchings of Muslims allegedly involved in slaughtering cows and trading beef in India. Such "cow vigilantism" is the policing of behaviour by Hindu nationalists against non-Hindus (mostly Muslims) in the name of protecting cows, which they consider sacred in Hindu religion. The slaughtering of cows is banned in most – but not all – Indian states, but beef trade is nevertheless a major industry. Hindu radicals take it upon themselves to enforce by violent means the ban on slaughtering cows and transporting and trading cow meat as a religious duty. Ahuja argues that the increase in such cow vigilantism must be seen in the context of the rising influence of *Hindutva*, a Hindu ethno-religious and nationalist movement that has gained political power in modern India, and a growing inter-religious and inter-caste intolerance. The cow vigilantes act on the basis of a perception (real or imagined) that non-Hindus are a threat to their religio-cultural identity if they breach their established norm of protecting cows. Such cow vigilantism is also a way to establish Hindu dominance over minority groups.

Chapter 5, "Violent attacks on migrants and minorities in the Russian Federation" by Martin Laryš describes how more than 600 people, mostly labour migrants from the Muslim regions of Caucasus and Central Asia as well as homosexuals, have been killed and several thousands have been injured by nationalists and neo-Nazis in Russia during a 17-year period. Although many of these murders can more appropriately be characterized as hate crimes or right-wing terrorism, a large proportion of the violence and killings have strong aspects of vigilantism to them. The perpetrators, mostly neo-Nazi skinheads and militant nationalists, often justified their violence as a way to defend the Russian people against rapists and criminal migrants. Homosexuals were also attacked in order to defend the moral order of society from delinquents subverting Russia's traditional values. For a long time, the police turned a blind eye on these lethal vigilante activities until a significant change in governmental policy repressed these movements and put a number of leaders in prison. This led to a sharp decrease in vigilante activities and violence from late 2013 onwards.

Daniel Koehler's overview of "Anti-immigration militias and vigilante groups in Germany" shows that although military sports groups ("Wehrsportgruppen") and groups of citizens defending their cities ("Bürgerwehren") have long traditions in Germany, it was only recently that these terms took on a vigilante dimension. Anti-immigrant violence and pogrom-like attacks have also been rife in Germany but only in a few cases has this violence had a distinct vigilante character. However, in recent years, a number of vigilante groups were formed and acts of vigilante violence were committed as a response to criminal acts (allegedly or actually) committed by immigrants. The sexual assaults on German women by mostly North-African migrants during the New Year celebration in Cologne 2015/16 and the passive police response became a watershed event, releasing a wave of vigilante movements in Germany (and beyond) against so-called "rapefugees". Some of these went in the direction of terrorist attacks on the homes of migrants. Yet, most of these movements remained in the social media only. Groups that started to function as a militia or alternative policing and committed criminal acts quickly became targeted by the authorities. However, lack of public trust in the police and other authorities creates an opportunity for right-wing extremist movements to mobilize on the claimed incompetence of the authorities, promoting vigilantism as an alternative.

A country with deep legacies of vigilantism is described and analysed in the chapter "Vigilante militias and activities against Roma and migrants in Hungary", written by Szilveszter Póczik and Eszter Sárik. The authors explain the traditions of fascist and nationalist vigilantism and their impact on the recent right-wing extremist scene. In August 2007, the Jobbik Party (Movement for a Better Hungary) founded the "Hungarian Guard Association for Protection of Traditions and Culture". This group won huge attention and it caused a rise of popularity of the Jobbik. It organized vigilante patrols and marches in Roma communities against alleged "Gypsy Crime". After its ban in 2009, several successor groups were established. These groups were fuelled by the migration wave of 2015–2017. However, they play a much more symbolic than effective role in the (anti)migration politics through marches, anti-Muslim protest and publication (Póczik and Sárik, this volume). The chapter also discusses a vigilante terrorist racist killer commando that was active in 2008–2009, killing six Roma people (and injuring many others). As in other East and Central European countries, we can see the dominance of anti-Roma vigilantism, enhanced by anti-Migrant vigilantism during the crisis in 2015 and later.

Miroslav Mareš and Daniel Milo deal with "Vigilantism against migrants and minorities in Slovakia and in the Czech Republic". The two former parts of the Czechoslovak federation have different traditions of vigilantism. However, after the fall of communism right-wing extremist militias as well as (mostly anti-Roma) skinhead racist groups were established in both countries. They justified their hate crimes by reference to alleged "ethnic crime" of the attacked minorities. Party militias are typical in both countries. The activities of the train patrols of the People's Party Our Slovakia (ĽSNS) – focused mostly on Gypsy crime – had a specific impact on the popularity of this party. Paramilitary groups are involved in anti-migrant patrols and in protection the borders. The Slovak Recruits are one of the strongest non-state paramilitary organizations in the region. Pro-Russian sympathy is typical of many vigilantes in the Czech Republic and Slovakia. Vigilantes from both countries cooperate closely.

The chapter "Vigilantism against ethnic minorities and migrants in Bulgaria", by Nadya Stoynova and Rositsa Dzhekova, analyses the rise of various formations in the country a, which is located on the "Balkan migration route" and has significant Roma minority. This migration route provides the reason for the most recent manifestation of vigilantism in the country, namely anti-migrant patrols and arrests at the Bulgarian–Turkish border. Nevertheless, ad-hoc and less organized manifestations of vigilantism, predominantly against the Roma, have been observed prior to the migrant crisis. The wider political context is crucial in understanding the phenomenon in Bulgaria, as vigilantism should be considered as a phenomenon emerging in the context of the political, societal and economic crisis in the country during the post-communist period of the nineties and its lingering implications (Stoynova and Dzhekova in this volume). The recent wave of anti-immigrant vigilante groups is also analysed within the context of a persistent "systematic crisis feeling", which remains endemic in the country and which was exacerbated by the scale and intensity of the crisis.

Anti-migration patrols are the topic of the chapter "The Minutemen: Patrolling and performativity along the U.S. / Mexican border" by Harel Shapira. Analysing the Minutemen paramilitary border patrol, he is struck by what he describes as the "militarized masculinity" within the context of "performed patriotism". The US government campaign to militarize the border, starting in the 1990s as a "new strategy to deter illegal immigration" (Shapira, this volume), is an important factor behind the establishing of anti-immigrant vigilante border groups. Shapira researched almost 200 Minutemen and he found out that they were composed of predominantly elderly white men who were almost exclusively military veterans. His study shows that a main motivation for the participants was that the Minutemen border patrols offered them an opportunity to relive their military past.

The dominant role of a political party in vigilante activities is analysed in the chapter "Vigilantism in Greece: The case of the Golden Dawn" by Christos Vrakopoulos and Daphne Halikiopoulou. They explain the political, social and economic environment of modern Greek vigilantism and many aspects of the party Golden Dawn. An analysis of the relations between this party and political groups and public agencies is a valuable part of this study. They stated: "Police officers tend to be Golden Dawn supporters and constituencies with high numbers of police voters tend to turn around higher Golden Dawn results" (Vrakopoulos and Halikiopoulou, in this volume). They also deal with far right vigilante activities beyond the Golden Dawn. The groups (such as Cryptheia) are responsible for violent anti-Immigrant attacks.

The most common form of vigilante activities in our collection of case studies is varieties of vigilante street patrols. These groups claim to prevent crime and deter criminals by patrolling alleged crime-infested streets or public transportation, thereby providing safety to ordinary citizens. These street patrols generally avoid the actual use of violence but they do display a capacity for violence by a show of strength, allegedly to enhance their crime deterring impact. Some of these street patrols are organized from below by concerned citizens but more commonly they are organized top-down by far-right organizations and parties. One example of the latter is analysed by Pietro Castelli Gattinara in his chapter on "Forza Nuova and the Security Walks: Squadrismo and Neo-Fascist Vigilantism in Italy". This extreme right party have organized "security walks" as one of their main activities. FN militants claim that they take the responsibility of patrolling local areas that are considered dangerous, thus serving a function that the decaying Italian state is unable – or unwilling – to fulfil. Vigilantism is thus framed not only as a response to criminality brought about by immigration, but also as a reaction to the inefficiency of state authorities. Security walks are also used as a recruitment strategy for the party by inviting concerned locals to join their patrols.

Pietro Castelli Gattinara's other chapter, "Beyond the hand of the state: Vigilantism against migrants and minorities in France", analyses two varieties of vigilante activities, one bottom-up initiative and one top-down. The former, calling themselves "Les Calaisiens en Colère" (The Angry People of Calais, LCC) emerged as a response to the large numbers of refugees that had gathered in the vicinity of Calais ("the Jungle") and the crime and disorder problems that accompanied this large mass of people. The LCC, which carried out nightly street patrols, claimed to be entirely non-political and non-violent. The top-down variety was a range of vigilante activities organized by the Identitarians, a far right nativist movement. They set up a number of "anti-scum" patrols in streets and public transport as well as other actions aimed at convincing the French people to "defend themselves" against insecurity caused by migrants. A special case of vigilante border patrol was the "Defend Europe" campaign, where Identitarian activists used web-based crowd funding to rent a ship that would patrol the Mediterranean Sea to dissuade illegal migration to Europe, in particular to expose the human smugglers and the NGOs helping migrants to reach Europe. Although the sea patrol did not stop any migrants, it was mainly a media stunt to influence policy, and it probably had some impact in Italian politics in particular.

The chapter by Elizabeth Ralph-Morrow on "Vigilantism in the United Kingdom: Britain First and 'Operation Fightback'" describes Britain First as a fringe far-right political party that carried out "mosque invasions" and "Christian patrols" in Muslim-dominated urban areas. The first "Christian patrols" started in 2014 as a response to a "Muslim patrol" video on YouTube, which featured three men who sought to enforce Sharia law in East London. Britain First patrols invaded several mosques and behaved in calculated insulting ways (drinking alcohol, refusing to take off shoes, alleging that Mohammed was a false prophet, etc.) to provoke and intimidate the congregation. Britain First's vigilante activities are characterized by making veiled threats, and do not involve actual use of violence. This threat is particularly conveyed through the organization's emphasis on militarism, wearing uniforms, and claiming that its activities are akin to those of a soldier at war. Although some of Britain First's vigilante activities are in response to alleged crimes such as immigrant "grooming gangs" (that had sexually abused large numbers of children). At other times the group is apparently acting mainly in response to the "Muslim occupation" of parts of British cities. Britain First activities were widely condemned and numerous criminal sanctions were also imposed on the group's leaders, including imprisonment for harassment and other charges, as well as bans to enter parts of specific cities or any mosque in England and Wales, or encouraging other persons to do so. However, in filming and uploading videos of its vigilante activities, Britain First have managed to promote the "Christian patrols" and "mosque invasions2 carried out by a handful of Britain First members to an audience of millions, and even receiving endorsement from president Donald Trump.

The most striking example of a trans-national vigilante movement is the Soldiers of Odin, which started in Finland in late 2015, and boosted by the stories about widespread sexual harassment during New Year's celebration in Cologne, spread to more than 20 countries within a few months. This phenomenon is analysed by Tommi Kotonen in his study of "The Soldiers of Odin in Finland: From a local movement to international franchise". The Soldiers of Odin (SOO) described itself as "a patriotic street patrol organization, which opposes harmful immigration, Islamization, EU and globalization". The members patrol on the streets especially late at night in order to protect people from violent behaviour and inform the police when something happens, emphasizing that they act as a non-violent preventive force. A main reason for the sudden international success of the Soldiers of Odin was its style – a black hoodie or sweater with a logo of a Viking-like god with the national flag as a beard, resembling the symbols ("colours") of outlaw MC clubs. As the Soldiers of Odin movement rapidly spread internationally, the original Finnish organization tried to maintain a certain control (and also get some incomes) by establishing a Soldiers of Odin World Wide leadership group and demanding that national chapters had to abide by the bylaws of the original Finnish SOO. However, case studies of Soldiers of Odin in Canada, Norway and Sweden shows that the various national chapters soon went their own ways.

Tore Bjørgo and Ingvild Magnæs Gjelsvik's chapter "Sheep in wolf's clothing? The taming of the Soldiers of Odin in Norway" analyses the rapid growth and the disintegration of the SOO in Norway. The Norwegian chapter gradually broke away from the Finnish mother chapter and later also with SOO World Wide, mainly because the SOO Norway leadership was uncomfortable with the increasingly right-wing extremist and anti-Islam profile of the mother organization. One main reason for this appears to be that the Norwegian SOO leaders and much of the membership had a different agenda than anti-immigration and anti-Islam activism. A large proportion of the members and leaders were young men known in their communities as petty criminals and troublemakers, and they saw SOO's street patrols as an opportunity to make up for their past and improve their tarnished identity and reputation. Any association with right-wing extremism or violent vigilantism would undermine that effort of identity change, making the SOO Norway strive hard to distance themselves from this. However, the police did not want to cooperate with Soldiers of Odin, and eventually banned the use of hoodies with SOO symbols during street walks, claiming that such uniforms would represent a breach of the police monopoly of patrolling streets to maintain public safety. Partly due to this ban on uniforms, in combination with internal conflicts over the high proportion of leaders and members with a criminal past within the organization, SOO Norway closed down after about a year of activity.

The chapter on "Soldiers of Odin in Canada: The failure of a transnational ideology" by Emil Archambault and Yannick Veilleux-Lepage describes how the Soldiers of Odin in Canada were marred by numerous breakups, internecine conflicts, and divisions, and analyse why this became so. More so than SOO elsewhere, the Canadian SOO combined vigilante street patrols with community building efforts and charity actions. They claimed, according to the SOO Canada bylaws, to exist because the higher authorities failed the Canadian citizens by the allowing of illegal aliens into the country, and their community minded activities were part of an effort to divert resources back to deserving Canadians and away from immigrants. Although all the activities of SOO Canada were within an anti-immigrant, xenophobic paradigm, several splits occurred over the ties to the Finnish mother organization and its anti-immigration and racist image, as well as over the priorities between vigilante patrolling and community building activities. There were also tensions between a strictly Canadian nationalist focus and the transnational "European" orientation of SOO Finland and World Wide.

Soldiers of Odin was only one among several varieties of "Pop-up vigilantism and fascist patrols in Sweden", as analysed by Mattias Gardell. He describes a surge of radical nationalist vigilantism between 2013 and 2017, fed by moral panic on migrant crime, no-go zones and alleged "rape jihad" of white Swedish women. The calls to vigilantism appears to have fizzled out for now, with the far-right turning its attention to other projects. Gardell describes four categories of vigilante activism: (1) Sweden's Citizens Militia emerged as a response to riots against police brutality in a stigmatized underclass suburb. The inner circle all had criminal records and links to radical nationalist groups. The loose group was involved in

26 Miroslav Mareš and Tore Bjørgo

several violent episodes. (2) Soldiers of Odin had a rapid growth but soon declined. They were ridiculed and met resistance from the police, local residents, Anti-fa and an outlaw biker gang, as well as embarrassing media exposure on the extremist ties, criminal records and violent behaviour of SOO members. (3) Gardet and several other autonomous vigilante groups also had a rapid growth in 2016 before they disappeared. (4) The patrols of the Nordic Resistance Movement (NRM), a pan-Nordic National Socialist organization, is probably the most organized and potentially most durable form of vigilante patrols in Sweden. They are disciplined and trained in knife fighting and other paramilitary activities. However, non-sanctioned violence is forbidden – except for self-defence (although the threshold for what is considered provocation is very low). NRM has engaged in numerous vigilante patrols in Sweden and Finland but this remains a limited part of the organization's activity. Gardell argues that vigilante activities in Sweden was mainly a ritual performance, either to promote the organization behind it, or to articulate the participants' white Swedish masculinity, and define public space as a white space.

In the concluding chapter, the editors will make use of the rich empirical data from the 17 case studies for comparative analysis of the research questions raised earlier in this introduction chapter.

Notes

1 There have also been cases of left-wing vigilantism, for example the "Lenin-boys" during the Commune of 1919 in Hungary, terrorizing the so called "bourgeois" middle classes. More recent examples of left-wing vigilantism are Antifa groups that surveilled and beat up people they considered to be fascists, and could be called upon if people observed neo-Nazis in their community. However, vigilantism from the far left is far less common than vigilantism from the far right.
2 The racist serial killer in Malmö, Peter Mangs, performed several of his attacks in ways that made the police believe this was violence among criminal immigrant gangs (Gardell 2015).
3 The DanerVærn web page, (www.danervern.net) is no longer available.
4 DanerVærn is not included in our sample of case studies. This Danish vigilante group was established in 2014. A main activity has been to protect bridges crossing highways, due to a rumor that some refugees had thrown stones on cars from such bridges. It has also done some street and border patrolling. In an interview, the leader stated: "Staten har et voldsmonopol. Vi udfordrer det Monopol" ("The state has a monopoly on violence. We challenge that monopoly"). *Jyllandsposten* 02.01.2016. The DanerVærn home page has been closed down but they do maintain a Facebook group with very limited activity.
5 That police officers may turn a blind eye to vigilantism or even be deeply involved is exemplified by several vigilante organizations in Latin America in the 1950s and 1960s. Besides police officers also military officers took part in these organizations in their free time (Sprinzak 1995: 30–31).

References

Abrahams, Ray G. (1998). *Vigilante citizens: Vigilantism and the state.* Cambridge: Polity Press.
Ajuha, Juhi and Pravin Prakash (2017). *Cow vigilantism in India: Modi's dilemma or legacy?* Singapore: Nanyang Technological University. Retrieved 31 January 2018 from, https://www.rsis.edu.sg/wp-content/uploads/2017/07/CO17131.pdf.

Barkun, Michael (1998). Conspiracy theories as stigmatised knowledge: The basis for a New Age racism? In: Jeffrey Kaplan and Tore Bjørgo (eds), *Nation and race: The developing Euro-American racist subculture* (pp. 58–72). Boston: Northeastern University Press.

Berg, Manferd and Simon Wendt (2011). Introduction: Lynching from an international perspective. In Manfred Berg and Simon Wendt (eds), *Globalizing lynching history: vigilantism and extralegal punishment from an international perspective* (pp. 1–18). New York: Palgrave MacMillan.

Bjørgo, Tore, and Rob Witte (eds, 1993). *Racist violence in Europe.* Basingstoke: Macmillan.

Bowling, Ben (1998). *Violent racism.* Oxford: Oxford University Press.

Button, Mark (2002). Voluntary policing. In Mark Button, *Private policing* (pp. 83–95). London: Willan.

Bötticher, Astrid and Miroslav Mareš (2012). *Extremismus. Theorien – konzepte – formen.* München: Oldenbourg Verlag.

Capoccia, Giovanni (2005). *Defending democracy. Reactions to extremism in interwar Europe.* Baltimore and London: The John Hopkins University Press.

Carey, Sabine C. and Neil J. Mitchell (2016). "Pro-government militias and conflict". In William R. Thompson, *Oxford research encyclopedia of politics.* doi: doi:10.1093/acrefore/9780190228637.013.33.

Cartwright, Mark (2016). *Vigiles.* In *Ancient History Encyclopedia.* Retrieved 31 January 2018 from https://www.ancient.eu/Vigiles/.

del Barrio Romero, F.; T. Bjørgo; H.-G. Jaschke; C. Kwanten; R.I. Mowby and M. Pagon (2009). *Police science perspectives: Towards a European approach. Extended expert report.* Frankfurt: Verlag für Polizeiwissenschaft.

Drmola, Jakub (2017). *Kybernetická bezpečnost. Systémový model protidžihádistického vigilantismu (dissertation thesis).* Brno: Masarykova univerzita. Retrieved 2 February 2018 from https://is.muni.cz/th/171810/fss_d/.

Gardell, Mattias (2015). *Raskrigaren: Seriemördaren Peter Mangs.* Stockholm: Leopard förlag.

Gazit, Nir (2015). State-sponsored vigilantism: Jewish settlers' violence in the occupied Palestinian territories. *Sociology,* 49(3), 438–454.

Gerstenfeld, Phyllis B. (2011). *Hate crimes: Causes, controls, and controversies.* Thousand Oaks, New Delhi: Sage.

Gerwarth, Robert and John Horne (2013). Paramilitarism in Europe after the Great War: An Introduction. In Robert Gerwarth and John Horne (eds), *War in peace. Paramilitary violence in Europe after the Great War* (pp. 1–18). Oxford: Oxford University Press.

Häggqvist, Linn (2017). *"Taking the law into your own hands". Violent vigilantism in post-war societies* (Master's thesis). Uppsala: Uppsala University. Retrieved 4 February 2018 from http://www.diva-portal.org/smash/get/diva2:1113108/FULLTEXT01.pdf.

Hall, Nathan (2013). *Hate crime.* London and New York: Routledge (2nd edition).

Haysom, N. Mabangalala (1986). *The rise of right-wing vigilantes in South Africa.* London: Catholic Institute for International Relations.

Hoffman, Bruce (2006). *Inside terrorism.* New York: Columbia University Press.

Holbrook, Donald and Max Taylor (2013). Introduction. In Max Taylor, P.M. Currie and Donald Holbrook (eds), *Extreme right wing political violence and terrorism* (pp. 1–13). London, New Delhi, New York, Sydney: Bloomsbury.

Huggins, Martha K. (1991). Introduction. Vigilantism and the state. A look south and north. In Martha K. Huggins (ed.), *Vigilantism and the state in modern Latin America. Essays on extra-legal violence* (pp. 1–18). New York: Praeger Publishers.

Johnston, Les (1996). What is vigilantism? *The British Journal of Criminology,* 36(2), 220–236.

28 Miroslav Mareš and Tore Bjørgo

Kirsch, Thomas G. and Tilo Grätz (2010). Vigilantism. State ontologies & encompassment. An introductory essay. In Thomas G. Kirsch and Tilo Grätz (eds), *Domesticating vigilantism in Africa* (pp. 1–24). Woodbridge: James Currey.

Kirschner, Andrea (2011). Putting out the fire with gasoline? Violence control in "fragile" states: A study of vigilantism in Nigeria. In Wilhelm Heitmeyer, Heinz Gerhard Haupt, Stefan Malthaner and Andrea Kirschner (eds), *Control of violence: Historical and international perspectives on violence in modern societies* (pp. 536–569). New York: Springer.

Kowalewski, David (2002). Vigilantismus. In Wilhelm Heitmeyer and John Hagan (eds), *Internationales Handbuch der Gewaltforschung* (pp. 426–440). Wiesbaden: Westdeutscher Verlag.

Kučera, Michal (2010). Antifašistická akce optikou teorie vigilantismu. In Ivo Svoboda (ed.), *Politický extremismus a terorismus jako ohrožení vnitřní bezpečnosti státu?* (pp. 26–38). Brno: Unverzita obrany.

Kučera, Michal (2017). *Informal policing v ČR: možnosti institucionalizace neformálních občanských iniciativ* (dissertation thesis). Brno: Fakulta sociálních studií Masarykovy univerzity. Retrieved 3 February 2018 from https://is.muni.cz/th/182226/fss_d/.

Kučera, Michal and Miroslav Mareš (2015). Vigilantism during democratic transition. *Policing and Society*, 25(2), 170–187.

Lehr, Peter (2017). Militant Buddhism is on the march in South-East Asia – where did it come from? *The Conversation*, Retrieved 3 February 2018 from http://theconversation.com/milita nt-buddhism-is-on-the-march-in-south-east-asia-where-did-it-come-from-86632.

Levin, Jack, and Jack McDevitt (1993). *Hate crimes: The rising tide of bigotry and bloodshed.* New York: Plenum Press.

Layton, Matthew, Mariana Rodríguez, Mason Moseley and Daniel Zizumbo-Colunga (2014). Citizen security, evaluations of the state, and policy preferences. In Elizabeth J. Zechmeister (ed.), *The political culture of democracy in the Americas, 2014: Democratic governance across 10 years of the Americas barometer* (pp. 73–116). Nashville: Vanderbilt University, Retrieved 3 February 2018 from https://www.vanderbilt.edu/lapop/ab2014/AB2014_Comparative_Report_English_V3_revised_011315_W.pdf.

Mareš, Miroslav (2012a). *Paramilitarismus v České republice.* Brno: Centrum pro studium demokracie a kultury.

Mareš, Miroslav (2012b). Vigilantism against Roma in East Central Europe. In Uwe Backes and Patrick Moreau (eds), *The extreme right in Europe. Current trends and perspectives* (pp. 281–296). Göttingen: Vandenhoeck & Ruprecht.

Mareš, Miroslav (2016). From subcultural groupings to actors of hybrid warfare: Current trends in conflicts in Eastern Europe. *Vojenské rozhledy*, 15 (special issue), 123–133, Retrieved from http://www.vojenskerozhledy.cz/en/kategorie-clanku/ozbrojene-kon flikty/cesti-bojovnici.

Mareš, Miroslav (2017a). Gegenwärtige rechtsextremistische Radikalisierung in Ostmitteleuropa aus Sicht der terroristischer Bedrohung. In Stefan Hansen and Joachim Krause (eds), *Jahrbuch terrorismus 2015/2016* (pp. 79–94). Berlin and Toronto: Verlag Barbara Budrich.

Mareš, Miroslav (2017b). Strategic impact of East Central European extreme right vigilantes: From subcultural fringes to instruments of hybrid warfare. *Paper presented at the ECPR General Conference, Oslo, 6–9 September 2017 in the panel Vigilantism Against Migrants and Minorities (Section Right Wing Extremism Beyond Party Politics).* Retrieved 9 January 2018 from https://ecpr.eu/Filestore/PaperProposal/3ca1881d-02fb-4eab-b9e5-c097cafabd1b.pdf

Mareš, Miroslav and Adam Veselý (2015). Sharia – Police v Německu: islamistický vigilantismus a nástroj propagandy. *Bezpečnostní teorie a praxe*, 21(2), 43–54.

Marx, Gary T. and Dane Archer (1971). Citizen involvement in the law enforcement process: The case of community police patrols. *American Behavioral Scientist*, 15(1), 52–72.

Monaghan, Rachel (2004). "One merchant, one bullet": The rise and fall of PAGAD. *Low Intensity Conflict & Law Enforcement*, 12(1), 1–19.

Moncanda, Eduardo (2017). Varieties of vigilantism: Conceptual discord, meaning and strategies. *Global Crime*, 18(4), 403–423.

Mudde, Cas (2000). *The ideology of extreme right*. Manchester: Manchester University Press.

Nečej, Elemír and Richard Stojar (2013). *Extremism vs. Armed Forces and Military Veterans in Slovakia and Czech Republic*. Bratislava: Centre for European and North Atlantic Affairs.

Osborne, Elizabeth (2005). *Latin and Greek Roots. A study of world families*. Clayton, DE: Prestwick House.

OSCE's Office for Democratic Institutions and Human Rights (2009): *Hate crime laws – A practical guide*. Warsaw: OSCE Office for Democratic Institutions and Human Rights (ODIHR) (author: Jernow Allison).

Page, Walker Thomas (1901). The real judge Lynch. *The Atlantic Monthly*, 88(530), December 2001, 720–743.

Perry, Barbera (2001). *In the name of hate: Understanding hate crimes*. London: Routledge.

Potočňák, Adam and Radka Vicenová (2015). Introduction. In Adam Potočňák and Radka Vicenová (eds), *Radicals in uniforms: Case studies of Austria, Czech Republic, Germany, Poland and Slovakia* (pp. 6–7). Bratislava: Centre for European and North Atlantic Affairs.

Ravndal, Jacob Aasland (2016). Right-wing terrorism and violence in Western Europe: Introducing the RTV dataset. *Perspectives on Terrorism*, 10(3), 2–15.

Ravndal, Jacob Aasland (2017). Explaining right-wing terrorism and violence in Western Europe: Grievances, opportunities and polarisation. *European Journal of Political Research*, 57(4): 845–866. doi: doi:10.1111/1475–6765.12254.

Rosenbaum, Jon and Peter C. Sederberg (1974). Vigilantism. An analysis of establishment violence. *Comparative Politics*, 6(4), 541–570.

Rubin, M. (2001). *Into the shadows: Radical vigilantes in Khatami's Iran*. Washington, DC: Washington Institute for Near East Policy.

Rydgren, Jens (2018). The radical right: An introduction. In Jens Rydgren (ed.), *The Oxford handbook of the radical right* (pp. 1–13). New York: Oxford University Press.

Schmid, Alex P. (2012). The revised academic consensus definition of terrorism. *Perspectives on Terrorism*, 6(2), 158–159.

Schmid, Alex P. (ed.) (2011). *The Routledge handbook on terrorism research*. London / New York: Routledge.

Schmid, Alex P., Albert J. Jongman, Michael Stohl and Peter A. Flemming (1988). Terrorism and related concepts: Typologies. In Alex P. Schmid and Albert J. Jongman (eds), *Political terrorism. A new guide to actors, authors, concepts, data bases, theories & literature* (pp. 39–59). New Brunswick, New Jersey, London: Transaction Publishers.

Scobell, Andrew and Brad Hammitt (1998). Goons, gunmen, and gendarmerie. Toward a reconceptualization of paramilitary formations. *Journal of Political and Military Sociology*, 26(2), 213–227.

Silke, Andrew (2007). Ragged justice. Loyalist vigilantism in Northern Ireland. *Terrorism and Political Violence*, 11(3), 1–31.

Sinclair, Kirstine (2013). *Muslim street patrols in London*. Odense: Center for Mellemøststudier. Retrieved 4 February 2018 from https://www.sdu.dk/en/om_sdu/institutter_centre/c_m ellemoest.

Smallridge, Joshua, Wagner, Philip, Crowl, Justin N. (2016). Understanding cyber-vigilantism. A conceptual framework. *Journal of Theoretical and Philosophical Criminology*, 8(1), 57–70.

Smith, Daniel Jordan (2004). The Bakassi Boys: Vigilantism, violence, and political imagination in Nigeria. *Cultural Anthropology*, 19(3), 429–455.

Sprinzak, Ehud (1995). Right-wing terrorism in a comparative perspective: The case of split delegitimization. *Terrorism and Political Violence*, 7(1), 17–43.

Stojarová, Věra (2012). Paramilitary structures in Eastern Europe. In Uwe Backes and Patrick Moreau (eds), *The extreme right in Europe. Current trends and perspectives* (pp. 265–279). Götttingen: Vandenhoeck & Ruprecht.

Trottier, Daniel (2017). Digital vigilantism as weaponisation of visibility. *Philosophy & Technology*, 30(1), 55–72.

Tyson, Adam (2013). Vigilantism and violence in decentralized Indonesia. The case of Lombok. *Critical Asian Studies*, 45(2), 201–230.

Waldmann, Peter (1998). *Terrorismus. Provokation der Macht*. München: Gerling Akademie Verlag.

Weber, Max (1922) *Wirtschaft und Gesellschaft*. Tübingen: Mohr.

2

KU KLUX KLAN

Vigilantism against blacks, immigrants and other minorities

Kathleen Blee and Mehr Latif

The Ku Klux Klan (KKK or Klan) is the most enduring form of vigilantism in United States history, extending from the 1870s through to today. The Klan is not historically continuous, despite the Klan's claims to the contrary in an effort to project an image of power and constancy (Blee, 2012). In fact, the Klan has appeared and then disappeared several times throughout U.S. history with different targets for its vigilante violence. Moreover, although the Klan presents itself as a unitary organization, in every Klan era there are separate and competing Klan groups and leaders. All Klan groups, however, are consistent in their efforts to organize vigilante violence and threats against racial, ethnic, religious, and national minority groups and non-white immigrants to the United States. Jews and those whose ancestry can be traced to the nations of Africa and Latin America, whether they are native-born or immigrants, are the most historically constant enemies of the Klan. Catholics, Mormons, Muslims, and those whose ancestry can be traced to the nations of Asia have also been the victims of Klan vigilantism in most eras, as have, at various times, labor union organizers, gay men, lesbians, and other sexual minorities, and employees and supporters of the federal (national) government.

To understand the Klan's agenda of fomenting vigilantism against particular groups of people, it is important to view each era of the KKK within the particular social, political, and economic context in which it arose and mobilized supporters and, upon occasion, voters. Four distinct eras witnessed significant mobilization by Ku Klux Klans in the United States: the 1870s, immediately after the Civil War over slavery; the interwar 1920s, which was characterized by high rates of immigration from Europe; the 1950s–1960s, which witnessed legal and political challenges to racial segregation or racially exclusive voting practices in the southern states; and the 1980s–2000s, during which the Klan allied with other far-right racist groups to forge a Pan-Aryan alliance. We discuss each era of the Klan within its historical context to explain how it justified and gained popular support for

32   Kathleen Blee and Mehr Latif

vigilante agendas and practices, which we define as actions or serious threats of extra-legal violence that replace or enhance the legitimated violence of the state such as the police, courts, and military. We pay attention to the wider context in which the Klan developed, how it was organized, its principle vigilante activities and strategies, and its relationship to electoral and government actors. In particular, we focus on how the Klan's use of violence was shaped by its relationship with the state.

Data

This paper draws on different sources of data for the different eras of the Klan. For the first Klan of the 1870s, we use information from the scholarly accounts that have reconstructed details of this Klan's wave of vigilante terror through a variety of historical sources, especially evidence gathered in the national government's investigation into the Klan's violent activities. For the second Klan of the 1920s we rely on data collected by the first author during the 1980s from unstructured oral histories of former women Klan members, local newspaper accounts of Klan activity in the state of Indiana where the Klan was large and politically powerful, documents from local, regional, and national male and female Ku Klux Klan organizations, and information published by anti-Klan organizations and newspapers, including details of Klan vigilante activities and the identities of Klan members (Blee 1991). Information on the third Klan comes from published research, largely based on evidence gathered by the police or federal investigators. For the Klan of the late twentieth and early twenty-first century, we draw on studies by the first author that secured insider information about the Klan's vigilante activities and plans through semi-structured interviews with Klan members and former members and observation of the Klan's public and private events (Blee, 1991/ 2009, 2002).

We present the best information available about the Ku Klux Klan's vigilantism, but it is important to note that data about the Klan is always partial. As a secret society that is often engaged in illegal actions or plans, the Klan takes care to obscure its leadership, structure, and locations and to exaggerate its size and influence. Even evidence about the Klan from law enforcement or government agencies can be suspect, as some state officials have been sympathetic to the Klan's violence or reluctant to reveal its ability to pursue vigilante actions with few legal consequences (Blee, 2017; Cunningham, 2012; McVeigh and Cunningham, 2012; (Wright, 1985). The sources on which we rely for data on vigilantism in the Ku Klux Klan thus required extraordinarily complex methods of research to surmount the Klan's secrecy, intimidation, and sharp difference between publicly available statements of plans and ideologies and what happens within its groups (Blee, 2002).

Klan vigilantism across historical periods

1st Klan: 1860s–1870s

The first Klan arose in the wake of the Civil War, which ended with the defeat of the Confederacy, a secessionist movement of southern states that sought to preserve their slavery-based economy and social order. The Klan emerged as a loosely organized association of white men, largely in the rural areas of the South, who wielded vigilante terrorism and violence to defend white supremacy and the racial state. Their name was meant to denote a circle of brothers, suggesting the racial fraternity that would long be a characteristic of Klan groups. Klan targets were primarily emancipated blacks and white northerners who had come to the south to reconstruct the state in the post-Civil War period. Its organization was limited, with officials holding titles such as Grand Dragon that were more symbolic than reflective of an actual integrated organization. Indeed, the Klan's locally based and largely uncoordinated groups mostly resembled loosely organized gangs.

Due to its loose organizational form, the Klan's vigilante violence was locally targeted with little overall strategy among groups beyond a shared antipathy toward both blacks and the northern, federally directed project of reconstructing the southern racial state. Indeed, it is difficult to identify precisely the acts of violence that are attributable to Klan groups, as white violence against blacks and their white allies was pervasive across the post- Civil war era South. Such violence was both vicious and extensive, taking the form of murders, arsons, lynchings, expulsion from homes and communities, robbery, and enslavement. In the state of Georgia alone, the Freedman's Bureau cited 336 murders or assaults in 1868, a significant proportion of which might have been related to the Klan, while the Klan was also responsible for burning schools and churches and numerous acts of political intimidation (Bryant, 2002). In one county in South Carolina, white vigilante violence, much likely attributable to Klan members, took the form of whipping, terrorizing, attacking, and even murdering and lynching former slaves who tried to leave their plantations (as well as those that hired them) or who showed disrespect to whites, (for men) approached white women, or were thought to be fomenting insurrection or resistance to white rule (Parsons, 2005; Tolnay & Beck, 1995). Moreover, the Klan in that county was responsible for two large scale raids on jails that ended in deaths after a black militia attempted to block the delivery of illegal liquor to a local hotel (Parsons, 2005).

The first Klan established an agenda that intertwined issues of race, gender, and region, a pattern that would recur in later Klans. Klan groups insisted that their vigilantism was necessary to protect Southern white women, who they saw as particularly vulnerable with the collapse of the former slavery state to what the Klan described as the vengeance and sexual depravities of now-freed black men. They especially highlighted fears about the plight of southern white women who were living without male protectors (as their husbands/fathers had died in the Confederate army) on often-isolated plantations across the South, and about the specter of interracial relationships as freed black men could now take advantage of innocent white southern women. Rejecting the idea that the southern state could be reconstructed by northern and federal government officials, the first Klan insisted that it was the only barrier against racial lawlessness and that its violent actions were the only effective means of controlling an uprising of freed blacks and their allies.

Vigilantism against migrants from the north was a strategy to protect the institutions of southern white supremacy against reform efforts by political organizers and politicians from the northern states that had been triumphant in the Civil War. These northerners were short-term settlers, arriving in the states of the defeated Confederacy to establish the institutions of governance that would replace the slave state and establish federal jurisdiction. To the Klan and its supporters, they were intruding on the rights of the southern self-determination by their efforts to upset the long-time social order of the South that had been based on white political and economic control and black exclusion and subordination.

The northern political agents who attracted the violent attention of the Klan were generally powerful and intentional travelers who were acting on behalf of the triumphant federal union, quite distinct from a general image of migrants as powerless and displaced people. In contrast, the Klan's vigilantism against blacks targeted a powerless group who, although legally free from slavery, rarely had any means of sustaining their livelihood or any legal claim to a residence. Many blacks fled to the northern states before, during, and after the Civil War. Those that remained in the South were swept into a system of debt peonage in which they were forced to work for very low wages, often on the very plantations on which they were earlier enslaved.

The Klan operated outside the official law but with the clear acquiescence of the white controlled law enforcement and judicial operations in the post-Civil War southern states. In this sense, the Klan's vigilante violence simply supplemented the racial violence that had long been a practice of southern slave states. After considerable outcry about its operations as a terroristic force, the first Klan was eventually the subject of investigation by the U.S. Congress, which passed an anti-Klan law that stripped southern states of legal authority over some crimes of violence and imposed a ban on wearing masks (targeted at Klan masks) in southern states. The Klan was disbanded in the 1870s, due both to federal pressure and to the reestablishment of a white political control in the south that made the Klan less necessary (Chalmers, 1981; Southern Poverty Law Center, 2011).

1920s Klan

The KKK re-emerged in late 1910s and grew to be the largest Klan by the mid-1920s at which point it had enlisted approximately 3–5 million white, native-born Protestant men and women across the country. Unlike the 1870s Klan, which operated at the margins of society, the 1920s Klan positioned itself simultaneously as a vehicle for white supremacism and a mainstream social club for white Protestants. And contrary to its predecessor, this Klan established itself largely in northern states and cities and towns (Jackson, 1967). The 1920s Klan also was different from the first Klan in its efforts to recruit women. Women were mobilized into the 1920s Klan for many of the same reason that brought men – a desire to preserve and extend the dominance of white Protestants over racial and religious minorities, and fears that immigration and the internal migration of blacks from southern to northern states portended a dangerous form of heterogeneity in communities that had long been dominated by white Protestants. Yet, some women joined the Klan to use their new voting rights to empower white women relative to black men who had earlier been formally enfranchised (Blee, 1991, 1996). Women's Klan chapters were separate from but allied with the men's Klans, eventually enlisting over a half-million women.

The second Klan began more as a sophisticated marketing scheme than an ideological campaign (Blee, 1991, 1996; Chalmers, 1981). It was designed by a couple of entrepreneurs who saw the potential for organizing a racist crusade through which they could make money by taking a share of members' dues and purchase of Klan robes, hoods, and other items. Their plan was a nearly-immediate success, with Klan groups appearing across the country and recruiting vast numbers of members through a coordinated strategy of modern marketing and public relations. Three aspects of their strategy were particularly effective in the Klan's explosive growth. One was its use of block recruiting. Instead of recruiting members by appealing to individuals, the second Klan absorbed groups of people by appealing to organizational leaders. Members of social clubs and fraternal organizations joined the Klan as a block, while the congregations of local Christian churches were swallowed into Klan chapters by the approval of their ministers. Second, the Klan's public self-presentation as an ordinary group enabled its ability to recruit large numbers of members. Despite its clear agenda of white supremacism and its calls to rid the country of blacks, Jews, Catholics, and others, the second Klan was so dominant in some communities that it was treated by white native-born Protestants as simply another club, with its activities routinely advertised and reported by local papers; it was often listed along with sewing clubs and fraternal associations in local directories (Blee, 1991). In this way, the Klan represented a social network, which an informant defined as a "friendly association"(Blee, 1991; 2001: 129). Third, the Klan employed sophisticated techniques to attract recruits, including massive public events, radio programming, and advertisements in the newspapers (often with the support of local businessmen) (Gordon, 2017). Its public events were particularly noteworthy for the time, featuring such crowd-attracting events as stunt airplanes, parachuting, beautiful (white) baby contests, parent–child sporting contests, and tents in which titillating tales of the alleged sexual depravities of Catholic priests and Jewish businessmen were recounted by alleged victims including so-called "escaped nuns" and white Protestant women whose virtue had been compromised by their Jewish employers. The Klan of the 1920s also staged enormous rallies and parades intended to bring new members as well as to terrorize its enemies. Klan members marched in large numbers down the main streets of many cities and towns and, in a particularly striking incident, paraded in formation along a main avenue in the nation's capital, Washington, D.C. Although clearly massive, the Klan's size and influence were often overstated by its leaders and supporters to intimidate mainstream politicians and those in its enemy groups as well to project an image of strength that would attract new recruits (Blee, 1991; Gordon, 2017). Moreover, the Klan's recruiting style, especially its block recruiting, meant that increases in size were often accompanied by increased group instability as many recruits had little commitment to the organization or, sometimes, even to its ideology and political agenda. As a result, their time in the Klan could be very brief.

While the Klan tried to position itself as a mainstream social organization, its agenda was explicitly that of white, native-born Protestant supremacism. Klan events combined aspects of a neighborhood block party, with bands, food, drinks, and a first aid station, with the raw politics of racial hatred, with speakers that harangued the crowd about the dangers of racial and religious minorities (Blee, 1999, 2001). In many ways, the Klan resembled a fraternal order of the 1920s, with elaborate rituals of clothing, secret passwords, oaths of commitment, and complex ceremonies that etched a firm boundary between insiders and outsiders. But the Klan's fraternal rituals were not intended solely to create solidarity among members; they were also meant to convey a sense of white Protestant power and strength to broader audiences of potential members, supporters, and victims (Blee & McDowell, 2012; MacLean, 1995; Parsons, 2005).

One strategy that the 1920s Klan used to increase its influence was a focus on electoral politics (McVeigh, 2009). Unlike the Klans that preceded and followed it, this second Klan made a major effort to win local and state political offices and to change national policies about immigration. The strategy had some success. Klan-backed candidates were successful in a number of locations, especially in the states of Indiana and Oklahoma, even at the level of the governor's seat in Indiana. Although the Klan did not seek national political office, it did rally its members and supporters to oppose the presidential candidacy of Al Smith, a Catholic, although they likely played only a minor role in Smith's defeat. More successful was the Klan's national legislative campaign to impose additional restrictions on immigration into the U.S., targeted at immigration of Catholics and Jews from southern and eastern Europe. Klan writers wrote and spoke about immigration as a moral, social, and economic menace to U.S. society, shaping a sense of white collective grievance. They also described outsiders—those not native-born and white and Protestant—as threatening U.S. interests by secretly championing the interests of outside agents. The most developed of these outsider threat narratives was the Klan's stance against Catholics claiming their loyalty to the Pope would outstrip their loyalty to the U.S. Such pronouncements, proclaimed without evidence, had a dramatic effect in the 1920s, shaping anger toward the Klan's enemy groups and mobilizing public opinion in favor of a revised policy on immigration with more restrictions and race-based quotas for immigrants.

Because the second Klan sought to wield its massive size to change public policy and assume public office, its vigilantism was less extensive and less dramatic, although still consequential for its enemies. Some members of the Klan were associated with acts of direct violence, especially lynchings, in the 1920s, but most of the violence of this second Klan took the form of threats, boycotts, and other efforts to force non-whites, immigrants, Catholics, and Jews out of their jobs and communities.

The Women's Klan was particularly effective in the 1920s Klan's new form of vigilante terrorism. Its Indiana chapters organized "poison squads of whispering

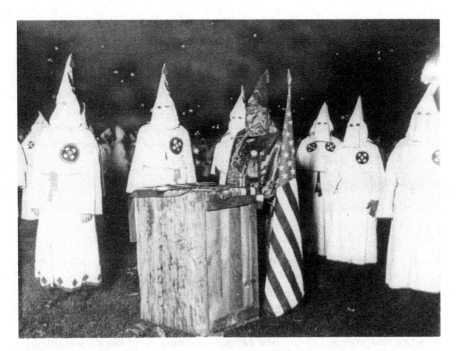

FIGURE 2.1 Ku Klux Klan night rally in Chicago around 1920 (from Library of Congress, unknown photographer).

women" who spread rumors about Jewish merchants and urged women to wield their power as consumers to boycott Jewish-owned stores, a strategy that collapsed businesses. In Blee's (1991: 147) analysis, "Organizing Klanswomen as consumers had an immediate and phenomenal effect. Businesses with Jewish owners, ranging from large department stores to small shops and professional services, went bankrupt throughout Indiana." Klanswomen also circulated rumors about Catholic schoolteachers that caused them to lose their jobs, and unfounded stories about the sexual crimes of black men that caused them to flee for their lives (Blee, 1991). Not all the efforts of the Women's Klan were aimed directly at non-white Protestants. Some also practiced what Linda Gordon (2017: 45) terms "black psywar" by distributing rumors that they attributed to Jews and Catholics to make their enemies appear unscrupulous. For example, the Denver Klan forged a document that suggested that Catholics were targeting 800 local Protestants for economic ruin (Gordon 2017). As Gordon notes, such stories could become more powerful by their lack of evidence, a common outcome of conspiratorial messages.

Unlike the first Klan whose vigilantism was exercised outside (but with the acquiescence of) the formal state because the southern states had become too weakened by the Civil War and its aftermath to ensure the foundations of white supremacy, the 1920s Klan tried to capture the state through electoral office and public pressure and enlist the formal state apparatus as an instrument for white and native-born Protestant dominance. The second Klan collapsed in the late 1920s, primarily because of internal issues that included prominent sexual and financial scandals that implicated its leaders, as well as because the introduction of national restrictions on Catholic, Jewish, and non-white immigration removed its central issue. Its collapse was also hastened by organized anti-Klan activities by Catholics, political progressives, and others who worked to expose the secret identities of Klan members and its secret plans for enacting white dominance in anti-Klan newspapers and publications and who organized mass resistance to some of its public appearances.

1950s–1960s Klan

The third Klan was largely centered in the South, like the first Klan, but it appeared in cities as well as rural areas. The impetus for its rebirth was the U.S. Civil Rights movement's success in dismantling some of the legal structure of racial segregation in schools and public accommodations in the South, known as Jim Crow laws. The Klan also built on white fear that the federal government would strengthen voting oversight and that federal courts would strike down as unconstitutional the set of laws and practices in the southern states that were enacted prevent black voting, such as literacy tests and poll taxes. Unlike the 1920s Klan, the Klans that emerged in the mid-twentieth century were largely populated by men, with women participating in the background, primarily as the wives of Klansmen (Cunningham, 2012).

The third Klan was neither as loosely organized as the first Klan, nor as bureaucratically organized as the second Klan. Rather, it existed as a set of local, state, and regional Klan organizations with rival leaders but a common agenda of racial exclusion and violence. Some were quite large: the U.S. Klans, Knights of the Ku Klux Klan formed by Eldon Edwards assembled an estimated 12,000 to 15,000 members by the late 1950s. Others were smaller but also intensely violent: members of a small Alabama Klan abducted a black man in the state, castrating him and dousing his wounds with hot turpentine (Southern Poverty Law Center, 2011). The Klan that attracted the most public attention was the highly secretive, medium-sized White Knights of Mississippi, which, among many acts of violence, was responsible for the 1964 murders of three civil rights workers, two of whom were white (Southern Poverty Law Center, 2011)

The Klans of the third era were intensely involved in vigilante violence against racial minorities, especially African Americans who they feared would dominate southern politics if they were allowed free access to voting, and those they termed civil rights "agitators," which included southern blacks and whites who sought racial equity and whites from the north who came to the South to register blacks to vote and encourage black turnout at the polls. The Klan paid less attention to migrants in this era, as there was little immigration to the southern areas in which the Klan was established although the Klan was hostile toward the relatively small number of Latino/a migrants to the South.

The third Klan's vigilantism was directly and intensely violent, using techniques that ranged from arson, murders, bombing campaigns, threats, assaults, and cross burnings to other forms of racial terror. A 1963 bombing of a church in Birmingham Alabama that killed four young black girls was long suspected to be the work of Klansmen, but only in recent years was a Klansman sentenced for this crime. In many instances in the 1950s and 1960s, Klan violence was closely coordinated with local law enforcement and judicial officers (some of whom were openly associated with the Klan, or later exposed as Klan members) who declined to arrest or prosecute Klan members for even very flagrant crimes and violence. David Cunningham (2012) suggests that in the heavily Klan-dominated state of North Carolina, the localities with larger Klan memberships were those in which the local state agencies (courts, police) were less involved in white supremacism. This indicates that the third Klan functioned as an alternative way to ensure white supremacy and racial segregation in locations in which this was perceived as changing or as less secure. This Klan thus took deepest root in areas of the South where the law was regarded by whites as no longer a reliable guarantor of white supremacy.

Although members of the third Klan participated in highly visible crimes and violence, the Klan was also integrated into and supported by the networks of mainstream white society. At times, the violence of the Klan and the power of mainstream white society worked in parallel, as when local pro-segregationist businesses, including radio shows and printing companies, supported Klan events and groups. At other times, the Klan and mainstream white society worked in complementary fashion; as when the Klan's violence was unable to prevent racial integration of southern schools, so segregationist whites simply established a parallel system of "white-flight" schools.

The vigilantism of the third Klan was in defense of a system of white supremacy that whites in the southern states supported but that was under threat from the federal government and the civil rights movement. This Klan largely collapsed in the late 1960s as the resistance of southern states to desegregation waned, in large part because of the emergence of new forms of school, residential, and political segregation through private white academies, racialized home mortgage practices by banks, and electoral districts drawn to dilute potential black electoral strength. The Klan also was eroded by significant anti-Klan resistance across the country, especially from the civil rights movement. However, as Rory McVeigh and David Cunningham (2012) find, the influence of the 1950s–1960s Klan was long enduring. Counties with strong Klans in the mid-twentieth century had higher homicide rates decades later than did counties with weak or no Klans, indicating that the Klan so effectively destroyed community life in southern localities that social disorganization lingered long after the Klan collapsed.

1970s–2000s

The Klan re-emerged as part of a surge in organized white supremacism in the late 1980s (Aho, 1990). It largely adopted the ideology of preceding Klans with two exceptions. One, it rarely espoused anti-Catholicism, and even admitted Catholic members. Two, it began to incorporate the virulent anti-Semitism associated with neo-Nazism and especially with the doctrines of Christian Identity, a pseudo-religious philosophy that argues that Jews are the literal descendants of the devil and that non-whites are nonhuman (Barkun, 1997). The fourth Klan also reinvoked the nationalism and nativism of the 1920s Klan to advance its agenda of opposition to immigrants and refugees from the countries of Africa, Asia, and Latin/Central America. Such opposition was expressed through vigilante violence, as in Klan attacks on Vietnamese fisherman working on the Gulf Coast, and immigrants from Mexico and Central America; each group was depicted as threatening the economic livelihood and future prosperity of white native born American citizens. Klan violence in the 1970s also targeted political leftists, most dramatically in a 1979 clash between the Klan and associated neo-Nazis with members of the Communist Workers Party (CWP) in North Carolina in which five CWP members were killed (Southern Poverty Law Center, 2011)

In the late 1980s and early 1990s, a number of Klans moved more underground to facilitate an agenda of terrorist violence. In the process, they made common cause with a variety of other white supremacist groups, including racist skinheads and neo-Nazis, the result of which was a modestly successful effort by several racist leaders to organize a single unified national racist movement. Although skinheads and neo-Nazis tended to deride the Klan as insufficiently aggressive in the defense of white supremacy and as an antiquated collection of older, ignorant, Southern men, a number of people who floated through the Klan and other networks of the racist right were associated with dramatic acts of racial terrorism. In the late 1980s, for example, members of the White Patriots were convicted in a plot to purchase stolen military explosives to blow up the offices of the antiracist organization, the Southern Poverty Law Center (Blee, 2002; Futrell, Simi, & Tan, 2018; Southern Poverty Law Center, 2011).

The alliance of the fourth Klan with other racist groups was not unproblematic for the racist movement. A number of neo-Nazi groups in the late twentieth century embraced a vision of global "Pan-Aryanism" that collided with the America-first nationalism of the Klan (Blee, 2003: 171). Yet, despite such differences, the Klan and other racist activists often appeared together at rallies and gatherings in this era, especially those held at the Aryan Nations headquarters in Idaho (since closed). Also, several prominent Klan leaders became Christian identity preachers, further linking them to other sectors of white supremacism.

The fourth Klan engaged in considerable vigilante violence against racial minorities and immigrants. This included symbolic violence such as cross-burnings and threats as well as violence against individuals and institutions such as community centers. Klan members also were involved in violence against the state itself, largely against the federal government, which the Klan regarded as an ally of civil rights and progressives and, for those Klan members influenced by Neo-Nazism and Christian Identity, as so dominated by Jewish elites such that it constituted a Zionist Occupation Government (ZOG) (Blee, 2002).

By the turn of the twenty-first century, the fourth Klan had become small and marginal even within white supremacism. Its demise is due to the successful efforts of anti-racist organizers and the legal strategies of anti-racist organizations such as the Southern Poverty Law Center, which bankrupted Klan chapters and cost them their property by filing civil suits on behalf of the victims of Klan violence. Its demise also reflected a general decline in the overall racist movement after the federal surveillance of the movement in the wake of the cataclysmic 1995 bombing of the federal office building in Oklahoma, as well as the Klan's inability to attract a younger and more geographically diverse membership.

Conclusion

The study of the Klan as a vigilante group provides two insights to the study of vigilantism more broadly. First, the Klan's use of rhetorical vigilantism against Catholics, Jews, and liberal northerners across much of its history suggests that non-physical violent tactics can be as consequential as physical violence in vigilantism. Further, the use of more indirect and non-physical forms of vigilantism allows racist groups to disguise their violent intentions while continuing to practice racial terrorism. Indeed, even as Klan members today are dwindling and quite incidental within modern U.S. white supremacism, Klan cross-burnings remain powerful and iconic forms of racial terrorism that send clear threatening messages to their intended targets and that inspire white supremacists more broadly (Blee, 2003; Blee, Simi, DeMichele, & Latif, 2017).

Second, the Klan's evolving vigilante strategies and targets underscore the importance of understanding how collective violence is positioned with regard to the state. With the exception of the 1920s, the Klan has maintained its hostility against the federal state as a threat to the dominance of the white southerners. In both the Klan eras of the 1870s and 1950s–1960s, it directly targeted the federal state or its agents, while perpetuating vigilante violence with the collusion of local and state-level officials; the 1920s Klan was an exception as it sought to directly influence federal policies and legislation. Vigilante movement are positioned with regard to the state in another way, as exemplified by the Klan's efforts in the 1920s and 1950s–1960s to support institutions such as schools, churches, and social institutions that would preserve a white dominant social order. In turn, such organizations further enabled racial vigilantism by channeling funds and resources to the Klan, providing them with a veneer of respectability and cover and allowing Klan members to evade state prosecution.

References

Aho, J. A. (1990). *The politics of righteousness: Idaho Christian patriotism.* Seattle: University of Washington Press.

Barkun, M. (1997). *Religion and the racist right: The origins of the Christian identity movement.* Chapel Hill: University of North Carolina Press.

Blee, K. (1991). *Women of the Klan: Racism and gender in the 1920s*. Berkeley: University of California Press.

Blee, K. (1991/ 2009). *Women of the Klan*. Berkeley: University of California Press.

Blee, K. (1996). Becoming a racist: Women in contemporary Ku Klux Klan and neo-Nazi groups. Gender & Society, 10(6), 680–702.

Blee, K. (1999). Ku Klux Klan. In N. L. Shumsky (Ed.), *The encyclopedia of urban America: The Cities and Suburbs*. New York: AFL-CIO Publishers.

Blee, K. (2001). Ku Klux Klan. In *Encyclopedia of fundamentalism*. New York and London: Routledge/Berkshire Reference Works.

Blee, K. (2002). *Inside organized racism: Women in the hate movement*. Berkeley: University of California Press.

Blee, K. (2003). Studying the enemy. In B. Glassner & R. Hertz (Eds.), *Our studies, ourselves* (pp. 13–23). New York: Oxford University Press.

Blee, K. (2012). Does gender matter in the United States far right. Politics, Religion & Ideology, 13(2), 253–265.

Blee, K., & McDowell, A. (2012). Social movement audiences. *Sociological Forum*, 27(1), 1–20.

Blee, K., Simi, P., DeMichele, M., & Latif, M. (2017). How racial violence is provoked and channeled. *Socio*, 9, 257–276.

Bryant, J. (2002). The Ku Klux Klan in the reconstruction era. In *New Georgia encyclopedia*. www.georgiaencyclopedia.org/articles/history-archaeology/ku-klux-klan-reconstruction-era.

Chalmers, D. M. (1981). *Hooded Americanism: The history of the Ku Klux Klan*. Chapel Hill: Duke University Press.

Cunningham, D. (2012). *Klansville, U.S.A.: The rise and fall of the civil rights-era Ku Klux Klan*. New York: Oxford University Press.

Futrell, R., Simi, P., & Tan, A. (2018). Political extremism and social movements. In D. A. Snow, S. A. Soule, H. Kriesi, & H. McCammon (Eds.), *The Wiley Blackwell companion to social movements*. Hoboken: Wiley.

Gordon, L. (2017). *The second coming of the KKK: The Ku Klux Klan of the 1920s and the American political landscape*. New York, London: Liveright Publishing Corporation.

Jackson, K. T. (1967). *The Ku Klux Klan in the city, 1915–1930*. New York: Oxford University Press.

MacLean, N. (1995). *Behind the mask of chivalry: The making of the second Ku Klux Klan*. New York: Oxford University Press.

McVeigh, R. (2009). *The rise of the Ku Klux Klan: Right-wing movements and national politics*. Minneapolis: University of Minnesota Press.

McVeigh, R., & Cunningham, D. (2012). Enduring consequences of right-wing extremism: Klan mobilization and homicides in southern counties. Social Forces, 90(3), 843–862.

Parsons, E. F. (2005). Midnight rangers: Costume and performance in the reconstruction-era Ku Klux Klan. *The Journal of American History*, 92(3), 811–836.

Southern Poverty Law Center. (2011). *Ku Klux Klan: A history of racism*. Montgomery, AL: Southern Poverty Law Center. https://www.splcenter.org/20110228/ku-klux-klan-history-racism.

Tolnay, S. E., & Beck, E. M. (1995). *A festival of violence: An analysis of Southern lynchings, 1882–1930*. Urbana: University of Illinois Press.

Wright, G. C. (1985). *Life behind a veil: Blacks in Louisville, Kentucky, 1865–1930*. Baton Rouge: Louisiana State University Press.

3

JEWISH VIGILANTISM IN THE WEST BANK

Nir Gazit

Introduction

On 29 August 2017, a group of Israeli settlers threw rocks and glass bottles at Palestinian homes in the area of Um al-Khair, east of the city of Yatta in the occupied West Bank. A Palestinian peasant, Suleiman Hathalin, said that he and his family were regularly attacked by the settlers from the nearby settlement of Carmel, who try to push them out of their land in order to seize it and expand their settlement.[1] Five months earlier, on 20 April 2017, a group of masked settlers attacked activists assisting Palestinians in the occupied West Bank near the Baladim settler outpost. Sarit Michaeli of Israeli human rights group B'Tselem said that about a dozen activists from the group Taayush – an Israeli and Palestinian non-violent direct action group – were accompanying Palestinian shepherds when they came under an "unprovoked" attack.[2] On 17 June 2017, settlers from Yitzhar, a radical West Bank settlement, called the army for help after a fellow settler suffered from dehydration.[3] According to the army, the ambulance came to Yitzhar "at the request of residents, to grant medical treatment. Afterwards, at the exit from Yitzhar, residents threw stones at the [military] ambulance, damaging its windshield."

Such illegal attacks take place almost on a daily basis in the West Bank, and range from acts of vandalism against Palestinian private property to brutal physical attacks that involve stone throwing and arson of Palestinian property. In addition, from time to time, Jewish vigilantes also target Israeli security forces that are deployed in the West Bank. While the raison d'être of the soldiers is to protect the settlers, they are occasionally attacked by the latter when they try to demolish illegal settler outposts or when they demonstrate a "soft hand" towards the Palestinians.

A previous article (Gazit 2015) discussed the political significance of the Jewish settlers' violence and the relationship between vigilantism, the state and other forms of political violence in the Occupied Palestinian Territories.[4] In the present chapter, I wish to outline in more details the characteristics of the Jewish vigilantism in the West Bank with a special emphasis on its various ideological and organizational features. The analysis would emphasize the diverse patterns of this phenomenon and the various agendas behind it.

As recently claimed by Moncada (2017: 404), within research on vigilantism, scholars often use varied conceptualizations without explaining how and why their constructs deviate from other variants. "This tendency might hinder our ability to reconcile findings across studies and, in turn, constrains our ability to advance knowledge regarding the relationship between vigilantism and a range of broader concerns, including state–society relations, crime and order" (ibid.). However, the magnitude and diversity of this phenomenon across time and place demand a more flexible conceptualization that would allow us to reveal the strong relationships between vigilantism and other forms of political violent mobilization.

Vigilantism is often conceptualized as a collective use or threat of violence by civilians that act "in the lieu of justice" (Caughey, 1957, p. 219) to impose a desirable moral order (see also: Abrahams, 1998; Brown, 1975; Pratten and Sen, 2008; Weisburd and Vinitzky, 1984). This definition, essentially interprets vigilantism as a mechanism of social control. But even vigilante groups that appear to be constituted primarily to maintain a desirable moral order often have political or economic agendas that in reality overshadow their concerns with problems of crime and disorder (Weisburd 1988: 139). Hence, vigilantism often extends social control and crime control and enters more political domains.

Using an individual act of vigilantism as a unit of analysis may help disclose the nature and scope of the varieties of vigilantism and ameliorate its definition (Moncada 2017: 416). The case of the Jewish vigilantism in the West Bank seems especially apposite for such an endeavour. Although this case takes place in unique historical and political circumstances of a prolonged military occupation, which might limit possible generalizations to other cases, the different patterns of the Jewish vigilantism make this case relevant beyond the limits of the particular Israeli case. As I shall demonstrate, the Jewish vigilantism takes many forms and is characterized by different levels of organization. While some of the vigilante activities in the West Bank are carried by loosely organized anti-establishment groups, other groups are much more organized and have strong relations with state authorities and political parties. Hence, even the general label "Jewish vigilantism" seems somewhat misleading given the diversity of this phenomenon.

It should be noted that given the unique political circumstances in the West Bank, the present analysis focuses only on Jewish vigilante activity in the occupied territories and not on similar phenomena that may take place in Israel.[5]

Methodology

Data for this research was obtained from various sources. Information on the frequency of the civilian violence come from Hebrew and English newspapers and research reports on the West Bank. It is important to note that this information is partial since many of the events are not documented by either official authorities or the media. Human rights organizations' reports (i.e. B'Tselem and Yesh Din) and UN agencies (i.e. OCHA – United Nations Office for the Coordination of Humanitarian Affairs) serve as substitutes as they supply reliable data on the magnitude of the phenomenon.[6]

In addition, I interviewed 71 Israeli soldiers and 30 Jewish settlers in the West Bank, between June 2004 and January 2006, November 2011, and throughout 2017. The interviews were conducted in Hebrew and English. They ranged from 45 minutes to three hours and occasionally continued over multiple sessions. Respondents were identified through a snowball sampling technique and during on-site observations. Their narratives uncover the motives of attackers and their interpretations regarding their violent activities. In addition, I also reviewed relevant internet sites that include movements' webpages and open access Facebook groups.

The analysis is mainly concentrated on the side of the Jewish settlers and Israeli soldiers. However, it also draws on testimonies of Palestinians collected by secondary sources, such as human rights organizations and Palestinian media.

Political and legal contexts

The political context of the Jewish settlers' violence is the Israeli prolonged military occupation of the West Bank. Since 1967, and particularly since the Oslo Accords (1993) between Israel and the Palestinian Liberation Organization (PLO), the Israeli occupation has been conducted in a framework of structural constraints that have maintained its under-institutionalized character (Gazit 2009, 2015). Israel has made no final decision regarding the political status of the Occupied Palestinian Territories; it neither annexed them nor declared its temporal rule there. This has generated a very complex, not to say a chaotic socio-political and legal environment – a "void of sovereignty" – a political order based on "illegality under the cover of legality", and on a wide interpretive space regarding what is "legal" and what is "not legal" – a situation that invites mechanisms of alternative extrajudicial political power (Gazit 2015).

According to international law, the Israeli control over these territories is defined as a "military occupation" and treated as temporary until "a just and lasting peace in the Middle-East" will allow a withdrawal of Israel's armed forces (Benvenisti, 2012; Kretzmer, 2002). Yet, since 1967, Israel has established over 130 Jewish settlements in the West Bank, appropriated Palestinians' lands and suppressed the Palestinian population (Zertal and Eldar, 2009). While most of these settlements were sponsored by the Israeli government and de facto enjoy a legitimate status in by the Israeli state, there are also dozens of "illegal outposts" [*ma'achazim*] – unauthorized small settlements that are built on Palestinian land and mainly inhabited by radical Jewish youth.[7]

Since 1995, and as a result of the Oslo Accords, the West Bank has been officially divided into three regional jurisdictions: Areas A and B (under Palestinian control) and area C (under Israeli control). About 400,000 Jewish settlers living in Area C (which constitutes about 60% of the West Bank with about 120,000 Palestinians (4% of the total Palestinian population in the West Bank).[8] While the Palestinians who reside in Area C are subjects of Israeli military law, the settlers, as citizens of the Israeli state, are subject to Israeli civilian law, although officially the "sovereign" in the West Bank is the commander of the IDF (Israeli Defence Forces) central command. Hence, in addition to the ambiguity around the international legal status of the occupied territories, it is also not clear what kind of legal system is active in these territories, is it the Israeli state law or the Israeli martial law.

The debate over the political status of the territories occupied by Israel in the 1967 Six-Day War, the Israeli policy vis-à-vis the Palestinians, and the legitimacy of the Jewish settlements, stand at core of the Israeli political discourse (Erlich, 1993). It also shapes the strained relationship between the Jewish settlers and the Israeli government. The Israeli government has always considered the settlements in the West Bank to be an important ingredient of the Israeli "Territorial Defence", against threats from the east (i.e. Jordan, Iraq, and Iran). Consequently, both right-wing and left-wing Israeli governments have subsidized most of the settlements since the late 1970s. In addition, right-wing parties consider the settlers an important political base (Zertal and Eldar, 2009). At the same time, the need to protect the settlements creates a security burden for the Israeli military, and thus torn the Israeli public.

The Israeli government's abstention from a formal annexation of the West Bank has fostered the settlers' revolutionary impulse and political activism (Feige, 2009; Zertal and Eldar, 2009 During peace negotiations with the Palestinians and when Israel shows willingness to remove settlements, the relationship between the Jewish settlers and the Israeli government turn conflictual. Moreover, when such ideas have been implemented (i.e. the withdrawal from northern Sinai in 1982 and the implementation of the Disengagement Plan in the Gaza Strip in 2005), or when the Israeli High Court has ruled against the illegal settlements, the settler violence also targets Israeli forces in the West Bank (Gazit, 2015).

At the same time, the Israeli government works in collusion with the violent settlers on different levels. First, the government tolerates illegal settlements and considers them an extension of the Israeli policy. This is done informally so as to bypass both international criticism and Israeli official regulations.[9] Second, and an extension of the first, the government's ground-level forces turn a blind eye on settler violence against Palestinians and occasionally even participate in it.

Similarly, the settlers have an ambivalent position vis-à-vis the Israeli state. On the one hand, the mainstream settlers are strongly integrated in the Israeli polity. They serve in the Israeli military, dominant in the government's bureaucracy, and their party, the Jewish Home –Habait Ha'Yehudi, is often part of the ruling coalition. Yet, the more marginal settlers' groups are much more critical of the, in their view, hesitated policy of the Israeli governments. This ambivalence is evident in the ideological and political agendas of the Jewish vigilantes.

Ideological and political agendas

The general stated purpose and justification for the Jewish vigilantes is threefold and combine security, political, and religious agendas. Security-wise, their activities are meant to increase the protection of the Jewish settlements and roads in the West Bank. Many of the settlers are dissatisfied by the quality level of security provided by the Israeli military and the soldiers' "soft hand" when treating the Palestinians. Many of them feel the military must do more in order to deter the Palestinians and increase the security of the Jewish settlers, as one of my interviewees explained:

> The soldiers do the best they can [protecting the settlements] but we believe the army should do more. [It should] be more assertive. Many times we find ourselves stand alone when Arabs get too close to the settlement. We won't wait for the soldiers to come and do nothing. We will take care of it ourselves. They [the Palestinian trespassers] know they should not have any business with us. When *we* act, they learn their lesson.

Yet, the main justification for their operation is politically framed; the need to demonstrate Jewish dominancy and Israeli sovereignty in the West Bank, or in what they term *"Judea and Samaria"*. This is especially evident in locations of intense friction between Israeli settlers and Palestinians, for example in the mixed city of Hebron. In Hebron Jewish vigilantes often penetrate the exclusively Palestinian neighbourhoods and drag the soldiers in to settle disputes. These provocations blur the official boundary between the two districts. This dynamic may be termed "spatial vigilantism", as the settlers' violent campaigns work as a mechanism of spatial and political deviation that extends the domain of Israeli effective control into new territories, even for a limited period of time (Gazit, 2015). An officer I interviewed revealed how this process takes place in Hebron:

> They [the settlers] go wherever they want, as if there are no no-go zones. It is like a childish chase game. Sometimes they are Jewish kids that like to tease the Palestinian locals but sometimes they are adult men and women who play these games. This is a real headache for us because we need to make sure they don't do much damage and at the same time we need to protect them when they enter Palestinian territory. Yet they do it on purpose to make a point that this is their city. All of it.

The informal cooperation between the Jewish settlers and the Israeli rule in the West Bank is based on the Zionist ideology and especially on religious interpretation of Zionism which considers the occupied territories an integral part of the biblical Land of Israel (*"Eretz Israel"*) (Aran, 1986, 2013). According to this ideology, the implementation of practical Zionism in settlement is simultaneously rooted in mainstream classical Zionist thought (Jamal, 2017) and simultaneously based on theological ideas of Jewish messianism. This ideological mixture is characterized by a revolutionary impulse and anti-establishment attitude that permits and even encourages informal political activity, which transcends institutional and legal limitations. These sentiments are actualized in the establishment of unauthorized settlements in remote places in the West Bank, in frequent clashes with the Israeli security forces, and in anti-Palestinian violence.

The religious motivation of the Jewish vigilantism has a special importance among the more radical vigilantes. Most if not all of the vigilantes in the West Bank are orthodox Jews, and the Jewish law of Halacha is important in giving justification for anti-Palestinian violence. While most settlers in the West Bank combine between religious beliefs and modern Zionism, the interpretation of some groups (i.e. the Hilltop Youth) is more radical and messianic. These groups often position themselves against the Israeli state and its authority and even use anti-Zionist rhetoric.[10]

Religious leaders play a key role in fostering these ideas. Rabbi Yitzchak Ginsburgh, for example, head of yeshiva *Od Yosef Chai* [11], often use concepts taken from Jewish mystic texts (such as Kabbalah) to justify contemporary radical activities. For example, he and his students support the idea of Jewish monarchy in the Land of Israel, oppose efforts to remove Jewish settlement from the West Bank, and encourage followers to attempt to dissuade soldiers and police officers from carrying out evacuations (Inbari 2009). Although Rabbi Ginsburgh does not directly promote violence, he received widespread criticism for his article "*Baruch Hagever*" (in English: "Baruch the Man" or "Baruch the Hero") in which he praised Baruch Goldstein who had massacred 29 Palestinian worshippers at the Cave of Patriarchs in Hebron in 1994.

Other rabbis, such as Yitzhak Shapira, Rabbi Ginsburgh's student, and Rabbi Yosef Elitzur, are more explicit in their support of anti-Palestinian vigilantism. Those two religious leaders published the book *Torat Ha'Melech* (in English: "The King's Torah"), which is a rabbinic instruction manual that outlines acceptable scenarios for killing non-Jews. In 2010, Shapira was arrested on suspicion of incitement to violence against non-Jews.[12] Israeli police investigated but made no arrests. In 2013, a month after the book's release, Rabbi Elitzur wrote an article in a religious bulletin saying that "the Jews will never win without [using] violence against the Arabs."[13] Again, while this extreme ideology is rejected by the majority of mainstream settlers and their institutional leadership, occasionally we can hear echoes of legitimation to Jewish vigilantism in right-wing and mainstream media.[14]

Who are the Jewish vigilantes in the West Bank?

The settlers in the West Bank are a heterogeneous population. The majority lives in the larger urban settlements (e.g. Ariel, Alfei Menashe, and Ma'ale Edomim) and consider themselves to be an integral part of Israeli mainstream society; they are not the ones actively involved in anti-Palestinian violence. By contrast, settlers who live in smaller, more isolated and ideological settlements, including the unauthorized outposts outside existing settlements (often referred to as *Noar Ha'Gvaot*, Hilltop Youth), are more politically radical and inclined to take part in violent activities against Palestinians and occasionally also against Israeli soldiers and policemen (Friedman, 2017).

We should differentiate between several groups of vigilantes in the West Bank, according to their level of organization and relations with the Israeli authorities:

The most organized and institutionalized are the settlements' defence squads ('*Kitot Konenut*'). These militias exist in most of the Jewish settlements and are organized, trained and armed by the IDF, as emergency response teams in case of Palestinian attacks (Vainer, 2005). They are mostly commanded by former IDF officers that often continue their military service in reserves. While these groups are the most passive in their interaction with the Palestinians, they often initiate violent friction by creating informal block roads and direct clashes with Palestinian shepherds and peasants.

Asymmetrical power balances characterize the figuration between these militias and the soldiers. Most of soldiers guarding the isolated settlements are temporarily separated from their organic military unit and the local civilian security officer often act as their direct supervisor. As a result, a reversed modality of patronage is created, in which the soldiers are subject to their civilian patrons (i.e. the settlers). The fact that some settlers are IDF officers in reserves strengthens the legitimacy of their patronage over rank-and-file soldiers, and thus encourages some soldiers to participate in their vigilante activities.

The second type of vigilantes is of those who belong to radical right groups such as "*Lehava*"[15] (in English: A Tongue of Fire) and remaining factions of past right-wing groups (that officially came apart because of they were declared illegal) such as "*Kach*" and "*Kahane Chai*".[16] These groups are believed to have an overlapping core membership of about 500 people. They are founded on Jewish supremacy ideas, radical anti-Arab sentiments, and racism, in the legacy of Rabbi Meir Kahane.[17] While they oppose Israeli mainstream politics, they do have informal cooperation with radical right-wing political parties, such as "*Otzma Yehudith*" (in English: Jewish Strength) and a faction of the coalition party the Jewish Home. The declared goals of these groups are preventing assimilation of Jews and Arabs in the Holy Land and oppose the presence of Christianity in Israel. While their main activity is in Israel, they are also active in Jerusalem and Hebron.

The less organized groups of Jewish vigilantes in the West Bank are those who are often tagged as the "*Noar Ha'Gvaot*" (in English: Hilltop Youth). Those are religious-nationalist teenagers and young adults who establish outposts without a formal authorization from the Israeli government. According to the ideology of the hilltop youth, the Palestinians are "raping the Holy Land", and thus must be expelled. The term "hilltop youth" is regarded by Daniel Byman (2011) as a misnomer, since the movement was founded mostly by married people in their mid-twenties. However, in recent years these groups mostly comprise marginal young people, some of them teenagers, who live in the more radical settlements (e.g. Itzhar and Tapuah) and in the illegal outposts such as Havat Gillad. These groups

50 Nir Gazit

are the most active in initiating anti-Palestinian violent attacks and in violent clashes with the Israeli security forces in the West Bank. Their numbers are estimated to be around 800, with approximately 5,000 others who share their ideological outlook. Many of the hilltop youth activists feel that the mainstream settler movement has lost its way (ibid.). Hence, they present themselves as more loyal to the political and theological ideology of Greater Israel (*Eretz-Israel Ha'shlema*).

Patterns of activity

The settlers' violent activities take many forms and range from blocking roads and acts of vandalism in Palestinian markets to violent attacks, such as arson of Palestinian fields, throwing Molotov cocktail at cars and houses, and beating. Rarely, they also include acts of manslaughter.[18]

The patterns of the Jewish vigilantism in the West Bank vary according to the various groups' agendas. The settlements' defence squads, which often maintain closer relationships and coordination with the IDF, usually restrict their activities to the outskirts of their settlements. When they attack or harass Palestinians, by blocking roads or damaging Palestinian property, these actions are usually framed as "active defence" (*Hagana Aktivit*) or acts of "retaliation and deterrence" (*Tguva Ve'Hartaa*). These acts usually develop in frontier zones and peripheral locations, both geographically and politically (Gazit, 2015). In such places, the state's institutional control is relatively weak, fostering alternative mechanisms of social control (Johnston, 1996). In the West Bank, the settlers' attacks usually take place in remote places in Area C, which according to the Oslo agreement is under Israeli jurisdiction. Over 90 per cent of all Palestinian villages that have experienced multiple instances of Israeli settler violence are located in those areas (Munayyer, 2012). Most severe attacks take place in geographically isolated areas where the military presence is scarce and where most radical settlements and unauthorized outposts are located – for example, in South Mt. Hebron and in the northern West Bank. In some remote and isolated settlements, where small groups of soldiers are stationed inside the settlements, soldiers and settlers often patrol the area together, and occasionally the soldiers are informally involved in the vigilante activity. A reserve solider stationed in an isolated settlement in Mt. Hebron area described this dynamic:

> It was really one big lawless place (*beit zonot*). Our officer commander rarely visited us there and we had great relationships with the settlers. We were like that [the interviewee crosses his fingers]. We visited their homes. We ate together. So, if [Palestinian] shepherds crossed in, it was obvious we would kick them away. Yes, we often did it together.

Such attacks usually take place in response to what the settlers consider "Palestinian provocation", for example when the Palestinian grazing their herds too close to the settlement, or in response to Palestinian attacks.

Many of such Jewish vigilantes are armed and often partially wear IDF uniform (e.g. military boots or pants). Thus, it may not be easy for the untrained eye to distinguish between them and the soldiers. Although the settlers are not official agents of the Israeli state, both the military and, presumably, the Palestinians consider them to be acting as state-agents in the West Bank. As a result, they contribute to the manifestation of the Israeli power in the West Bank, even if their original motivation is to promote what at times is represented as their sectional political interests.

Acts of retaliation are more frequent by more radical settlers that use violent clashes with the Palestinians to demonstrate Jewish dominancy in the West Bank. For example, after a group of teenage Jewish hikers were attacked by Palestinians near the village of Qusra in the West Bank, activists of the radical right-wing party "*Otzama Yehudit*" arrived at the scene to provoke violence and "demonstrate Jewish presence".[19] Although members of such parties and organizations are often involved in these activities, they are not always formally initiated by these movements but carried out spontaneously by their supporters. For example, in Hebron, activities such as graffiti writing on Palestinians' shops, vandalism and physical harassment are done almost on a daily basis by local settlers who are associated with these political movements and their ideological milieu.

A more organized activity is that of *Lehava* movement. The organization has a permanent booth that is manned in the centre of Jerusalem every Thursday night. The activists use the booth to spread their messages, to recruit new supporters, and to deter Arab presence in "Jewish Jerusalem". Occasionally, they also march the avenue nearby, wearing black shirts with their logo, waving Israeli flags and the movement's banners, and shouting racist slogans. From time to time, they also verbally intimidate and physically abuse random Arab victims they come across during their marches. The movement also has an internet website it uses to disseminate its ideology and to report its activities.[20]

The activities of the Hilltop Youth, which tend to be the most violent, are also the most subversive. The Hilltop Youth is an informal epithet to loosely organized groups of young males (and occasionally females) roaming the West Bank. While some of these groups are informally sponsored by older radical settlers that host them in their homes, others do not have any senior leadership and are comprised of a band of about a dozen members that may perish after a certain time. The hostility to the Israeli establishment and its agents is only second to their hatred to the Palestinian Arabs in the West Bank, and a result of their suspicion and anti-establishment spirit they seek to remain underground. They rarely use phones (and especially smartphones) to communicate. Their symbolic identifying marks are long and wild sideburns and large yarmulkes. Their sloppy attire signifies their anti-materialist ideological devotion.

In parallel to their anti-Palestinian activity, they also seek to ridicule the Israeli authorities. Being arrested for questioning by the Israeli security agencies is considered a badge of honour. This hostility also echoes in the soldiers' and Israeli politicians' narratives who describe the Hilltop Youth as Jewish terrorists.[21] This labelling has triggered some of the activists to go out of the shadows and allow mainstream media to cover some of their non-violent activities.[22] Recently, they also opened an open Facebook page by the name "Hilltop Youth – A closer acquaintance" to gain wider public support.

Despite these efforts, the Hilltop Youth are notoriously known for their violent attacks against Palestinian civilians and property. In parallel to the establishment of unauthorized outposts in Palestinian densely populated areas and playing hide-and-seek with the soldiers, activists linked to these groups have been accused of engaging in vandalism of Palestinian schools[23] and mosques,[24] the rustling of sheep from Palestinian flocks and the extirpation of olive groves, or stealing their olive harvests. Their activities are mostly associated with the *Price Tag* slogan due to the graffiti they usually leave behind after they attack.

Conclusion

The ambiguity surrounding the formal status of the Israeli state in the OTP creates a governmental void. This void is filled, inter alia, by greater freedom of action of the settlers, who, in effect, act as informal agents of the state, behaving as vigilantes and taking the law into their own hands.

Since the end of the second Intifada, the Palestinian uprising in 2005, there has been a proliferation of Jewish violent attacks against Palestinian civilians and property and in the number of Palestinian casualties of Jewish civilian violence (Gazit 2015). This increase ran parallel to a significant decline in the level of Israeli military violence, in a period when no large-scale operation was carried out by IDF forces in the West Bank. These trends, although not statistically significant, suggest a correlation between the two forms of Israeli violence – institutional military violence and non-institutional civilian violence. In times and places of low military presence and violence, unofficial civilian political mechanisms come into play. These reproduce Israeli dominance through direct violence or through initiating Palestinian hostility resulting in provisional active military involvement.

The collusion of the official Israeli control system in the West Bank and the mundane vigilantism that is carried out by civilian settlers partly explain the relative tolerance of the Israeli state to this phenomenon. While civilian violence is often characterized as a force that challenges state monopoly over the legitimate use of violent means, in our case the Israeli state seems to compromise its monopoly in favour of alternative sources of power, compensating for its lack of ability to base its rule on official and legitimate political institutions.

However, this policy comes with a price. In parallel to settler militias that are more controlled by the state, and thus more restricted in their violent activities, other more radical vigilante groups in the West Bank also develop. Such groups are not only more violently extreme but also develop an anti-establishment ethos and thus do not hesitate to clash with the Israeli security force to advance their agendas. Hence, while the Jewish vigilantism in the West Bank has many forms and faces and

Jewish vigilantism in the West Bank **53**

each group seems to have a unique character, they are certainly connected. One cannot discuss the activities on any of the groups without examining the wider political context in which these activities take place. Consequently, it seems that we should a more contextual analysis of contemporary vigilantism, which would not only illuminate its diversity but also enable us to disclose the interconnection between various expressions.

Notes

1 http://www.maannews.com/Content.aspx?id=778906.
2 http://www.aljazeera.com/news/2017/04/israeli-settlers-attack-activists-west-bank-170 421172750896.html.
3 https://www.timesofisrael.com/yitzhar-residents-stone-army-ambulance-called-to-settle ment/.
4 In the Israeli political discourse, this phenomenon is often referred to as "Price Tag" activities. This tag is somewhat misleading as it neglects the differences between the violent activities that take place in Israel and the attacks in the West Bank. Here, I will concentrate mainly on the vigilante activities in the West Bank.
5 Interestingly, in recent years we witness first signs of vigilante organization in Israel. An example is the organization *HaShomer HaChadsah* (the "New Gourd") that mainly focuses on protecting agricultural property and land in Israel.
6 For more information on scale and magnitude of the phenomena, see Gazit 2015.
7 http://www.pmo.gov.il/SiteCollectionDocuments/PMO/Communication/Spokesma n/sason2.pdf (in Hebrew).
8 https://www.cia.gov/library/publications/the-world-factbook/geos/we.html.
9 http://www.pmo.gov.il/SiteCollectionDocuments/PMO/Communication/Spokesman /sason2.pdf (in Hebrew).
10 https://www.youtube.com/watch?v=BLrojKbmp9I (in Hebrew).
11 Yeshiva is a Jewish institution that focuses on the study of traditional religious texts. Od Yosef Chai is a yeshiva situated in the West Bank settlement of Yitzhar, which is considered as one of the radical strongholds of the settlement movement.
12 https://www.ynetnews.com/articles/0,7340,L-3925115,00.html
13 https://www.inn.co.il/News/News.aspx/348453.
14 https://www.timesofisrael.com/rights-group-calls-for-investigation-of-tv-host-for-incitem ent/.
15 https://leava.co.il/.
16 Kach was a radical orthodox movement that was established and lead by Rabi Meir Kahane. The movement existed between 1971 and 1994, when it decaled illegal by the Israeli authorities. In 1968, Kahane established the American Jewish vigilante group the Jewish Defense League (JDL) to protect Jews from local manifestations of anti-Semitism. The vigilante ethos of these past organization still lives in the new movement of Lahava.
17 https://forward.com/news/breaking-news/211725/racist-jewish-group-offers-dilemma -to-israel-as-an/.
18 https://www.haaretz.com/israel-news/1.709792.
19 https://www.makorrishon.co.il/nrg/online/1/ART2/537/781.html.
20 https://leava.co.il/.
21 https://www.makorrishon.co.il/nrg/online/1/ART2/316/196.html.
22 https://www.youtube.com/watch?v=BLrojKbmp9I.
23 Tovah Lazroff (21 October 2010). "Palestinians blame 'hilltop youth' for school arson". The Jerusalem Post. Retrieved 11 January 2012.
24 https://www.haaretz.com/1.5219163.

References

Abrahams, R. (1998). *Vigilant citizens: Vigilantism and the state.* New York: Polity Press.

Aran, G. (1986). From religious Zionism to Zionist religion: The roots of Gush Emunim. *Studies in Contemporary Jewry,* 2, 116–143.

Aran, G. (2013). *Kookism: The roots of Gush Emunim, settler culture, Zionist theology, and contemporary messianism.* Jerusalem: Carmel Publishers.

Benvenisti, E. (2012). *The international law of occupation.* Oxford: Oxford University Press.

Brown, R. M. (1975). *Strain of violence: Historical studies of American violence and vigilantism.* New York: Oxford University Press.

Byman, D. (2011). *A high price: The triumphs and failures of Israeli counterterrorism.* New York: Oxford University Press.

Caughey, J.W. (1957). Their majesties the mob: Vigilantes past and present. *Pacific Historical Review,* 26, 217–234.

Erlich, A. (1993). *Israeli society: Critical perspectives.* Tel Aviv: Breirot Publishers, 253–274.

Feige, M. (2009). *Settling in the hearts: Jewish fundamentalism in the Occupied Territories.* Detroit, MI: Wayne State University Press.

Friedman, S. (2017). *The hilltop youth: A stage of resistance and counter culture practice.* London: Lexington Books.

Gazit, N. (2009). Social agency, spatial practices, and power: The micro-foundations of fragmented sovereignty in the occupied territories. *International Journal of Politics, Culture, and Society,* 22(1), 83–103.

Gazit, N. (2015). State-sponsored vigilantism: Jewish settlers' violence in the Occupied Palestinian Territories. *Sociology,* 49(3), 438–454.

Inbari, M. (2009). *Jewish fundamentalism and the Temple Mount: Who will build the Third Temple?* Albany: SUNY Press.

Jamal, A. (2017). Neo-Zionism and Palestine: The unveiling of settler-colonial practices in mainstream Zionism. *Journal of Holy Land and Palestine Studies,* 16(1), 47–78.

Johnston, L. (1996). What is vigilantism? *British Journal of Criminology,* 36(2), 220–236.

Kretzmer, D. (2002). *The occupation of justice: the supreme court of Israel and the Occupied Territories.* Albany: State University of New York Press.

Moncada, E. (2017). Varieties of vigilantism: Conceptual discord, meaning and strategies. *Global Crime,* 18(4) , 403–423.

Munayyer, Y. (2012). *When settlers attack.* The Palestinian Center. Retrieved from http://www.theje-rusalemfund.org/ht/a/GetDocumentAction/i/32678.

Pratten, D., and Sen, A. (2008). *Global vigilantes.* London: Hurst.

Vainer, A. (2005). *Permanent temporariness or temporary permanence? The organization and action of the territorial security system of the Sameria settlements.* MA thesis, Jerusalem: The Hebrew University of Jerusalem.

Weisburd, D. (1988). Vigilantism as community social control: Developing a quantitative criminological model. *Journal of Quantitative Criminology,* 4(2),137–153.

Weisburd, D., and Vinitzky, V. (1984). Vigilantism as rational social control: The case of the Gush Emunim settlers. *Political Anthropology,* 4, 69–87.

Zertal, I., and Eldar, A. (2009). *Lords of the land.* Philadelphia, PA: Nation Books.

4

PROTECTING HOLY COWS

Hindu vigilantism against Muslims in India

Juhi Ahuja

Introduction

On 28 September 2015, a Muslim man named Mohammed Akhlaq and his son Danish were brutally attacked by a Hindu mob in their home in Dadri, Uttar Pradesh, India. The mob, which beat up both father and son with sticks and bricks, accused them of storing and consuming beef. As they had no way of proving otherwise, the violent episode resulted in the unfortunate death of Akhlaq. Danish was seriously injured. Despite the family's pleas that the meat in question was actually goat meat, not beef, the police sent samples to a laboratory for testing. It indeed turned out that the meat was mutton, not beef. Several individuals were arrested for the crime, to which local villagers protested. At least two of the arrested were affiliated to the local village temple, and at least one was linked to the ruling Bharatiya Janata Party (BJP) (Huffpost 2017).

The aftermath of the incident was deeply politicized in a climate already fraught with inter-communal tensions and politics. Media coverage of the attack was widespread and stoked religious sentiments. National and local political parties were quick to capitalize on the attack as politicians visited the home of Akhlaq's family – all of which was reported on and even televised. Despite the arrests made, little was done to allay the fears of Muslims who form India's largest religious minority group. Given the local authorities' delayed treatment of the attack (police were rather slow to respond) and determination to verify the type of meat, it seems almost as if should the meat indeed have been beef, the crime committed against Akhlaq and Danish may not have been treated by the state as too severe or reprehensible. Even though the slaughtering of cows is banned in the state of Uttar Pradesh, the lynching of Akhlaq and Danish by vigilantes is certainly not justified by any means. The targeting of Muslims by some sections of the Hindu community raises critical questions of the state of majority-minority religious and communal relations in India. It also raises concerns about rising incidents of vigilantism in the name of religion.

The abovementioned incident of Hindu vigilantism against Muslims is one of many that have occurred since 2014. This chapter aims to delineate the modern phenomenon of Hindu vigilantism in India and explain the socio-political context in which it is able to take root and life. It is able to manifest in India because of the intermingling of (1) the rising influence of *Hindutva*; and (2) growing inter-religious and inter-caste intolerance. Placing Hindu vigilantism in the context of the wider academic study of vigilantism, I argue that Hindu vigilantism against Muslims in India is expressed most commonly in the public sphere in the form of "cow vigilantism". Cow vigilantism, which will be explained in detail below, is the policing of behaviour by Hindu nationalists against non-Hindus (mostly Muslims) in the name of protecting cows, which they consider sacred. It is not, however, within the scope of this chapter to discuss ongoing debates about the sanctity of the cow in Hindu traditions, both historically and in contemporary times.[1]

Given existing contestations surrounding the legality of vigilante activity within definitions of vigilantism, this chapter does not purport that Hindu vigilantism is or is not extra-legal or illegal. Instead it highlights the context within which it is able to take place and proliferate. Tacit support from the BJP and its affiliates is illustrated by their glaring support for *Gau Raksha Dals* or cow protection committees, and lack of a clear public commitment by its elites in addressing cow vigilantism. The analyses provided in this chapter brings to the fore how the relationship between the state and civil-society creates space for vigilantism and other forms of political violence.

The observations and analyses are based on media reports, case studies, and scholarly articles (few, as this is an under-studied phenomenon).

Setting the context

The study of vigilantism in India had received little attention as a phenomenon per se by both academia and mainstream media before Narendra Modi's ascension to power as Prime Minister in 2014. Destructive episodes in the public sphere tended to be defined and analysed in terms of inter-communal violence, mob violence, riots, and terrorism – by academics and the media alike. Although such incidents obviously still occur and should be defined as such, vigilante activity carried out in the name of Hinduism is on the rise.[2] It is "Hindu vigilantism" precisely because groups of civilian Hindus attempt to forcefully police certain activities and practices of Muslims (and Dalits), who form the largest religious minority in India.[3] As will be explained further below, this vigilantism is a result of the rising influence of right-wing politics led by the BJP and its affiliates, coupled with religious and ideological motives of Hindu nationalist groups.

As Modi and the Bharatiya Janata Party (BJP) came to power in 2014, numerous Hindu nationalist organizations and cultural groups across the country have been emboldened. Modi's election to office can be attributed largely towards the support he and his party receives from the Sangh Parivar, the family of Hindu nationalist organizations in India including the Rashtriya Swayamsevak Sangh (RSS), Vishwa Hindu Parishad (VHP), and Bajrang Dal, among others. The RSS, the ideological backbone of the BJP, is where Modi earned his credentials as a grassroots leader. Hence, his coming to power and his desire to remain in power depends to a large extent on his reliance on the Sangh Parivar for its support and influence over the huge Hindu support base (Jaffrelot 2015). Individual groups within the Sangh Parivar have expanded across the country and their activities have become more overt since the BJP returned to power in 2014 (Michael 2018). While the proliferation of Hindu nationalist organizations is not surprising, tensions arise when these very organizations instigate intolerant attitudes and political violence in the name of protecting the Hindu religion, culture, and state. It is evident that such organizations and their ideologies (please refer to explanation on *Hindutva* below) have been emboldened when the statistics illustrate that the number of violent episodes carried out in the name of Hinduism have increased manifold since 2014 (IndiaSpend 2018) and little is being done by the government to curb their violent activities.[4]

A major consequence of the invigoration of Hindu nationalist and fundamentalist groups has been the rise of Hindu vigilantism. While "Hindu vigilantism" in itself is a fairly new term, gaining public attention only since 2014, it is arguably historically based in the 1966 cow protection movement. At the time, mobs of Hindu *gau rakshaks* or self-proclaimed cow protectors attempted to attack the Indian Parliament in a bid to ban the slaughter of cows nationwide. Although a blanket ban on cow slaughter has never been implemented, cow protection continues to be an instrumental political tool and point of communal contention.

The Indian Supreme Court suspended a law in 2017 that would have banned the sale of cattle for slaughter nationwide. Instead, each state has the constitutional right to enforce its own laws on cattle slaughter. Most Indian states ban the slaughter and consumption of beef, barring the Southern state of Kerala where beef is widely consumed by even Hindus, and north-eastern Indian states such as Nagaland, Tripura and Sikkim (among a few others). It must be noted that the ban on cow slaughter has been a bone of contention since the drafting of India's constitution at the time of Independence. An ideological spat arose when India was to be conceived of as a democratic, secular nation with freedom of religion and expression, yet the sentiments of the majority Hindu population had to be appeased on the topic of cow protection. Indian independence leader M.K. Gandhi himself believed in cow protection, as much as he believed in secularism.[5] As such, Article 48 of the Indian Constitution states,

> The State shall endeavour to organise agriculture and animal husbandry on modern and scientific lines and shall, in particular, take steps for preserving and improving the breeds, and prohibiting the slaughter, of cows and calves and other milch and draught cattle.[6]

As illustrated above, there is no legislated ban against cow slaughter, only a vague directive to work towards the prohibition of cattle slaughter. Right-wing Hindu groups have time and again attempted to change this. The 1966 cow protection movement, which failed to institutionalize the ban of cow slaughter, is often cited by cow protection committees and Hindu organizations as an example of the state's unwillingness to protect the rights of the Hindu majority. For example in 2016, several radical Hindu and cow protection groups (with affiliation to the RSS and/or the VHP) organized a memorial to commemorate the 50th death anniversary of those "martyred" in front of Parliament (Rai 2016).[7] It was also a public event to continue the advocacy of a nationwide ban on cow slaughter. Such events and justifications are expected given the RSS, VHP, and Bajrang Dal's agenda of banning cow slaughter (Jha 2002, 20).[8] It is not surprising then, that activism for cow protection has increased since the BJP (and by extension the RSS and VHP) gained power in 2014. Unfortunately, such activism in the name of cow protection has instigated an increase in the number of attacks on minorities (namely Muslims and Dalits) as well. While there are no official government statistics, independent journalistic website IndiaSpend.com estimates that 97% of all cow related violent incidents since 2010 have occurred after the BJP's ascension in 2014, and 86% of those killed since 2010 were Muslim (IndiaSpend 2018).

Framing Hindu vigilantism within the wider study of vigilantism

Studying Hindu vigilantism in its modern form is useful in helping us to understand the behaviour of certain Hindu groups against minority groups, and helps us explore the nexus between right-wing politics and expressions of Hindutva on the ground. Also, it allows for the analysis of what political and societal conditions enable vigilante activity to occur repeatedly.

Hindu vigilantism in India manifests itself in several forms. While the most prominent and violent form is cow vigilantism, other types include sporadic violent action against inter-religious couples (where Hindu mobs attack Muslim or Christian partners of Hindu individuals), "honour killings" against inter-caste couples, and moral policing – where members of right-wing Hindu organizations such as the Shiv Sena allegedly beat up young, unmarried couples in public on Valentine's Day.

This chapter looks closely at cow vigilantism because it is an example of Hindu vigilantism that illustrates best the tacit approval of the state in the policing of behaviour by civilians of civilians. It must be noted however, that although the state and legal framework does punish perpetrators of cow vigilantism, the perpetrators are usually affiliates or members of right-wing Hindu groups or cow protection committees with ties to the BJP, RSS, and/or the VHP. The phenomenon of cow vigilantism highlights the complex relationship between the state, civil society groups such as the cow protection committees, and minority groups such as Muslims and Dalits. Furthermore, it illustrates the dynamic power struggle between Hindus and Muslims in India, and their fight for communal identity based on mutual, reciprocal bashing of one another.

While there is no one set understanding of vigilantism in academic literature, it fundamentally entails certain assumptions and questions about state-society relations (Pratten and Sen 2008; Moncada 2017). In the case of India, political culture is unique such that, the Congress and BJP as the main rival political parties establish certain norms where and when each is in power. For the BJP, its cadre-based right-wing organizations such as the RSS, VHP, and affiliated groups form the powerful grassroots by sheer numbers. As such,

> vigilantism is not a response to an exceptional situation, but a permanent condition of the way that the relation between party and state is organized, with the cadre and the ruling party relationship dividing up the space of civil society and state by themselves.
>
> *(Sundar 2010, 115)*

Hence, it is not as useful to delve into the legality or extra-legality of cow vigilantism as it is to analyse the manner in which perpetrators and supporters justify their motives and enforce their actions. In a post-colonial multicultural state such as India, political culture determines that the government will not be fully able to ever eradicate communal strife. Such a culture absolves the state of taking responsibility of managing inter-communal relations – which both encourages vigilante activity (as people can blame their actions on state inaction), and a top-down punitive approach (as the state can blame citizens for taking the law into their own hands as a show of power and righteousness) (Sundar 2010, 114).

Individuals and groups who perpetrate cow vigilantism in India tend to benefit from both outcomes as they have the agency to maintain the established laws or norms of Hindutva. While they may be punished for their actions before the law, they are regarded as martyrs by fellow cadres and supporters of Hindutva. As will be explained below, their ideological beliefs transcend any violent actions taken to achieve their ambitions and therefore justify how they publicly legitimize their behaviour (Moncada 2017, 407). They engage in such vigilantism because they believe their ambitions will not be met by the state. Nevertheless, it is crucial to note that the state provides the necessary conditions for the activities to take place in the form of institutions (Jaffrelot 2017). The RSS and VHP support cow protection committees, which invariably harbour echo chambers of radical Hindu ideologies, where the so-called protection and promotion of Hindu identity is paramount. In this regard, protecting the cow and establishing social control over minority groups are effective means. Cow vigilantism in India, then, is concerned more with social control and the enforcement of hegemony by Hindu nationalists to dominate communal order (Johnston 1996, 228).

As Johnston (1996) suggests, conceptualizing vigilantism as merely a means of social control broadens its definition so much so that it renders itself no different from any other types of political violence. As such, cow vigilantism fits perfectly within Johnston's notion that it is a "reaction to real or perceived deviance" (Johnston 1996, 229). As will be illustrated in the case studies below, cow vigilantes

60 Juhi Ahuja

act based on a perception (real or imagined) that non-Hindus are a threat to their religio-cultural identity if they breach their established norm of protecting cows. Hence even if there is slight suspicion of carrying or transporting beef or cows respectively, so-called cow protectors perpetrate violent vigilante activity.

In this regard, some actual cow vigilante acts may be spontaneous in the sense that certain episodes draw mobs of people into the violence. However, cow vigilantism as a social phenomenon is certainly not spontaneous, it is the result of a deliberately planned strategy and infrastructure of right-wing Hindutva groups. The institutionalization of cow protection committees and their affiliations to the state by way of the RSS and VHP provide agency and capital for vigilante activity to take place – also owing to its predisposition and premediation (Johnston 1996, 222). Given that the perpetrators are not from vigilante groups per se (they are first Hindutva groups), cow vigilantism for them is a means of establishing social control and policing minority groups where they have transgressed out of the norm. It is a reaction to social deviance (Johnston 1996, 231), rather than an end in itself. For example, if cow slaughter is successfully banned, believers of the Hindutva ideology may find other avenues to establish dominance over minority groups and assert their Hindu identity.

Case studies

Following the fatal lynching in Dadri mentioned above, another violent vigilante episode took place this time near the tumultuous Kashmir Valley, in Udhampur on 9 October 2015. Zahid Ahmed (who eventually died of injuries) and Showkat Ahmed, two local Kashmiri Muslim men, were driving a truck into the Kashmir valley when their truck was attacked and hit by petrol bombs. The alleged attackers were self-styled Hindu vigilantes who took advantage of the stationary truck due to traffic on the Jammu-Srinagar National Highway because of a strike called by Hindu outfits over rumours that three cows were killed by Muslims in the area (Masoodi and Iqbal 2015). It was later discovered that the cows had died from food poisoning. Although the perpetrators of this cow vigilantism were not found to have connections to the BJP, RSS, VHP, or cow protection committees (Sharma 2015), they attempted to exploit existing communal disharmony in the area on the pretext of maintaining the established norms of cow protection.

On 13 January 2016, a Muslim couple was assaulted at a railway station in the central Indian state of Madhya Pradesh by members of the *Gau Raksha Samiti* of the locality, for allegedly objecting to having their baggage checked on suspicion of them carrying beef (Ghatwai 2016). This occurred after the vigilantes found an unclaimed bag containing meat in it, which they believed to be beef. It was later found that the meat in question was buffalo (The Hindu 2016). Although two Samiti members were arrested after the incident, deterrence seems low as such violent episodes continue.

In April 2017, dairy farmer Pehlu Khan was travelling from Rajasthan to Haryana when he along with his associates were brutally attacked in Alwar by an

Protecting holy cows in India **61**

alleged mob of around 200 Hindu cow vigilantes. They were accused of smuggling cows, despite their pleas that they possessed the necessary documentation to prove that they legally purchased the cows for their dairy business (Sarkar 2017). Pehlu Khan did not survive the violent thrashings. Upon further investigations, it was found that the accused were members of local cow protection committees. The Alwar police registered a case against the accused for the murder of Pehlu Khan, and against the deceased Pehlu Khan and his associates for allegedly smuggling cows (Mukherjee 2018).

On 11 June 2017, a convoy of trucks carrying cattle by Tamil Nadu government officials from Rajasthan was attacked by around 50 vigilantes, who blocked the highway and beat up the drivers while pelting stones at the vehicles. The officials, who were from Tamil Nadu's Animal Husbandry Department had allegedly purchased the cows with all the required documentation and permissions (News18.com 2017). While several arrests were made in relation to the attacks, it remains to be seen if any strong action will be taken against groups inciting vigilante activity.

The above incidents illustrate the severity of the matter with regards to violence perpetrated by self-style cow vigilantes. They also indicate that be it cow smuggling, trafficking, possession of beef or the mere *rumour* or suspicion of any of the above, Muslims in many parts of India are vulnerable to attack by cow vigilantes. These examples also illustrated the massive role of disinformation in these attacks, as many take place on false pretexts of cow smuggling or possession. Yet, as seen from the attack on Pehlu Khan and the Tamil Nadu officials, the self-styled cow vigilantes are not interested in the truth. For them, the ideal of protecting the cow physically and symbolically is so great and pertinent to protecting Hindu identity, that violence becomes justified as a means to their desired end (Ahuja and Prakash 2017). Given the numerous cow vigilante episodes since 2014, there is the risk that such episodes may become normalized (Anand 2007).

At this juncture, it is important to note also that there exists an economic dimension to cow vigilantism in India as well. While the self-styled cow vigilantes are fighting for their religio-cultural identity and hegemony, it must also be pointed out that India is one of the world's largest exporters of beef (Iyengar 2015). As a consequence of the wealthy industry, cattle smuggling is rife (Cons 2016). That cow vigilantes are interested in the sole protection of cows, of all animals in India's meat industry, is of note.

In this regard, cow vigilantism falls under the wider phenomenon of Hindu vigilantism, which in itself is a means to achieving the Hindutva ideal. Hindu vigilantes are motivated by a desire to (1) weaken their enemies (namely non-Hindus) in a perceived ethnic conflict; (2) to enhance their own social standing; and (3) to forge a superior religio-cultural identity to ensure their communal power ensures their political prowess.

Hindutva and its rising influence

In order to better understand Hindu vigilantism against Muslims in India, it is crucial to understand the political, social and ideological motivations of extreme right-wing Hindu groups or Hindutva groups, as they are popularly known.

62 Juhi Ahuja

The term *Hindutva* is often used in Hindu nationalist discourse to represent the idea that native Indians should be loyal to their ancestral roots and that they should recognize the great civilizational history of India, while honouring Hindu culture (Juergensmeyer 2008). It is religiously fundamentalist in its ideology because there is an insistence on exclusivity, in terms of what constitutes Hinduism and what defines a Hindu person. It is an attempt to hijack the religion and enforce a particular type of Hinduism – one that is defined by one's loyalty to the land or sense of nationalism (Juergensmeyer 2008). It purports that Hindus should consider India as both their Fatherland and Holy Land. There is a clear conceptualization of history in its own terms, the belief that the subcontinent is sacred to the Hindu "race" and has the ambition of unifying all Hindus under this ideal which is perceived to be greater than the religion itself. This is problematic because although Hindutva ideologues are clear that the Hindu race referred to people who resided in the region of the Indus river (irrespective of their beliefs), it excludes Indians who identify themselves as non-Hindu in religious terms. By default, other religious groups in India – namely Muslims and Christians who make up the largest minorities – are excluded from the Hindutva ideal (Schied 2011, 80). Buddhist, Sikhs, and Jains fall within the Hindu cultural group for most Hindutva ideologues, as these religions were founded on Indian soil. As a result, there is clear ideological basis for intolerant attitudes towards Muslims and Christians – who arguably may not view India as their holy land (Jaffrelot 2010).

While the objective and consequence of Hindutva is to instil a sense of (ethnoreligious) nationalism, it is still a form of religious fundamentalism because it employs religious texts (not necessarily scriptural texts) to justify the need to expound its mission, and embarks on a mission to semantically and symbolically give its pursuit divine qualities (Lipner 2016, 111).[9] The fact that even the cultural Hindu belongs to the Hindu (religious) tradition in modern terms blurs the boundaries of who a Hindu is.[10] As such, this Hindu political fundamentalism was focused on a nationalizing goal, not committed to propagating Hinduism per se (Lipner 2016, 104–5). It is true that the term "Hindu" carries much religio-cultural baggage, as it originated in meaning to refer to the Indic populations who lived beyond the River Indus; it has since colonial times, come to be defined and articulated more in terms of a religious category in Western discourse, similar to the constructs of the Christian, Muslim, or Jew (Lipner 1994, 7–8; Keppens and Bloch 2010; Sugirtharajah 2003).

As with religious fundamentalisms, the attempt to provide a nuanced meaning of "Hindu" and to re-capture it from the grips of the imperialists, is striking in the Hindu fundamentalists' pursuits. Although Hindu political fundamentalists attempt to homogenize the term "Hindu" such that it adheres to only one meaning, there is an attempt to re-capture it from the western, colonial, religiously laden meanings of the term (Sugirtharajah 2003).[11] With the belief and promotion of this alternative narrative, there is the intention to create a sense of social solidarity, albeit an organic, cosmic one that pre-exists, in order to realize the unity of the people in India, and to establish a formidable nation (Savarkar 1969). In essence, Hindu nationalism is the political expression of Hindu fundamentalism expressed in a variety of forms by political and cultural parties in India such as the Rashtriya Svayamsevak Sangh (RSS), Bajrang Dal, Vishwa Hindu Parishad (VHP), and by extension the current ruling party, the Bharatiya Janata Party (BJP) (Oberoi 1995, 101; Lipner 2016, 104–107).

Labelling certain activities as "vigilantism" in the Indian context may have cultural implications as certain behaviour may not be considered vigilantism, but rather "protection" or "self-defence", depending on the context. For instance, protecting cows in India has become institutionalized such that there are dedicated cow protection committees and shelters that look after the welfare of the cattle. The individuals who run these committees are known as *gau rakshaks* or cow protectors. It is also true that some shelters function purely for the protection of animal rights, while others are motivated by religio-cultural reasons.

Proponents and ideologues of Hindutva are immersed in their own ideology such that their entire worldview is aimed at achieving their mission. Central to the Hindutva idea of the "nation" is the notion that it should be made up of Hindus who are allegiant to the subcontinent, and were once united during a Golden Age before the land was invaded by Muslim Mughals and then the Christian British (Jaffrelot 2007, 98).

The so called "Vedic golden age" that pervaded until the Mughals invaded the subcontinent was considered a sacred time, and it was desirable to return to that period in the present, modern day (Jaffrelot 2007, 30; Liu and Khan 2015; Guichard 2010, 29). Given that Hindu political fundamentalism is a modern phenomenon, it is not separate from its scriptural variant; meaning that the ideologues of Hindutva were largely influenced by Hindu reform and revivalist movements of the nineteenth century (Lipner 2016, 97). For example, scriptural fundamentalists such as Dayananda Sarasvati played a critical role in essentializing Vedic scriptural authority, and asserting the superiority of Hindu thought. Further, Hindu nationalism gained much traction from the Arya Samaj; which is a reform movement that emerged in the nineteenth century in the context of colonial rule, based on the teachings of Sarasvati (Zavos 1999). The Arya Samaj played a critical role in the development of the fundamentals of Hindu nationalist ideology; with its key principles of the Vedas holding utmost truth, and the *time* of the conception and practice of Vedic religion (before foreign invasion) as the "Golden Age" (Jaffrelot 2007, 9; Zavos 1999, 63). By constructing a narrative based on a glorified past, the ideologues of Hindutva attempted to justify not only the geographical significance to the native Hindus, but also their racial or cultural superiority.[12] Hindutva is ideologically radical due to its insistence on unity based on a particular Hindu identity.

Within this context of the increasing popularity of Hindutva as a right-wing ideology and expressions of it in India since the establishment of the Modi government, the meaning of Hindu identity has become further politicized. While the notion of "communalism" is unique to the Indian context wherein religious groups tend to identify themselves along ethno-nationalist lines, the rise of Hindu nationalism and the popularity of its resultant right-wing politics have created the ideal circumstance and space for the empowerment of Hindu nationalists. Moreover, in an effort to assert Hindu superiority, Hindu nationalists assume it to be their ordained duty to contribute to society in a way that will help them in their aspiration to construct a *Hindurashtra* or Hindu nation. Given the sacredness of the cow to the Hindutva project, any perceived attack on the cow is seen as an attack on the pursuit towards the *Hindurashtra*. This gives rise to Hindu vigilantism in the name of protecting cows, and the *nation*.

It must also be noted that many of the reports on vigilante activity due to cow slaughter and consumption indicate that in many cases, the victims were only rumoured or suspected to have slaughtered or consumed beef. Furthermore, in several reported cases, the victims of vigilante violence were merely transporting cattle. There is reasonable evidence to suggest that the cow is being used as a political tool to conduct hate crimes against the Muslim minority, as a method of intimidation and establishment of cultural superiority. The ideological justification of Hindutva to commit vigilante activity against Muslims is further propounded by a rising sense of religious intolerance in India.

Intolerance

As these vigilantes grip on to their fixed idea of history and ideals, attitudes of intolerance against others manifest. Recent incidents of inter-religious clashes on a national scale have been deeply polarizing and raise important questions about the meaning of constitutional secularism in India. For example in January 2018, a medieval epic film by the name of *Padmaavat*, directed by the acclaimed Sanjay Leela Bhansali, drew massive controversy over whether the film should be banned in its entirety because of certain themes it featured. Some Hindutva groups had deep objection to the film's portrayal of Rajput culture and Mughal ruler Alauddin Khilji. Mass demonstrations ensued prior to the film's release in the state of Rajasthan, where the epic film was contextually set. Hindutva outfits such as the Karni Sena threatened to inflict harm on the cast and makers of the film, and organized protests to get the film banned. It resulted in widespread coverage by domestic and international media – deeply dividing the nation in terms of the "correct" version of history, and whether or not mainstream film-makers should have the agency to portray subjects which may be culturally sensitive.

Although the film was not eventually banned, a censored version was released. The episode illustrates the sensitivities of and strength that Hindutva groups have in India. Moreover, it highlights the deep-rooted sensitivities around the conceptualization of Hindu identity and culture – for which Hindu nationalists exploit issues of Muslim reformism and Islamist extremism, caste politics, and the state's apparent inability to effectively manage communal disharmony to justify their motivations.

As Hindu nationalists attempt to define and create their own nation, a *Hindu rashtra*, anything that deviates from it is labelled foreign. For the case of Muslims, since they are perceived to not consider India their holy land, they immediately

Protecting holy cows in India **65**

become foreign (despite them being in India for centuries). This fuels already hostile feelings.

While it is not within the gambit of this chapter to discuss the history of Hindu–Muslim relations in India, a modern conception of it began during the partition and independence of India and Pakistan 1947, and has carried on since. Specific points of infliction include the crisis in Kashmir, the Babri Masjid/Ram Janma-Bhumi controversy, and the Shah Bano case.

The most widely discussed incident in India among scholars and politicians is the Ram Janma-Bhumi controversy, often viewed as the epitome of Hindu nationalist and communalist politics in India (Liu and Khan 2015, 211). The term "communalism" in India is widely used to refer to the various religious groups, and was constituted at the time when the British first conducted the Indian census (Sarkar 2014, 269; Guichard 2010, 19). Given the theoretical precedence of the Hindutva ideologues regarding the disruption of the golden era by Muslims, Hindu fundamentalists and nationalists in contemporary times have justified the demolition of the Babri mosque in the Indian city of Ayodhya with the argument that it was illegitimately built by the Mughal invaders in 1528 at the site where Lord Ram was born (Liu and Khan 2015, 231). Although this is an oversimplified account of the controversy, the example has further solidified the above argument that the mixing of religious scripture and mythology with political ambition is indicative of religious fundamentalism, which leads to social exclusion, intolerance, and sometimes violence.

Conclusion

The conditions within which Hindu vigilantism, and especially cow vigilantism, are able to manifest have ripened since the BJP gained power in 2014. Nevertheless, this chapter does not propound that the BJP, or RSS, or any one politician for that matter, is solely responsible for the rise in such violent episodes against minorities. Rather, the Hindutva ideology that has been given space and fuel to smoulder by the state, along with strong intolerant attitudes, enables the radicalisation of youth to commit vigilante activity as described above. Many sections of Hindu society may have allegedly legitimate or rational fears, as do sections of American and British society who voted for Trump and Brexit respectively. However, when the state creates the space for toxic ideologies which spread intolerance and instigate violence, it threatens democracy and undermines the rights of minorities.

This study provokes the study of immigration in India as well, as the Hindu nationalism render religious minorities as immigrants (though they may have been there for generations).

Disinformation has a huge role to play, but is that really a saving grace? If full, complete, true information was available, it does not remove the potential for such attacks to take place in the future. Perhaps due to disinformation, these intolerant sentiments are out in the open. It indicates that deep social cleavages exist in Indian

66 Juhi Ahuja

society and that they run much deeper than just inter-communal tensions. In addition to the institutionalization of "cow protection", there is the risk of the institutionalization of cow vigilantism. Gau Raksha dals and Samitis need to be better managed, and laws surrounding mob violence need to be tightened.

However, there is no near or easy solution. The desire for a Hindu *rashtra* or nation for Hindu nationalists is so strong, that cow vigilantism is a convenient public avenue for their activism. It is unfortunate that fellow Indian citizens are made victim. It is not just Muslims, but Dalits are attacked too. These attacks show the might of the majority against minority groups, and what ensues is a real or imagined power struggle. Attacks on Dalits as well shows that the discrimination is not only against Muslims. It is worth exploring further whether the motivations of Hindu vigilantes are based more on a hatred for minorities, or for a desire to portray hegemony and establish in their view a superior religio-cultural identity – one which defines and maintains all social norms, as the state is inept to do so. Whatever the case, in today's context, Hindu vigilantism seems to serve the ruling party's interests (Jaffrelot 2017).

Notes

1 For more context on the sanctity of the cow in Hindu tradition, please refer to Jha, D. N. 2002. *The Myth of the Holy Cow*. London, New York: Verso.
2 For statistical evidence on the number of documented cow-related hate crimes in India since 2010, please refer to the IndiaSpend database, http://data.indiaspend.com/hate-crime.
3 Although the term "Dalit" is a highly contested and politicised term, it is often used to refer to castes in India of traditionally lower socio-economic status. Caste in India is still very much prevalent and is dependent on one's family lineage, profession, and background.
4 This is illustrated by increased Hindu militancy by groups such as the Hindu Yuva Vahini and Bajrang Dal.
5 Please see compilation of views of Mahatma Gandhi on cow protection, https://web.archive.org/web/20111125093504/http://dahd.nic.in/ch2/an2.6.htm "Compilation of Gandhi's views on Cow Protection". Dahd.nic.in. 7 July 1927.
6 Please see "The Constitution of India", https://www.india.gov.in/sites/upload_files/npi/files/coi_part_full.pdf.
7 Please see also Hindutva websites http://www.hinduhumanrights.info/remembering-the-7th-nov-1966-gopastami-hindu-massacre-in-delhi/; and https://hinduexistence.org/2016/11/07/remembering-the-50-years-of-largest-hindu-killing-by-indira-gandhi-in-goraksha-abhiyan-in-delhi/.
8 The Bajrang Dal is the youth-wing of the VHP and is affiliated to the RSS.
9 Religious texts can include written, oral, pictorial, and physical artefacts, which are used to make sense of religious tradition.
10 It is not within the gambit of this chapter to explain conceptual differences in the terms "culture" and "religion".
11 See Sugirtharajah, Sharada. 2003. *Imagining Hinduism: A Postcolonial Perspective*. London: Routledge, for the construction of Hinduism as a modern religious category, and the derivative term "Hindu" as a person who identifies as belonging to the religion.
12 Some scholars argue that methods and ambitions of Hindutva ideologues and those of reform movements such as the Arya Samaj are essentially attempts to "Westernise" Hindusim and mimic the models of Abrahamic faiths. Please see Jaffrelot, Christophe. 2010. *Religion, Caste & Politics in India*. Delhi: Primus Books, 164.

References

Ahuja, Juhi, and Pravin Prakash (2017). *Cow vigilantism in India: Modi's dilemma or legacy?*. Singapore: RSIS Commentaries. Retrieved from https://www.rsis.edu.sg/rsis-publication/cens/co17131-cow-vigilantism-in-india-modis-dilemma-or-legacy/#.WwuKb0iFOM8.

Anand, Dibyesh (2007). The violence of security: Hindu nationalism and the politics of representing 'the Muslim' as a danger. *The Round Table*, 94(379), 203–215.

Cons, Jason (2016). *Sensitive space: Fragmented territory at the India–Bangladesh border*. Seattle: University of Washington Press.

Ghatwai, Milind (2016, January 15). Muslim couple on train beaten in MP over beef suspicion. *The Indian Express*. Retrieved from http://indianexpress.com/article/india/india-news-india/muslim-couple-on-train-beaten-in-mp-bags-searched-over-beef-suspicion/.

Guichard, Sylvie (2010). *The construction of history and nationalism in India: Textbooks, controversies and politics*. Abingdon: Routledge.

Huffpost (2017, August 1). Of the 18 accused in the Dadri lynching case, only 3 are in jail. *Huffington Post India*. Retrieved from https://www.huffingtonpost.in/2017/08/01/of-the-18-accused-in-the-dadri-lynching-case-only-3-are-in-jail_a_23059249/.

IndiaSpend (2018). Hate crime: Cow-related violence in India. Retrieved from http://data.indiaspend.com/hate-crime.

Iyengar, Rishi (2015, April 24). India stays world's top beef exporter despite new bans on slaughtering cows. *Time*. Retrieved from http://time.com/3833931/india-beef-exports-rise-ban-buffalo-meat/.

Jaffrelot, Christophe (2007). *Hindu nationalism: A reader*. Oxfordshire: Princeton University Press.

Jaffrelot, Christophe (2010). *Religion, caste & politics in India*. Delhi: Primus Books.

Jaffrelot, Christophe (2015). The Modi-centric BJP 2014 election campaign: New techniques and old tactics. *Contemporary South Asia*, 23(2) (May), 151–166.

Jaffrelot, Christophe (2017, May 13). Over to the vigilante. *The Indian Express*. Retrieved from http://indianexpress.com/article/opinion/columns/over-to-the-vigilante-gau-rakshak-cultural-policing-beef-ban-4653305/.

Jha, D.N. (2002). *The myth of the holy cow*. London, New York: Verso.

Johnston, Les (1996). What is vigilantism. *Brit. J. Criminol*, 36(2) (Spring), 220–236.

Juergensmeyer, Mark (2008). Political targets of rebellion: South, Central and Southeast Asia. In *Global rebellion: Religious challenges to the secular state, from Christian militias to Al Qaeda* (pp. 84–106). Berkeley and Los Angeles: University of California Press.

Keppens, Marianne and Esther Bloch (2010). Introduction: Rethinking religion in India. In Esther Bloch, et al. (Eds) *Rethinking religion in India: The colonial construction of Hinduism*, Oxon: Routledge.

Lipner, Julius (1994). *Hindus: Their religious beliefs and practices*. London: Routledge.

Lipner, Julius (2016). Hindu fundamentalism. In J. D. G. Dunn (Ed.), *Fundamentalisms: Threats and ideologies in the modern world* (p. 111). London: I.B. Tauris & Co. Ltd.

Liu, James H. and Sammyh S. Khan (2015). Nation building through historical narratives in pre-independence India: Gandhi, Nehru, Savarkar, and Golwalkar as entrepreneurs of identity. In M. Hanne et al. (Eds), *Warring with words: Narrative and metaphor in politics*. New York: Psychology Press.

Masoodi, Nazir, and Sheikh Zaffar Iqbal (2015, October 19). Kashmir tense after trucker attacked over beef rumours dies. NDTV. Retrieved from https://www.ndtv.com/india-news/clashes-in-jammu-as-trucker-targeted-over-beef-rumours-dies-1233569.

Michael, Arndt (2018). India's foreign policy and Hindutva: The new impact of culture and identity on the formulation and practice of Indian foreign policy 2014–2017. In M.

Rehman (Ed.), *Rise of saffron power: Reflections on Indian politics* (pp. 62–83). Oxon, New York: Routledge.

Moncada, Eduardo (2017). Varieties of vigilantism: Conceptual discord, meaning and strategies. *Global Crime*, 18(4), 403–423.

Mukherjee, Deep (2018, February 1). Pehlu Khan lynching case: Alwar police charge all victims with cow smuggling. *The Indian Express*. Retrieved from http://indianexpress.com/article/india/pehlu-khans-lynching-case-alwar-police-charge-all-victims-with-cow-sm uggling-5046962/.

News18.com (2017, June 12). Vigilantes beat up Tamil Nadu officials transporting cows from Rajasthan. *News18.com*. Retrieved from https://www.news18.com/news/india/vigilantes-attack-tamil-nadu-officials-transporting-cows-from-rajasthan-1430489.html.

Oberoi, Harjot (1995). Mapping Indic fundamentalisms through nationalism and modernity. In M. Marty & R. S. Appleby (Eds.), *Fundamentalisms Comprehended*, Volume 5. Chicago: The University of Chicago Press.

Pratten, David, and Atryee Sen (2008). *Global vigilantes*. New York: Columbia Press.

Rai, Siddhartha (2016, October 20). Holy cow: RSS, VHP to revive 1966 Gau Rakshaks' movement. *India Today*. Retrieved from https://www.indiatoday.in/mail-today/story/holy-cow-rss-vhp-1966-gau-rakhshaks-movement-349224-2016-10-30.

Sarkar, Ipsita (2017, April 7). As minister's comment sparks outrage, a new video of attack by cow vigilantes. *NDTV*. Retrieved from https://www.ndtv.com/india-news/as-ministers-comment-sparks-outrage-a-new-video-of-attack-by-cow-vigilantes-1678325.

Sarkar, Sumit (2014). *Modern times: India 1880s–1950s*. Ranikhet: Permanent Black.

Savarkar, V. D. (1969). *Hindutva*. 5th edition. Bombay: Veer Sarvarkar Prakarshan.

Schied, Michael (2011). The turn to fundamentalism: The significance of religious ideology in state-formation and nation building in South Asia. In U. Martensson et al. (Eds.), *Fundamentalism in the modern world volume 1, Fundamentalism, politics and history: The state, globalisation and political ideologies*. New York: I.B. Tauris & Co Ltd.

Sharma, Arun (2015, October 12). Udhampur truck attack part of larger plan to engineer communal tension: Police. *The Indian Express*. Retrieved from http://india nexpress.com/article/india/india-news-india/udhampur-truck-attack-police-attack-pa rt-of-larger-plan-to-engineer-communal-tension/.

Sugirtharajah, Sharada (2003). *Imagining Hinduism: A postcolonial perspective*. London: Routledge.

Sundar, Nandini (2010). Vigilantism, culpability and moral dilemmas. *Critique of Anthropology*, 30(1), 113–121.

The Constitution of India (1950). *Government of India*. Retrieved from https://www.india.gov.in/my-government/constitution-india.

The Hindu (2016, January 15). Muslim couple assaulted on train over beef suspicion. *The Hindu*. Retrieved from http://www.thehindu.com/news/national/other-states/Muslim-couple-assaulted-on-train-over-beef-suspicion/article14001428.ece.

Zavos, John (1999). The Arya Samaj and the antecedents of Hindu nationalism. *International Journal of Hindu Studies*, 3(1) (April), 58–63.

5

VIOLENT ATTACKS AGAINST MIGRANTS AND MINORITIES IN THE RUSSIAN FEDERATION

Martin Laryš

Introduction

This chapter analyses the period from Putin's coming to power in 2000 as the president of the Russian Federation until now. It examines a heavily under-studied dynamics of the violent tendencies of Russian radical nationalist organizations and informal groups. In the first decade of this century, more hate murders happened in Russia than in all European countries combined.

Most of these murders were committed by racist street gangs, lacking a sophisticated ideology and strong organizational structure.

Vigilantism in Russia has lately had several forms. The most dangerous one has been vigilante terrorism in the form of bomb attacks or demonstrative racist murders, which sent underlying messages to the state authorities. Another one was created by Movement Against Illegal Immigration (and later copied by other nationalists) with the aim of performing as a "defender of Russians against criminal immigrants, terrorizing the common Russian people". This movement was pressuring the central and local authorities to fight more decisively against migration. The "raid" movements against immigrants and homosexuals, organized by both grass-roots and well-known nationalist organizations, were the main form of vigilantism in Russia for quite a short period of time around 2012–2014.

Putin's entering office and renewing Chechnya's war campaign coincided with the rise of violence of racist groups, mostly connected to skinhead subculture. It was directed against people of "non-Slavic" (i.e. "non-white") appearance who were easily recognized on the streets. The first skinhead gangs, formed in the second half of the 1990s in the largest cities, have laid the foundation for what later became radical militant autonomous nationalist organizations, and even terrorist groups. Members of these gangs were responsible for the first pogroms against non-Slavic immigrants and became a subject to nationwide media interest. The assaults

70 Martin Laryš

were occasionally fatal but they were not as frequent as several years later. Skinheads and football hooligans often targeted marketplaces and dormitories of non-Russian workers (Litoi 2015, Shnirelman 2007, Tarasov 2005, for football hooligan violence see more in Tarasov 2010). The peak of racist violence took place between 2006–2010 when racist street gangs were to a substantial extent responsible for at least 386 hate murders and almost 2500 injured people (mostly from Caucasus and Central Asia), according to data from the Non-Governmental organization SOVA Center, monitoring racist violence in Russia (Kozhevnikova 2007, 2008, 2009, 2010, Verkhovskii & Kozhevnikova 2011). Real numbers would probably be even higher (Interview A. Verkhovskii 2009).

Forms of vigilantism in Russia

Vigilantism in Russia has three main forms: vigilante terrorism, "people's gathering" (organized by radical nationalists for protection of local Russian communities) and "raid" movement (divided into two subcategories because of the different methods and targets of their activities – migrants vs homosexuals).

Vigilante terrorism

The main motive for the acts of vigilante terrorism is the fight against "occupants" and "colonists" (as nationalists call immigrants and some ethnic minorities, originating mainly from Northern Caucasus) who came, according to them, with the intention to replace the ethnically Russian population and had the unspoken consent of the Russian state authorities. This terror was in some cases aimed not only against the immigrants. There was also an insurgent component of the fight against the state, which in their view had ignored the suffering of Russian people in the hands of immigrants without any interest in protecting ethnic Russians.

The first group attempting to use terrorist methods was the neo-Nazi Combat Terrorist Organization ("*Boevaya terroristicheskaya organizatsiya*", BTO) from St Petersburg, active between 2003 and 2006 (see more in Falkovskii and Litoi 2013, Sidorov 2006, Lvov 2006). At different times, the group consisted of 6–11 people. They perceived themselves to be a neo-Nazi elite. "If the skinheads are infantry, the BTO are new SS soldiers," wrote one of the BTO leaders (Sidorov 2006). In their printed materials, the members wrote: "We are running the war on the system. We understand that the main enemy is ZOG (Zionist Occupation Government, term popular with western neo-Nazis), not 'blacks'" (ibid.). It was clear to them that they could not get close to the "ZOG leaders" and that the revolutionary coup was unrealistic. The only possible way of fighting for them was "destabilizing terror". This terror took the form of murders and physical attacks on "non-white" inhabitants. The gang was well-organized, exploiting tactics of acting in illegality. In total, the members of BTO were accused and sentenced for seven murders, eight physical injuries, armed assaults on post offices, attempted bomb attacks at a café in which foreign students were meeting, and illegal possession of weapons and explosives (Abarinov 2006, News.ru 2009).

The bombing at Cherkizovsky Market in the summer of 2006, leaving 14 dead and 61 injured, is the second important case of vigilante terrorism. The attack was perpetrated by SPAS group and its main leader neo-Nazi Nikola Korolev, responsible for several other murders of immigrants. It was committed in the biggest marketplace in Moscow (Cherkizovskiy rynok), considered a kind of "sin city" – hotbed of ethnic crime and illegal immigration because most of the market sellers there have Caucasian and Central Asian origins (Zheglov 2007). According to Korolev, the Cherkizovsky Market was bombed because it was a centre of illegality – a state within the state where "the Southern occupants" ruled on all markets (Falkovskii and Litoi 2013).

The third most notable movement inclining towards vigilante terrorism was Combat Organization of Russian Nationalists (*Boevaya organizatsiya russkikh natsionalistov*, BORN), consisting of Moscow veterans from the skinhead neo-Nazi scene and with close ties to the nationalist Russian Image (*Russkiy obraz*) organization, founded around 2008. This group killed several Antifa leaders, a judge who was dealing with prosecution of the racist gang White Wolves, left-wing advocate Stanislav Markelov and journalist Anastasia Baburova. The last case received international media coverage. Among BORN's targets were also randomly chosen immigrants killed in a retaliation attack for immigrants' "crimes against the Russian people". The most brutal assault was committed as a revenge attack for the rape and murder of a Russian teenage girl in a Moscow suburb by an Uzbek migrant worker. In December 2008, members of BORN caught a random Tajik guest worker, killed him, cut his head off and put it in front of the administrative building of the Mozhaiskiy district in Moscow. Subsequently, they sent a letter to the media and NGOs in which they explained their motives, which were typical for almost all racist gangs in Russia:

(This) surprise for the Moscow officials has been prepared by the non-indifferent Russian people, who are tired of the invasion of foreigners into their hometown. Caucasians and Asians rape Russian women, children, and rob and kill peaceful people. A blind man is one who does not notice what an unprecedented wave of crime has swept the capital. But, apparently, the suffering of ordinary Russian citizens does not concern the official authorities. They continue to bring in foreign migrant workers and support Caucasian speculators. They attract migratory flows to our house and are going to grant Russian citizenship to any resident of the former USSR, regardless of nationality and knowledge of the Russian language. They wanted to spit on the popular opinion on this matter. We will have to declare it as harshly as possible. We do not need millions of Caucasians and Central Asians here! If officials continue to populate Russia with aliens, then we will have to start eliminating officials! There is no enemy worse than a traitor with authority, selling his

Russian origin. State officials, if you do not start evicting blacks, we will begin to avenge their crimes to you! And then your heads will already fly.

(Falkovskii and Litoi 2013: 30)

BORN's last murder was executed in September 2010. The victim was an Armenian taxi driver whom the propaganda website *Life News* accused (falsely, as it later transpired) of having beaten a pregnant Russian girl.

The most prominent case of the well-organized racist gang as the border case of vigilant terrorism is National-Socialist Society (*Natsional-sotsialisticheskoe obshchestvo*, NSO). After Maxim Bazylev became leader of this organization in 2007, he declared:

> [...] to cover this country with corpses (...) the NSO must become the most radical organisation that will set the direction of all national and national socialist movements, it must become an example worth following, it must ignite a total terrorist war.
>
> *(Falkovskii and Litoi 2013: 98)*

The aim of Bazylev and NSO was provoking racial war in Russia by executing street terrorism targeting non-Russian citizens. Bazylev argued that active steps must be taken, i.e. the movement must kill "non-white" people. He claimed that only when the situation in the country is unstable, involving mass unrests, large-scale murders and terrorist acts, would it be possible to take over the power. In his opinion, murders and bombings were necessary to force state authorities to resign. The most notorious fraction, known as NSO-North (*NSO-Sever*) killed almost 30 people from Caucasus and Central Asia in 2007–2008. One of the NSO-North members explained the reasons for his murderous activity in court:

> I believe that only the indigenous population of Russia has the right to live on the territory of the Russian Federation, the visiting people should not reside on the territory of the Russian Federation, these people, in my opinion, are occupants who need to be physically exterminated.
>
> *(Falkovskii and Litoi 2013: 110)*

In this period there were other racist gangs such as Ryno-Skachevskii, White Wolves, Nevograd 14/88 etc. who killed 10–30 immigrants, stabbing them with knives several dozen times. They were chosen randomly in housing estates or around metro stations. Their vigilantism was based on their racial hatred towards the "non-white" immigrants with the aim of stopping them from coming to Russia and "protecting the Russians against the immigrant threat". One of the perpetrators of the racist murders said in court:

> The ruling regime is hostile to the Russian nation, and judges are merely servants of the regime. We do not recognize their right to judge neither our

comrades, nor the enemies of our nation. From now on, we ourselves are judges on our land, and there is no such power that would forbid us to protect the Russian people.

(Falkovskii and Litoi 2013: 32)

This level of racist violence began to decrease at the end of 2009, under serious police pressure and because of a certain disillusionment within militant groups, which were usually perpetrating racist attacks. They have gradually started to realize that beatings and murders of "aliens" had no impact on the pace of migration, government policies, or public opinion – such methods would not bring the "white revolution" any closer (Verkhovskii 2016: 84).

Out of all the cases described above, only SPAS and BORN terrorist activities could be characterized as forms of vigilantism. These were mostly cases of crime control vigilantism, protecting the identity of the "own threatened group" against "the others", perceived as a deviant and/or criminal threat (Waldmann 1998: 92–94). Their actions were intended to force the state authorities to do something about the immigration "to protect the Russian people". Activities of BTO and NSO-North had a more insurgent character with the aim of overthrowing the current political regime and bringing the "white revolution" with the help of terrorist violence against random "non-white" people. Immigrants were only meant to be the instrument to their final political goal.

Anti-immigrant "raids"

Over the past years, raids inspired by various ethnic and "social" issues have been an important part of the activities undertaken by nationalist groups with the aim of demonstrating their active "civic" position to the public. Between 2012 and 2014/15, aggressive raids on illegal migrants, homosexuals and drug dealers were particularly popular among the nationalists. Nevertheless, since late 2013 their numbers have decreased steadily thanks to the repression from the security forces (Yudina and Alperovich 2016). In the context of severe police crackdowns on "traditional" racist violence and the failure of political actions, raids of different types began to be seen by many nationalists as the most promising type of activity. Some managed to work closely with the police and migration services, the others less so, as they were organized to enforce "law and order" and fight with illegal immigration. They were not planning to undermine the state law enforcement structures but to strengthen them and help them to be more efficient. Also, the tolerance of police was significantly higher than in cases of ordinary street racist violence (Verkhovskii 2016: 88–89).

Incursions that were mostly carried out on the workplaces and living quarters of those considered to be illegal immigrants were attractive as they were aggressive but not too dangerous at the same time. They required little risk-taking by leaders or ordinary participants. Raids could have been advertised, and were often covered on television as well as on videos distributed via the Internet. They became a

74 Martin Laryš

powerful way of attracting supporters, too. The rise of such activities came from the "grassroots" beyond the main radical nationalist organizations like Igor Mangushev's Bright Rus (*Svetlaia Rus'*) and Shield of Moscow (*Shchit Moskvy*) in Moscow (Verkhovskii 2016: 88). Members of these organizations, typically about 10–15 participants, broke into dormitories for immigrants, demanding their documents and sometimes expelling them to the streets (Nikulin 2013). The organizers of other raids (in St. Petersburg it was Nikolai Bondarik, Dmitryi Evtushenko and Dmitriy Bobrov from National-Socialist Initiative) focused on searching illegal market stalls, demanding permits for sale and other documents from vendors, sometimes smashing their products – usually fruits and vegetables. These vendors were targeted because they were immigrants (Stekolshchikova 2013, RBC.ru 2013). Eventually, the main radical nationalist organizations set up their own "raid projects", as did "Russkie" (the Russians) movement (banned for extremism in 2015), who called their project "Guestbusters".

Assaults, or other forms of limited violence, have had more potential than efforts to instigate pogroms or simple backstreet murders because the public was more accepting of them – as a rather unusual, but nevertheless necessary, form of civic activism (Verkhovskii 2016: 88–89). The campaign was eventually almost stopped in 2014 with the beginning of the political mass mobilization against the West and the "Kiev junta" (the new authorities in Ukraine after the revolution). The impact of the anti-migrant raids was completely smoothed over. The new propaganda campaign led to a complete political consolidation around the Kremlin to the detriment of ethno-centric nationalist ideas. In spring 2014, ethno-xenophobia declined rapidly as did the support for ethnic nationalist slogans (Verkhovskii 2016: 82). The Guestbusters project was closed already in autumn 2014. Bright Rus has changed its focus to cooperation with the private military group E.N.O.T. Corp., which is officially sending humanitarian help to Donbass, but is unofficially taking active part in the war (at least until the first half of 2017). Former leader of Shield of Moscow, Alexei Khudyakov, also switched from raids to support of pro-Russian separatists in Eastern Ukraine. Some other activists formed military-sport groups and stopped organizing raids in 2016 (Yudina & Alperovich 2016).

"Single-issue" vigilantism against homosexuals

There were other organizations attacking homosexuals (and alleged drug dealers) by vigilante squads in the same period of 2012–2014. In an ideological way, the main reason was to defend moral order of the society from delinquents subverting the traditional values. The level of tolerance towards the LGBT community in Russia is constantly very low and homophobia is felt throughout all social strata, including in the law enforcement agencies. In the beginning of March 2012, the infamous law against "homosexual propaganda" was adopted in St. Petersburg and some other regions. Radicals of all stripes (Sol 2017) perceived this as an unspoken show of support for anti-LGBT violence.

The main organization involved in homophobic vigilantism was the Restrukt movement founded by well-known neo-Nazi Maksim Martsinkevich. In 2005 Martsinkevich founded Format-18, which recorded videos of its members' physical assaults on non-Slavic (non-white) victims and ideological (left-wing) opponents, posting them on the internet. Restrukt originated as an attempt to give the radical nationalist front new form with the main focus on "protection of the traditional values" (Lutykh 2017). This new form gave the "raid movement" a powerful boost (Verkhovskii 2016: 88). Restrukt had two subsidiaries named *Okkupai-pedofilyai* and *Okkupai-narkofilyai* – the former focused on alleged sexual delinquents, a category which included gays. People wishing to participate in the "hunt for paedophiles" (called "safari") had to send a certain sum of money to Martsinkevich for whom this generated a handsome income as these projects were unbelievably popular. *Okkupai-pedofilyai* has had 220,000 followers on the *VKontakte* social network (Yudina and Alperovich 2014).

Martsinkevich presented his supporters as the guardians of morality, protecting children from sexual violence. They usually shot videos about the capture of "paedophiles on the live bait". Performing on social networks under the guise of minors, his supporters lured "paedophiles" to a date with a young man (aged 14–16) where they were in turn met by group of young nationalist homophobes. Afterwards, they mocked them and interrogated the victims on camera. They accused them of being gay or paedophile, showering them with homophobic insults as well as bullying them. The records were posted on the internet and allegedly sent to relatives and friends of "paedophiles". It turned out to be a sadistic reality show in which viewers could savour someone else's humiliation, covering their ecstasy with the banner of fighting paedophiles. These "safaris" were accompanied by violent threats, abuse, beatings and humiliation of the victims. Victims of these attacks have often suffered depression and psychological damage later on. Martsinkevich and others tried to exploit the high level of homophobia in the society under the guise of fighting paedophilia, assuming that most homosexuals are paedophiles as well. The regional cells of *Okkupai-pedofilyai* numbered several dozens and the movement even reached other neighbouring countries like Kazakhstan, Ukraine or Belarus (Turovskii 2013, Human Rights Watch 2014, Sputnik i pogrom 2013).

The Restrukt movement was later banned. Together with other members who got sentences from three to ten years, its leader, Martsinkevich, was sentenced to ten years in prison in 2017 (Lutykh 2017). Between 2012 and 2013, one of Martsinkevich's teenage sympathizers, Filipp Razinskii, founded a similar homophobic vigilante group called *Okkuai-gerontophilai*. The group pursued young gay boys who went to meetings with older men. Razinskii held the boys by force, scoffed at them and shamed them. It was accompanied with bullying. The publication of videos on the Internet followed. The purpose of the campaign was announced publicly: "Make reposts, break their lives!" (Human Rights Watch 2014). There were also some regional imitations of the homophobic violent vigilante squads like for example The Frontier of the North ("Rubezh severa") in

76 Martin Laryš

Syktyvkar (Komi Republic). Its members were arrested and sentenced after 2014. The level of anti-LGBT violence has decreased since then. However, this was not caused by decrease of homophobia in the society but rather by lowering the public profile of LGBT activists and banning the vigilante homophobic groups (Yudina and Alperovich 2015, Human Rights Watch 2014). After 2014, homophobic violence lost its vigilante nature and now mostly consists of ad hoc attacks by homophobes on people publicly defending their right of sexual orientation, which is not happening very often because of the fear of being attacked.

"People's gatherings" as a vigilante strategy

Another form of vigilantism was based on attempts to instigate pogroms after the clashes (mostly street fights) between ethnic Russians and "aliens" (non-Slavic people) that took place in Russian regions. Nationalists tried to characterize these cases as inter-ethnic conflict and show them to the people as the proof of the oppression of ethnic Russians by immigrants and non-Slavic minorities. Their tactics were to publicise violent incidents involving people from the Caucasus and Central Asia to get political benefits and a reputation as the defenders of the common Russian people. This strategy was created by the Movement against Illegal Immigration (*Dvizhenie protiv nelegalnoi immigratsii*, DPNI). It was founded in 2002 and later, after being banned in 2011, it became the main part of the Russkie coalition.

The former leader of DPNI, Alexandr Belov, who was sentenced to 7.5 years in prison in 2016, confirmed that DPNI at first began to collect and analyse information about the negative role that immigrants played in our life.

> We are monitoring their crimes and learning about the methods of fight against illegal immigration in many regions in Russia and abroad. The main goal of our mass action is to pressure the state authorities for some action in the interests of the local people.
>
> *(Belov 2007)*

The official goal was to force state authorities to adopt a tough approach towards immigration. The informal aim was to score political points and advertise their activities.

DPNI members and other activists usually arrived in towns and distributed leaflets discriminating the target group. A "people's gathering" ("*narodnyi skhod*") of locals and nationalist activists was organized. Unlike a rally, it could legally be called without authorization by the government officials. The turning point in the incitement of riots came with the events in Karelian Kondopoga in September 2006. A brawl between Russians and Caucasians in a pub developed into a mass affray during which two Russians were killed and six persons injured. DPNI managed to encourage violence. It called a "people's gathering" in which about 3,000 people participated. It was followed by pogroms on the property of

Caucasians in the city (looting and arson attacks) and calls for deportation. The police were unable to control the situation for several days. DPNI recorded its greatest-ever success, which it sought to repeat over the following years. The Kondopoga scenario was never successfully repeated, however. The law enforcement agencies were aware of these plans and able to prevent the spreading of violence (Kozhevnikova 2008). Notwithstanding, attempts to repeat Kondopoga attack were occasionally accompanied by inflexible and unprofessional police action and a lack of credible information about what was actually happening when the unrest had taken place. Ordinary conflicts developed into larger clashes; if culprits were not punished (due to corruption, for instance), people were fuelled by righteous anger, and information vacuums facilitated the spread of rumours, myths and conspiracy theories which the nationalists exploited and turned ordinary conflict into inter-ethnic clashes (Yudina, Alperovich & Verkhovskii 2013). An essential part of this strategy was the nationalists' claim that the Russian government and police are always on the side of the non-Russians. Through a wave of police repressions against leaders and ordinary members of militant nationalist organizations these efforts have been halted and there are no such events at present. With the last attempt around 2015, radical nationalists lost their interest in similar activities. It happened also because of their fear of police actions.

End of vigilante activities in Russia (2014–2018): police repressions, banning, fragmentation and marginalization of the radical nationalists

After the main wave of racist violence taking place around 2009–2010, no leading political activists were imprisoned. However, their sense of not being punishable evaporated. The large-scale arrests of those involved in racist violence led to a reduction of hate crimes. The aim of state authorities was to marginalize the entire stream of Russian radical nationalism. Alternatives were created for radical nationalists who wanted to break away from the groups that had come under pressure, like Kremlin youth organizations (Verkhovskii 2016: 80–81). Since 2014, the war in Ukraine has caused the split in the ranks of radical nationalists. It was followed by more vigorous police repressions against pro-Ukrainian opposition nationalists in Russia. The Russian state took very harsh measures against all of them, criminalizing things such as sharing posts on social media. Since that time, almost all militant radical nationalist organizations were banned and their leaders arrested or exiled. The number of murders decreased tenfold compared to 2007–2008, although anti-immigrant violence did not disappear from Russian streets completely (9 killed and 72 injured in 2016 and 6 killed and 71 injured in 2017) (Yudina & Alperovich 2017, Yudina 2018). The main radical nationalist coalition movement Russkie (The Russians) was banned in 2015 and its leaders arrested and jailed (Baklanov 2014, Dzhapoladova 2016, Yudina & Alperovich 2015). Several new and less-known groups, theoretically capable of vigilante activities against migrants and minorities, have emerged on the ruins of the Russkie movement but they were not very successful in attracting people to its circles. Turf wars between the last few radical nationalist leaders in Russia started during 2017, when they accused each other of being provocateurs working for Russian special services (Yudina & Alperovich 2017). The last anti-immigration raid was organized in Moscow in February 2017 by Vladimir Komarnitskii who led the Tsitadel project (one of the small network communities based on the ruins of the "Russkie" coalition). The ambush happened in the underground subway at the vegetable stalls – no violence took place and police took away the trays of vegetables to their station for control (Vkontakte: Avtonomnye NS Moskvy 2017).

Political, social and economic context

A swift rise of xenophobia in Russian society in 2000s has been linked to the wave of migration coming mainly from the Caucasus and Central Asia, and to the conflict in Chechnya. The Chechen conflict spread into Russian cities through terrorist attacks. Terrorism has played a significant role in reducing the sense of security in Russian society, corresponding to the rise of fears, anxieties and aversion to all Caucasians, disrespecting their nationality (Laryš & Mareš 2011: 133–134, Prusenkova 2017).

After 1991, a serious demographic crisis led to a growing demand for unskilled or low-skilled guest workers and labour immigration from the former Soviet republics. The great migration treks from Central Asia were a relatively new phenomenon, gaining momentum only after the differences in living standards between Russia and the southern tier of former Soviet republics began to widen drastically in the first decade of the 2000s. Estimating how many illegal workers are in Russia nowadays is a matter of anybody's guess. According to Tatiana Moskalkova, Russia's Commissioner for Human Rights, there were between 8 and 10 million illegal immigrants in Russia in 2017 (Vashchenko 2017). Real figures, however, are less important for the nationalistic discourse in Russia than the perception that the country is being engulfed with the people who are not only culturally foreign, but dangerous. Moreover, the ethnocultural distance between the new migrants and local population was increasing: Ukrainians, South Caucasians and Moldovans were being replaced increasingly by Tajiks, Kyrgyz and Uzbeks (Kolstø 2016: 3). Most of these guest workers belong to the young generation, born after the Soviet Union disintegrated. They were not educated in the Soviet system, do not speak Russian very well and do not know Russian culture. Immigrants can help each other and co-operate within their communities, unlike Russians, whose society is mostly atomized (Laryš & Mareš 2011: 133). It helps them to negotiate with the state authorities (including the police) more effectively, sometimes even enabling them to evade punishment for crimes by buying themselves out thanks to omnipresent corruption in the Russian state structures and possible financial resources of distant relatives. In these cases, the nationalists are talking about "ethnic mafias". Major complaints from the Russian society towards immigrants are related to their perceived responsibility for the high crime rates, such as robberies, rapes, etc. directed against the Russian majority and "ethno-cultural threat" towards the host society and its, variously conceived, values (Kosmarskaya & Savin 2016: 140–141). Russian nationalists traditionally see ethnic Russians as marginalized by the state and other nationalities as favoured. They claim that state fails to defend the Russians from systematic abuse (Hutchings & Tolz 2016: 309–325).

In the past, the state authorities had largely condoned radical Russian nationalism. The Putin regime had apparently calculated that they could harness nationalist sentiments in the population and exploited them for their own purposes, as for instance the establishment of the pro-Putin youth movements. Nevertheless, around 2009/2010, Kremlin strategists seemed to have second thoughts about the wisdom of this strategy. The disenchantment was mutual: Russia's nationalists felt that Putin has betrayed them by welcoming immigrant labourers and sending billions of dollars in subsidies to the Muslim regions in North Caucasus. When the hard-line nationalists were driven out of the Kremlin´s embrace, some of them transferred to the anti-Putin opposition. This became clear when huge anti-Putin protests erupted in Moscow and other Russian cities after the fraudulent parliamentary elections in December 2011. In these demonstrations, pro-Western democrats marched together with vociferous nationalists (Kolstø 2016: 2–3).

In addition to an influx of people from the "near abroad", all major Russian cities also have a population stemming from the "inner abroad" – the string of ethnically non-Russian republics north of Caucasian Range. High fertility rates and low standards of living have induced many people from these areas to migrate to other parts of Russia. Russian nationalist discourse often does not distinguish between labour (im)migrants from the near and the inner abroad, but puts them together as one group of "aliens" or "colonists" who allegedly threaten to dilute the (ethnic) Russian character of their neighbourhoods. Widespread and growing migrantophobia in the Russian population soon became the main motor behind the nationalist mobilization (Kolstø 2016: 4–5). Due to an increase in xenophobic rhetoric in many media outlets, dislike of foreigners was especially wide-spread in 2013. Supported by the anti-immigrant riots in Biryulevo (blue-collar suburb in Moscow) in October 2013, they were very quickly replaced by the official hatred against the West and new Ukrainian government during the annexation of Crimea and war in Donbass as old–new "external threat". Ethno-xenophobia in the society has decreased since 2014 because the state authorities have found a very comfortable enemy, embodied in the West and its values (Gannenko 2017, Strzelecki 2017).

Xenophobia and migrantophobia have been almost eliminated from the public space (especially internet) by criminalizing everything remotely resembling incitement to hatred on racial, ethnical or nationalistic grounds. Increasingly restrictive "anti-extremist" laws in an authoritarian regime are problematized by the fact that any political opposition to the regime may be now labelled as extremist and criminalized (the liberal "anti-system" pro-western opposition is also being called "extremist"). In 2016, more than 1650 accusations of extremist crimes were reported. It was 416 more than in 2014 and 121 more than in 2015, but only the number of non-violent "crimes" has risen while the level of violent hate crimes is constantly decreasing – from 115 crimes in 2015 to 77 in 2016 (Vyzhutovich 2017).

Organization and communication

Due to the authoritarian character of the current political regime, electoral policy for radical nationalists is completely closed as a way of communication with its potential electorate or as an instrument for societal mobilization. The young autonomous nationalists were the main asset of key nationalist organizations for public events until 2014–2015, when they acted as street soldiers demonstrating the power of radical nationalists.

The attendance at the traditional political nationalist meetings never exceeded a few hundred (Verkhovskii 2016). The main nationalist event is the Russian March ("*Russkii marsh*") taking place every year since November 2005. In 2011–2013, around 5,000 to 6,000 radical nationalists and neo-Nazis took part in this event, compared to just 300 in 2017. After the pressure of state authorities, nationalists were forced to refrain from most of public activities while rank-and-file radical nationalists ceased to attend public events. Some radical ethno-nationalist organizations solved this problem by cooperating with liberal opposition structures and came to the streets with civic slogans. The others completely ceased public activities (Alperovich 2017).

Criminalization of posting and sharing anything with supposedly extremist content (or what is defined by authorities as such) has greatly hampered nationalist online communication. As the word "extremism" has no clear legal definition in Russian laws, its ambiguity was widely used against any opposition (more on this in Kalajdžić 2016, Meduza 2016, Kochetov 2017, Krivets 2016, Torocheshnikova 2018). The social media profiles of active organizations display a main focus on the support for imprisoned nationalists, radical opposition to Putin's regime, militant anti-communism, and solving their international disputes. Only rarely will an anti-immigrant post emerge. Usually, they assume that Putin's regime is attempting to replace ethnic Russians with the "more obedient" immigrants from post-soviet non-Slavic countries (Vkontakte: Partiya natsionalistov 2017).

No radical nationalist organization in Russia is registered as a political party. During the all-opposition, anti-regime protests in 2011–2012, part of the radical nationalist structure has approached the liberal opposition. The liberal PARNAS party was their first choice to turn to because it shared a similar political agenda – opposition to the authoritarian regime in Russia and its aggressive foreign policy. Some radical nationalist activists were even nominated to this party in the 2016–2017 parliamentary and local elections (Yudina & Alperovich 2017). This does not mean that PARNAS leadership shares the racist and/or xenophobic agenda. It rather resembles a "marriage of convenience", using the nationalist organizational structures and personal resources for achieving their goals on the principle the "enemy of my enemy is my friend". Part of the radical nationalists also support well-known opposition figure Alexei Navalnyi by attending his meetings. An anonymous participant of the Russian March in 2017 explains the beliefs of most of these activists:

> I support Navalnyi because he is fighting Putin. Putin is the symbol of Russophobia. During Putin's rule, they (police) arrest nationalists. Putin is mixing us with Chinese and Caucasians.
>
> *(Yakovlev 2017)*

The main political opponent for most of radical militant nationalists is Russian president Vladimir Putin. He is being accused of anti-Russian policy, "Rusophobia" and personal responsibility for immigrant influx and financial preferences for Northern Caucasian republics, especially Chechnya. For state-oriented, neo-imperial nationalists the major political opponents in Russia are the liberal political structures and international/pro-western NGOs. They are perceived as a "fifth column", aiming to destroy "traditional values and orthodox faith", which according to them is to be replaced with "homosexuality, multiculturalism, political correctness and cultural decay". These state-oriented nationalists do not attack migrants, but they can be occasionally involved in anti-LGBT violence (see more in Human Rights Watch 2014).

The ties and contacts that Russian radical nationalists maintain with their Western counterparts are not essential for the growth of this movement. Some anti-immigrant groups resemble their western peers, but they do not maintain immediate links to them. The closest ties of radical nationalists are with Ukraine, where part of the leadership emigrated, and to their nationalist structures – primarily National Corps ("*Natsionalnyi korpus*"), a political party that emerged in 2018 from Azov regiment with its own vigilante groups "National Militia" ("*Natsionalni druzhyny*").

Ambiguously, more immediate connections with far-right groups and parties in Europe are maintained by the Russian state through some loyal organizations and government organized non-governmental organizations (GONGOs) even supporting them financially (see Shekhovtsov 2017). Most of the European far-right parties perceive Putin's authoritative regime as a vital alternative to multi-cultural liberal European values. Moreover, the Putin regime is attempting to legitimize itself ideologically by sticking to ultra-conservative ideas to cover its kleptocratic nature (see more at Rodkiewicz & Rogoza 2015). The majority of the European far-right parties sympathize more with the Dugin anti-western ideas rather than with pro-Ukrainian and anti-Putin Russian nationalists.

Conclusion

Most of the anti-immigrant violence was committed between 2006 and 2010 against visually distinguishable "ethnic aliens" from Caucasus and Central Asia. It was executed mostly by racist teenage gangs but there were also vigilante tendencies within the radical nationalist groups. The vigilante terrorism could be identified in several medially known cases, often inter-connected with the insurgent terrorism. Other vigilante movements were not so violent, but the "people's gatherings" initiated and organized by nationalists for "the defence against the criminal migrants" threatened with political destabilization in some regions. The "raid movement" gained traction in 2012, after the "people's gatherings" had been suppressed by state authorities and abandoned by nationalists. This time it focused on limited violence to avoid police pressure and to win public sympathies. Nonetheless, this method was not very successful and these movements were either banned or started to turn their attention to other activities around 2014. Hate crimes have decreased almost tenfold since 2008. The main reason is not an increase of tolerance within the Russian society, but the shift of attention to other issues accompanied by the crackdown against radical nationalists. There is still a high general level of xenophobic violence compared to European countries but it is more related to an overall high level of violence and criminality in Russia. Radical ethno-nationalists are cut off from all important means of communication within the Russian society. In fact, public activity is almost non-existent while their focus is directed to the opposition of the authoritative regime in Russia, keeping down racist rhetoric within the all-opposition front. Without access to the media and ability to organize public events it is very hard for radical ethno-nationalists to spread their message among ordinary Russians. Their public image has been further damaged by their association with liberal political organizations. These groups became unpopular because of their fight against Putin and his aggressive foreign policy, after an effective anti-western propaganda campaign.

Finally, Russia was not affected by the migrant crisis as Europe was since 2014. On the contrary, the migrant crisis was used by Russian authorities for both domestic and foreign policy goals. In the domestic policy, it was applied for media coverage of the mortal crisis in Europe, shattering apart thanks to its decadent liberal values and exaggerated tolerance to non-European immigrants. In general, its aim was reducing the attractiveness of an economically advanced and culturally attractive West in Russian society. In its foreign policy, the immigration crisis appeared as a suitable pretext for supporting vigilante and/or far right movements in European countries with the aim to destabilize and undermine liberal democracies. Part of this campaign was presenting a contemporary Russian authoritarian model based on "traditional values" as an alternative to the decadent and politically correct West.

References

Abarinov, V. (2006) "Russkaya bolezn", Sovershenno sekretno, 2. Retrieved from https://www.sovsekretno.ru/articles/id/1489/ .

Alperovich, V. (2017, December 26). Eto fiasko gospoda. Dvizhenie russkikh natsionalistov letom-osenyu 2017 goda, *Informatsionno-analiticheskiy tsentr SOVA*. Retrieved from http://www.sova-center.ru/racism-xenophobia/publications/2017/12/d38558/.

Avtonomnye NS Moskvy (2017, February 1). "Tukhlaya rybka" – Proekt "Tsitadel", *Vkontakte*. Retrieved from https://vk.com/blacknsblock?w=wall-118555608_253.

Baklanov, A. (2014, October 16). Osnovatelya DPNI zaderzhali po delu o khishchenii pyati milliardov dollarov, *Snob*. Retrieved from https://snob.ru/selected/entry/82356?preview=print&v=1452779894.

Belov, A. (2007, October 25). Ideologiya bolshinstva, *Polyarnaya zvezda*. Retrieved from http://zvezda.ru/politics/2007/10/25/belov.htm.

Chawrylo, K. (2014, December 29). Russian nationalists on the Kremlin's policy in Ukraine, *Centre for Eastern Studies, OSW Commentary*. Retrieved from https://www.osw.waw.pl/en/publikacje/osw-commentary/2014-12-29/russian-nationalists-kremlins-policy-ukraine.

Dzhapoladova, N. (2016, March 15). Russkiy natsionalist i "Zloi kazakh", *Radio svoboda*. Retrieved from http://www.svoboda.org/a/27611013.html.

Falkovskii, I. & Litoj, A. (2013). *Grazhdanskaya voyna uzhe nachalas*. Moscow, Algoritm.

Gannenko, V. (2017, September 20). Krymnash protiv ksenofobii: Kak Rossiya stanovitsya terpimee Evropy, *Sobesednik.ru*. Retrieved from https://sobesednik.ru/obshchestvo/krymnash-protiv-ksenofobii-kak-rossiya-stanovitsya-terpimee-evropy.

Human Rights Watch (2014, December 15). License to harm – violence and harassment against LGBT people and activists in Russia. Retrieved from https://www.hrw.org/report/2014/12/15/license-harm/violence-and-harassment-against-lgbt-people-and-activists-russia.

Hutchings, S. & Tolz, V. (2016). Ethnicity and nationhood on Russian state-aligned television: Contextualising geopolitical crisis. In: Kolstø, P. & Blakkisrud, H. (eds). *The new Russian nationalism – imperialism, ethnicity and authoritarianism 2000–15*. Edinburgh, Edinburgh University Press, pp. 298–336.

Kalajdžić, P. (2016, June 3). Desyatki lyudei v Rossii sazhayut v tyurmy za "laiki" i ssylki v sotssetyakh, *Inosmi.ru*. Retrieved from http://inosmi.ru/social/20160603/236751298.html.

Kochetov, N. (2017, July 24). Repostnul, laiknul – v tyurmu, *Rosbalt*. Retrieved from http://www.rosbalt.ru/russia/2017/07/24/1633123.html.

Kolstø, P. (2016). *Introduction: Russian nationalism is back – but precisely what does that mean?* In: Kolstø, P., & Blakkisrud, H. (eds). *The new Russian nationalism – imperialism, ethnicity and authoritarianism 2000–15*. Edinburgh, Edinburgh University Press, pp. 1–18.

Kosmarskaya, N. & Savin, I. (2016). *Everyday nationalism in Russia in European context: Moscow residents' perceptions of ethnic minority, migrants and migration*, In: Kolstø, P. & Blakkisrud, H. (eds). *The new Russian nationalism – imperialism, ethnicity and authoritarianism 2000–15*, Edinburgh, Edinburgh University Press, pp. 132–160.

Kozhevnikova, G. (2007, April 1). Radikal'nyi natsionalizm v Rossii i protivodeistvie emu v 2006 godu, *Informatsionno-analiticheskii tsentr SOVA*. Retrieved from http://www.sova-center.ru/racism-xenophobia/publications/2007/04/d10516/.

Kozhevnikova, G. (2008, February 7). Radikal'nyi natsionalizm v Rossii i protivodeistvie emu v 2007 godu, *Informatsionno-analiticheskii tsentr SOVA*. Retrieved from http://www.sova-center.ru/racism-xenophobia/publications/2008/02/d12582/.

Kozhevnikova, G. (2009, February 19). Radikal'nyi natsionalizm v Rossii i protivodeistvie emu v 2008 godu, *Informatsionno-analiticheskii tsentr SOVA*. Retrieved from http://www.sova-center.ru/racism-xenophobia/publications/2009/02/d15326/.

Kozhevnikova, G. (2010, February 2). Pod znakom politicheskogo terora. Radikal'nyi natsionalizm v Rossii i protivodeistvie emu v 2009 godu, *Informatsionno-analiticheskii tsentr SOVA*. Retrieved from http://www.sova-center.ru/racism-xenophobia/publications/2010/02/d17889/.

Krivets, A. (2016, June 24). Kodeks blogera. Kak zhit v mire, gde sazhayut za repost vo "Vkontakte", *Medialeaks.ru*. Retrieved from http://medialeaks.ru/2406nastia-kodeks-blogera-kak-zhit-v-mire-gde-sazhayut-za-kartinku-vkontakte/.

Laryš, M. & Mareš, M. (2011). Right-wing extremist violence in the Russian Federation. *Europe-Asia Studies*, 63(1), 129–154.

Litoi, A. (2015, June 3). Delo Ilii Goryacheva: ot BORNa do Antimaydana, *The Insider*. Retrieved from http://theins.ru/politika/8873.

84 Martin Laryš

Lutykh, S. (2017, June 28). Devyat' druzei Tesaka, *Lenta.ru*. Retrieved from https://lenta.ru/articles/2017/06/28/tesak/.

Lvov, A. (2006, May 24). Peterburg vyzdoravlivaet ot "korichnevoi chumy", *Fontanka*. Retrieved from http://www.fontanka.ru/2006/05/24/165427/.

Meduza (2016, July 5). "VKontakte" so sledovatelyami – Pochemu dela ob ekstremizme vozbuzhdayut tolko za posty v etoi sotsseti, *Meduza*. Retrieved from https://meduza.io/feature/2016/07/05/vkontakte-so-sledovatelyami.

News.ru (2009): Peterburgskie militsionery "poteryali" spisok chlenov bandy neonatsista Borovikova eshche 5 let nazad, 29. 9. 2009, *News.ru*. Retrieved from http://www.newsru.com/crime/29sep2009/miltloseganglistsp.html.

Nikulin, P. (2013, October 31). "Bessmyslennoe makhanie flazhkami", *Russkaya planeta*. Retrieved from http://rusplt.ru/society/russkij_marsh_storonniki.html.

Partiya natsionalistov (2017, December 27). Politika genotsida korennogo naseleniya Rossii prodolzhaetsya, *Vkontakte*. Retrieved from https://vk.com/partiyanatsionalistov?w=wall-106619597_16563.

Prusenkova, N. (2017, September 20). Voina vyshla iz podvoroten, *Novaya gazeta*. Retrieved from https://www.novayagazeta.ru/articles/2017/09/20/73910-voyna-vyshla-iz-podvoroten.

Rodkiewicz, W. & Rogoza, J. (2015). *Potemkin conservatism – An ideological tool of Kremlin*. Warsaw, Centre for Eastern Studies, Point of View.

Shekhovtsov, A. (2017). *Russia and the western far right: Tango Noir*. Abingdon, Routledge.

Shnirelman, V. (2007). *'Chistilshchiki moskovskikh ulits'—skinkhedy, SMI i obshchestvennoe mnenie*. Moscow, Russian Academy of Science.

Sidorov, P. (2006, June 2). Beshennye psy Peterburga, *Moskovskii komsomolets*. Retrieved from http://www.mk.ru/editions/daily/article/2006/06/02/181810-beshenyie-psyi-peterburga.html.

Sol (2017, May 17). Gde predstavitelyam LGBT zhivetsya "nekhorosho"? V Rossii poyavilas "karta nenavisti", *Sol*. Retrieved from https://salt.zone/radio/7491.

Sputnik i pogrom (2013, December 13). "Oskorblenie pobedy, edy i Vali": za chto obyavili v mezhdunarodnyi rozysk skinkheda Tesaka? *Sputnik i pogrom*. Retrieved from https://sputnikipogrom.com/politics/7190/dont-insult-food-and-valya/.

Stekolshchikova, E. (2013, August 1). "Russkie zachistki": natsionalisty prodolzhat gromit nelegalnye rynki, *Argumenty i fakty*. Retrieved from http://www.spb.aif.ru/society/136562.

Strzelecki, J. (2017, August 8). Russian nationalism three years after the annexation of Crimea, *Centre for Eastern Studies, OSW Commentary*. Retrieved from https://www.osw.waw.pl/en/publikacje/osw-commentary/2017-08-08/russian-nationalism-three-years-after-annexation-crimea.

Tarasov, A. (2005). Natsi-skiny v sovremennoi Rossii, *Byuro po pravam cheloveka moskovskoi-khel'sinskoi gruppy*. Retrieved from: http://scepsis.net/library/id_605.html.

Tarasov, A. (2010). *Subkultura futbolnykh fanatov v Rossii i pravyi radikalizm*, In: Verkhovskii, A. (ed.) *Russkiy natsionalizm mezhdu vlastyu i oppozitsiei*. Moscow, Tsentr "Panorama", pp. 18–51.

Torocheshnikova, M. (2018, January 8). Srok za repost, *Radio svoboda*. Retrieved from https://www.svoboda.org/a/28943937.html.

Turovskii, D. (2013, July 5). Obraztsovo-pokazatelnoe unizhenie – Kak "Okkupai-Pedofilyai" boretsya s "izvrashchentsami" na Urale, *Lenta.ru*. Retrieved from https://lenta.ru/articles/2013/07/05/kamenskuralsky/.

RBC.ru (2013, August 22). Uchastniki "russkikh zachistok" v Peterburge okazalis za reshetkoi, *RBC.ru*. Retrieved from https://www.rbc.ru/spb_sz/22/08/2013/5592a89f9a794719538d030a.

Vashchenko, V. (2017, May 17). Rossiya pereschitala migrantov, *Gazeta.ru*. Retrieved from https://www.gazeta.ru/social/2017/05/17/10677761.shtml.

Verkhovski, A. (2009). Interview, Moscow.

Verkhovskii, A. (2016). Radical nationalists from the start of Medvedev's presidency to the war in Donbas: True till death? In: Kolsto, P. & Blakkisrud (eds). *The new Russian nationalism – imperialism, ethnicity and authoritarianism 2000–15*, Edinburgh, Edinburgh University Press, pp. 75–104.

Verkhovskii, A. & Kozhevnikova, G. (2011, March 11). Prizrak Manezhnoi ploshchadi: Radikal'nyi natsionalizm v Rossii i protivodeistvie emu v 2010 godu, *Informatsionno-analiticheskii tsentr SOVA*, Retrieved from http://www.sova-center.ru/racism-xenophobia/publications/2011/03/d21140/.

Vyzhutovich, V. (2017, June 8). Ksenofobiya: smena obiekta, *Rossiyskaya gazeta* Retrieved from https://rg.ru/2017/06/08/vyzhutovich-uroven-ksenofobii-v-rossii-zametno-ponizilsia.html.

Waldmann, Peter. 1998. *Terrorismus. Provokation der Macht*. München: Gerling Akademie Verlag.

Yakovlev, D. (2017, November 4). Za russkikh i Navalnogo, *New Times*, Retrieved from https://newtimes.ru/articles/detail/125657/.

Yudina, N. & Alperovich, V. (2016, February 20). Dvizhenie ultrapravykh v situatsii davleniya. Ksenofobiya i radikalnyi natsionalizm i protivostodeistvie im v Rossii v 2015 godu, *Informatsionno-analiticheskiy tsentr SOVA*, Retrieved from http://www.sova-center.ru/racism-xenophobia/publications/2016/02/d33886/#_Toc443492086.

Yudina, N. & Alperovich, V. (2017, March 22). Starye problemy i novye soyuzy. Ksenofobiya i radikainyi natsionalizm i protivostodeistviie im v 2016 godu v Rossji, *Informatsionno-analiticheskiy tsentr SOVA*, Retrieved from http://www.sova-center.ru/racism-xenophobia/publications/2017/03/d36630/.

Yudina, N. & Alperovich, V. (2014, July 14). Ukraina sputala natsionalistam karty: Ksenofobiya i radikal'nyi natsionalizm i protivodeistviye im v Rossii v pervoi polovine 2014, *Informatsionno-analiticheskiy tsentr SOVA*, Retrieved from http://www.sova-center.ru/racism-xenophobia/publications/2014/07/d29887/.

Yudina, N. & Alperovich, V. (2015, March 26). Zatishie pered burei? Ksenofobiya i radikalnyi natsionalizm i protivodeistvie im v 2014 godu v Rossii, *Informatsionno-analiticheskiy tsentr SOVA*, Retrieved from http://www.sova-center.ru/racism-xenophobia/publications/2015/03/d3157ize5/.

Yudina, N., Alperovich, V. & Verkhovskii, A. (2013). Ultrapravye na ulitsakh: s plakatom za demokratiyu ili s nozhom v karmane. Ksenofobiya i radikalnyi natsionalizm i protivodeistvie im v 2012 godu v Rossii, *Informatsionno-analiticheskii tsentr SOVA*, 15. 3. 2013, Retrieved from http://www.sova-center.ru/racism-xenophobia/publications/2013/03/d26655/.

Yudina, N. (2018, January 31). Ksenofobiya v tsifrakh: Prestupleniya nenavisti i protivodeistvie im v Rossii v 2017 godu, *Informatsionno-analiticheskiy tsentr SOVA*, Retrieved from http://www.sova-center.ru/racism-xenophobia/publications/2018/01/d38732/ .

Zheglov, A. (2007) "Studentov-terroristov vydal dnevnik", *Kommersant*, 8 August, Retrieved from https://www.kommersant.ru/doc/793804.

6

ANTI-IMMIGRATION MILITIAS AND VIGILANTE GROUPS IN GERMANY

An overview

Daniel Koehler

Introduction

On 21 May 2016, in the small East German town of Arnsdorf, located in the state of Saxony, a conflict between a 21-year-old Iraqi refugee and cashiers in a local grocery store was escalating. He had repeatedly entered the store that day to report problems with a prepaid cell phone card he had bought. Not being able to make himself understood, he was accused of harassing the store clerk. The police, who were called two times, brought the Iraqi citizen back to a psychiatric hospital, where he was treated for multiple mental health issues. When he returned to the store the third time, a self-proclaimed vigilante group physically apprehended him. This resulted in a struggle ending with the refugee being beaten and tied to a nearby tree until the police arrived. Everything was filmed by another person watching the scene, and the recording of the encounter later found its way onto the Internet resulting in a nationwide outcry. Almost one year later, in May 2017, the same person was found dead in a nearby forest, almost at the same time as the trial against four members of the vigilante group from Arnsdorf for illegal restraint and physical assault was beginning. The trial was ended after a couple of hours and all suspects acquitted (Maxwill, 2017).

The Arnsdorf case brought the issue of extreme right-wing or anti-immigration vigilante groups to a wider public attention. As a reaction to the large increase of numbers of refugees seeking asylum in Germany between 2015 and 2017, far-right anti-immigration mobilization and violence also reached the second highest peak since the early 1990s, when, following the German reunification, a wave of racist and xenophobic violence swept across the country. A key component of far-right and right-wing populist propaganda in their efforts to mobilize against the government's immigration policies was the notion of an existential physical and cultural threat for every German citizen materializing through the stream of refugees crossing the borders. Exploding crime rates (especially focusing on rape and other forms of sexual assault by refugees) were prophesized over and over again by far-right groups, which systematically organized street protests and resistance whenever possible and usually in the vicinity of newly opened or designated refugee housing units.

Vigilantism as a new mobilization strategy by extreme right-wing groups aims to capitalize on feelings of existential threats posed by refugees and disappointment with the perceived German government's inability to address these threats and provide adequate protection. This newly opened critical space for criticizing the government as impotent, corrupt or even conspiring against its own population provided a chance to offer alternative and extra-legal solutions to these perceived problems.

While vigilante groups as such are a rather fringe phenomenon in Germany, some cases of crossover even into right-wing terrorism have become public. Hence, this chapter will provide an overview of what is known about far-right and anti-immigration vigilantism in Germany and their context within the overall violent organized extreme right-wing milieu in the country. A main argument of this chapter is that far-right vigilantism as a more or less new form of anti-immigration mobilization has not yet established itself as a significant aspect of the German far-right movement. Even though perceived existential threats and anti-government conspiracy theories have resulted in an increase of far-right vigilantism, Germany appears to be withstanding and constraining the many attempts to create functioning and lasting vigilante groups, with a few local exceptions. One reason for that might be the strong rule of law and monopoly of force in Germany, which has a comparatively strict legislation regarding possession of weapons by citizens and posing as alternative policing force. Whether that remains the case in the future as well depends on the one hand on the impact of highly polarizing events, such as terror attacks or high impact crime scenarios. On the other hand, the long term success of right-wing populist movements and parties, such as the Alternative for Germany (AFD), which use their anti-establishment platform to erode trust in the German government, will also play a significant role.

This chapter will give an overview of far-right and anti-immigration oriented vigilantism in Germany. It will address its historic roots and role within the current right-wing landscape, as well as permissive and repressive factors of the cultural and legal context. The chapter will also introduce some specific case studies highlighting how such groups might organize and operate in the future and whether they add a distinctive new threat to other forms of extremist or anti-immigration mobilization. As there is currently no qualitative or quantitative research about far-right or anti-immigration vigilante groups in Germany and no official governmental statistics exist (except on answer by the Federal Government to a parliamentary inquiry), the following observations and hypotheses are based largely on secondary sources, for example on press reports, and selected case studies.

88 Daniel Koehler

Militias and vigilante groups in Germany: a historical and definitional note

Vigilante groups, called "Bürgerwehren"[1] in Germany, have their historical roots in the nineteenth century, when citizens were called upon to form defence forces based on the duties associated with the legal status of citizenship. These paramilitary units played a significant part in the German March Revolution of 1848/1849 but lost their relevance with the subsequent implementation of standing professional armies. Mostly, these groups have a folkloristic and traditional function in Germany, where "citizen guards" (Bürgergarde) perform displays of local culture and history at festivities.

Partially referring back to this historic tradition of citizens defending their cities, modern far-right influenced "Bürgerwehren" or vigilante groups have a very different common characteristic, which is to provide extra-legal and non-sanctioned parallel policing and protection against crime. This protection is typically offered for a rather exclusively understood notion of "the people", usually meaning other citizens or somehow legitimate inhabitants of a certain area as opposed to external foes. The existence of such vigilante groups implies a lack of trust by their members in the abilities of the German government and legitimate law enforcement to adequately provide protection and public safety and the urgent need to "take matters into their own hands". While clearly different types of such groups in this sense need to be differentiated (e.g. those just alerting the police of suspicious activities or those actively pursuing forms of lynching justice), no official definition and statistics regarding anti-immigration vigilante groups exist in Germany so far.

Nevertheless, it is important not to confuse vigilantism with another form of paramilitary far-right activity with a long tradition in Germany: military sports groups or so called "Wehrsportgruppen". These clearly militaristic forms of organization reached their peak in the 1980s and crossed the border into terrorism on multiple occasions. The most infamous case was the "Wehrsportgruppe Hoffmann" (WSG), which was established 1973 by the trained graphic designer Karl-Heinz Hoffmann and banned as a militant anti-constitutional organization in 1980. The group is connected (even though this is rarely legally proven) with a number of individual acts of violence (killings, bombing attacks and arson). After the group's prohibition for example, the former WSG-member Gundolf Köhler committed the most lethal terrorist attack in post Second World War Germany: the bombing of the Munich Oktoberfest 1980, causing 13 deaths and wounding 211 victims. With about 440 members, divisions all over Germany, a military infrastructure and hierarchy (including uniforms, ranks and insignia) and members extensively trained in guerrilla warfare, including the handling of explosives, insurgent tactics, and raids on military targets, the WSG actively prepared to overthrow the German government. The WSG regularly acted as a security force for other extreme right-wing events during which WSG members violently clashed with opponents or the police on multiple occasions. Its ideology was based on a militant rejection of democracy rooted in neo-Nazism and portrayal of being the spearhead of the right-wing revolution (Koehler, 2016c).

In a similar way, vigilante groups can also not be compared with militias of World War I veterans during the time of the Weimar Republic in the interwar period, which played a significant role in undermining democratic governance and helping National Socialism to gain power. In addition, paramilitary organizations like the SA (Sturmabteilung) provided specific protection for political events such as speeches and rallies of the National Socialists and were also used to engage in open street fights against Communists. All these activities did not have pre-dominantly the goal to provide security for citizens as an alternative police force but either to directly attack political opponents and defend against them or to provide an organizational structure for war veterans and resisting demobilization.

The military sports groups or militias of the post-World War II Germany had the preparation for a violent struggle against a perceived oppressive illegal occupation government as their main goal and did not care about the protec-tion of private citizens against crime (and immigrants). "Bürgerwehren" is still a somewhat ambiguous term in German, which only recently caught a strong anti-immigration and xenophobic connotation, following increasing public attention to incidents of far-right violence involving such self-organized and self-proclaimed amateur policing forces.

However, the difficulty in measuring the impact of specifically extreme right-wing or anti-immigration oriented vigilante groups is increased by lack of defini-tional clarity and ways to distinguish them from other groups, like, for example, neighbourhood watches or other associations supported by local police. This pro-blem became clear in January 2017, when the German government replied to an official parliamentary inquiry on that matter, stating that it only had knowledge about seven vigilante groups with ties into the right-wing extremist movement but also had to admit that crimes of such organizations is not separately captured by any current police statistic (Bundesregierung, 2016). Nevertheless, it is clear and was pointed out in the same government document, that far-right propaganda sees vigilantism as a key recruitment tool and actively calls for the creation of such groups across Germany. It seems, that the majority of vigilante activism in Ger-many might still be confined to the online space, for example to the creation of dedicated Facebook groups. In February 2016, a journalistic investigation by *Vice Magazine* looked at a sample of 15 local interest far-right vigilante groups on Facebook with membership between 500 and 14,000. It was striking though, that almost all of these groups were displaying serious struggles to translate any online sympathy into offline activism, for example to organize patrols or strategy meetings (Locker & Neifer, 2016). Groups operating at the national level, such as the "German Defence League" have a visible and comparatively strong presence on Facebook, and their symbols can be observed regularly in far-right rallies. Never-theless, their role remains comparatively marginal. They were only mentioned once in the annual intelligence report of 2012, after members of the GDL clashed with Salafists during demonstrations (BMI, 2013, p. 269). Extreme right-wing parties like the "Nationaldemokratische Partei Deutschland" (NPD) (National Democratic Party of Germany) or "Der Dritte Weg" (The Third Way) have tried to raise the importance of vigilante groups through their own propaganda. The comparatively limited success in that regard must be seen within the context of the far-right as such in Germany.

One of the very few studies on modern German vigilante groups and their crossover with far-right milieus identified four different types: (1) "cooperative security initiatives"[2], (2) "pre-political interest groups"[3], (3) "protest groups"[4] and (4) "right-wing extremist violence groups"[5] (Quent, 2016, pp. 18–30). While type 1 is characterized by close cooperation with the police and the authorities without a specific political agenda (usually created after certain events) (ibid., p. 19), type 2 vigilante groups do not cooperate with law enforcement. They in turn use this form of activism as a tool to further their own particularistic interests, for example by changing their public image or gaining access to new resources (ibid., p. 21). Type 3 groups do not cooperate with the police and authorities either, exist mainly in the virtual space and have predominantly the political goal to challenge the status quo and delegitimize established political parties, political opponents or the police (ibid., p. 25). Finally, type 4 groups usually comprise known members of the extreme right-wing movement, previously convicted extremists and other activists from radical groups. They try to be active offline and use vigilantism as an opportunity to commit violence against their opponents or to control social and geographical areas (ibid., p. 29).

Context: the far-right in Germany

The far-right in Germany is, on the one hand, composed of extreme right-wing and right-wing populist parties taking part in elections with varying degree of success. On the other, a vibrant subcultural milieu partially overlaps with official political organizations but also forms a separate contrast society (Koehler, 2015) with distinct varieties of subcultural products and styles but also with significant relevance for clandestine political violence and terrorism.

On the official political side, the most important extreme right-wing parties are the National Democratic Party of Germany (Nationaldemokratische Partei Deutschlands – NPD), The Third Way (Der Dritte Weg), and The Right (Die Rechte). For the year 2016 German authorities estimated the overall extreme right movement at about 23,100 persons of which 12,100 were considered to be violent (BMI, 2017).

Over the last years, far-right activism and mobilization has shifted away from political parties to subcultural forms of organization. Numbers of official extreme right-wing party membership have steadily declined and are by now surpassed by those active in subcultural milieus, even though of course both categories are not mutually exclusive.

This shift might also be partially due to the rise of anti-immigration focused right-wing populist parties, such as the Alternative for Germany (Alternative für

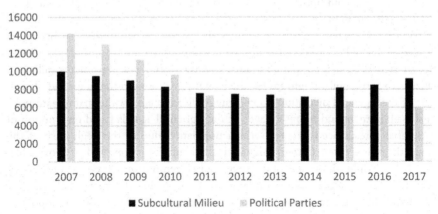

FIGURE 6.1 Number of right-wing extremists in political parties and sub-cultural groups (Germany)

Deutschland – AfD) or grass roots movements, such as Patriotic Europeans Against the Islamization of the Occident (Patriotische Europäer gegen die Islamisierung des Abendlands – PEGIDA). In particular, these two types of political activism have campaigned with a major focus on the government's lack of capability or intent to protect the German population against immigrants' crimes and by that the attempt to instil a widespread fear against immigration as such.

Germany's subcultural far-right mobilization, on the other hand, makes up for a significant percentage of the activism and right-wing motivated crimes. The boundaries between these networks, associations and subcultural milieus, on the one hand, and political parties on the other, are fluid, depending on personal networks and contacts as well as collaboration between groups and individuals. In addition, the ideological and personal differences between groups such as, for example, the Ku Klux Klan, Aryan Brotherhood, Hammerskin Nation, Autonomous Nationalists or Reichsbürger (sovereign citizens) are partially significant and have prevented a tighter, more cohesively organized collaboration for the most part.

Another aspect of the German far-right is extreme right-wing motivated terrorism and clandestine violence, which has a long tradition in this sphere almost since the end of the Second World War. To detail the history and characteristics of right-wing terrorism goes beyond the scope of this chapter and has been addressed elsewhere (Koehler, 2014, 2016a, 2016c). Nevertheless, organized clandestine violence, such as for example arson attacks, assassinations or explosive attacks not only involve hierarchically organized groups of long time extreme right-wing activists, but also individuals previously unknown to the authorities forming rather spontaneous associations for their attacks (called "hive terrorism": Koehler, 2016b). The extent of violent extreme right-wing motivated acts with an underlying tendency

92 Daniel Koehler

to "terrorize" if not outright falling into the "terrorism" category (for a detailed discussion about the difficulties of defining right-wing terrorism, see: Koehler, 2016c), shows a continuous potential for significant threats for the public safety by the German far-right.

Within this diverse political and subcultural spectrum, vigilantism has become a propaganda tool for attempted recruitment and mobilization from multiple sides of the far-right. Right-wing populist and extremist parties and movements call upon citizens to form vigilante groups for their own protection on the one hand. This is part of their general delegitimization strategy directed against the mainstream political establishment and a consequence of their political agenda based on a notion of existential threats faced by the German population due to the negligence of the currently ruling elites. Extreme right-wing subcultural groups and networks, like neo-Nazis, skinheads or parts of the sovereign citizen movement on the other hand have tried to use vigilantism as a new form of organizing clandestine political violence and influence the local status quo, as well as to challenge the monopoly of force by democratic institutions.

Watershed moment: New Year's Eve in Cologne

One specific event during New Year's Eve 2015/16 became a watershed moment for far-right and anti-immigration vigilantism in Germany and even in other European countries. During the last hours of 2015 an estimated 1,000 male persons with a predominantly North African or Arabic background between 15 and 35 years old gathered around Cologne's central station and cathedral area. Around one hour after midnight the first reports about large numbers of serious crimes reached the police. Nevertheless, local police officials reported no highly unusual activities during the first days of January, while on social media and some news outlets reports of victims of widespread sexual assaults and robberies started to appear. City officials, including the mayor, Henriette Reker, started to officially recognize the scale of unfolding events between two press conferences on 5 and 8 January, which also resulted in relieving police chief Wolfgang Albers of duty. By 16 June 2016 1182 charges (including 497 for sexual assault) had been filed with the local prosecutor and police and 1276 victims had been identified (ZeitMagazin, 2016). Five charges for rape and 16 for attempted rape were filed as well. Of the 183 suspects identified by investigators, 55 were Moroccan, 53 Algerian, 22 Iraqi, 14 Syrian and 14 German. Seventy-three suspects had applied for asylum, 36 were illegally residing in Germany and 11 had a residence permit (ibid.). Until late November 2016 only six suspects had been convicted, mostly for theft and to sentences with probation due to lack of evidence and problems with clearly identifying perpetrators (dpa, 2016b).

A special investigation by the German Federal Criminal Police (BKA) found that nationwide similar events of mass sexual assault had taken place, albeit nowhere on the same scale as in Cologne. In July 2016, the BKA counted 881 cases of sexual assault across Germany at New Year's Eve with around 1200 female victims and an

Militias and vigilante groups in Germany **93**

estimated 2000 perpetrators. Only a tiny minority of suspects were identified (62 by February and 120 by July 2016) but those were predominantly very recent immigrants and had mostly already committed various criminal acts before New Year's Eve. The BKA attempted to explain the events with group-dynamics based on cultural misogyny, frustration with lack of perspectives, mutual pressure, perceived anonymity and non-visible reaction of law enforcement, rather than organized and pre-arranged joined criminal acts (Mascolo & von der Heide, 2016).

The reactions of policy makers and the police were subjected to a parliamentary commission, which in its final report pointed out the missing early and decisive intervention by police forces to stop the unfolding events and misleading information provided by leading officials (NRW, 2017). It were exactly those two points – lack of police intervention and lack of governmental transparency – that were picked up widely by far-right and anti-immigration propaganda in an attempt to scandalize the perceived lack of ability of the authorities to enforce the law and protect German citizens. It was also portrayed as deliberate act of misinformation about the perpetrators' ethnicity out of a dictated sense of political correctness or as part of a large scale governmental conspiracy against the German population. Hence this series of events across the country were of key importance of for shaping the far-right and mainstream discourse on vigilantism. Many (if not most) anti-immigration vigilante groups currently active in Germany refer to the New Year's Eve events in their main mission statements and the threat-based rhetoric combined with fuelling distrust of the authorities might have had some effect. In 2016 for example, the number of applications for permit to carry small defensive weapons (called "kleiner Waffenschein" – small weapons permit in Germany, includes teargas or alarm pistols) rose by 63 per cent compared with 2015 (dpa, 2016a). far-right propaganda introduced the term "rapefugee" after this watershed moment, which belongs to the standard repertoire of extreme right-wing and anti-immigration rhetoric and visual materials by now.

Case studies

FTL/360

One of the most significant cases of a far-right anti-immigration vigilante group, which also crossed over into right-wing terrorism, is the "FTL/360" or, as it is called by the German authorities, the "Freital group".

As a type 4 vigilante group ("right-wing extremist violence groups"), it developed during daylong anti-immigration protests and violent clashes with the police in the small town of Freital in Saxony starting in March 2015. As described on the group's Facebook profile, FTL/360 was founded by a bus driver after Moroccan refugees had allegedly harassed German teenagers on a bus. Narratives like these are typical for vigilante groups, trying to establish themselves as legitimate reactions after traumatic events, while it is now uncommon for these groups to invent such narratives for their own purposes (Quent, 2016, p. 25). The group's name was

94 Daniel Koehler

composed of the vehicle licence plate code for the town of Freital ("FTL") and 360, which was the bus line on which the alleged incident took place. The goal of FTL/360 was to patrol in busses, specifically during weekends at night, and to establish law and order. The group's Facebook page reached 2,600 followers until November 2015. FTL/360's founder, Timo S., moved to Freital from Hamburg in 2014 and was known to the police and intelligence for having participated in various neo-Nazi rallies. He allegedly was also active in the periphery of a militant neo-Nazi network banned in February 2016 ("Weiße Wölfe Terrorcrew") (Polke-Majewski, 2017; Spiegel, 2016).

On 19 April 2016, 200 German police officers, including elite GSG9 anti-terror units, searched various premises in Freital and arrested four members of FTL/360. As part of the searches a three-figure number of explosives was secured by the police. In total, eight members were charged by the Federal Prosecutor General with attempted murder, physical assault and forming a terrorist organization (Schlottmann & Schawe, 2015). The trial against seven male and one female FTL/360 members started on 7 March 2017. Prosecutors connected the group with at least five attacks in Saxony, including explosive attacks against a refugee home in September and November and against a left-wing alternative housing project in October 2015. In addition, the group, which closely cooperated with other militant extreme right-wing networks, is thought to have played an important role in an explosive attack on the car of a left-wing politician and a left-wing party office in Freital (dpa, 2017). On 7 March 2018, all eight defendants were found guilty of forming a terrorist organization and sentenced to between four and ten years in prison (Rietzschel, 2018). Most of the defendants have filed a motion for revision of the sentence with the Federal German High Court (Bundesgerichtshof BGH) in an attempt to reduce the prison terms. However, this motion does not challenge the basic guilty verdict. A decision of the BGH was not available before this chapter was finished.

Another aspect that kept the Freital case under wide public scrutiny was that the group allegedly received information from local police officers, which provided them with knowledge about law enforcement operations and when it was comparatively safe to conduct their attacks. Investigations against three officers were concluded without yielding evidence for prosecutions, albeit under circumstances receiving heavy public criticism (Biermann, 2017).

FTL/360 is a noteworthy case study, since it is the only known vigilante group that developed into an alleged right-wing terrorist organization. It seems that some key factors played an important role in that process. First, the group's leader, Timo S., has a past in the organized neo-Nazi milieu and was active in the periphery (at least) of other militant right-wing extremist networks. After becoming active in Freital, the vigilante group quickly started cooperating with other highly militant and longer established extreme right-wing organizations, such as, for example, the "Freie Kameradschaft Dresden" (Free Comradeship Dresden) or with members of the "Skinheads Sächsische Schweiz" (SSS), which was outlawed in 2001 as one of the most dangerous neo-Nazi groups in East-Germany (LVZ, 2017). FTL/360 members also participated alongside other extreme right-wing activists at other violent incidents, for example in clashes with the police during anti-immigration protests in Heidenau in August 2015 (ibid.) or during a large-scale hit and run attack on a left-wing dominated district in Leipzig (mdr, 2016).

Second, the vigilante group was formed at the peak of anti-immigration protests and clashes with the police in Freital, which means local public support for alternative policing and protection was arguably very high. Also, public anger with established political parties provided group members with a strong legitimizing narrative and motivational backup. Third, the group, according to statements by members, even received support from local police officers and seemed to have been well embedded in the local community.

This indicates that the level of interaction and overlap with more established extreme right-wing networks and milieus, as well as the perceived degree of public support and legitimacy, is key to understand a vigilante group's trajectory into organized clandestine violence.

"Deutsches Polizei Hilfswerk" (German Police Assistance Association – DPHW)

The "German Police Assistance Association" DPHW was active between April 2012 and June 2013 mainly in the three East-German states Brandenburg, Thuringia and Saxony. It was founded by a former member of a police union (Volker S.), who himself only had the status of supporter and was not a police officer. The DPHW saw itself as the executive arm of the sovereign citizen "Reichsbürger" movement (Reichsbürger Bewegung – RBB), which usually does not engage in public patrolling or law and order activism, especially since their members commonly reject the current German rule of law. At its peak, the DPH had about 100 members and was organized strictly hierarchically, using ranks adopted from the former military of the German Democratic Republic (Nationale Volksarmee NVA). The group's main stated goal was to prevent police brutality and failing of the authorities (Meiborg, 2013). In this sense, the DPHW could have been focused on controlling the police instead of providing security for private citizens.

Nevertheless, Volker S., who recruited the DPHW members predominantly from the RBB and rejected any legitimacy of the German state and legislation, promised to provide law and order for the population, as well as detect and investigate and prevent any breaking of the law. Seeing itself as a true police force responsible in areas where other law enforcement could not provide security, the DPHW based their own legitimacy on the constitutional right to resist against any form of illegal occupation or removal of democratic government (§20 GG).

In over 50 educational workshops for new recruits, the DPHW claimed to both cooperate with the police but also provide checks and balances on their conduct. DPHW members were uniformed and used, whenever possible, names, symbols and codes closely aligned with local police in an obvious attempt to appear legitimate in the eyes of the population. Main activities of the DPHW included patrolling and counselling of members in lawsuits (ibid.). The DPHW was involved in numerous confrontations with the authorities and legitimate law enforcement agencies. On 23 November 2012, for example, DPHW members tried to "arrest" an official court appointed bailiff to prevent seizure of premises used by the group (dpa, 2015). Other incidents involved DPHW members trying to interfere with police arrests or other actions taken by the authorities against sovereign citizens. Even though numerous legal charges were filed against DPHW members, most were dropped, especially those directed against low-ranking activists. Leading DPHW members received convictions for illegal restraint, coercion, assumption of authority, physical assault and other crimes (Locke, 2016) but the trials are partially still ongoing in late 2017.

After this wave of lawsuits against the DPHW starting in 2012 the group remained passive until it was dissolved in June 2013. As of November 2017, the DPHW still maintains a Facebook page with regular activity and 629 likes. According to the typology of vigilante groups presented above, the DPHW appears to have been a mixture of type 2 ("pre-political interest groups") and type 3 ("protest groups"). As part of the sovereign citizen RBB movement, the group's main intent was to rebrand the wider movement into a more pro-population and legitimate actor, while at the same time directly seeking conflict with the established authorities and undermine the rule of law.

As a vigilante group, the DPHW came closest to forming an alternative police force, with uniforms, training courses for their recruits, strict hierarchies and activism resulting in clashes with the authorities. Similar to the FTL/360 group, the DPHW had multiple links and overlap with a radical milieu, in this case the sovereign citizen "Reichsbürger" movement. It was observed that this milieu initially greeted the establishment of the DPHW with great enthusiasm but seemed to have become predominantly disappointed with it due to the DPHW's self-proclaimed goal to also cooperate with the police when necessary (Rathje, 2014, p. 23). Contrary to the FTL/360 though, the DPHW did not receive significant local public support and was active before the far-right and right-wing populist networks had started to take an interest in the "existential threat through refugees" narrative.

To provide some context to the DPHW: the Reichsbürger Bewegung (sovereign citizen movement – RBB) developed in the 1980s in Germany and became increasingly active from 2010, moving from the fringes of the German far-right to the centre of public attention. When in October 2016 a German SWAT police officer was fatally shot during an attempted arrest of a RBB member, authorities realized the potential threat of that long-underestimated movement (Clauß, Friedmann, & Menke, 2016). After the incident, police systematically searched RBB members' homes and premises for weapons, which they had been acquiring for years. The overall movement, which is very diverse and does not have a unified structure or leadership, was estimated at about 16,500 members across Germany in January 2018, including about 900 right-wing extremists (dpa, 2018). With an ideology denying any legitimacy of the German government and its branches at all levels, invoking pseudo-legal arguments referring to laws of the German Reich passed before the end of the Second World War (Rathje, 2014), the RBB has gained momentum and has significantly radicalized during the recent years. Seeing the German government in all its forms as an illegitimate occupation force, it legitimizes organized violence to remove that oppression. This attitude became visible to the public in January 2017, for example, when a group of six RBB members around a self-styled "Druid" was arrested for allegedly plotting terror attacks against police officers, refugees and Jews (Biermann & Geisler, 2017).

Soldiers of Odin

German chapters of the Soldiers of Odin (SOO) vigilante group, which was founded in October 2015 in Finland, became active in late 2016, mostly in southern Germany (e.g. Bavaria). In November 2017 multiple different Facebook groups with names referring to a SOO Germany chapter existed. The two largest in terms of likes and followers (SOO Bavaria with 751 likes and SOO Germany support chapter with 2,497 likes), however, explicitly claimed not to be associated with the Finish mother organization and declared not to be bound by its rules and leadership. SOO have a comparatively low profile and only rarely become visible through offline activities such as patrols or charity events. If so, hotspots for SOO seem to be the cities of Würzburg and Munich, both in Bavaria. Activities in Würzburg involve regular (weekly) patrols of usually four-person teams with dogs (to avoid police intervention due to breaking German laws regulating open assembly), charity food runs for animal shelters (Jung, 2017) and applying stickers with "Schutzzone" ("protective zone") (Zöller & Winkelmann, 2017). In Munich the first SOO patrol was noted by the press in November 2017 (Bernstein, 2017). Based on SOO members' profiles in social media and their offline backgrounds, multiple links into the organized neo-Nazi milieu, as well as to PEGIDA were observed (Bernstein, 2017; Grassl, 2017). As a consequence of SOO's increased activity in late 2017, the Bavarian domestic intelligence service ("Landesamt für Verfassungsschutz") announced to start monitoring the SOO as an extreme right-wing group (mho/dpa, 2017). So far, however, SOO seems to be active (offline) to a notable scale only in Bavaria and has otherwise not taken any prominent role in the German far-right. Applying the above mentioned typology of vigilante groups once more, it is difficult to classify the SOO, as currently not much is known about its goals and membership structure. They have so far not acted violently, but it seems to be the case that a significant share of members has ties to the organized extreme right-wing movement in Germany. Hence, the SOO in Germany does hold the potential to become a type 4 vigilante group ("right-wing extremist violence groups").

Repressive and permissive factors for vigilante groups in Germany

As anti-immigration or extreme right-wing vigilante groups are still a fringe phenomenon in Germany, with most groups mostly active online and only a few examples that have achieved some form of offline life, it seems that Germany has a more repressive than permissive environment for vigilantism. Starting with weapons and gun regulations, Germany prides itself on having one of the most restrictive legislations regarding private gun and weapons ownership. Separating into "small" (for teargas and alarm pistols) and "large" (firearms) gun permits, the latter one is generally only available for hunters, professional sport shooters, licensed security personnel and money transport services. Requirements regarding eligibility are considered to be very restrictive, including a broadly defined concept of "reliability", which is reviewed at least every three years. Authorities have significant freedom to withdraw a gun permit if any circumstances that could be considered to change a person's reliability (e.g. ideological, psychological, substance abuse, criminal behaviour) arise. After the October 2016 killing of a police officer by a sovereign citizen Reichsbürger, German authorities included that specific ideology as a significant aspect reducing reliability and have since then systematically revoked gun permits and removed weapons from members of that milieu (Gensing, 2017).

Another repressive factor in Germany lies within the comparatively strict association laws, which allow authorities to target organizational structures effectively through group prohibitions or lawsuits against whole groups on the basis of criminal or anti-constitutional goals (e.g. §129 and 129a of the criminal code). As long as vigilante groups form hierarchically structured organizations, which is common as they try to mimic the police or the military, they become an easy target for law enforcement and prosecutors in the case of criminal activity.

Finally, Germany is still considered to be a country with a culture of obedience and respect towards authorities and law enforcement, which might be a barrier for the widespread establishment of vigilante groups.

Nevertheless, some permissive factors can also be identified. The German code of criminal procedure, for example, allows for every citizen to apprehend any suspect of a crime and hold the person in limited custody until the police arrives (§127 StPO). This paragraph, however, does not include the right to use weapons, physical force or even attempt an identification of the suspect. Still, vigilante groups regularly base their activities on this so called "every person's right" ("Jedermannsrecht"), which also includes the right to self-defence.

Another permissive factor can be seen in the strong focus of the German criminal code on structural aspects of organizations and not so much on subcultural milieus. Mobilization tactics, such as, for example, leaderless resistance, are much more difficult to prosecute and to target with legal measures.

In addition, the restrictive gun and weapons regulations do have loopholes. Of the currently estimated 15,000 sovereign citizen Reichsbürger in Germany, at least 1,000 were in possession of a full gun permit, arguably having themselves licensed as hunters or sportsmen to get legal access to firearms (Jansen, 2017). A similar problem might arise from private security corporations, which saw continuously rising numbers in Germany during the last decade and also can have access to weapons permits. There regulation and training, as well as screening of personnel

Militias and vigilante groups in Germany   99

has been criticized as insufficient, especially after numerous incidents involving extreme right-wing employees of private security corporations guarding asylum centres abusing and even torturing refugees (Lasarzik & Leurs, 2014).

Conclusion

Summing up this chapter, the limited research and available data on the phenomenon of anti-immigration or far-right vigilante groups in Germany only leaves limited space for scientific exploration. Governmental statistics about this form of political mobilization do not exist and most information comes from press sources. Only very few vigilante groups (e.g. FTL/360 and DHPW) have had significant impact beyond their local context either through the severity of their criminal acts or through their (short lived) visibility. While hundreds of groups and initiatives claiming to be vigilante groups exist on social media sites (e.g. Facebook), the vast majority of them do not seem to have any significant offline impact. Nevertheless, this is difficult to verify, since rural areas for example could be experiencing a strong social dominance and control by such groups. As no comprehensive studies about the real extent of vigilante activism in Germany have been done so far, one can only refer back to press and governmental (e.g. court verdicts) sources to estimate its impact.

From the current situation in Germany, it seems fair to say that vigilantism has become a major propaganda tool for far-right and anti-immigration movements, parties and networks. The major push to call for formation of vigilante groups came after the watershed events around New Year's Eve 2015/16 in Cologne and other major cities. Vigilantism was and still is presented as the natural right to self-defence for the German population against an existential threat of mass migration bringing crime and erosion of German culture with it. In addition, the call for vigilantism has become a manifestation of the outcry against the claimed incompetence and corruption of the establishment and the subsequent empowerment of the population against the ruling elites. Different special interests within the far-right and anti-immigration milieus have resulted in various types of vigilante activism, which are used for various political or non-political goals (Quent, 2016).

Vigilantism, however, remains a fringe phenomenon in Germany so far. Restrictive gun and association laws, as well as a strong culture of obedience to established authorities, seem to have limited the space for vigilante groups to spread and reach a critical mass. Groups who reached some significance beyond their local context had active and strong relationships with existing extremist or radical milieus (e.g. the neo-Nazi or Reichsbürger movement). Some groups enjoyed strong local support and took advantage of conflicts, frustration and anger with mainstream politics in some communities. When they increased organizational sophistication to function as a militia or alternative policing force and committed various criminal acts, they quickly became targeted by the authorities.

Nevertheless, established extreme right-wing groups as well as right-wing populist and anti-immigration movements have increasingly become interested in

100 Daniel Koehler

vigilantism as a tool to mobilize parts of the population they were unable to penetrate before. Eroding trust in the authorities' abilities to provide law and order, which is facilitated through far-right and anti-immigration propaganda, goes hand in hand with the call for vigilantism. The future of this form of mobilization depends on additional watershed events and the police's ability to win back trust from the population where they have lost it.

Postscript

After this chapter was completed, riots with vigilante dimensions took place in the city of Chemnitz in East Germany, in response to a brawl and a fatal stabbing of a local man, with an asylum seeker as suspected perpetrator. Violent anti-refugee riots led by hooligans and neo-Nazis took place there on August and September 2018. A group called "Revolution Chemnitz" formed by local extreme right-wing activists started to patrol Chemnitz as self-declared vigilantes, attempted to check passports and immigration status of presumed refugees and violently attacked other immigrants. Eight members of that group were formally charged with plotting a terrorist attack against leading politicians and journalists, among others. According to the charges, the group was in the process of acquiring firearms and compared itself to the National Socialist Underground (NSU) terror group, which they described as "kindergarten pre-school" level in chat conversations.

Notes

1 Meaning literally citizen defence force.
2 "Korporatistische Sicherheitsinitiativen"
3 "Vehikel für vorpolitische Eigeninteressen"
4 "Protestgruppen"
5 "rechtsextreme Gewaltgruppen"

References

Bernstein, M. (2017, November 17,). Rassistische Bürgerwehr in Pasing. *Süddeutsche Zeitung*. Retrieved from http://www.sueddeutsche.de/muenchen/rechte-gruppierung-rassistische-buergerwehr-in-pasing-1.3754490.

Biermann, K. (2017, July 21,). Verfahren gegen Polizisten aus Mangel an Beweisen eingestellt. *Zeit Online*. Retrieved from http://www.zeit.de/gesellschaft/zeitgeschehen/2017-07/gruppe-freital-polizei-helfer-verfahren-eingestellt.

Biermann, K., & Geisler, A. (2017). Der Nazidruide aus Schwetzingen. Retrieved from http://www.zeit.de/gesellschaft/2017-01/rechtsextremismus-schwetzingen-druide-terrorzelle-razzia-bundesanwaltschaft.

BMI. (2013). *Verfassungsschutzbericht 2012*. Berlin: Bundesministerium des Innern.

BMI. (2017). *Verfassungsschutzbericht 2016*. Berlin: Bundesministerium des Innern.

Bundesregierung. (2016). *Aktivitäten von so genannten Bürgerwehren im Zusammenhang mit Neonazis und Flüchtlingsunterkünften*. (Drucksache 18/7189). Berlin: Regierung der Bundesrepublik Deutschland.

Clauß, A., Friedmann, J., & Menke, B. (2016). Die krude Welt des Wolfgang P. Retrieved from http://www.spiegel.de/panorama/justiz/reichsbuerger-aus-georgensgmuend-die-krude-welt-des-wolfgang-p-a-1117421.html.

dpa. (2015, December 13,). Reichsbürger vor Gericht. *Sächsische Zeitung*. Retrieved from http://www.sz-online.de/sachsen/reichsbuerger-vor-gericht-3274544.html.

dpa. (2016a, November 25,). Anträge für Kleine Waffenscheine um 63 Prozent gestiegen. *Die Welt*. Retrieved from https://www.welt.de/politik/deutschland/article159743562/Antraege-fuer-Kleine-Waffenscheine-um-63-Prozent-gestiegen.html.

dpa. (2016b, November 25,). Bisher nur sechs Verurteilungen. *Frankfurter Allgemeine Zeitung*. Retrieved from http://www.faz.net/aktuell/politik/inland/bisher-wurden-nur-sechs-taeter-der-koelner-silvesternacht-verurteilt-14545141.html.

dpa. (2017). Generalbundesanwalt klagt Terrorgruppe "Freital" an. Retrieved from http://www.spiegel.de/politik/deutschland/freital-generalbundesanwalt-erhebt-anklage-gegen-terrorgruppe-a-1120189.html.

dpa. (2018, January 25,). Zahl der "Reichsbürger" stark gestiegen. *Spiegel Online*. Retrieved from http://www.spiegel.de/panorama/gesellschaft/reichsbuerger-16-500-menschen-gehoeren-der-szene-an-a-1189854.html.

Gensing, P. (2017, June 1,). "Reichsbürger" sollen entwaffnet werden. *Tagesschau*. Retrieved from https://www.tagesschau.de/inland/reichsbuerger-waffen-imk-101.html.

Grassl, T. (2017, November 23,). Breiten sich in Deutschland aus „Soldiers of Odin": Rechte Bürgerwehr patrouilliert jetzt auch in München. *Focus*. Retrieved from http://www.focus.de/politik/deutschland/breiten-sich-in-deutschland-aus-soldiers-of-odin-rechte-buergerwehr-patrouilliert-jetzt-auch-in-muenchen_id_7883621.html.

Jansen, F. (2017, October 12,). Deutlich mehr Reichsbürger als gedacht. *Tagesspiegel*. Retrieved from http://www.tagesspiegel.de/politik/zahlen-des-verfassungsschutzes-deutlich-mehr-reichsbuerger-als-gedacht/20447404.html.

Jung, W. (2017, November 22,). "Soldiers of Odin" sind in Würzburg unerwünscht. *Mainpost Regional*. Retrieved from http://m.mainpost.de/regional/wuerzburg/Buergerwehren-Hilfsorganisationen-und-Hilfseinrichtungen-Tierfutter-Tierheime;art735,9802899.

Koehler, D. (2014). German right-wing terrorism in historical perspective. A first quantitative overview of the 'database on terrorism in Germany (right-wing extremism) – DTG rwx project. *Perspectives on Terrorism*, 8(5), 48–58.

Koehler, D. (2015). Contrast societies. Radical social movements and their relationships with their target societies. A theoretical model. *Behavioral Sciences of Terrorism and Political Aggression*, 7(1), 18–34. doi:10.1080/19434472.2014.977325.

Koehler, D. (2016a). Political violence from the far right in Germany; terrorism, hate crimes and dynamics of escalation. In J. Jamin (Ed.), *L'extrême droite en Europe* (pp. 181–200). Brussels: Bruylant.

Koehler, D. (2016b). Right-wing extremism and terrorism in Europe. Developments and issues for the future. *PRISM*, 6(2), 84–104.

Koehler, D. (2016c). *Right-wing terrorism in the 21st century. The National Socialist underground and the history of terror from the Far-Right in Germany*. Oxon/New York: Routledge.

Lasarzik, A., & Leurs, R. (2014, September 29,). Misshandlungen in Burbach. Die Fakten über Sicherheitsdienste in Flüchtlingsheimen. *Spiegel Online*. Retrieved from http://www.spiegel.de/panorama/misshandlung-in-fluechtlingsheim-burbach-fakten-ueber-sicherheitsfirmen-a-994378.html.

Locke, S. (2016, January 15,). Amtsgericht in Meißen verurteilt "Reichsbürger". *Frankfurter Allgemeine Zeitung*. Retrieved from http://www.faz.net/aktuell/gesellschaft/kriminalitaet/amtsgericht-meissen-verurteilt-sechs-reichsbuerger-zu-freiheitsstrafen-14016090.html.

102 Daniel Koehler

Locker, T., & Neifer, A. (2016, February 13,). Von Maulhelden und Ein-Mann-Kiezstrei-fen: Wo sind all die Bürgerwehren hin? *Motherboard Vice*. Retrieved from https://motherboard.vice.com/de/article/z43apy/rohrkrepierer-buergerwehr-111.

LVZ. (2017, April 18,). Staatsanwältin sagt im Terrorprozess um "Gruppe Freital" aus. *Leipziger Volkszeitung*. Retrieved from http://www.lvz.de/Mitteldeutschland/Polizei-ticker-Mitteldeutschland/Staatsanwaeltin-sagt-im-Terrorprozess-um-Gruppe-Freital-aus.

Mascolo, G., & von der Heide, B. (2016, July 10,). 1200 Frauen wurden Opfer von Silve-ster-Gewalt. *Süddeutsche Zeitung*. Retrieved from http://www.sueddeutsche.de/politik/uebergriffe-in-koeln-frauen-wurden-opfer-von-silvester-gewalt-1.3072064.

Maxwill, P. (2017). Großes Spektakel, kurzer Prozess. Retrieved from http://www.spiegel.de/panorama/justiz/arnsdorf-fluechtling-gefesselt-kurzer-prozess-in-kamenz-a-1143924.html.

mdr. (2016, September 1,). "Exakt": Hooligans, Neonazis und Kampfsportler überfielen Connewitz. *mdr Exakt*. Retrieved from http://www.mdr.de/presse/exklusiv/press-einformation-exakt-connewitz-100.html.

Meiborg, M. (2013, September 5,). Eins, zwei, falsche Polizei. *Zeit Online*. Retrieved from http://www.zeit.de/2013/37/polizeihilfswerk-sachsen-brandenburg/komplettansicht.

mho/dpa. (2017, December 29,). Verfassungsschutz beobachtet "Soldiers of Odin". *Spiegel Online*. Retrieved from http://www.spiegel.de/politik/deutschland/bayern-verfas-sungsschutz-beobachtet-rechtsextreme-soldiers-of-odin-a-1185424-amp.html.

NRW. (2017). *Schlussbericht des Parlamentarischen Untersuchungsausschusses IV zu dem Auftrag des Landtags Nordrhein-Westfalen vom 27. Januar 2016 Drucksache 16/10798*. (Drucksache 16/14450). Landtag Nordrhein Westfalen Retrieved from https://www.landtag.nrw.de/portal/WWW/dokumentenarchiv/Dokument/MMD16-14450.pdf.

Polke-Majewski, K. (2017, March 22,). Ein beschriebenes Blatt. *Zeit Online*. Retrieved from http://www.zeit.de/gesellschaft/zeitgeschehen/2017-03/gruppe-freital-prozess-ter-rorismus-verfassungsschutz-timo-s.

Quent, M. (2016). *Bürgerwehren. Hilfssheriffs oder inszenierte Provokation?* Retrieved from Berlin: https://www.amadeu-antonio-stiftung.de/w/files/pdfs/buergerwehreninternet.pdf.

Rathje, J. (2014). *"Wir sind wieder da!. Die "Reichsbürger": Überzeugungen, Gefahren, Hand-lungsstrategien*. Berlin: Amadeu Antonio Stiftung.

Rietzschel, A. (2018, March 7,). Lange Haftstrafen gegen Terror-Gruppe Freital. *Süddeutsche Zeitung*. Retrieved from http://www.sueddeutsche.de/politik/eil-lange-haftstrafen-im-prozess-gegen-rechte-gruppe-freital-1.3895872!amp.

Schlottmann, K., & Schawe, A. (2015). Sondereinheit hebt Bürgerwehr aus. Nach Spreng-stoffattacken auf Flüchtlinge und ihre Unterstützer sitzt der mutmaßliche Freitaler Drahtzieher in Haft. Retrieved from http://www.sz-online.de/sachsen/sondereinheit-hebt-buergerwehr-aus-3243757.html.

Spiegel. (2016, February 1,). Timos Hass auf die Flüchtlinge. Die Karriere eines rechten Brandstifters. *Spiegel TV*. Retrieved from http://www.spiegel.de/video/buergerwehr-freital-timos-hass-auf-die-fluechtlinge-video-1646417.html.

ZeitMagazin. (2016, June 22,). "Vielleicht habe ich den Frauen zu wenig Trost gespendet". *Die Zeit*. Retrieved from http://www.zeit.de/zeit-magazin/2016-06/henriette-reker-armlaenge-aeusserung-fehler.

Zöller, J., & Winkelmann, A. (2017, December 12,). Soldiers of Odin Bayern - Bürgerwehr setzt auf Angst. *Bayerischer Rundfunk*. Retrieved from https://www.br.de/nachrichten/soldiers-of-odin-bayern-buergerwehr-setzt-auf-angst-100.html.

7

VIGILANTE MILITIAS AND ACTIVITIES AGAINST ROMA AND MIGRANTS IN HUNGARY

Szilveszter Póczik and Eszter Sárik

Introduction

As a country, Hungary has witnessed a long tradition of far right movements and political parties as well as paramilitary and military organizations. Together they represent combatant nationalist and social conservative reactions to diverse political and social trends in different historical periods. The goal of these Janus-faced movements who considered themselves *vigilante organizations* was much less about the prevention of crime than the persecution of persons and groups they called "parasites", "degenerates" or "internal enemies" (Gellner, 2009). These groups were considered to oppose the majority's value set and to represent a threat to the ruling political and ethnic community. The roots of such movements go back to the end of the nineteenth century when in the course of capitalist development, social tensions widened, and nationalism became the leading idea of politics in whole of Europe. In a certain parallelism, a number of political movements came to life that claimed to unify and achieve social and national goals through a great "national social" revolution, destroying the cosmopolite communists and the not less destructive power of finance capitalism at the same time (Szabó, 2015).

This was particularly typical in Eastern-Middle-Europe because this region was not only multiethnic but also suffered under heavy social antagonisms and continuous waves of immigration. Attracted to the intensive economic development, liberalism and safety of the Austro-Hungarian monarchy, Jewish immigrants arrived in large numbers from politically, economically and socially underdeveloped regions of Eastern Europe, particularly from Russia. In Austria, the Jewish Emancipation Law of 1890 and in Hungary, the Law XLII of 1895 secured the equal status of the Hebrew community with other confessions. The Jewish community contributed far more to the economic development of Hungary than its population rate would have suggested. However, the immigration of Jews and their fast and

104 Szilveszter Póczik, and Eszter Sárik

spectacular social rise triggered resentments within a social strata who felt threatened by capitalism (Komoróczy, 2012). Even though, at the time, Hungary was witnessing a great capitalist transition; this phenomenon had its dark sides too. Both the capitalist economic modernity and the early socialist movements attacked and weakened the old social structure rooted in late feudal circumstances, particularly the ruling position of the conservative agrarian, the catholic aristocracy and gentry landowners. With the Jewish minority being overrepresented in the finance and investment business and at the same time playing an active role in socialist movements, they soon became the personalized symbol of both the destructive and cosmopolite economic liberalism and the anti-national and cosmopolite i.e. internationalist communism. Beyond them, other ethnic groups with separatist aims were treated as potential threats too. In this era a great number of Romany (called Gypsy, Zigan, Cigány at that time) immigrated to Hungary from Eastern regions who sustained their vagrant (peripatetic) ways of life and according to the public opinion were overrepresented in criminality (Póczik, 2016).

The ideologies of xenophobia, anti-minority and anti-migratory far right initiatives in today's Hungary are rooted in the historical development described above. These protest movements do not essentially differ from other current extreme right movements of neighbouring countries (Slovenská národná strana, Partidul România-Mare etc.), but definitely show some variability in their presence and weight from other countries' far right movements. They communicate in terms of an anti-democratic and anti-modernist political agenda – including anti-finance capitalism, anti-liberalism, anti-feminism (anti-genderism) and homophobic attitudes. Their attitudes are determined by sharp anti-communism, racism, as well as racial or cultural anti-Semitism, militant nationalism, ethno-centric attitudes and a deep-seated antipathy towards foreigners. These groups demand "law and order", national and political unity and closed and regulated national economy based on small enterprises instead of corporations. They also demand the maintenance of a great power vision including the idea of – biological or cultural – national superiority (supremacy) based on pre-eminent national (ethnic) abilities, a heroic past determined by religious and family values and symbols of rigorous military organizations. The core elements of the activities of these movements are a kind of *social control, political(ly) motivated violence* and *other hate crimes* as well as propaganda.

The Hungarian far right and the Fascist tradition

The lost war of 1918, the post-war chaos and the power takeover by the Communists (known as Commune or Hungarian Soviet Republic of 1919) combined with the "red terror"[1] led partly by persons of Jewish ethnic background intensified the anti-Semitic climate in Hungary. In 1920, Hungary lost more than two thirds of its territory and 65% of its population, among them 3.3 million ethnic Hungarians, due to the Trianon Peace Treaty (Macartney, 1962; Bernstein, 2003). So it was not a surprise that – like the Freikorps in Germany – a number of special military branches and associations (Zinner, 1989; Ormos, 1990; Ujváry, 1991; Pelle, 1998) came to life intending to take revenge and to regain the lost territories. But they first wanted to frighten the "renegades of the nation", particularly the left wing and Jewish juveniles. The so-called Irredentist (Redeeming) Movement for the restoration of Hungary's "historical" borders (Zeidler, 2002) linked different forms of anti-Semitism and completed it with the motive of "stab-in-the-back myth", which is similar to the German conspiracy theory "Dolchstosslegende" (Watson, 2008). In the period of the white terror (August 1919 – December 1921), the persecution of Communists was connected with anti-Semitic pogroms (Kulcsár, 2010).

After this period, in a nearly 20-year era of the relative consolidation secured by Regent Admiral Miklós Horthy (Sakmyster 1994), these paramilitary groups became part of the Hungarian Fascist (Hungarist) Movements. At first, they were split into several small parties but later unified under the Arrow Cross Party – Hungarist Movement (Lackó, 1969; Karsai, 2016) having about 300,000 party members and winning 15% of the mandates (29) in the Parliament in 1939. The former quasi-military units became active again before WWII and participated in correcting the borders in cooperation with the Army and Gendarmerie. They directed their activities against the foreign ethnic groups living in the occupied territories, mainly the Jews. Later, in WWII, they were integrated into the regular Army and Gendarmerie. On 19 October 1944, in a coup d'état the Arrow Cross Party took power and in the last month of the war they organized the deportation of Jews by handing them over to the Nazi authorities determined to carry out the Holocaust. The Arrow Cross Armed Service (organized on the model of the German SS) started mass murdering Jews in the Capital by shooting many persons into the Danube River.

After 1945, the Paris Peace Treaty prohibited establishing or re-establishing any Fascist organization. The top Fascist leaders and other ringleaders were sentenced to death but the so-called "deceived Nazi Party members" were granted a "pardon". They were integrated into the newly formed Communist Party, which was preparing for coming to power at that time (Vámos, 2011). In spite of the definite anti-Fascist ideology of Communists, some of the aforementioned persons managed to make carriers in the era of the Communist dictatorship achieving relatively high positions. The former Fascist leaders and other Arrow-Cross movement members emigrated and were able to avoid the Nuremberg Trial.

In the epoch of the suppressive communist dictatorship, the ruling Communist party (MSZMP – Hungarian Socialist Labour Party) intended to break the ethnic and national solidarity. They propagated proletarian internationalism and carried out ideological campaigns against the Hungarian ethnic minorities who were being forced to live outside Hungary. The Communists were also opposed to the historical inter-ethnic sympathies of the Hungarians towards Poland and Croatia (Póczik & Sárik, 2018).

The political and social transition 1990–2000 and the rebirth of far right political tradition

The promising – but eventually quite unfortunate – political and economic changes that have occurred as part of the transition since 1990 found the Hungarian

106 Szilveszter Póczik, and Eszter Sárik

society highly fragmented. As shown by polls and crime latency research, the fear of crime, the mistrust in police and state administration as well as the fear and hate against the underprivileged Roma minority and vice versa was growing (Tóth, 2010; Póczik, 2004). "The general mistrust to the public institutions is a basic trait of the society until today" (Péterfi, 2014).[2] Hungary was only partly able to utilize the economic chances given by the capitalist (re)transition and EU-membership and suffered great losses in the crisis of 2008. Currently, Hungary is the poorest country even in the Visegrad-4 group, showing relatively low economic growth and extremely low salaries. The society is highly polarized in all respects, a thin upper class started to become disproportionately rich whilst the lower middle classes experienced intensive impoverishment. The working class of the communist era turned out to be the absolute losers due to the transition. Currently, 40% of the total population lives at the edge of poverty and more than 400,000 persons in total poverty (Havasi, 2017).[3] This social group living in absolute poverty is made up almost entirely of people with Roma origins (Cserti & Orsós, 2015). This means that both social poverty and ethnic poverty exist simultaneously featuring deprived and segregated social neighbourhoods with the usual additional problems of aggression, violent crime, crime against property, mental and physical disease, high number of children, low rates of education, eliciting fear and hate by the majority society (Tökés, 1996).

The first steps towards the far right

After the transition of 1990, the extreme left-wing movements diminished from the political scene, whilst the extreme right swung into action as small and fragmented but very active groups. These groups were concerned partly with the continuation of the Hungarian chauvinistic and Fascist tradition and partly with the rootless racist juveniles (skinheads, rockers, football hooligans) who conducted verbal propaganda and committed aggressive excesses against allegedly criminal or deviant Roma. In spite of their activism they were unable to build an effective political force and remained in political quarantine. A number of legal NGOs and underground organizations maintaining close contact with parliamentary far-right party sections were active, but mostly on the level of propaganda. However, it was well known that they were behind occasional violent acts, too (Bíró Nagy, Boros & Varga, 2012).

The political rivalry during the Hungarian transition was followed by violent attacks (beating, stabbing, murder, bombing) directed partly against politicians and partly against businessmen involved in politics, illegal trade as well as transnational organized crime. In some of these cases, political hatred was also a motive for attacking politicians and hate motivated violent attacks were committed against Roma and Jewish political activists too. In other cases, skinheads or right-wing extremists attacked non-white immigrants and members of the LGBTQ community.

Beyond the democratic parties and NGOs, new right-wing, extreme right-wing and semi-Fascist organizations came to life fuelled by the regained democratic freedom to establish political and non-political organizations. Despite the international treaties that prohibited establishing or re-establishing Fascist organizations, they had the newly experienced right to express any opinions without censorship or restraint. Some former emigrants of the Arrow Cross Movement and fighters of the Revolution of 1956 moved back to Hungary from abroad and began to establish nationalist organizations and parties on the periphery of the mainstream democratic policy that orchestrated social reforms.

Polarization of the right wing in the Parliament

In the period of transition, the leading political force and first government party MDF (Hungarian Democratic Forum) unified all national and anti-communist reform-oriented groups but they got fragmented very soon. In 1993, an excommunicated parliament deputy of MDF established the Party of Hungarian Interest (Magyar Érdek Pártja) and tried to form a *militant youth organization of (right-wing) skinheads* calling them "nationally thinking juveniles", which was financed – as later turned out – by the Baath Party of Saddam Hussein.[4] The national radicals led by the dramatist István Csurka, established the new nationalist Party for Hungarian Justice and Life (MIÉP – Magyar Igazság és Élet Pártja) in 1993 representing a (cultural) anti-Semitic and anti-Zionist/anti-Israel position. MIÉP won 5.5% of the votes and gained parliamentary representation with 14 seats in the 1994 election but in the next elections the party scored only 4.4% and won no seats in the Parliament. In 2005, MIÉP joined Jobbik in a party coalition. The Jobbik Party was the newly established radical Hungarian nationalist political party of the youth. A new political formation was registered under the name of the MIÉP–Jobbik Third Way Party Alliance. It stood up for Christian values and for the rights and autonomy of Hungarian minorities in the neighbouring countries. The MIÉP–Jobbik Party Alliance's program was based on a "law and order" agenda, focusing on growing crime, wide spread fear of crime, necessity of crime prevention and repressive criminal policy. In the aftermath of the 2006 elections when the alliance broke up, MIÉP lost its relevance.

Semi-Fascist movement fragments and militias outside of the political scene

In the period 1989–2000, various neo-Fascist organizations were established on the initiative of former Fascist leaders living abroad (Tóth, 2008). Good examples of these organizations are the Hungarian National Socialist Action Group, which was later renamed the Hungarian National Front Line (Magyar Nemzeti Arcvonal – MNA), which cooperated with the World-National People's Power Party chaired by the emissary of the Australian-based Hungaro-Fascist emigration group, the Association of Victims of Communism (Eörsi, 2004) and the Hungarian Hungarist Movement (Magyar Hungarista Mozgalom), which was later renamed the Hungarian People's Welfare Association.

In 2001, the renegades of the above mentioned organizations and small skinhead groups founded the (Hungarian) Blood and Honor Cultural Association (BHCA)

108 Szilveszter Póczik, and Eszter Sárik

which became a member of an international network operating under the same name. They not only declared their loyalty to the Hungarian national ethnic community and to the Christian ethical value set but also declared the intention to pursue a cultural fight. Previously, they organized the Day of Honor in memory of the attempted break out by Hungarian troops, German military and SS units from the Buda Castle while being shelled by the Red Army on 11 February 1945. Afterwards, they also organized a 60 kilometre long memory march called "Kitörés 60" every year, but it was prohibited in 2006. Later on, the Unified Movement for our Homeland continued the activities of the Hungarian Blood and Honor (Domokos, 2005; Marsovszky, 2012). This incorporates numerous groups, among others the Outlaws' Army described below.

Advancement of the current militant far right

In the years after 2000, all these organizational initiatives became more or less insignificant. They could not become parliamentary parties, nor could they gather an active mass basis and nor could they build an attractive ideological profile. In 2004, Hungary – governed by a new coalition of Socialists and Liberals – became an EU member state and was optimistic about the future. Nevertheless, this optimistic climate ended shortly and by 2006 the Socialist-Liberal governments became totally discredited. They consciously deluded their voters, ruined the economy, drove the country into a debt-trap and pushed their citizens, particularly the descendants of the relative winners of the Communist era, into deeper and deeper poverty. The unemployment rates grew beyond 10%. When the Prime Minister in 2006 admitted his political dishonesty and the catastrophic financial situation of the country, violent riots broke out in Budapest and other towns. Different juvenile groups, organized football hooligans and extreme right wing organizations took part in street fights. These demonstrations were repressed brutally by the police using unlawful means and methods. This meant the de facto end of left wing politics. However, the Socialist-Liberal coalition managed to remain in power until 2010.

As predicted the elections of 2010 brought a great success for the conservative parties. The coalition of the hardliner conservative centre-right wing FIDESZ and Christian Democrats established their government with a two thirds majority in the Parliament. The formerly chanceless (2006: 119,000 votes) far right Jobbik Party also gained a strong position, winning 12.2% of the deputy seats (47 deputies).[5] In the elections of 2014 Jobbik became even stronger: it polled more than one million votes, securing 20.55 percent of the total, making them Hungary's third largest Parliament party having 23 deputies, i.e. 11% of all deputies.

The Jobbik Party – the wolf in sheep's clothing

In 2002, the Jobbik Party (Movement for a Better Hungary – Right-Wing Youth Association / Jobbik Magyarországért Mozgalom – Jobboldali Ifjúsági Közösség) was established by both Catholic and Protestant university students and became a political party in 2003. As mentioned earlier, the Jobbik Party also tried to operate jointly with MIÉP. Jobbik described itself as "a principle-based conservative and radically patriotic Christian party" whose 2fundamental purpose" was the protection of "Hungarian values and interests". They emphasized the importance of the Christian values – partly because they treated it as a source and framework of crime prevention (Sárik, 2011). However, the Jobbik party was ostracized from the "political class" and was described by other legal parties and the mainstream Hungarian and European media as a neo-Nazi, extremist, racist, anti-Semitic, anti-Ziganist, xeno- and homophobic organization with strong masculine (macho comradeship) tendencies.

Until its spectacular "transfiguration" since 2016, Jobbik's ideology was a combination of ethno-nationalism with an anti-elitist populist rhetoric and a radical critique of existing political institutions. Anti-globalist and sceptic of European integration, Jobbik specifically opposes Israeli and Jewish investments in Hungary. On a practical level, Jobbik demands territorial autonomy for Hungarians living in Slovakia, Ukraine, Romania, and Serbia, but on an ideological level, Jobbik is an adherent of irredentism (reconstruction of the ancient Hungarian Empire) calling for revision of the Trianon Peace Treaty. This attempt is underlined with a historical revisionism: the relativization of the Holocaust and the rehabilitation of ultra-conservative and Fascist governments of the period 1919–1945, particularly the role of Admiral Horthy.

The party also pursued intensive international organizational activities. In May 2008, a delegation of Jobbik's Committee of Foreign Affairs met Nick Griffin, chairman of the British National Party in London. The Alliance of European National Movements (AENM) was formed in Budapest in October 2009. The founding members of the alliance were the Jobbik, the National Front in France, the British National Party in UK, the Tricolour Flame in Italy, the National Democrats in Sweden and Belgium's National Front. According to research conducted by the Political Capital Institute, over the last few years Jobbik has served Russian interests. They did so by social and political destabilization at country-, EU- and NATO-level for the external legitimacy of Russia and for the purposes of gaining information and spreading disinformation for and by Russia led by Putin. The Russian influence extends to other right-wing extremist organizations (64VM Youth Movement, Hungarian National Frontline, Conquest 2000) as well as to social media surfaces (Juhász, Győri, Krekó & Dezső, 2015).

Jobbik had several ideas that attracted votes such as their demand for repressive crime prevention, for tightening up punishment, the criminalization of promoting "sexual deviancy" in order to "protect public morals and the mental health of the young generations" and the idea of the reestablishment of the Gendarmerie[6] was also popular. Since the beginning of the migration crisis in 2015, they wanted to re-establish a separate Border Guard that was integrated into the police during the preparation for Hungary's integration into the Schengen Area.

Jobbik discovered and identified a new enemy: namely the Roma minority when they racially characterized this population as "genetically determined" or

FIGURE 7.1 Hungarian Guard's memorial march in honour of Governor Horthy, 19 November 2009
(Photo: Béla Szandelszky)

"born" criminals. Jobbik launched a campaign against the so-called *Gipsy crime*: a notion used by the police of the Communist era for ethnic profiling. This way Jobbik instrumentalized the main ethnic resentment of the Hungarian population:

the anti-Ziganism (Harper, Steger & Filcak, 2009). "Earlier no organization dared to propagate it publicly. The action of Jobbik changed this situation making racism openly presentable again" (POLCAP, 2008).

Based on our own field research (Póczik, 2011), we can state that the social character was the main driver in attracting great masses to Jobbik. This could be concluded on the basis of voters' composition. They were nationalist juveniles, partly students with a high degree of perceived insecurity (about 16%), social groups of the lower middle classes threatened by crime and social misery, losers from the social changes of the transition and the EU-membership, unstable existences and par excellence racist groups from the metal-rock music scenes and football-freaks, etc. (REP, 2015).

Janus-faced vigilantism – the Hungarian Guard

To highlight the attempt to recover public safety, the Jobbik Party founded the "Hungarian Guard Association for Protection of Traditions and Culture" (Magyar Gárda Mozgalom Hagyományőrző és Kulturális Egyesület) in August 2007. The Hungarian Guard as a top-down organization served as the unarmed but uniformed (para)military wing of Jobbik. The party militia was chaired by the Jobbik party leader Gábor Vona himself. According to the Foundation Declaration[7] of the Guard, it set the goal to protect the Hungarian culture and history. The Guard (and later its successor UMGM) aimed to take part in crime prevention and protection of the citizens as well as in charity actions such as park cleaning, soup kitchen, flood protection etc. Under the slogan "Faith, force and will!" and the salutation "Wish a brighter future!" – borrowed from juvenile organizations of the period between the two World Wars – the Guard declared that they would aim to "defend the physically, spiritually and intellectually defenseless Hungary" (Kerepeszki, 2010). They aimed to substitute the dismantled Hungarian Army and also to act against the criminals who

> keep terrorizing the Hungarian citizens [...] if the Jobbik gains power [...] the members of the Hungarian Guard will form the backbone of the new Hungarian gendarmerie, will be invested with public authority, and will march here, on the streets [...] with weapons on their side.

The Guard's uniform was composed of black boots, black trousers with a white shirt and black vest that had a lion figure on its back and an escutcheon on the front side, a shielded black cap and a red-white striped scarf. The Guard's escutcheon was based on the escutcheon shield of King Emeric of Hungary which features the Árpád-stripes[8] with nine golden lions in four red stripes (3–3–2–1 lions per stripe). The Guard's uniform was similar to the Arrow Cross uniform.

The social composition of the Guard was quite heterogeneous. The vast majority of the members were male (but some were also female), nationalist juveniles of the (lower) middle class, former military and police officers, soldiers of the French

FIGURE 7.2 Swearing in and inauguration of new members of the Hungarian Guard, October 2007
(Photo: Béla Szandelszky)

Foreign Legion and other mercenaries, entrepreneurs and different weapon freaks and militarists appeared in its ranks, too. Until the dissolution of the Guard, more than a thousand people became members of the Guard in public inauguration ceremonies in "comradeship" with other smaller or local paramilitary organizations, i.e. the right-wing quasi military National Civic Guard Association (Nemzeti Őrsereg)[9] established in 2007, later the 64VM and the Outlaws' Army (Betyársereg). In the period 2007–2009, six inauguration ceremonies took place on historically prominent sites of Budapest (Royal Palace, Square of the Heroes) always in March or October.[10] The Guard also had youth and children's organizations in which the members were called *cadets* and *lion whelps*.

In September 2007, the Guard started a nation-wide "anti-crime tour" in the bigger towns of Hungary. They held citizen forums and protest demonstrations in Romany settlements against "Gypsy crime" for "safety in the province". All these were followed by protests from left-wing organizations. Clad in uniform, the Guard also marched against "the terror by Gypsy criminals" that took place in smaller settlements. These were villages where the segregated Roma communities had serious conflicts with the Hungarian majority or where individual Roma perpetrators committed serious violent crimes. In December 2007 in Tatárszentgyörgy, in April 2008 in Nyírkáta and Vásárosnamény, June 2008 in Pátka and in

March 2009 in Sarkad, uniformed units of the Guard of 100–200 persons held so called protest demonstrations with threatening intent. The function of these marches was more about political propaganda for the Jobbik Party and intimidation of the Roma minority than vigilant activity. In reality, the Guard's effective vigilant activity was quite limited, though in a couple of cases the local units of the Guard prevented illegal occupation of dwellings and also the expansion of conflicts between Roma and non-Roma. Still in several cases, the anti-criminal demonstrations and marches ended up in violent conflicts between the Guard members and Roma persons or counter demonstrators.

By the end of 2008, the Guard split into two parts having different "captains" but the same ideology and goals. In December 2008, based on a motion by the Prosecutor General, the Metropolitan Court Budapest disbanded the Guard explaining that the activities of the organization were against the human and minority rights guaranteed by the Constitution. The Guard appealed against the verdict, but in July 2009, the Budapest Tribunal upheld the prohibition on the Guard and the Supreme Court did the same. In 2013, the European Court of Human Rights in Strasbourg upheld the ban on the Guard, ruling that it was "the least violent manner" to deal with a group that posed a clear threat to minority groups. Since its dissolution the Guard has attempted to re-organize itself as the New Hungarian Guard, but the government acted against the so called "criminals in uniform" and in February 2010 the Parliament passed a law that significantly raised the punishment for participating in a dissolved organization.[11]

FIGURE 7.3 Uniformed units of the Hungarian Guard march through the Roma community of Tatárszentgyörgy
(Photo: Bela Szandelszky)

114 Szilveszter Póczik, and Eszter Sárik

Some parts of the prohibited Hungarian Guard attempted to re-organize themselves as legal unarmed auxiliary police NGOs.[12] In Hungary, the Civic Auxiliary Police (Polgárőrség) is a state controlled and state supported association of NGO-volunteers having limited policing powers to participate in crime prevention and crime control. Some groups of the dissolved Guard joined them or established their own auxiliary police NGOs for legal purposes and to step into the circle of respectable people. One of the successor organizations was the Auxiliary Police Association for a Better Future (Szebb Jövőért Polgárőr Egyesület). This group was involved in a bloody mass tussle between Roma and participants of an anti-Roma demonstration in April 2011 in the settlement of Gyöngyöspata (Miklósi, 2011). As a consequence, the Auxiliary Police Association for a Better Future was dissolved by the court in 2014 (Janecskó, 2014). The Government labeled them "uniformed criminals" and the Parliament issued a law on "prohibited policing activity". This also led to the law on the civic auxiliary police being sharpened.

Anti-vigilante legislation – dilemmas of law making and judicial practice

In studying vigilantism, there are two types of crimes which should be examined due to their strong relation to the phenomenon. Private Justice, on the one hand, and acts that can be interpreted under the umbrella-category of hate crimes, on the other. These two types together are more or less able to describe vigilantism as a whole, the first from the control aspect of it and the other from the content side which means hate and bias motivation in the activities examined.

The crime called "Private Justice" represents the classical interpretation of vigilantism; when the vigilante action or behavior reacts to real criminal actions, in spite of alleged wrong-doings or perceived legal or moral disorder. This crime was formulated in order to punish those offenders who use violence to enforce their legal or allegedly legal *material* (!) claims. In other words, this behavior was legislated as a crime in the Criminal Code to hinder those aggressive behaviors that were definitely conducted for enforcing nothing but concrete financial claims. However, Private Justice cannot be purely identified as a homogeneous crime in the terms of its legal dogmatic position. It was introduced into the Criminal Code in 1948 in Hungary, but due to its double-faced character, its position remained uncertain. Though its property-protective aspect is dominant in its character, Private Justice-activities endanger both private property and public peace, due to which the crime was placed under different titles in the Penal Code from time to time. It necessarily implies that the legislator intended to suggest different meanings and approach. From 1961, it was regulated under the title of "Crimes against the Social and Private Property" later the Act IV of 1978 positioned it among the "Crimes against the Public Peace". Currently, the Hungarian Criminal Code[13] classifies it as a "Violent Crime against Property". Regarding the fact that from 1998 Private Justice also holds "offending in a group"[14] as a qualifying circumstance, those vigilante activities which aim to take revenge on certain crimes committed against property, can be punished for Private Justice (Radnai, 2015).

Vigilantism and militias in Hungary **115**

Nevertheless, most of the vigilante acts do not necessarily reflect to actual property crimes,[15] but rather perceived or imaginary anti-social behaviors by minority groups who are generally associated with the phenomenon of criminality. In the last decades, several ethnic groups became targets of artificially induced hate campaigns. In the 1980s, the Poles were described as lazybones, in the 1990s the Russians as Mafiosi and the Chinese as smugglers and illegal traders serving the Triads. But the constant target of spontaneous ethnic hate was and still remained the Roma minority. To protect the vulnerable groups from any illegal and endangering actions, the Hungarian legislators defined several behaviors as hate crimes: Apartheid, Incitement against a Community, Open Denial of Nazi and Communist Crimes, Use of Symbols of Totalitarianism, the Degrading Treatment of Vulnerable Persons, Violence against a Member of a Community and the qualified forms of Harassment. The crimes listed contain features that would definitely cover jeopardizing or harming the status or the existence of a certain community, but in reality Violence against the Member of a Community (Section 216), Incitement against a Community (Section 332) and Use of Symbols of Totalitarianism (Section 335) should be relevant with regards to the topic of vigilantism.

The section "Violence against the Member of a Community"[16] covers different modi operandi of crimes and lists sensitive groups who might be subject of violent crime due to features such as their nationality, ethnicity, race or religion, or in particular, on the grounds of disability, gender identity or sexual orientation. The legislation can be titled sufficient to protect the listed minorities from any definite violence and threat used against them, explicitly because of their group features.

Section 216(1) – Any person who displays an apparently anti-social behaviour against others for being part, whether in fact or under presumption, of a national, ethnic, racial or religious group, or of a certain societal group, in particular on the grounds of disability, gender identity or sexual orientation, of aiming to cause panic or to frighten others, is guilty of a felony punishable by imprisonment not exceeding three years. (2) Any person who assaults another person for being part, whether in fact or under presumption, of a national, ethnic, racial or religious group, or of a certain societal group, in particular on the grounds of disability, gender identity or sexual orientation, or compels him by force or by threat of force to do, not to do, or to endure something, is punishable by imprisonment between one to five years. (3) The penalty shall be imprisonment between two to eight years if violence against a member of the community is committed: a) by displaying a deadly weapon; b) by carrying a deadly weapon; c) by causing a significant breach of interest; d) by tormenting the aggrieved party; e) in a gang; or f) in criminal association with accomplices. (4) Any person who engages in the preparation for the use of force against any member of the community is guilty of a misdemeanor punishable by imprisonment not exceeding two years.

However, in many cases the given criminal act does not reach the level of violence. The vigilante group often represents danger purely because of its features of a well-organized and symbolically (and sometimes physically) armed community. This is well illustrated by the infamous *march in Gyöngyöspata* (see above in

116 Szilveszter Póczik, and Eszter Sárik

subchapter III.2) when the criminal act could be judged as "Incitement against a Community". Article 332 (Hungarian Criminal Code) provides people with protection against non-violent conduct motivated by racism, xenophobia or other bias motive (e.g. homophobia), according to which anyone publicly inciting hatred against the Hungarian nation or any national, ethnic, racial or other groups of the population shall face punishment for a felony offence with imprisonment for up to three years (Balogh, 2011). This regulation reflects verbal actions generating hatred towards protected communities, which could be applicable in most of vigilante situations. In cases when the incitement to hatred is strengthened by visual representations, "Use of Symbols of Totalitarianism" can also be applied in legal cumulation with it.

For the clear and comprehensive interpretation of the Gyöngyöspata case, it is important to note that the Hungarian Civil Liberties Union (TASZ) filed a civil action against the Hungarian police for breaching the right of equal treatment of the Roma inhabitants. In 2015, the Municipal Civil Court of Eger accepted the case and declared that the police was responsible for the breach of the aforementioned rights of citizens as they did not protect the Roma inhabitants from Auxiliary Police Association for a Better Future, who was invited to Gyöngyöspata by the Jobbik in order to threaten the Roma inhabitants. The Court of Eger stated that the police's passivity induced a situation in which the Roma were discriminated against and harassed. Though the application was accepted at the first stance, the Court of Appeal of the town Debrecen rejected it in April 2016. Upon the request for review, the final decision was taken in 2017 by the Curia of Hungary,[17] which stated that the night marches with torches, the organization of soldier training camps and their permanent stay in Gyöngyöspata definitely threatened the inhabitants of the village and the passivity of police and the lack of police action fulfilled the requirements of the violation of human dignity (Pap, 2017).

Still, dubious decisions were made by the courts regarding the scope of the victims of "Violence against the Member of Community". In 2013, a small village witnessed Roma perpetrators attack members of a vigilante group.[18] The attackers were sentenced to two years' imprisonment because of "Violence against a Member of a Community" since the perpetrators expressed that they attacked the victims due to their Hungarian nationality. Though their crime was related to the nationality of the victims, the text of the sentence did not highlight the importance of the threat that the offenders suffered from the vigilante groups of the Hungarian National Guard and Auxiliary Police Association for a Better Future, both successors of the Hungarian Guard, who had organized a protest demonstration in the settlement two days before the criminal act mentioned above. A similarly pronounced criminal case was when the perpetrators in Sajóbábony attacked Hungarians, yelling "You will die, Hungarians! We will kill you!" and damaged the car of one the victims with metal bars. The victims were connected to the Jobbik Party. The verdicts were in line with Decision No. 96/2008. VII.3 by the Constitutional Court, which set that the crime of "Violence against a Member of a Community" is not a minority protective regulation but the scope of the protection refers on any group identities and not exclusively on the membership to a certain ethnic minority. Due to this, the judgments were formally accurate but the decisions were criticized by the Hungarian Civil Liberties Union (TASZ) on the ground that they lacked any background information on the political orientation of the victims and threat the offenders suffered, which definitely influenced the criminal act.

Despite making use of the available hate crime regulations, the government decided to formulate a new paragraph in order to hinder vigilante grouping and marching. In 2011, as a response to the events in Gyöngyöspata (see subchapter III.2.), the Criminal Code[19] was amended to prevent such activities in the future by enacting the crime of "Prohibited Policing Activity". According to this,[20] to *establish an organization* without legal authorization in order to enforce public order and safety or to organize an activity with the appearance of such, and/or to fail to fulfil the obligation to cooperate with the authorized organizations, is a misdemeanour punishable by imprisonment not exceeding two years. The new crime neither got loud public attention nor serious reflections from the legal sphere. Even in the "Commentary", the Official Legal Explanation of the Criminal Code, only half a page was devoted to discussing this law. Belovics, Molnár and Sinku (2016) discussed it in only half a page.[21] The regulation's novelty lay in the fact that the fake policing activities could be punished automatically, however the penal consequences apply only to the organizers and not to other participants. The textualization of the crime lacks any hint of hate propaganda or hostile attitudes of marching against minorities. The legislation simplifies the problem of vigilantism and equalizes it with forbidden policing activities. Thus, this crime can form a legal cumulation with "Incitement against a Community", and together, the joint indictment of these crimes would be able to hinder vigilantism.

Though the enactment of this regulation suggests that the government implements strict legislative measures against vigilantism, we believe that it would be more important to enforce serious judicial reactions on hate crimes and on hate-speech rather than creating new sections in the Criminal Code. It also means that if the legal responses were consequent enough and the judicial practice would not suffer from the problems of under-qualification of hate motives[22] and sometimes from doubtable sentences, these crimes would be sufficient to keep vigilantism under control.

Meanwhile, the appearance of hate speech (or at least remarks on hate) is not uncommon in political communication and media, which acts hardly ever have criminal consequences or if yes, they suffer delay. The rigorous tackling of vigilantism (which is unquestionably sympathetic) is regrettably in line with the efforts of the ruling government to gain control over all segments of the society, they intend to hinder particularly those civil initiatives which are independent, critical and oppose the government's agenda.

Vigilante terrorism – a racist death squad hunts down Roma

The saddest chapter in the history of the far right militant activity is the unprecedented series of murders of Roma in the period 2008 to 2009 committed by a death squad of four perpetrators (Vágvölgyi, 2016). Without any certain reasons and based on the idea of equating Roma with criminality, they killed six Roma persons in ten attacks, among them one child, living in peripheral slum settlements. The perpetrators did not know their victims and chose them randomly. Based on the whole perception of the so called "Gypsy crimes", the killers' intent was to take revenge through their actions. For them, the aim was to provoke violent reactions by the Roma that would lead to an ethnic civil war, which was fueled by their speculation that the police and penal justice handled the Roma criminal offenders too indulgently. The ethno-chauvinist offenders had loose contacts with the Jobbik and Hungarian Guard but they acted independently. They were linked much more to skinheads and football hooligan groups. A particularly strange element of the case was that one of the four charged persons was a former informant of the Military Security Agency (Katonai Biztonsági Hivatal) (Pilhál, 2015). In January 2016, the Supreme Court sentenced three offenders to life long (min. 40 years) imprisonment and one perpetrator to 13 years of prison. According to the reasoning of the judgment, this series of crimes was "advance planned multiple homicides committed particularly cruelly by a criminal organization upon malicious motive, against adults and minors unable to defend themselves" (Csona, 2016).

New far right organizations between militarism and vigilantism, and the decline of the Jobbik Party

In the meantime, other militant far-right associations also came to life such as the Defense Force (Véderő) (Dezső, 2011) and the so-called 64VM. The Defense Force organized basic military tactical trainings for youngsters, but after the suicide of its commander it fell apart. The Sixty-Four Counties Youth Movement (Hatvannégy Vármegye Ifjúsági Mozgalom, abbr. as HVIM/64VM) named in memory of Greater Hungary which was divided into 64 counties, is an irredentist movement claiming for the unification of all ethnic Hungarians that live outside of Hungary and the revision of the Peace Treaty of Trianon. This group was until 2013 chaired by László Toroczkai who later became the vice chair of Jobbik. Currently, the mayor of Ásotthalom at the southern border to Serbia is the chair. 64VM is acting mainly in Hungary but is also present in the surrounding countries on the level of communication, ideology and propaganda. In December 2015, two members of the organization were arrested by the Romanian authorities based on the false accusation of planning to detonate an improvised explosive device in Kézdivásárhely / Târgu Secuiesc during the Great Union Day[23] Parade on 4 July 2018. The "offenders" were finally sentenced to five years' imprisonment.

In 2016, the Jobbik Party began its transition to become a people's party positioned in the political centre. Its chairmen disowned the party's earlier radical features, such as their anti-Semitism and anti-Ziganism stand. The de-radicalization obviously caused sharp debates within the Jobbik Party and a great loss in the elections of 2018. In reaction to this phenomenon, persons formerly closely linked with Jobbik established new alternative radical parties to keep the radicals together.

Examples include Force and Intrepidity (Erő és Elszántság),[24] Identitesz – Association of Identitarian Students (Identitárius Egyetemisták Szövetsége) and Order and Justice (RIA – Rend és Igazságosság).[25] The chairman of the latter, Mihály Zoltán Orosz, former Jobbik member and radical anti-Ziganist mayor of the village Érpatak,[26] established the Legion of Honor (Becsület Légiója) in 2016,[27] which was a local vigilante guard-association to keep the Roma population under control.

These groups are interlinked with other organizations such as the Outlaws' Army (Betyársereg).[28] The Outlaw's Army represents a new wave of vigilante organizations, as it is a grass-root group having no political party as a background supporter. Unlike the Hungarian Guard, the Outlaws' Army is more conspiring and generally avoids media and spectacular mass demonstrations. Their modest uniform is much cheaper and simpler than that of the one-time Hungarian Guard. It consists of black T-shirts and hoodies with their emblem showing two battle axes with the motto "Do not hurt the Hungarian if you want good". Their romantically designed parade uniform is similar to the clothing of the horse herds and bandits (called "betyár") of the nineteenth century.

The Outlaws' Army presents its program in their declaration. The document titled "The way of recovery – ideological lines of the Hungarian new right wing movement", issued in September 2017, contains a detailed and relatively coherent ideology of a new conservative radicalism. Its starting point is the decadence of the Occident that is to be reversed. The elements of the decadences are liberalism, democracy, materialism, lost norms and identities, left-wing movement, demographic decline,

FIGURE 7.4 László Balázs, leader of Identitesz, on the left behind him the flag of the Outlaws' Army
(Photo: Gábor Bankó)

120 Szilveszter Póczik, and Eszter Sárik

expansion of ethnic and racial minorities and self-destruction of the youth. The recovery can be achieved by uncompromising radical right-wing activism against liberalism, conservativism and progressivism, refusal of equality, gender philosophy and political correctness, self-defense for the Hungarian and European future and "metapolitics" for a change of attitudes. Their goals are focused on ethnic and cultural homogeneity in Europe and Hungary, termination of multiculturalism, order, hierarchy, communities, autocracy as the organic way of life, unity of European patriots, continuous self-education and activism by the members and acting as police if the authorities are unable the defend the citizens. The Outlaws' Army is now the biggest militant network with 300–400 members organized in so-called clans at a regional basis and in activity fields. Their network as such is quite clandestine, so they give little information about themselves.[29]

Migration crisis and vigilantism reloaded

In July 2016, Human Rights Watch (HRW) reported[30] that illegal civil vigilante groups were active at the southern border of Hungary and attacked asylum seekers. HRW called the authorities "to check up the news that the border police cooperates with patrolling units of the Outlaws Army in harassing migrants". The TV channel ATV obtained the information that Zsolt Tyirityán, top leader of Outlaws' Army, boasted among his friends that the Ministry of the Interior, the Defense Ministry and the National Police Headquarters requested his organization to participate in border control and they successfully took part in it. ATV asked both ministries on this issue but received no answer. According to reliable information, the Outlaws' Army organized protest demonstrations against migrants and pro-migration NGOs such as Migration Aid and MigSzol. In some cases, violent conflicts happened in which the police intervened.[31]

According to other sources, the members of Field Patrol Service (Szlavkovits, 2014) of the settlement Ásotthalom took part in the detection of illegal migrants on behalf of the mayor László Toroczkai[32]. The Field Patrol Service[33] is a legal local armed policing organization that can be established if there is need for that by the villages in order to defend agrarian lands and plants. Obviously, as a propaganda video attests[34], Toroczkai misuses the local Field Patrol Service and intends to form it into "migrant hunters". That is why the liberal party Együtt, reported Toroczkai to the police because of committing "Private Justice" (Haszanz, 2017).

Analysis and conclusions

In our research, we used primary and secondary sources, among others historical and sociological studies, media interviews, reports and videos, as well as empirical scientific studies and surveys, from which we ascertained that three types of vigilantism can be observed in Hungary today.

(a) The party-supported and -managed nationwide top-down organization based on the subordination principle with definite hierarchy (as the Jobbik-supported

Hungarian Guard was). (b) The local or regional and subregional vigilant groups, supported and managed by local administrative leaders (as the Legion of Honor, led by a village mayor) and (c) the decentralized grass-root organizations consisting of more or less independent sub-groups (such as the Outlaw's Army). Finally, there is a fourth type, which is quite difficult to classify. This category contains the cases where local administrative leaders use, or rather misuse, legal security organizations to implement actions to which they are not authorized. This happened with Field Patrol Services (in the village of Ásotthalom, led by mayor László Toroczkai) in the border region. These mentioned leaders and their more or less decentralized organizations represent very different levels of political and social embeddedness, influence and efficiency as well as a deep rooted political tradition and continuity of militarist far right movements of vigilante character. These organizations react to negative social trends and appear in periods of real or alleged crisis, which sharpens the discrepancies of national identity.

The core ideas of these movements lie in the heroic military tradition, particularly that of WWI and WWII. They call for a "national revolution" conducted by a militarily organized avant-garde with the mission to clean up all noxious social groups, including criminals. Other central elements in their ideology are: anti-modernism, anti-globalism, racial, ethnic, cultural homogeneity and supremacy, termination of social parasites and/or certain foreign ethnic groups (Jews, Germans, Slavs, Romany), anti-multiculturalism, order, hierarchy, autocracy, meritorism, community-based productive (agrarian) society, organic way of life, unity of patriots, self-education and quasi military activism (squadrismo, arditismo). Some varying elements are enemy images, in relation to Europe and the neighboring ethnic groups etc. The basic elements and frames of this mindset have existed since 1920, as mentioned in the Introduction.[35]

The broadest interpretational frame of the current development is the post-Communist period, when the state lost the ability to protect the citizens. Criminality expanded radically. This lead to an urgent demand for citizens to organize privately in pursuit of crime prevention (vigilantism). The disastrous consequences of the Communist dictatorship and the social changes of the last 30 years amplified the latent energies resulting from social dissatisfactions and channelled this energy into (quasi) violent movements. In these movements, which adhere to old and outdated ideologies, the protest of the youth of the (lower) middle classes was articulated. These far right oriented political efforts found echo and popularity, particularly in regions of Hungary where the population was extremely endangered by (long-lasting) unemployment, uncared neighbourhoods, poor and segregated but demographically booming Romany settlements and diffused social anxieties summing up in fear of crime (Korinek, 1995). According to DEREX (Demand for Right-Wing Extremism Index, a measurement developed by the Political Capital Institute), in the period 2002 to 2009, the rate of citizens (older than 15 years) showing sympathy for right extremist efforts grew from 10 to 21%. This result was in line with the growing mistrust in the democratic institutional system (Krekó & Juhász & Molnár, 2011).

The extending criminality and growing fear of crime, the extremely disadvantageous social status of the Roma minority and the migration crisis of 2015 helped the extremist groups to find a new "enemy image" and to initiate activities that meet the sympathy of broad social strata. So, the Hungarian Guard can be considered the "mother" of the current vigilante groups. It was established as the party militia of the far right Jobbik Party in a period of left-wing governments of Socialists and Neoliberals. Their mission was to restore "law and order" and to persecute the Roma minority stereotyped as criminal. In the course of the fragmentation of the top-down organized Hungarian Guard and its party background, new bottom-up structured vigilant groups such as the Outlaws' Army grew. While earlier organizations such as the Hungarian Guard sought wide publicity and media coverage (TV, radio, print media), this latter organization does not operate publicly. It is mainly active on social media (Facebook, Twitter), or communicates through covered channels (WhatsApp etc.). They make use of personal contacts, since many members of the Outlaws' Army have criminal records.

After the economic crisis of 2008 had passed and the government of Viktor Orbán came to power, these groups were fuelled by the migration wave of 2015–2017. The role they play in (anti-)migration politics, by publishing texts and organizing marches and anti-Muslim protests, is more symbolic than effective. Despite its anti-migration policy and resentments against Muslims and Islamic customs, the current Hungarian government does its best through the state authorities to suppress any spontaneous or planned incidents as well as vigilant activities. However, the rare attempts in some municipalities at the state border to expand the scope of different local legal police-like organization for migration control is legally questionable.

With regards to the notion and interpretation of vigilantism, a hard debate is going on in the literature of criminology (Moncada, 2017). If the essence of vigilantism is using illicit collective violence (or threatening with it) against criminals for securing social justice and conservative/traditional morality (when the failed state and its authorities are incapable of doing so, or to do it efficiently), then most of the Hungarian groups represent a "non-vigilante" vigilantism. In these cases, vigilantism does not signify a real readiness to act violently. Rather, it is a kind of demonstration of aggressive emotions that serves to sustain or enhance the internal cohesion of a (political) community. In most cases, symbolic aggression is directed partly towards one or more target groups stamped as enemies mainly for social, ethnic or criminal reasons. It is not the crime-preventing vigilant activity but the common set of political values and attitudes that keep these groups together. On the other hand, this non-vigilante vigilantism expresses or underlines the hate of the population against the weak state on behalf of a power-hungry political party. These far right based semi-violent organizations avoid violating the law as aggressive actions rarely take place. Their activity usually remains on the level of hate speech and hate propaganda. This does not mean that these groups are harmless, as symbolic aggression can easily turn into effective violence – into vigilante terror – if the proper conditions are given.

We can also state that such organizations represent a typical phenomenon in the period of the political and social transition of 1990–2010 in the countries of Eastern Central Europe. Despite their local differences, these groups show quite similar features: they are paramilitary organizations and are established generally by political parties who (more or less) accept the existing parliamentary frames but contest the authority and power monopoly of the state. The main function of these semi-violent groups is to aid their background parties in extending their electoral basis. The role of the militants remains marginal, however. Their organizations can be dissolved relatively easily: "The Moor has done his duty, the Moor can go". This is why it seems inaccurate to treat them as equivalent to the Nazi storm troops SA or SS.

Although the Hungarian Guard was the most powerful and best organized of all and achieved the most intensive media coverage worldwide, it is quite difficult to define which organization served as a model for others in Eastern Europe. Was it the Slovakian Brotherhood (Slovenská pospolitost') that came to life in 2003 and declared Hungarians, Jews and Roma enemies or was it the National Guard established by the Czech National Party in 2007 for the implementation of the "final solution" (sic!) of the Roma problem, or the Bulgarian National Guard, which was formed by the party called Bulgarian National Guard to intimidate the Romany minority? Even though these organizations don't thrive for long, one should reasonably be afraid of the rebirth of these or similar organizations in future periods of crisis.

Notes

1 The notion "red terror" stems from the times of the Communist revolution attempts, particularly from the Soviet Revolution in Russia of 1917 when the Communist rulers tried to stabilize their dictatorship with unlawful terroristic methods to which the conservative groups reacted with the so called "white terror". (See https://en.wikipedia.org/wiki/Red_Terror).
2 The total mistrust in police amounts to 48.5%.
3 According to the official statistics the proportion of people living in so called "income poverty" is 14.5%, 26.5% are "at the risk of poverty and exclusion" and 40% of the Hungarian population live under the poverty threshold. The "income poverty" means 78 HUF/month/ one adult person. The official calculation of poverty threshold was changed in 2014 as the 40% seemed impossible to handle within the context of social policy.
4 (Admin – editorial article): Tudott a politika Király B. Izabella olajáról, [Political circles were conscious of the oil business by Izabella Király B.] 2 February, 24.hu, https://24.hu/belfold/2004/02/09/tudott_politika_kiraly_b/.
5 It is notable that the Arrow Cross Party had 15% of mandates (29 deputies) in the Parliament in 1939.
6 The Hungarian Gendarmerie was a professional policing organization operating in the province before 1945 but since it was involved in the deportation and extradition of Jewish citizens to the Nazi authorities it was disbanded after WWII.
7 Currently not accessible in electronic form.
8 Basic motives of the dynasty of Árpád, first monarch of Hungary (845–907 AD).
9 National Civic Guard Association for Heritage Protection and Civic Defense (Nemzeti Őrsereg Hagyományőrző és Polgárőr Egyesület). Official website: http://nemzetiorsereg.hupont.hu/.

124 Szilveszter Póczik, and Eszter Sárik

10 March and October are connected with revolutionary events (1848 and 1956) in the Hungarian history.
11 See Act LXXXVI of 2010, Section 13.
12 Establishing and activity of these NGOs are regulated in the Act CLXV of 2011 on the Civic Auxiliary Police.
13 Act No. C of 2012, English translation: http://thb.kormany.hu/download/a/46/11000/Btk_EN.pdf.
14 Which means three or more people together in the terms of the Criminal Code.
15 The group of the so called Thief Busters (Tolvajkergetők) – see below – can be regarded as an exception.
16 Section 216(1) in the Hungarian Criminal Code.
17 The Curia is the highest judicial authority in Hungary.
18 Known as Case of Valkó.
19 Valid at that time: Act IV of 1978.
20 Section 217 in Act IV of 1978. This law entered into force immediately the day after it was accepted and enforced two amendments in Decree No.218/1999 (XII.28.) on Administrative Offences. Two new administrative offences came into force, both of which belonged to the legal scope of the police.
21 Currently the crime is regulated under Section 352 in Act C of 2012 (the new Criminal Code). The actual Commentary to the Criminal Code edited (Belovics, Molnár & Sinku, 2018) does not contain added information compared to the previous one.
22 The vast majority of the Hungarian legal scientific literature and NGO guidelines formulate criticism on legal practice with regard to the legal practice handling hate-crimes, in terms of false qualification and disguised crimes, which means that the judicial decisions tend to qualify these actions as public vandalism or other crime without the element of bias. (See: Jovánovics, 2015; Balogh, & Dinók, & Pap, 2012).
23 National Day of Romania.
24 Website: https://eroeselszantsag.net/.
25 Website: http://rendesigazsagossag.hu/.
26 He lost his mayor position in the interim local elections in March 2018.
27 NGO registration number 00 18 335400.
28 Website: http://betyarsereg.hu/.
29 An interview with the leader of the Outlaws' Army. https://www.youtube.com/watch?v=stDtqxMVN3g.
30 Why the Police is silent about the events at the Southern border? HVG editorial article, 22 July 2016. http://hvg.hu/itthon/20160722_deli_hatar_menekultek_toroczkai_betyarsereg.
31 The Outlaws' Army marching to Szeged. HVG editorial article, 6 July 2015. http://hvg.hu/itthon/20150706_Kivonult_a_Betyarsereg_Szegedre.
32 László Toroczkai was former vice chair of Jobbik and in 2018 he established a new radical political party named Our Homeland Movement (Mi Hazánk Mozgalom).
33 See: Law No. CXX of 2012 and Decree of the Agrarminister No. 29/1998. (IV. 30.) about the Field Patrol Service. Field Patrols are allowed to use a pellet gun against animals if unavoidable, but never against humans.
34 https://www.youtube.com/watch?v=42Vyelz698k and https://www.youtube.com/watch?v=fgJRjy2Xc0c.
35 To give a comprehensive picture on the Hungarian scene of vigilantism we have to mention the group of Thief Busters (Tolvajkergetők, www.tolvajkergetok.hu, www.youtube.com/watch?v=XRxTucrU4Q4) which focused solely to prevention and persecution of bicycle thefts and other petty crimes and had no political ideology. In spite of their effort to close cooperation with Police and law-abiding behavior, the leader of the group was sentenced because of illicit use of violence and other crimes and his group fell apart.

Vigilantism and militias in Hungary **125**

References

Balogh, Lídia (2011) Racist and related hate crimes in Hungary – recent empirical findings. *Acta Juridica Hungarica.* 52(4), 296–315. http://real.mtak.hu/43756/1/ajur.52.2011.4.2.pdf

Balogh, Lídia & Dinók, Henriett & Pap, AndrásLászló (2012) A jog által láthatatlan? A gyűlölet-bűncselekmények szabályozási kérdései és gyakorlati problémái [Not visible by law? The regulation dilemmas and practical problems of hate crimes]. *Fundamentum,* 4.

Bernstein, Richard (2003, August 9) East on the Danube: Hungary's tragic century. *The New York Times.* Retrieved from http://www.nytimes.com/2003/08/09/world/east-on-the-danube-hungary-s-tragic-century.html.

Belovics, Ervin & Molnár, Gábor Miklós & Sinku, Pál (2016) *Büntetőjog II. (Criminal law, Part II).* (Edited and peer-reviewed by Béla Busch) Budapest: HVG-ORAC.

Belovics, Ervin & Molnár, Gábor Miklós & Sinku, Pál (2018) *Büntetőjog II. Különös Rész (Criminal law, Part II).* (Edited and peer-reviewed by György Vókó) Budapest: HVG-ORAC.

Bíró Nagy, András & Boros, Tamás & Varga, Áron (2012) *Right-wing extremism in Hungary. International policy analysis.* Berlin: Friedrich Ebert Foundation.

Cserti, Csapó Tibor & Orsós, Anna (2015) Mélyszegénység – gyermekszegénység - a cigányok / romák helyzete és esélyegyenlősége [Extreme poverty, poverty of children, situation and equal opportunities of Roma]. *Gypsy Studies,* 31. ISSN 1586–6262. http://www.kompetenspedagogus.hu/sites/default/files/cserti-csapo-tibor-orsos-anna-melyszegenyseg-gyermekszegenyseg-a-ciganyok-romak-helyzete-es-eselyegyenlosege.pdf.

Csona, Árpád (2016, January 12) Romagyilkosságok – Hat év elteltével jogerősen lezárult az ügy [Roma killers – Final sentence after six years]. Retrieved from http://www.romnet.hu/hirek/2016/01/12/romagyilkossagok_8211_hat_ev_elteltevel_jogerosen_lezarult_az_ugy.

Dezső, András (2011, April 28) Alátett a Jobbiknak a Véderő [Defence force's unpleasant surprise for the Jobbik Party]. Retrieved from http://hvg.hu/itthon/20110428_jobbik_vedero_gyongyospata.

Domokos, Endre János (2005) A Vér és Becsület rövid, de zivataros története [The short and conflictful history of blood and honour]. *Vérés Becsület Kulturális Egyesület.* Retrieved from http://www.paxhungarica.org/vbke/irodalom/vbkestory.html.

Eörsi, László (2004) *A Széna-tériek 1956. [Fighters on the Széna Square].* Budapest: 1956-os Intézet.

Gellner, Ernest (2009) *Nations and nationalism.* Ithaca, NY: Cornell University Press.

Harper, Krista & Steger, Tamara & Filcak, Richard (2009) Environmental justice and Roma communities in Central and Eastern Europe. *Environmental Policy and Governance,* 19(4), 251–268. Retrieved from http://works.bepress.com/krista_harper/2/.

Haszanz (2017, June 26) Önbíráskodás miatt feljelentik a menekülteket földre kényszerítő ásotthalmi mezőőröket [Field Patrol Service members denounced at police ...]. Retrieved from https://444.hu/2017/06/26/onbiraskodas-miatt-feljelentik-a-menekulteket-foldre-kenyszerito-asotthalmi-mezooroket.

Havasi, Éva (2017): Szegénység: számolva és számolatlanul [Poverty: Counted and uncounted]. Retrieved from http://kettosmerce.blog.hu/2017/01/08/havasi_eva_szegenyseg_szamolva_es_szamolatlanul.

Janecskó, Kata (2014, October 8) Jogerős: feloszlatták a Szebb Jövőért Egyesületet [The "For a Better Future Association" dissolved finally and definitely]. Retrieved from https://index.hu/belfold/2014/10/08/jogeros_feloszlatjak_a_szebb_jovoert_egyesuletet/.

Jovánovics, Eszter (2015, May 7): A Társaság a Szabadságjogokért álláspontja a gyűlölet-bűncselekmények szabályozásáról, [Summary of the Hungarian Civil Liberties Union on

126 Szilveszter Póczik, and Eszter Sárik

the legislation on hate crimes]. Retrieved from https://tasz.hu/files/tasz/imce/ta sz-gybcs-allaspont-final_.pdf.

Juhász, Attila & Győri, Lóránt & Krekó, Péter & Dezső, András (2015) *"I am Eurasian" The Kremlin connections of the Hungarian far-right.* Budapest: Political Capital Kft. Retrieved from http://www.politicalcapital.hu/wp-content/uploads/PC_SDI_Boll_study_IamEurasian.pdf

Karsai, László (2016) *Szálasi Ferenc – Politikai életrajz [Ferenc Szálasi – A political biography].* Budapest: Balassi Kiadó Publ.

Kerepeszki, Róbert (2010) A Levente mozgalom [The "Levente" movement]. *Rubicon* 4–5, 104–115. Retrieved from http://www.rubicon.hu/megrendelheto/termek_cikkek/kerep eszki_robert_a_levente_mozgalom/66/14/0.

Komoróczy, Géza (2012). *A zsidók története Magyarországon [History of the Jews in Hungary],* Vol. 2. Bratislava: Kalligram Publ.

Korinek, László (1995) *Félelem a bűnözéstől [Fear of crime].* Budapest: Közgazdasági és jogi kiadó Publ.

Krekó, Péter & Juhász, Attila & Molnár, Csaba (2011) A szélsőjobboldal iránti társadalmi kereslet növekedése Magyarországon [Growing Demand for Right-Wing Extremism in Hungary]. *Politikatudományi Szemle* 20(2), 53–79. Retrieved from http://www.poltuds zemle.hu/szamok/2011_2szam/kjm.pdf.

Kulcsár, Árpád (2010) A megfélemlített ország. Terrorhullámok a 20. századi Magyarországon [Intimidated country – terror waves in Hungary in the 20th century]. *Hetek.* February 19.

Lackó, Miklós (1969) *Arrow-cross men: National Socialists 1935–1944.* Budapest: Akadémiai Kiadó.

Macartney, Carlile Aylmer (1962) *Hungary and her successors: The Treaty of Trianon and its consequences 1919–1937.* Oxford: Oxford University Press.

Marsovszky, Magdalena (2012, December 6) Tag der Ehre, *Progress Magazin,* Retrieved from https://www.progress-online.at/artikel/tag-der-ehre.

Miklósi, Gábor (2011, March 6) Cigány- és gárdaterror Gyöngyöspatán [Terror by Roma and Guard members in Gyöngyöspata]. Retrieved from https://index.hu/belfold/2011/ 03/06/ciganyterror_es_gardaterror_gyongyospatan/.

Moncada, Eduardo (2017) Varieties of vigilantism: Conceptual discord, meaning and strategies. *Global Crime,* 18(4), 403–423.

Ormos, Mária (1990) *Civitas Fidelissima – Népszavazás Sopronban 1921 [Civitas Fidelissima – The referendum in Sopron 1921]* Publ. by Gordiusz Kiadó, Győr. See chapter: A nyugat-magyarországi felkelés [The Insurgence in West-Hungary]. Retrieved from http://www. sopron.hu/upload/varos/nepszavazas1921/Felkeles.html.

Pap, András László (2017, June 11) Jogalkalmazási fejlemények (és adalékok) a zaklatás tárgykörében (Development of legal practice in the topic of harassment). JTIblog, Retrieved from http://jog.tk.mta.hu/blog/2017/06/jogalkalmazasi-fejlemenyek-es-ada lekok-zaklatas.

Pelle, János (1998, December 19) Egyetemi antiszemitizmus a két világháború között [Antisemitism at the universities between the two World Wars]. *Hetek.* Retrieved from http://www.hetek.hu/velemeny/199812/egyetemi_antiszemitizmus_a_ket_vilaghaboru_ kozott.

Péterfi, Ferenc (2014) Közbizalom 2014 [Public confidence 2014]. Retrieved from https:// www.cka.hu/blog/2015/03/10/arh-2014-orszagos-kozbizalom-felmeres-eredmenyek/.

Pilhál, Tamás (2015, April 14) Gyilkosságok és titkosszolgálati kérdőjelek [Muders and doubts concerning secret services]. *Magyar Nemzet.* Retrieved from https://mno.hu/bel fold/gyilkossagok-es-titkosszolgalati-kerdojelek-1281716.

Póczik, Szilveszter (2004) Romany minority opinions and aspects in the 2003 National Victimological Data Collection. In: Irk, Ferenc (ed.) *Victims and opinions, Vol. II.* pp. 156–209. Budapest: OKRI/NIC – Hungarian National Institute of Criminology Publ.

Póczik, Szilveszter (2011, July 3) Szabályozott szabadság, egzisztenciális biztonság, kiszámítható jövő. Főiskolás fiatalok személyes, társadalmi és spolitikai attiűdjei egy empirikus kutatás tükrében [Regulated freedom, existential safety, calculable future – individual and political attitudes of university students in the mirror of an empirical research] *Polgári Szemle.* pp. 74–86. Retrieved from http://polgariszemle.hu/archivum/130-2011-juniu s-7-evfolyam-3-szam/a-valtozasok-dinamikaja/442-szabalyozott-szabadsag-egzisztencialis-biztonsag-kiszamithato-joevo.

Póczik, Szilveszter (2016) Roma-Gruppen in Ungarn bis Anfang des 20. Jahrhunderts – Eine historische Skizze. In: Kropf, Rudolf / Polster, Gert (Hg.) (2016) *Die Volksgruppe der Roma und Sinti bis 1938.* Tagungsband der 34. Schlaininger Gespräche, 14–18. September 2014. Wissenschaftliche Arbeiten aus dem Burgenland (WAB). Bd. 157. Eisenstadt. pp. 29–44.

Póczik, Szilveszter & Sárik, Eszter (2018) Law and (B)Order: Will border fence and transit zones stop the asylum seekers wave on the Balkan route? In: Kury, Helmut, & Redo, Sławomir (eds.) (2018) *Refugees and migrants in law and policy. Challenges and opportunities for global civic education.* (pp. 75–109) Cham, Switzerland:International Publishing AG. http s://doi.org/10.1007/978-3-319-72159-0, Study accessible: https://link.springer.com/chapter/10.1007/978-3-319-72159-0_3.

POLCAP (2008) *Political capital: A növekvő romaellenesség nemzetbiztonsági kockázatainak előrejelzése a Political Capital Nemzetbiztonsági Hivatal számára készített elemzéseiben 2006–2008 – összefoglaló. [Prognosis of the national security risks caused by the growing anti-Ziganism in analytic reports by Political Capital made for the Constitution Protection Office – Summary]* Retrieved from http://www.politicalcapital.hu/wp-content/uploads/PoliticalCapital_Kozlemeny_160421_Melleklet.pdf.

Radnai, Veronika (2015) Az önbíráskodás és a vagyonvédelem elhatárolása (The differentation of private justice and property protection). In: *Jogi Fórum Publikáció*http://www.jogi forum.hu/files/publikaciok/radnai_veronika__az_onbiraskodas_es_a_vagyonvedelem_el hatarolasa[jogi_forum].pdf.

REP (2015) A Jobbik szavazói [Jobbik voters] An analysis of the Republikon Institute, Budapest. http://republikon.hu/media/21048/republikon_a-jobbik-szavazo%CC%81i.pdf.

Sárik, Eszter (2011) A büntetőjogi gondolkodás és a vallás kérdései a posztmodern tükrében [Penal law considerations and questions of religion in the mirror of the post-modernity]. *Belügyi Szemle,* 59, 82–122.

Sakmyster, Thomas (1994) *Hungary's admiral on horseback: Miklós Horthy 1918–1944.* New York: Columbia University Press.

Szabó, Miklós (2015) *Az új konzervativizmus és a jobboldali radikalizmus története 1867–1918 [History of the new conservativism and right wing radicalism 1867–1918].* Budapest:Új Mandátum. Retrieved from http://mek.oszk.hu/14000/14078/14078.pdf.

Szlavkovits, Rita (2014) "Vétlen embert lőttek meg" – Megosztott Toroczkai faluja a fegyveres mezőőrök miatt [A harmless man has been shot]. In: *Magyar Narancs,* 31 May. Retrieved from http://magyarnarancs.hu/kismagyarorszag/eloszor-vaktolteny-csak-utana -az-eles-tragediat-okozhat-toroczkai-fegyveres-otlete-a-helyiek-szerint-90322.

Tökés, Rudolf (1996) Political transition and social transformation in Hungary. *Afers Internacionals,* 34–35, 79–101. Retrieved from http://www.raco.cat/index.php/revistacidob/a rticle/viewFile/28011/27845.

Tóth, István György (2010) A társadalmi kohézió elemei, bizalom, normakövetés, igazságosság és felelősségérzet [Elements of social cohesion trust, norm conformity, justice and

128 Szilveszter Póczik, and Eszter Sárik

responsibility]. In: Kolosi, Tamás & Tóth, IstvánGyörgy (eds.) *Társadalmiriport 2010* [*Social report 2010*]. (pp. 254–287). Budapest: TÁRKI Publ.

Tóth, Tibor (2008) *A hungarista mozgalom emigrációtörténete. Az "Út és Cél" és a "Hungarista tájékoztató" című sajtótermékek tükrében* [*History of the Hungarist emigration in the mirrors of its print media* ...]. Debrecen: Multiplex Media–Debrecen University Press.

Ujváry, Gábor (1991): Egyetemi ifjúság a "neobarokk társadalomban" – A bajtársi szövetségekről [University students in the new Baroque society – about the comrade assocoations], *Valóság* 5, 64–73.

Vágvölgyi, B.András (2016) *Arcvonal keleten* [*Frontline in the East*]. Budapest: Konkrét Könyvek Kiadó Publ.

Vámos, György (2011, July 30): Nyilasok a kommunista pártban [Arrow Cross men in the Communist Party]. *Nemzeti Internet Figyelő.* Retrieved from https://internetfigyelo.wordp ress.com/2011/07/30/nyilasok-a-kommunista-partban/.

Watson, Alexander (2008) Stabbed at the front. *History Today*, 58(11), 21–27.

Zeidler, Miklós (2002) *A magyar irredenta kultusz a két világháború között.* [*Hungarian irredentism between the two World Wars*]. Budapest: Teleki László Alapítvány / Foundation.

Zinner, Tibor (1989) *Az ébredők fénykora 1919–1923* [*The golden age of the "Awakening Hungarians"*]. Budapest: Akadémiai Kiadó Publ.

8

VIGILANTISM AGAINST MIGRANTS AND MINORITIES IN SLOVAKIA AND IN THE CZECH REPUBLIC

Miroslav Mareš and Daniel Milo

Introduction

Vigilantism against migrants and minorities has won huge public attention in the Czech Republic and in Slovakia in recent era. Governmental documents on extremism or reports of intelligence services analyse this issue, media inform in headlines about home guards or anti-immigrant paramilitaries. This form of vigilantism has a long tradition in both these countries and it was connected mostly with extreme right politics. Currently, the pro-Kremlin spectrum, which mixes nationalist motives with legacies of the communist era, is active alongside traditional right wing extremism. Many common trends characterize the development of the vigilante strategy and tactics in Slovakia and in the Czech Republic. Parts of the scenes in both countries cooperate closely. On the other hand, some specific features can be found in both parts of former Czechoslovakia. This chapter describes the extreme right legacies and the recent development separately in each country (however, we do not describe Hungarian groups in Slovakia), then we deal with the profiles of individual important organizations and, finally, we try to analyse and to compare selected contemporary development trends of vigilantism.

Historical legacy of extreme right vigilantes in the Czech Republic

Modern forms of extreme right paramilitaries can be found on the territory that is now the Czech Republic in the interwar period. Czech fascists as well as Sudeten-German Nazis established their own party militias. The government prohibited some of them, such as "Scouts of the National Community of Fascists" (Junáci Národní obce fašistické) (Pejčoch 2009, 31–32). The "Order Service of the Sudeten German Party" (Ordnerdienst der Sudetendeutschen Partei) served as a member base for recruitment of pro-Hitler insurgents in the late 1930s (Burian

130 Miroslav Mareš and Daniel Milo

2012, 306–327). The official Czechoslovak governmental paramilitary forces from this era are used as a model by some of the current Czech nationalist vigilantes. In the Second World War militias of Czech collaborationists operated with vigilante purposes, mostly against the Jews and against anti-Fascist resistance.

During the Cold War, the communist regime eliminated serious activities of right-wing extremists. Since the mid-1980s, a new generation of the extreme right grew up in Czechoslovakia. Small gangs of youngsters attacked Roma people and foreign students from African and Arabian countries. The attackers, among others, justified these attacks by reference to the alleged criminal activities of their victims. The expansion of racist skinhead subculture at the turn of the 1980s and 1990s led to various skinhead "anti-Gypsy" patrols and even to the lynching of some Roma accused of crime (as Emil Bendík who was murdered in the town Klatovy in 1991). Associations and neo-Nazi groupings established from "post-skinhead" circles continued with this form of vigilantism also later, as the patrols of the "National Resistance" (Národní odpor) against "Gypsy crime" in Orlová in 2005 show (Mareš 2012b, 137–139).

A new era of Czech extreme right vigilantism started in 2007–2008, under the influence of the successful political marketing of the Hungarian Guard. In 2007, the "National Guard of the National Party" (Národní garda Národní strany) was founded. However, this party and its militia had a very limited member base (despite huge media attention) (Stojarová 2012, 275). With the exception of one patrol of two men outside a primary school in the town Karlovy Vary (where the children were allegedly attacked by "Gypsy youngsters"), the activity of the National Guard proceeds mostly on the internet. Regular patrols of the "Protection Corps of the Workers' Party" (Ochranné sbory Dělnické strany) and their involvement in anti-Roma riots in Northern Bohemia in 2008–2009 were more important. However, the real member base of this group is estimated to be only around 40 persons. The existence of this unit played a significant role in the ban of the "Workers' Party" in 2010; together with the spread of racial hate and the interconnection with the neo-Nazi underground (Mareš 2012a). Smaller extreme right vigilante groups, such as the "The Kin Defenders" (Rodobrana) of the organization "Czech Lions" (Čeští lvi), were active also during anti-Romani riots in the years 2011 and 2013 (Mareš 2014). The name "Rodobrana" was also used by the Slovak extreme right vigilante organization from the interwar period (see below).

Current vigilantism against migrants and minorities in the Czech Republic

Current Czech vigilantism has its roots in the middle of the second decade of the twenty-first century. At that time, a new type of vigilante groupings was established, without links to previous right-wing extremist scenes. In contrast, some founders came from the ex-communist milieu. They combined nostalgia for the communist regime with a veneration for Putin's Russia and after the start of the migration crisis also with anti-immigrant politics. The first of these groupings was the paramilitary-focused group the "Czechoslovak reserve soldiers against the war planned by the NATO command" (Českoslovenští vojáci v záloze proti válce plánované velením NATO), founded at the beginning of 2015. At the end of 2015, after internal disputes, the new "Czechoslovak reserve soldiers for peace" (Českoslovenští vojáci v záloze pro mír – ČVVZPM) split from this original group. At the same time, another group of former members joined the organization "National Home Guard" (Národní domobrana – ND), founded in the summer 2015 (Ministerstvo vnitra České republiky 2017b, 12–14). At the end of 2017, several dozens of members left the "National Home Guard" and they established a new organization – the "Land Home Guard" (Zemská domobrana). These four organizations are more deeply analysed in the next part of this chapter (including explanation of their internal disputes). They are the most important contemporary vigilante organizations in the Czech Republic.

However, during the peak of the migration crisis in 2015–2016, several small vigilante groups were established, but usually they existed only for a short time. They were formed from the spectrum of new anti-Islamic organizations, which were founded as a reaction to a wave of Islamist terrorist attacks in Western Europe and as a reaction to subjectively perceived "migration threat". Small groups, such as the "Czechoslovak Patriotic Guard" (Československá vlastenecká garda) or the "Voluntary Public Patrols" (Dobrovolné občanské hlídky), served mostly as protection for political meetings. However, they were trained also for anti-criminal vigilante activities (Hřebenář 2016). Patrols of the trains were organized rarely – one known case is connected with members of the initiative "We don't want Islam in the Czech Republic" (Hloušek 2017, 31–32).

In 2016, the political party "Dawn – National Coalition" (Úsvit – Národní koalice) initiated the "Foundation of the Guard of the Defence of the State" (Nadace Stráže obrany státu – SOS). The aim of this foundation was establishing a paramilitary corps (called SOS) for border protection within the structures of the Ministry of the Interior (Zelená 2016). It was named after a governmental paramilitary corps from the 1930s, which protected the Czechoslovak borderlands against German Nazis at that time. In the end, this corps was not founded due to a weak position of the party and due to lack of interest on the part of the government (which considered the "Dawn – National Coalition" an extremist party at that time) (Ministerstvo vnitra České republiky 2017b, 11).

These groupings were affiliated with the Czech nationalist spectrum, including its anti-Nazi traditions. On the other hand, a group of former activists of the neo-Nazi spectrum founded the "Soldiers of Odin Czech Republic" in 2016, as part of a transnational network with roots in the Nordic countries (Ministerstvo vnitra České republiky 2017a, 5). The Germanic orientation of this group was criticized by the pan-Slavic pro-Kremlin spectrum.

Neo-Nazi gangs with vigilante tendencies operated clandestinely in the Czech Republic besides publicly active and usually uniformed vigilante groups. A wave of anti-Romani skinhead violence culminated in the 1990s. Many violent acts were also committed later, however. In April 2009, a group of four young neo-Nazis, at

132 Miroslav Mareš and Daniel Milo

least partially inspired by the Hungarian death squad (see chapter on Hungary), attacked a house with a Roma family in Vítkov (ČT 24 2010). A two-year-old Roma girl was burned on more than 80% of her body. Luckily, she survived. While the perpetrators were sentenced to harsh punishments, they are celebrated in the far-right scene (Honus 2010). Similar attacks without seriously injured or fatal victims occurred in the town Aš in 2011. Two members of the "Blood & Honour/Combat 18 Bohemia/Sudetenland" set fire to the door and threw a Molotov cocktail into the window of a residential hotel with Roma residents. Fortunately, the fire was quickly extinguished (Nejvyšší soud České republiky 2017). The Czech neo-Nazi scene propagated positively also individuals who acted in self-defence or misused self-defence and who killed people from the Romani community (Nutil 2017), despite the fact that courts do not find a racist motive behind these acts.

Historical legacy of extreme-right vigilantes in the Slovak Republic

Contemporary vigilantism in Slovakia is present mostly in the form of groups either directly connected to extreme-right political groups or at least with close affinity to such ideologies. This comes as no surprise, since the historical legacy of vigilantism in Slovakia dates back to groups operating in the interwar period. In the 1920s and 1930s several vigilante and paramilitary groups existed in Slovakia (as part of Czechoslovakia) and it was usual for political parties to have paramilitary wings. Political violence at meetings and demonstrations was commonplace and following a number of deaths resulting from fights at political meetings, "Slovak People's Party" (Slovenská ľudová strana – SLS) (later on "Hlinka`s Slovak People`s Party") set up its paramilitary wing called "Rodobrana" (The Kin Defenders), modelled on Mussolini's black shirts in 1923 (Sokolovič 2009, 23–25). It was disbanded by the authorities twice (in 1923 and in 1929), but later resurfaced and was transformed into the infamous Hlinka's Guard. This was a paramilitary wing of the ruling "Hlinka's Slovak People's Party" (Hlinkova slovenská ľudová strana – HSĽS), but also performed security related and even counter-insurgency functions during the wartime fascist Slovak State (Sokolovič 2009, 447–449).

The resurrection of vigilantes came with the fall of communism and was mostly associated with the skinhead subculture. Since one of the characteristic features of the skinhead subculture in Slovakia was the heavy influence of neo-Nazi ideology, which was dominant in the whole movement (SHARP and RASH skinheads were a tiny fraction of the whole subculture), manifestations of anti-Gypsyism were commonplace (Milo 2005). On several occasions, the hatred towards Roma was manifested in attempts to carry out organized attacks or patrols "cleaning the streets" of Roma, but also any other foreign-looking elements. Such activities often led to serious injuries, or even deaths of attacked Roma (Cahn 1997)

An important milestone in the history of vigilantism in Slovakia was the formation of "Slovak Togetherness" (Slovenska Pospolitosť), which later became the hegemon of not only the right-wing extremists scene, but also marked the ascent of the modern day vigilantism. "Slovak Togetherness", officially established in the mid-1990s (Milo 2005), attracted public attention due to their use of uniforms resembling those of "Rodobrana" and their use of symbols closely resembling the ones used during the fascist Slovak State. Although the group did not carry out typical vigilante activities such as patrolling the streets, this was a first attempt at the revival of a paramilitary/vigilante group with direct ideological and visual reference to "Hlinka`s Guard". During the ethnic riots in Eastern Slovakia in 2004, the group leader Marián Kotleba claimed the right of Slovak citizens of self-defence against rioting Romani people. While several dozens of racist skinheads expressed their will to counter these riots, they remained in their homes (Mareš 2012b, 253).

After the Supreme Court disbanded the political wing of this organization ("Slovak Togetherness – National Party" – Slovenska Pospolitosť – Národná strana) in 2006, several independent guards were formed in different regions of Slovakia (the "Stropkov guard" – Stropkovská stráž and the "Orava guard" Oravská stráž) (Mareš 2012b, 252, Mareš 2013, 33). These guards were loosely affiliated to Slovenská pospolitosť and were used for conducting various paramilitary activities.

A third important group, which was active in the first ten years of the twenty-first century, was National Resistance Nitra (Národný Odpor Nitra) based on the principle of autonomous nationalism. Individuals associated with this group conducted vigilante activities (such as street patrolling against drug users and Roma people) and were allegedly involved in several high-profile attacks against so-called alternative youth, but also against a Hungarian-speaking girl, Hedviga Malinová (Majchrák & Hanus 2007).

Current vigilantism against migrants and minorities in the Slovak Republic

The current forms of vigilantism against migrants and minorities have their roots at the beginning of the second decade of the twenty-first century. They developed in three main, partially interconnected streams. The pillar of the first stream is the political party "People's Party – Our Slovakia" (Ľudová strana Naše Slovensko – ĽSNS), which was registered under this name in 2009. However, the leader of the party, Marián Kotleba, has in previous years chaired the above-mentioned organization the "Slovak Togetherness". In this sense, the party belongs to the neo-Clergy-Fascist spectrum, inspired by the Slovak state from the years 1939–1945. The ĽSNS developed from a marginal neo-Fascist party and became a party with parliamentary representation (Kluknavská & Smolík 2016). Vigilante activities, predominantly their train patrols in 2016, enabled the rise of the ĽNSN.

The second stream is connected mostly with the legacies of the neo-Nazi spectrum. In the regional part of this spectrum, the paramilitary group "Kysuce Resistance" (Vzdor Kysuce) was formed in 2007. It was named after the peripheral region Kysuce. The most visible person of this group was Marián Magát. In 2011, it was renamed into the "Action Group Kysuce Resistance" (Akčná skupina Vzdor), and

134 Miroslav Mareš and Daniel Milo

after the enhancement of its activities, the national "Action Group Slovak Resistance" (Akčná skupina Vzdor Slovensko) was founded in 2015. While this group was trained mostly for military combat, it was also prepared for vigilante activities.

The third stream is connected with the group "Slovak Conscripts" (Slovenskí branci), which was founded by nationalist teenagers at the turn of 2011/ 2012 and which step by step grew into one of the best organized and well-trained non-state paramilitary groups in East Central Europe. The ideological background of this group is based on a mixture of Slovak nationalist traditions and the ideas of Slavic cooperation. Despite the predominantly military drill, the group also provides vigilante street patrols.

Beside these three main groups (which are described in the next section), also other forms of vigilantism are typical of contemporary Slovakia. As in the Czech Republic, brutal racist violence against Roma occurred in Slovakia after the 1990s. Hate violence is often justified by alleged "Gypsy crime". During the migration crisis, a part of the racist propaganda was re-directed from Romani people against the immigrants. In 2015, a young man on the internet offered 20 euros for each killed migrant. He was later sentenced due to this declaration and he later also denied the Holocaust (Majerová 2016).

In the Slovak right-wing extremist scene, people who killed Roma during serial shootings are celebrated. Examples include Ľubomír Harman in Devinska Nova Ves in 2010 (he killed seven people) or the incident in Hurbanovo in 2012 (city policeman Milan Juhász killed three Roma and two injured). These acts were not considered racist hate crimes by the police or judicial bodies. However, right-wing extremists, such as the Slovak white power band "Cirhoza 88", celebrate their perpetrators. Brutal acts of revenge are propagated as a recommended approach towards the so called "Gypsy criminals" (as they are called by racists) (Janíček 2015, 53).

Profiles of the most important contemporary vigilante groups in the Czech Republic and Slovakia

Czechoslovak reserve soldiers against the war planned by the NATO command and the Czechoslovak reserve soldiers for peace

The paramilitary group "Czechoslovak reserve soldiers against the war planned by the NATO command" (Českoslovenští vojáci v záloze proti válce plánované velením NATO – ČVZVPVPVN) was established at the beginning of 2015. Its creation was caused mostly by the crisis in Ukraine. The main founder of this group was Ondřej Hrčiak. Retired colonel and former military physician Marek Obrtel was named as its first leader. Originally, this group's raison d'être was the rejection of Czech and Slovak participation in a possible NATO war against Russia. It served mostly reserve soldiers (compulsory military service was ended in 2004 in the Czech Republic). In the spring of 2015, a part of the organization started to use a modified name "Czechoslovak reserve soldiers for peace" (Českoslovenští vojáci v záloze pro mír (ČVVZPM)(Mareš 2017a, 86).

With the development of the migration crisis (and decline of the Ukrainian crisis), a turn to the migration issue was visible. The group organized meetings of members in various regions (so called "Advisory fires" in countryside landscape) during the first half of 2015 and it started paramilitary training, aiming at, among other things, protection of borders against irregular migrants (Ministerstvo vnitra České republiky 2017b, 12–14). A ceremonial parade in uniforms during a mass demonstration to support President Miloš Zeman (popular in the scene due to his pro-Kremlin, anti-immigrant and anti-Muslim statements) was organized by a group in Prague on 17 November 2015 (Wirnitzer 2015). It offered the president protection patrols to save the borders; however, it was not accepted (Bukač 2015).

In 2015, Czech television broadcast a report about the activities of the group. One member – a veteran from Bosnian campaign, Martin H. – cited a misinterpreted quotation by Ernest Hemingway from his novel *A Farewell to Arms*. In this TV report he said that "people should shoot their own government on the first day of the war" (but the real words written by Hemingway are different), and he added some threats to the current Czech government and parliament. These words were aimed against politicians in case they support the NATO war against Russia (Landa 2017). Martin H. was charged for threatening a public office. However, the regional court in České Budějovice acquitted him, deciding his statement was protected by the right to free speech (Krajský soud v Českých Budějovicích 2017).

Gradual radicalization of one group of members and other personal disputes led to splits and loss of members of the original organization at the end of 2015 (at that time the organization had around 500 members) (DVTV 2015). The first group around Marek Obrtel left this organization and joined the National Home Guard, founded in summer 2015 (see below). The second faction remained in the organization, which still uses the original name "Czechoslovak reserve soldiers against the war planned by the NATO command". However, its activities declined significantly and currently they are limited to online propaganda (Českoslovenští vojáci v záloze proti válce plánované velením NATO 2018).

The third faction continued their activity under the name "Czechoslovak reserve soldiers for peace" (ČVZPM). Colonel in reserve Ivan Kratochvíl (former officer of the Czechoslovak People's Army from the communist era) became leader of this group. According to the Czech law, the organization was officially registered as an association in April 2016. The goals declared are improvement of education in civil defence and education in patriotism. The top of this association is the Supreme command (Českoslovenští vojáci za mír z. s.) (Českoslovenští vojáci za mír z. s. 2016). Czechoslovak soldiers in reserve for peace probably have only around 20 members. They organize regular drills. The group participated in some "Military education days" for school children, mostly in Northern Moravia. However, some statements of the sympathizers of the group on its profiles on social networks are objects of concern of security experts. Pro-Kremlin, anti-EU and anti-NATO expressions are typical (Jelínková 2018). This organization does not organize direct vigilante activities, but the skills from its training activities can be useful for potential future vigilantes.

National Home Guard and the Land Home Guard

The organization "National Home Guard" (Národní domobrana – ND) was founded in the summer of 2015 by the right-wing extremist party "National Democracy" (National Democracy). It was registered as an association in December 2015, with the official goal to support education in the field of home guard, prevention of crime, crisis management and help to people in need (Národní domobrana 2015, 1). The first commander of the ND was David Buchtela. At the turn of 2015/2016 several dozens of former members of the Czechoslovak soldiers in reserve (including Marek Obrtel) joined the ND. In 2016, the ND declared its autonomous status and it is no more affiliated to the National Democracy. The symbol of the ND is the Czech lion and two crossed swords. It is used on the uniform of the group (Národní domobrana 2016). In 2016, the ND became the most important Czech extreme right vigilante group with several tens of local organizations in the whole Czech Republic.

In January 2016, the previous commander was substituted by a free collective body. The Coordination council of the National Home Guard played the free regulatory role over the spectrum of local groups. The three members of the council

FIGURE 8.1 Members of the Land Home Guard in the Czech Republic during the ceremonial pilgrimage to Říp Mountain on 22 April 2018
(Photographer: Dalibor Puchta)

since January 2016 have been Marek Obrtel, František Krajča and Nela Lisková (the last named person is active also as a self-styled consul of the Donetsk People's Republic in the Czech Republic). In 2016, the National Home Guard declared approximately 2,500 members (Malát 2017), organized in more than 100 active local groups in the Czech Republic. At the end of 2017, the number declined to 62 groups (Malecký 2018). However, many of them were or are active only on the internet; the real number of active members is around 100–200 (Zelenka & Kropáček 2017).

National Home Guard organized paramilitary trainings and shooting exercises. Its members were encouraged to get their own weapons. They were meant to patrol and monitor the security situation in their localities (Malát 2017). The local group of the ND "Ore Dogs" (Krušní psi), named after the Ore Mountains (Krušné hory), patrolled at the Czech-German border. This group claimed to protect the border against migrants (Malecký 2017), which seems to be paradoxical, because migrants rarely cross the border from Germany to the Czech Republic.

In September 2017 a case from the town Orlová attracted huge media attention. Uniformed members of the National Home Guard participated at the public "Military Day", where they trained children. This event was organized at the municipal playground (Zelenka & Prchal 2017).

At the end of 2017 the newly created "Land Home Guard" (Zemská domobrana – ZD) split off from the ND. The reasons for this split were personal tensions and disputes about the organizational structure. The "old" National Home Guard had a free network with central command, while the split "Land Home Guard" prefers a strictly hierarchical structure (Malecký 2018). However, some local groups from each of the organizations cooperated after the split. Commander of the new group ZD is David Buchtela, who, after meeting with other members, dissolved the original registered ND in May 2018 (Národní domobrana 2018).

However, the "National Home Guard" is still active also without this registration, but in 2018 its activities declined significantly (Marek Obrtel – see above – stood in October 2018 as a candidate for the Senate of the Parliament of Czech Republic in Prostějov, nominated by the Czech National Socialist Party).

The official goals of the newly founded ZD (Zemská domobrana – ZD, which was registered as an association in January 2018 under the name ZEM-DOM z. s.) are similar to those of the ND. The organization wants to act within the scope of the Czech law and to educate in civil defence, preparedness for crisis situations and prevention of crime (ZEM-DOM z. s. 2018). The number of members is around 40.

The "Land Home Guard" started active patrolling in some cities, mostly in middle Bohemia at the turn of 2017/2018 (mostly in the town Nymburk, where the level of crime is very low, paradoxically) (Zemská domobrana 2018a). Its members offered assistance to the local police; however, they were rejected. The ZD published materials about survival after disasters (Janouš 2018).

Uniformed members of the ZD also visited public meetings, for example the Pilgrimage to the Říp Mountain in April 2018 (this mountain plays an important role in the Czech national mythology) (Zemská domobrana 2018b). A message to the "sunny people" (popular pejorative nickname for leftist and liberal humanists, mostly for migration supporters) was written on their website in August 2018. They were warned that similar punishment that was used for the Nazis and collaborators with German occupants in 1945 could be used in case they do not stop their treasonous activities and offense of "real patriots" (Zemská domobrana 2018c).

Soldiers of Odin Czech Republic

The Czech branch of the "Soldiers of Odin" was founded at the beginning of 2016. They are an unregistered, freely structured group of approximately 30 people from Northern Bohemia (this geographical location allows for a self-perception as "Nordic" activists and the local national socialist scene often uses Scandinavian far-right motifs). They mobilized mostly members from the neo-Nazi spectrum (Hloušek 2017, 19). Some "Soldiers of Odin" are former activists of the Protection Corps of the Worker's Party (see above).

This group is focused on crime committed by Muslims and Roma in Northern Bohemia. In 2016, they organized patrols, among other places in the spa Teplice, visited by many tourists from Arabian countries. They wanted to monitor potential disturbances of public order (such as waste disposal on public places, night-time noise disturbing the peace etc.) (Ministerstvo vnitra České republiky 2017b, 8). Soldiers of Odin participated also as "a protective unit" during incidents of unrest in the town Žatec in 2016. A Roma youngster was killed after a clash with local men and as a consequence ethnic protest of Roma people broke out (Ministerstvo vnitra České republiky 2017b, 10). They wear T-shirts with the logo of the group (Zelenka 2016).

This small branch of the transnational network still exists; however, due to imprisonment of one of the leaders (due to hate crime without a direct link to the activity of the Soldiers of Odin), a decline of activities since the autumn 2017 was evident and was limited mostly to activities in social networks (Ministerstvo vnitra České republiky 2017a, 5).

Vigilante activities of the People's Party Our Slovakia (Ľudová strana Naše Slovensko – ĽSNS)

Various vigilante activities are connected with the People's Party Our Slovakia (Ľudová strana Naše Slovensko – ĽSNS). As written above, this name of the party was registered in 2009 (in fact, activists of the association Slovak Togetherness took over control over an older marginal "Party of Wine Friends", which already had the legal registration). The real leader of the party was and is a charismatic long-term veteran of the right-wing extremist scene Marián Kotleba (born 1977), despite the fact that officially also some other chairmen were registered during the history of this party. Kotleba's name was even officially added into the name of the party ("Kotleba – ĽSNS").

With strong criticism of the governmental establishment, hard-line-statements against the Roma community and rejection of migration, the party won 8% of the votes in national elections in 2016 (209,000 votes absolutely), while in 2012 it received only 1.58% (Kluknavská & Smolík 2016). The party made the first unexpected break-through in 2013, when Kotleba won the post of regional governor of Banská Bystrica. He kept this position until 2017. The clever use of vigilantism targeting segregated Roma settlements was actually one of the main reasons for a surge of public support of this previously marginal political party. Strong anti-Roma statements continue to dominate its rhetoric.

It was actually the vigilante style march to the Roma part of the village of Šar-išske Michalany in 2009 and a violent police action against Kotleba and his sup-porters, which prompted the political resurrection of Marián Kotleba. Public meetings and gatherings and attempts to march through Roma settlements brought a lot of media attention to Marián Kotleba and his party.

One of the long-standing promises of Marián Kotleba was to establish the so-called Domobrana (Home Guard). The first attempt officially to organize such a structure dates back to 2012, when Marián Kotleba tried, unsuccessfully, to register a civic association "Guard of ĽSNS". The registration was rejected by the Ministry of the Interior and this decision was upheld by the Supreme Court in 2016 (Mesežnikov & Bránik 2017,17).

However, this did not prevent the ĽSNS from including the same proposal into the official party election programme. The programme openly stated that "We will set up Homeguard, which will protect all decent people where the police failed ... Every criminal should know that we will hit them hard not only with the police, but also with Homeguard" (ĽSNS 2016a). Although the programme did not spe-cifically mention Roma, it was clear from the context that it was supposed to act against the so called "gypsy criminals". This was a first openly stated attempt by any political party in Slovakia to create a parallel security structure, replacing the police force or working alongside the police. However, the most successful vigilante action of the ĽSNS were the so-called train patrols.

The train patrols of the "People's Party Our Slovakia" became a significant issue of Slovak politics in 2016–2017, thanks to their interconnection with the successful extreme right party. The activities of these patrols started in summer 2016. Their main goal was to protect "white" passengers in Slovak trains against the so-called "Gypsy crime" (Mareš 2017b). These are patrols composed of two to four ĽSNS members dressed in T-shirts with the party logo, patrolling in the trains frequented by Roma, but in general any trains they deem necessary. These patrols were organized by one of the most vocal and visible members of the ĽSNS of the Slovak parliament – Milan Mazúrek (ĽSNS 2016b). He became notorious in 2015 for his verbal attack on a Muslim family in Bratislava during an anti-immigration march (Kyseľ 2015). Train patrols are unarmed. However, other ĽSNS MPs joined the patrols, some of them even carrying legally owned guns such as Peter

140 Miroslav Mareš and Daniel Milo

Krupa (Teraz.sk 2016), which only added to the controversy. The patrols stated that they would act within the scope of the Slovak law. As a reaction to their activity, the state-owned train company adopted changes in its regulations, and in Parliament, the change of criminal procedure was initiated with the goal to stop the patrols, however, without much success (TA3 2017).

Despite huge media attention, the patrols did not manage to apprehend any criminal, but were seen, quite rightly so, as the most effective PR exercise of the L'SNS. According to surveys, the popularity of the party was growing at that time (Mesežnikov & Bráník 2017, 57). They patrolled in Romani settlements, and used the slogan "For polite Slovakia. Against asocial extremists" in areas with Romani villages were also activities with a strong media impact in 2017 (Vražda 2017). However, in 2018 the activity of these patrols declined.

The "Action Group Kysuce Resistance" (Akčná skupina Vzdor Kysuce)

The "Kysuce Resistance" (Vzdor Kysuce) was formed in 2007 on the basis of previously existing local neo-Nazi groups, in the relatively poor region of Kysuce in Northern Slovakia. The most important phase of its existence started in 2011. After that, it was renamed the "Action Group Kysuce Resistance" (Ministerstvo vnútra Slovenskej Republiky 2016, 81). The group announced that it had not had a commander (Struhár 2016, 20). However, the real leader was Marián Magát. Lukáš Kováč significantly shaped the character of the group (Mesežnikov & Bráník 2017, 30). The group enhanced its activities on the whole Slovak territory, and in 2015 the umbrella organization "Action Group Resistance Slovakia" (Akčná skupina Vzdor Slovensko) was founded with Magát as its spokesman (Struhár 2016, 20).

Kysuce Resistance became known, following a series of interviews and videos, in which the leaders of this group tried to portray themselves as a skilled, well-trained paramilitary force performing physical exercises, shooting practices and other paramilitary activities. They wear field uniforms. The number of members is around 30. In its logo, the group uses the wolf's head in the same form as the Russian group "Resistance" (Soprtivlenye) (Ministerstvo vnútra Slovenskej Republiky 2016, 81, 108). Ideologically, the group uses legacies of Slovak collaboration with the Third Reich from WWII. The group announced its readiness to substitute the official Slovak army and police with its own "elite units" (Cuprik 2015).

This strictly paramilitary nature of "Kysuce Resistance" began to change as the group leadership participated in several elections in 2014 and 2016 and as such tried to change its public profile. Instead of paramilitary style trainings, the group collected and distributed food to poor Slovak families, cleaning the forests from debris and attending public rallies. Some senior members of this group even developed close contacts with Marián Kotleba, leader of "People's Party Our Slovakia" and ran on its candidate list in 2016 parliamentary elections (including Marián Magát, ranked 88th on the candidate list). Members of the AG also joined the train patrols of the L'SNS. However, in the middle of 2016, leaders of the AG

Kysuce stopped their support for the ĽSNS after personal disputes with Kotleba (Mesežnikov & Bráník, 2017, 30).

Despite this change of public appearance, "Kysuce Resistance" keeps its paramilitary core and is regarded as the most dangerous paramilitary and vigilante group operating in Slovakia. A noteworthy development happened in 2016, when leaders of the "AG Kysuce Resistance" urged its members and sympathizers to join the military and the police force and act as sleeping agents, acquiring skills, information and access to weapons and equipment within these security structures (Mesežnikov & Bráník, 2017, 31). Public activities of the group were strongly limited after 2016, however, its structure remains and training of the group is still ongoing. Allegedly also anti-crime patrols are organized in some regions, ridiculed by anti-fascist activists in social networks (Naše Slovensko 2017). According to some sources, at least part of the "AG Kysuce Resistance" wants to support the nationalist "Slovakian Revival Movement" (Slovenské hnutie obrody – SHO) in the next parliamentary elections in 2020 (Mesežnikov & Bráník, 2017, 30).

The Slovak Conscripts (Slovenskí branci)

Perhaps the best-known organization in Slovakia when it comes to vigilante and paramilitary groups is "Slovak Conscripts" (Slovenskí Branci). Slovak Conscripts were set up in December 2011 when they organized their first exercise. They started public activities in 2012. They originally cooperated with the organization "Slovakian Revival Movement" (SHO) and they supported its activities (including the commemorative demonstration by the statute of Josef Tiso, the president of the Slovak state from 1939–1945 on 16 March 2012) (Holúbek 2012).

However, they left this cooperation after several months and have acted autonomously since this time. Contacts with the ĽSNS and other right-wing extremist organizations were also temporarily and regionally limited. From the ideological point of view, they abandoned the legacy of the Slovak clergy-Fascist war state and they use various legacies from modern Slovak history, including national democratic traditions and Slavic ideas. Strong patriotism is typical of this organization.

The initial idea to set up such a group was the outcome of an intense, several weeklong military training for young people. Peter Švrček (at that time aged 16), one of its founding members, undertook training in the Russian Federation with the patriotic military Stjag association, closely linked to Cossacks military structures, in the summer of 2011 (Mikušovič 2015). Another founding member, who played a crucial role in the positioning and orientation of Slovak Conscripts, was Marek Rusyniak. After several years of study in the Russian federation, Rusyniak became interested in the Russian system of patriotic military education and joined several such organizations. Following his return to Slovakia, he used his knowledge and connections to set up Slovak Conscripts and invite Russian ex-military or ex-SPETZNAZ instructors to train the newly created group (Mesežnikov, Bráník, 2017, 22).

FIGURE 8.2 March to the Ceremonial Act of the Slovak Conscripts in Trnava on 5 January 2019
(Photographer: Marty Surma)

"Slovak Conscripts" organize paramilitary trainings, including training for partisan warfare. They expanded their activity from the town Trnava, where they were established, to the whole Slovak territory (they have 17 local units) (Struhár 2016, 25). The real number of people involved is around 250. The "Slovak Conscripts" also established their political wing called Our Homeland – Our Future (Naša Vlasť – Naša Budúcnosť), which was registered in April 2016 by the Ministry of Interior as a civil society organization (Mesežnikov & Bránik 2017, 25).

They became a hotly debated issue in the media and among decision-makers, due to the participation of one of its former members in the conflict in Eastern Ukraine. Martin Keprta, one of the founding members of Slovak Conscripts was identified speaking on Russian TV as one of the members of the international brigade of pro-Russian separatists fighting against the Ukrainian Army in the Donetsk region (Bránik, 2015). However, Slovak Conscripts announced that Keprta was excluded from the organization, as were more than 40 members with extremist beliefs (Struhár 2016, 22).

In addition to their public proclamations of readiness to protect Slovakia from any external threat, the "Slovak Conscripts" carried out several vigilante-style patrols during the migration crisis in 2015 and summer 2016. The first attempt was patrolling the Slovak–Austrian border, followed by patrols in the vicinity of the refugee camp in Gabčíkovo. However, due to low the age of the participants and lack of any meaningful show of force, their activities were ridiculed (Aktuality.sk 2015).

On a separate occasion "Slovak Conscripts" arrived in the Slovak spa resort Piešťany, frequented by foreign guests, including Arabs, in an attempt to protect the natives from "violent Arabs" only to realize that there were no violent Arabs to protect from (Kyseľ 2016). In September 2018, members of the group protected vineyards in Dražovice. They were invited by a parliamentary deputy from this region (Hopková 2018). The "Slovak Conscripts" were uniformed but unarmed during the above-mentioned patrols.

In 2018, the documentary movie about the group "When the War Comes" (Až přijde válka) was made by director Jan Gebert. It was presented at the film festival Berlinale. The hierarchical and militarist character of the group is shown in the movie (Berlinale 2018). Members of the group strongly rejected the message of this documentary (Slovenskí branci 2018).

According to their official statements, the "Slovak Conscripts" try to improve the security system and situation in Slovakia. They try to cooperate with governmental bodies. They are usually rejected, with the exception of some lectures at primary schools in Slovakia (Struhár 2016, 22). In the summer of 2018, cooperation and common exercises of the "Slovak Conscripts" with the Slovak branch of Russian motorcycle gang "Night Wolves", with heavy military weapons (armoured cars etc.), won media attention. It led the Ministry of the Interior, Ministry of Defence and Ministry of education to an announcement of repressive measures against the "Slovak Conscripts". The Ministry of education published a statement for schools, in which it did not recommend them to cooperate with the "Slovak Conscripts". The Minister of defence asked the General state prosecutor to determine the legal status of the "Slovak Conscripts". The participation of professional soldiers in the activities of the "Slovak Conscripts" was strongly criticized by the minister of defence, and such soldiers should be released from the army (Šnídl 2018). However, at the time of writing, legal changes have not been adopted. Various protest activities by anti-Fascists are organized against the "Slovak Conscripts" (such as a provocative marching of a clown in military uniform with toy trumpet during the ceremonial act of the unit in Trnava on 5 January 2019) (Mareš 2019).

Transnational cooperation of the Czech and Slovak vigilante groups

Czech and Slovak vigilante groups are often closely connected and they also develop various transnational contacts outside the territory of former Czechoslovakia. The Czechoslovak soldiers in reserve even tried to build ex-federal Czecho-Slovak structures. They also cooperated with the "Slovak Conscripts". On the other hand, in the eastern part of the Czech Republic the group "Moravian Conscripts" (Moravští branci) was independently established by Slovak students as a branch of the "Slovak Conscripts" in 2015 (Gebert 2015). One year later the establishment of the "Czech-Moravian Conscripts" (Česko-moravští branci) in the Czech Republic was announced (Mesežnikov & Bráník 2017, 25).

144 Miroslav Mareš and Daniel Milo

The chair of the "Czechoslovak reserve soldiers for peace", Ivan Kratochvíl, and the former leader of the "Action Group Resistance Kysuce", Marián Magát, published a joint interview on YouTube (Kratochvíl & Magát 2016). It is a dialogue between a former officer of the communist army and a former activist of the neo-Nazi spectrum. AG Kysuce Resistance also cooperated with the "Hungarian National Front" (Ministerstvo vnútra Slovenskej republiky 2016, 91). Slovak Conscripts had close links to Russia, as described above.

The Czech National Home Guard cooperates also with the "Bulgarian National Movement Shipka" (БНД ШИПКА). Leaders of both these pro-Kremlin groupings visited their partners and the Czech ND organized a collection of winter clothes for Bulgarian guardians patrolling at the Bulgarian–Turkish border (Národní domobrana 2017, see also the chapter on Bulgaria in this volume). As mentioned above, one of the leaders of the "National Home Guard", Nela Lisková, is also the so-called honorary consul of the Donetsk People's Republic in the Czech Republic. She also visited the separatist regions in Eastern Ukraine (Ministerstvo vnitra České republiky 2017b, 13). While "Soldiers of Odin" feel that they are part of the transnational network, they are connected with their foreign partners mostly on social networks (Hloušek 2017).

Analysis of context, justification and modus operandi of vigilantism in the Czech Republic and Slovakia

The major cause of vigilante activities in the Czech Republic and in Slovakia until the mid-2010s was connected with strong anti-Gypsyism in both countries. Vigilante militias of political parties as well as racist (often neo-Nazi) gangs with terrorist tendencies used this issue for radicalization of their own members as well as for mobilization of supporters in the broader public. Paramilitary groups, focused originally only on paramilitary training with combat goals, were established in Slovakia and later also in the Czech Republic beside these party militias and racist gangs, originally under strong influence from Russia. In Slovakia, they started activities at the beginning of the second decade of the twenty-first century, in the Czech Republic several years later (as a consequence of the so called "Ukrainian crisis"). When the migration crisis in 2015 broke out, traditional militia vigilante groups as well as paramilitary units adopted themselves to the new situation. Paramilitaries started patrolling in towns, outside refugee houses or along the borders.

Immigrants from the Middle East and Africa, particularly Muslims, became the main enemy of the extreme right (at least temporarily). It is a paradox of East Central European countries, that despite a very low number of Muslims in this area (approximately 15,000 Muslims in the Czech Republic with 10 million inhabitants and approximately 3,000 in Slovakia with 5 million inhabitants), the level of Islamophobia and anti-immigrant attitudes is very high (Ostřanský 2015).

Due to a real absence of refugees and immigrants, the traditional "Gypsy-card" was again present in the extreme right agenda. The use of this card was connected mostly with the rise of the "Kotleba – People's Party Our Slovakia" and this party turned to this issue with creation of its train patrols in 2016. However, also in the Czech Republic it has re-emerged as an important trope (among others in the activity of "Soldiers of Odin").

The rise of pro-Kremlin vigilante and paramilitary groups is connected also with a strong position of the political forces with anti-Western and pro-Russian orientation in Czech and Slovak politics in the recent era. Pro-Russian vigilantes criticize the European Union and the North Atlantic Treaty Organization (NATO) for their inability to protect Europe against "criminal migrants" and terrorism. Czech and Slovak pro-Western politicians are labelled as "puppets" of the so-called New World Order. On the other hand, the existence of pro-Kremlin paramilitary units was strongly criticized by pro-Western forces in Czech and Slovak politics (Mesežnikov & Bráník 2017, Vejvodová, Janda & Víchová 2017).

The official positions and statements of registered vigilante groups are within the boundary of the law. The existence of the vigilante groupings should create something like an "alternative security system", which can be used – according to public statements – for cooperation with the governmental system in case of emergency. However, the activities of the vigilante groups serve also as subversive factors towards the democratic regime, and within the context of the pro-Kremlin spectrum, these groupings are part of the so called hybrid campaign (Mareš 2017b).

The political measures against vigilante activities are focused mostly on monitoring potential lawbreaking and aimed at official rejection of cooperation with vigilante groups. However, in some areas, mostly at local level, vigilantes are in touch with local authorities (usually with some directors of primary schools due to civil defence education). The participation of professional soldiers and policemen in vigilante structures is considered a security threat.

From the organizational point of view, there are varieties of organizations of Czech and Slovak vigilante groups in the current era, depending on their strength and aim. The largest groups are currently the "Slovak Conscripts" with around 250 members; other important groups consist of approximately 50 members (the real number members of the Czech groups "National Home Guard" and "Land Home Guard" is unclear after tensions in years 2017–2018). The level of hierarchy is different. While the "Slovak Conscripts", the "Land Home Guard" and the train patrols of the ĽSNS have clear leaders, the "AG Kysuce Resistance", the "National Home Guard" and the "Soldiers of Odin" are more freely structured.

With the exception of the train patrols of the ĽSNS, all imported groups in both countries act autonomously without any long-term party political affiliation. However, the "National Home Guard" was established by the "National Democracy" and all groupings have short-lived contacts with some political parties and movements. The "Czechoslovak soldiers in reserve" support President Miloš Zeman.

Regarding the modus operandi, the most visible activity of the vigilante groups in the Czech Republic and in Slovakia are public patrols, which should monitor and record crime and illegal migration. Members of the vigilante groups receive training in policing and military fighting (also with real weapons). Many individual members possess their own light weapons (Malát 2017). These weapons are not owned by the organization because armed associations are prohibited in the Czech Republic and in Slovakia. However, patrols in towns are unarmed. Guns are carried by some vigilantes during border patrols. Symbolism and uniforms play an important role in the activities of Czech and Slovak vigilante groups. Paramilitaries usually wear military uniforms, while party militias and Soldiers of Odin don T-Shirts with their logos.

The activities of the Czech and Slovak vigilante groups combine online-activism with real activities on the streets and in the country. Vigilante groups have their own internet pages and profiles on social networks (Facebook and Vkontakte) and they usually present their activities for propagandist purposes. Social networks also serve as a communication platform about politics. Various posts deal with recent political events and issues. "Echo chambers" are created for members of these groups (Hloušek 2017, 20).

Conclusion

Czech and Slovak extreme-right vigilante groups have a long tradition from the inter-war and war period and they were established also in the post-communist period in successor countries of former Czechoslovakia. The anti-Roma focus of party militias and racist gangs was typical of most vigilante activities until the mid-2010s, when the anti-immigrant and anti-Muslim attitudes caused a new wave of vigilantism in both countries. Anti-Gypsyism remains an important part of the ideology of vigilantes. Several paramilitary groups with combat training started vigilante activities during this crisis, mostly border patrols and patrolling in various localities against the alleged "immigrant" and "Gypsy" crime. While in Slovakia the most important paramilitaries ("Slovak Conscripts" and the "AG Kysuce Resistance") were established in 2011, roots of current Czech paramilitary groups can be found in the years 2014/2015. The use of party militias in the form of train patrols by the ĽSNS caused a growth of popularity of this right-wing extremist party with parliamentary representation (this party was inspired by the party militias and anti-Roma marches of the Czech "Workers' Party" in previous decade). The most serious growth of vigilante activities in the recent era can be observed in both countries in 2015/2016. Despite a slight decline in 2017/2018 (more in the Czech Republic than in Slovakia due to decline of the "National Home Guard"), the vigilante and paramilitary spectrum remains strong and it is considered a security threat in the Czech Republic as well as in Slovakia.

References

Aktuality.sk (2015). Pri tábore pre utečencov v Gabčíkove sa objavili Slovenskí branci. Retrieved from https://www.aktuality.sk/clanok/306788/pri-tabore-pre-utecencov-v-ga bcikove-sa-objavili-slovenski-branci/.

Berlinale (2018). Až prijde válka (When the War Comes), Berlinale. Retrieved from https://www.berlinale.de/en/archiv/jahresarchive/2018/02_programm_2018/02_Filmdatenblatt_2018_201813888.html#tab=video.

Bránik, R. (2015, February 24). Rozhovor s dôstojníkom armády Doneckej ľudovej republiky Martinom Keprtom. Retrieved from https://branik.blog.sme.sk/c/375808/roz hovor-s-dostojnikom-armady-doneckej-ludovej-republiky-martinom-keprtom.html.

Bukač, I. (2015). Vojáci v záloze nabídli prezidentovi pomoc při ostraze hranic v uprchlické krizi. Retrieved from http://www.jcted.cz/vojaci-v-zaloze-nabidli-prezidentovi-pom oc-pri-ostraze-hranic-v-uprchlicke-krizi/?discussion-paginator-page=3.

Burian, M. (2012). *Sudetoněmecké nacionalistické a tělovýchovné organizace a československý stát v letech 1918 až 1938*. Praha: Karolinum.

Cahn, C. (1997). Time of the Skinheads: Denial and Exclusion of Roma in Slovakia, ERRC. Retrieved from http://www.errc.org/cms/upload/media/00/15/m00000015.pdf

Cuprik, Roman (2015). Skupina Vzdor pritvrdzuje, hrá sa na políciu Sme. Retrieved from https://domov.sme.sk/c/7921605/skupina-vzdor-pritvrdzuje-hra-sa-na-policiu.html.

Českoslovenští vojáci v záloze proti válce plánované velením NATO (2018). Úvod. Retrieved from https://csla.komuna.cz/.

Českoslovenští vojáci za mír z. s. (2016). Stanovy. Retrieved from https://or.justice.cz/ias/ui/vypis-sl-firma?subjektId=941592.

ČT 24 (2010). Útok ve Vítkově měl být vzorovou akcí neonacistů. Retrieved from http://www.ceskatelevize.cz/ct24/domaci/1332737-utok-ve-vitkove-mel-byt-vzorovou-akci-neonacistu.

DVTV (2015). Česko je vazalem Spojených států, říká bývalý člen misí NATO ČAktuálně. cz Retrieved from https://video.aktualne.cz/dvtv/cesko-je-vazalem-spojenych-statu-rika-byvaly-clen-misi-nato/r~02c457cc9c1011e49e4b0025900fea04/?redirected=1538321843

Gebert, J. (2015). Na válku připraveni! Slovenská "domobrana" chce pobočku v ČR. Tyden.cz. Retrieved from https://www.tyden.cz/rubriky/domaci/na-valku-pripraveni-slovenska-domobrana-chce-pobocku-v-cr_335587.html.

Hloušek, Z. (2017). *Vigilantismus v ČR v souvislosti s migrační krizí (bachelor thesis)*. Brno: Fakulta sociálních studií Masarykovy univerzity. Retrieved from https://is.muni.cz/th/407053/fss_b/.

Holúbek, Tomáš (2012). Tisa velebili mladučkí branci v kanadách a maskáčích. My. Retrieved from https://mynitra.sme.sk/c/6303944/tisa-velebili-mladucki-branci-v-kana dach-a-maskacoch.html#ixzz5SaTVTe4W.

Honus, A. (2010). Ostravský stadion zhanobili rasistickým nápisem. Novinky. Retrieved from https://www.novinky.cz/domaci/203626-ostravsky-stadion-zhanobili-rasistickym -napisem.html.

Hopková, D. (2018). Na nitrianske vinice mali dohliadať Slovenskí branci, zavolal si ich poslanec. Aktuality.sk. Retrieved from https://www.aktuality.sk/clanok/624985/na-nitrianske-vinice-mali-dohliadat-slovenski-branci-zavolal-si-ich-poslanec/.

Hřebenář, J. (2016). Černohorský si hrál na občanské hlídky. Hrebnar.eu. Retrieved from https://www.hrebenar.eu/2016/09/cernohorsky-si-hral-na-obcanske-hlidky/.

Janíček, T. (2015). *Súčasné krajne pravicové násilie na Slovensku*. Brno: Fakulta sociálních studií Masarykovy univerzity.

Janouš, Václav (2018). Domobranci chtějí mít vlastní vojsko, sbližují se s policií, varuje BIS Idnes, Retrieved from https://www.idnes.cz/zpravy/domaci/domobrana-policie-bis-cesko.A180831_205038_domaci_ane.

Jelínková, A. (2018). NATO je teroristická organizace, hlásá spolek, který učí žáky brannou výchovu. Idnes. Retrieved from https://www.novinky.cz/domaci/472093-nato-je-teror isticka-organizace-hlasa-spolek-ktery-uci-zaky-brannou-vychovu.html.

Kluknavská, Alena – Smolík, Josef (2016). We hate them all? Issue adaptation of extreme right parties in Slovakia 1993–2016. *Communist and Post-Communist Studies*, 49(4), 335–344.

Krajský soud v Českých Budějovicích (2017). Rozsudek 14 To 100/2017–168.

148 Miroslav Mareš and Daniel Milo

Kratochvíl, I. & Magát, M. (2016). Za obnovení svobodného Československa. www.Svo bodnaTelevize.cz for the Výbor veřejného blaha z. s. Retrieved from https://www.you tube.com/watch?v=kG0zcVdknjQ.

Kyseľ, T. (2015). Extrémisti hádzali kamene na arabskú rodinu s dieťaťom v kočíku. Retrieved from https://www.aktuality.sk/clanok/278213/video-extremisti-hadzali-kam ene-na-arabsku-rodinu-s-dietatom-v-kociku/.

Kyseľ, T. (2016). Slovenskí branci sa zľakli Arabov, ich hliadky chceli v Piešťanoch nastoliť poriadok. Aktuality.sk. Retrieved from https://www.aktuality.sk/clanok/362784/slo venski-branci-sa-zlakli-arabov-ich-hliadky-chceli-v-piestanoch-nastolit-poriadok/.

Landa, L. (2017). Nebezpečná hra na vojáky. Česká televize. Reportéři ČR. Retrieved from http://www.ceskatelevize.cz/ivysilani/1142743803-reporteri-ct/217452801240020/titulky.

Ľ'SNS (2016a). Parliamentary Election Pogramme of Kotleba-Ľudová Strana Naše Slovensko. Retrieved from http://www.naseslovensko.net/wp-content/uploads/2015/01/Volebn%C3%BD-program-2016.pdf.

Ľ'SNS (2016b). Train patrols are working. Retrieved from http://www.naseslovensko.net/nasa-praca/vlakove-hliadky-ls-nase-slovensko-prinasaju-vysledky/.

Majchrák, J. & HanuM. (2007). Štát versus Hedviga II. Týždeň. Retrieved from https://www.tyzden.sk/casopis/321/stat-verzus-hedviga-ii/.

Majerová, S. (2016). Za inzerát o strieľaní migrantov dostal iba podmienku, teraz skončil vo väzbe. aktualne.sk. Retrieved from.

https://www.aktuality.sk/clanok/322923/odmena-za-zabitie-migranta-davidovi-k-opat-hro zi-basa/.

Malát, Š. (2017). Národní domobrana se chystá na partyzánské boje proti NATO a migrantům. Forum.24. Retrieved from http://forum24.cz/pripravte-plany-postupu-na rodni-domobrana-se-chysta-na-partyzanske-boje-proti-nato-a-migrantum/.

Malecký, R. (2017). TOP 2017: Haf! Jsme Krušní psi. Jak Národní domobrana loví nelegální migranty na zelené hranici. Aktualne.cz, Retrieved from https://hlidacipes.org/top -2017-haf-krusni-psi-narodni-domobrana-lovi-nelegalni-migranty-zelene-hranici/?hilite= %27domobrana%27.

Malecký, R. (2018). Těžké časy extrémistů z Národní domobrany. Pro některé členy je málo radikální, začíná se štěpit. HlidaciPes.org. Retrieved from https://hlidacipes.org/tezke-ca sy-extremistu-narodni-domobrany-nektere-cleny-malo-radikalni-zacina-se-stepit/?hilite=% 27domobrany%27.

Mareš, M. (2012a). Czech militant democracy in action : Dissolution of the Workers' Party and the wider context of this act. *East European Politics and Societies*, 26(1), 33–55.

Mareš, M. (2012b). *Paramilitarismus v České republice*. Brno: Centrum pro studium demokracie a kultury.

Mareš, M. (2013). *Rozpoznávanie politického extrémizmu na Slovensku, Príručka pre identifikáciu extrémistických symbolov*. Bratislava: CENAA.

Mareš, M. (2014). *Základní trendy a perspektivy soudobého extremismu. Paper presented at the Senate Public Hearing "Extremismus a role elit"*. Praha: Senát Palamentu České republiky, Retrieved from http://www.senat.cz/xqw/webdav/pssenat/original/80367/67499.

Mareš, M. (2017a). Gegenwärtige rechtsextremistische Radikalisierung in Ostmitteleuropa aus Sicht der terroristischen Bedrohung. In Stefan Hansen and Joachim Krause (eds.) *Jahrbuch Terrorismus 2015/2016* (pp. 79–94). Berlin and Toronto: Verlag Barbara Budrich.

Mareš, M. (2017b). Strategic Impact of East Central European Extreme Right Vigilantes: From Subcultural Fringes to Instruments of Hybrid Warfare. Paper presented at the ECPR General Conference, Oslo, 6–9 September 2017 in the panel Vigilantism Against Migrants and Minorities (Section Right Wing Extremism Beyond Party Politics), Retrieved from https://ecpr.eu/Filestore/PaperProposal/3ca1881d-02fb-4eab-b9e5-c097cafabd1b.pdf.

Mareš, M. (2019). Observation of the Ceremonial act of the Slovak conscripts in Trnava, 5 January 2019 (documentation in author's archive).

Mesežnikov, G. & Bráník, R. (2017). *Hatred, violence and comprehensive military training. The violent radicalisation and Kremlin connections of Slovak paramilitary, extremist and neo-Nazi groups.* Budapest: Political Capital. Retrieved from http://www.politicalcapital.hu/pcadm in/source/documents/PC_NED_country_study_SK_20170428.pdf.

Mikušovič, D. (2015). Rozhovor s brancami: Čo je zlé na cvičení so zbraňou v lese? Denník N. Retrieved from https://dennikn.sk/57900/rozhovor-s-brancami-co-je-zle-na-tom -cvicit-v-lese-zbranou/.

Milo, D. (2005). *Rasistický extrémizmus na Slovensku.* Bratislava: Ludie proti rasizmu - Friedrich Ebert Stiftung. Retrieved from http://library.fes.de/pdf-files/bueros/slowakei/04215.pdf.

Ministerstvo vnitra České republiky. (2017a). *Extremismus. Souhrnná situační zpráva 3. čtvrtletí roku 2017.* Praha: MVČR. Accessed January 9 2018, http://www.mvcr.cz/clanek/ ctvrtletni-zpravy-o-extremismu-odboru-bezpecnostni-politiky-mv.aspx.

Ministerstvo vnitra České republiky (2017b). *Zpráva o problematice extremismu na území České republiky v roce 2016.* Praha: MVČR. Retrieved from http://www.mvcr.cz/clanek/extrem ismus-vyrocni-zpravy-o-extremismu-a-strategie-boje-proti-extremismu.aspx.

Ministerstvo vnútra Slovenskej republiky (2016). *Symbolika využívaná extrémistickými a radikálnymi skupinami.* Bratislava: MVSR.

Národní demokracie (2016). Národní demokracie předala agendu Národní domobrany. Retrieved from http://narodnidemokracie.cz/narodni-demokracie-predala-agendu-narod ni-domobrany/.

Národní domobrana (2015). Stanovy. Retrieved from https://or.justice.cz/ias/ui/vypis-sl- detail?dokument=41655863&subjektId=918483&spis=1003971.

Národní domobrana (2016). *Domovinu ubráníme.* Praha: Národní domobrana. Retrieved from http://narodnidomobrana.cz/images//BROZURA/ND_brozura.pdf.

Národní domobrana (2017). Národní domobrana pořádá sbírku zimního oblečení pro bulharské domobrance. Retrieved from http://www.narodnidomobrana.cz/243-narodni- domobrana-porada-sbirku-zimniho-obleceni-pro-bulharske-domobrance.

Národní domobrana (2018). Zápis z členské schůze spolku Národní domobrana ČR z. s. Retrieved from https://or.justice.cz/ias/ui/vypis-sl-detail?dokument=53666110&sub jektId=918483&spis=1003971.

Naše Slovensko (2017). Akčná skupina Vzdor Kysuce. Retrieved from https://it-it.facebook. com/beznenavisti/photos/akčná-skupina-vzdor-kysuce-dnes-opäť-hliadkovala-na-lúke- v-okolí-turzovky-všetko/1318068851595149/.

Nejvyšší soud České republiky (2017). Usnesení 4 Tdo 1630/2016.

Nutil, P. (2017). Teroristický útok v Chomutově? Manipulátoři. Retrieved from http://ma nipulatori.cz/teroristicky-utok-chomutove/.

Ostřanský, B. (2015). Czech Islamophobia: The manifestations, paradoxes and perception of anti-Muslim sentiments in the Czech Republic. In Kusek, R., Purchla, J. & Sanetra- Szeliga, J. (Eds.), *Nations & Stereotypes 25 Years After: New Borders, New Horizons* (pp. 208– 219). Krakow: International Cultural Centre.

Pejčoch, I. (2009). *Armády českých politiků.* Cheb: Svět křídel.

Slovenskí branci (2018). Generální predstavitelia síl SB o filme od HBO "Až přijde válka". Slovenskí branci. Retrieved from http://www.slovenski-branci.sk/generalni-predstavitelia -sil-sb-o-filme-od-hbo-az-prijde-valka/.

Šnídl, V. (2018). Minister priznal, že so Slovenskými brancami cvičia aj profesionální vojaci. O pomoc požiadal prokuratúru. Denník N. Retrieved from: https://dennikn.sk/ 1186231/minister-obrany-kritizoval-slovenskych-brancov-ziada-generalnu-prokuraturu-a by-ich-preverila/.

Sokolovič, P. (2009). *Hlinkova garda 1938–1945*. Bratislava: Ústav pamäti národa.

Stojarová, V. (2012). Paramilitary structures in Eastern Europe. In Backes, U. & Moreau, P (Eds.), *The extreme right in Europe. Current trends and perspectives* (pp. 265–279). Götttingen: Vandenhoeck & Ruprecht.

Struhár, P. (2016). Vývoj neoficiálnej pravicovo-extrémistickej scény na Slovensku od roku 1989. *Rexter*, 14(1), 1–43, Retrieved from http://casopis.rexter.cz/rexter_01_2016.pdf#page=4.

Teraz.sk (2016). Kotleba zavádza vo vlakoch hliadky, prvú viedol pišťoľník Krupa. Retrieved from http://www.teraz.sk/slovensko/kotleba-zavadza-vo-vlakoch-hliadky-p rv/191382-clanok.html.

TA3 (2017). Nový zákon Kotlebove hliadky z vlakov nevyhnal. Tvrdia, že sú len cestujúci. Retrieved from https://www.ta3.com/clanok/1098034/novy-zakon-kotlebove-hlia dky-z-vlakov-nevyhnal-tvrdia-ze-su-len-cestujuci.html.

Vejvodová, P., Janda, J. & Víchová, V. (2017). *The Russian connections of far-right and paramilitary organizations in the Czech Republic*. Budapest: Political Capital. Retrieved from http://www.politicalcapital.hu/pcadmin/source/documents/PC_NED_country_study_ CZ_20170428.pdf.

Vražda, D. (2017). Kotlebovci si značkovali región. Denník N. Retrieved from https:// dennikn.sk/857365/kotlebovci-si-znackovali-region/.

Wirnitzer, J. (2015). V Česku roste proruská polovojenská milice. Chce si "vzít vlast zpět". Idnes. Retrieved from https://zpravy.idnes.cz/profil-ceskoslovensti-vojaci-v-zaloze-obr tel-foo-/domaci.aspx?c=A151123_123952_domaci_jw.

Zelená, H. (2016). Domobrana: Armády politických stran se šikují. Armadní noviny.cz Retrieved from http://www.armadninoviny.cz/domobrana-armady-politickych-stra n-se-sikuji.html.

Zelenka, J. (2016). V Česku se formují Ódinovi vojáci, Teplicemi už prošla hlídka. Kvůli muslimům. Lidovky.cz. Retrieved from https://www.lidovky.cz/v-cesku-se-form uji-odinovi-vojaci-teplicemi-uz-prosla-hlidka-kvuli-muslimum-1vd-/zpravy-domov. aspx?c=A160714_171425_ln_domov_jzl.

Zelenka, J. – Kropáček, J. (2017). Mapa domobran: Buněk je skoro stovka, cvičí i hledají migranty. Na schůzi stačí vzít drobné na pivo, Aktualne.cz. Retrieved from https://zpra vy.aktualne.cz/domaci/mapa-domoobrana/r~82af0b0c687411e7b56e002590604f2e/.

Zelenka, J. & Prchal, L. (2017). Domobranci v Orlové učili děti střílet ze zbraní. Nejsou to extremisté, brání se pořadatel akce, Aktualne.cz. Retrieved from https://zpravy.aktua lne.cz/domaci/domobranci-v-orlove-ucili-deti-strilet-ze-zbrani-nejsou-to-e/r~d43fd53a9 d3c11e79c7c002590604f2e/.

Zemská domobrana (2018a). Ani sníh ani mráz nás nezastaví. Občanské patroly. Retrieved from http://www.zemskadomobrana.org/.

Zemská domobrana (2018b). Pouť na slavnou horu Říp. Retrieved from https://zemskadom obrana.org/prakticka-domobrana/ze-zivota-skupin/44-pout-na-slavnou-horu-rip.

Zemská domobrana (2018c). Tip na výlet a jedno ponaučení pro sluníčkáře. Retrieved from https://zemskadomobrana.org/clanky/z-domova/57-tip-na-vylet-a-jedno-pona uceni-pro-slunickare.

ZEM-DOM, z. s. (2018). Stanovy. Retrieved from https://or.justice.cz/ias/ui/vypis-sl-deta il?dokument=52055762&subjektId=1006728&spis=1102982.

9

THE MINUTEMEN

Patrolling and performativity along the U.S. / Mexico border

Harel Shapira

Introduction

In an age of globalization, borders have become lighting rods for the politics of belonging. On the one hand, borders are legal boundaries; but they are also physical and symbolic objects that promote new kinds of social practices, shared projects, and collective identities. One example of the role of borders in contemporary identity formation is found along the U.S. / Mexico border, where, since 2002, the militia group known as the Minutemen has been undertaking patrols.

How are we to understand these patrols? In part, the Minutemen's patrols can be understood by focusing on the ideology of group members – an expression of the kind of right-wing and racist political views that have re-entered the American political mainstream over the past couple of decades. Such xenophobic and racist attitudes form an important dimension of who the Minutemen are, as they talk about immigrants as criminals; say that Mexican culture is backwards; and, more often than not, speak of immigration as an "invasion." But at the same time, the Minutemen's attitudes about immigration exceed simple hatred and xenophobia. When I tell Robert, who, like most Minutemen was a white military veteran in his 60s, that I feel bad for the people coming across the border, this is what he tells me:

> You're wanting to put yourself in the plight of the immigrant that's coming here. And feel their pain. And I can understand that ... There have been times in my life when I needed a job. Where I couldn't afford to pay the bills. And I can understand about wanting to make a better life. We are Americans and that's what we do. That's what we are raised to do, that is the American dream. Get an education, get a career, get a job. To better ourselves.

152 Harel Shapira

Robert's identification with the plight of immigrants suggests that patrolling is sustained by much more than racism. Robert is aware of structural forces and of immigrants' economic hardships. He even constructs the people coming across as emblematic of the American ideal. It is not that the Minutemen don't understand what is driving immigration, or that they lack sympathy. They do, and they still go to the border.

While ideology offers us a limited account of the Minutemen, there are other things that can help us make sense of the group and what it is that they are doing on the border. In this chapter, I follow the work of Erving Goffman (1959), and analyze the Minutemen's patrols as a set of identity performances. Analytically, it means that rather than focusing on the underlying set of attitudes and beliefs of the group, I look at the actual practices and experiences they have in order to make sense of who they are. Specifically, I draw on my three-year long ethnographic study of the Minutemen (Shapira 2013), to show that these patrols are organized around performances of patriotism, connected to enactments of soldiering and masculinity. Through these performances – from putting on camouflage, to calling each other by their old military nicknames, to being part of a masculine space – the Minutemen seek to escape their current lives as aging veterans, put their old skills to use and reclaim a lost sense of purpose, status, and meaning.

Setting the stage

In Erving Goffman's dramaturgical approach to social life, identities – be they gender, class, or race – are not essences that people simply have inside them, but rather something accomplished through a "performance." Goffman's approach is helpful for understanding the Minutemen's patrols along the border. Instead of just seeing them as simply an expression of xenophobic ideology (though that is certainly one important element), or as being driven by quantifiable goals such as stopping or reducing the number of people who cross the border illegally, we should consider these patrols as a set of performances organized around the practice of soldiering which seek to reconstitute the lost sense of meaning and purpose connected to these men's previous lives as soldiers and current lives as aging veterans. Importantly, the majority of the Minutemen are white male military veterans for whom notions of purpose, status, and meaning were deeply enmeshed with being a soldier. Consequentially, reclaiming these as well as the identity of a patriot, entails being a militarized space and engaging in military style activities.

What are the spaces in the contemporary world where one can engage in such activities? What are the spaces in the contemporary world which serve as "stages," as Goffman would call them, for the enactment of soldiering?

In Goffman's account, the "setting" or "stage" is a precondition for the performance of identity; without a stage upon which to act the actor cannot perform. Moreover, not all stages are the same, and particular stages are generative of particular identities, creating the conditions which enable a particular performance to take place, and a specific identity to be realized. Like all performances, the

Minutemen's performance of patriotism is contingent upon what Goffman calls "controlling the setting" (1959: 22). By "controlling the setting," that is, by managing the stage, actors are able to promote a particular "definition of the situation," which refers to the way the context in which the performance takes place is framed. This framing is consequential because it renders the performances that take place in that context meaningful. In order for patrolling the U.S./Mexico border to be rendered a performance of patriotism, the border, the stage on which the performance takes place, must be framed as dangerous and unguarded, and hence, a privileged stage on which one can perform patriotism.

In this section I examine how the U.S./Mexico border emerged as a stage upon which the Minutemen could engage in performances of patriotic masculinity and soldiering. In order to understand the establishment of the U.S./Mexico border as such a stage it is important to consider two interconnected dynamics: first, the militarization of the border starting in the 1990s; and second, the terrorist attacks of 9/11. Each of these elements played a key role in not only mobilizing the Minutemen, but also providing them with both a discursive and physical stage upon which to act.

The border as a battlefield

Until the year 2000, the Arizona section of the United States / Mexico border was not yet a stage for the performance of patriotism. Starting in the 1990s the United States government initiated a campaign to militarize the border as a new strategy to deter illegal immigration. "Operation Gatekeeper," which commenced in 1993 in San Diego, California and "Operation Hold the Line," which began the following year in El Paso, Texas, were the two main initiatives of this campaign. The campaigns transformed the border from a loosely defined zone to a militarized border.

Beyond actual physical infrastructure, in the form of walls and barbed wire fences, these initiatives dramatically increased the size of the federal Border Patrol. Between 1986 and 2002, the Border Patrol's budget grew from $151 million to $1.6 *billion*. At the same time, the number of Border Patrol agents more than doubled. The growth in the budget and size of the Border Patrol coincided with dramatic changes in its very mission. The Immigration and Naturalization Services (INS) – the agency of which the Border Patrol is a part – was renamed as the Department of Homeland Security (DHS) a change that marked the larger discursive and political shift in how America conceptualized and responded to immigration. As Joseph Nevins (2002) has argued, the militarization of the border entailed promoting a definition of the "illegal immigrant" as a deviant and as the root cause of various social and economic problems, and increasingly immigration was cast as a matter of national security. Consider, for example, the following quote outlining the changed "mission" of the Border Patrol reveals, in which immigration was defined as a matter of "homeland security," and "illegal immigration" was conceived of as a criminal matter alongside terrorism:

In the wake of the terrorist attacks of September 11, 2001, the Border Patrol has experienced a tremendous change in its mission. [...] The Border Patrol has as its priority mission preventing terrorists and terrorist weapons from entering the United States. The Border Patrol will continue to advance its traditional mission by preventing illegal aliens, smugglers, narcotics, and other contraband from entering the United States as these measures directly impact the safety and security of the United States.[1]

The border militarization initiatives of the 1990s focused on the California and Texas sections of the border, but they left untouched the 370 miles of the Arizona border. Consequentially, the movement of illicit people and goods simply shifted away from California and Texas and towards Arizona. And it was the area around Southern Arizona known as the "Tucson Sector" specifically which became the most heavily traveled route: whereas in 1993 there were only 92,639 apprehensions of "illegal immigrants" reported by the Border Patrol in this area, by 2000 the number was 616,346, accounting for over one-third of the total number of apprehensions on the entire U.S. / Mexico border, by far the largest share of any of the sectors. Beyond this, according to the Department of Homeland Security, 1.7 million pounds of marijuana was seized along the border with Mexico in 2006, over a third in the Tucson Sector alone.[2] In other words, by 2000 Southern Arizona had more "illegal immigrants" and drugs coming through it than the rest of the border combined.

All of this, of course, was motivated and made possible by the National Free Trade Agreement (NAFTA) signed into law on January 1, 1994. NAFTA led to a dramatic movement of capital between the U.S. and Mexico, increasing push and pull factors that led to immigration and that made Mexican workers need and want to come to the United States in the first place. As it had done previously in California and Texas, in response to increasing traffic of people and drugs, in 2004 the U.S. government initiated a series of campaigns – Arizona Border Control Initiative, the Secure Fence Act, and the Secure Border Initiative – to militarize Arizona's border. Suddenly, the Southern Arizona border took on the appearance of a war zone. Armed Border Patrol agents were everywhere, checkpoints were set up along the roads, and surveillance towers dotted the otherwise barren skylines. It was in 2002, within this militarized political context, that the group which eventually came to be known as the Minutemen first emerged in the town of Tombstone, Arizona.

Like much of Southern Arizona, Tombstone grew to prominence in the late nineteenth century, thanks in large part to the mining boom that took place in the area. While the mines have long closed, Tombstone continues to be connected to its past, with the town occupying a central place in the American mythology of the "Wild West." The site of numerous stories of cowboys fighting Indians and vigilante justice, these days, Tombstone's economy is based on a tourism industry organized around cowboy themed stores and restaurants. It was in this symbolic heart of the American frontier, that on October 24, 2002, Chris Simcox published

The Minutemen 155

a call in the local newspaper for volunteers to patrol the U.S / Mexico border with him: "Enough is Enough!" Simcox wrote in the front pages, "A Public Call to Arms! Citizens Border Patrol Militia Now Forming!"[3]

The formation of the Tombstone Militia came almost exactly one year after the terrorist attacks of 9/11. It was a time when America was deeply enmeshed in establishing what would come to be a seemingly never ending "War on Terror." Indeed, Simcox's call to arms echoed many sentiments expressed by then President George W. Bush who himself made a public call to arms on national television shortly after the terrorist attacks, "Every American is a soldier, and every citizen is in this fight."[4]

Framed in the post-9/11 discourse of America being under attack from terrorists, a discourse the state had itself promoted, the mobilization effort was filled with indictments of the government for failing to protect America by failing to "secure the border." Simcox turned the state's own language against it. "The bottom line," he wrote, is that "the government is not doing their job to protect our borders. I call on American citizens to do the job for them [...] It is time we the citizens band together to show our inept Homeland Security Department a thing or two about how to protect National security and the sovereignty of our Democratic Republic." Patrolling the border was a right granted to all citizens, Simcox argued, and was about taking the initiative to do what the state had failed to do. "It is time to help out our constitution by acting on the liberties and powers it gives us, the citizens, to come to the aid of our republic in times of duress."

Transforming the border into a stage for patriotism involves conveying impressions of the border as an insecure and vulnerable space which needs defenders because it is not being adequately guarded by the state. As one of the organization's pamphlets indicates, rendering such an impression is, in itself, one of the groups' objectives:

> Your fellow U.S. citizens ... are asking for your help in bringing attention to the disgraceful situation on our border. We have been called to serve our country once again ... With your participation ... we WILL call attention to the problem of open borders.

Paradoxically, it is within the context of increased government expenditure on the border that an opposite sense has emerged among the Minutemen. They see themselves as living in a moment of a scaled back government, in which the latter is derelict in its task of securing the border. Joining the many socially progressive groups that critique the programs of neoliberalism, the Minutemen hold that the government is failing adequately to take care of its citizenry. As Chris Simcox put it in his first "call to arms":

> The government is not doing their job to protect our borders. I call on American citizens to do the job for them [...] It is time we the citizens band together to show our inept Homeland Security Department a thing or two about how to protect National security and the sovereignty of our Democratic Republic.

156 Harel Shapira

In such a manner, the Minutemen frame the state as a failed institution, and hence the need for the patriot, constituting his mission: "to protect National security." Beyond the failure of the state to "secure the border," the Minutemen seek to define the border as a dangerous place, and in order to achieve this impression the Minutemen depict the people coming across the border as dangerous. The following recruitment campaign offers a typical expression of this effort:

> It is unjust to leave law-abiding American citizens helpless to defend themselves against well-organized international crime cartels and violent foreign gangs, rapists, murderers and drug dealers who are terrorizing our neighborhoods and exploiting the prosperity and generosity of this great nation.

In the above, the illegal immigrant is not mentioned as such, instead proxy categories such as "well-organized international crime cartels," "violent foreign gangs," "rapists," "murderers and drug dealers," are used to characterize the people coming across the border. Through such figurations the Minutemen project their patrol of the border as aimed at protecting "helpless" "American citizens."

The fantastic danger that is projected onto the border, where even the smallest, most ambiguous signs evince danger and help establish the Minutemen's own actions as patriotic deeds, is keenly represented by what the Minutemen refer to as "rape trees." Located in places known as "lay up sites" where illegal immigrants camp out before making the final leg of their "invasion," the "rape trees" are believed to be places where the "coyote," the guide for the illegal immigrants on their journey, rapes women who are traveling in the group. The "rape tree" is recognized by a bra hanging from its branches. Below is a text regarding "rape trees," which was circulated to members.

> On Tuesday, April 17th, a routine event took place on the border. The victim, statistics show, was young, female, and of Latin American descent [...] 'Rape Trees' are a visible reminder of the dangers of our unsecured borders [...] The 'coyote' committed a crime when he took advantage of a defenseless woman in his care. He raped the young woman and went away bragging about his machismo to his peers. He left his mark, the woman's bra, cut between the 'cups', on the tree for all to see how big a man he is [...] This is part of his culture and an accepted part of his business.

The depiction of the coyote is filled with images of savagery and a depraved masculinity. We are told he "raped the young woman and went away bragging about his machismo to his peers ... He left his mark ... for all to see how big a man he is." The "rape trees" promote the border as a stage of competing masculinities, where the Minutemen's virtuous masculinity, based on protecting the troubled female, is pitted against the coyote's vile "machismo." For the Minutemen, the "rape trees" are a powerful symbol of the Mexican male's immorality, and simultaneously, imbues their own actions with valiancy; by patrolling the border they are defending not just America, but women, and not just American women. In Goffman's terms, the border is assembled as the stage of a "character contest" where manhood can be achieved. The process involves taking signs whose status is ambiguous and rendering them as evidence of danger through an active process of interpretation. Beyond the public, the definition of the situation along the border as dangerous also targets fellow members and potential recruits, as it is intended to develop what Goffman calls a "working consensus," that is a shared definition of the situation among the Minutemen themselves. By projecting an image of the border as dangerous and patrolling as an activity in which one can ward off danger, the group seeks to sustain its mobilization effort. The following announcement seeking volunteers for a patrol operation illustrates this aspect of the impression management:

> Never has the border situation here in Arizona been so dangerous ... The Border Patrol is undermanned and under funded. This country needs you to be the third line of defense [...] Volunteers need to be keenly aware that the bad guys are emboldened – never has the chance of encountering violent criminals been higher .

The descriptions of the situation, filled with hyperbolic characterizations of danger, show the constant effort undertaken to sustain the image of the border as dangerous and patrolling as patriotic. Another example of the way that a "working consensus" of the situation is transmitted to volunteers is given in a short essay circulated among group members entitled "Heavy Traffic Continues":

> The Three Points, AZ area continues to be the hot spot along the border for illegal crossings. The trend is slowly pushing towards the west deserts of Arizona, but foot prints don't lie. Most of the trails in the Three Points area are being heavily traveled [...] The pictures below are of 2 of the trails on our new lines. Come check it out for yourself, we would love to have you come down and join us!

As with previous comments, the above focuses on underscoring the extent to which patrolling the border includes a high potential for "encountering" the "bad guys." Importantly, the above text and image of "footprints," offers a window into the way in which the Minutemen must translate the landscape to convey an impression of the border as dangerous. While the writer acknowledges that the "trend is slowly pushing West," he uses the photographs to indicate that they have located "new lines" where illegal immigrants are crossing and there is a good chance of encountering them. As the writer puts it, "footprints don't lie." In such ways, through these theatrical practices and military semiotics, as well as the framing of the border as a dangerous and unguarded place, the Minutemen set the stage for their performance of patriotism.

Performing patriotism

So what happens on this stage? How is it that the Minutemen perform their patriotism on the border?

As previously mentioned, the Minutemen are composed of predominantly elderly white men who are almost exclusively military veterans. In my own survey of 193 members who were actively engaged in patrols, I found that the average age was 65, 85% were men, and of those men, 84% had previously served in the military. Moreover, not only had they served in the military, but most of them had extensive military careers, serving many years beyond their mandatory tour of duty. After retiring many went on to work in law enforcement jobs such as private investigators, police officers, or parole officers. Membership in the group needs to be situated within these life histories, life histories dominated by previous participation in military life and current status as aging veterans. To invoke Pierre Bourdieu (1977), the Minutemen have a political habitus infused by militarism, one that structures both how they feel loss and also how they feel at home. Consequently, their border patrols are organized not simply around a set of beliefs about immigration, but a desire to participate in a militarized social world, infused with hierarchy and masculinity, that recreates their earlier lives as soldiers.

Militarized masculinity

Before outlining what happens on the actual patrols, it is important to highlight the centrality of the Minutemen "base camp" to the group. In each of the border locations where the Minutemen undertook patrols, they would have a central area – normally a ranch that belonged to a private individual supportive of their cause – where they would camp out and base their operations. In Southern Arizona, where I conducted the majority of my research, and which served as the center of all Minutemen operations, the "base camp" is located on a stretch of land in the middle of the desert which belongs to a local rancher. The volunteers camp out on the land during the course of their patrols – whether for a weekend or for an entire month. Some use tents while others drive to the border in motor homes (RVs) and sleep in those. Consequentially, the camp consists of a number of tents and motor homes spread across an otherwise vast and mostly empty desert terrain.

Beyond these the Minutemen camp is filled with nationalistic and militaristic symbols – from countless U.S. flags, to flags of various military regiments – such as the Marine Corps. or Air Force. Indeed, everything in the camp is organized in militaristic ways, meant to reproduce the feeling of a military outpost – from the appearance of things to the language used to describe the space – from meetings which are called "strategy briefings" to the naming of toilets as "latrines," to the naming of their patrol operations as "musters," to the organizational hierarchy known as a "chain of command," to naming patrol lines using military code. And on their actual patrols they engage in putting on camouflage, of working in the "comms room," of doing "recon work," and being able to call each other by their old "handles" from their days in the military. From Goffman's dramaturgical point of view, all of these aspects, in particular the military clothing and military gear constituted the Minutemen's "identity kit" – clothes and related accessories, signifiers of the self, which are an integral part of the way we present ourselves to the world (1961). For the Minutemen that presentation is directed towards a soldiering self.

The actual patrols take place throughout the day along various locations nearby to the base camp and are organized into three "shifts": the "morning shift" from 9AM–5PM; the "swing shift" from 5PM–12AM; and the "graveyard shift" from 12AM–9AM. There is an understanding that the work of patrolling, particularly the "graveyard shifts" are not meant for women. As another volunteer, whose wife often also participated in the patrols, explains to me, "You know a lot of this just isn't cut out for women." The volunteer says that he enjoys having his wife join him on the border, but that when she is there he feels compelled to, "do the boring day shifts, because she can't do the night ones and I don't want to leave her alone." But the reality of patrols is that it involves very little physical work. It isn't difficulty that organizes these different spaces at the camp, but an idea of the past, a memory of life in the military that the partitions in the camp are meant to reproduce. On the front lines in Vietnam, Korea, or Iraq, where these men were previously, there are no women, and to relive that experience, it needs to be that way on the patrol line.

FIGURE 9.1 A Minuteman walks towards his assigned patrol location after finishing putting camouflage over his car which is located on the top right corner of the photo
(Photo: Andrea Dylewski).

160 Harel Shapira

The roles we occupy as members of a nation are gendered. As Joane Nagel puts it, women are defined as "supporting actors whose roles reflect masculinist notions of femininity and of women's proper place" (1998: 243). In the battle for the nation, women have a mostly symbolic role to play; either as caretakers or as representatives of ideas to be defended. The real actors and agents of the nation are the men.

In her work on the relationship between gender and nationalism, Nira Yuval-Davis (1993) notes that a significant feature of the gendered division of nationalism is the geographic partitioning of national space, both physical and symbolic space, into the "home front" and the "battle front." Each space is gendered: the women are relegated to caring for the "home front" and men, for waging war on the "battle front." The Minutemen reproduce this gendered partitioning of the national space in their camp, where the campground functions as a feminine "home-front" and the patrol line constitutes the masculine "battle front." While the women have no place on the patrol line, they do have a place at the camp – preparing sandwiches for the men to take to the line, making coffee in the morning, keeping the latrines clean, and so forth. Importantly, while many men came to the border by themselves, almost no women came alone, rather, they came with their husbands. But many husbands didn't want their wives around. Gender identities are the products of practices. As West and Zimmerman put it, gender identities are the result of a process of "doing gender" in which gender is a continual performance that involves, "routine, methodological, and recurring accomplishment" (1987:126). The division of the masculine space of the patrol, and the feminine space of the camp allows the Minutemen to metonymically situate themselves in the nation. They are the men: brave, potent, protecting their home front.

Normally, there would be between 14–20 people going out on a given patrol, and they would be paired into teams of two. There would be a person in charge, known as the "line leader" who determine where these pairs of two would be positioned, though the entire patrol would almost always be organized in a line, with each pair being spread about 100 yards apart. The volunteers would almost always be dressed in some form of camouflage or military uniform, they would be armed with at minimum one firearm (almost always a handgun though some would also bring rifles though this was a point of contention and debate among members), they would carry powerful, large hand-held flashlights, and have binoculars. And then, for hours they would sit, motionless, on folding chairs they will have brought with them, looking out into the desert with their binoculars. And when it became dark, most had military grade "night-vision" binoculars, which allowed one to see in images in the dark.

Although media stories and images about the Minutemen patrols focused on instances where they would encounter "illegal immigrants" crossing the border, the truth of the matter is that such instances were extremely rare. Furthermore, when the Minutemen did encounter "illegal immigrants" they were restricted by the Border Patrol as well as by national and local laws from directly apprehending anyone.[5] What the Minutemen would do if they saw an "illegal immigrant" was

FIGURE 9.2 A Minuteman on patrol, sitting on a folding chair with a radio by his side ready to communicate with the Border Patrol in the event that he sees an "illegal." Note another Minutemen on the top right corner of the photo who is sitting on top of a structure normally used when hunting animals. (Photo: Andrea Dylewski)

shine their bright flashlight at them. The use of this flashlight was intended to disorient the people crossing the border and frighten them, with the hopes that it would lead them to stop, without the Minutemen actually breaking any laws because they were not legally authorized to coerce people into stopping or detain them. From my experiences, if and when people crossing the border were encountered, what would happen is that the Minutemen would shine their flashlights, the immigrant would run, and the Minutemen would use their radio (which everyone had) to communicate with the "line leader". The line leader would then use their own radio to call the Border Patrol and ask them to come to the scene and attempt to locate and detain the person or persons who had run.

More than anything, the typical activity of patrols involved simply sitting on a chair with very little "action" taking place. Patrolling the border, you need to understand, is like fishing. The catch is a rare occurrence. Most of time is spent preparing for an encounter that will not happen. That, to quote Goffman, is not where the action is (1967). And when you do see an immigrant, it usually involves seeing him race past you while you pick up the phone and call the border patrol. Quite simply, the Minutemen do not catch immigrants, and their impact on stopping immigration, at least through enforcement, is negligible. This leads to a simple truth: patrolling the border is not about enforcing immigration policy. The project the Minutemen are engaged in is, first and foremost, a project of the self,

162 Harel Shapira

not a project in support of a government policy. Theirs is a project whose meaning comes from the practices it is organized around. As one of the volunteers explains to me about being a "line leader" organizing the patrols:

> When I'm line leader I'm not really focused on catching anyone. I've got to make sure the thing runs smoothly, and that means concentrating on the volunteers on the line [...] It's kind of like you're in charge and when its done with and it was a good shift, and everyone gets back safe, you feel good about yourself, and you feel like you've earned the confidence of the people on the line.

This volunteer doesn't catch any immigrants, but he does get to have a sense of self-respect and worth. And, through this, he gets to extend his former life: on one arm this volunteer has an old Marine Corps tattoo, and now, on the other arm, he has added a new Minuteman tattoo.

As the Minutemen interpret the situation, if they see migrants crossing, they say it is evidence that they are needed. If they do not see anyone crossing, they say it is evidence that they have done their job effectively. No matter what the "data," as it were, the Minutemen render the practice of patrolling important and meaningful.

It was, in fact, the moments when the Minutemen did encounter migrants face to face that their patrols were in a sense most greatly threatened. One day, as I was sitting around having coffee, one of the volunteers said that he hasn't seen any terrorists come across the border, that the only people he has seen are hardworking people looking for a better life. Another volunteer jumps in and says, "Yes, but it only takes one."

What is the significance of such a statement, "it only takes one"? In saying "it takes only one," the Minuteman is not simply rescuing the belief that immigrants are terrorists but, rather, he is rescuing the sets of practices and social worlds connected to those beliefs. That is, the beliefs matter but only insofar as they support a social world—in this case, a militarized social world with an incidental, but consequential, connection to the border itself.

Conclusion

While we may think that patrolling the border is defined by stopping immigrants, what matters for the Minutemen are not the "practical" impacts of their patrols – that is, the extent to which their presence on the border helps stop immigrants. Yes, stopping "illegal immigration" matters to the Minutemen, but it matters first and foremost because through it these men have created a culture, a camp, a set of heroes, a set of enemies, an entire social world, through which their past is extended, resurrected, and in the case of some, even invented. "Illegal immigration" matters, the war on terror matters, but they matter because they have enabled a world to get created down on the border and a stage on which to enact a set of identity performances. And if we are to understand what border patrols are about, we need to understand the appeal of this militarized stage. We need to understand that the U.S. / Mexico border is constitutive of, and at the same time constituted by, a set of practices and experiences by which white, working-class men have found community and purpose—and an otherwise elusive sense of entitlement—through military service.

Notes

1 United States Customs and Border Protection, National Border Patrol Strategy (Washington, DC: Office of the Border Patrol, September 2004), 2.
2 See United States Department of Homeland Security, Statistical Yearbook (Washington, DC: Department of Homeland Security, 2005), Table 35. See also Eric Swedlund "Drug Seizures on Border Soar," Arizona Daily Star, July 10, 2006.
3 Chris Simcox, "Enough Is Enough!" Tombstone Tumbleweed 16, 17, October 24, 2002.
4 These remarks came following a meeting between President Bush and the Homeland Security Council, October 29, 2001. e full transcript is available at John T. Woolley and Gerhard Peters's American Presidency Project, University of California, Santa Barbara. http://www.presidency.ucsb.edu/ws/index.php?pid=63772&st=&st1=.
5 It should be noted that the Minutemen would negotiate with the local Border Patrol sector chief and so there was some variation on what they were authorized to do, depending on who the chief was. For example, in some cases they were told they could not form a circle and shine flashlights when surrounding an immigrant. But in no instance were they authorized to directly touch and forcefully detain an immigrant.

References

Bourdieu, P. (1977). *Outline of a Theory of Practice*. Cambridge, UK: Cambridge University Press.
Goffman, E. (1959). *The Presentation of Everyday Life*. New York: Anchor Books.
Goffman, E. (1961). *Asylums: Essays on the Social Situation of Mental Patients and Other Inmates*. New York: Anchor Books.
Goffman, E. (1967). "Where the Action is." in *Interaction Ritual* (pp.149–270). Garden City: Anchor Books.
Nagel, J. (1998). Masculinity and nationalism: gender and sexuality in the making of nations. *Ethnic and Racial Studies*, 21(2), 242–269.
Nevins, J. (2002) *Operation Gatekeeper: The Rise of the 'Illegal Alien' and the Remaking of the U.S. – Mexico Boundary*. New York: Routledge.
Shapira, H. (2013). *Waiting for José: The Minutemen's Pursuit of America*. Princeton: Princeton University Press: 2013.
West, C. and D. Zimmerman. (1987). Doing gender. *Gender and Society*, 1(2), 125–151.
Yuval-Davis, N. (1993). Gender and nation. *Ethnic and Racial Studies*, 16(4), 621–632.

10

VIGILANTISM AGAINST ETHNIC MINORITIES AND MIGRANTS IN BULGARIA

Nadya Stoynova and Rositsa Dzhekova

Introduction

Xenophobia and discrimination against ethnic minorities and migrants in Bulgaria have taken different shapes and forms, including intimidation, violence and hate speech. Vigilante activities against minorities and migrants have also occurred intermittently since the fall of the socialist regime in 1989.

Vigilantism in Bulgaria can roughly be divided in two categories – ad-hoc vigilantism and organized vigilante activities. Ad-hoc vigilantism generally lacks significant pre-meditation and is often a reaction to (alleged) criminal activity by representatives of a vilified community. Different activities can be subsumed under this type of vigilantism, which is not associated with stable organizations, being perpetrated instead by individuals, local informal groups and angry mobs which form spontaneously. Instances of ad-hoc vigilantism in Bulgaria tend more often to be associated with violence against the target community.

On the other hand, organizations from the far-right spectrum have often been the driving forces behind organized vigilantism. These activities are often aimed at increasing the appeal and political clout of the formations by exploiting popular fears and prejudices but have had variable degrees of success and durability. The preeminent form of organized vigilantism are patrols aimed at countering minority and migrant criminality as well as irregular migration through the state border. Since the organizations engaged in such vigilante activities seek popular support, they tend to avoid outright violence. The actors involved are diverse. The more prominent far-right parties have largely eschewed direct engagement in vigilantism, opting instead to support patrolling activities in principle and to call for their legalization. Organized vigilantism has mostly been carried out by non-partisan far-right organizations. For these actors, vigilantism was a more ancillary activity, carried out infrequently and with little success. More recently, however, the migrant crisis has given rise to two paramilitary formations and two non-partisan activist organizations for whom vigilantism was a core activity, which received significant popular support.

Until 2013, the Roma have been the most important target of vigilante activities. The roots of anti-Roma vigilantism can be traced to the transition period which was marked by social, economic and political crisis, which had profound effect on the majority population, but even more so on the Roma, leading to their further marginalization. More recently, the intensification of the migrant crisis has provided another community which conveniently has been construed as an existential threat. The sustained migratory pressure fuelled the establishment of formations whose primary activities included vigilante patrols at the border targeted at irregular migrants. The period since 2013 was marked by a number of political crises and an overall increase in negative attitudes towards migrants and minorities, creating significant opportunities for actors using simplistic, populist arguments to gain support and publicity.

This chapter offers an account of vigilantism in Bulgaria which has recently generated significant public attention nationally and internationally, but has so far not been systematically investigated.[1] The chapter examines both manifestations of vigilantism, focusing in more detail on the four new vigilante organizations that emerged as a result of the migrant crisis.

Socio-economic and political context

Macro-level factors such as sustained socio-economic dissatisfaction and political disaffection, radicalization of public opinion, widespread and unchallenged hate speech in public discourse, coupled with external shocks and developments such as the migrant crisis, drive the emergence and popularity of vigilante groups and agendas. The rise of populist nationalism in recent years has further provided an impetus to such activities. Due to the lack of a stable political party system, populist parties with nationalist agendas and rhetoric have been on the rise in recent years, offering quick solutions to pressing social problems. However, this type of short-term populism has also had the opposite effect – raising the electorate's expectations for quick fixes and noticeable changes, resulting in further political frustration, anti-establishment sentiments and overall disaffection with the political class, leading the population to look for alternative solutions (Zankina, 2014; see also Dzhekova et al., 2015).

Vigilantism should be considered as a phenomenon emerging in the context of the political, societal and economic crisis prevalent in the country during the post-communist period of the nineties and its lingering implications. Vigilante activities in the country have usually occurred in response to a specific event or series of events that lead to an escalation of inter-ethnic tensions. The Roma community has traditionally been the prime target. The poorly handled process of privatization, together with the outdated legal framework could not fulfil the expectations of Bulgarian society for a fair transition towards a stable democracy and market economy. The retreat of the state was felt strongly by minorities, especially the Roma. The rise in unemployment was not offset by sufficient social security measures and corresponded with increases in property crimes perpetrated by Roma (Bezlov, 2007), straining relations with the majority population significantly.

In addition, during the first months of 1990 large numbers of law enforcement and judiciary personnel exited institutions and for the rest of the decade the police, prosecution and the court system barely functioned. The reduced capacity of law enforcement, especially in smaller localities, coupled with the often unclear ownership of public property during the period meant that often such crimes could not be properly handled, increasing the sense among sections of the Roma community that these activities are not illegal (ibid.). Such developments, together with the general feeling of anomie during the period, led to a deterioration of perceptions of the Roma both among Bulgarians and even among the other large minority in the country, ethnic Turks. The earliest data available shows that in 1992, 90.3% of Bulgarians and 92.3% of ethnic Turks saw the Roma as "criminally inclined" (Nakova, 2011).[2] Similar sentiments have been documented among police officers (Bezlov et al., 2006).

Subsequent efforts to bring about the successful integration of the Roma community have had dubious success and despite research suggesting a period of decrease in social distances between different ethnic groups in the country (Pamporov, 2012), ethnic tensions continue to simmer and occasionally erupt.

Anti-migrant vigilantism also emerged in the context of what Avramov (2015, p. 300) has termed "systematic crisis feeling" – the persistent and deep-seated dissatisfaction with the political class, the socio-economic state and living standards in the country observed during transition which persisted after entry to the European Union (EU, see list of acronyms in Appendix I). In this social climate, the intensification of the migrant pressure gave rise to concerns about migrants among a significant proportion of the population.[3] These anxieties were exploited and fuelled by far-right organizations, which stepped up their anti-migrant alarmist rhetoric (Institute for Social Integration (ISI), 2017).

Ad-hoc vigilantism

A number of vigilante activities in the country have been ad-hoc, spontaneous and/or self-organized initiatives by locals in response to what is viewed as excessive Roma criminality. In 1992, the residents of a village in Northern Bulgaria, fed up with burglaries and police inaction, burned down Roma houses. Subsequently, volunteers patrolled the streets to prevent retribution and the Roma were eventually expelled (Kodinova, 2013). In 2001, the same group of Roma were evicted by the residents of another village after a Roma woman was involved in the murder of an elderly man (Dencheva, 2001). Other attempts at forceful expulsion have been recorded as well (Bulgarian Helsinki Committee (BHC), 2001). In another case of vigilante violence in 1997, an angry mob tied up and lynched five Roma after they were accused of stealing livestock (BHC, 1997). During the same year, another group of Roma accused of a similar crime were tied up to a tractor and paraded across the village as punishment (ibid.).

In many localities, self-organized patrols formed to tackle crime claim no minority bias even though focus on Roma criminality is often implied. This is evident in cases where patrols have been organized against pickpocketing (Yordanova, 2015), which is closely associated with Roma women or to prevent illicit activity in places where Roma petty criminality is perceived as the predominant problem ("Roma thieves lynched", 2016).

The Roma have also traditionally been a frequent target of violent attacks such as hate crime perpetrated by skinhead gangs (e.g. BHC, 2001). Other ethnic and religious minorities, including immigrants, have also fallen victims to vigilantism, violence and discrimination. However, in terms of both spread and intensity, biases against the Roma are much more pronounced (Kirilov, 2012). For this reason, actions against this community have been more vicious and frequent. Nevertheless, since the advent of the migrant crisis, ad-hoc vigilantism with the aim to prevent illegal border crossing (so-called "migrant hunters" like Dinko Valev[4]) has also been observed.

While self-organized and spontaneous vigilante activities showcase the fundamental lack of trust in state institutions and deeply ingrained prejudices against minorities, with some exceptions, they are usually local, short-lived and have not received widespread media or popular attention.

The development of the far-right scene and the rise of organized vigilantism

Actors in the far-right spectrum have been important drivers of organized vigilante activities against migrants and Roma in the country. Nevertheless, prior to 2013, vigilante activities organized by far-right actors were rare. The period since 2013 presented favourable conditions leading to the recovery and growth especially of populist far-right organizations, the emergence of new formations and the rise of organized vigilantism.

The far-right scene in Bulgaria includes a spectrum of actors roughly falling in the following three categories (Dzhekova et al., 2015): political parties, non-parliamentary activist organizations and informal groupings. The political actors include both important political parties who have (had) representation in Parliament and a plethora of smaller parties. Informal groups represent gatherings mostly involved in hooligan acts and hate crimes without a particularly crystallized ideological foundation (e.g. Blood and Honour Bulgaria, skinhead movements). Last but not least, there are non-partisan activist formations which exhibit a more sophisticated degree of organization, ideological argumentation and political ambitions. One prominent example is the Bulgarian National Union (BNU), the longest-running organization of this type.[5]

In Bulgaria, a far-right party emerged as a political force only in 2005, despite significant political crisis and turbulence during the nineties. Due to this relatively late consolidation of a recognizable far-right political actor, Bulgaria has been considered as an "odd case" compared to the rest of Eastern Europe (Beichelt and Minkenberg 2002, p. 15). The electoral success of the Ataka (Attack) party was unexpected, since it was formed only shortly before the elections (Krasteva, 2016). While other far-right organizations existed before 2005, they were considered "fringe, small and politically irrelevant" despite widespread prejudice and violence against different ethnic and religious minorities (Ivanov and Ilieva, 2005).

The years between 2009 and 2013 marked a period of diminished public visibility of far-right organizations. Ataka, the most successful party in the far-right spectrum experienced a decline and subsequent stagnation in election results after a high point in 2006 (Todorov, 2013). Similarly, the Bulgarian National Union suffered a setback after its leader Boyan Rasate left the group in 2010 and the membership declined significantly (Doichinova and Derelieva, 2015). Nevertheless, already in 2011, there were signs of intensification of the activity of far-right groups including attempts to recruit new members (Council of Ministers, 2012). The protests and political unrest that Bulgaria experienced in 2013–2015,[6] coupled with the migrant crisis,[7] provided a suitable environment for the re-invigoration of some existing far-right organizations and the emergence of new actors (Mircheva and Zahariev, 2013). The last parliamentary elections of 2017 resulted in the entry of the far-right coalition Patriotic Front (PF)[8] in the governing coalition, which marked the first time the far-right became a decisive factor in government.

Nevertheless, not all far-right actors experienced a boost in activities and popularity. The BNU's former leader Rasate's subsequent political project, the Bulgarian National Union – New Democracy (BNU-ND) did very poorly in the 2014 elections (Purvanov, 2009). Similarly, the Nationalist Party of Bulgaria, including individuals associated with the BNU and groups like Blood and Honour, National Resistance and different football fan factions, was denied registration by the Sofia City Court in 2014.

While almost all far-right organizations in Bulgaria have a comparable view on the issue of Roma criminality and irregular migration, both of which are used extensively for securing support from the population, not all far-right organizations have engaged in vigilante activities. Political actors, including more prominent parties, generally eschew direct involvement in vigilantism and have instead called for the legalization of civilian patrols (Cvetanova, 2016). Prior to 2007, there were sporadic instances of far-right organizations initiating and orchestrating vigilante activities on their own. In cases where they were involved, they appear to have taken advantage of and galvanized popular discontent, partnering with other actors instead of independently carrying out vigilante activities. One such example is the 2001 intimidation and attack of Protestants from the United Church of God by a crowd of local people, led by an Orthodox priest and a representative of one of the smaller far-right parties (BHC, 2001).

The BNU was the first far-right organization that attempted to launch a more stable vigilante initiative. In 2007, it formed a "national guard" squad to patrol and protect Bulgarians from alleged Roma raids after tensions erupted in a Sofia neighbourhood with a significant proportion of Roma inhabitants. A BNU activist admitted that these vigilante groups were formed for populist purposes and aimed to show off belonging to a group with specific views as well as to increase the visibility of the organization and to make the logo of the organization recognizable. This populism was introduced by the BNU's then leader Boyan Stankov-Rasate copying tactics employed by the leader of Ataka, the largest far-right party in the country. Thus, it appears that vigilante activities were largely a personal project in this case. However, despite widespread prejudice and inter-ethnic tensions and some expressed support (Chipeva, 2007), the initiative did not have any lasting impact.

Since 2013, the intensification of the migrant crisis led to the establishment of organized vigilante activities by both established far-right organizations and new formations. Upon leaving the BNU in 2010, through his other organizations Rasate kept advocating for the legalization of civilian patrols. In 2013, he also organized short-lived patrols in the centre of Sofia with the aim to counter migrant criminality. He failed to receive significant support or exposure and the patrols were quickly rejected by the authorities stating that the reaction to vigilantism will be strengthened police presence ("The Prosecution and the Ministry of the Interior will react", 2013). For both the BNU as well as Rasate's subsequent organizations vigilantism can be described as an ancillary activity, organized sporadically and aimed at generating public attention and recognition.

On the other hand, four formations emerged in response to the migrant crisis that have become known in the public domain for their patrolling activities near the Bulgarian border with Turkey, the main entry point for the migration flow from the Middle East (Stoilova, 2016). The Vasil Levski Military Union (MU), along with the Shipka Bulgarian National Movement (BNM) and their umbrella organization, the Vasil Levski Committee for National Salvation (CNS), are para-military nationalist organizations which share the same leadership. Two other acti-vist formations emerged as well – the Organization for the Protection of Bulgarian Citizens (OPBC) and the Civil Squads for the Protection of Women and the Faith (CSPWF). In the following sections, these new vigilante organizations will be examined in more depth.

Organized vigilante groups

Activities

The organization of civilian patrols against irregular migrants are among the main activities of the new formations. These patrols would stop migrants they encounter and alert the authorities, even though there have been cases when the migrants were unlawfully detained. However, all of the new vigilante organizations have engaged in other activities as well, which have become important with the dissipation of the migrant crisis.

In addition to border patrols, BNM Shipka and the MU also claim to regularly organize voluntary military and combat trainings presented as "land navigation and first-aid trainings" (BNM Shipka, n.d.b). The BNM Shipka and the MU further-more claim to have established an elite antiterrorist squad to be trained abroad by world class professionals in the field of counterterrorism and security (BNM Shipka, 2016). The two organizations have also taken part in different protests (e.g. against the incarceration of CSPWF's leader Petar Nizamov[9]). Probably the most important event for the organizations was a protest planned for 20 April 2016 in front of the Parliament, which was supposed to put the so-called operation "Lib-eration"[10] in motion and attract numerous supporters from all over country. In fact, the protest was attended by as little as 50 people in total (Grozev, 2016) and thus failed to deliver the definitive social statement its organizers had hoped for. Members of the organizations claimed that the low turnout was due to the arrest of twenty of the protest coordinators prior to the event (Kojuharov, 2016).

The members of the BNM and MU refrain from violent clashes with other groups or with the police since they risk to undermine their legitimacy by appearing as just another group of hooligans. However, on 30 June 2016 members of BNM Shipka attacked a group of Ukrainian and Bulgarian demonstrators pro-testing against the arrival of the members of the Russian bikers club Night Wolves, closely affiliated with Vladimir Putin. Despite being a singular case this incident demonstrates that members of the BNM and MU are willing to use violence.

Vigilante activities on the border were also key activities for the two activist formations, the OPBC and CSPWF. Nevertheless, aside from organizing migrant patrols, the OPBC also engages in protests, marches commemorating historical personalities, charity (gathering and donating clothes, blood) and volunteer work (e.g. assisting in putting out forest fires) (OPBC, n.d.). OPBC members have downplayed their activities in border areas, stating that they take walks and day trips and if they happen to come across migrants would alert the Border Police ("Civilian patrols", 2016). The CSPWF has taken part in protests and charitable activities. While the CSPWF's leader became infamous for the 'citizen arrest' of a group of migrants, the CSPWF and OPBC also tend to avoid violence. The OPBC has publicly renounced citizen arrests (Stoilova, 2016).

The civilian border patrols have generated support and publicity for the four organizations. However, in 2017 with the decrease in migration pressure, patrol activities have ceased, leading the organizations to focus on other activities to sus-tain their public profile and relevance, without significant success. The OPBC and CSPWF have focused mostly on charitable activities. The latter formation has also attempted to generate publicity and support by organizing another vigilante action against an individual who attacked an elderly woman without provocation ("Perata calls for retribution", 2017). On the other hand, the BNM and MU appear to have scaled down their activities significantly during 2017. Their last public event for that year was a demonstration against shale gas extraction by foreign companies in the Dobrudzha region. Similar protests from previous years have been attributed to Russian funding and attempts to stop reduction of Bulgarian energy dependence on Moscow (Hope, 2014).

Ideology, narratives and goals

The new vigilante formations largely share similar ideas, with some notable differences in focus. Significant overlap with ideas espoused by older far-right formations can also be identified.

The BNM Shipka and MU Vasil Levski argue against foreign interference in Bulgarian affairs – more specifically against the US, Turkey, the EU and NATO. However, the BNM Shipka and MU Vasil Levski largely eschew criticism and even demonstrate sympathies for Russia as exemplified by the involvement of former Russian soldiers in the training of BNM Shipka members (Papakochev, 2016). The anti-immigration, anti-refugee, populist-nationalist ("Bulgaria for the Bulgarians") and anti-Zionist rhetoric is also strongly represented. Interestingly, compared to older far-right organizations and the two new activist formations, the paramilitary organizations are more nuanced in their use of anti-Roma rhetoric. While they acknowledge "Roma terror", the BNM and MU see the stoking of inter-ethnic tensions as a ploy by Western powers to further the genocide against the Bulgarian nation (BNM Shipka, 2017).

In addition, the BNM and MU engage more heavily in what Avramov (2015, p. 300) has termed "hard" populism or populism which "represents a challenge to the model of representative democracy", as opposed to the predominantly "soft" populism of the majority of older far-right organizations and the two new activist formations, which is more of a "challenge to the party system within the democratic framework".

The BNM and MU espouse strong anti-establishment ideas, with some leftist elements. Citing the corruption of the current political elite and system and a number of international human rights documents, the organizations advocate for the abolition of the constitutional order and parliamentary democracy and introduction of a direct democracy (carried out through referenda) (BNM Shipka, n.d.c). However, the transition is to begin with the creation of an interim government led by the Vasil Levski CNS (BNM Shipka, n.d.a) with the aim to help the people organize their self-rule. For the purposes of establishing the new order, peaceful means are to be used, provided the current political class submits to their demands. Violence is justified in case the government fails to bring about the change of the political system. Despite a strong condemnation of the party system, in May 2018 the BNM Shipka announced the formation of a political party, the "Shipka People's Court" (BNM Shipka, 2018).[11] The contradiction between the establishment of a party and the often repeated argument that all parties should be dissolved, is not addressed.

Aside from their goal for direct democracy, the BNM Shipka and Vasil Levski MU present no concrete roadmap for the government of this political system. By their own admission, the organizations do not adhere to "the national socialism of German Jews,[12] capitalism, Judeo-Bolshevism, Trotskyism, liberalism, the Marxism of the Jewish Rabbis, to fake democracy or any other criminal or false ideology or –isms" (BNM Shipka, n.d.b). This mash-up of different or non-existing ideological strands is indicative of the haphazardness of the underlying ideology of the formations.

172 Nadya Stoynova and Rositsa Dzhekova

As paramilitary organizations, the BNM Shipka and MU Vasil Levski's rhetoric is heavily focused on themes of militarization, creating parallel structures and urgency of taking action. Uniforms are often worn during different activities and their insignia are designed to induce a feeling of a genuine military formation. The messages that the two organizations share are bombastic and grandiose, often presented in capital letters, and generally fall in four categories: condemnation of the treacherous political elite, glorification of the struggle against it, calls to join the revolution and warnings of the impending doom brought by migrant conquerors.

On the other hand, the other two new vigilante organizations, the OPBC and CSPWF, can be described as single-issue activist formations, being mostly pre-occupied with irregular migration. According to the CSPWF their mission is to "not let any new migrants in and to return the very last one who managed to cross" (CSPWF, 2016). Despite criticism towards the government (Kostadinov, 2016) these two groups do not appear to share the same degree of animosity towards the overall political system.

All of the organizations disseminate their views and other important information through social media and their own websites. Social media and the internet are preferred both for communication with existing members and for the recruitment of new ones. However, a notable difference in the communication strategy of the organizations is that while CSPWF and especially the BNM and MU frequently share fake or heavily distorted news articles, the OPBC generally eschews such content.

The dissipation of the migrant crisis has reduced the visibility of these new organizations, necessitating a calibration in rhetoric in order to stay relevant and justify their continued existence. The BNM and MU focus heavily on the detri-mental effect on foreign interference in Bulgaria with the help of the corrupt political elite, such as shale gas exploration by foreign companies. On the other hand, the OPBC and CSPWF have largely returned to the evergreen topic of Roma criminality and government corruption.

Beyond any ideological arguments, preconceptions against the irregular migrants as criminals and a threat to security or the desire to counter illicit activity, however, identifying other possible motivations behind engagement in vigilantism is not straightforward. With regard to the two paramilitary organizations, the indications of foreign financing (see Group alliances below) undermines the stated motivation to counter crime and foreign interference in service of the Bulgarian people, especially with regard to the leadership of the organizations.

Similarly, two of the infamous "migrant hunters", the independent Dinko Valev[13] and the CSPWF's leader Petar Nizamov both gained significant personal fame which likely to some extent motivated continued engagement in vigilantism. It should, however, be noted that there are speculations that "migrant hunters" were paid by human smuggling networks to pursue migrants who refuse to pay for facilitation (Galabov, 2017; Krasteva, 2018) even though they have not been substantiated. Considering the Bulgarian criminal underground's widespread involvement in human smuggling during the crisis (Bezlov and Stoynova, 2017) and the associations

Vigilantism in Bulgaria 173

with organized crime which surfaced with regard to both Valev (Rusev, 2016) and Nizamov (Shtilianova, 2016), such a motivation is at least plausible.

Organizational structure, membership and sources of financing

A common feature of Bulgarian vigilante organizations is the tendency to highly overstate their membership base and complexity of organizational structure. While this is done with the goal to appear as a more credible actor, the exaggerations are often outlandish and implausible.

Beyond a few front figures, little is known about the members of MU Vasil Levski, Shipka BNM and their umbrella body. The MU aims to unite current and former military and police officers, even though the Ministry of Defence has denied working with these organizations (Stoyanov, 2016). The Shipka movement accepts everyone else (volunteers without military or police background). Between them, the paramilitary formations claim to have 29,000 supporters (Kojuharov, 2016). A report by the German ZDF channel indicated that there were about 800 people involved in border patrolling activities ("Bulgarian volunteer army", 2016). The claims by the formations are likely highly exaggerated, since the real membership and popularity is estimated by law enforcement and intelligence agencies as significantly lower and diminishing with the dissipation of the migrant crisis towards the end of 2016.

The MU and BNM claim to have branches in 22 Bulgarian cities (including two in Sofia) as well as abroad in the US, the UK and the Czech Republic (BNM Shipka, n.d.c). The CNS acts as the joint leadership for the other two organizations and is responsible for setting goals and managing the network of branches under its command. The BNM Shipka claims a very sophisticated structure, including a counterintelligence subdivision, a financial service, an information analysis centre, a centre for legal and economic analyses and legal protection as well as a centre for countering hostile propaganda, psychological warfare and other such anti-Bulgarian campaigns (Ibid).

The OPBC's stated structure of the organization includes a general assembly, a management board, chairman and a vice chairman, head of department and deputy and members, whose number is not disclosed (OPBC, 2014). On the other hand, the CSPWF's mostly revolves around its leader, Petar Nizamov, a. k.a. Perata, and likely has limited membership. Nizamov's reinvention into an active nationalist appears to be relatively recent, as he was previously connected to organized crime activities in Bourgas and has three convictions for bodily injury and one for hooliganism (Shtilianova, 2016).

The BNM, MU and the OPBC are officially registered as non-profit organizations which receive membership fees. All of the organizations are actively seeking donations, but the BNM and MU are particularly aggressive, attaching the call on every subsection of their website. Nevertheless, there are indications that the BNM and MU receive foreign funding. The Bulgarian Helsinki Committee has claimed that the organizations' sources of financing are non-transparent and that for their first year of existence, the formations declared no activity or income (Papakochev, 2016). Similarly, an advisor to the Minister of Defence has indicated that these organization are financed by Russian intelligence services (Ibid). Unsurprisingly, members of the formations refute such claims and a representative even denied that the formations receive donations at all ("Zdravko Velev: BNM Shipka", 2016).

Group alliances

Bulgarian vigilante organizations showcase differences in the connections they have with other actors in the far-right milieu, both domestically and internationally. Generally, despite sharing much of their ideas, the new vigilante groups do not appear to have direct connections to the traditional far-right in Bulgaria. The reaction of established organizations to the new formations in the non-parliamentary spectrum has been very limited, with few outright declarations of support. This is possibly prompted by anxieties about the new formations drawing a portion of the membership or supporters (especially more extreme members who might be frustrated by inaction) of the older non-partisan organizations. This process as posited by McCauley and Moskalenko (2008) involves outbidding and group competition "in which groups who are more radical or more extreme may be perceived as more committed or devout which may make them more attractive to potential members and supporters" (McCauley and Moskalenko, 2008, cited in Borum, 2011: 22). The relations between the new vigilante formations themselves can be described by a variable degree of conflict and support, including rifts between actors with previously amicable relations.

Importantly, there is evidence of ties with a number of foreign far right organizations and personalities. BNM and MU, in particular, openly emphasize international connections and activities, intended to create the impression of a well-developed network and support from the wider far-right scene in Europe. BNM and MU claim the support of foreign organizations such as the French Nuit debout movement, the German and Dutch PEGIDA and the American network Veterans Today.

In 2016, together with PEGIDA and 12 other far-right organizations, the BNM and MU took part in a conference organized by the Czech Bloc against Islam. The meeting resulted in the formation of the group Fortress Europe and the release of the Prague Declaration, warning of the demise of Western civilization at the hand of Islamic conquerors ("PEGIDA meets with European allies", 2016). The host of the conference was claimed to be the Czech Parliament (BNM Shipka, 2016). In 2016, former Pegida and Alternative for Germany activist Tatjana Festerling, Edwin Wagensveld from the Dutch PEGIDA and the founder of Britain First, Jim Dowson joined the MU Vasil Levski patrols in Bulgarian border areas ("Camouflage comrades", 2016). CSPWF's Petar Nizamov joined a far-right protest in Dresden, where he could be seen posing with Tatjana Festerling (Todorova, 2016). Nevertheless, it is difficult to judge the closeness of these relations due to the tendency of the organizations to overstate the support they receive.

Government and (civil) society reaction

The reaction of the authorities and political actors towards the vigilantism of the new formations have been ambivalent. Initially, the Prime Minister Boyko Borissov thanked them for supporting the work of the government institutions ("Borissov thanked refugee patrols", 2016). However, after the release of Petar Nizamov's video showing tied up migrants, which gained international notoriety, the reaction was more unequivocally condemnatory, as evidenced by statements of the Minister of Interior and Chief Prosecutor ("The 'migrant hunter' Petar Nizamov is renown", 2016).

Where criminal justice action was undertaken it was circumscribed. Petar Nizamov was indicted for the unlawful detainment of migrants even though he was subsequently acquitted. On the other hand, the BNM and MU have so far mostly escaped official scrutiny. Perhaps the most serious action against the formations was a preventive arrest of "regional coordinators" on suspicions of planning to act as provocateurs at a protest organized by Ministry of Interior employees in late 2015.[14] For the altercation with the protesters demonstrating against the arrival of the Russian motor club "Night Wolves", pre-trail proceedings for hooliganism were opened against two persons from each side, even though there is evidence that BNM and MU were acting more aggressively (Atanasova, 2016).

Most importantly, however, the paramilitary formations' rhetoric about overthrowing the current political system with violence if necessary is prohibited by the Criminal Code. On the basis of this, in June 2016, two NGOs have demanded the ban of the organizations by the prosecution (Papakochev, 2016). Some tentative investigative actions were undertaken by the State Agency for National Security (SANS) (ibid.) and the prosecution (Krastev, 2017), but did not result in indictments and had no effect on the BNM and MU. Officials from specialized security and defence commissions in the Parliament have also largely refused comment with regard to these organizations (Georgiev, 2016).

With the entry of a far-right political formation in the governing coalition, the push for the adoption of a legal framework regulating civic security patrols was renewed more actively and a number of draft legislative acts were proposed in 2017. Nevertheless, key figures from the PF have in 2013 and later in 2016 also condemned unsanctioned anti-migrant border patrols as attempts at personal glorification and as undermining serious nationalism ("Valeri Simeonov, PF", 2016; Georgieva, 2013). It is difficult to estimate whether legalization of vigilante activities will strengthen the organizations currently associated with such activities. However, possible legalization of civilian patrols is concerning in light of the negative trends in popular opinion against migrants and minorities. Research shows that there is decline in anti-Roma attitudes in the period 2013–2016 (Kirilov, 2016), while hate speech against migrant and minorities is becoming more prevalent (Ivanova, 2016).

While institutional reactions to the new vigilante organizations have been ambivalent, surveys have shown significant popular support for vigilante activities

176 Nadya Stoynova and Rositsa Dzhekova

with civilian arrests enjoying support by 54,8% of the population ("Alpha research: More than 50%", 2016) and civilian patrols by 65% (Angelov, 2016). However, favourable views of vigilante activities cannot necessarily be taken to represent support for the organizations which engage in them. Indeed, active support for the vigilante formations appears scarce as evidenced by the failure of the BNM and MU's failed Operation "Liberation". Instead, favourable presentation of 2migrant hunters" by the media (Nikolova et al., 2016; Krasteva, 2018), together with widespread anxieties about the threat posed by migrants (Kyuchukov, 2016) likely played a role in fostering support for anti-migrant vigilantism.

Conclusion

The current analysis demonstrates that vigilantism in Bulgaria is a recurring phenomenon. The Roma have mostly been the target of ad-hoc, self-organized or spontaneous vigilantism, to a large degree fuelled by the widely held prejudice against the community and the perceived inability of institutions to effectively counter crime. These vigilante activities have taken place in a number of towns and villages but remain diffused and haphazard.

Well-established far-right groups have thus far failed to harness the popular anti-Roma sentiment in support of organized vigilante activities, which remained ancillary and infrequent. However, the migrant crisis, coupled with significant political instability and popular dissatisfaction served as the necessary fertile soil for the establishment of new vigilante organizations with a strong anti-migrant agenda. For these formations vigilante activities can be described as an integral feature of their action repertoire. The widespread dissatisfaction with the political status quo coupled with the presentation of the migrants as an immediate and existential threat conferred legitimacy to the rhetoric and actions of the new vigilante groups.

Compared to skinhead type gangs, football hooligans or other similar far-right groupings that are ideologically unsophisticated and often involved in violent hate crime, formations such as the BNM and MU avoid violence and at the very least create the impression of having a structure and spelled-out goals including clear political ambition, while still using simplified populist rhetoric and leaving behind more refined ideological arguments. The actual extent to which the two formations are in the process of becoming well organized paramilitary formations, which can present a viable threat to democracy and social cohesion requires further research. It is, however, very likely that their claims both in terms of membership, preparedness and structure are highly exaggerated.

Nevertheless, the changes in rhetoric they represent, namely the focus on immediate action to change the status quo as well as indications of foreign financing are notable and should not be dismissed lightly. The BNM and MU try to recruit former and current police, army and security services personnel. The number of active law enforcement and security personnel combined with those that experienced early retirement or dismissal during the nineties is large, representing a significant potential pool for recruitment. Last but not least, many of those that exited the army and law enforcement in that period can be described as alienated and resentful since given their privileged status under socialism, many of them have not fared well during the transition. The potential for wider recruitment as well as of the instrumentalization of this population by populist political actors in a manner similar to the way football fan factions were used in the period 2013–2014 for escalating public protests and generating social tensions, poses a risk for galvanization under favourable conditions.

Notes

1 The analysis is based on desktop research, review of online content produced by vigilante groups, observation of groups' online presence and behaviour, interviews with law enforcement experts and far-right activists.
2 During communism, despite government policies aimed at assimilation, conflicts between the majority Bulgarian population and the Roma occurred as well (Pashova, n.d.).
3 According to a study from 2016, 60% of the population consider migrants as a security threat (Kyuchukov, 2016).
4 The infamous anti-migrant vigilante Dinko Valev patrolled near the Southern border of Bulgaria and apprehended migrants before calling the police. (Tomlinson, 2016). His activities are not associated with any organisation.
5 Even though it is supposedly non-partisan, the BNU was initially closely associated with the Ataka party and has produced affiliated parties, such as the Guard party (Avramov, 2008).
6 In 2013–2014, the country experienced a string of large-scale anti-government protests and changes in government. In this period far-right groupings such as football fan factions were used by political actors for escalating public protests and counter-protests and for generating social tensions (Bezlov, 2015).
7 For a more in-depth overview of the development of the migrant crisis in Bulgaria see Bezlov and Stoynova (2017).
8 A coalition between two far-right parties, NFSB and IMRO-BNM.
9 He was briefly charged with the unlawful detainment, after he posted a video online showing tied up migrants.
10 According to the leader of the formations, Doncho Rusev aka Valter Kalashnikov, Operation Liberation was supposed to initiate the execution of the organisation's detailed plan to bring power to the people and radically change the political order (Grozev, 2016).
11 The name People's Court alludes to the People's Court which was set up in 1944 Communist Bulgaria. The Court was set up outside of the framework of constitutional law and charged and subsequently sentenced (including to death) members of the political, military and royal elite of the country and enemies to the communist regime (Chorbadzhiyski, 2018).
12 In line with the strong anti-Jewish and anti-Zionist Rhetoric of the BNM Shipka and Vasil Levski MU, this phrase, "the national socialism of German Jews", can be considered to propagate arguments typical of Holocaust denial theories, which consider the rise of National Socialism and the Holocaust as a Jewish conspiracy.
13 Valev was the subject of a number of media articles, interviews and shows, including in foreign media (Tomlinson, 2016) and later starred in reality TV shows.
14 The protest was prompted by government plans to cut social benefit packages of the MoI staff. According to representatives of the paramilitary formations, the arrested were going to support the rightful protest of police officials (Georgiev, 2016).

178 Nadya Stoynova and Rositsa Dzhekova

Bibliography

Angelov, K. (2016, April 22). Динкё, Перата, граждански ётряди... Хёрата им симпатизират [Dinko, Perata, civilian patrols...People sympathise with them]. Днес, Retrieved from https://www.dnes.bg.

Atanasova, M. (2016, June 30). Бёй в Бургас заради Рёкерите на Путин [Fight in Burgas because of Putin's rockers]. Мёнитёр, Retrieved from http://monitor.bg/.

Avramov, K. (2015). The Bulgarian radical right: Marching up from the margins. In Minkenberg, M. (ed.) *Transforming the transformation? The East European radical right in the political process* (pp. 299–319). London: Routledge.

Beichelt, T. and Minkenberg, M. (2002). *Explaining the radical right in transition: theories of rightwing radicalism and opportunity structures in post-socialist Europe*. Working Paper No. 3/02. Frankfurt: Frankfurter Institut fur Transformationsstudien.

Bezlov, T. (2007, February 26) Рёмите и престъпнёстта: пёлицейска статистика и реалнёсти [The Roma and criminality: Police statistics and realities]. Дневник, Retrieved from https://www.dnevnik.bg.

Bezlov, T. (2015). Football hooliganism. In R. Dzhekova et al. *Radicalisation in Bulgaria: Threats and Trends*. (pp 101–143). Sofia: CSD.

Bezlov, T. and Stoynova, N. (2017). *Transnational organised crime: Bulgaria and Norway in the context of the migrant crisis*. Sofia: Center for the Study of Democracy.

Bezlov, T. et al. (2006). *Police checks and the use of ethnic profile in Bulgaria*. Sofia: Center for the Study of Democracy (CSD).

BNM Shipka (n.d.a) Кёмитет за Нациёналнё Спасение „Васил Левски"[Committee for National Salvation Vasil Levski]. Retrieved from https://www.bnoshipka.org/index.php?cat=1&subcat=0.

BNM Shipka. (2016, July 7). Дейнёст [Activity]. Retrieved from https://www.bnoshipka. org/index.php?special=deinost&cat=1&id=51.

BNM Shipka (n.d.b) Вёински съюз: Структура, цели и задачи [Military Union: Structure, goals and tasks]. Retrieved from https://www.bnoshipka.org/index.php?cat=2&subcat=3.

BNM Shipka (n.d.c) Българскё Нарёднё Опълчение "Шипка": Цели и задачи [Bulgarian Peoples' Army of Volunteers "Shipka": Objectives and tasks]. Retrieved from https://www.bnoshipka.org/index.php?cat=3&subcat=6.

BNM Shipka (2017, July 7). Умишленё създават етническа вёйна в България, за да ни унищёжат! Замислете се [There are deliberate attempts to stoke an inter-ethnic war in Bulgaria in order to destroy us! Think about it]. Retrieved from https://www.bnoshipka. org/index.php?special=videos&cat=1&id=26.

BNM Shipka (2018, May 1). Окёнчателнётё Освёбёждение на Нарёда и истинскё Нациёналнё възраждане на България вече запёчна! [The Final Liberation of the People and true National Rebirth of Bulgaria has begun!]. Retrieved from: https://www.bnoshipka.org/index.php?special=publikacii&cat=3&id=141.

Borum, R. (2011). Radicalization into violent extremism I: A review of social science theories. *Perspectives on Radicalization and Involvement in Terrorism* 4 (4): 7–36.

Bulgarian Helsinki Committee (BHC) (1997). *Human rights in Bulgaria in 1997*. Sofia: BHC.

Bulgarian Helsinki Committee (BHC) (2001). *Human rights in Bulgaria in 2001*. Sofia: BHC.

Bulgarian Helsinki Committee (BHC) (2002). *Human rights in Bulgaria in 2002*. Sofia: BHC

Bulgarian Helsinki Committee (BHC) (2006). *Пет гёдини пё-къснё: Неправителствените прёекти за десегрегация на рёмскётё ёбразёвание в България [Five years later: The non-governmental projects for the desegregation of the Roma education]*. Sofia: BHC.

Bulgarian Volunteer Army On Border Patrol Defending Against Migrants (Pics and video). (2016, August 15). *NDL News*, Retrieved from http://www.norwegiandefenceleague.info

Chipeva, N. (2007, August 24). Да гасиш пёжара с вентилатёр [Putting out the fire with a fan]. Капитал, Retrieved from https://www.capital.bg.

Chorbadzhiyski, M. (2018, January 31). Нарёдният съд – кървавата машина на Отечествения фрёнт [The People's Court – the bloody machine of the Fatherland Front]. Retrieved from https://bulgarianhistory.org/narodniat-sud/.

Council of Ministers. (2012). *Гёдишен ётчет за изпълнение на пёлитиките и прёграмите на Министерския съвет за 2011 г.* [*Annual report on the implementation of the policies and programs of the Council of Ministers for 2011*]. Sofia: Council of Ministers.

CSPWF (2016, January 4). About Отряди на Петър Низамёв за защита на жените и вярата [Civil squads of Petar Nizamov for the protection of women and the faith] In Facebook. Retrieved13 November 2016 from https://www.facebook.com/pg/Цивилни-ётряди-за-защита-на-жените-и-вярата-746589968774726/about/?entry_point=page_nav_about_item.

Cvetanova, K. (2016, March 29). ВМРО иска: Дёбрёвёлни ётряди срещу рёмите пё селата [IMRO wants volunteer corps against the Roma in the villages]. Днес, Retrieved from https://www.dnes.bg.

Dencheva, D. (2001, August 20). Циганите през глава избягаха ёт Стежерёвё. Желаниетё за мъст ёстана [The Gypsies ran from Stejerovo. The desire for revenge remained]. Сега, Retrieved from https://www.sega.bg.

Doichinova, M. and Derelieva, L. (2015). Right-wing and left-wing radicalisation. In R. Dzhekova et al. *Radicalisation in Bulgaria: Threats and trends.* (pp 55–99). Sofia: CSD.

Dzhekova, R. et al. (2015) *Radicalisation in Bulgaria: Threats and trends.* Sofia: Center for the Study of Democracy.

Galabov, A. (2017). Roundtable presentation at the event "Бежанската криза – предизвикателствё пред българските институции" [The refugee crisis – challenge for the Bulgarian institutions]. Retrieved from http://borkor.government.bg/bg/page/485.

Georgiev, I. (2016, July 1). Игра на вёйници, или кёй дърпа дявёла за ёпашката [Playing soldiers or who is pulling the tail of the devil]. *Сега5619* (148).

Georgieva, C. (2013, November 11). Нёщна стража [Night watch]. *Уебкафе*, Retrieved from https://www.webcafe.bg/.

Grozev, K. (2016, April 20) Накрая ще се питаме: Къде сбъркахме? [In the end we will be asking ourselves: Where did we go wrong?]. Уебкафе, Retrieved from https://webcafe.bg.

Hope, K. (2014, November 30). Bulgarians see Russian hand in anti-shale protests. *Financial Times*, Retrieved from https://www.ft.com/.

Institute for Social Integration and Friedrich Ebert Stiftung. (2017). *Езикът на ёмразата – прёблем № 1 на бежанците в България* [*Hate speech – problem № 1 for refugees in Bulgaria*]. Sofia: Institute for Social Integration.

International Center for Minority Studies and Intercultural Relations (IMIR). (1992) *Етнёкултурната ситуация в България* [*Ethno-cultural situation in Bulgaria*]. Sofia: IMIR.

IMIR. (1994). *Връзки на съвместимёсти несъвместимёст между християни и мюсюлмани* [*Intersections of compatibility and incompatibility between Christians and Muslims*]. Sofia: IMIR.

Ivanov, C. and Ilieva, M. (2005). Bulgaria. In Mudde, C. (ed.) *Racist extremism in Central and Eastern Europe.* London: Routledge.

Ivanova, I. (2016). *Обществени нагласи спрямё речта на ёмразата в България през 2016 г.* [*Public attitudes towards hate speech in Bulgaria during 2016*]. Sofia: Open Society Institute.

Kirilov, N. (2016). *ROMED external evaluation report: Country findings, Bulgaria.* Strasbourg: Council of Europe.

Kirilov, S. (2012). Рёми срещу българи – сблъсъкът в Красна пёляна в медийнётё ёгледалё [Roma against Bulgarians: The Krasna Polyana clash in the media mirror]. *Медии и ёбществени кёмуникации* 13.

Kodinova, E. (2013, November 22). Прегрупиранетё на нациёналистите. [The regrouping of the nationalists] В. Преса. Retrieved from http://epicenter.bg/?p=article&id=28861&cat_id=11&sub_id=33.

Kojuharov, G. (2016, September 11). Прёпёведниците на светёвния загёвёр срещу България [The prophets of the international conspiracy against Bulgaria]. *Капитал.* Retrieved from https://www.capital.bg.

Kostadinov, T. (2016, April 13). ОЗБГ пред Topnovini.bg: Акё държавата беше наред, нас нямаше да ни има [OPBC in front of Topnovini.bg: If the state was in order, we would not have existed]. *Топнёвини,* Retrieved from http://burgas.topnovini.bg.

Krasteva, A. (2016). The post-communist rise of national populism: Bulgarian paradoxes. In Lazaridis, G., Campagni, G. and Benveniste, A. (eds.). *The rise of the far right in Europe: Populist shifts and 'othering'* (pp. 161–200). Basingstoke: Palgrave Macmillan.

Krasteva, A. (2018, February 9). Прёф. Анна Крръстева: Ние виждаме нациёнал-пёпулизма на улицата, нё тёй е изключителнё мёщен в дигиталната сфера. Интервю за Маргиналия [Prof. Anna Krasteva: We see national-populism on the street, but it is incredibly powerful in the digital sphere]. Retrieved from https://annakrasteva.wordpress.com.

Krastev, B. (2017, February 20). За каквё плачат българските паравёенни ёрганизации? [What are the Bulgarian paramilitary organisations complaining about?]. *Клуб "Z",* Retrieved from https://clubz.bg/.

Kyuchukov, L. (2016). *Impact of the refugee crisis on Bulgarian society and politics: Fears but no hatred.* Sofia: Friedrich Ebert Stiftung.

McCauley, C. and Moskalenko, S. (2008). Mechanisms of political radicalization: Pathways toward terrorism. *Terrorism and Political Violence* 20(3): 415–433.

Mircheva, N. and Zahariev, L. (2013, December 23). Най-значимите събития в България за 2013-та [The most notable events in Bulgaria in 2013]. Икёнёмик БГ, Retrieved from http://www.economic.bg.

Nakova, A. (2011) Динамика на етническите предразсъдъци [Dynamics of social prejudice]. *Social Studies* I (7), 1–7.

Nikolova, Y., Spasov, O. and Daskalova, N. (2016). *Езикът на ёмразата в България: Рискёви зёни, уязвими ёбекти.* [Hate speech in Bulgaria: Risk zones and vulnerable subjects]. Sofia: Center for Policy Modernisation and Foundation Media Democracy.

OPBC. (2014, November 9). Йерархия [Hierarchy]. Retrieved from http://ozbg.bg/yerarhiya/.

OPBC. (n.d.). Дейнёст [Activity]. Retrieved from http://ozbg.bg/deynost/.

Pamporov, A. (2012) *Сёциални дистанции в България в периёда 2008–2012 г. [Social distances in Bulgaria in the period 2008–2012].* Sofia: Bulgarian Helsinki Committee.

Papakochev, G. (2016, July 6). Имат ли Васил Левски и Шипка мястё в България [Do Vasil Levski MU and Shipka BNM a place in Bulgaria]. Дёйче Веле, Retrieved from http://www.dw.com/bg/.

Pashova, A. (n.d.) *"Всички цигани да се преёбразят в българи" /Пёлитики на тёталитарната власт към рёмите в България / 1944–1989г./* ["All Gypsies will be transformed into Bulgarians"/Policies of the totalitarian government towards the Roma in Bulgaria /1944–1989/]. Blagoevgrad: Southwestern University.

Pegida meets with European allies in the Czech Republic. (2016, January 23). *Deutsche Welle*, Retrieved from http://www.dw.com.

Purvanov, K. (2009, May 17). Нёвият шифър на Расате [Rasate's new cypher]. *В. Тема 18* (393).

Rusev, H. (2016, April 2). Динкё ётвъд границата. На закёна [Dinko beyond the boundry. Of the law]. Капитал, Retrieved from https://www.capital.bg.

Shtilianova, T. (2016, April 16) Лёвецът на мигранти Низамёв студент пё правё с 3 присъди [The migrant hunter Nizamov is a law student with three convictions]. *168 часа*, Retrieved from http://www.168chasa.bg.

Stoilova, Z. (2016, April 15). Камуфлажните патриёти на Странджа [Stranzha's camouflage patriots]. *Капитал*, Retrieved from https://www.capital.bg.

Stoyanov, S. (2016, July 8). Паравёенните – игра на вёйници или реална ёпаснёст [The paramilitaries – playing soldier or a real danger]. Инфёрмациёнен център, Министерствё на ётбраната, Retrieved from http://armymedia.bg.

Todorov, A. (2013). *The extreme right wing in Bulgaria*. Sofia: Friedrich Ebert Foundation.

Todorova, K. (2016, October 3). Петър Низамёв–Перата на сбирка на патриёти в Дрезден [Petar Nizamov-Perata attends a meeting of patriots in Dresden]. *24 Часа*, Retrieved from https://www.24chasa.bg/.

Tomlinson, T. (2016, March 10). Bulgarian 'migrant hunter' leads vigilante patrols in armoured vehicles to round up and terrorise refugees along the Turkish border... and boasts 'it's a sport'. *Daily Mail*, Retrieved from http://www.dailymail.co.uk.

Yordanova, M. (2015, January 28) Джебчийките във Варна с брутални заплахи срещу ётрядите (снимки) [The pickpockets in Varna with brutal threats against the volunteer corps (pictures)]. *Днес*, Retrieved from https://www.dnes.bg.

Zankina, E. (2014, January 30) Лявётё и дяснётё в Изтёчна Еврёпа. [The Left and Right in Eastern Europe]. *В. Култура*.

"Алфа Рисърч": Над 50% ёт българите ёдёбряват "гражданските арести" на бежанци [Alpha Research: More than 50% of Bulgarians approve of the "civilian arrests" of refugees]. (2016, April 16). *Капитал*, Retrieved from https://www.capital.bg.

Бёрисёв благёдари на хайките за бежанци, всяка пёмёщ била дёбре дёшла [Borissov thanked refugee patrols, every help is welcomed]. (2016, April 10). *Офнюз*, Retrieved from https://offnews.bg.

Валери Симеёнёв, ПФ: В нашата прёграма имаме залёженё създаванетё на дёбрёвёлни ётряди [Valeri Simeonov, PF: In our program we have included the creation of regulated volunteer corps]. (2016, April 26). *Инфёрмациённа агенция Фёкус*, Retrieved from http://m.focus-news.net/.

Граждански патрул тръгна на лёв за бежанци(видеё) [Civilian patrols go on refugee hunts (video)]. (2016, April 4). *Епицентър*, Retrieved from http://epicenter.bg/.

Здравкё Велев: БНО "Шипка" няма нищё ёбщё с "Нёщни вълци" [Zdravko Velev: BNM Shipka has nothing to do with the Night Wolves]. (2016, July 24). *БНР*, Retrieved from http://bnr.bg/.

Камуфлажни другари [Camouflage comrades]. (2016, October 28). *Капитал*, Retrieved from https://www.capital.bg.

"Лёвецът на мигранти" Петър Низамёв е дёбре пёзнат в пёдземните кръгёве на Бургас [The "migrant hunter" Petar Nizamov is renown in the Burgas underground]. (2016, April 12). *БТВ Нёвините*, Retrieved from http://btvnovinite.bg.

Перата зёве за ётмъщение: "Да гё пребием!". Причаква с приятели Живкё, ритнал зверски възрастна жена в Бургас [Perata calls for retribution: "Let's beat him up!". Waits with friends for Jivko, who severely kicked an elderly woman in Burgas]. (2017, May 18). *168 часа*, Retrieved from http://www.168chasa.bg/.

Прёкуратурата и МВР ще реагират с пёвече пёлицаи срещу "гражданските патрули" [The Prosecution and the Ministry of the Interior will react with more police against the "civilian patrols"]. (2013, November 13). Дневник, Retrieved from https://www.dnevnik.bg/.

Рёми-крадци линчувани в Нёви хан [Roma thieves lynched in Novi Han]. (2016, June 15). *Канал 3*, Retrieved from http://www.kanal3.bg

Appendix I

Acronyms

BHC – Bulgarian Helsinki Committee
BNM Shipka – Bulgarian National Movement Shipka
BNU – Bulgarian National Union
BNU-ND – Bulgarian National Union – New Democracy
CNS – Committee for National Salvation
CSPWF – Civil Squads for the Protection of Women and the Faith
EU – European Union
IMIR – International Center for Minority Studies and Intercultural Relations
IMRO – BNM – Internal Macedonian Revolutionary Organization – Bulgarian National Movement
ISI – Institute for Social Integration
MoI – Ministry of Interior
MU Vasil Levski – Military Union Vasil Levski
NFSB – National Front for the Salvation of Bulgaria
NGO – Non-governmental Organization
OPBC – Organization for the Protection of Bulgarian Citizens
PEGIDA – Patriotic Europeans against the Islamization of the West
PF – Patriotic Front
SANS – State Agency for National Security

11

VIGILANTISM IN GREECE

The case of the Golden Dawn

Christos Vrakopoulos and Daphne Halikiopoulou

Introduction

This chapter focuses on vigilantism in Greece. Specifically, it examines the Golden Dawn, a group that beyond engaging in vigilante activities is also the third biggest political party in the country. The Golden Dawn is distinct from a number of other European parties broadly labelled under the 'far right' umbrella in that it was formed as a violent grass-roots movement by far-right activists, its main activities prior to 2012 confined to the streets. It can be described as a vigilante group, which frequently uses violence, engages in street politics, has a strong focus on community-based activities, and whose members perceive themselves as 'street soldiers'. Since 2013 a number of its leading cadres, who are also members of the Greek parliament, have been undergoing trial for maintaining a criminal organization and other criminal acts including murder and grievous bodily harm.

The progressive entrenchment of this group in the Greek political system has raised a number of questions about its potential implications on the nature of democracy and policy-making. This chapter examines various dimensions of the Golden Dawn's vigilante activities. Following a brief overview of the Greek socio-political context, it proceeds to examine the party's ideology, its organizational structure, its various operations, communications activities and relationships with other political actors and groups in Greece.

The political, social and economic environment

Political violence and the history of vigilantism in Greece

Vigilante and paramilitary activities have a long tradition in Modern Greek history. According to Psychogios (2013), political violence, including terrorism, clashes between protesters and the police, and neo-Nazi racist attacks, is not infrequent in Greece because it is ingrained in Greek political culture. The civil war (1946–1949) and military junta (1967–1975) are pertinent examples of political violence. Vigilantism during these periods was primarily aimed, not against ethnic minorities or migrants, but against political opponents. For example, the military regime often targeted political dissidents, and in turn left-wing activist groups and/ or individuals perpetuated violent acts directed against the regime (Voglis 2011). The legacy of both events has been the maintenance of this culture of violence that characterizes Greek society, as political consensus among political parties remained at a minimum level after the restoration of democracy (Papasarantopoulos, 2014).

Vigilantism during the metapolitefsi era

The period between the restoration of democracy in 1974 and the eruption of the economic crisis in 2008 was characterized by relative political stability. Nonetheless, the adversarial nature of Greek politics maintained the deeply engrained culture of confrontation. During this period, the Greek political system was characterized by a competition between two main parties, the centre-left Panhellenic Socialist Movement (PASOK) and the centre-right New Democracy (ND), which together occupied the majority of the 300 seats in the Greek Parliament (Vasilopoulou and Halikiopoulou, 2013). Most small parties were excluded from parliamentary representation and vigilante activities took place mainly on the streets.

During this era, political violence was perpetrated by vigilante groups of both the right and the left, some targeting political opponents and others targeting minorities. Most notably, right-wing extremist groups during the early metapolifsi era (1970s and 1980s) targeted mostly the so-called 'internal enemies' (Psarras 2012), i.e. left-wing activists. Michaloliakos, the leader of the Golden Dawn, was a protagonist in those attacks. Notable examples include an attack against five journalists during the funeral of a well-known military junta supporter police officer; a series of bomb explosions in various areas of Athens, most importantly in two cinemas that showed Union of Soviet Socialist Republics (USSR) movies on the 4th anniversary of the restoration of Democracy. Michaloliakos was arrested in both instances (Psarras 2012). During the 1990s, and after the creation of the Golden Dawn, attacks against internal enemies as well as against migrants, increased. Psarras (2012) identifies at least 27 violent attacks against left-wing individuals, workers and immigrants by members of the Golden Dawn. Also, after the collapse of the USSR and the Warsaw Pact, there was an influx of immigrants from those countries, mostly Albanians, who suffered from a large number of racial attacks (Lazaridis and Skleparis, 2015). An example is the mass attacks against Albanians after an international football game between Greece and Albania (Karamanidou, 2016).

Vigilantism post-2008: the Golden Dawn and the Greek crisis

The eruption of the economic crisis in 2008 altered the dynamics of party competition, as it resulted in a grand coalition between PASOK, ND and the far right Popular Orthodox Rally (LAOS). During this period, the Greek government signed the first Memorandum of Understanding with the European Union (EU) and the International Monetary Fund (IMF), which offered Greece financial aid and set economic policy conditionality between the country and its creditors (Vasilopoulou et al., 2014). This Memorandum became the target of a number of small, anti-establishment Greek parties, which blamed it for the accentuation of the economic crisis because of the austerity measures that accompanied it. As a result, in 2012 representation increased for small parties. A total of seven parties entered parliament, including the Golden Dawn. This trend continued in the 2014 European Parliament elections and the subsequent January and September 2015 national elections, indicating the party has consolidated a secure voting base of circa 6–7%.

Therefore, Greece's severe economic crisis was in many ways pivotal for the changing dynamics in Greek politics. What is key about the Greek case, however, is the extent to which the economic crisis became translated into a problem of governance and a broader crisis of legitimacy and democratic representation (Halikiopoulou and Vasilopoulou 2018), indicated by lack of trust in political institutions and an overall dissatisfaction with democracy. Notably, trust in political parties, trust in government and parliament, and satisfaction with democracy declined dramatically in the period between 2007 and 2013, dropping well below the EU average (European Commission, 2018) (for details, see Appendix A1).

At the same time, trust in institutions that employ violence, such as the army and the police, remain high in Greece. Notably, trust in the army and trust in the police both increased during the period 2010–2014. This is a broader illustration of support for authoritarianism, which partly explains the authoritarian attitudes expressed in the support for Golden Dawn. The political crisis in Greece was not just a rejection of the established political parties, but rather a rejection of the political system as a whole (Halikiopoulou and Vasilopoulou 2018), which created fertile ground not only for smaller parties in general, but specifically vigilante groups defined by authoritarian attitudes and an endorsement of violence.

Immigration and the treatment of minorities in Greece

The deeply engrained culture of violence (Psarras 2012) as well as support for authoritarian values and nationalism (Fragkoudaki 2013) are often manifested in a deep-seated intolerance against a number of minority groups, including homosexuals, people with left-leaning attitudes, members of other religions and different ethnic groups. The treatment of minorities in Greece has often been criticized by international human rights organizations, including Human Rights Watch and Amnesty International (Human Rights Watch, 2013). This discrimination intensified post-2012, partly legitimated by the fact that violent, vigilante groups such as the Golden Dawn enjoyed parliamentary representation. This can be illustrated by both non-institutionalized activities that have taken place on the streets, such as the events that unfolded outside the Hytirio theatre in Athens in 2012, when a Greek theatre company was verbally and physically abused by members of the public, Golden Dawn MPs and members of the Greek Orthodox Church for attempting to stage a version of Terence McNally's Corpus Christi; and in the institutionalized form of discriminatory policies, for example 'Hospitable Zeus', a policy introduced in 2012 as part of an initiative to reduce the number of illegal immigrants. The racism and overt discrimination characterising the policy have led to severe criticisms with regards to the extent to which human rights are respected in Greece (Vasilopoulou and Halikiopoulou, 2015). These examples suggest that attitudes towards minorities may be understood as part of a broader xenophobia that pervades Greek political culture (Lazaridis and Skleparis, 2015).

It is important to note that this scepticism and intolerance towards minorities is to a degree separate from actual levels of immigration in Greece. While this issue has been increasing in salience across Europe, and constitutes one of the key factors to which the rise of the far right is attributed in a series of comparative studies (see e.g. Ivarsflaten 2008; Inglehart and Norris 2016), in Greece, immigration figures are generally low compared to other European countries, and actually declined during the period of economic crisis (see Appendix A1). In addition, research on party manifestos before and after the eruption of the crisis has shown that immigration is not one of the three most salient issues in the Golden Dawn's agenda (Halikiopoulou et al., 2016). Indeed, immigration is ranked as the 4th or 5th most important issue facing the country from 2005 onwards (European Commission, 2018).

With regards to the refugee crisis, Greece is one of the most greatly affected countries in Europe. Between April 2015 and September 2015 Greece received approximately 400,000 new asylum seekers (Dinas et al. 2017). Exposure to the refugee crisis was much greater in certain islands of the eastern Aegean, given their proximity to the Turkish coast, such as Lesvos, which during the same period received over 200,000 asylum seekers (ibid.: 2). Research illustrates that in those Greek islands that faced a massive inflow of refugees just before the September 2015 election, vote shares for Golden Dawn did indeed increase, but only moderately, by 2 percentage points (Dinas et al., 2017). Beyond voting patterns, refugee camps in islands such as Lesvos have frequently become the target of extreme right-wing violence (see e.g. ekathimerini.com, 2018).

The ideology and organizational structure of the Golden Dawn: justification and motivation

Given the centrality of violence in both its ideology and practices, the Golden Dawn can be described as a vigilante group. The party endorses 'the collective use of extra-legal violence' (Moncada, 2017) and fulfils most of Johnston's (1996) criteria for vigilantism, including the planning of the act of violence, the voluntary participation by private citizens, the exercise of autonomous citizenship and the use and frequent threat of violence. More specifically, in accordance to Moncada's (2017) classification, the Golden Dawn acts as a vigilante group in terms of its social organization, identified targets, its repertoire, justification and motivation. In terms of social organization, the planning and execution of vigilante activities take place at the group level, involving leading cadres of the party and members. In terms of targets, in accordance with its Nazi ideology (see below), the Golden Dawn identifies two sets of enemies, internal and external. The former are usually members of left-wing groups and organizations; the latter are immigrants or refugees. In terms of its repertoire, the party adopts both lethal and non-lethal tactics, which include a range of physical and psychological forms of violence. The justification lies in nationalism (Vasilopoulou and Halikiopoulou, 2015); and their motivation, more narrowly, can be found in the party's palingenetic (Griffin, 1991) vision: i.e. the need to cleanse the Greek nation of its internal and external enemies, so to facilitate its rebirth.

Its leader, Nikolaos Michaloliakos, founded the Golden Dawn in 1980 as a bulletin (Bistis, 2013), which openly supported Nazism (Hasapopoulos, 2013). Although the party has increasingly denied the 'Nazi' label, promoting itself instead as a Greek Nationalist Party (Ellinas, 2013; Psarras, 2012; Vasilopoulou and Halikiopoulou, 2015), its ideology fulfils all the criteria for what constitutes a fascist, and specifically Nazi, group (Halikiopoulou and Vasilopoulou, 2015). In line with Mann's (2004) definition of fascism, the Golden Dawn is pan-nationalist, authoritarian, statist, and militarist. It seeks to transcend social cleavages and cleanse the nation of internal (i.e. political dissidents) and external (i.e. those not belonging to the 'organic' nation) enemies (Vasilopoulou and Halikiopoulou, 2015). The two key ideological themes in its programmatic agenda include a focus on societal degeneration and a proposed final solution, which encompasses the necessity for national rebirth through a collective movement from below. In other words, while the party itself may reject the Nazi label, it nonetheless espouses all core Nazi principles.

Nationalism is a central principle in the Golden Dawn's ideology and the basis of justification of its violent and vigilante activities. In its manifesto the party makes clear that to be a member of Golden Dawn one must accept the principle of establishing the state in accordance with nationalism, which it defines in ethnic-organic terms as the supremacy of the 'ethnos-race' (Vasilopoulou and Halikiopoulou, 2015: 55). In this regard the party places great emphasis on biological and ascriptive determinants of national belonging, including blood, genealogy, race and common ancestry. The party's nationalism is linked to its palingenetic vision (Griffin, 1991; Vasilopoulou and Halikiopoulou, 2015), i.e. the need for the Greek nation to be reborn from the ashes of the old degenerate order for which corrupt domestic and external elites are responsible. It presents itself as the saviour and defender of the Greek nation, which is unique and superior to all other nations (Vasilopoulou and Halikiopoulou, 2015: 71). The party is racist and indiscriminately anti-immigrant, portraying all others as 'barbarians' who must be cleansed so that the nation can be reborn.

The party's organizational structure reflects its ideology. It can best be described as a top-down political organization (Ellinas and Lamprianou, 2017a), highly concentrated, strictly hierarchical and militaristic (The Economist, 2013). As noted above, the Golden Dawn openly endorses and employs violence. Militarism is key to the Golden Dawn in both ideological and organizational terms. The party sees the army as the ultimate value, both because it is the protector of national security and because it embodies the ultimate value of collective sacrifice for the nation (Vasilopoulou and Halikiopoulou, 2015: 61). Members are seen as 'street soldiers' fighting for the nationalist cause. They are known for the organization of local paramilitary groupings, which train and carry our raids against a variety of target groups, including immigrants, Roma groups and left-wing groups (Hasapopoulos, 2013; Vasilopoulou and Halikiopoulou, 2015).

Golden Dawn's organization expanded after the party's entry in the Greek parliament in 2012. From just 4 local organizations in Athens, Thessaloniki, Piraeus and Kalamata in previous years, the party had developed a total of 69 local branches and 9 local cells across the Greek territory in 2015 (Ellinas and Lamprianou, 2017a). Their activities also increased, with 3594 recorded during the 2012–2015 period (Ellinas and Lamprianou, 2017a).

Many Golden Dawn members and leading cadres of the party, including the leader Nikolaos Michaloliakos, are well known for their activities in the right-wing extremist community and have criminal records (Psarras, 2012). Many were previously members of the extreme right party August 4th, which was dissolved in 1977, and also of the National Political Union that openly supported the extreme right junta regime. Michaloliakos has been linked to a series of bombings in bookstores that sell books related to Soviet Union and cinemas showing 'left-leaning' movies (Hasapopoulos, 2013: 13); he was arrested for possession of weapons and bombs in 1976, when he spent ten months in prison (Psarras, 2012). The more recent examples of the criminal activities and records of Golden Dawn officials are discussed in the 'Operations and activities' section of this chapter.

Support and membership

Electoral support: According to the vast literature on far-right voting behaviour, certain socio-demographic and attitudinal characteristics are shared by far right voters. Far-right supporters tend to be economically and culturally insecure voters with authoritarian attitudes, often disillusioned with the system and untrusting of democratic institutions (e.g. Norris, 2005). Far-right supporters are most commonly male, either unemployed or in precarious employment. They tend to be working class and/ or low-income individuals who compete with immigrants for jobs and social status (Lucassen and Lubbers, 2012) and they have low levels of education. They are the losers of modernization (Kriesi et al., 2006), those most vulnerable to social change who have come to resent the political establishment that left them behind. An examination of the Golden Dawn voter profile shows some consistency with the findings of this broad literature, but also some differences, notably in terms of the socio-demographic dimension. Using data from the Hellenic Panel Component of the 2014 European Election Study (EES), Vasilopoulou and Halikiopoulou (2015) find that attitudinal variables are more significant in determining the propensity for the Golden Dawn than socio-demographic variables. The Golden Dawn voter is unlikely to have a university degree, is highly disaffected by the political system, has little trust in the government and most likely belongs to the right of the political spectrum (Vasilopoulou and Halikiopoulou, 2015:47–48). Lamprianou and Ellinas (2017) confirm that economic grievances have a limited, and cultural grievances a moderate, effect on GD voting, while the strongest correlates of GD voting are those capturing institutional grievances.

In terms of socio-demographic variables, we know from the June 2012 exit poll (Georgiadou, 2013) that the voters of the party are mainly male (76%) and 44 years old or younger. The September 2015 exit poll shows a similar picture (www.metronanalysis.gr). Interestingly, Golden Dawn supporters vary across different occupations (Vasilopoulou and Halikiopoulou, 2015). The only occupations that the Golden Dawn is underrepresented amongst are pensioners and housewives, which is also captured from the gender and age group categories. The fact that Golden Dawn's supporters come from a broad range of occupational sectors is in contrast with the main findings from the existing literature on extreme-right voting and supports the political grievance model.

Membership: Data with regards to the membership of the organization is less readily available. As the Golden Dawn is an official political party with fairly broad electoral support, it would be incorrect to assume that all its voters automatically take part in vigilante activities. This requires a closer look at the party's membership. To a great extent, the composition of Golden Dawn's membership confirms the 'angry white men' paradigm (Bistis, 2013; Psarras, 2012). The majority of members are males under the age of 50. Female membership, however, has been increasing, with a substantial number of women having joined the party (REF). In terms of gender representation, women tend to have their own Golden Dawn forums where they come together to discuss issues and organize a variety of activities (e.g. White Women Front: www.whitewomenfront.blogspot.uk)

Operations and activities

The Golden Dawn operates on three different levels: as a political party, as a protest and pressure group and as a vigilante group. While it adopts violence at all levels, only in the latter can its activities be explicitly described as vigilante. We may also distinguish between those activities the party undertakes indoors to communicate with activists and those it organizes outdoors to communicate with voters (Ellinas and Lamprianou, 2017b). In terms of its activities as a political party, the Golden Dawn runs in national, European and local elections. Despite its participation in democratic procedures, the party is generally critical of democracy and disrespectful of democratic institutions. The party's dismissal of liberal democracy is reflected by the behaviour of Golden Dawn MPs in parliament and their disrespect of other elected officials. Examples abound. Following their election, the party leader and leading cadres performed a Nazi salute upon their entry in Parliament. During the same year and in a public display of violence, Ilias Kasidiaris threw a glass of water on SYRIZA MP Rena Dourou and slapped KKE MP Liana Kaneli live on Greek television (Telegraph.co.uk, 2012).In 2016, Golden Dawn MEP Lampros Fountoulis violently interrupted an event organized to discuss the situation with ethnic Turks living in Thrace (Crisp, 2016). In 2017, Golden Dawn party spokesman Ilias Kasidiaris attacked ND MP Nikos Dendias on the pretext that the latter walked in front of him while Kasidiaris was talking (Ekathimerini.com, 2017). And, in June 2018 Golden Dawn MP Konstantinos Barbarousis called for a military coup d'état during his talk in Parliament on the Macedonia question (Kathimerini. gr, 2018). The MP was subsequently charged with treason and arrested.

In terms of protest and pressure group activities, the Golden Dawn is highly active, especially following its electoral success in 2012. For example, Ellinas and Lamprianou (2017a) show that, within the time span of three years, the party organized a total of 3594 activities, including speeches and 'debates' where Golden Dawn members discuss current affairs, historical and ideological issues and electoral campaigns; political activities, such as celebrations, demonstrations and even camps and exercises for their members; and social charity activities, such as the organization of job centres, food and clothes collections, blood donations (Ellinas and Lamprianou, 2017a). It is important to note here that these latter activities were intended only for Greeks, a status to be confirmed by the presentation of a Greek identity card to one of the Golden Dawn members on site, and are part of a broader Golden Dawn initiative to offer an alternative service of state and welfare provisions reminiscent of the Nazi 'Winterhilfswerk' (Vasilopoulou and Halikiopoulou, 2015).

In terms of its vigilante activities, Golden Dawn members have been consistently involved in violent acts since the group's establishment. The group was notorious for a range of violent acts in the 1980s, 1990s and 2000s. Group members often wear black uniforms and military trousers, reflecting the group's military-style organization, in an attempt to instil fear. As noted above, their targets are those groups they identify as internal and external enemies; in other words, left-wing activists and immigrants. An exhaustive list of recorded cases would take up the space of this entire chapter. An indicative list of well-known cases includes the murder of left-wing student Dimitris Kousouris in 1998; numerous attacks against immigrants and pro-immigrant organizations; threats and vandalism at the Chytirio theatre in Athens in 2012 to 'protest' against the staging of the play 'Corpus Christi'; the murder of the 26-year-old Pakistani immigrant Shehzad Luqman, who was stabbed by members of Golden Dawn in Athens in 2013 (To Vima, 2015); and the murder of left-wing activist Pavlos Fyssas in 2013, which triggered the arrest of 20 or so Golden Dawn MPs.

Golden Dawn operations continue. They patrol neighbourhoods in order to provide security to Greeks and carry out attacks. They even carry out visits to workplaces to encourage employers to hire Greeks instead of foreign workers

(Margaronis, 2012). Since the emergence of the refugee crisis, Golden Dawn members introduced another vigilante activity, which is common in other countries, namely boat patrols, to push back the refugees who try to enter Greece from the Aegean Sea (Xchange.org). Despite the notoriety of their violent activities and pending indictment, the Golden Dawn continues to run for election as its leading cadres continue to serve as elected representatives.

Communication activities: Golden Dawn propaganda offline and online

The Golden Dawn has a very elaborate propaganda strategy. The party is particularly active in disseminating its message, both verbally and visually, through online and offline means of communication. The message they try to convey is the following: the Golden Dawn is a Greek nationalist party, not a Nazi party. While, for example, the party's logo (see Figure 11.1 below) is reminiscent of the Nazi Swastika (Halikiopoulou and Vasilopoulou, 2015), the Golden Dawn itself insists it is the Meander – an ancient Greek symbol – and completely unrelated to Nazism. As noted above however, despite the party's denial of Nazism, its ideology and practices well fit all the criteria of what constitutes a Nazi group. Like other Nazi organizations, the group sees its ultimate goal as the eradication of the corrupt social order through the cleansing of the nation's enemies. The Phoenix-like rebirth of the Greek nation from its ashes can only be made possible through the Golden Dawn, a movement from below which embodies the Greek nation and whose mission is to salvage it from extinction and restore its former glory (Vasilopoulou and Halikiopoulou, 2015). Their motto, 'blood and honour' is a well-known Nazi motto; their organization of soup kitchens and blood donations are

FIGURE 11.1 The Golden Dawn logo

reminiscent of the Nazi 'Winterhilfswerk'; and their practice of standing and saluting the leader upon entry is clearly a Nazi practice.

In terms of its online presence, the Golden Dawn has a frequently updated website (http://www.xryshaygh.com) whose prime aim is to disseminate the party's nationalist message and justify its stance on a broad range of issues. The website is elaborate, with a series of sub-sections including the party's positions and manifesto, news and current affairs, history, local government and EP party activities. There is a special 'dedications' page, which offers short articles on Greek historical events, prominent Greek figures and popular heroes as well a commemorative texts on anniversary dates for important national events. Online pages are updated on a regular basis, and it is clear the Golden Dawn invests time and resources for these activities. News and current affairs are framed in terms of nationalism, taking advantage of various issues such as events to do with the country's relationship with Turkey and FYROM/Macedonia among others. Interestingly there are many references to Cyprus and the activities of the Cypriot sister party to the Golden Dawn – ELAM. The Golden Dawn also has a radio station (radio.antepithesi.gr) and publishes a number of bulletins, magazines and newspapers that can also be accessed online, including ethnikismos.net, and https://emprosnews.wordpress.com. Finally, the party has set up a number of online and on-site stores where one can purchase a range of paraphernalia including books often authored by Golden Dawn members, flags, calendars mugs, T-shirts, jewellery and key rings with the party's logo (http://www.xakatastima.gr).

Relationship to political groups and public agencies

Overall, other actors have progressively marginalized the Golden Dawn in the Greek system. Initially, after the party's election in parliament, its reception was varied with some political groups actively opposing it and others not taking an active stance. It was only after the murder of left-wing activist Pavlos Fyssas and the in-depth examination of the case from the police, that the Golden Dawn started facing a more repressive environment. This has a visible impact on party activities. For example, the number of activities the group organized after the 2013 arrest was halved, from 200 activities per month prior to 2013 to 100 (Ellinas and Lamprianou, 2017a). However, the party has retained its electoral support, which, considering the increasingly repressive environment the party operates in, as well as the fact that it hardly campaigned for the 2015 elections because of imprisonment and impending trial, is alarming.

Because of its anti-democratic profile and links to violence, no other political party in Greece has agreed to co-operate or enter a coalition with the Golden Dawn. The party does not participate in any European Parliament group. It is affiliated with the Alliance for Peace and Freedom (APF), which is an alliance of ultranationalist far right parties and politicians including the German National Democratic Party (NPD), Italy's Roberto Fiore, the leader of Italy's Forza Nuova (FN), and Nick Griffin, the former leader of the British National Party (BNP).

With regards to the media, the party is often no-platformed. This, however, was not always the case. Following the initial success in Athens mayoral elections in 2010, mainstream media began to pay attention to the Golden Dawn as a political party, frequently covering stories about its members and activities. Much of this initial media focus was on the Golden Dawn's charity activities, for example the blood donations and soup kitchens, while completely ignoring the party's vigilante activities and attacks against immigrants and left-wing activists (Prinos, 2014; Kandylis and Kavoulakos , 2011). Often the media even indirectly promoted the Golden Dawn, portraying its members as modern day Robin Hoods – muscular skinheads in uniforms whose main goal was to protect the vulnerable members of the Greek population from the criminal activities that mass immigration brought to Greece and thus restore law and order (TVXS, 2014). This changed after 2013, following a series of incidents, which exposed the violent tendencies of Golden Dawn members, including Ilias Kasidiaris' attack against KKE MP Liana Kaneli and SYRIZA MP Rena Dourou live on Greek television (Gilani, 2012).

Last but not least, it is important to discuss the relationship between the Golden Dawn and the police, which remains a matter of contention in Greece and has attracted a lot of attention. This issue is sensitive and data is scarce. It is often suggested that the Golden Dawn is particularly appealing to the police. Police officers tend to be Golden Dawn supporters and constituencies with high numbers of police voters tend to turn around higher Golden Dawn results. For example, in their study of police voting behaviour in Athens, Papanicolaou and Papageorgiou (2016) find that Golden Dawn's presence has been much more emphatic among police personnel than among the general public. In addition, according to the Golden Dawn itself, the number of police officers who voted for the party during both 2015 elections was approximately 60% (Golden Dawn, 2015). Beyond voting preferences, the Greek police has frequently been criticized for entrenched racism, endemic violence and unlawful conduct, sometimes linked with Golden Dawn activities. In December 2013, among those arrested alongside with Golden Dawn officials were two police officers; ten police officers were found to have direct or indirect links with criminal activities attributed to Golden Dawn members (Amnesty International, 2014). However, systematic data on this issue is absent.

Far-right vigilante activities beyond the Golden Dawn

From 2015 onwards two new extreme-right vigilante groups appeared in Greece, namely Cryptheia and C18. Both groups appear to be affiliated with the Golden Dawn (Krithari, 2018) Specifically, Cryptheia is a vigilante group created after a breakaway from the Golden Dawn (Dettmer, 2017). The group's purpose is to force all migrants and refugees out of Greece (Dettmer, 2017). The group became known after an attack against the residence of an 11-year-old Afghan boy, just because the boy was selected by his school to carry the Greek flag at a national parade (Dettmer, 2017). Members of Cryptheia also claimed responsibility for an arson attack in a refugee centre in Athens' town centre (Daily Sabah, 2018). With regards to the C18, this is another neo-Nazi vigilante group, whose members have participated in approximately 30 attacks against leftists, anarchists and others (Krithari, 2018). Some have linked this group with the Golden Dawn, as they stress that C18 replaced Golden Dawn, after the Golden Dawn's trial started (Krithari, 2018).

The actions of these groups can be subsumed under the concept of vigilantism as they meet Johnston's (1996) criteria mentioned earlier in this article, including the planning, use and frequent threat of violence. Such groups often attempt to take law enforcement upon themselves (Heitmeyer, 2005). For example, Cryptheia's objection to a non-native carrying the Greek flag for whatever reason, led to the violent attack against the residence of the 11-year-old Afghan boy. In addition, their attack against the Athens refugee centre is premised on their refusal to accept the existence of migrants or refugees in Greek territory. Finally, C18's attacks against leftists and anarchists are premised on the alleged inability of the legal system – and law enforcement – to prevent building occupations.

Conclusion

Far-right vigilante groups, operating at the street level, are not uncommon. The Greek case is particularly interesting, however, as the main vigilante group against migrants and refugees is also the third biggest party in the Greek parliament. The rise of the Golden Dawn can be seen as part of a broader trend towards the far right across Europe. At the same time it is set apart from other European far right parties precisely because of its vigilante nature and activities: the party openly endorses and uses violence, which it justifies on the basis of its racist and organic nationalist ideology. What is striking about the Golden Dawn is the extent to which it continues to generate electoral support despite the notoriety of its vigilante activities, the imprisonment of its leading cadres and its impending trial.

Note

1 All the data on trust gathered from the European Commission, as it is yearly and also comparable to the other European Union countries.

References

Amnesty International (2014, April 3). Impunity, excessive force and links to extremist Golden Dawn blight Greek police. Retrieved from https://www.amnesty.org/en/latest/news/2014/04/impunity-excessive-force-and-links-extremist-golden-dawn-blight-greek-police/ [accessed 25 January2018].

Bistis, G. (2013). Golden Dawn or democratic sunset: The rise of the far right in Greece. *Mediterranean Quarterly*, 24(3), 35–55. Retrieved from http://muse.jhu.edu/journals/med/summary/v024/24.3.bistis.html.

Crisp, J. (2016, March 3). Golden Dawn thugs disrupt European Parliament meeting. [online] EURACTIV.com. Retrieved from: https://www.euractiv.com/section/eu-priorities-2020/news/golden-dawn-thugs-disrupt-european-parliament-meeting/ [Accessed 11 Dec. 2017].

Daily Sabah. (2018, March 24). Neo-Nazi group claims responsibility for arson attack on Afghan refugee center in Greece. Retrieved from: https://www.dailysabah.com/europe/2018/03/24/neo-nazi-group-claims-responsibility-for-arson-attack-on-afghan-refugee-center-in-greece [Accessed 25 Jun. 2018].

Dettmer, J. (2017, November 8). Gang with suspected neo-Nazi links vows to force migrants from Greece. VOA. Retrieved from: https://www.voanews.com/a/gang-with-suspected-neo-nazi-links-vows-to-force-migrants-from-greece/4106386.html [Accessed 25 Jun. 2018].

Dinas, E., K. Matakos, D. Xefteris and D. Hangartner (2017), *Waking up the Golden Dawn: Does exposure to the refugee crisis increase support for extreme-right parties?*. mimeo.

Ekathimerini.com. (2017, June 15). GD ejected from House after spokesman assaults Dendias | Kathimerini. Retrieved from: http://www.ekathimerini.com/218445/article/ekathimerini/news/gd-ejected-from-house-after-spokesman-assaults-dendias [Accessed 30 Jan. 2018].

Ekathimerini.com. (2018, 23 April) Far-right hooligans attack migrants on Lesvos, turn town into battle ground. Retrieved from: http://www.ekathimerini.com/227956/article/ekathimerini/news/far-right-hooligans-attack-migrants-on-lesvos-turn-town-into-battleground [accessed 7 August 2018].

Ellinas, A.A. (2013) The rise of Golden Dawn: The new face of the far right in Greece. *South European Society and Politics*, 18(4), 543–565.

Ellinas, A.A. and Lamprianou, I. (2017a) How far right local party organizations develop: The organizational buildup of the Greek Golden Dawn, *Party Politics*, 23(6), 804–820

Ellinas, A.A. and Lamprianou, I. (2017b), Far right activism and electoral outcomes, *Party Politics*, First Published September 8, 2017.

European Commission. (2018). Public Opinion – European Commission. Retrieved from: http://ec.europa.eu/commfrontoffice/publicopinion/index.cfm/Chart/index [Accessed 16 Jan. 2018].

Fragkoudaki, A. (2013) *Ο εθνικισμός και η άνοδος της ακροδεξιάς (Nationalism and the rise of the extreme right)*. Athens: Alexandria.

Georgiadou, V. (2013). Right-wing populism and extremism: The rapid rise of "Golden Dawn" in crisis-ridden Greece. In: R. Melzer and S. Serafin, ed., *Right-wing extremism in Europe: Country analyses, counter-strategies and labor-market oriented exit strategies*. (pp. 75–102) Berlin: Friedrich-Ebert-Stiftung.

Gilani, N. (2012, June 11). Far-right Greek MP who punched woman in the face on live TV sues his victims for defamation. *Mail Online*. Retrieved from: http://www.dailymail.co.uk/news/article-2157770/Ilias-Kasidiaris-Greek-MP-punched-woman-face-live-TV-sues-victims.html [Accessed 16 Jan. 2018].

Golden Dawn. (2015, September 22). Υψηλά ποσοστά της Χρυσής Αυγής στα τμήματα που ψήφισαν οι Έλληνες αστυνομικοί. Retrieved from: http://www.xryshaygh.com/enimerosi/view/sarwse-gia-allh-mia-fora-h-chrush-augh-sta-swmata-asfaleias [Accessed 16 Jan. 2018].

Golden Dawn. (2018). Golden Dawn | Information. Retrieved from: http://www.xryshaygh.com/en/information [Accessed 16 Jan. 2018].

Griffin, R. (1991) *The nature of fascism*. London: Routledge.

Halikiopoulou, D. and Vasilopoulou, S. (2015, June 23) Why the Golden Dawn is a neo-Nazi party. *The Huffington Post*, https://www.huffingtonpost.co.uk/daphne-halikiopoulou/golden-dawn_b_7643868.html [last accessed 26 June2018].

Halikiopoulou, D., K. Nanou and Vasilopoulou, S. (2016) Changing the policy agenda? The impact of the Golden Dawn on Greek party politics, *Hellenic Observatory Papers on Greece and Southeast Europe*, GreeSE Paper No.103.

Halikiopoulou, D., and Vasilopoulou, S. (2018). Breaching the social contract: Crises of democratic representation and patterns of extreme right party support. *Government and Opposition*, 53(1), 26–50. doi:10.1017/gov.2015.43.

Hasapopoulos, N. (2013) *Golden Dawn: The history, the people and the truth*. Athens: Livani (in Greek).

Heitmeyer, W. (2005). Right-wing terrorism. In T. Bjørgo, *Root causes of terrorism : myths, reality and ways forward*. Oxford: Routledge.

Human Rights Watch. 2013. Greece: Abusive crackdown on migrants. Retrieved July 19, 2013 (http://www.hrw.org/news/2013/06/12/greece-abusive-crackdown-migrants).

Inglehart, Ronald and Pippa Norris. 2016. *Trump, Brexit, and the rise of populism: Economic have-nots and cultural backlash*. Harvard Kennedy School Faculty Research Working Paper Series [accessed on 26/01/17].

Ivarsflaten, E. (2008). What unites right-wing populists in Western Europe? Re- examining grievance mobilization models in seven successful cases. *Comparative Political Studies*, 41, 3–23.

Johnston, L. (1996) What is vigilantism? *British Journal of Criminology*, 36(2), 220–236. doi: doi:10.1093/oxfordjournals.bjc.a014083.

Kandylis, G. and Kavoulakos, K. (2011) Framing urban inequalities: Racist mobilization against immigrants in Athens. *The Greek Review of Social Research*, 136, Special Issue, 157–176.

Karamanidou, L. (2016). Violence against migrants in Greece: Beyond the Golden Dawn. *Ethnic and Racial Studies, 39*(11), 2002–2021. doi: doi:10.1080/01419870.2015.1124124

Kathimerini.gr. (2018, June 15). Επεισόδιο με βουλευτή της Χρυσής Αυγής στην Ολομέλεια (βίντεο) | Kathimerini. Retrieved from: http://www.kathimerini.gr/969574/gallery/epikairothta/politikh/epeisodio-me-voyleyth-ths-xryshs-ayghs-sthn-olomeleia-vinteo [Accessed 26 Jun. 2018].

Kriesi, H., Grande, E., Lachat, R., Dolezal, M., Bornschier, S., and Frey, T. (2006) Globalisation and transformation of the national political space: Six European countries compared. *European Journal of Political Research, 45*(6): 921–956.

Krithari, E. (2018, March 24). Tracing fascist crime online: How Greek bloggers exposed neo-Nazis. Medium. Retrieved from: https://medium.com/athenslivegr/tracing-fascist-crime-online-how-greek-bloggers-exposed-neo-nazis-9d9a36eaac16 [Accessed 25 Jun. 2018].

Lamprianou, I. and Ellinas, AA. (2017) Institutional grievances and right-wing extremism: Voting for Golden Dawn in Greece, *South European Society and Politics*, 22(1), 43–60.

Lazaridis, G., and Skleparis, D. (2015). Securitization of migration and the far right: The case of Greek security professionals. *International Migration*, 54(2), 176–192. doi: 10.1111/imig.12219.

Lucassen, G. and M. Lubbers. 2012. Who fears what? Explaining Far-right-wing preference in Europe by distinguishing perceived cultural and economic ethnic threats. *Comparative Political Studies*, 45(5), 547–574.

Mann, M. (2004) *Fascists*. Cambridge: Cambridge University Press.

Margaronis, M. (2012, October 26). Fear and loathing in Athens: The rise of Golden Dawn and the far right. Retrieved from: https://www.theguardian.com/world/2012/oct/26/golden-dawn-greece-far-right.

Moncada, E. (2017) Varieties of vigilantism: Conceptual discord, meaning and strategies, *Global Crime*, 18(4), 403–423.

Norris, P. (2005). *Radical right: Voters and parties in the electoral market*. Cambridge: Cambridge University Press.

OECD (2018a), Foreign-born population (indicator). doi: doi:10.1787/5a368e1b-en (Accessed on 16 January 2018).

OECD (2018b), Permanent immigrant inflows (indicator). doi: doi:10.1787/304546b6-en (Accessed on 16 January 2018).

Papanicolaou, G. and Papageorgiou, I. (2016) The police and the far right in Greece: a case study of police voting behaviour in Athens. *Crime, Law and Social Change* 66: 397. https://doi.org/10.1007/s10611-016-9633-7.

Papasarantopoulos, P. (2014). *Εξτρεμισμός και Πολιτική Βία στην Ελλάδα (Extremism and Political Violence in Greece)*. Thessaloniki: Epikentro.

Psarras, D. (2012) *The black bible of Golden Dawn*, Athens: Polis, (in Greek).

Psychogios, D. (2013). *Η πολιτική βία στην ελληνική κοινωνία (The political violence in greek society)*. Thessaloniki: Epikentro.

Smith, H. (2013, October 3). Golden Dawn leader jailed ahead of Greek criminal trial. *The Guardian*. Retrieved from: https://www.theguardian.com/world/2013/oct/03/golden-dawn-leader-jailed-nikos-michaloliakos [Accessed 16 Jan. 2018].

Telegraph.co.uk. (2012, June 7). Greece: far-right Golden Dawn politician slaps female MP on live TV. Retrieved from: http://www.telegraph.co.uk/news/worldnews/europe/greece/9316355/Greece-far-right-Golden-Dawn-politican-slaps-female-MP-on-live-TV.html [Accessed 4 Jan. 2018].

The Economist. (2013, October 4). Cite a website – cite this for me. Retrieved from: https://www.economist.com/blogs/economist-explains/2013/10/economist-explains-1 [Accessed 16 Jan. 2018].

To Vima. (2015, September 24). Courts rule that racist motives were behind the murder of Shehzad Luqman. Retrieved from: http://www.tovima.gr/en/article/?aid=740315 [Accessed 16 Jan. 2018].

TVXS. (2014, April 5). Η πραγματική ιστορία πίσω από το στημένο ρεπορτάζ για τις γριούλες και την Χρυσή Αυγή. Retrieved from: http://tvxs.gr/news/blogarontas/i-pragmatiki-istoria-piso-apo-stimeno-reportaz-gia-tis-grioyles-kai-tin-xrysi-aygi [Accessed 16 Jan. 2018].

Vasilopoulou, S. and Halikiopoulou, S. (2013). In the shadow of Grexit: The Greek election of 17 June 2012. *South European Society and Politics*, 18(4), 523–542.

Vasilopoulou, S., Halikiopoulou, D. and Exadaktylos, T. (2014). Greece in crisis: Austerity, populism and the politics of blame. *Journal of Common Market Studies*, 52(2), 388–402.

Vasilopoulou, S. and Halikiopoulou, D. (2015). *The Golden Dawn's 'nationalist solution': explaining the rise of the far right in Greece. Reform and Transition in the Mediterranean*. London: Palgrave Pivot.

Voglis, P. (2011). The junta came to power by the force of arms, and will only go by force of arms. *Cultural And Social History*, 8(4), 551–568. doi: doi:10.2752/147800411x13105523597922.

Xchange. (2015). Armed vigilantes attacking migrant boats off Greece: HRW. Retrieved from: http://xchange.org/armed-vigilantes-attacking-migrant-boats-off-greece-hrw/ [Accessed 25 Jun. 2018].

Appendix A1

Trust in institutions: Prior to the crisis (in 2007), trust in political parties was 20.5% (European Commission, 2018).[1] In 2011, this number dropped to 5.1% and in 2013, it declined further to 4.1%. Similar dynamics apply for levels of trust in government and parliament. In 2007, trust in government was 45.5%. However, in 2011 this was reduced to 8.5%. Trust in the national parliament declined from 51.85% in 2007 to 12% and 11.89% in 2011 and 2013 respectively. Dissatisfaction with democracy also confirms the above argument. In 2007, 62.8% of Greek citizens were satisfied with democracy in their country. However, in 2011 only 17% were very or fairly satisfied with democracy; in 2013 this number slightly increased to 18% (European Commission, 2018).

Trust in army and the police: In 2010 trust in the army in 2010 (2011 is not available) was 66.73% and trust in the police was 52% (European Commission, 2018). In 2014 (2013 is not available either) both figures had increased to 71.53% and 58.93% respectively.

Immigration: With regards to actual immigration figures, the stock of foreign-born population in Greece is low compared to other European countries. It declined from 7.4% (or 828.4 thousands) in 2010 to 6.6 (or 727.5 thousand) in 2014 (OECD, 2018a). The number of inflows of foreign population also declined in recent years. In 2005 the number of inflows of foreign population in Greece was 65.3 thousand; in 2009 this number dropped to 35.8 thousand; and in 2011, a year before the national elections that saw the entry of the Golden Dawn in the Greek parliament for the first time, the number further decreased to 33 thousand (OECD, 2018b).

12

FORZA NUOVA AND THE SECURITY WALKS

Squadrismo and extreme-right vigilantism in Italy

Pietro Castelli Gattinara

Introduction

If we define vigilantism as a response to the perceived inability of the state to enforce security and the rule of law within its territory, Italy can arguably be considered a particularly ripe context for the emergence of such practices. On the one hand, the legitimacy of state executive agencies has been eroded by years of political crises, and especially so since the beginning of the Great Recession. On the other, perceived insecurity and ethnic competition have been on the rise in concomitance with the so-called European migration crisis, and the related moral panic that this caused in the Italian public debate since 2015 (Castelli Gattinara, 2017). As we shall outline in this chapter, however, these circumstances built on pre-existing factors delimiting the opportunities for vigilante mobilization in Italy, especially under the initiative of extremist right-wing actors. In particular, we focus on political and cultural factors, focusing on the discursive and legal framework regulating urban security and vigilantism in Italy, as well as the historical heritage of Italian fascism and the *squadrismo* movement (cf. e.g. De Felice, 1969; Gentile, 2011).

This chapter analyses vigilantism looking at the case of one of the actors that have engaged the most in anti-refugee mobilization in Italy: the extreme right party *Forza Nuova* (New Force, FN). FN was first formed as a grassroots branch of pre-existing extreme right political parties, and subsequently splintered to pursue a more organic collaboration with political and subcultural groups of the neo-fascist right in Italy (including skinhead organizations). As will be discussed, the party's ideology is ultra-nationalist and conservative, and it is articulated primarily in opposition to immigration, globalization and Islam. For several years, FN has organized the so-called 'security walks' (*Passeggiate della sicurezza*), which are considered here as a paradigmatic case of vigilante mobilization. Indeed, they are promoted to ensure street security 'in response to demands by Italians that do not feel safe at home' (Forza Nuova, 2016). The basic rationale is one in which FN militants take the responsibility of patrolling local areas considered dangerous, thus serving a function that the decaying Italian state is unable – or unwilling – to fulfil. Vigilantism is thus framed not only as a response to criminality brought about by immigration, but also as a reaction to the inefficiency of state authorities (Forza Nuova, 2017a).

The empirical analysis is based on the investigation of the repertoires of protest of Forza Nuova, with a special focus on the activities of street patrolling promoted in the wake of the refugee crisis. While anti-refugee mobilization in Italy integrates different types of actors, including unaffiliated citizen assemblies, far-right political parties, as well as social movement organizations engaged primarily in grassroots politics. We focus here on organized collective actors only, which includes several groups mobilizing on migration and security, such as the *Lega Nord*, the radical right *Fratelli d'Italia*, as well as more extremist groups like *Forza Nuova* and *Casa-Pound Italia*. While Lega Nord were the first to introduce citizen squads patrolling the streets in northern Italy, many other groups followed suit in the late 1990s and 2000s. Our choice to focus on Forza Nuova is motivated by the fact that this is the group that invested the most in promoting and diffusing vigilantism in Italy in recent years. To the contrary, other organizations, most notably CasaPound, have long neglected the issue of migration and this specific repertoire of action in their agenda of contention, at least until recently (Albanese, Bulli, Castelli Gattinara, & Froio, 2014).

More specifically, we investigate the nature of their vigilante activism, in terms of organization, purposes and self-proclaimed values. To this goal, we use original data from five in-depth interviews with Forza Nuova activists, which we triangulate with the analysis of the content of newspaper reports on their mobilization. Face-to-face interviews were conducted in early 2017. We identified interviewees by snowball sampling to ensure variety in the location, starting from grassroots organizations that had promoted highly mediatized initiatives against refugees over the previous months in Italy (Castelli Gattinara, 2018). Prior to the interviews, we established a rapport with participants through regular contact via telephone and email. The interviews were then conducted in public settings such as bars, shops and restaurants. Albeit the interviews included questions about strategies of opposition to migration, most of the interview relied on an unstructured format intended to generate unsolicited narratives.

We integrate this data with information from media reports of Forza Nuova's vigilante actions, retrieved from news stories extracted from the daily broadsheet *Il Corriere della Sera,* retrieved from the Factiva digital archive (1996–2015). Newspaper articles were selected using a search string intended to capture all articles that contain implicit or explicit reference to the security walks, the main vigilante campaign promoted by the group. Finally, additional sources – such as written, photographic, and audio-visual material produced by the group – were used to contextualize this information.

The chapter is structured as follows, first, we will provide a general overview of the context in which these vigilante activities developed, focusing on economic and political circumstances, with special attention to the opportunities for far-right mobilization that have been triggered by public debates on migration with the beginning of the refugee crisis. We will then introduce the case of Forza Nuova, contextualizing its political worldview and value system in the Italian extreme right milieu. Building upon this framework, we shall illustrate how favourable political opportunities have incentivized the development of vigilante activities throughout the Italian territory, and describe their main features in terms of organization, goals and targets. In doing so, the chapter starts to sketch out some of the crucial meanings that have come to characterize grassroots street activism in FN, assessing the extent to which it was successful in spreading the values of its far-right initiators, and underlining the cultural and political factors that have limited its impact on the Italian public sphere.

Opportunity structures: the political, social and legal context

Italy can be considered a suitable case for the study of vigilante groups. As I shall illustrate in the next section, this has much to do with the cultural embeddedness of vigilantism in the history of Italy's fascist direct activism. But there is more to it. There are, in fact, specific political, social and legal factors that make Italy a case of special interest to observe the emergence and development of vigilantism in Europe. I shall focus here on the main political crises that Italy had to face in its recent history, which are likely to have produced favourable circumstances for the emergence of vigilante groups, and then address more specifically national political opportunities for far-right mobilization in Italy, as well as the legal framework regulating vigilante activities in the country.

To begin with, the 2008 Global Financial Crisis, resulting in at least two full years of recession (2013–2015), heavily affected Italy's economy. Although Italy is considered to have recovered from recession, the growth is still below both the Italian Government's expectations and the Eurozone average. Besides, the Great Recession had a profound impact on the country's political system, with dramatic consequences in terms of the legitimacy of representative institutions and government. The perceived lack of progress on the economic front has progressively eroded the popularity of the large coalition governments since 2011 (Monti; Letta; Renzi; Gentiloni), allowing the main challengers of Italy's mainstream parties, the populist Five Star Movement and the far-right Lega Nord, to take on the anti-establishment mantle and gain much public support. Most indicators on the level of trust in institutions tend to confirm that. According to recent surveys, political trust in public institutions is in a steep decline compared to few years ago: in the period 2010–2016, trust in the judiciary system declined by 12%, and trust in the Italian State by 10 percentage points. As of 2016, only 22% of Italians declared to have at least some trust in the State, and only 10% expressed trust in the parliament (Diamanti, 2016). While people express a much higher level of confidence in law enforcement agencies, the scores for Italy are still considerably lower than the European average: 68% vs 75% (European Commission, 2017). Most strikingly, if in 2005 the aggregate trust in political institutions in Italy was over 40%, by 2016 this figure had fallen to 26%, after reaching a minimum of 21% in 2014 (Diamanti, 2016).

The public perception of state institutions as either weak or absent was only aggravated with the beginning of the so-called refugee crisis in 2015. Of the one million refugees that crossed the Mediterranean in 2015 alone, 154,000 landed in Italy, resulting in a 31 percentage-point increase in annual asylum application rates (EASO 2016). While holding a position of crucial importance in the Mediterranean migration route to Europe, however, Italy generally represents a country of transit for most asylum seekers. As a result, most political and humanitarian tensions emerged at the borders, since the EU treaties on asylum issues require refugees to stay in the country of first arrival. This had profound humanitarian consequences in the north of the country, as migrants waiting for opportunities to pass into France, Austria, and Switzerland concentrated in border towns lacking appropriate structures to accommodate them, while neighbouring countries strengthened the controls at their borders. The EU government's unwillingness to relax the strict principles of the Dublin treaty, combined with the long-lasting unpreparedness of the Italian authorities in coping with migrant reception, triggered the emergence of a series of small reproductions of the Calais Jungle across the country, especially in border towns and around the train stations of major cities (cf. the Chapter on France in this volume). This provided many opportunities to far-right actors to campaign on law and order. Even though right wing and far political parties have long campaigned on immigration as a source of insecurity, the situation has greatly deteriorated since the beginning of the crisis. If in 2012 'only' 26%t of Italians considered immigration a danger for individual security and public order, the amount of people agreeing with this statement reached 33% in 2015 – the year of the 'long summer of migration' – and then further increased to 40% the following year, and reached 46% in 2017 (Demos, 2017).

In terms of political opportunities, right-wing street movements in Italy have regained legitimacy after the so-called 'Years of Lead', and since the mid-2000s they enjoy a rather privileged channel of communication with the electoral arena. In terms of protest and subcultural politics, far-right actors take advantage of the inefficient implementation of anti-racist and anti-fascist sanctions, and mobilize based on a mix of anti-democratic, autocratic, and ultra-nationalist political concepts, mainly borrowed from the ideology of fascist and right-wing authoritarian regimes of the interwar period. In the electoral arena, the right-wing populist Lega Nord and Fratelli d'Italia have long been allied with the political mainstream, and thus receive intensive coverage by the mass media and considerable popularity in opinion polls. In so doing, they enlarge the opportunities for mobilization of other actors in the same area, providing resonance to issues like immigration, security, and opposition to the establishment. Thus, even extremist movements of the far right (such as Forza Nuova) manage every so often to get the attention of the mass media.

The success of the Lega Nord at the local level (in city and regional administrations) and national level (in coalition governments), further increased the political opportunities for vigilantism in Italy. In 2009, the Minister of Internal Affairs in the fourth Berlusconi cabinet – Roberto Maroni, a prominent member of the Lega Nord – took advantage of the public clamour for the access of Bulgaria and Romania to the EU to pass a Security Package. The Package would set urban security at the core of the Italian public agenda, *de facto* legalizing vigilantism. The security package was in reality focused mainly on illegal immigration: it provided new competences to city mayors to intervene in case of urgent security threats, and it was motivated by the allegedly exceptional security circumstances caused by the multiplication of illegal immigrant and Roma camps throughout the territory. A specific clause of the package, moreover, legalized civil patrols, by introducing the possibility to set up citizen committees of volunteers with the goal of patrolling the territory in support of law enforcement and police services in order to relieve situations of urban insecurity and social discomfort. While the measure clarified that these patrols must be activated and coordinated with law enforcement agencies, and that they cannot be equipped with any form of weapon, but only with mobile phones to get in touch with the police and signal episodes of violence to the authorities, it nevertheless elicited much outraged reactions. If opposition parties and left-wing organizations accused the law of facilitating the activities of extremist right-wing organizations, the government insisted that the goal of the measure was precisely that of regulating street patrols, thus integrating civilian citizens in the management of urban security and preventing the diffusion of loose paramilitary groups.

Forza Nuova: ideological profile and background

As illustrated by the debate ensuing the introduction of the security packages outlined above, vigilantism in contemporary Italy cannot be explained without reference to an Italian tradition of considerable political and historical importance: fascist squadrismo, i.e. the fascist movement based on armed squads.[1] To date, historians disagree as to whether the historical experience of squadrismo can be understood as a distinct and specific category of non-state violence, thus comparable with non-European vigilantism and terrorism. Some address squadrismo as a form of ritual violence – promoted by paramilitary groups with the consent of local and economic élites – against trade union leaders and other 'subversives' (Clark, 1988). To the contrary, others underline that there is a difference between party-militias, or vigilante groups complementing the legal activities of a political party, and militia-parties understood as self-standing political movements, such as Italian fascism in its 'blackshirt' phase (Suzzi Valli, 2000). What matters for the purposes of this chapter, however, is that the myth of squadrismo and its revolutionary purity survived the fall of the fascist regime, especially among young fascists. On the one hand, thus, the memory of the fascist action squads is often used to stigmatize right-wing activism and street patrolling, to the extent that the very concept of 'vigilantism' bears a pejorative connotation in its Italian use. On the other, the reference to the blackshirts also works as an internal motivational incentive for mobilization by young right-wing extremist, especially in terms of direct activism (see e.g. Albanese et al., 2014; Froio & Castelli Gattinara, 2017).

The crucial role played by squadrismo in Italy's fascist culture can be appraised in terms of the concept of 'fascism-movement' advocated by Renzo De Felice (1969). Accordingly, fascism must be understood in terms in two different streams, distinguishing between a form of revolutionary, anti-capitalist, and overwhelmingly secular movement phase, and the more conservative, institutional fascism of the regime. In the post-war years, the interpretation of fascism-movement came to be identified with radical factions pursuing revolutionary ideals and vitalistic dynamism, while rejecting the decadent democratic system (Ignazi, 2003). Forza Nuova can be located in this stream of Italy's post-war fascism. Its origins, in fact, date back to the 1990s, which marked the transformation of what had once been the most successful extreme right party in Europe – the *Movimento Sociale Italiano* (MSI) – into a party of government (Ignazi, 2003; Rao, 2014). Rejecting the moderate turn imposed by the party leadership, a number of prominent members belonging to the 'movement' faction of MSI founded the neo-fascist *Fiamma Tricolore* (Tricolour Flame, FT). At first, Forza Nuova represented the grassroots branch of the newly born party, reproducing the traditional differentiation between street activism and engagement in the institutional arena of the Italian extreme right. In 1997, Forza Nuova officially splintered from FT and set out its own agenda, in direct competition with FT for hegemony over direct activism in the Italian far right milieu.

While a strong portion of Italian post-war fascism was traditionally secularist, a trademark of FN's politics was its strong identification with the Roman Catholic tradition, combining ultra-religious values with the legacy of Italian fascism. Based on the idea that politics should regain its spirituality, this resulted in a series of campaigns on cultural liberalism and civil rights issues, especially with respect to abortion, euthanasia and same-sex marriages. Over the 1990s and early 2000s, FN infiltrated organized soccer clubs to recruit militants and radicalize Italian hooliganism, as well as the subcultural music and skinhead milieu to attract young people towards the movement (Caldiron, 2013). While the interpenetration between extreme right ideology, hooliganism and skinhead culture soon became the trademark of FN, the group also tried to gain legitimacy in the electoral arena. Originally, it did so by collaborating with other splinter groups of this political area. From 2008 onwards, however, FN runs its own independent candidates in national and local elections, generally with little success. Similar to the factions that have characterized Italy's post-war fascism, FN displays a double tendency, seeking respectability as a political party, while claiming to be 'revolutionary' in the protest arena (Campani, 2016). As a street movement, it engaged in protests against globalization and migration, including the storming of demonstrations for gender equality, as well as other political initiatives organized in cooperation with skinhead organizations. From 2008 onwards, however, FN has run its own independent candidates in national and local elections, generally with little success.

Forza Nuova's political proposals are summarized in its eight programmatic points, which largely configure its general ideological worldview. First, the group demands the withdrawal of the Italian legislation on abortion (1), the development of new family policies aimed at demographic growth (2), and the recognition of the Roman Church as the spiritual leader of the nation (3). In addition, it asks that all forms of free masonry and secret societies are abolished (4), and that the national public debt is cancelled (5). While FN understandably opposes the legislation criminalizing fascist organizations in Italy (6), it also demands the introduction of a corporatist system replacing trade unions (7). Still, the issue on which FN mobilizes the most is certainly immigration (8), calling for a total shutdown of Italian borders, alongside the 'humanitarian' repatriation of all migrants currently residing in Italy. Immigration is, in fact, considered a threat to the 'harmonious coexistence among peoples', 'a disturbance to public order' and a source of 'cultural heritage loss'.

Since its origins, FN showed a predilection towards engaging in protest against migrants and immigration, which represent by far the top priority of the group. This only increased with the beginning of the so-called 'refugee crisis', which offered the group new opportunities to mobilize at the local as well as national level, while also being able to set up alliances with grassroots organizations engaged in anti-refugee protest (Castelli Gattinara, 2018). It is in this framework that FN rediscovered the practice of the so-called *Passeggiate della Sicurezza* –'security walks', which represent the instance of vigilantism that we will address in detail in the next section.

The security walks: Forza Nuova's vigilante activism

The security walks are one of the main political activities promoted by the central organization of Forza Nuova. While, as we have seen, the Italian legal system is rather permissive towards private citizen squads patrolling the streets, the security walks promoted by FN do not qualify as legal for two main reasons. First, the law was meant to legalize already existing groups – specifically the patrols of the Lega Nord in northern regions – whereas it tended to discourage the creation of new ones. The irregular and non-continuous nature of FN's patrols, which emerge at times mainly in response to criminality news stories, could hardly fit this legal framework. Second, patrols must be organized in active cooperation between private citizens, mayors and law enforcement agencies. Also in this respect, FN's walks can hardly meet existing regulations.

There are, in fact, strong promotional motivations behind the organization of the security walks, which FN hopes to use to increment its public image as well as its rooting in local settings. The group differentiates its political action in a set of areas of intervention, each of which is allocated a specific page in the web portal of the organization. We find there FN's international allies (the Alliance for Peace and Freedom), its youth section and the media it uses for internal and external communication, including a web radio, a dedicated magazine, and a website selling clothing, merchandise and accessories of FN. In addition, there are four thematic areas of political intervention: environmental action (e.g. ethical consumerism),

206 Pietro Castelli Gattinara

sport activities (gyms and leisure time), solidarity (distribution of food, charity, and support for the disabled and the unemployed) and security. Specifically, the security walks are presented as follows:

> Responding to the demands of so many Italians who feel less and less safe at home, Forza Nuova has launched the Security Walks across the areas most at risk of dozens of small and large cities: when the state abandons its citizens, our militants engage in patrolling the most dangerous streets at night. Our goal is to give confidence back to citizens, and to reach the deterrent effect that the absence of institutions fails to guarantee.
>
> *(Forza Nuova, 2017b)*

Throughout its political life, the FN promoted multiple good-will activities to improve its public image, especially by means of solidarity actions and direct social initiatives addressing Italian citizens only. The security walks are understood as a similar form of engagement. On the one hand, this enables the group to increase its visibility and legitimacy at the local level. On the other, it provides FN with leverage to be used when negative news stories concerning its members and supporters are published, including ones having to do with the security walks. Indeed, while there have been multiple episodes of violence promoted by far-right activists in Italy, there has been little evidence directly connecting the use of physical violence to groups engaged in security walks initiatives. As I shall illustrate, FN appraises security walks as having two combined, and complementary, functions. On the one hand, they offer a 'concrete' help to citizens, *de facto* replacing the inefficiency and unresponsiveness of the state and law enforcement agencies. On the other, they are expected to offer an 'example' of virtuous behaviour, which citizens ought to follow in view of a mass revolt against the elites.

The security walks were originally launched in the mid-2000s, taking advantage of the opportunities made available by the abovementioned security packages introduced by the government, which legalized the patrolling of streets by private citizens. At that time, in fact, the moral panic that followed the EU enlargement induced other right-wing political entrepreneurs to promote similar initiatives, especially among Northern League mayors and local politicians. Operatively, security walks gather 5 to 15 people, including members of FN and unaffiliated citizens, who meet in allegedly dangerous neighbourhoods, and patrol the streets by walking across the area (Interview IT5). Participants are unarmed and they do not wear specific uniforms. Yet, they are recognizable, as they wear reflective bibs to increase their visibility at night and to mark membership in the patrolling group. The idea is that participants carry with them a mobile phone in order to call the police in case they get across a critical situation, while they are not supposed to intervene directly to restore public order.

The rationale for these actions is that while insecurity and criminality have grown in Italy, the state has given up on its responsibility of punishing deviance. In this respect, a crucial discursive function is played by the notion of 'dissuasion', in

Extreme-right vigilantism in Italy **207**

that vigilante activism is framed as a form of dissuasion against criminals willing to commit offenses (Interview IT3). Typically, the patrols take place in response to mediatized crime stories and local debates about urban decay and illegality. Participants understand these initiatives as dissuasive of potential criminal offenses and thus complementary to the activities of law enforcement agencies (Interview IT2). Accordingly, the vigilantes involved in security walks do not operate covertly, and generally publicize the initiatives in order to get support from the local citizenry and visibility in the media. At the same time, the security walks are hardly ever organized in coordination with law enforcement agencies and prefectures. To circumvent these restrictions and avoid legal sanctions, FN normally promotes vigilante activities such as distribution of pamphlets by groups of a maximum of three people, so that the group does not have to get prior authorization from the police (Interview IT3).

Territorial branches are thus in charge of setting up the patrolling activities at the local level. Among the self-proclaimed ideological motivations for their engagement, there is the logic of 'order against chaos' and the 'need to defend the people' (Interview IT4). Since law and order issues represent a core feature of far right political agendas, ideological reasons explain why political practices of street surveillance have represented a constant feature in FN activism from the very early days of the movement. At the same time, strategic reasons connected with the legitimacy of far-right political mobilization explain the varying diffusion and visibility of this form of direct activism over time. In FN's rhetoric, citizens understand the patrols as a response to the increasing demands for security:

> We only go where we are called: every day we receive emails, warnings and calls, from people who want to drag our attention to particular situations of illegality. Yet, these people live there, so they are afraid to get exposed ... because the state gives them no protection. And thus us, Forza Nuova, takes the street. And then, slowly but increasingly, citizens find the bravery and they join us in the security walks.
>
> *(Interview IT3)*

FN's vigilantism has escalated in concomitance with favourable political opportunity structures at the national level (e.g. when the security packages were approved), as well as advantageous discursive opportunities at the local level, especially in terms of moral panics over the relocation of asylum seekers and criminality stories involving migrants and ethnic minorities. Indeed, in some circumstances (e.g. following public controversies on the management and location of asylum seekers in Italy), some groups also engaged in guarding specific facilities at the risk of being assigned to host migrants, as well as train stations (Interview IT1 and Interview IT6). The analysis of the media visibility of this form of vigilantism tends to confirm that. Using the FACTIVA database for the mainstream quality newspaper *Il Corriere della Sera*, I identified 146 news stories mentioning FN and the security walks, covering a period ranging from early 2007 to late 2017. The mentions, however, are distributed unequally over this period, since 93 of these news stories (corresponding to 65 per cent of the total) were published in the last two years only, and in particular from summer 2015, i.e. the beginning of the so-called refugee crisis. Indeed, the news stories on security walks often report claims-making by FN activists and high-rank officials, which promote these initiatives by taking positions on related issues. Accordingly, migration should be stopped because Italy's border towns cannot become the 'dump of Europe'; the citizenship regime based on *Ius Soli* should be rejected because it leads to 'multicultural chaos, Islamic predominance and imported mafias'; and refugees are 'not welcome' because Italy's resources must be devoted to help the citizens who suffered from earthquakes in 2016.[2]

While officially the target of these initiatives is 'criminality' in general, it has been clear since the beginning that the real targets are migrants, refugees, and the Roma, whose presence in Italian cities and neighbourhood is associated with criminality, illegality and decay. With the beginning of the European migration crisis, moreover, FN has slightly changed the way in which it presents its security walks, declaring that their objective is to stop anyone who commits crimes 'against Italians' (Forza Nuova, 2017c). In a recent call for participation, FN quite straightforwardly appraised the patrols as 'security walks against extra-communitarian criminality', and adding that people must come to the streets to avoid 'the Islamization of our cities and neighbourhoods'. In recent months situation has been deteriorating as public attention to migration, integration and asylum issues has increased. The context of the urban peripheries of Rome is a case in point, as FN has increasingly organized its street patrols in areas that host reception centres and shelter facilities for asylum applicants. Rumours about tensions between native and immigrant residents have acted as triggers for the mobilization of FN, leading first to the organization of vigilante groups, and then to the promotion of demonstrations demanding that the reception centres are shut down.[3] In this context, there have been multiple reports of street violence against migrants as well as clashes between the police and FN's militants.[4] The groups that were originally formed in the framework of FN's vigilante patrols have also been responsible for confrontational actions and violence against asylum centres and the NGOs in charge of hosting migrants.[5]

> When the citizens saw the truck with the people from the cooperative approaching, they startled, they took on the street and blocked it. I think we can say it was basically an uprising. [...] There were no clashes with the police. The cooperative workers ran away, and left the camion with the supplies there ... and then someone set on fire the televisions and the mattresses.
>
> *(Interview IT1).*

As can be noted from the above quotation, the narrative about security walks focuses primarily on the role of 'citizens'. Yet, there are no official numbers on the participants and supporters engaged in the patrols, neither at the local nor at the national level. As of today, FN can count on a few thousand militants throughout the country (the last official data for 2001 reported little more than 2000 members). Accordingly, we can say little about the specific characteristics and socio-economic background of the people engaging in vigilantism. In our interviews, FN activists declare that the operations of street patrolling at night also helps promoting the visibility of FN in degraded neighbourhood, with the goal of spreading propaganda and possibly attracting new recruits. Yet, FN militants also acknowledge that it is very rare that citizens that are not already politically engaged with FN take part to this type of activities (Interview IT1 and Interview IT2). In September 2017, FN called for a nation-wide set of patrols in all neighbourhoods 'out of control', and where the elderly and women are considered to be in danger. The stated objective of the initiative combined propagandistic messages concerning the need to restore 'hope' for Italians, with considerably more threatening messages: 'we want to send a warning to criminals: Italians have run out of patience and they will not tolerate that their sisters are touched' (Forza Nuova, 2017c). Accordingly, the national headquarters asked territorial branches to invite the following categories of people to take part to patrols: football supporters, 'because they feel a strong and lively attachment to their cities'; taxi drivers 'for their knowledge of the territory and civic engagement'; boxers, 'for their bravery and discipline'.

In conclusion, the analysis shows that FN is careful in not using – at least explicitly – the stigmatizing vocabulary of vigilantism, and presents its street patrolling activities in a way that is compatible with the political and discursive context of Italy. At the same time, the framing of vigilantism must be coherent with FN's ideological and programmatic apparatus. Accordingly, I suggest conceptualizing this form of activism in the framework of the notion of direct activism. Previous literature appraises direct (social) actions as a specific form of political contention aiming to offer a direct solution to phenomena perceived as dysfunctional, which accordingly can be distinguished from traditional repertoires addressing representative institutions and demanding the mediation of the state for the solution of public problems (Bosi & Zamponi, 2015; Froio & Castelli Gattinara, 2017). The group claims to provide a service to the community, replacing the inefficiency of state authorities in delivering security and preventing crime, and thus reinforcing the link between the 'movement and the people' (Interview IT4). At the same time, vigilantism transforms the very meaning of political participation in FN, as militancy becomes a form of 'patriotic Christian solidarity' (Interview IT4). This has to do with an organicist understanding of the nation, in which each individual is conceived as a parcel of the same body of the people. By organizing the patrols, FN militants show the way in which Italians ought to behave, setting up the example for the behaviour of others. In this respect, vigilantism is expected to 'shake the conscience of the citizens, giving them a sense of nation, land, of homeland' (Interview IT1). In short, while vigilantism is to be understood as a political repertoire based on direct activism, its deep ideological and symbolic implications perfectly fit with fascist world-views and especially with FN's self-proclaimed investment in 'a revolutionary project based on an idea of counter power' (Interview IT4).

Concluding remarks

This chapter analysed vigilantism as a response to the perceived inability of the state to enforce security and the rule of law. Empirically, it looked at *Forza Nuova*, which stood out in recent years for its aggressive campaigning against migrants and refugees, and at the specific case of the security walks, promoted to ensure street security for Italian families. Considering the political and economic turmoil that Italy has suffered in recent decades, and the ensuing crisis of legitimacy characterizing its political system, it was suggested that Italy would offer fertile grounds for the development of vigilante activities. Indeed, vigilantism is facilitated by political and discursive opportunities available for collective street action by extreme right organizations. On the one hand, Italy displays a favourable legal framework for street patrolling by groups of private citizens, which were inherited from the security policies implemented by centre-right and Lega Nord coalition governments in the late 2000s. On the other, the historical legacy of Italian fascism and squadrismo triggers motivational incentives for street mobilization by extreme-right activists, especially in terms of direct activism, albeit arguably also representing a discursive constraint for the legitimization of vigilantes in the public sphere.

At the most basic level, the rationale of vigilantism by Forza Nuova is that of serving a function that the Italian state is unable – or unwilling – to fulfil. Yet, the specific content of vigilantism is framed depending on external circumstances, so that at times of economic distress the focus is on the lack of resources for law enforcement agencies, whereas during political crises street patrolling is understood as a response to the unresponsiveness of the government and the inefficiency of the state. Unsurprisingly, therefore, recent public debates on asylum have contributed to making the linkage between vigilantism and opposition to migration more explicit and visible. In this context, the impression is that the moral panic that followed the so-called refugee crisis facilitated the radicalization of FN militants and supporters. In this respect, while Forza Nuova ostensibly has been one of the first actors engaging in this form of activism, and despite being the group engaging in it most systematically, it is certainly not alone. Vigilante patrols are increasingly embedded in broader cycles of demonstrative protests, so that the groups that had originally formed to ensure neighbourhood watch become an integral component of anti-refugee collective action. By integrating street patrolling with political contestation, vigilantism in Italy has thus also progressively turned to political confrontation with – and at times even violence against – opponents and the police.

Notes

1 Squadrismo consisted of fascist squads organizing strikebreaking, punitive missions and vigilante reprisals against revolutionary socialist and communist groups in the period 1918–1924. The rationale of these actions was precisely that public authority was either absent or too timid in disciplining criminal acts, strikes, seizures and occupations (Suzzi Valli, 2000).

2 M. Sasso, *L'Espresso,* 20 September 2016: 'Forza Nuova e la festa sul campo dei partigiani'. Retrieved from http://espresso.repubblica.it/attualita/2016/09/20/news/forza-nuova-e-la-reunion-sul-campo-dedicato-ai-partigiani-1.283453.
3 L. Matarrese, *Huffington Post Italia,* 8 September 2017: 'La ronda di Forza Nuova al Tiburtino terzo. Tensione con la polizia, rimbombano gli slogan: Roma ai romani'. Retrieved from http://www.huffingtonpost.it/2017/09/08/la-ronda-di-forza-nuova-al-tiburtino-terzo-in-cerca-di-migranti_a_23202125/.
4 *Il Messaggero,* 9 September 2017, 'Roma, Forza Nuova sfida la Questura: "La passeggiata di sicurezza si farà"'. Retrieved from http://www.ilmessaggero.it/roma/cronaca/forza_nuova_passeggiata-3226845.html.
5 M. Cifelli, *Roma Today,* 3 September 2017: 'Tiburtino III: migranti assediati dai fascisti nella chiesa di Santa Maria del Soccorso'. Retrieved from http://www.romatoday.it/cronaca/assedio-fascisti-chiesa-migranti-tiburtino.html.

References

Albanese, M., Bulli, G., Castelli Gattinara ,P., & Froio, C. (2014). *Fascisti di un altro millennio? Crisi e partecipazione in CasaPound Italia.* Roma: Bonanno Editore.

Bosi, L., & Zamponi, L. (2015). Direct social actions and economic crises: The relationship between forms of action and socio-economic context in Italy. *Partecipazione e Conflitto,* 8(2), 367–391. https://doi.org/10.1285/i20356609v8i2p367.

Caldiron, G. (2013). *Estrema destra.* Milan: Newton Compton Editori.

Campani, G. (2016). Neo-fascism from the twentieth century to the third millennium: The case of Italy. In G. Lazaridis, G. Campani, & A. Benventiste (Eds), *The Rise of the Far Right in Europe. Populist Shifts and 'Othering'* (pp. 25–54). London: Palgrave Macmillan UK.

Castelli Gattinara, P. (2017). The 'refugee crisis' in Italy as a crisis of legitimacy. *Contemporary Italian Politics,* 9(3), 318–331.

Castelli Gattinara, P. (2018). Europeans, shut the borders! Anti-refugee mobilization in Italy and France. In D. della Porta (ed.), *Contentious moves: Solidarity Mobilizations in the 'Refugee crisis'* (pp.271–297). London: Palgrave Macmillan.

Clark, M. (1988). Italian squadrismo and contemporary vigilantism. *European History Quarterly,* 18(1), 33–49.

De Felice, R. (1969). *Le interpretazioni del fascismo* (1995 ed.). Bari: Laterza.

Demos (2017). *Osservatorio Europeo sulla Sicurezza.* Retrieved from http://www.demos.it/a01427.php.

Diamanti, I. (2016). *XXI Rapporto Gli Italiani e lo Stato (Gli Italiani e lo Stato).* Demos. Retrieved from http://www.demos.it/a01341.php.

EASO (2016). European Asylum Support Office – Annual report on the situation of asylum in the European Union 2015. Retrieved from https://www.easo.europa.eu/sites/default/files/public/EN_%20Annual%20Report%202015_1.pdf.

European Commission. (2017). *Eurobarometer.* Eurobarometer. Retrieved from http://ec.europa.eu/commfrontoffice/publicopinion/index.cfm/Chart/getChart/themeKy/18/groupKy/88.

Forza Nuova (2016). Programma Politico 'Per Uno Stato Nuovo': Rivoluzione. Retrieved from www.forzanuova.eu.

Forza Nuova (2017a). Area Stampa. Retrieved 16 November 2017, from http://www.forzanuova.eu/area-stampa/.

Forza Nuova (2017b). Passeggiate per la Sicurezza. Retrieved 16 November 2017, from http://www.forzanuova.eu/passeggiate-la-sicurezza/.

Forza Nuova (2017c, January 9). Passeggiate per la Sicurezza contro la criminalità extra-comunitaria. Retrieved 16 November 2017, from https://www.facebook.com/RobertoFiorePaginaUfficiale/photos/a.801427453237672.1073741831.702795233100895/1431096716937406/?type=3&theater.

Froio, C., & Castelli Gattinara, P. (2017). Direct social actions in extreme right mobilisations. Ideological, strategic and organisational incentives in the Italian neo-fascist right. *Partecipazione e Conflitto*, 9(3), 1040–1066.

Gentile, E. (2011). *Le origini dell' ideologia fascista (1918–1925)*. Bologna: Il Mulino.

Ignazi, P. (2003). *Extreme right parties in Western Europe*. Oxford: Oxford University Press.

Rao, N. (2014). *Trilogia della celtica*. Milan: Sperling & Kupfer.

Suzzi Valli, R. (2000). The myth of squadrismo in the fascist regime. *Journal of Contemporary History*, 35(2), 131–150. https://doi.org/10.1177/002200940003500201.

List of interviews

IT1: Local activist Forza Nuova, 17 January 2017.

IT2: Local Activist Forza Nuova, 17 January 2017.

IT3: National-level official Forza Nuova, 23 January 2017.

IT4: National-level official Forza Nuova, 24 January 2017.

IT5: National-level official Forza Nuova, 6 February 2017.

13

BEYOND THE HAND OF THE STATE

Vigilantism against migrants and refugees in France

Pietro Castelli Gattinara

Introduction

So far, vigilantism has attracted remarkably little scholarly and public attention in France. While sporadic research has focused on popular justice (Michel, 2011; Brodeur and Jobard, 2005) and citizen participation in policing operations (Favarel-Garrigues and Gayer, 2016), the empirical study of contemporary practices of vigilantism taking place in France is in its infancy at best. Even though France has a long tradition of popular violence following political unrest, especially in the midst of the French Revolution, in fact, the central state has been effective in enforcing a monopoly over the system of criminal justice since the second half on the nineteenth century (Michel, 2011). In this sense, France follows a common pattern among Western European countries, where strong state institutions and efficient law-enforcement systems have progressively neutralized most of citizens' substitutes for legal justice.

Contemporary practices of vigilantism, however, are not only the result of the negotiation between public actors and aggregated private interests, but are also indebted to the various configurations and historical trajectories by which state actors have contended to citizens the right to maintain public order. If in other countries, most notably in the US, contemporary vigilante actors can at least try to legitimize their practices in light of their historical embeddedness, the opposite holds true in France. Within the European context, France has been singled out as a paradigmatic case for the development of "court rationality" standards in the legal system, as well as for the monopolization of the legitimate means of violence by growing state apparatuses (Elias, 1969). Since, historically, vigilante groups have faced the structural tendency of the French State to centralize police powers, invoking the past has proved not only an inefficient strategy, but also a rather powerful source of disqualification for these actors (Favarel-Garrigues and Gayer, 2016).

214 Pietro Castelli Gattinara

Yet, despite these structural constraints to vigilante mobilization, there have been numerous spontaneous outburst of anti-migrant violence, with the tacit approval of local communities. As citizens progressively lose faith in law enforcement agencies, France witnessed a series of episodes in which groups of individuals try to take the law in their own hands, or at least evoke to resorting to "do-it-yourself" justice when other established means fail. In past years, notable cases of lynching justice have concerned in particular the French Roma community. In 2008, unsubstantiated rumours about the Roma community of Marseille led to an attack against three Roma men. Assaulted by a mob of about a hundred persons, their car was set on fire and only the intervention of the police avoided worse consequences.[1] The voicing of discriminatory and stereotypical views of Roma by politicians and governmental representatives legitimized intimidation of Roma people by French citizens, with the result that attacks by private citizens and groups continued unabated in France in the following years (Amnesty International, 2014). In 2014, a 16-year-old Roma boy accused of burglary by local residents in a small town of the Paris region was abducted and tortured in a cellar, beaten into a coma, and left unconscious in a shopping trolley (Naydenova, 2014).

A similar scenario has emerged in more recent years, in concomitance with the emergence of the so-called refugee "crisis". Public debates on migration hit France at a time of permanent state of exception, as the country experienced two consecutive years of state of "emergency" from 2015 to 2017, allowing for unprecedented restrictions on civil society. In this context, the perceived failure of the French immigration and security regime, as well as the effects of the political crisis following the 2008 Recession, had a profound impact on the political climate of the country, fuelling not only hostility against migrants, but also anti-establishment sentiment and distrust in state institutions. The perceived unresponsiveness of French authorities grew exponentially in response to heated debates on humanitarian emergencies at the French borders, most notably concerning the Calais "Jungle", and following the hesitant steps taken by the French government to address the crisis. This further reflected mounting sentiments of anxiety, and frustration against public authorities among local communities. The combination of declining trust in State authorities and growing concerns about individual and collective security is likely to offer today new political opportunities to contest the monopoly over the legitimate use of violence, paving the way to vigilante practices.

This chapter offers a first, explorative analysis of vigilante practices in contemporary France. It offers an overview of the activities of street patrolling promoted in the wake of the so-called refugee crisis by two different types of actors: the citizen association *Les Calaisiens en Colère* and the political association *Les Identitaires*. The chapter highlights crucial organizational factors in their vigilante activism, focusing on the stated purposes and values of citizen activists. Empirically, it uses original data from three in-depth interviews with French activists, and media reports on far-right and anti-immigration mobilization. Additional material collected during fieldwork is used to contextualize the interview and media data. The findings show that attempts to take charge of the implementation of the law in France do not configure a blatant challenge to the authorities or the state monopoly of law and order. To the contrary, extreme right and anti-refugee movements present themselves as complementary law enforcement agencies, mobilizing strategically using the notion of "dissuasion".

Political and cultural opportunities for vigilantism in France

As vigilantism is still largely understudied in France, it is difficult to assess the political opportunities for this form of mobilization. If vigilantism originates from two major transformation of contemporary nation states – the progressive deregulation of security and the outsourcing of state repression (Rosenbaum and Sederberg, 1974) – the French tradition of monopolizing institutions has certainly inhibited the formation of private forms of citizens justice, at least in a historical perspective. The French state in fact displays a structural tendency towards the centralization of police powers, which constitutes a strong deterrent for the development of vigilante activism.[2] Furthermore, unlike in other countries (such as the US), in France political actors cannot claim any historical embeddedness of this type of practice.

Still, vigilantism can also be understood as a form of collective interest articulation, or bottom-up citizen movement, emerging against the perceived inability of the state to enforce the law (Johnston, 1996; Froio and Castelli Gattinara, 2016; Pratten and Sen, 2008). Traditionally, trust in the police and in law enforcement agencies in France is very high, scoring consistently above 60% since the mid-2000s, and increasing in recent years to 80% (European Commission, 2017). In contrast, trust in government has been declining over time. Although the pattern is in line with European trends, the French public opinion displays strikingly little trust in the national government by the end of Hollande's mandate (19% in 2015; 17% in 2016), and a steep decline in trust in local authorities (from more than 60% before 2010, to 45% in 2015). Most important to explain the motivations for vigilantism, a similar decline can be observed with respect to trust in the justice system: if in 2004 the majority expressed confidence in the French justice system (56%), this score was down to 41% in 2017.

These circumstances might facilitate the emergence of autonomous vigilante groups aiming to bypass state inefficiency in providing security and justice. It must be noted, however, that vigilantism is not conceivable without at least a minimum of social support from some specific audiences to which these actors can address their security discourse (see e.g. Buzan, Wæver, and Wilde, 1998; Balzacq, 2011). Actors articulating security discourses in response to everyday demands for security, thus, have to motivate their action on shared understandings of what constitutes a threat and what is the best way to tackle it (Doty, 2007; Huysmans, 1998). They must be able to claim that *the people* support their activities, be that for the sake of the general population or for that of specific local constituencies. This explains why the security problems that visible vigilante groups across Europe aim to tackle systematically coincide with public priorities of security management at the state level, often linking perceived citizen insecurity to immigration and minority issues.

Even though the state does not directly participate or promote vigilantism, in fact, there is often convergence between its objectives and the ones of actors who challenge its monopoly over law enforcement (Jarman, 2008). State and non-state articulations of threat often share the same underlying logic, so that similar issues and rationales resonate across distinct understandings of societal and state security. This is most striking when it comes to the issue of migration, at the core of much research on securitization (Buzan, Wæver, and Wilde, 1998). Tensions between majority populations and minority groups, including migrants and refugees, characterize the internal politics of most European countries, creating fertile grounds for the far right, and increasing public tolerance towards vigilantism and direct engagement of citizens in solving security problems.

France has certainly not been immune to these developments. In January 2017, the presidential campaign had already begun, and the designation of candidates featured prominently on the political agenda. The political system was experiencing a deep transformation, with the demise of the two mainstream socialist and conservative parties, the emergence of a new centrist catchall party led by Emmanuel Macron, and the stabilization of populist left wing and right wing challengers. Over the previous years, the right-wing populist *Front National* (FN) acquired a remarkable influence in French politics and society, albeit without managing to get a stable representation in parliament, at least so far. The new leader Marine Le Pen opened up a process of 'de-demonization' of the party, taking distance from her father's acknowledged racism and anti-Semitism with the goal of diversifying the party's electoral audience (Mayer, 2013; Crépon, Dézé, and Mayer, 2015). Enjoying great media attention, Marine Le Pen's agenda on migration, security and Islam (Odmalm, 2014), represents a crucial resource for far-right movements, which otherwise suffer by the presence of various laws that forbid religious, ethnic and racial discrimination, allowing the banning of anti-democratic and anti-Semitic parties.

Traditionally, the visibility of other groups on this area depends on the issue at stake. High mediatization is enjoyed by a restricted set of political movements, or networks of networks, which mobilize on secularist values and demand the exclusion of specific religious minorities, such as *Riposte Laique* (Froio, forthcoming; Mondon, 2015). The same applies to groups that are primarily engaged in street politics but often coordinate their activities with the Front National, such as Les Identitaires. Besides these exceptional cases, however, most grassroots organizations, which may be susceptible to promoting vigilante activism, normally remain confined to subcultural milieus. The 2015–2016 terrorist attacks in Paris and Nice, however, sparked new discussions on issues related to security and the state of emergency, polarizing political debates on refugees and the place of religious signs in the public space, thus offering new opportunities for mobilization against migrants and minorities.

Vigilantism and the "refugee crisis" in France

Debates about immigration in France have been centred on issues of citizenship especially concerning the perceived "crisis of integration" of migrants from former Maghrebi colonies (Geddes and Scholten, 2016). After 2014, however, the politicization of migration witnessed a sharp twist, in response to the events connected with the Arab Spring, the Paris terror attacks, and the media portrayals of asylum seekers trying to reach the EU. This revitalized debates on two alternative conceptions of migration which were first introduced by French president Nicolas Sarkozy (Simon, 2014), according to which France must favour the "chosen" immigration (*immigration choisie* – such as highly skilled migrants) over endured immigration (*immigration subie* – such as family reunification). Furthermore, France had to cope with humanitarian and security emergencies at its borders (especially the French–Italian one), and at the entrance of the port of Calais and the nearby Eurotunnel terminal. If migrants trying to reach France from Italy found themselves stuck as France temporarily restored controls at its southern border, migrants in northern France could not pass into Britain due to the tightening of controls, which led to a dramatic increase in the population of the migrant encampment that would come to be known as the Calais "jungle".

The French response to the refugee crisis rapidly took a highly politicized tone. While French President Francois Hollande pledged support for Europe-wide solidarity, the Front National and the French right criticized the proposal for a European quota system for asylum migrants (Geddes and Scholten, 2016). Simultaneously, the disproportionate growth of the Calais Jungle, and the deterioration of its living conditions, draw the attention of public authorities, the mass media, and NGOs in the Calais area. This ultimately triggered two forms of vigilantism that are relevant to this study. First, small groups emerged at the local level, under the initiative of citizens that grew concerned by the presence of migrants, organized via social media, and promoted activities to preserve individual safety and street security in the area of Calais. Second, organized political groups took advantage of increasing perceived insecurity to relaunch their security campaigns against migration.

Calais, its "Jungle" and its vigilantes: Les Calaisiens en Colère

In October 2013, the centre-right mayor of Calais announced the set-up of a dedicated email address, which citizens could use to report on "No-border" activists and migrants residing illegally in the city area.[3] If the goal was to raise attention about the conditions in Calais, the result was to legitimize various initiatives against migrants by private citizens and grassroots organizations. In a few weeks, multiple Facebook pages appeared with the goal of organizing and coordinating citizens' initiatives against refugees (Gardenier, 2016). The two most notable groups were *Sauvons Calais* [Let's Save Calais] and, a few months later, *Les Calaisiens en Colère* [The Angry People of Calais, LCC].

218 Pietro Castelli Gattinara

According to its promoters, LCC is a grassroots initiative by disenfranchised citizens in Calais, with the stated purpose of responding to aggressions by migrants and the degradation in the city area due to illegal refugee settlements. Despite frequent accusations by migrant solidarity organizations, the group always proclaimed itself non-political and non-violent. Activists claim to be completely disenfranchised from any existing political organizations in France, not least the *Front National*, and they do not recognize themselves as either left or right wing (Interview FR1). In its early days, the group was active online only, giving voice to citizens to express their grievances against migrants by producing short videos and reportages about the Jungle. LCC's first street mobilization took place in October 2015, when the group organized a street march to "Stop irregular migration". The demonstration gave the group, and its narrative of "abandonment by the state", much visibility: by December 2015, the Facebook page reached 35,000 likes (at the time of the interviews, it reached 75,000).[4]

The motivations for the rally, which gathered 500/1000 people, encompass some elements of relevance to understand the emergence of citizens patrols over the following weeks:

> We struggle to show you the sad reality of our everyday life, denouncing the blatant injustice that we suffer, and supporting the people who are in distress. [...] It's touching to see so many people gather here today: people who suffer here are abandoned by the state.[5]

The interviews with LCC activists confirm that individual life experiences represent a crucial motivation for getting involved in direct action, as a response to the perceived unsustainability of living conditions in Calais, and the unresponsiveness of state and local authorities.

> The first group was created in 2013, under my initiative, and it was called "Let's defend Calais". I had been aggressed by an illegal migrant in 2012. I was stabbed ... I have a lifetime illness because of it. Hence, I decided to open this page to discuss my aggression and other aggressions that I heard about.
>
> *(Interview FR1)*

> We created a Facebook page to talk of the aggressions taking place in Calais. There have been rapes, thefts, houses have been squatted, degradation ... Some animals have been stolen, killed, eaten.
>
> *(Interview FR2)*

By December 2015, LCC had already started organizing its night watch through the streets of Calais, not without raising concerns among solidarity activists and the mass media about the nature of their patrols. The stated goal of activists was to make citizens "feel safe" by offering a "presence" in the streets. The overnight patrols covered a rather wide area considered "at risk" of migrant intrusion, including the city outskirts, the entrance of the Eurotunnel, and the main highway connecting to the border. First, LCC activists aimed at preventing migrants who could not find shelter in the Jungle, to have access to the summerhouses at the outskirts of Calais. Second, they wanted to avoid roadblocks by migrants aiming to reach into the UK. Third, they aimed at preserving security in general, against theft, violence and rapes.

After the dismantlement of the Jungle, however, LCC's vigilante strategy was partially reformulated, focusing instead on preventing the formation of new refugee campsites:

> Originally, the main objective of *Les Calaisiens en Colère*, when there was the Jungle, was to avoid theft, aggressions and migrants squatting our houses … but even more to avoid roadblocks on the highway because the life of road users was hard back then. Now, considering that the Jungle is gone, our mission is to look for the new camps and at the same time to avoid the aggressions in parking spaces on the highway.
>
> *(Interview FR1)*

As far as the organizational aspects are concerned, prior to each watch, the vigilantes gathered next to the French police truck in downtown Calais. Law-enforcement agencies are the only actor with whom LCC activists acknowledge to relate, declaring to be "unofficially" in contact with the police for coordination purposes, to demand permission to access specific areas, and to call for intervention when necessary. The patrols normally took place from 20:30 to early in the morning, and the groups were composed of no more than 8–10 people, moving around by car. The interviewees report that the maximum mobilization was reached in 2015 ("when the situation had become unsustainable", Interview FR2), with 80 persons involved in patrolling for several consecutive nights. By January 2017, the group was composed of no more than a few dozen young residents of Calais, which met irregularly and took rounds for participating in the patrols. Some of them reported working – or having worked – for private security agencies. Participants were aged 17 to 60, and they were overwhelmingly male, albeit there have been reports of women taking part in the night watches.[6]

> The women are our drivers, they are our eyes. They stay inside the car while we go out in the ground. They have their eyes on our back, for our security, and they stay in touch with us with walkie-talkies, so that in case of troubles, we get out. It would be a pity to leave a man behind in the car, because he is certainly more useful on the ground than in the car.
>
> *(Interview FR1)*

The patrols generally take two different forms. Normally, the vigilante group moves to a number of specific areas that they consider "at risk" of migrant intrusion, thus patrolling across different places. Occasionally, however, they can also act

220 Pietro Castelli Gattinara

in response to specific requests by private citizens, thus engaging as a private security agency, patrolling the surroundings of a house, gathering video material to send to law enforcement agencies, or directly scaring away migrants from illegal camps that formed in someone's property.

> People call us, we come and we install ourselves. We tape what we see, so that we can signal it to law enforcement authorities, telling them at this address is happening this and that, you must take action.
>
> *(Interview FR2)*

In the early days of their mobilization, LCC's vigilantes did not have an official dress code. Yet, the media clamour surrounding the night watches led them to wear reflective bibs with the name of the organization, to be more easily identifiable during night actions.[7] Officially, participants are unarmed, as they might only bring a flashlight to "dissuade" migrants from pursuing illegal activities. These are allegedly "much stronger than those used by the police" and are intended to scare migrants by convincing them that vigilantes are the police. The cars also serve the same function, but from a distance. In case the abovementioned dissuasive measures are not sufficient to disperse migrants, the activists call for the intervention of the police. Even though the media has frequently reported of open confrontations between LCC activists and groups of migrants, the official position of the group concerning risks of confrontation is the opposite, as reported by one of our interviewees:

> Concretely, in reality, we cannot do much if something happens: we cannot beat them up, we cannot arrest them, we can do nothing. We can only scare them, that is all.
>
> *(Interview FR1)*

Two crucial concepts stand out in the analysis of vigilantism by *Les Calaisiens en Colère:* "dissuasion" as a strategy to avoid migrant criminality, and "complementarity" of vigilantism and police action. These two elements play a fundamental role in the narratives of vigilante groups; in constructing their credibility within the local community; and in legitimizing its activities. If, in fact, the motivations for engagement have to do with the feeling of abandonment by the authorities, mobilization does not aim at replacing the state in the operation of its crucial function of maintaining collective security. To the contrary, direct engagement in LCC is framed in terms of dissuasion, so that vigilantism is understood as complementary, rather than alternative, to the usual administration of law enforcement. This framing allows vigilantes to articulate mobilization without creating an overlap, or a conflict, with the role of the state as the unique holder of the monopoly of violence and the enforcement of order.

Mediatized vigilantism across France (and beyond): Les Identitaires

A well-known protagonist of the extremist right-wing scene in France are the groups inspired by the French New Right (Bar-On, 2012). We focus here on the *Bloc Identitaire* (Identitary Bloc, BI), a nativist-regionalist movement founded in 2003 by a group of sympathizers of the outlawed group *Unité Radicale* and the Front National, and on its youth organization *Génération Identitaire* (Identitary Generation, GI). While BI represents one of the main networks of right-wing street movements in France since the early 2000s (Blum, 2017), its youth section came to be known in more recent years thanks to showcase activism against Islamization, mass migration and multiculturalism, most notably the occupation of a mosque in Poitiers in 2012.

The Identitaires address primarily young generations, privileging community-building activities such as concerts, sports, collective training, and excursions. From 2016, BI has suspended all electoral activities to focus exclusively on street protest and grassroots actions, being aware that the Front National already represented the group's issues and stances in the party system. Although no official alliance was ever signed, this ultimately resulted in a "division of labour" between the two actors. Les Identitaires thus considers themselves as the "street-based" branch of Marine Le Pen's campaign. Although the FN is considerably more cautious in recognizing linkages with grassroots groups of this sort, a number of high officials of BI obtained important positions within the party.[8] In January 2013, the GI promulgated a "declaration of war", a video in which it expresses its ideological antagonism to Europe's multicultural society (Génération Identitaire, 2013). The video has been translated in various languages, so that today the symbols and colours of the Identitaires have become a brand identity for spin-off groups in Austria, Italy, the Netherlands, Switzerland and Czech Republic (Blum, 2017).

The *Identitaires* promote numerous anti-immigration initiatives, including vigilante actions. First, they organize the so-called "Anti-Scum" patrols (*Génération anti-Racaille*), which are part of a broader set of actions aimed at convincing the French people to "defend themselves" against insecurity (Génération Identitaire, 2014). These actions mainly focus on securitizing public transport, but parallel initiatives include training courses in self-defence, legal assistance for victims of violence, and courses targeting specifically high school students. Although the framing of the actions focuses on all types of criminal activities, their main target are migrants and religious minorities in France, in line with the broader political activity of the group.

> The objective was to show to public transport users that there is a youth that promotes solidarity and self-defence against insecurity caused by those scum and the resignation of the police. We also wish to challenge the candidates for mayor of Lyon on the theme of insecurity in transport. Awareness, prevention and deterrence are the watchwords of this action.
>
> *(Génération Identitaire, 2014)*

222 Pietro Castelli Gattinara

> A group of militants go on public transport and simply take care that everything goes fine. [...] Our goal is to avoid problems, rather than causing them. Our objective is prevention.
>
> *(Interview FR3)*

The campaigns are promoted by the Bloc Identitaire, but delegated to local militants in charge of participating, gathering supporters and managing the logistics. The usual format involves 10 to 20 voluntary activists, who jump on trains and metro lines considered "dangerous", and distribute flyers to passengers. The underlying logic is that the militants remain on the train until the last stop, so that their presence makes sure that nothing happens during the transit. The distribution of flyers has two functions: on the one hand, it works as propaganda for the group, making its mission and symbol visible among a broader audience and potential supporters. On the other, it is a protective measure against legal sanctions. While the promoters do not act in coordination with police, they nevertheless make sure that their activities are within the boundaries of the law (such as leaflet distribution by small groups), or they ask for prior authorization for some form of standardized political activity.

> Sometimes they distribute flyers to passengers to make them aware and to inform them that if they witnessed something that is not normal, they could call a given number. To tell them that we are there in support of the police and not to replace it.
>
> *(Interview FR3)*

Participants are not armed and they do not wear official uniforms, but they make sure to be recognizable by wearing reflective bibs with the logo of the Identitaires. The branding of the action and the immediate recognizability of the promoters fits well with the broader strategy of the group. Vigilantism, in fact, does not represent only a form of direct social activism aimed at offering a concrete, material, solution to an urgent problem. Rather, it also helps presenting the group as crucially different from actors engaged in traditional forms of protest addressing third parties (e.g. the state, the media), and demanding their mediation for the solution of a public problem. This is the same logic driving the groups' solidarity actions:

> This is also the theme of what we call "Génération Solidaire": every winter, the Identitarians take on the streets throughout France to distribute soups, warm clothes and other goods to homeless people from Europe. That's because migrants are already hosted by the State in relatively luxurious centres, while native-born French have to sleep in the streets.
>
> *(Interview FR3)*

By means of vigilante engagement, the Identitaires invest in direct engagement against something perceived as dysfunctional, in this case migration and insecurity.

Furthermore, the patrols also serve the function of promoting the "identitarian brand" and its activities. The promoters of these campaigns, in fact, try to maximize the media impact of their actions, through the careful selection of colours and symbols, and through the staging and – when possible – the spectacularization of protest. Mediatized vigilantism also relates to the broader agenda setting strategy of the Identitarians.[9]

This second nature of vigilantism also emerges from another campaign by the Identitaires: *Defend Europe*. Launched in 2017, this campaign aimed at setting up a search-and rescue mission, documenting the misbehaviour of NGOs in the Libyan coast, and hampering their cooperation with human smugglers (Defend Europe, 2017). The idea originated in the network of the French *Génération Identitaire*, in cooperation with its affiliated groups across Europe. Together, they raised about €75,000 through web-based crowdfunding, and used it to hire a vessel and a crew, and set sail to the Mediterranean Sea. The campaign offers a straightforward example of the mediatized logics of vigilantism, as it combines the ambition of setting up a patrol, with the media-oriented spirit that drives much of the Identitarians' politics. Indeed, Defend Europe was presented using typical narratives of direct activism, such as the need to act "here and now", and the desire of acting on behalf of law enforcement agencies, offering the citizenry a service that the state is either unable, or unwilling, to fulfil. In this respect, the logic is the same as in night watches and vigilante squads: the Mediterranean patrol is understood as the functional equivalent of the building-up of a wall, with the goal of dissuading the pursuit of illegal migration to Europe.

At the same time, the Defend Europe promoters had very clear in mind that the real objective of the mission was in the media, rather than at sea. The action does not exclusively address migrants, but also the media system, with the goal of breaking the mainstream consensus concerning "search and rescue" operations and the role of NGOs in the Mediterranean. Activists thus engage in patrolling, but also in reporting with video and pictures the reality about immigration to Europe, offering alternative material and uncovering the collusion between the NGOs and human smugglers.

> The main Goal of DEFEND EUROPE is to reveal the outrageous activities of NGOs to the entire world.
>
> *(Defend Europe, 2017)*

The promoters of Defend Europe claimed numerous victories while sealing in the Mediterranean, as they considered that their presence, their documentation activity, and their patrols, not only inhibited NGOs by unveiling their alleged criminal actions, but also set in motion a number of reactions, especially in Italian politics. Most notably, Defend Europe campaigners took credit for the Italian government's choice to threaten to shut its ports to NGOs who failed to sign to a controversial code of conduct implying, among other things, that the Italian army would be allowed to accompany the rescue missions. It is true, indeed, that by the

224 Pietro Castelli Gattinara

end of the summer numerous humanitarian NGOs had withdrawn their ships, in disagreement with the code of conduct. Similarly, it is undeniable that the Italian executive endorsed the tenets of a prominent xenophobic conspiracy theory, insinuating that NGOs act in cooperation with human smugglers. Whether this can be linked to the concrete activity of Defend Europe, however, is more questionable. As a matter of fact, the vessel ultimately spent only a week monitoring the sea by Libya. The anti-immigrant vessel had to cope with a number of problems: first, they were denied the docking rights in Sicily, after mounting clamour by local anti-racist movements; then, they had to renounce refuelling in Greece and Tunisia, because of local opposition; finally, having failed to provide a satisfactory crew list, the vessel was stopped in the Suez Canal. Some crew members were ultimately arrested in Northern Cyprus over people smuggling allegations, and subsequently released on the claim that crew members on board were apprentice sailors.[10]

In this sense, Defend Europe configured a performative action, based on a specific mix of agenda setting and direct activism logics. The group hailed the action "a political success, a media success, and a success in activism" (Defend Europe, 2017), because of its indirect impact via the mass media, as well as its direct impact on the management of search and rescue missions:

> Defend Europe has received an enormous amount of media coverage. While almost all were hostile, and several were lying, these articles and TV reports brought our action to the minds of millions of people. It is this media impact which allowed our political success. Only two months ago, many NGO ships were cruising near Libyan coasts like taxis waiting for their customers. Right now, the 20th of August, there's only one left.
>
> *(Defend Europe, 2017)*

In sum, vigilantism by the Identitarian movement shows that some of the motivational elements in their direct campaigning are common to previously observed vigilante practices, such as the perception of unresponsiveness by state authorities and the perceived inefficiency of law enforcement agency. Similarly, the main focus is on how to prevent and deter violence and insecurity, which resonates with the previous discussion on vigilantism as a form of dissuasion. Yet, the rationale is remarkably different, in that the logic is not one of direct engagement by citizens that aim at solving "here" and "now" a critical situation or problem, but rather that of staging a display to the public and the mass media. In this sense, the logic is much closer to the media-oriented agenda setting practice of social movements than to one of direct activism and vigilantism.

Concluding remarks

This chapter analysed vigilantism understood as acts of coercion in defence of an established political order, albeit in violation of its formal boundaries of security enforcement and rule of law. It focused on the vastly understudied context of France, where vigilante experiences can count on virtually no historical embeddedness, and have to cope with a strong state tradition of centralization of police powers. Despite these structural constraints to vigilante mobilization, it showed how declining faith in law enforcement agencies and state institutions has facilitated some episodic experiences by groups of individuals that have tried to take the law in their own hands. Empirically, the chapter thus focused on the case of the Calaisiens en Colère and the Identitarian movement, with a special focus on anti-refugee and anti-migrant mobilization. In so doing, it showed that vigilante practices represent a viable strategy for different types of groups in contemporary France, paving the way not only for disenfranchised grassroots campaigns by local citizens, but also for organized political initiatives by more established far right organizations.

As was discussed, there are a number of common features to the very different vigilante practices set forth by the two groups under observation. Most notably, in both cases the underlying rationale is that vigilantism is made necessary by the state's inability and unwillingness to fulfil its duties towards citizens. The feeling of "abandonment" by the state, and the critique to the establishment, however, does not go as far as to promote activities intended to replace the state function of ensuring security. In all circumstances, vigilantes avoid running the risk of creating a conflict between their practices and the state as the unique holder of the monopoly of violence. To the contrary, the logic is the one of "complementarity" and "dissuasion", so that direct activism enables citizens to engage on urgent problems in support of police action, so that vigilantism is promoted as complementary to the usual administration of law enforcement by the state.

Some differences between various approaches to vigilantism emerge, however, if we compare the practices by grassroots citizen groups and organized political movements. Only the latter, in fact, have successfully combined the strategies of direct activism with the logics of agenda setting. The Identitarian movement seems to be interested in vigilantism primarily because it enables a to bridge between the logics of direct engagement aimed at solving "here" and "now" a situation perceived as critical, with a mediatized understanding of contentious politics. In this respect, vigilante activities are not much about providing a material answer to a problem. As shown by the Defend Europe campaign, vigilantism often configures a staged performance, by which anti-immigrant actors try to impose a certain scenario to attract the attention of the public and the mass media. Rather than vigilante actions, thus, these events represent vigilante performances. This might explain why vigilantism is often so appealing to relatively small and weak far-right street movements: because it allows them to invest simultaneously in audiences at the local level (in the territories where they engage), as well as at the national and transnational level (thanks to the media resonance of vigilante performances).

Notes

1 L. Leroux, Le Monde, 13 August 2008: Les Roms de Marseille En Butte À Une Vague D'hostilité.
2 As a matter of fact, all forms of "private militias" have been forbidden in France for a long time. The law of 10 January 1936, subsequently abrogated and reiterated in the Article L212–1 in 2012, allows the French state to dissolve by decree all associations or groups who "by their military form and organization, have the character of combat groups or private militia" or "whose activity tends to defeat measures concerning the reestablishment of republican legality". https://www.legifrance.gouv.fr/affichCode.do?idSectionTA=LEGISCTA000025508340&cidTexte=LEGITEXT000025503132.
3 Huffington Post. 24 October 2013: La Maire de Calais Incite Ses Habitants a "signaller" les Squats de Migrant. Available at: http://www.huffingtonpost.fr/2013/10/24/migrants-maire-calais-natacha-bouchart-facebook_n_4158094.html (11/03/2018).
4 France Info, 4 October 2015:Calais: La Manifestation Des "Calaisiens En Colère" a Bien Eu Lieu Available at: https://france3-regions.francetvinfo.fr/hauts-de-france/calais-la-manifestation-des-calaisiens-en-colere-bien-eu-lieu-822299.html (22/01/2018).
5 France Info, 4 October 2015: Calais: La Manifestation Des "Calaisiens En Colère" a Bien Eu Lieu.
6 La Voix Du Nord, 5 January 2016: Migrants de Calais: Les Rondes Nocturnes Controversées Des Calaisiens En Colère. Available at: www.lavoixdunord.fr/archive/recup%3A%252Fregion%252-Fmigrants-de-calais-les-rondes-nocturnes-controversees-ia33b48581n3248794 (6/2/2018).
7 La Voix Du Nord, 12 January 2016: Migrants: Les Calaisiens En Colère Arretent Provisoirement Leurs Rondes Nocturnes. Available at: http://www.lavoixdunord.fr/archive/recup/region/migrants-les-calaisiens-en-colere-arretent-ia33b48581n3264028.
8 G. Rof, Le Monde, 2 January 2017: Les Identitaires Investissent Le Front National. Available at: http://www.lemonde.fr/politique/article/2017/01/02/les-identitaires-investissent-le-front-national_5056584_823448.html (15/02/2018).
9 R. Herreros, Planet France, 14 May 2014: Rondes "anti-Racailles": Qui Sont Les Militants de Génération Identitaire? Available at: http://www.planet.fr/societe-rondes-anti-racailles-qui-sont-les-militants-de-generation-identitaire.620403.29336.html (22/01/2018).
10 M. Oppenheim, The Independent, 21 August 2017: Defend Europe: Far-Right Ship Stopping Refugees Ends Its Mission after a Series of Setbacks. Available at: www.independent.co.uk/news/world/europe/ defend-europe-far-right-ship-stop-refugees-mediterranean-end-mission-c-star-setbacks-migrant-boats-a7904466.html (31/01/2018).

References

Amnesty International (2014). Europe's failure to protect Roma from racist violence. Retrieved from: https://www.amnesty.org/en/documents/EUR01/007/2014/en/. (25/02/2018).

Balzacq, T. (2011). *Securitization theory: How security problems emerge and dissolve*. London: Routledge.

Bar-On, T. (2012). The French new right's quest for alternative modernity. *Fascism*, 1(1), 18–52.

Blum, A. (2017). Men in the battle for the brains: Constructions of masculinity within the 'identitary generation'. In M. Köttig, R. Bitzan, and A. Petö (eds), *Gender and far right politics in Europe* (pp. 321–335). Basingstoke: Palgrave Macmillan.

Brodeur, J-P. and Jobard, F. (2005). *Citoyens et Délateurs*. Paris: Autrement.

Buzan, B., Wæver, O. and de Wilde, J. (1998). *Security: A new framework for analysis*. Boulder: Lynne Rienner Publishers.

Crépon, S., Dézé, A. and Mayer, N. (2015). *Les faux-semblants du Front National*. Paris: Presses de Sciences Po.

Defend Europe (2017). The mission. Retrieved from http://defendeurope.net/en/the-mission_fr/.

Doty, R. (2007). States of exception on the Mexico–U.S. border. *International Political Sociology* 1(2), 113–137.

Elias, N. (1969). *The civilizing process*. Oxford: Blackwell.

European Commission (2017). Eurobarometer. Retrieved from http://ec.europa.eu (25/02/2018).

Favarel-Garrigues, G. and Gayer, L. (2016). Violer la loi pour maintenir l'ordre. *Politix*, 115, 7–33.

Froio, C. and Castelli Gattinara, P. (2016). Direct social actions in extreme right mobilisations. *Partecipazione e Conflitto* 9(3), 1040–1066.

Geddes, A., and Scholten, P. (2016). *The politics of migration and immigration in Europe*. London: Sage.

Froio, C. (forthcoming) Race, religion or culture? Framing Islam between racism and neoracism in the online network of the French far-right. *Perspectives on Politics*.

Gardenier, M. (2016). Vigilante groups and the refugee situation in Calais. *Localities*, 6(16), 33–58.

Génération Identitaire (2013). Déclaration de guerre. Retrieved from http://www.youtube.com/watch?v=5Vnss7y9TNA (25/02/2018).

Génération Identitaire (2014). Tournée anti racailles: Après Lille, Lyon! Retrieved from https://www.facebook.com/generationidentitaire/posts/502857523156395 (25/02/2018).

Huysmans, J. (1998). The question of the limit. *Millennium* 27(3), 569–589.

Jarman, N. (2008). Vigilantism, transition and legitimacy. In D. Pratten and A. Sen (eds), *Global vigilantes*. New York: Columbia University Press.

Johnston, L. (1996). What is vigilantism? *The British Journal of Criminology*, 36(2), 220–236.

Mayer, N. (2013). From Jean-Marie to Marine Le Pen: Electoral change on the far right. *Parliamentary Affairs*, 66(1), 160–178.

Michel, J. (2011). Popular justice, class conflict, and the lynching spirit in France. In M. Berg and S. Wendt (eds), *Globalizing lynching history* (pp. 137–152). New York: Palgrave Macmillan.

Mondon, A. (2015). The French secular hypocrisy: The extreme right, the Republic and the battle for hegemony. *Patterns of Prejudice*, 49(4), 392–413.

Naydenova, V. (2014). For Roma in France, is climate of intolerance fueling violence? *Open Society Foundation*. Retrieved from: https://www.opensocietyfoundations.org/voices/roma-france-climate-intolerance-fueling-violence (24/02/2018).

Odmalm, P. (2014). *The party politics of the EU and immigration*. New York: Springer.

Pratten, D. and Sen, A. (2008). *Global vigilantes*. New York: Columbia University Press.

Rosenbaum, HJ. and Sederberg, P.C. (1974). Vigilantism: An analysis of establishment violence. *Comparative Politics*, 6(4), 541–570.

Simon, P. (2014). Contested citizenship in France: The Republican politics of identity and integration. In A. Cole, S. Meunier, and V. Tiberj (eds), *Developments in French Politics* (pp. 203–217). Basingstoke: Palgrave Macmillan.

14

VIGILANTISM IN THE UNITED KINGDOM

Britain First and 'Operation Fightback'

Elizabeth Ralph-Morrow

Introduction

Britain First was a fringe political party best known for its 'mosque invasions', 'Christian patrols' and – more recently – being at the centre of a 2017 international dispute between President Donald Trump and Prime Minister Theresa May. This chapter charts the brief history to date of Britain First, beginning with its post-British National Party origins and ending with the imprisonment of its leaders and suspension of their social media accounts.

Drawing on original qualitative data and online materials, this chapter provides an overview of Britain First's ideology, vigilante activities, and supporter base. Britain First is not the first UK far-right organization to fuse direct action with formal politics. However, its vigilante activities, religious allusions and savvy social media use set it apart from the parties and movements that came before it. In filming and uploading videos of its uniform-clad supporters storming mosques, distributing British army bibles and departing in a camouflaged Jeep, Britain First has managed to simultaneously threaten violence to British Muslims – and reach an audience of millions. However, it remains to be seen whether the organization can sustain its vigilantism and vast social media reach in the face of increasing censure from technology companies and the UK's legal system.

The ideology, origins and supporters of Britain First

Britain First was founded in 2011 by James Dowson, a former member of the far-right British National Party (BNP) who split from the party in 2010 following allegations that he had made unwanted sexual advances towards a female colleague (Allen, 2014). Dowson was joined by Paul Golding, a former BNP councillor, in launching Britain First in 2011, and the two used contacts they had from the BNP

Vigilantism in the United Kingdom **229**

to recruit supporters (Allen, 2014). In 2014 Dowson resigned after objecting to the 'mosque invasions' organized by Golding (Sommerlad, 2014). Jayda Fransen, a former member of the English Defence League, was elevated to the deputy leadership the same year (Wright, 2016c).

In its mission statement, Britain First (Britain First) describes itself as 'a patriotic political party and street movement that opposes and fights the many injustices that are routinely inflicted on the British people'. Apparently hinting at vigilante activities and revealing that its involvement in politics is nominal, the mission statement claims that Britain First 'is not just a normal political group, we are a patriotic resistance and "frontline" for our long suffering people' and asserts that it has a 'proven track record of opposing Islamic militants and hate preachers and this fightback will continue'.

Britain First claims it will 'defend our nation, our heritage and culture'. What constitutes British heritage and culture and how it will be defended is unclear, although the mission statement suggests that Christianity is 'the bedrock and foundation of our national life' and makes the nostalgic appeal that Britain First 'will make Britain a beautiful country once again where you can leave your door unlocked and your children can play in the streets'. The organization reveals its desire to prevent 'our people' being made second class citizens and to respect, promote and teach young people about British traditions and history.

Like other far-right organizations, Britain First singles out immigrants and Muslims as threatening the UK's economy and women. The organization claims that immigration has damaged healthcare, housing and the environment and calls for its end. The group also asserts that '[t]he rapid growth of militant Islam is leading the suppression of women, freedom of speech and racist attacks'. Britain First is also 'overtly proud' of its stance in putting 'our people' first, before 'foreigners, asylum seekers or migrants', thereby suggesting that the latter category do not constitute true British citizens.

Britain First was nominally a political party and contested elections before deregistering in 2017 (Booth, 2017). It stood two candidates in the 2014 European Parliamentary elections in Wales and Scotland who attracted 0.9 per cent and 1.02 per cent of the vote respectively (BBC, 2017c, 2017d). Golding also stood as a candidate during London's mayoral election in 2016 where he attracted 1.2 per cent of the vote (BBC, 2017b; Blair, 2016). Although the majority of UK citizens tend not to trust the government, Britain First's electoral results suggest that most voters do not see it as a credible alternative to the political mainstream (European Commission n.d.).[1]

Although Britain First has fared badly at the polls, many voters share the organization's concerns about immigration and Islam. UK voters have consistently ranked immigration as being among the most important issues facing the country (and in 2016 it was ranked as the most important issue), although the public remains divided on the topic. There are particularly stark divisions between professional and managerial workers and unskilled workers: a majority of the former believe that migration enriches British culture and benefits the economy, whereas less than a third of unskilled workers believe that there are economic or cultural benefits (Blinder & Allen, 2016; Ford & Lymperopoulou, 2017). The UK is also characterized by high levels of Islamophobia. In 2015, 40 per cent of YouGov respondents had a negative impression of Muslims, and in 2016 nearly half of the YouGov respondents agreed that '[t]here is a fundamental clash between Islam and the values of British society' (Dahlgreen, 2015; YouGov, 2016).

Because Britain First does not release membership lists, the demographics of its supporter base is unknown. However, fieldwork and observation at three Britain First demonstrations suggests that, similar to other far-right movements, the organization's supporters are mostly white men.[2] Numerous supporters at Britain First demonstrations admitted to having previously engaged in right-wing activism (for example, in the English Defence League or its splinter groups, the South East Infidels or North East Infidels, and PEGIDA UK) and two participants had family members who had engaged in National Front activism. Some supporters – such as a former Conservative party councillor, UK Independence Party (UKIP) candidate and UKIP member – have also engaged in formal politics.

Britain First supporters recognize that participating in the organization can attract stigma that may jeopardize employment. A male factory worker who attended the 2017 Telford demonstration said that his wife supports the ideas of Britain First but is 'an NHS school nurse and attending the demonstration wouldn't be a good look'. Other participants admitted that their attendance could lead to 'professionally damaging consequences' and asserted that their friends and neighbours support the organization but will not attend demonstrations due to a fear of losing their job. The unemployment rate in the UK is currently 4.5 per cent and wages dropped by nearly 10 per cent after the financial crisis (Financial Times, 2017; Office for National Statistics, 2017).[3]

Britain First and the UK far right

Britain First's fusion of direct action and formal politics is not a new phenomenon in the UK and was similarly employed by the British Union of Fascists. Formed in 1932, its leader, Sir Oswald Mosley, advocated the creation of a British economy that could survive without external trade (Cullen, 1993). Like Britain First, the British Union of Fascists displayed paramilitaristic traits and utilized a paramilitary structure, with members wearing a black shirt that symbolized, in the words of Mosley, 'young men dedicated to the salvation of great nations from decadence and degradation' (Pugh, 2013). Mosley also established a uniformed and disciplined Fascist Defence Force (Thurlow, 1998a). The recruits to the Fascist Defence Force lived a semi-military life, residing in barracks and participating in drills in order to have the physical capability of preventing groups on the left from driving it by force from the streets (Pugh, 2013). Prior to being banned in 1940 for its pro-German propaganda, the BUF marched through areas of London with a high concentration of Jews in a bid to intimidate and anger the community (Thurlow, 1998b).

The National Front, formed in 1967, marked the next wave of British right-wing extremism (Copsey, 2004). Ideologically, the party promoted nationalist-racism, with National Front policies advocating the compulsory repatriation of non-white immigrants and their offspring, and the promotion of a eugenic consciousness among the nation's white inhabitants (Taylor, 1982). The National Front staged demonstrations characterized by an undercurrent of violence, chaos and fear (Taylor, 1982). However, the party's relentless focus on white nationalism did not resonate with the electorate and it polled only 1.3 per cent of the vote in the general election (Copsey, 2004).

Ideologically, Britain First has much in common with the BNP, a far-right party founded in 1982 by John Tyndall, a former member of the National Front. (Goodwin, 2011). The BNP experienced its greatest degree of electoral success under the leadership of Nick Griffin, who homed in on the threat that multiculturalism posed to the 'native British', and argued that white cultural expression was being curtailed on the grounds that it was considered offensive to minority groups (Rhodes, 2011). Following the September 11 attacks, the BNP distributed leaflets that warned that Britain was being turned into an Islamic republic (Goodwin, 2011). The BNP's mobilization of Islamophobia and anti-immigration sentiment, was temporarily successful. By the end of 2006, it had 46 elected local councillors (Wood & Finlay, 2008). However, despite this initial success and persistent voter concerns about immigration and Islam, the 2010 general election dashed the BNP's hopes of widespread electoral breakthrough when the party failed to capture a parliamentary seat (Copsey, 2012).

In 2009, the anti-Muslim street protest organization, the English Defence League, was established. Unlike the British Union of Fascists, National Front, and BNP, the EDL never entered formal politics and remained a street-based movement (Stocker, 2017, p. 106). The organization's Facebook page and mission statement claim that the EDL seeks to 'peacefully protest against militant Islam' and utilize the United Kingdom's courts and legislature to achieve its aims of protecting and promoting human rights, democracy and the traditions of England. However, in reality the organization favours hostile, direct action and has staged over 50 demonstrations that often involve public disorder, aggressive anti-Muslim chanting, and clashes with counter-demonstrators and police (Meadowcroft & Morrow, 2016).

While the EDL shares similar ideological concerns to Britain First and engages in direct action, the two organizations also differ in their approaches to managing crowds at demonstrations, alcohol consumption and religion. Further, the EDL does not organize vigilante activities, although some of its supporters have engaged in anti-Muslim violence (Treadwell & Garland, 2011).

Although both Britain First and the EDL stage street-based demonstrations – ostensibly to raise awareness of problems such as 'grooming gangs' and terrorism – the two organizations take different approaches to managing these events. Britain First circulates a code of conduct to participants on its mailing list, which provides them with instructions that prohibit: the display or consumption of alcohol; masks, balaclavas, and face coverings; profane, abusive, or racist language; and 'engaging in moronic, hooligan and drunken behaviour that brings Britain First into disrepute'. These rules appear to be enforced; a Britain First steward asked attendees at a Dewsbury demonstration in January 2016 if they were carrying alcohol and participants were not wearing face coverings.

Although alcohol consumption is a noted feature of EDL demonstrations (Busher, 2015; Pilkington, 2016), Britain First's prohibition on alcohol appears to be favourably received by participants at its demonstrations. One supporter revealed that he had not gone to EDL demonstrations because 'they seem like drunken idiots'. Two former EDL participants suggested that the organization was undermined by drunkenness; and another supporter compared the EDL unfavourably to Britain First, saying that 'Britain First are a respectable group of people and aren't lagging by 11am'.

Britain First's emphasis on Christianity distinguishes it from the EDL and its other far-right predecessors. Britain First members have distributed British army bibles during 'mosque invasions'; its mission statement claims Christianity is a 'bedrock and foundation', and its founder, James Dowson, is an evangelical Christian (Allen, 2014, pp. 357–358). Observation at Britain First demonstrations also revealed multiple references to Christianity: speeches delivered by Golding and Fransen began with the Lord's Prayer; the leaders claimed that Muslims worship a satanic God; Golding asserted that Britain is a modern Knights Templar; and Fransen called for volunteers to help carry large white crosses.

Britain First vigilante activities and legal sanctions

Britain First's vigilante activities began in 2014 and, initially, were reactive. In January 2014 the organization staged a 'Christian patrol' in response to 'Muslim patrol' videos posted on YouTube, which featured three men who sought to enforce Sharia law in East London (Allen, 2014, p. 358). Golding and other members of Britain First assembled out the front of East London Mosque where they filmed themselves drinking alcohol, distributing leaflets and unfurling a 'We are the British resistance' banner (East London Mosque and London Muslim Centre, 2014; Gye, 2013). Britain First was condemned by the mosque director, who referred to the 'relentless' efforts to intimidate and marginalize their community. *The Daily Mail* also criticized the stunt and the 'far-right thugs' who had orchestrated it (Robinson, 2014). The Bishop to Stepney condemned the patrol and stated that '[t]here is no place for vigilante patrols' and a spokesman for East London Mosque referred to Britain First as 'neo-Nazis' (Robinson, 2014). These condemnations did not deter the group from staging further 'Christian patrols' throughout 2015 and 2016.

In May 2014, Britain First began to engage in proactive and confrontational vigilante activities when members 'invaded' ten mosques in Bradford. The videos filmed and uploaded by Britain First show members wearing a uniform consisting of a waterproof jacket and flat cap, refusing to remove their shoes and confronting worshippers and imams about the failure of the Muslim community to stop 'grooming gangs', alleging Mohammad was a false prophet and insisting that mosque attendees read the bible (Allen, 2014, p. 358). Golding has described the 'invasions' as being 'part of Operation Fight Back' (Fransen, 2016a; Muslim First, 2014). Britain First has since conducted 'mosque invasions' in Luton, Bradford, London, and Cardiff with stated reasons for the invasions including the need for a mosque to remove 'sexist signs' that designate separate entrances for men and women and to confront 'a hate preacher ... who said it's okay for Muslims to keep sex slaves' (Britain First, 2016a; Dearden, 2014).

Britain First's vigilante activities are characterized by the threat, rather than use, of violence. This threat is particularly conveyed through the organization's emphasis on militarism, including the wearing of uniforms, use of a camouflaged vehicle when conducting patrols, distributing British army bibles; and describing its activities as amounting to an 'invasion' and 'Operation Fight Back' (Allen, 2014, p. 360). Although some of Britain First's vigilante activities are in response to alleged crimes such as 'grooming gangs', at other times the group is apparently acting in response to the 'Muslim occupation' of parts of London. The group's 'mosque invasions' and 'Christian patrols' therefore involve 'the collective use or threat of extra-legal violence in response to an alleged criminal act' and constitute vigilantism (Moncada, 2017, pp. 408–410).

Unlike Britain First's demonstrations, which are promoted in advance and open to the public, the group's vigilante activities are unadvertized and conducted by a small number of members. The videos typically feature Golding and Fransen accompanied by fewer than ten, mostly male, Britain First members and are captioned with text identifying the participants as being part of a 'battalion' engaging in 'Operation Fightback'. This emphasis on militarism may be an attempt by Britain First to portray its vigilante activities as akin to those undertaken by a soldier of war, thereby bestowing grandeur on its 'mosque invasions' and 'Christian patrols' (Bennett Furlow & Goodall Jr, 2011).

Britain First was initially suspected to have engaged in violent vigilantism when Jo Cox, the Labour Member of Parliament for Batley and Spen, was murdered on 16 June 2016. Cox was shot and stabbed by Thomas Mair, a member of her constituency, who was claimed to have shouted 'Britain first, keep Britain independent, Britain will always come first' during the attack (Cobain, Parveen, & Taylor, 2016). These reports led Britain First to deny any connection to Mair and Golding released a statement on Facebook claiming 'We had nothing to do with it ... this kind of thing is disgusting' (York, 2016).

Britain First's vigilante activities have resulted in numerous criminal sanctions being imposed on the group's leaders. In 2016 Bedfordshire Police successfully applied to the High Court to ban the leaders of Britain First from entering parts of Luton or any mosque in England or Wales, or instructing or encouraging any other person from doing so, for three years (Wright, 2016a). In explaining their unusual decision to apply for an injunction, an Assistant Police Constable of Bedfordshire Police said 'we decided to take action following a number of incidents where these parties came into areas of Luton and caused tension ... we will not tolerate any individual who seeks to cause disharmony or provoke tensions within our communities' (Bedfordshire Police, 2016). At the time of the case, Golding claimed that Britain First was facing a '6k legal bill' and 'crippling injunction conditions' and asked for donations to cover their legal fees (Fransen, 2016b).

Golding and Fransen's vigilante activities have resulted in their imprisonment. Golding was imprisoned for eight weeks for contempt of court when he drove four members of Britain First to the Al-Manar Centre in Cardiff (BBC, 2016; Colley, 2016). When sentencing Golding the judge said that his conduct was 'calculated to increase tensions between different members of the community ... particularly to affront the Muslim community in relation to their religion' (Colley, 2016). In 2016, Fransen was found guilty of religiously aggravated harassment for telling a Muslim woman she encountered during a 'Christian Patrol' that Muslim men 'cannot control their sexual urges' and are 'raping women across the continent' (Osborne, 2016).

Golding and Fransen were jailed again in 2018 for 18 and 36 weeks respectively for religiously aggravated harassment. The charges arose from an incident when they banged on the windows and doors of a pizza takeaway shop located beneath a flat where a gang rape was committed by Muslim men while shouting 'paedophile' and 'foreigner' at those inside the shop. Fransen was also convicted of abuse for visiting a home believed to be connected to one of the rape trial's defendants and yelling racist abuse through the door (BBC, 2018a).

Golding and Fransen have also been fined for wearing a political uniform in a rare enforcements of the Public Order Act 1936, which prohibits 'the wearing of uniforms in connection with political objects and the maintenance by private persons of associations of military or similar character' (Osborne, 2016; Wright, 2016b). The Public Order Act was originally passed to target the Britain Union of Fascist's 'Blackshirts' (Wright, 2016b).

Britain First's international contacts have also been subject to law enforcement scrutiny. Jacek Miedlar, a former Polish priest accused of anti-Semitism and Islamophobia, had been promoted as a speaker at Britain First's 2017 Telford demonstration. However, Fransen claimed Miedlar was unable to attend the rally because he had been detained at the airport for questioning. Fransen also said that some of their Bulgarian friends, who act as a border patrol to stop immigrants entering Bulgaria, had been told that if they entered the UK they would be arrested.

The institutions responsible for sanctioning Britain First – the police and courts – are generally trusted by the public. The 2013/14 Crime Survey for England and Wales showed that 76 per cent of adults tended to or strongly agreed with, overall, having confidence in the local police (Office for National Statistics, 2015). Confidence is also high in the courts, with 70 per cent of respondents agreeing that the UK courts are 'very good' or 'fairly good' in terms of ensuring the independence of courts and judges.

Online communications

Britain First has managed to promote its vigilante activities effectively through posting videos of its 'Christian patrols' and 'mosque invasions' on Facebook and YouTube. Its videos are watched by a large audience, with some attracting over four million views (Britain First, 2016b). Additionally, the organization's Facebook page had over two million 'likes' – more than double that of the Labour Party (Hern & Rawlinson, 2018).

Britain First's social media accounts attracted international attention in November 2017 when US President Donald Trump retweeted three videos posted by Fransen that purported to show violent acts committed by Muslims: a young man on crutches being attacked by a 'Muslim migrant'; a man smashing a statue of the Virgin Mary; and footage of a man being pushed off a building in Alexandria during the 2013 Egyptian riots (BBC, 2017a). The spokesman of UK's Prime Minister Theresa May responded by saying that it was 'wrong for the president to have done this' (BBC, 2017a). President Trump initially responded by tweeting '@Theresa_May, don't focus on me, focus on the destructive Radical Islamic Terrorism that is taking place within the United Kingdom. We are doing just fine!' (BBC, 2018c). He later admitted that he was prepared to apologize for the retweets (BBC, 2018b).

Britain First's online presence has also been used to form, and promote, the organization's alliances with far-right organizations and individuals in Europe. Some of these alliances – especially with Jacek Miedlar and Marian Lukasik from the nationalist Polish Wielka Polsta Nicpodlegla – are promoted by Britain First in a bid to attract UK-based Poles to its demonstrations (Devlin, 2017).

However, in recent years, Britain First's online presence has been significantly reduced due to Facebook and Twitter suspending its accounts, and YouTube restricting access to some of its videos. As a result, much of the online content it previously shared is no longer available. Golding and Fransen have responded to their social media suspensions by opening accounts on Gab, a US-based social networking service that is marketed as a 'free speech alternative' to existing social media options.

Conclusion

Britain First shares some ideological and tactical similarities with its far-right predecessors. Its fusion of formal politics and direct action, and militaristic traits, have previously been employed by the UK far-right. However, the organization is distinguished by its religiosity, social media savviness and vigilante activities.

In likening its organization to the Knights Templar and distributing British army bibles during its 'mosque invasions', Britain First's leaders may seek to conjure images of a religious battle. Additionally, because Britain First's vigilante activities are conducted by a group of uniformed members who travel in a camouflaged Jeep and describe their actions as being part of 'Operation Fightback', the organization suggests its activities are akin to those of a soldier at war. This analogy may simultaneously bestow grandeur on Britain First's activities in the eye of their supporters while increasing the perceived threat of Britain First from those on the receiving end of its vigilantism. In filming and uploading videos of its vigilante activities, Britain First have managed to promote the 'Christian patrols' and 'mosque invasions' carried out by a handful of Britain First members to an audience of millions.

Although Britain First's social media accounts received an unexpected boost of publicity when President Trump retweeted anti-Muslim videos posted by Fransen, the organization has since found itself on the receiving end of censure from the social media sites it relies on to promote the organization and its vigilante activities. Twitter, Facebook and YouTube have taken steps to suspend Britain First accounts and reduce access to content produced by the organization. Although Britain First has opened an account on the new social networking site Gab, it remains to be seen whether the organization can still promote its activities to a large audience via social media, and, indeed, whether Fransen and Golding are still prepared to engage in vigilantism when to do so may lead to their imprisonment.

FIGURE 14.1 Britain First leaders Paul Golding and Jayda Fransen at a demonstration in Telford, 2017. The organization's leaders often carry crosses during demonstrations and 'patrols' and its mission statement claims that Christianity is a 'bedrock' and foundation.

(Photo: *The Shropshire Star*)

Notes

1 There have been three governments that have been in power since Britain First was founded in 2011: a coalition between the Conservatives and Liberal Democrats from 2010–2015; a Conservative government from 2015–2017, and a coalition between the Conservatives and Democratic Unionist Party from 2017. Over that time, the number of respondents who agreed they tend not to trust the UK government has declined from 74 per cent in 2011 to 62 per cent in 2017.
2 Data for this chapter was gathered through attendance at three Britain First demonstrations in Dewsbury, Telford, and London throughout 2016 and 2017, and conducting formal and informal interviews with supporters during and after demonstrations. Ethical approval was obtained from King's College London prior to data collection.
3 The unemployment rate was 8.1 per cent in 2011 when Britain First was founded (The National Archives, 2011).

References

Allen, C. (2014). Britain First: The 'frontline resistance' to the Islamification of Britain. *The Political Quarterly*, 85(3), 354–361.
BBC. (2016, December 15). Ex-Britain First leader Paul Golding jailed over mosque ban. Retrieved from http://www.bbc.co.uk/news/uk-politics-38326446.
BBC. (2017a, November 29). Donald Trump retweets far-right group's anti-Muslim videos. Retrieved from http://www.bbc.co.uk/news/world-us-canada-42166663.
BBC. (2017b, 2017). London Elections 2016. Retrieved from http://www.bbc.co.uk/news/election/2016/london/results.
BBC. (2017c, March 15). Scotland Vote 2014 Europe. Retrieved from http://www.bbc.co.uk/news/politics/eu-regions/S15000001.
BBC. (2017d, June 6). Wales Vote 2014 Europe. Retrieved from http://www.bbc.co.uk/news/politics/eu-regions/W08000001.
BBC. (2018a, March 7). Britain First leader and deputy leader jailed for hate crimes. Retrieved from http://www.bbc.co.uk/news/uk-england-43320121.
BBC. (2018b, January 26). Donald Trump prepared to apologise for Britain First retweets. Retrieved from http://www.bbc.co.uk/news/uk-42829555.
BBC. (2018c, January 19). Theresa May to meet Donald Trump in Davos. Retrieved from http://www.bbc.co.uk/news/uk-42755632.
Bedfordshire Police. (2016, August 16). Bedfordshire Police obtain full High Court injunction against Britain First organisers. Retrieved from http://www.bedfordshire.police.uk/about_us/news/latest_news/2016/160816_-_bedfordshire_police_o.aspx?theme=textonly.
Bennett Furlow, R., & Goodall Jr, H. (2011). The war of ideas and the battle of narratives: A comparison of extremist storytelling structures. *Cultural Studies? Critical Methodologies*, 11(3), 215–223.
Blair, O. (2016, May 25). Britain First threatens to target London Mayor Sadiq Khan with 'direct action'. Retrieved from http://www.independent.co.uk/news/people/sadiq-khan-britain-first-london-mayor-threaten-direct-action-a7047991.html.
Blinder, S., & Allen, W. L. (2016, November 28). *UK public opinion toward immigration: overall attitudes and level of concern*. Retrieved from http://www.migrationobservatory.ox.ac.uk/wp-content/uploads/2016/04/Briefing-Public_Opinion_Immigration_Attitudes_Concern.pdf.
Booth, R. (2017, November 29). Britain First: Anti-Islam group that bills itself as a patriotic movement. Retrieved from https://www.theguardian.com/world/2017/nov/29/britain-first-anti-islam-group-that-bills-itself-as-a-patriotic-movement.

Britain First. (n.d.) Britain First mission statement. Retrieved from http://www.britainfirst. org.uk//mission-statement/.

Britain First. (2016a, December 15). Breaking! Britain First leader Paul Golding sent to prison! Retrieved from https://www.facebook.com/OfficialBritainFirst/photos/a. 346633882148546.1073741826.300455573433044/1208766382601954/?type=3.

Britain First. (2016b, January 23). Britain First carries out Christian Patrol in Islamist hotspot Bury Park, Luton. Retrieved from https://www.youtube.com/watch?v=fA6XcyXsxXU.

Busher, J. (2015). *The making of anti-Muslim protest: Grassroots activism in the English Defence League*. Abingdon: Routledge.

Cobain, I., Parveen, N., & Taylor, M. (2016, November 23). The slow-burning hatred that led Thomas Mair to murder Jo Cox. Retrieved from https://www.theguardian.com/uk-news/2016/nov/23/thomas-mair-slow-burning-hatred-led-to-jo-cox-murder.

Colley, J. (2016, December 15). Ex-Britain First leader jailed after Cardiff 'mosque invasion'. Retrieved from http://www.walesonline.co.uk/news/wales-news/ex-britain-first-leader-jailed-12326200.

Copsey, N. (2004). *Contemporary British Fascism*. Hampshire: Palgrave Macmillan.

Copsey, N. (2012). Sustaining a mortal blow? The British National Party and the 2010 general and local elections. *Patterns of Prejudice*, 46(1), 16–39.

Cullen, S. M. (1993). Political violence: The case of the British Union of Fascists. *Journal of Contemporary History*, 28(2), 245–267.

Dahlgreen, W. (2015, June 15). Roma people and Muslims are the least tolerated minorities in Europe. Retrieved from https://yougov.co.uk/news/2015/06/05/european-attitudes-minorities/.

Dearden, L. (2014, July 15). Britain First 'battalion' invades mosque demanding removal of 'sexist' entrance signs. Retrieved from http://www.independent.co.uk/news/uk/home-news/britain-first-battalion-invades-mosque-demanding-removal-of-sexist-entrance-signs-9607978.html.

Devlin, K. (2017, July 11). The anti–immigration party trying to recruit immigrants. Retrieved from http://www.bbc.co.uk/news/blogs-trending-40509632.

East London Mosque and London Muslim Centre. (2014, February 2). Extremist patrols unwelcome in Tower Hamlets. Retrieved from http://www.eastlondonmosque.org.uk/news/extremist-patrols-unwelcome-tower-hamlets.

European Commission. Public opinion. Retrieved from http://ec.europa.eu/commfrontoffice/publicopinion/index.cfm/Chart/getChart/themeKy/18/groupKy/98.

Financial Times. (2017). How wages fell in the UK while the economy grew. Retrieved from https://www.ft.com/content/83e7e87e-fe64-11e6-96f8-3700c5664d30?mhq5j=e3.

Ford, R., & Lymperopoulou, K. (2017). *Immigration*. Retrieved from http://www.bsa.natcen.ac.uk/media/39148/bsa34_immigration_final.pdf.

Fransen, J. (2016a, September 22). Britain First invades Luton mosques. Retrieved from https://www.youtube.com/watch?v=oYCMCqoFAyw.

Fransen, J. (2016b, September 28). Urgent update from Paul Golding and Jayda on Luton Injunction application. Retrieved from https://www.youtube.com/watch?v=Y-9yAv80pes.

Goodwin, M. J. (2011). *New British Fascism: Rise of the British National Party*. Abingdon: Routledge.

Gye, H. (2013, February 1). 'Muslim Patrol' jailed for harassing couple holding hands and men drinking in a bid to enforce Sharia law in East London. Retrieved from http://www.dailymail.co.uk/news/article-2519519/Muslim-Patrol-jailed-harassing-couple-holding-hands-men-drinking-bid-enforce-Sharia-law-East-London.html.

Hern, A., & Rawlinson, K. (2018, March 14). Facebook bans Britain First and its leaders. Retrieved from https://www.theguardian.com/world/2018/mar/14/facebook-bans-britain-first-and-its-leaders.

Meadowcroft, J., & Morrow, E. A. (2016). Violence, Self-Worth, Solidarity and Stigma: How a Dissident, Far-Right Group Solves the Collective Action Problem. *Political Studies*, 65(2), 373–390.

Moncada, E. (2017). Varieties of vigilantism: conceptual discord, meaning and strategies. *Global Crime, 18*(4), 403–423.

Muslim First. (2014, May 16). Britain First trying to invade Mosques in Bradford. Retrieved from https://www.youtube.com/watch?v=pfFQDT7x7GU.

Office for National Statistics. (2015). Compendium: Crime Statistics, Focus on Public Perceptions of Crime and the Police, and the Personal Well-being of Victims: 2013 to 2014. Retrieved from https://www.ons.gov.uk/peoplepopulationandcommunity/crimeandjustice/compendium/crimestatisticsfocusonpublicperceptionsofcrimeandthepoliceandthepersonalwellbeingofvictims/2015-03-26.

Office for National Statistics. (2017). Unemployment. Retrieved from https://www.ons.gov.uk/employmentandlabourmarket/peoplenotinwork/unemployment#timeseries.

Osborne, S. (2016, November 3). Jayda Fransen guilty: Britain First Deputy Leader convicted after abusing Muslim woman in hijab. Retrieved from http://www.independent.co.uk/news/uk/crime/jayda-fransen-guilty-britain-first-deputy-leader-convicted-court-muslim-woman-hijab-a7395711.html.

Pilkington, H. (2016). *Loud and proud: Passion and politics in the English Defence League*. Manchester: Manchester University Press.

Pugh, M. (2013). *Hurrah for the Blackshirts!: Fascists and fascism in Britain between the wars*. London: Random House.

Rhodes, J. (2011). Multiculturalism and the subcultural politics of the British National Party. In N. C. a. G. Macklin (Ed.), *The British National Party: Contemporary Perspectives* (pp. 62–78). Abingdon: Routledge.

Robinson, M. (2014, February 6). 'We are the CHRISTIAN patrol!': Far-right thugs swill Stella outside east London mosque in bid to confront Muslims who object to their behaviour. Retrieved from http://www.dailymail.co.uk/news/article-2552894/We-CHRISTIAN-patrol-Far-right-thugs-swill-Stella-outside-east-London-mosques-bid-confront-Muslims-object-behaviour.html.

Sommerlad, N. (2014, July 27). Britain First founder quits over mosque invasions which attract "racists and extremists". Retrieved from http://www.mirror.co.uk/news/uk-news/britain-first-founder-quits-over-3923810.

Stocker, P. (2017). *English uprising*. London: Melville House UK.

Taylor, S. (1982). *The National Front in English politics*. London: Macmillan.

The National Archives. (2011). Labour market statistics, October 2011. Retrieved from http://webarchive.nationalarchives.gov.uk/20160109123912/http://www.ons.gov.uk/ons/rel/lms/labour-market-statistics/october-2011/statistical-bulletin.html.

Thurlow, R. C. (1998a). *Fascism in Britain: From Oswald Mosley's Blackshirts to the National Front*. London: I.B. Tauris.

Thurlow, R. C. (1998b). The straw that broke the camel's back: Public Order, Civil Liberties and the Battle of Cable Street. *Jewish Culture and History, 1*(2), 74–94.

Treadwell, J., & Garland, J. (2011). Masculinity, marginalization and violence – a case study of the English Defence League. *British journal of criminology, 4*(1), 621–634.

Wood, C., & Finlay, W. M. L. (2008). British National Party representations of Muslims in the month after the London bombings: homogeneity, threat, and the conspiracy tradition. *British Journal of Social Psychology, 47*(4), 707–726.

Wright, P. (2016a, August 19). Britain First banned from Luton and all mosques in England and Wales after police High Court victory. Retrieved from http://www.ibtimes.co.uk/brita in-first-banned-luton-all-mosques-england-wales-after-police-high-court-victory-1576355.

Wright, P. (2016b, August 1). Britain First leader Paul Golding convicted for wearing 'intimidating' fleece. Retrieved from http://www.ibtimes.co.uk/britain-first-leader-paul-gol ding-convicted-wearing-intimidating-fleece-1573621.

Wright, P. (2016c, January 26). Female face of Islamophobia: Britain First's Jayda Fransen threatens civil war between Muslims and Christians. Retrieved from http://www.ibtimes. co.uk/female-face-islamophobia-britain-firsts-jayda-fransen-threatens-civil-war-between-m uslims-1540013.

York, C. (2016, June 17). Britain First Leader Paul Golding releases statement on Facebook over the death of MP Jo Cox. Retrieved from http://www.huffingtonpost.co.uk/entry/ britain-first-jo-cox_uk_5762f6a6e4b0681487dcdcc1.

YouGov. (2016, February 19). Tracker: Islam and British values. Retrieved from https:// yougov.co.uk/news/2016/02/19/tracker-islam-and-british-values/.

15

THE SOLDIERS OF ODIN FINLAND

From a local movement to an international franchise

Tommi Kotonen

The Soldiers of Odin Finland (SOO) is a street patrol organization that has or has had chapters in most of the cities in Finland, and which at its peak was also present in more than 20 countries. The members patrol on the streets, especially late at night, in order to protect people from violent behavior and inform the police when something happens. However, they see the purpose more broadly than sheer auxiliary policing, emphasizing that they act as a preventive force, and also work in the "grey zone," on cases that are not directly illegal but more like "bad behavior." Especially, young refugees are seen as a security threat, and SOO sees itself as their "physical counter-force" (interview, SOO 1). Besides patrolling, the SOO has also taken part in demonstrations and done charity work.

According to its official rules, approved by the Finnish authorities, the Soldiers of Odin aims "to maintain and to support the security culture at its territory, and to enhance voluntary maintenance of the secure environment by the citizens" (PRH, 216.621). Their programmatic statement draws a more nuanced picture: they are "a patriotic street patrol organization, which opposes harmful immigration, Islamization, EU and globalization, and aims at tackling the byproducts caused by the aforementioned problems, like weakening of the security." To negative developments they add also "multiculturalism," which brings "foreign cultures to Finland, cultures that are incompatible with Finnish culture" (SOO Finland, 9.6.17). As a nationalist, anti-immigration program, the SOO statement is pretty similar to those of other movements born in the wake of 2015 refugee crises (cf. e.g. Finland First: PRH 217.654).

A local SOO leader who has been active in writing their political statements has stressed that what all members share "100%" is anti-Islamism, and that "Islam should be declared as a political ideology instead of a religion" (interview SOO 1). An anti-Muslim leaflet they have distributed lists several fundamental cultural and psychological differences between Finnish society and Islam, emphasizing the lower

242 Tommi Kotonen

level of civilization in Islamic countries. The Soldier of Odin sees the integration of the Muslims as impossible. According to them "the Islam is both a bellicose religion and a political system seeking world domination"(Muslimit on ongelma n.d.). SOO chapters often deny their apparent racism, but this depends to some extent on definitions: As has been pointed out, SOO does not see its all-encompassing anti-Islamism as racism (ADL 2016; cf Hafez 2014; Cleland et al. 2017).

In this chapter I will analyze the growth and development of the Soldiers of Odin in Finland in the light of online observation, court and police files, interviews with both rivaling street patrolling organizations and representatives of the Soldiers of Odin, and the official statements and media interviews given by the members of the SOO. As a part of my research I have also analyzed the Facebook profiles of 26 SOO leaders. In this analysis, political opportunity, organizational resources, and communication strategy are scrutinized more closely in order to highlight reasons behind the growth of the SOO.

Founding the Soldiers of Odin and its connections to Nordic Resistance Movement

The Soldiers of Odin was reportedly founded in October 2015 in Kemi, a small town in Northern Finland (Yle 2016b). According to some reports, it was initially a spin-off from a Facebook-based closed group "Kemi vapaakeskustelu" ("Kemi non-restricted discussion"), founded in July 2015 by Mika Ranta, a truck driver from Kemi who is now in his early thirties. That new group was founded after the immigration discussion at the open Facebook group Kemi got heated and discussion on immigration was banned (see the guidelines for Facebook group Kemi). The group had among its first members several of those people who would later form the Kemi chapter of the Soldiers of Odin (Kemi vapaa keskustelu, list of members, Facebook).

The SOO was born as a part of the anti-immigration protest movement in Finland, which had its peak of mobilization during the summer and autumn 2015, when refugees arrived in unprecedented numbers. Arrival of the refugees was followed by mass demonstrations demanding closing the borders, and some violent attacks followed too, like throwing Molotov cocktails against the refugee reception centers. To counter some unwanted behavior some people expected especially by the refugees, several street patrols were created as well. The most successful of these became the Soldiers of Odin, which was soon labeled in the media as a far-right or even neo-Nazi organization.

The early history of SOO shows several links to the national socialist Nordic Resistance Movement. Chairman and founder of the SOO, Mika Ranta, used to be a member of NRM, although probably, as he claims, just in the role of a supporter (Yle 2016b). Ranta says he is still a national socialist. Besides a connection to NRM, he has had some other radical initiatives: for example, in November 2015 Ranta asked for a permit to create a chapter of Combat 18 in Kemi, emphasizing it is a national socialist group. C18, a group of British origin that promotes racial war,

The Soldiers of Odin in Finland 243

was shortly visible in Finland in relation to anti-refugee demonstrations in Southern Finland, with one former B&H activist as a leader (Mika Ranta, Facebook).

Ranta had written anti-Islamic messages against refugees in Kemi already in 2009 (discussion forum Suomi24). This was related to growing tensions between local youth and refugees in 2009, when the number of refugees in Kemi rose sharply, and some anti-refugee attacks followed (Kemi Police, 8690/R/5910/09, 8690/R/5908/09). The number of hate-crimes also peaked in Kemi in 2009 (Police College of Finland 2010). Following clashes in 2009, a group of men from Kemi came up with a plan to start a local NRM chapter, and a meeting took place between them and NRM (interview Holappa). However, for reasons unknown, nothing came of this idea.

The refugee situation escalated in Finland in 2015, and during the summer and early autumn, the number of asylum applications in Kemi increased twelvefold (MTV 2015).[1] In Kemi as well as in other places the number of hate-crimes peaked again (Police College of Finland 2016; cf. Kemi-Torniio district court R09/260). A group from Kemi came up with a new idea, street patrols. They contacted NRM again, asking for a permit to organize patrols (interview Holappa; cf. Yle 2016b). This was possibly due to the fact that NRM had its own patrols too and overlapping of the activities was something to be avoided.

The connection to NRM has not disappeared since; in early 2016 SOO withdrew from cooperation with Finnish Defence League – an anti-Islamic organization based on the British model – right after NRM claimed FDL was a covert Zionist organization (Vastarinta.com 2016). In 2017 SOO participated in at least two demonstrations organized by NRM, members and chapters share Facebook posts by the NRM, and some members even spread NRM propaganda during the SOO patrols. The cooperation with the NRM is something they are currently quite open about, although a local leader emphasized that "we do cooperate to some extent, but it concerns topics we agree upon" (interview SOO 1). These topics include shared anti-EU and anti-immigration positions. Unlike in the case of NRM, anti-Semitism does not seem to stand out in the communication of the SOO – which is, besides the lack of a coherent political program, one of the reasons NR supporters have criticized SOO (Dahlberg-Grundberg 2017 cf. Bjørgo 1995).

For the purposes of this article, 26 online-profiles of SOO leaders have been analyzed. The analysis shows that unlike NRM, key members of the SOO do not have a clear background in skinhead subculture. Typically, a SOO leader has a wife and kids, works in a blue collar job, and quite often has been or is a member of some motorcycle club or similar group. Membership in motorcycle clubs is common – however, these seem not to be "outlaw" style groups like Hells Angels or Bandidos. The age of the leaders analyzed is most commonly between 25 and 35 years, although especially among the rank and file there are much older people too – some of them are over 50. The skinheads have also shown some interest in joining the SOO, but in most of the cases they have not been accepted because, as an interviewee claimed, they "try to recruit people who know how to behave."

This may at least partly explain the relatively non-violent behavior, especially when compared to NRM: even if many of the SOO members are former petty-criminals with violent behavior, they have no such organizational and cultural experience of violence as in skinhead subculture where violence is an essential part of the cultural heritage.

The organizational schema of SOO follows a structure with local chapters, regional divisions and the leadership at the hands of a board-like group. Local groups may decide independently on their activities, as long as they follow the rules and some general guidelines given by Kemi. The recruiting process runs a path from a supporter to prospect and ending in full membership. A common way of joining is by invitation from friends, but SOO recruits people via social media too. They also take part in discussions and debates, and join other movements at their demonstrations. What is, to some extent, also remarkable is that SOO did not have a proper web page at all until 2017, apart from a couple of chapters that have created modest pages for selling SOO items. This reflects the development of the field in Finland also more generally: in contrast to NRM and several other groups created during the 2000s, SOO represents the new form of mobilization via social media, alongside with other similar new phenomena like the Close the Borders movement. Establishing a local chapter is also based on social media: one asks a permit from the HQ, creates a Facebook group, and starts to invite new members and organize patrols via support pages. Communication between leaders used to happen via Messenger groups, but these were shifted to the Telegram-messaging platform after some leaks in 2016 (interview SOO 1; online-observation.)

Expansion and decline

The Soldiers of Odin started as a modest local group, but a few months after its establishment it gained large media attention, and soon also international media took a notice of the group. The growth snowballed in late 2015 and in early 2016. The count of local chapters reached 27 by the end of January 2016. The number of international chapters grew similarly.

The boom in January 2016 happened to some extent due to the escalating media attention, and even if the news were negative, initially it seemed to create more support for the SOO – and they even claim they did not avoid controversy but added fuel to the fire on purpose (interview SOO2; cf. Castelli Gattinara and Froio 2018). A local leader has commented this by noting that "the group Ranta got together in Kemi, it was something exciting, it was great. There was something mystical about it" (interview SOO 1). The first reports on street patrol groups were not all negative either, and, among others, even the chair of the national police board showed his support for them (Helsingin Sanomat 2016a), although back-pedaling later. To the horror of her party comrades, one city council member of the Social Democratic Party in Oulu gave even the NRM patrols her support (Kaleva 2015). If a sign of anything, it perhaps tells of initial chaos and confusion at the face of a new situation. The "mystique" started to vanish soon, however.

After a rapid start, the growth of the SOO stabilized during the spring of 2016, and new chapters were created only at a similar pace as that with which others were closing down. It is noteworthy that two of the original division centers ceased their operation, too. The decline in membership and number of chapters reportedly occurred when some local groups saw their patrolling as meaningless and recruiting new members, or even keeping the old ones active, appeared difficult (Helsingin Sanomat 2016b; Satakunnan Kansa 2016).

One factor in the decline may have been that the SOO officially distanced itself from the more moderate groups, such as Finnish Defence League. At about the same time as the stagnation, a promotional video was shown on their Facebook account, with logos of the NRM visible (YouTube 2016a). These developments were followed by internal fighting, which led to some chapters closing their activities and in some cases starting to patrol under different banners (YouTube 2016b). For example, in Helsinki one member who left the SOO established his own group, Sons of Nemesis, which was inspired by SOO but appeared as more violent, and later faced charges for running a criminal organization (Helsinki District Court, R16/8576). Several counter-movements were also created, the most well known of these being the Loldiers of Odin, a group of clowns following the SOO patrols.

Establishing new chapters during the summer of 2016 may be explained also as a reaction to news claiming the SOO is in decline; SOO calls these "fake-news" (e.g. SOO Finland, Facebook 24.8.2017). Revitalization by uniting the forces of several cities, thereby gathering bigger patrols, was probably also one of these efforts to counter the news. That way they could show their force, and collect more than the usual handful of patrollers. SOO has also acknowledged in public that the number of activists peaked in the spring, the number of members growing to about 600, and then diminishing by about 25% (SOO Finland, Facebook 6.1.2016). As stated by the Finnish Security Intelligence Service, some of the leaders have apparently reacted to the decline by radicalizing their message (Etelä-Suomen Sanomat 2016; cf. Della Porta 1995, 84): they started to share national socialist material without restraints. But some members were also fired due to the negative publicity even if they thought they were only doing what was expected from them. One fired member, who was convicted and fined for an assault, explained his ending up in a fight with quarrelling drunken people: "I was then a member of Soldiers of Odin, and saw it as my duty to intervene" (Imatra Police Station, 5620/R/4495/16). Since the start of the SOO, quite a lot of people have indeed left active participation, partly due to their behavior: "At the start there came people who were very short-tempered. There were some fights [...] but those disappeared quite soon. Here in Jyväskylä there is only one original member left" (interview SOO 1).

Decline in activity is clearer when analyzing the reports on patrolling. The silent period in the SOO activities during the summer was reported in several newspapers and has been confirmed by observation. It is striking that especially in the summer of 2016 there was an obvious gap in several otherwise active localities. For example

246 Tommi Kotonen

in Joensuu, patrols were reportedly organized between February and April, and after a long silent period the activity started again in October 2016.

Soldiers of Odin as an international phenomenon

Originally, the idea of the Soldiers of Odin was to focus on the Kemi area; there was no intention to spread the organization to the whole of Finland, let alone grow the movement into an international phenomenon. As later became apparent, this unpreparedness to lead an international organization was the cause of many of problems – not to mention the fact that the SOO leaders did not have much previous leadership experience whatsoever.

The international dimension of the far right may be seen to act in two different ways, international or transnational: building an actual international organization or creating a loose transnational network for sharing ideas and patterns of action (Virchow 2013). To some extent SOO has both dimensions, but at the practical level it works more as a network and brand than as an organization. On the ideo-logical level the issue that binds chapters in different countries together, is their anti-Muslim prejudice, which, according to some analysts, is also the lowest common denominator on which the European radical right can agree (Caiani 2018). Very often, the anti-Muslim messages are shared via images, so called memes, which makes it easier also to overcome the language barriers (cf. Doerr 2017).

The international franchise of the Soldiers of Odin started to grow especially fast after international media noticed the presence of the group:

> Partly with the help of the media the knowledge was spread all over the world, and then came requests [for permit to form a chapter], but this was mainly via Facebook through foreign acquaintances. Later we started to look more carefully at who are suitable to join, and started to weed out those who did not follow the rules.
>
> *(interview SOO 2)*

The weeding out has been quite heavy: currently, in April 2018, officially recognized foreign groups exist only in eight countries, with Finland included. This is a remarkable decline from the highest figures presented: in the autumn of 2016 they claimed to have groups in 22 countries. In the USA, SOO claimed to have chapters in more than 40 states, but now only two remain.

The organization has indeed seemingly suffered problems with foreign groups not fulfilling their obligations and submitting themselves to the command of Kemi. Kemi has tried to control groups abroad by moderating their Facebook groups, some Finns being members in several groups and leading the franchise (interview SOO 1.). Currently, the foreign contacts are taken care of by a team of members, mostly Finns but also one Maltese member, and they also make occasional visits to foreign chapters. Some foreign groups, especially Swedish ones, have also visited Kemi HQ, but most of the communication happens via Facebook, and sometimes

The Soldiers of Odin in Finland **247**

by phone. A peculiar case is the Estonian chapter, which is led by Estonians living in Finland. In some cases, like in Russia, language problems have prevented the building of new foreign chapters. They have also avoided making official connections with countries where the activity may be found to be illegal (interview SOO 2.)

According to some foreign chapters Kemi acts in a dictatorial manner, and tries to bully other groups to make them pay for the costs of the Finns and, as they claim, their new clubhouse. But like local chapters in Finland, SOO claims the foreign groups are relatively independent as long as they follow the rules (interview SOO 1). However, some foreign groups dissociated from the Finnish SOO have been dissatisfied with public image of the SOO, distancing themselves from the racism of the Finnish group, and have also been unhappy with membership fees (SOO Finland, 2.8.2017, Facebook; interview SOO 1). The Finnish SOO members have acknowledged some mistakes were made in this respect:

> It was actually a fundamental mistake, that when this [SOO] was spread abroad, there were no payment obligations. [...] Then there was a lot of work for those, who lead this foreign thing, and we thought one has to somehow compensate them for their efforts, and had to create a fee.

Afterwards, the SOO leadership noticed there were actually very many chapters, for example in the USA, so the amount of money to be paid was huge. Demands for payments caused fights, and allegedly in some cases the leaders disappeared with the money. Too much money caused problems in Finland too: "Then came the fights: We have 10,000 on our bank account, what shall we do with it? At some stage money is counterproductive."

Building an international "franchise" or an actual organization has faced similar problems elsewhere too, as can be observed in, for example, the cases of organizations like the World Union of National Socialists and brands like Combat 18. Groups abroad may be interested in the "brand," but not in following the foreign leadership, and there may be suspicions that the foreign leaders are just making money for themselves. Stealing money and mismanagement are common accusations (Jackson 2014, 15, 26). Problems faced by the SOO are thus in no way unique.

Reasons for the early success of the SOO in Finland: political opportunity and organizational resources

The Soldiers of Odin was born in the middle of the mobilization wave around the refugee-issue. Even though other street patrol organizations were founded, the SOO became the market leader in Finland, outbidding its rivals, and soon was the only one left on the streets. The growth of the SOO happened in interplay with local authorities, media and counter-movements (cf. Quent and Schulz, 2015), but was also helped by the political climate, which created political opportunity.

Open access to political decision-making and institutions tend to facilitate protest, but moderate its form. Where these opportunities are lacking, the protest

248 Tommi Kotonen

often takes more radical, sometimes violent form (Caiani et al. 2012, 11). This suggests that when radical right parties have electoral support and thus larger share in political decision making, they work as a safety valve, moderating the protest. But in order to channel the protest, the party in question needs to be a credible alternative to the ruling elite.

In Finland, the anti-immigration Finns party had already in previous elections gained much new ground, and managed to hold their positions in 2015 as well, becoming a government party. Due to their shift from opposition to a party in government, the "safety valve" effect was to some extent diminished. As a member of a coalition government the Finns party had to compromise some of their relatively radical positions on immigration, and instead of channeling the protest, they became a target of criticism from anti-immigration circles (interview Street Hawks; interview SOO 1; cf. Hatakka 2016).

Discussions at the largest Finnish anti-immigration forum Hommaforum exemplify their disappointment and search for new alternatives (see e.g. Hommaforum 2016). Behind the electoral success of the Finns was to a large extent extra-parliamentary groups, especially the anti-immigration organization Suomen Sisu, which itself saw the representative form of democracy as a "travesty" (Vaarakallio 2015). In 2015 the protest started to channel away from the Finns Party – which sank heavily in the polls – and outside the representative political system. Relatively large demonstrations during the refugee crisis in the autumn 2015 were one sign of this development. Also, the Suomen Sisu got hundreds of new members – most of them without any previous political or organizational activity – the growth was "explosive" (interview Suomen Sisu).

At the local level, SOO found an early supporter from a Finns Party city-council member in Kemi, Harri Tauriainen, who is also a member of Suomen Sisu. Tauriainen had promoted anti-Islamic views, and wrote messages supporting "white power" in his blog and in social media. For example, one of his blog posts stated it bluntly: "100% white, 100% proud" (Kunnollisvaalit 2013). Before the SOO made its first appearance in 2015, Tauriainen took part, he claimed as a private citizen, in a demonstration against "uncontrollable refugee policy" organized by Mika Ranta (Lapin Kansa 2015). Tauriainen labeled the immigration as an "invasion by the Islamists" and, despite being a member of a government party, acted like an opposition politician and claimed he and the crowd were sending a message to the government against their refugee policies (YouTube 2015).

Protest channeled via extra-parliamentary routes and through internal opposition of the Finns Party thus also enabled the establishment of the SOO. In some cases local representatives of the Finns Party acted as organizers, even if occasionally the party members started their own, rivaling patrols too (Ilta-Sanomat 12.1.2016). Since 2017, after the split within the Finns and the anti-immigration faction of the party went into opposition, SOO has publicly supported their candidate Laura Huhtasaari in the 2018 presidential election and spread leaflets for her support, and in some cities local representatives of the party meet regularly with the SOO (interview SOO 1).

The Soldiers of Odin in Finland **249**

One of the keys to the success of SOO in Finland was also how it resonated with society's larger interpretational frames on immigration and refugee crisis. How the other movement organizations and especially the politicians defined matters was highly relevant. An older example by Ruud Koopmans shows, that when "the extreme right suddenly found support for its view of foreigners and refugees as an unbearable burden for Germany, [it] was able to reach a number of substantive victories, which encouraged further mobilization" (Koopmans 1996). A similar growth of support for anti-refugee statements occurred in Finland during the autumn 2015.

Political discourse on the refugee crisis in Finland echoed themes present in the SOO community. It is notable, that also the members of the government started to use language referring to uncontrollable crisis soon after the first refugees arrived in Finland. The prime minister used metaphors relating to natural disasters, like the dehumanizing term "refugee flood" (Yle 2015d), and the Minister of the Interior spoke of the situation as an uncontrollable phenomenon (Yle 2015c; STTK 2015). President Niinistö noted that all of the refugees came with good intentions and that some of them are just seeking better life (Office of the President of the Republic of Finland, 2016). As Jouni Tilli (2016) has noted, framing the debate on refugees in Finland in 2015–2016 had three differing dimensions: discourses focused on economic aspect, threat, or humanitarian viewpoints. Welfare chauvinist statements or those seeing a potential threat did not follow party lines. Current needs of the refugees were to some extent sidelined and focus was on their future potential. One may also note that in speeches of the political elite, a certain kind of nationalism was present: Questions regarding refugees were usually framed from national perspective, i.e. how Finland as a nation is going to survive this crisis.

Instead of focusing just on anti-immigration rhetoric and security issues, SOO provided people with possible culprits, and also a solution to the Islamization: At the core of the problem lay, according to them, the ideology of multiculturalism, which caused the flow of refugees and was seen as a cultural threat to original, white Finnish culture. Other groups, like Streetpatrols or Katuhaukat (Street Hawks), seemed to avoid the deeper political interpretations (Helsingin Uutiset 2016; Oulu-lehti 2016). From the perspective of the SOO, those groups have been "too cautious" in their activities and in avoiding racist language (interview SOO 1). Rival groups, on the other hand, saw the activities of the SOO as counter-productive from a security perspective (interview Suomen Sisu), and some even avoided using the term "street patrol" and talked instead of outdoor activities or jogging, and did not use any signs or vests (interview Street Hawks). There was no "mystique" or confrontational aspect in their work, and politics as well as use of discriminating or racist language was avoided – the lack of counter-movements underlines this issue.

A more radical, openly political message and militant appearance secured the media attention for SOO, which was seen as a reason why they won the out-bidding between rivaling patrol-organizers (interview Suomen Sisu; cf. Castelli Gattinara and Froio 2018). Among the SOO the demand for more openly political

250 Tommi Kotonen

position-taking is still present, and has even increased. According to an interviewee, the majority of the SOO members see, that "nothing will change if they only patrol, even if 24/7." One needs to go more political, "otherwise we cannot influence the root causes of the problems" (interview SOO 1).

Values, language and violence

Especially after first setbacks in organizing patrols, SOO seems to have focused on community issues, and references to brotherhood and unity are very common. Self-promotion constitutes a large part of the communication: out of the images shared by the SOO Finland via Facebook almost one quarter depict their troops on patrol (analysis of the images, 17.8.2017). The use of similar clothing with SOO logos also helps in creating group solidarity and to show loyalty. The significance of common logos was shown in return of some members who left the SOO in 2016. After a year of trying to organize patrols under their own label, Finnish Home Guards, they rejoined the SOO, and one of the returnees justified this, claiming that patrolling under no visible logos was just not satisfying: they "did not stand out, because there was no common dress code" (Facebook 29.5.2017). Visible presence on the streets and demonstrations differentiates SOO from other street patrol groups, which act without any recognizable sings or outfits.

The appeal to potential members is increased by showing solidarity among the members and active community building (cf. Meadowcroft and Morrow 2017). The Soldiers of Odin has created what resembles a subculture of its own.[2] Unlike other street patrol movements in Finland, the SOO has been able to bond its members into a common cause, even if there have been inevitable internal schisms. There are lots of similarities with the values of the skinheads as observed e.g. by Mark Hamm (1994, 25; on Finnish skinheads, see Lähteenmaa 1991, 34–36): skinheads were proletarian, puritanical, chauvinistic, clean-cut, and aggressive, with rough machismo demeanor, had traditional working class community values and pride in the neighborhood territory. Besides local security culture, which is emphasized in their program, concern about local community is also a broader issue: "If the decision making is taken away from homes and villages and apartment buildings and municipalities and cities, and even outside the state, people lose their ability to decide on their own lives" and become "apathetic zombies." Smaller and larger worries are shared between members, who may spend time together also outside the SOO activities (interviews SOO 1 and SOO 2).

To support the local community, the Soldiers of Odin also does occasional charity work –echoing the Finnish political discourse on the refugees, which did not lack the welfare chauvinist aspect. Referring to SOO in Canada, Emil Archambault (2017) has summed the goals of the charity work: "The group purports to help 'Canadians' (defined largely as white, 'European'); excluding migrants and refugees is part of the same ploy: for 'Canadians' to win, Muslims and refugees must lose." Or as a Finnish Odin member argued, the issue was that "the welfare services and health care, they must work, they are for us Finns. Our dads and mothers and grandparents have built this system" (interview SOO 1).

Loyalty has been a central theme in the SOO communication and is often repeated using visual elements. In their recruiting they also stress this point: "Trust and loyalty between the members must be steadfast" (SOO Joensuu, Facebook 13.2.2016). When these principles are broken, the response may be aggressive. This had its most dramatic manifestation when a former Southern Division capital city Kouvola decided to cut its ties to SOO. A photo of a burning clothing item, apparently a SOO jacket of Kouvola chapter, was circulated within SOO media, alongside with text "Kouvola batch. Our rat city. Fuck you guys."[3]

Reactions may be similar when an individual leaves the group. For example, when one of the leading members announced he will no longer be active within SOO due to family reasons and apparently also due to fighting at the local SOO club, most of the commentators understood the decision. But one member commented he will "come and nail those signs back," another one agreeing and writing that he has "a nail gun in his car, and a box of 9mm nails, if needed … So that those signs surely will stay" (Facebook 22.9.2016; cf. North-Carelian district court, R 17/731).

The SOO employs a dual communication strategy when appealing both to "concerned citizens" as well as more radical elements, which may also be a factor explaining their success within the Finnish far right. In itself, the strategy is not new, but, as Luca Tateo (2008, 290) has pointed out, has been used for example in the online communication of the Italian far right already in the 2000s. The strategy aims at "self-legitimating toward the outgroup and increasing the cohesion toward the ingroup." A similar type of dual communication can also be found in action within the Finns Party and especially within its extra-parliamentary wing Suomen Sisu. Tuula Vaarakallio (2015) has described their communication as a hybrid model using calculated ambivalence and differing ways of appeal to ingroup and outgroup.

Analyzing the profiles of the Finnish SOO leaders, one may note that white nationalism (Beirich and Hicks 2009) is one of the commonly shared ideological themes among them, and it is especially often shared in the form of memes. Regarding direct, written references to white nationalism, in one of the first public statements by Odins their Joensuu chapter claimed they are a "patriotic organization fighting for the white Finland" (Yle 2016a). Later their leader Ranta tried to minimize this statement, arguing "white Supremacists are welcome to join the Odins, but only five per cent of Odins hold these views" (Daily Mail 2016). Analysis of the leaders' profiles shows, however, that the number of those leaders who have promoted white nationalism or white supremacy is actually around 20 percent – and may even be higher when considering the figure is based solely on their public profiles.

It is also notable, that even the official national support groups share messages and memes promoting white nationalism: among many others, the German national chapter has published an image which includes the unofficial slogan of the white nationalists, "14 words" by David Lane (Michael 2009), with only the minor modification of having "white children" changed to "our children" (SOO

252 Tommi Kotonen

Germany Support, 19.7.2016): "We must secure the existence of our people and a future for our children."

As a "physical counter-force" and echoing themes of white nationalist ideology, the SOO Finland has an obvious violent potentiality. However, the analysis of the leader profiles shows, that, in most of the cases, they are not a part of the violent subcultures, and they also avoid recruiting members who may be seen as too aggressive. Violent inclinations have so far been channeled through violent messages and internal fights; there are only a handful of cases where SOO members have used violence towards outsiders. Also, in their public statements the SOO has stressed that they use violence only for self-defense and that they do not allow any illegalities.

The concept of self-defense seems to be flexible though (cf. Lööw 1993). Among others, one local chapter commented on Facebook that "stopping the harmful immigration, multicultural hell and islamization is no longer possible by democratic means" (SOO Jyväskylä Support 7.4.2017). Statements by the leader of SOO, Ranta, have been even more direct: "Our Fatherland, arm your sons and ask us to drive away those strangers, preferably right away" (Facebook 16.11.2015).

Militant outlook and militant rhetoric emphasize the Odins' conviction Finland is under invasion.[4] Loyalty, unity and brotherhood are needed at the battle against invaders, and those who are ruining the traditional Finnish lifestyle and culture and eventually the national unity, are seen as traitors. Fittingly a common theme in memes is the Winter War (1939–1940), which has often been depicted as an exemplary case of national unity against a common enemy (cf. Bjørgo 1995).

Ranta is – like many right-wing extremists – influenced by the so called Islamophobes who consider civil war with Islam as inevitable (cf. Ekman 2015), and he has brought this ideology to SOO too:

> If Civil War is needed to make our streets safe again, then a Civil War it will be, but we will never withdraw. If you want to take part in the fight for our living space, make contact and join us.
>
> *(Facebook 5.4.2016)*

After the Turku incident in August 2017, currently investigated as an Islamist terrorist attack, Ranta declared that "this means war, Finland will have revenge" (Facebook 18.8.2017). So far, this war has been waged only on paper.

Notes

1 At that time hundreds of refugees travelled through Kemi and neighboring Tornio, which already belonged to the cities that had received most refugees per capita Finland during the past 20 years (Yle 2015a; Yle 2015c; Yle 2016c). Also, the unemployment rate was high in the Kemi-Tornio region.
2 The British subcultural theory has during the last 20 years been under debate, and several of its original assumptions have been either denied or shown to be incompatible with

The Soldiers of Odin in Finland 253

later developments, and its relevance outside the "original," British subcultures, like punks, may be questioned. Not going into that debate here, it suffices to say that some elements of the theory may be useful in analyzing the extremist movements as well. Cf. Daniela Pisoiu (2015): "Subcultural Theory Applied to Jihadi and Right-Wing Radicalization in Germany," Terrorism and Political Violence, 27:1, 9–28.
3 Maybe worth noting but burning ones "colors" is also a tradition within MC-clubs when resigning from membership.
4 This is also reflected in terms used at the extreme right in general: before 2015 perhaps the most common derogatory term for refugees in Finland was "pakoloiset," a Finnish word referring to refugees as parasites, but since then it has been replaced by "matut," short for "maahantunkeutujat," invaders.

References

Official sources

Helsinki District Court, judgment in case R16/8576.
Imatra Police Station, pre-trial investigation file 5620/R/4495/16.
Kemi Police Station, pre-trial investigation files 8690/R/5910/09 and 8690/R/5908/09.
Kemi-Tornio District court, judgment in case R09/260.
North-Carelian district court, judgment in case R17/731.
Police College of Finland (2010). Report on suspected hate crimes reported to the police in Finland in 2009. Police College of Finland: Tampere.
Police College of Finland (2016). Report on suspected hate crimes reported to the police in Finland in 2015. Police College of Finland: Tampere.
PRH: Finnish Patent and Registration Office, The Official Rules of the Soldiers of Odin, registration number 216.621.
PRH: Finnish Patent and Registration Office, The Official Rules of the Suomi Ensinry (Finland First), registration number 217.654.

Online sources

ADL (2016). Soldiers of Odin USA. The extreme European anti-refugee group comes to America. Anti-Defamation League, Retrieved from https://www.adl.org/sites/default/files/documents/assets/pdf/combating-hate/Soldiers-of-Odin-USA-Report-web.pdf.
Archambault, Emil (2017, April 15).The Soldiers of Odin and Canadian politics. Retrieved from https://politicsdistilled.wordpress.com/2017/04/15/the-soldiers-of-odin-and-canadian-politics/.
Daily Mail (2016, February 2). Exclusive – Nazi daggers, SS hats and a hangman's noose: On night patrol with the 'Soldiers of Odin', neo-Nazi led vigilantes vowing to 'keep Europe's women safe from migrant sex attacks'. Retrieved from http://www.dailymail.co.uk/news/article-3426685/Nazi-daggers-SS-hats-hangman-s-noose-night-patrol-Soldiers-Odin-neo-Nazi-led-vigilantes-vowing-Europe-s-women-safe-migrant-sex-attacks.html.
Etelä-Suomen Sanomat (2016, July 4). Soldiers of Odinin rivit harvenevat ja ärhäköityvät – Supo huolestunut. Retrieved from http://www.ess.fi/uutiset/kotimaa/art2283647.
Helsingin Sanomat (2016a, January 5): Poliisiylijohto hyväksyy kansalaisten katupartioinnin – suojelupoliisi seuraa ilmiötä huolestuneena. Retrieved from http://www.hs.fi/kotimaa/art-2000002878195.html.

254 Tommi Kotonen

Helsingin Sanomat (2016b, May 26). Katupartioiden toiminta hiipuu Suomessa – Soldiers of Odinin aktiivi: "Pitäisi sattua jotain huonoa, että ihmiset aktivoituisivat." Retrieved from http://www.hs.fi/kotimaa/art-2000002903098.html.

Helsingin Uutiset (2016, January 28). Uuden katupartion taustoista paljastui hämäriä piirteitä. Retrieved from http://www.helsinginuutiset.fi/artikkeli/359539-uuden-katupartion-taustoista-paljastui-hamaria-piirteita.

Hommaforum (2016,February 5): Perussuomalaisten gallup-kannatus. Retrieved from https://hommaforum.org/index.php/topic,110745.0.html.

Ilta-Sanomat (2016, January 12) Perussuomalaisten kunnanvaltuutettu aikoo johtaa katupartiota Iisalmessa – Puoluesihteeri: kannattaisi harkita uudelleen. Retrieved from https://www.is.fi/kotimaa/art-2000001064519.html.

Kaleva (2015, July 31) "Painajaismainen ajatus" – SDP – vaikuttajat irtisanoutuvat oululaisen valtuutetun katupartiokannasta. Retrieved from. http://www.kaleva.fi/uutiset/oulu/painajaismainen-ajatus-sdp-vaikuttajat-irtisanoutuvat-oululaisen-valtuutetun-katupartiokannasta/703448/.

Kunnollisvaalit (2013, January 14) Harri Tauriainen, Kemi, PS. Retrieved from http://kunnollisvaalit-2012.blogspot.fi/2012/10/harri-tauriainen-kemi-ps.html.

Lapin Kansa (2015, September 17). Kemissä ja Torniossa osoitetaan mieltä. Retrieved from https://www.lapinkansa.fi/lappi/kemissa-ja-torniossa-osoitetaan-mielta-15129018/.

MTV (2015, August 29) Kemiin tulee turvapaikanhakijoita kolmessa päivässä yhtä paljon kuin viime vuonna. Retrieved from https://www.mtv.fi/uutiset/kotimaa/artikkeli/kemiin-tulee-turvapaikanhakijoita-kolmessa-paivassa-yhta-paljon-kuin-viime-vuonna/5285106#gs.cTOtseU.

Office of the President of the Republic of Finland (2016, January 1). Tasavallan presidentti Sauli Niiniströn uudenvuodenpuhe 1.1.2016. Retrieved from http://www.presidentti.fi/public/default.aspx?contentid=339634&nodeid=44810&contentlan=1.

Oulu-lehti (2016, January 12). Ouluun puuhataan katupartiota. Retrieved from http://www.oululehti.fi/?app=NeoDirect&com=6/255/70799/362f0332a6.

Satakunnan Kansa (2016, June 20). Soldiers of Odinin toiminta lopahti Porissa – harkitsee paikkakunnan vaihtoa. Retrieved from https://www.satakunnankansa.fi/satakunta/soldiers-of-odinin-toiminta-lopahti-porissa-harkitsee-paikkakunnan-vaihtoa-13808621/.

STTK (2015, October 11). Sisäministeri Petteri Orpo: Vihapuheelle laitettava piste. Retrieved from https://www.sttk.fi/2015/10/11/sisaministeri-petteri-orpo-vihapuheelle-laitettava-piste/.

Tilli, Jouni (2016, August 12): Talousapuja, elintasosurffareita, Ismaelinjalkelaisia – maahanmuuttajat poliittisessa retoriikassa. Politiikasta.fi 12. 8. 2016. Retrieved from http://politiikasta.fi/talousapuja-elintasosurffareita-ismaelin-jalkelaisia-maahanmuuttajat-poliittisessa-retoriikassa/.

Vastarinta.com (2016, March 11) Soldiers of Odin teki pesäeron sionistiseen FDL: ään. Retrieved from http://www.vastarinta.com/soldiers-of-odin-teki-pesaeron-sionistiseen-fdlaan/.

Yle (2015a, September 2): Kemiin Lapin kaupungeista suhteellisesti eniten pakolaisia. Retrieved from https://yle.fi/uutiset/3-8273857.

Yle (2015b, September 14): Video: Sadat turvapaikanhakijat kansoittivat taas Kemin keskustan. Retrieved from https://yle.fi/uutiset/3-8305169.

Yle (2015c, September 14). Orpo: Pohjois-Suomen pakolaistilanne hallitsematon – pohjoisessa aloitetaan tehostettu valvonta raja-alueilla. Retrieved from https://yle.fi/uutiset/3-8304601.

Yle (2015d, September 16). Katso ja lue Sipilän puhe tästä kokonaisuudessaan. Retrieved from https://yle.fi/uutiset/3-8311098.

The Soldiers of Odin in Finland 255

Yle (2016a, January 4) "Valkoisen Suomen puolesta taisteleva järjestö" aloitti katupartioinnin Joensuussa. Retrieved from https://yle.fi/uutiset/3-8568968.

Yle (2016b, June 7). Henkilökuva: Kemin katujen pikkukingi – kuinka Mika Ranta tuli perustaneeksi Soldiers of Odinin. Retrieved from http://yle.fi/uutiset/3-8822027.

Yle (2016c, December 1). Varkaus vastaanotti yhden pakolaisen samassa ajassa kuin Kemi yli 700 – "Ehkä olemme tässä viiveellä liikkeellä." Retrieved from https://yle.fi/uutiset/3-9320676.

YouTube (2015, September 19). Speech by Harri Tauriainen in Kemi, September 19, 2015 (starting at 6:00) (seen 3. 8. 2017, later removed). Retrieved from https://www.youtube.com/watch?v=GzX3FHR5dX4.

YouTube (2016a, March 16). Soldiers of Odinin ja Suomen Vastarintaliikkeen mainosvideo. Retrieved from https://www.youtube.com/watch?v=Qex-Qw3PeQs.

YouTube (2016b, September 19). Suomi Ensin – Heinola. Retrieved from https://www.youtube.com/watch?v=prKMBuRNaHM.

Printed sources

Beirich, Heidi and Kevin Hicks (2009).White nationalism in America. In Barbara Perry, *Hate Crimes. Vol.1* (pp. 109–132). Westport, CT: Greenwood Publishing.

Bjørgo, Tore (1995). Extreme nationalism and violent discourses in Scandinavia: "the resistance", "traitors," and "foreign invaders." *Terrorism and Political Violence*, 7(1), 182–220.

Caiani, Manuela (2018). Radical right cross-national links and international cooperation. In Jens Rydgren (ed.), *The Oxford handbook of the radical right* (pp. 394–411). New York: Oxford University Press.

Caiani, Manuela, Donatella della Porta, and Claudius Wagemann (2012). *Mobilizing on the extreme right: Germany, Italy, and the United States.* Oxford: Oxford University Press.

Cleland, Jamie, Chris Anderson and Jack Aldridge-Deacon (2017). Islamophobia, war and non-Muslims as victims: an analysis of online discourse on an English Defence League message board. *Ethnic and Racial Studies*, 41(9), 1541–1557.

Dahlberg-Grundberg, Michael (2017). Internet som politiskt verktyg. In: Heléne Lööw, Mattias Gardell and Michael Dahlberg-Grundberg, *Den ensamme terroristen?*Stockholm: Ordfront.

della Porta, Donatella (1995). *Social movements, political violence, and the state. A comparative analysis of Italy and Germany.* Cambridge: Cambridge University Press.

Doerr, Nicole (2017). Bridging language barriers, bonding against immigrants: A visual case study of transnational network publics created by far-right activists in Europe. *Discourse & Society*, 28(1), 3–23.

Ekman, Mattias (2015). Online Islamophobia and the politics of fear: Manufacturing the green scare. *Ethnic and Racial Studies*, 38(11), 1986–2002.

Castelli Gattinara, Piero and Froio, Caterina (2018). Getting 'right' into the news: grassroots far-right mobilization and media coverage in Italy and France. *Comparative European Politics.* [Online First] https://doi.org/10.1057/s41295-018-0123-4.

Hafez, Farid (2014). Shifting borders: Islamophobia as common ground for building pan-European right-wing unity. *Patterns of Prejudice*, 48(5), 479–499.

Hamm, Mark (1994). *American skinheads – the criminology and control of hate crime.* Boulder: Paladin Press.

Hatakka, Niko (2017). When logics of party politics and online activism collide: The populist Finns Party's identity under negotiation. *New Media & Society*, 19(12), 2022–2038.

Jackson, Paul (2014). Accumulative extremism: The post-war tradition of Anglo-American Neo-Nazi activism. In Paul Jackson and Anton Shekhovtsov. *The post-war Anglo-American far right: A special relationship of hate* (pp. 2–37). Basingstoke: Palgrave Macmillan.

Koopmans, Ruud (1996). Explaining the rise of racist and extreme right violence in Western Europe: grievances or opportunities? *European Journal of Political Research*, 30(2), 185–216.

Lähteenmaa, Jaana (1991). Hip-hoppareita, lähiöläisiä ja kultturelleja. Nuorisoryhmistä 80-luvun lopun Helsingissä. Helsingin kaupungin nuorisoasiainkeskus.

Lööw, Heléne (1993). The cult of violence: The Swedish racist counterculture. In Tore Bjørgo and Rob Witte (eds.), *Racist violence in Europe* (pp. 62–79). London: Macmillan.

Meadowcroft, John and Elizabeth A. Morrow (2017).Violence, self-worth, solidarity and stigma: How a dissident, far-right group solves the collective action problem. *Political Studies*, 65(2), 373–390.

Michael, George (2009). David Lane and the fourteen words. *Totalitarian Movements and Political Religions*, 10(1), 43–61.

Muslimit on ongelma [Muslims are the problem]. Leaflet produced by the Soldiers of Odin. No date.

Pisoiu, Daniela (2015). Subcultural theory applied to Jihadi and right-wing radicalization in Germany. *Terrorism and Political Violence*, 27(1), 9–28.

Quent, Matthias and Peter Schulz (2015). *Rechtsextremismus in lokalen Kontexten. Vierverglei-ichende Fallstudien*. Wiesbaden: Springer VS.

Tateo, Luca (2008). The 'fascist' discourse in computer mediated communication: the 'dual strategy' model of the Italian extreme right. *Psicologia & Sociedade*, 20(2), 287–296.

Vaarakallio, Tuula (2015). The borderline between parliamentary and extra-parliamentary rhetoric: The case of the populist (True) Finns Party. In Suvi Soininen, Tuula Vaarakallio (Hrsg.) *Challenges to parliamentary politics: Rhetoric, representation and reform* (pp. 99–124). Baden-Baden: Nomos Verlag.

Virchow, Fabian (2013). Creating a European (neo-Nazi) movement by joint political action? In Brian Jenkins, Andrea Mammone and Emmanuel Godin (Eds.) *Varieties of right-wing extremism in Europe* (pp. 197–214). London: Routledge.

16

SHEEP IN WOLF'S CLOTHING?

The taming of the Soldiers of Odin in Norway

Tore Bjørgo and Ingvild Magnæs Gjelsvik

Soldiers of Odin Norway have tried very hard to communicate that they were *not* vigilantes and *not* right-wing extremists. Although they obviously have displayed some traits of vigilantism and anti-Islam opinions, they were clearly less militant and right-wing extremist than their original role model, the Soldiers of Odin in Finland. This chapter will explore why the Norwegian chapter of the Soldiers of Odin (SOO) turned out as a rather moderate variety of the phenomenon but also why it – in its stated mission to provide public safety in the streets – attracted a particular type of participants: young men with a criminal past.

Data

This study[1] is based on several sources of both primary and secondary data. We have had extensive interviews with the two main national leaders, and previously also the first spokesman.[2] We have been participant observers during one of the first SOO patrols in Drammen on 20 February 2016 and talked with several participants during that event. We have followed a few open Soldiers of Odin support sites on Facebook (but not their closed Facebook sites). Furthermore, we have interviewed (and communicated more informally with) several police officers who have handled different aspects of SOO activities. Some court documents and police data have also been made available to us. And finally, a huge amount of news coverage on SOO activities and activists have provided massive amounts of secondary data.

The emergence of Soldiers of Odin in Norway

Norway is characterized by a relatively low level of crime, and a high level of social trust as well as a high level of trust in the police and other public institutions,

258 Tore Bjørgo and Ingvild Magnæs Gjelsvik

according to the European Social Survey.[3] The Norwegian police is well educated, but it has one of the lowest ratios of police officers per capita in Europe.[4] The police are considered professional, fair and honest, but score lower on capacity and effectiveness.[5]

Like in many other European countries, the so-called "refugee crisis" became a hot political issue in Norway. 31,135 refugees, mostly from Syria and Afghanistan, applied for asylum in Norway in 2015. The following year, the numbers were down to 3460,[6] partly due to a very restrictive asylum policy by the government, which consisted of a coalition between the Conservative Party and the right-wing populist Progress Party, whose party platform is distinctly restrictive on immigration. Beyond the Progress Party, the far-right scene in Norway is small and weak. Anti-immigration sentiments have a considerable following on social media but have a very limited impact on the street level. Far right political parties generally fail in elections. The Norwegian branch of the neo-Nazi Nordic Resistance Movement have only a few dozen activists but lean heavily on support from their Swedish partners when organizing demonstrations in Norway. Their activities are increasing, though.

Opponents of accepting in a rapidly rising number of refugees from the Middle East and Africa into Europe claimed that the "flood of refugees" constitutes a threat along several dimensions: There were concerns about the economic costs, and some were also worried about demographic and cultural impact of the arriving refugees. Some pointed to the potential risk of terrorist infiltration into Europe, and the possible negative consequences of immigration for public safety and crime – and in particular the fear of rape of European women by Muslim males.

What turned more or less well-founded worries into a moral panic was the events that took place in Cologne and several other cities on New Year's Eve 2015/2016: several hundred women became victims of sexual assaults, mainly committed by recently arrived male refugees from the Middle East and Northern Africa.[7] During the following days, there were reports of similar incidents on a smaller scale in Kalmar, Sweden, and unsubstantiated accounts from several other places. Claims (partly substantiated) that the police and the media initially tried to cover up the assaults to avoid stigmatizing refugees contributed to a widespread anger against refugees as well as distrust towards authorities. Anti-Islam and anti-immigration movements obviously tried to reinforce such emotions, claiming that Muslim men are coming to Europe not only to conquer our lands for Islam, but they are also sexually aggressive predators coming here to molest our women.[8]

During the days and weeks after the New Year events, there were intensive discussions on several Norwegian Facebook pages about the need to do something to protect "our women" against the criminal and sexually over-charged male refugees. The Soldiers of Odin group of Finland and their "uniform", black hoodies (sweaters with a hood) with symbols combining Norse symbolism, national flags, a militant name and the style of outlaw MC club back patches clearly appeared as an attractive approach. Some contacted the leaders of the original SOO groups in the town Kemi in Finland, and got permission to make use of a

The Soldiers of Odin in Norway **259**

Norwegian variety of the SOO symbols on condition of abiding with the by-laws of the Finnish SOO. The Finnish mother organization had admin status of the Facebook pages of the Norwegian chapter during the first establishment phase but lost (or relinquished) this control after a while. Gradually the Norwegian SOO chapter distanced itself from the Finnish SOO but it regained its ties with the international SOO organization, which was controlled by a Finnish and a Maltese leader.[9]

The Norwegian chapter started to organize, recruit and plan activities on Facebook during late January 2016. They staged their first patrol ("walk") in the city of Tønsberg on a Saturday night on 13 February 2016, with around 14 participants.[10] The first (allegedly self-appointed) spokesman was a former leading activist in Norwegian Defence League, Ronny Alte. There were also a couple of well-known neo-Nazi activists among them. However, most of the participants had no ties to far-right groups but they were well known by the police for many other issues. The event attracted huge media interest and controversy, which probably helped to fuel recruitment and spread the idea to new places. Within the next ten months, SOO staged more than 100 "walks" in more than 20 different locations in Norway, mostly in smaller cities and towns. Many of these were one-off events with few if any local participants but with "guest appearances" of SOO activists from chapters elsewhere. The most frequent walks were concentrated in five cities: Arendal, Tønsberg, Lillestrøm, Drammen and Fredrikstad.[11]

The start-up phase as well as the continuation became highly chaotic for Soldiers of Odin Norway. Within the first months, two factions split off and established their own organizations: "Sons of Odin"[12] (which included some of the founders of "Soldiers" in Norway) as well as "Guardian Angels".[13] In addition, the self-appointed spokesman of SOO, Ronny Alte, was excluded from the organization because he acted on his own on behalf of the group without a mandate to do so, and due to his known ties to anti-Islam organizations. He gave SOO an image of being right-wing extremist, which was not the case, his opponents claimed.

A more formal national organization with an elected leadership started to emerge in late February 2016. A kind of general assembly meeting was held in Drammen on 12 March 2016.[14]

A typical SOO "walk" in the areas where they were most active when the organization was at its peak could consist of 5–12 people gathering at an appointed place on a late Friday or Saturday night, but sometimes they were fewer.[15] Full members would wear the SOO hoodies whereas newcomers had normal clothes. They also emphasized the importance of mustering a sufficient number of participants in order to make the group look strong.

> Small groups (2–4 persons) will often be perceived as provocative out in the streets; therefore it is a rule to walk in larger groups of around 10 people. This will give a strong signal-effect which as such will contribute to prevent or "drive away" unwanted behaviour/persons. If you plan to do walks in

troubled neighbourhoods or near big events this is particularly important – the more people, the better![16]

The group would then walk together in the outskirts of the town centre – but usually not in the main entertainment areas of the town where they risked getting into confrontations with opponents, or where they were more likely to be approached by the police. They argued that rape, robbery and drug dealing were more likely to take place in the back alleys than in the main streets. Since many of the SOO members were "streetwise" they knew where in town crime was likely to happen. During the first weeks after SOO Norway emerged in February 2016 there were hints that they might intervene if they come across something criminal.[17] However, very soon they took care to emphasize that they would not be any kind of "extra police" but only observe, document and report to the police. They would only intervene if lives were in danger or serious harm could be prevented.

They did concede that their intimidating appearance was intended to have a deterring impact on potential offenders, and that even a bad (and undeserved) reputation as right-wing extremists could have some advantages:

> Soldiers [of Odin] got a very intimidating reputation, partly from abroad. [... SOO] is pretty radical in Finland, and it caused a rumor among the immigrants [here in town], in particular among the criminal immigrants, because we know more or less who among the immigrant gangs are criminal. And as soon as they saw us [i.e. SOO] they left the city center, and that was of course excellent! We did not talk to them or anything, they just saw us and then we did not see them anymore that evening. [...] Yes, it was a bad reputation, but in just this context it was a good thing that the criminal elements disappeared when they knew we were in town, and that was great![18]

This SOO leader claimed that they received many positive responses from the locals when they were patrolling his hometown, Arendal. However, when we observed the SOO group walking in Drammen, we found it rather striking that most people avoided contact and appeared to find them frightening. This intimidating image was reinforced by the two rather scary dogs the group brought with them.[19]

There was a striking contradiction between what the Soldiers of Odin communicated verbally – distancing themselves totally from anything having to do with violence, right-wing extremism or vigilantism – and what they communicated visually and symbolically. The name refers to the Norse god Odin's mythological fighters, about whom Snorre's saga states that

> [Odin's] own men [...] were crazy like dogs and wolves, they were biting in their shields, were strong like bears and oxes; they killed all people, and neither fire nor iron could harm them, it was called to go berserk ...[20]

FIGURE 16.1 Soldiers of Odin posing for the photographer before they start a night patrol in Drammen, Norway, 20 February 2016
(Photo: Heiko Junge).

Images of Vikings or Norse gods have long traditions in right-wing extremist circles and the combination with the flag reinforces the nationalist connotations. The stylistic elements were obviously put together to mimic the back patches of outlaw motorcycle gangs, adding to the intimidating image.

To our knowledge, there have not been any reports in the news media nor by the police that the Soldiers of Odin have committed any acts of violence or made any explicit threats during any of their more than 100 "walks". However, there is no evidence that SOO through their many walks have disrupted any specific acts of crime either.[21]

Who were recruited to Soldiers of Odin Norway – and why?

During the first weeks after SOO Norway emerged, leaders claimed that they got support from all kinds of people, and that their members included dentists and police officers. However, mainstream middle class people were rarely seen among those who turned up for walks with Soldiers of Odin.

Given the fact that Soldiers of Odin was initially established as a reaction to the refugee crisis in 2015, it was hardly surprising that several well-known right-wing extremists and anti-Islam activists turned up as participants in the first Soldier of Odin walks in February 2016. However, as SOO Norway gradually established itself as a formal organization, persons with overt extremist or racist views were swiftly excluded from the group.

> People who turned up and thought we were real racists who were out to beat up "negroes"; they were immediately weeded out and excluded. [...] at least 50 people were excluded during my time in the board.[22]

Although many members of SOO continued to hold views critical to immigration and some clearly had ties to far right groups,[23] expressing such views during SOO walks was met with strong disapproval.[24] Whereas right-wing extremists eventually became far less visible in SOO than one might expect, another type of participants became far more prominent in the organization: young men with a criminal past, typically in their twenties and thirties.

The first formally elected leader, Steffen André Larsen, did not hide the fact that he had a background from a criminal milieu and had an extensive criminal record.[25] He resigned as a leader in December 2016 when he faced trial for a violence case (unrelated to his SOO activities). When the new leader, Jan Tellef Aanonsen, took over, he was frustrated by the fact that the previous leader had recruited a number of local SOO leaders with the same kind of criminal background as himself, and also let in a lot of members who were (former) criminals or drug abusers.

> It should be the task of the leader to sort out such people. Instead [the former leader and his side-kick] were appointing their pals, including a regional leader who was a drug addict. I went mad! And then they wonder why the police are so much against them?! I have no problems understanding that! [... When you have local leaders like that], young 20-somethings with criminal records and who are drug addicts, they will not get [law-abiding] adults in their 40s or 50s [like me] to go out on walks with them, they don't want to be seen with such people, it's as simple as that![26]

After only a couple of weeks as the leader of SOO Norway, Jan Tellef Aanonsen resigned and closed down the organization in early January 2017, claiming that the main reason was that Soldiers of Odin had attracted "the wrong kind of people". He also asserted that he refused to adhere to the anti-Islam approach of the international leaders of the Soldiers of Odin, and that this position displeased these international leaders (op. cit.).[27]

An interesting question is why so many young men with a criminal past joined an organization that had as its stated purpose to help the police to maintain peace and order in the streets. Many of them had been charged with violence and unruly behaviour, carrying illegal weapons, drug dealing and abuse, robbery and violence against the police – the kinds of behaviours they were now setting out to prevent. The former leader (op. cit.) claimed that even if they excluded many people for being unfit for SOO, around 70 per cent of the active members had such a criminal background. So why did these former offenders then join the Soldiers of Odin?

The Soldiers of Odin in Norway   **263**

Part of the explanation is that much of the recruitment was based on pre-existing social networks that in this case happened to be networks between young offenders. However, the Soldiers of Odin was obviously attractive to this type of young men, for several reasons. The black hoodie with the SOO symbols provided the participants with a cool identity, standing out as a strong, uniformed group with an image associated with nationalism, manly warrior ideals, outlaw MC clubs and a strong group identity based on masculine ideals. The organizational structure and the recruitment process was a simplified version of the outlaw biker club model. It required some effort to be accepted as a full member and be permitted to use the hoodie with the SOO logo. That this status was something to be achieved made it even more attractive for certain young men to join. The admission requirements were moderate, though: participate in three walks and three meetings and behave in an acceptable way.[28]

Another explanation was that many young men with a tainted criminal record considered participation in the Soldiers of Odin as an opportunity to make amends for some of the bad things they had done in the past. This interpretation was confirmed by the former leader, Steffen Larsen:

Many of the Soldiers of Odin have been in jail, they are fed up with the system and how things function around them, and now they have a desire to do something really positive for society. We have experience with the criminal scenes. [...] We have a uniform which enables people to recognize us, a very simple logo, so that people cans say, "Oh yes, there they are; these are the people we may ask for help".[29]

[... That people in SOO have a troubled background] is something I am well aware of. [... This] has been quite a big theme [in our group]. That "yes, I have been involved in some criminal stuff and I have been finished with that several years ago and now I feel I have to give something back". It's a really nice way to give something back [to society], by joining something like [Soldiers of Odin].[30]

When the fuss around the "flood of refugees" and stories about their alleged sexual assaults of European women spread like a moral panic during winter and spring 2016, many of these young men grasped the opportunity to make a positive contribution by protecting women and other vulnerable people against this alleged threat. At the same time, it was an opportunity to turn a negative identity and a tarnished personal reputation into something positive: Rather than being known as the town's troublemakers and petty criminals they could now become heroes from whom people could seek protection. The SOO participants were mainly young men,[31] and many were at the end of a career of juvenile delinquency. Soldiers Of Odin could provide them with an attractive exit from their stigmatized identities. Because they knew street life and had experience from the criminal environment they believed they were in a better position to know where and when criminal incidents and rapes were likely to take place.

FIGURE 16.2 Soldiers of Odin in Norway are helping two young girls safely home on a late Saturday night in Tønsberg, Norway, 13 February 1916. This was the first SOO patrol in Norway
(Photo: Luca Kleve-Ruud)

Soldiers of Odin frequently claimed they were "a kind of night ravens". They were then often challenged with the question of why they could not just join the official, well-established Night Ravens [*Natteravnene*], an organization of volunteers that encourages adult, sober citizens to walk around in the city in groups during weekend nights. Participants are typically parents of youths or children, or elderly, concerned citizens. Their task is to be visible and available for the public, based on the idea that the presence of sober adults will prevent violence and anti-social behaviour. The Night Raven volunteers will also assist people who are unable to take care of themselves. They do not intervene in cases of violence or unruly behaviour but call the police. Like the Night Ravens, they claim to be preventative, not interventionist.[32] The Night Ravens have been in operation since 1990, sponsored by an insurance company, and working closely with the police.

The Soldiers of Odin claimed their tougher image gave them some extra "respect" that ordinary Night Ravens were lacking:

– But why can't you just join the ordinary "Night Ravens"? [...]
– Because they have to stand there watching if someone are beaten up. They cannot intervene.
– But can you intervene without being vigilantes?

The Soldiers of Odin in Norway **265**

- Yes, if life or health is at stake, then it is our duty. But it is not merely about that. We have more respect than two ladies in their sixties wearing a yellow reflex vest,[33] replies [the local SOO leader].
- [Another SOO activist] adds that several members of the group have been convicted for offences and therefore feel that they do not fit in as ordinary Night Ravens.[34]

The leader of SOO Norway, Steffen Larsen, discussed how they differ from the ordinary Night Ravens:

[The Night Ravens] do not walk around where things happen. And that's what we try to do; we walk in [back] streets where things are likely to happen [...] And many people claim that "you are so big and scary". If that can have a preventive affect against a rapist, I think that is fine. I will honestly admit that. Because people who observe us should not become scared of us unless they have a reason to be.[35]

Distancing themselves from the traditional Night Ravens, the Soldiers of Odin nevertheless continued to present themselves as "a kind of private night raven service". The official Night Ravens were highly critical to the ways SOO were exploiting their reputation and legitimacy as a politically and religiously neutral organization. "The Soldiers of Odin grew out of a right-wing extremist milieu. If you want to contribute to more safety for all groups in the population, it is critical that you act with credible neutrality", the general secretary [of the Night Ravens] states.[36]

Responses to the Soldiers of Odin

Receiving some kind of recognition from their social surroundings for doing something good was obviously important to many of the participants in Soldiers of Odin – in particular because many of them had a rather tarnished reputation in their local communities. The responses at the street level varied considerably, however, from expressions of disapproval and ridicule to statements of support.

The Facebook group "Support Soldiers of Odin Norway" had around 4000 members. In the general public debate and in the new media critical and negative views on SOO dominated. All the political parties in Parliament spoke out against the Soldiers of Odin and similar vigilante movements. Only one single MP from the right-wing populist Progress Party supported SOO, Jan Arild Ellingsen, who was the party's spokesperson on justice politics. However, the party leader, Siv Jensen, disagreed with her party colleague, and the Progress Party's Minister of Justice at the time, Anders Anundsen, stated that "It is the police that shall secure our streets. [...] I cannot see that the Soldiers of Odin has any role in this context". Prime Minister Erna Solberg stated that Soldiers of Odin "looks like a vigilante group, and we are against that. There are no others who should patrol and provide safety in Norwegian towns, this is a task for the police alone".[37]

The media coverage of the SOO was also generally very negative, frequently portraying them as right-wing extremists, which stigmatized those who participated in SOO walks.

> After the media went out so badly against us, many [of our participants] almost lost their jobs. Many employers told them that "you have to choose, either being a neo-Nazi or work here". [...] One member was married to a priest, and he was told that unless he reined in his wife he might lose his job. It's pretty sick, if you ask me.[38]

The police were also generally outspoken about not wanting any help from the Soldiers of Odin to maintain law and order in the streets.[39] However, there was great variation in how the police in different cities and police districts actually responded to SOO activities after they started their "walks" in February 2016, and the police appeared rather uncertain and fumbling about how to respond. In some cities they were promptly turned away by the police and not allowed to walk around in the streets with their uniforms. In Kristiansand, for example, they were refused to patrol the streets but they were permitted to hand out coffee and cakes.[40] The local police made a public statement that they considered private patrolling to be a criminal offence. Elsewhere, groups of uniformed SOO members were permitted to walk around in the streets but under strict police supervision.[41] Obviously, the SOO activities were not of much help to the police in making the city safer, as they, in effect, tied up considerable police resources that could have been put to better use. In some towns, the police did not respond at all to SOO walks.

A couple of weeks after the first Soldiers of Odin walks, in late February 2016, the police chiefs in all the police districts agreed on a common policy. They referred to the so-called "vigilantism paragraph" in the Police Law:

> According to the Police Law § 26, "It is illegal for any other than the police to organise or participate in private operations with the purpose of maintaining public order or in any other forms of law enforcement in public areas."[42]

The police chiefs agreed that activities appearing like "patrolling", with the use of joint "uniforms", without any affiliation to the police or similar institutions, will be considered by the police to be in violation of the Police Law § 26. When the Soldiers or Odin or similar groups appeared in the streets as a group in uniforms, this was considered punishable by law and the group would be instructed to stop this activity, meaning to disband or to remove their uniforms. The activity could be considered illegal and punishable in itself, regardless of whether the activity will disturb the public order or not.[43]

The Soldiers of Odin in Norway **267**

Although the police chiefs in principle had agreed to stop Soldiers of Odin and similar groups from patrolling the streets on the basis of the Police Law's § 26, the police practice continued to vary considerably in different parts of Norway. In some places the SOO continued to patrol uniformed without any police intervention; elsewhere, they were ordered by the police to take off or turn inside out their hoodies in order to hide the symbols.

Elsewhere, the local police tried to prevent the SOO from walking around in the streets with their uniforms with a *different* legal basis, namely the Police Law's § 7 on disturbing public law and order. When the police in the town Kongsvinger in November 2016 on this basis fined the SOO leader for refusing to take off (or reverse) the hoodies they were wearing, he was freed from the charges in the local court. The judge "could not see that removing the group's logo from the attire alone could stop any disturbances of the public order, safeguard the safety of individuals or the public, or disrupt or stop acts of crime, cf. the Police Law § 7".[44]

This verdict was, of course, interpreted as a victory by the Soldiers of Odin, believing that they now had a legal verdict giving them the right to carry out their walks dressed in their hoodies with visible symbols. However, Kai Spurkland, a police lawyer and leading expert on the legal framework for police operations and private policing argued in a paper widely distributed in the police that the verdict was probably correct, given the legal basis the local police had referred to (the Police Law § 7). However, had they instead justified their intervention by claiming that the Soldiers of Odin's uniformed patrolling was a breach of the Police Law § 26 on banning private law enforcement, this would probably have prevailed in court.[45]

Increasingly, the police used the latter approach to order the SOO to disperse or take off their uniforms, and on several occasions, SOO participants were fined. The last known case took place in the city of Tønsberg in early May 2017 when ten Soldiers of Odin were ordered by the police to take off their hoodies. They initially obeyed but when the police came across them again later the same night – dressed in their hoodies – the police fined three of them. "When they appear as a group and are uniformed, it is against the Police Law", the police stated.[46] This was the last known attempt of the Soldiers of Odin to organize a "walk" in a Norwegian city, with or without their hoodies and symbols.

Concluding remarks

There are few permissive conditions that could make Norway conducive to the emergence of vigilantism. Norway is a stable and affluent democracy with a high trust in public institutions, the police and the rule of law among the large majority of people – although there are some pockets of more distrustful groups. There are no cultural traditions of people taking the law in their own hands in Norway (unlike e.g. the USA).[47] The "offer" by the Soldiers of Odin to help the police to maintain safety in the streets was promptly turned down – by the police as well as by leading politicians from all the major parties. Those who expressed support to

268 Tore Bjørgo and Ingvild Magnæs Gjelsvik

the Soldiers of Odin were few and marginal. The main permissive factor that might contribute to the emergence of vigilantism is the low level of visible policing – police officers are rarely seen in the streets, and they are not necessarily available when you need them.

The main repressive response – that the police eventually banned the SOO from patrolling the streets with their "uniforms" (the hoodies with symbols) and fined them if they refused to take them off – took time to establish consistently in different police districts and cities. In many towns, the local police fumbled on how to handle the Soldiers of Odin. However, when the police finally established a more consistent practice of fining the SOO if they continued to walk as a group with their hoodies, the Soldiers of Odin disappeared from the streets in Norway. The last Soldiers of Odin "walk" took place in Tønsberg on 6 May 2017, one year and three months after they had their first "walk" in the same city.

Thus, the main cause of the downfall of the Soldiers of Odin in Norway was most likely the increasingly consistent approach of the police to ban them from walking as a uniformed group. Thereby they lost their cool image and the identity symbol that obviously was very attractive and important to many of the participants. However, the internal conflicts, organizational problems and strife about who should be leaders and members, and the stigmatization of participants also contributed to the disintegration of the Soldiers of Odin in Norway.

The Soldiers of Odin in Norway was clearly part of a transnational movement of vigilantism in Europe, responding to the "flood of refugees" in 2015 and onwards, and, in particular, to sexual assaults on women on New Year's Eve in Cologne. Organizationally and visually, it was inspired by the Soldiers of Odin in Finland and their style. However, the Norwegian branch developed in a more moderate direction, playing down the anti-immigration and anti-Islam views of the mother organization, and excluded participants who expressed overt racist or right-wing extremist views. Why did SOO Norway move in this direction?

One part of the explanation is probably related to the people who gained control over the organization. After a brief period of splits and exclusions, the emerging leaders were people who had other agendas than fighting immigration and Islam. They seemed to be very concerned about achieving public recognition for being "good guys" who wanted to do something beneficial and noble. Many of the most active members had a tarnished reputation in their local communities for being criminals and troublemakers. The Soldiers of Odin's effort to make the streets safer for women and others was their opportunity to make up for some of the bad things they had done in the past. If the SOO became associated with right-wing extremism, this would stigmatize them, and undermine their effort to gain recognition and improve their standing in society.

Notes

1 This chapter is based on the research we did in connection with our study on right-wing extremism in Norway: Tore Bjørgo and Ingvild Magnæs Gjelsvik (2018). Utvikling og

utbredelse av høyreekstremisme i Norge. In: Tore Bjørgo (ed.). *Høyreekstremisme i Norge: Utviklingstrekk, konspirasjonsteorier og forebyggingsstrategier*. Oslo: PHS Forskning: 4.

2 Steffen Larsen was interviewed twice, 20 February 2016 (during a SOO patrol we observed) and on 18 August 2016. He was the national leader from late February 2016 until December 2016. Jan Tellef Aanonsen had been a deputy national leader until he took over as leader on 19 December 2016 but retired and (in effect) closed down the organization on 6 January 2017. He was interviewed on 17 October 2017. These two plus the first (self-appointed) spokesman were highly public figures and are the only SOO activists to be named in this study.

3 See e.g. https://www.academia.edu/2215329/Trust_in_justice_-_Topline_findings_from_the_European_Social_Survey?auto=download.

4 See: https://www.reddit.com/r/europe/comments/6dggqx/police_officers_per_capita_in_europe/.

5 Gunnar Thomassen, Jon Strype and Marit Egge (2013). Trust no matter what? Citizens' perception of the police 1 year after the terror attacks in Norway. *Policing*, Volume 8, Number 1, pp. 79–87.

6 https://www.regjeringen.no/no/tema/innvandring/innsikt/statistikk-om-innvandring/id2339904/.

7 For a discussion of the New Year incidents in Cologne, see the chapter by Daniel Koehler in this volume.

8 See https://www.theguardian.com/world/2016/feb/18/polish-magazines-islamic-of-europe-cover-sparks-outrage, discussing the cover page of a Polish magazine with a picture of a white woman draped in the EU flag, being molested by several "brown hands", headlined "Islamic Rape of Europe" (*wSieci*, No. 7, 2016).

9 This is based on information from our separate interviews with the two national leaders of SOO Norway.

10 https://www.vg.no/nyheter/innenriks/asyl-debatten/her-patruljerer-soldiers-of-odin-for-foerste-gang-i-norge/a/23616953/.

11 Based on information from former SOO leader Jan Tellef Aanonsen. According to him, the police were unaware of many of these walks.

12 The Sons of Odin was quite active with "walks" in Bergen and a few other towns during winter/spring 2016. It is not clear to us what the differences between them and "Soldiers" were, and whether one was more extremist than the other. The media and the police tended to confuse the two groups.

13 The Guardian Angels had a softer image than SOO, using light blue hoodies without symbols associated with right-wing extremism. However, this group did not succeed and soon faded away.

14 https://www.dt.no/nyhet/drammen/soldiers-of-odin-mottes-i-drammen/s/.5-57-319582. See footage from the meeting: http://www.aftenbladet.no/tv/#!/video/101164/her-legger-ledelsen-i-soldiers-of-odin-planen-for-gruppen-videre.

15 This description is based on our own participant observation of a SOO walk in Drammen on 20 February 2016 and our discussions with two SOO leaders and the police.

16 Cited from the bylaws of Soldiers of Odin Norway, made available to us by the SOO leader at the time.

17 Example: http://www.agderposten.no/nyheter/soldiers-of-odin-aksjonerer-i-arendai-sentrum-onsker-a-bli-arrestert-1.1557302.

18 Interview with SOO leader Jan Tellef Aanonsen, 17 October 2017, talking about SOO walks in his hometown.

19 During a stop and check by the police in Drammen the SOO members were told to take the dogs back to the cars.

20 From Snorre Sturlason's *Saga of the Kings of Norway: Heimskringla*, Chapter 6, written in the first half of the thirteenth century.

21 In interviews with police officers, we were informed about a single case where the Soldiers of Odin had notified the local police about a drunk man who was laying out in the cold. The police subsequently brought him to safety.

22 Former SOO leader Jan Tellef Aanonsen, interview 27 October 2017.
23 For example, a young man who repeatedly appeared in the media as a local SOO leader in 2016 was marching with the national socialist Nordic Resistance Movement's demonstration in Kristiansand on 29 July 2017.
24 One telling episode took place during our observation of a SOO walk in Drammen on 20 February 2016: a man approached the SOO group and presented himself as an "Islam critic", holding a brief monologue about his anti-Islam ideas. The SOO group stayed silent until he left. It is possible that our presence influenced the situation but our feeling was that his views were not welcome, and that they did not want to invite him to join the group.
25 https://www.vg.no/nyheter/innenriks/odins-soldater/ny-odins-soldater-leder-til-vg-jeg-har-sonet-min-straff/a/23627125/.
26 Former SOO leader Jan Tellef Aanonsen, interview, 27 October 2017.
27 According to Aanonsen, it was the Finnish and Maltese leaders of SOO worldwide who declared that "Soldiers of Odin in Norway does not exist anymore", and that this happened as a consequence of him resigning as a leader of SOO Norway.
28 According to the bylaws of Soldiers of Odin Norway, § 4.
29 Film interview in Aftenposten TV 31.03.2016: http://www.aftenposten.no/webtv/#!/video/111303/man-faar-ikke-stoppet-en-folkebevegelse-som-soldiers-of-odin. This URL does not work anymore, but the following does: http://www.aftenbladet.no/tv/#!/video/101164/her-legger-ledelsen-i-soldiers-of-odin-planen-for-gruppen-videre. This film from an internal national meeting of leaders and activists in SOO shows several interesting aspects of who participates in SOO and how they behave.
30 Our interview with former SOO leader Steffen Larsen, 18 August 2016.
31 There were some female members of SOO in Norway; some of these were the girlfriends of male members.
32 Tammy Castle and Tara Parsons (2017). Vigilante or Viking? Contesting the mediated constructions of Soldiers of Odin Norge. *Crime Media Culture*, 1–20. DOI: 10.1177/1741659017731479. To our knowledge, this is the first scholarly study on the Soldiers of Odin on Norway.
33 A yellow reflex vest is the "uniform" of the Night Ravens, making them easily visible at night.
34 Interview in the local newspaper Agderposten 23.07.2016 http://www.agderposten.no/nyheter/soldiers-of-odin-aksjonerer-i-arendai-sentrum-onsker-a-bli-arrestert-1.1557302
35 Interview with SOO-leader Steffen Larsen, 18 August 2016.
36 https://www.aftenposten.no/norge/i/M3wo/Natteravnene-tar-avstand-fra-Odins-soldater.
37 Several central politicians were negative to SOO: *VG* 23.02.16: https://www.vg.no/nyheter/innenriks/asyl-debatten/erna-solberg-om-odins-soldater-ligner-en-borgervern gruppe-og-det-er-vi-imot/a/23623556/.
38 Interview with former SOO leader Steffen Larsen, 18 August 2016.
39 The only exception was one single leading police officer in northern Norway who stated that "much of what the Soldiers of Odin plan to do is unproblematic from the police point of view". https://www.nrk.no/finnmark/politisjef-om-odins-soldater_-_-uproblematisk-at-de-trygger-byer-og-tettsteder-1.12810642.
40 https://www.nrk.no/sorlandet/politiet-holdt-oye-med-odins-soldater-1.12814198
41 When the authors walked with the Soldiers of Odin in Drammen on 20 February 2016, the police spent considerable resources on keeping around 12 participants under close supervision, making use of uniformed police officers as well as plain-clothes officers. The police checked the participants for weapons, registered their IDs and ordered two big dogs to be locked up in the cars. http://drm24.no/nyheter/her-patruljerer-soldiers-of-odin-i-drammen-1622048.
42 https://lovdata.no/dokument/NL/lov/1995-08-04-53#KAPITTEL_8.
43 This summary of the consensus between the police chiefs is based on a policy document produced by the Oslo Police District, made available to us.

44 Cited from the verdict in Glåmdal tingrett, case no. 17–004234MED-GLOM, page 4.
45 Kai Spurkland: Kommentar til dom i Glåmdalen tingrett om "Odins soldater". Paper dated 7 February 2017.
46 https://www.tb.no/odins-soldater/politi/nyheter/tre-far-bot-etter-odins-soldater-patrul jering/s/5-76-531878?key=2017-12-12T13:44:19.000Z/retriever/3721444a5963529f45 598be7d0d7b7792bbfd7b0.
47 However, there have been historical incidents of collective "hunting of travelers" ("fantejakt") in Norway, Olav Rune Ekeland Bastrup and Aage Georg Sivertsen (1996). *En landevei mot undergangen. Utryddelsen av taterkulturen i Norge*. Oslo: Universitetsforlaget: 54–55, summarized in Tore Bjørgo & Ingvild Magnæs Gjelsvik (2015). *Forskning på forebygging av radikalisering og voldelig ekstremisme: En kunnskapsstatus*. Oslo: PHS Forskning 2015:2. http://hdl.handle.net/11250/284584|.

17

THE SOLDIERS OF ODIN IN CANADA

The failure of a transnational ideology

Emil Archambault and Yannick Veilleux-Lepage

The Soldiers of Odin first established a Canadian presence in March 2016, five months after the foundation of the group in Finland. As in other countries, the group experienced rapid growth in Canada, establishing a number of chapters throughout the country. Yet, as is common with far-right groups in Canada (Perry & Scrivens, 2016, p. 823; 831–832), the presence of the Soldiers of Odin in Canada has been marred by numerous breakups, internecine conflicts, and divisions.

In this chapter, we trace and assess the six internal splits that marred the group during its first 14 months of existence in Canada, between March 2016 and April 2017. One apparent central point of contention and divergence among Canadian members, we argue, was the significance and perceived value of belonging to the wider transnational network of the Soldiers of Odin, particularly of the Canadian chapters' relationship to the Finnish leadership. As such, this chapter examines the spread and decline of the Soldiers of Odin in Canada through this transnational lens, and argues that the relationship of the Canadian Soldiers of Odin to the wider movement provided a focal point around which internal disagreements coalesced, leading to the failure of the movement to establish a lasting presence. We suggest that the experience of the Canadian Soldiers of Odin is the result of a disjuncture between a transnational rhetoric and ideology emphasizing transnational communities and local presence and concerns.

Ideology of the Soldiers of Odin in Canada[1]

The first chapter of the Soldiers of Odin was created by the self-avowed white supremacist Mika Ranta in October 2015, in what is generally taken to be a response to the influx of refugees settling in Finland or transiting through Finland to reach Sweden (Lamoureux, 2016a). By December 2016, the SOO claimed 20 national chapters all around the world (Montpetit, 2016), including Australia, the United States, Canada, and throughout Europe, from France to Estonia. As Tommi Kotonen's chapter in this volume details, the Finnish founding chapters quickly faced accusations of racism, neo-Nazism, and white supremacism, due both to the group's anti-immigrant, anti-Islam stances, and the composition of its membership (see Rigatelli, 2016a and 2016b; Lamoureux, 2016b; Simons, 2016). Most notably, while the group claims to be overtly non-racist and open to all (Lamoureux 2016b), the organization's founder, Mika Ranta, self-identifies as a "National Socialist" and is well known for his support of white supremacist ideology (Rigatelli, 2016a).[2]

The group spread to Canada as early as March 2016,[3] with its initial chapter reportedly established in Gimli, Manitoba, a town with significant Icelandic heritage (Biber, 2016). The group quickly spread across the country, with chapters being established over the summer in Quebec, British Columbia, Ontario, Saskatchewan, Alberta, and even Yukon. Unlike in Finland, the official emphasis in Canada seems to have been put on community-building efforts, such as shovelling snow (CBC News, 2016), organizing food drives for local charities and shelters (CBC News, 2017a), cleaning up parks (Lamoureux, 2016a), etc. In order to spread rapidly, the Soldiers of Odin in Canada established a particularly strong online presence, through a number of Facebook pages and groups. Indeed, through its main Facebook page which, at its peak, counted over 10 000 "fans",[4] as well as a large number of province- and city-focused Facebook groups, the Soldiers of Odin were able to effectively communicate and transmit propaganda and organizational messages. For this reason, the spread of the group was extremely rapid. Shortly after the foundation of the group in March 2016, the Soldiers of Odin already counted chapters in most Canadian provinces (Andersen & Fedec, 2016, p. 2).

The Canadian Soldiers of Odin, in line with other branches of the movement, conduct "observe-and-report styled patrols" in order to act, in their words, as "the eyes and ears of the police" (Soldiers of Odin, 2016b, p. 1). The vigilantism that defines the group's *modus operandi* worldwide remains a significant part of the Canadian Soldiers of Odin's operations. These patrols very often have an overt or covert Islamophobic or xenophobic *raison d'être*. For instance, in December 2016, the leader of the Quebec chapter was ousted as he "insisted on patrolling the 'politically correct' areas of Quebec City, like Saint-Roch, where the group was less likely to confront the city's immigrant population", according to the leader who replaced him. She, in turn, stated that they used to "avoid that, on patrols, we go into areas where there are a lot of Muslims or Islamization. But, when it comes down to it, that's where we should be patrolling" (Montpetit, 2016). Thus, while the patrols are officially about preventing crime, the group draws a very direct link between Islamophobic sentiments, anti-immigration discourse, and crime prevention, which it displays and enforces through vigilante-style patrols.

In combination with these vigilante street patrols, however, Canadian Soldiers of Odin also emphasize a commitment to community-building and charity actions. The bylaws thus note that they want "to help make local communities better", and to this end "will also host family friendly events and give back to the local charities in [their] communities" (Soldiers of Odin, 2016b, p. 1). Indeed, branches of the Soldiers of Odin have conducted a number of charitable actions, collecting goods and food for the homeless, cleaning up public parks, even offering free snow shovelling (CBC News, 2016, 2017a). The Canadian Soldiers of Odin, by and large, seem to consider these two activities – vigilante patrolling and community and charity work – as complementary, and part of a single ideological and rhetorical frame.

The group's bylaws, once again, offer insight into this ideological framing. The group overtly claims to exist because "the higher authorities are failing the Canadian citizens". The authorities do so by "the allowing of illegal aliens into this country", by "accepting refugees from countries that hate us", and by "releasing confirmed terrorists back to their organizations". From these points, the racist, xenophobic, and Islamophobic justification for street patrols is made clear: refugees and immigrants are equated with security threats, and lead to crime and violence, which vigilante patrols are meant to counter. Indeed, the bylaws continue, "we as Soldiers of Odin realize that it is time to take back our streets, provinces, and country". The "other", from whom the "streets, provinces, and country" are meant to be reclaimed, is clearly construed as immigrants-qua-criminals (encouraged by friendly authorities). Crucially, however, the bylaws specifically denounce government authorities for accepting refugees and immigrants "while Canadians are on the streets" (Soldiers of Odin, 2016b, p. 1); this framing recurs regularly in Canadian Soldiers of Odin propaganda, often with a specific focus on veterans as the disadvantaged and disenfranchised party.

In other words, Canadian Soldiers of Odin frames immigration and social care as part of a zero-sum equation, where providing assistance to refugees means taking away resources from (real) Canadians. As such, protests against immigration, vigilante patrols, and charity work are part of a single, xenophobic, ideological mindset: immigration constitutes the problem, and the group's community minded activities are part of an effort to divert resources back to deserving Canadians and away from immigrants who illegitimately appropriate resources while "caus[ing] more harm against Canada" (Soldiers of Odin, 2016b, p. 1). The whole activities of Canadian Soldiers of Odin remain within an overwhelmingly anti-immigrant, xenophobic paradigm, and as such are consistent with the rest of the Soldiers of Odin movement, despite the focus on community work, which distinguishes them from other branches of the movement.[5]

Nevertheless, this focus on local communities points at a tension within the ideological framework of the movement. The group's bylaws, as cited above, point to a specifically Canadian focus, with Canadian Soldiers of Odin endeavouring "to keep Canadians safe [...] and protect our Constitutional Rights"; similarly, the emphasis on community action points to a specifically Canadian nationalist outlook. The bylaws, however, immediately undercut this nationalist mindset by accusing Canadian authorities of "demonizing anything that has to do with European Culture to try and create racial tensions to turn citizens on one another"

(Soldiers of Odin, 2016b, p. 1). This mention of "European Culture" points to the larger significance of the Soldiers of Odin's transnational network, the majority of which is indeed (geographically) European. In the case of the Canadian Soldiers of Odin, it remains unclear where they fit within this Soldiers of Odin network's "European" focus, particularly when key figures of the network such as Mika Ranta post on Facebook exhortations to "Build the European Homeland" (Ranta, 2017). While "European" here definitely ought to be taken as an ideological (and racial) term rather than as a strictly geographical denomination, it does nevertheless indicate a tension within Soldiers of Odin Canada between Canadian nationalism and transnational ethnonationalism.[6]

These ideological tensions are also made manifest in disagreements between branches of the Canadian Soldiers of Odin over tactics. The Quebec Soldiers of Odin, for instance, seem to put more emphasis on street patrols, and put less emphasis on charitable actions (Montpetit, 2016).[7] In contrast, Mack Lamoureux, attending an Edmonton meeting, noted that "while [the leaders] assured the group that patrols will happen, the meeting focused primarily on volunteerism at a local homeless shelter and cleaning up garbage. The men around the pool table seemed dedicated to staying on the straight and narrow," even quoting one of them as stating "We're not criminals, and we're not fucking vigilantes" (Lamoureux 2016b). Thus, it seems that the tension between community-building activities and vigilante patrolling represented a pressing concern within the group, fragilizing its ideological unity; this tension, in turn, mirrored the fragile balance between Canadian and "European" ethnonationalist identities.

Divisions within the movement

This tension between a strictly Canadian nationalist focus and a transnational civilizational, "European" orientation has proven to be a major point of contention throughout the existence of Canadian Soldiers of Odin, with numerous splits occurring as a result. Already from the start, Canada's Soldiers of Odin have had an ambiguous relationship to the Finnish group: the group's bylaws identify Canadian Soldiers of Odin as "a Division of the original Soldiers of Odin Finland" (Soldiers of Odin, 2016b, p. 1); yet, in an interview, the national leader in Canada stated that "What they do over in Finland and in Europe, they have all sorts of different issues altogether. That's not really what we are. We're an independent charter of Soldiers of Odin; we're a community watch group" (Biber, 2016). While, as argued above, vigilante patrols and community building activities are part of a single anti-immigrant, xenophobic ideology, the Canadian Soldiers of Odin struggled in finding a balance between overt and covert xenophobia, emphasizing or downplaying the affiliation to the Soldiers of Odin Finland in response to pressure from their members, a largely sceptical public, and watchful authorities.

The first group to split from the Canadian Soldiers of Odin seems to have been the Canadian Sentinels, in November 2016, although the group seems to have been rather short-lived and marginal. The second breakup, however, was more consequential, as a number of Albertan chapters left shortly after to form the Guardians of Alberta. The founder of the Guardians of Alberta, claiming black and native American ancestry, explicitly attributed the split to "the racist overtones" in Canadian Soldiers of Odin "and its ties to neo-Nazi organizations" (Johnson, 2017).[8] As such, while not mentioned explicitly, it seems that the Canadian Soldiers of Odin's connection to the Finnish Soldiers of Odin did play a role, given Mika Ranta's and other members' avowed neo-Nazi ties (Rigatelli, 2016a, 2016b; Simons, 2016).[9] Nonetheless, it should be mentioned that the Guardians of Alberta's social media presence and communiqués are far from devoid of Islamophobic overtones (see for instance Guardians of Alberta, 2017).

Shortly thereafter, a leadership shakeup in the Quebec wing of Canadian Soldiers of Odin saw the removal of the Quebec president and national vice-president Dave Tregget in December 2016. By both his account and that of the new Soldiers of Odin Quebec leaders, the main cause of his removal was attributable to the contentious association with the Finnish Soldiers of Odin: "Tregget felt the group's success in Quebec depended on softening its anti-immigration image and putting some distance between the founding Finnish members, who have been accused of having ties with neo-Nazis" (Montpetit, 2016). Tregget himself stated that he was "finished with the racist image of Finland"; the new leadership, meanwhile, specifically targeted "areas where there are a lot of Muslims or Islamization" and sought to "return the Quebec branch of the Soldiers of Odin to its Finnish roots" (Montpetit, 2016). Tregget, meanwhile, went on to found Storm Alliance, a group which rose to (relative) prominence in 2017 as it conducted protests against illegal immigration, particularly Muslim immigration (Tasker, 2017).

In a further split, in February 2017, the Saskatchewan chapters broke off from Canadian Soldiers of Odin to constitute the "Patriots of Unity". As with the earlier groups breaking off, the focal point of contention seemed to consist in perceptions of racism, associations with neo-Nazism, and particularly the affiliation to the Finland leadership. In their statement announcing the split, the Patriots of Unity explicitly announced the end of their affiliation with "Soldiers of Odin Canada, or Finland" (Ward, 2017a). As with the Guardians of Alberta, they reoriented their activities to focus on community assistance, although they continued to conduct street patrols. Furthermore, the Patriots of Unity borrowed almost verbatim the Soldiers of Odin bylaws, although they deleted the few sentences about opposing immigration and the Canadian government (Ward, 2017b).

Around the time of the secession of the Saskatchewan chapters in February 2017, there seems to have been a move to emphasize the connection of Finnish and Canadian Soldiers of Odin.[10] Possibly in response to this statement, Canadian Soldiers of Odin strengthened the rhetoric relating to the Finnish-Canadian connection, as well as to the transnational network of Soldiers of Odin. The slogan "United we Stand, Divided we Fall" became more prominent; profile or cover pictures showing the "Soldiers of Odin Worldwide", or lapel pins of Canadian and Finnish flags started appearing, in conjunction with or replacing the standard Soldiers of Odin images. Yet, this is in tension with another prominent slogan used by the Soldiers of Odin in Canada, namely "We stand on guard for thee", lifted from the Canadian National Anthem, emphasizing the local outlook of the Canadian Soldiers of Odin.

As the history of these splits demonstrates, the presence of a link between Canadian and Finnish Soldiers of Odin chapters proved to be quite contentious as issues of racism and xenophobia have coalesced around the significance of this transnational connection. While Soldiers of Odin Canada is by no means devoid of racism, xenophobia, and Islamophobia (see, for instance, the excerpts from the bylaws discussed above), ideological disagreements have tended to be blamed on the transnational relationship and its role in dragging the Canadian Soldiers of Odin away from its nationalist and community-based roots. As Dave Tregget noted, the presence of the transnational affiliation was routinely considered as holding back the Canadian Soldiers of Odin by tainting the whole movement with overt racism, which these splinter groups would rather see downplayed.[11] While these splinter groups often display similar Islamophobia and anti-immigration sentiments as the Soldiers of Odin do, they acknowledge that the presence of a connection to the Finnish leadership may contribute to both radicalize the movement and infuse it with more overt racist ideology.

The Canada–Finland split

The final straw came at the end of April 2017, as Soldiers of Odin Canada, following a change in leadership, announced its separation from the international Soldiers of Odin movement. In turn, the Quebec chapter split from Soldiers of Odin Canada in order to remain affiliated to the Finnish leadership. Since then, (independent) Soldiers of Odin chapters have continued to exist in Canada in a much more subdued and less visible form, retaining the name and logo of the Soldiers of Odin while separate from the Finnish leadership, except for Quebec, where affiliation was retained.

The statement published by Soldiers of Odin Canada explaining the reasons for their departure is quite clear (although somewhat misleading). They state that they "officially Denounce the Finland and the international leadership of SOO", as they "are against their racist agendas". They continue to assert that Soldiers of Odin Finland's "ridiculous beliefs in racism has always been a huge issue for us in Canada as we do not support or share their views on race", and that "We do not and have not ever abided by these twisted beliefs or the Racist entities in SOO" (Soldiers of Odin Canada, 2017). The Canadian Soldiers of Odin, therefore, clearly attempted to portray this latest splinter as the result of a significant ideological disagreement with the Finnish leadership, attributable to the racist views of the latter.

That being said, there are several reasons to doubt this official narrative as presented by the Canadian Soldiers of Odin. First of all, it is somewhat odd that they would have waited a full year before discovering Soldiers of Odin Finland's racist ideology, even more so given that their racist discourses, iconography, and commitments were widely reported (Simons, 2016). The number of previous splits

278 Archambault and Veilleux-Lepage

from Soldiers of Odin Canada rather show that a large number of people were aware of the implications of the association with Soldiers of Odin Finland and left as they felt that the movement was too closely aligned with its overseas counterparts. While the former leader of Soldiers of Odin Canada had emphasized that they are "an independent charter of Soldiers of Odin" (Biber, 2016), Soldiers of Odin Canada was aware of the ideological commitments of Soldiers of Odin Finland and chose to embrace their association for over a year before the split. As Katy Latulippe, the Quebec leader, wondered, "[Bill Daniels, the Soldiers of Odin Canada President] spent one year as a leader, saying that the Finnish chapter wasn't racists. And then suddenly, after a little conflict, he starts using the term racist? It doesn't hold" (Montpetit, 2017).

Second, as established above, xenophobia and Islamophobic ideology are present at the core of Soldiers of Odin Canada and are not as foreign to the group as the statement quoted above suggests. In Canada, the group repeatedly associated with other far-right, Islamophobic, and anti-immigration groups and speakers (Bell, 2017), in addition to propagating messages in line with the anti-immigration positions quoted in the group's bylaws. Rather, it would seem that the dispute was partly over money, as the Finnish group sought to collect membership fees from members (Montpetit, 2017).

It seems much likelier that, in addition to the dispute over membership fees, the main disagreement concerned methods, pointing to the dichotomy between local concerns and transnational ideology identified in the first part of this chapter. As such, Soldiers of Odin Canada's statement on the break states that they want "the ability to run [their] own countries without being micromanaged by another country"; more clearly, they assert that they "are against their racist agendas and only doing Street patrols and not helping our fellow countrymen and women" (Soldiers of Odin Canada, 2017). It seems therefore that the distinction between community-building work – though inspired by xenophobic sentiments, as explained above – and vigilante patrols became untenable, as the two conflicting orientations indicated the presence of an increasing rift between a xenophobic Canadian hyper-nationalism and identification to a transnational, civilizational struggle. Significantly, it suggests that Soldiers of Odin Canada failed to mobilize on the basis solely of the transnational affiliation, and that local Canadian dynamics in the end mattered more than the affiliation to the transnational network of the Soldiers of Odin.

The Soldiers of Odin and the extreme right in Canada

In addition to the difficulty in forging a coherent group ideology and the resulting splitting of Soldiers of Odin Canada, the movement, despite its initial momentum, appears to have struggled to retain its members and to contain defections to other far-right groups. A preliminary analysis of the online activities of 265 individuals in Canada with clear and demonstrable evidence of membership in the Canadian Soldiers of Odin conducted by the authors of this chapter between January and September 2017, allows us to assess the effects of the breakaway from Finland and

The Soldiers of Odin in Canada **279**

the following decline of the group (Veilleux-Lepage and Archambault, 2019). This preliminary study examined the Facebook profiles of members displaying clear iconography – logos, clothing, slogans, etc. – associating them to the Soldiers of Odin; a repeat examination of the previously identified profiles was conducted in September 2017 to assess variations in group affiliation. This allows us to garner insights into the groups joined by former Soldiers of Odin members and what these individuals sought by joining the Soldiers of Odin, and how they perceived their former group.

This research paints a rather clear portray of the scale of defections amongst the group members. Out of the 265 members, 61 individuals appear to have consciously removed all traces of their previous Soldiers of Odin affiliations, 49 had joined another far-right group, and 54 remained active within Soldiers of Odin chapters.[12] Among the 49 members who joined other groups, most of them either joined a group which resulted from a splinter from Soldiers of Odin; *La Meute* [trans. The Wolf Pack], a Quebec-based, anti-immigration group founded in October 2015; or Canadian chapters of The Three Percenters, an American paramilitary movement which pledges armed resistance against attempts on the restriction of private gun ownership (Lamoureux, 2017b).

The poor retention of members by Soldiers of Odin Canada is unsurprising and conforms to Perry and Scrivens' observation that members of far-right groups tend to "try on different coats", moving "from group to group throughout their lives" as a result of various factors, including personal disagreement and infighting between group members, increase in attention by law enforcement, weak leadership; or changes in members personal or financial circumstances (Perry & Scrivens, 2016, p. 831). However, the defections from Soldiers of Odin to La Meute and to The Three Percenters are rather telling and can potentially be attributed to the aforementioned tension within Soldiers of Odin Canada between Canadian nationalism and transnational European ethnonationalism. Unlike the Soldiers of Odin or the short-lived PEGIDA Quebec, La Meute is an entirely domestic far-right movement, and more particularly a Québécois movement. The Three Percenters, similarly, emphasize the defence of local communities against a government perceived as illegitimate.

La Meute was founded in 2015, by Eric "Corvus" Venne and Patrick Beaudry, Canadian Forces veterans determined to combat what they perceived as a threat posed by Islamic extremism as Canada began accepting the first of 25,000 Syrian refugees. It has become Quebec's biggest, most rapidly growing far-right group with 45,000 members in their Facebook group, and up to an estimated 5,000 to 10,000 active members (PRI World Staff, 2017). In a province where cultural issues are at the front and centre for every political party, the appeal of La Meute can be attributed to its leveraging of profoundly local concerns, often overlapping concerns expressed by mainstream political parties in Quebec. In August 2013, the government of the *Parti Québécois* first introduced the idea of what was to become Bill 60 – also known as the Quebec Charter of Values[13] – which aimed primarily to affirm the secular nature of the state, along with gender equality. The bill, which

280 Archambault and Veilleux-Lepage

amongst the suggested measures, prohibited employees of the public and para-public sectors from wearing an "object which ostensibly displays one's religious affiliation" (art. 5); required employees and users of public services to provide and receive services with their "face uncovered" (art. 6 and 7), and banned activities and practices in childcare and schools "such as dietary practices stemming from a religious precept" (art. 30), received initial support amongst the wider population (La Presse Canadienne, 2015).

As keenly observed by Nadeau and Helly, the debate surrounding the Bill 60 served to crystalize anti-immigration and anti-Muslim sentiments in Quebec in a fashion akin to that of European extreme right parties such as Le Front National and UKIP (Nadeau & Helly, 2016). Moreover, Nadeau and Helly observed that support for the bill was essentially based on general themes: (1) the fear of a return of religion in the public space; (2) the emergence of a Muslim enemy whose values are perceived as irreconcilable with those of Quebec culture; (3) the inertia of the political class and its complicity with media and minorities; (4) the predominance of legal over political powers and of individual over collective rights; and (5) multiculturalism, as a factor of denationalization and social fragmentation (Nadeau & Helly, 2016). The theme of Islamic religious practice being irreconcilable with Quebec's values and multiculturalism as a source of denationalization and social fragmentation represents a central component of La Meute's discourses and actions. For example, La Meute was heavily involved in campaigning against the establishment of the Muslim cemetery in St-Apollinaire (Peritz, 2017). Furthermore, it organized jointly with Storm Alliance – the Soldiers of Odin splinter group founded by Dave Tregget – two large-scale protests (in August and November 2017) in Quebec City opposing illegal immigration and policies of the Quebec government (CBC News, 2017b; HuffPost Quebec, 2017; Pineda, 2017).

The other group that has attracted the largest number of former members of the Soldiers of Odin is The Three Percenters, which first emerged as a largely decentralized American paramilitary group that organized after Barack Obama was elected president in 2008 and built around strong anti-government and pro-gun views. The Canadian origins of The Three Percenters can be traced back to late 2015, shortly after Justin Trudeau became prime minister. While, in many ways, The Three Percenters are a direct copy of an American militia that has been adapted to fit into a Canadian worldview – even the name "Three Percenter" comes from an American myth that it was 3 percent of the American population that fought against the British in the War of Independence – their success in recruiting individuals in Canada, particularly in Alberta and Quebec, can also be attributed to its ability to leverage local concerns effectively, particularly with regards to firearm deregulation (Lamoureux, 2017b).[14] As such, with its vehemently anti-Islam views – the group was after all described as "anti-Islam" by Beau Welling, the president of the Alberta chapter and national vice-president of The Three Percenters in Canada – and its strong emphasis the creation of an armed militia, it appears that The Three Percenters appealed to members of the Soldiers of Odin, who might have felt disenchanted by the group's efforts to reduce its Islamophobic

The Soldiers of Odin in Canada **281**

hard-line, members who believed that armed preparation was necessary, or members who prioritized firearm deregulation, particularly during a liberal tenure (Lamoureux, 2017b).[15] Indeed, it is worth noting that in December 2018, The Three Percenters appointed a new national leader who is a former local leader of the Soldiers of Odin (and also openly Islamophobic) (Lamoureux 2018b).

In summary, while a significant number of Soldiers of Odin members seem to have disengaged – at least for the time being – from involvement with the far right following the disintegration of the group, the majority of members surveyed continued to be involved in far-right movements in Canada, either in the Soldiers of Odin themselves or in other groups. The transfer of members to The Three Percenters should be of particular concern, as it indicates at the very least a willingness to prepare for potential violence combined with anti-immigrant, xenophobic ideology.

Conclusion

This chapter has provided a survey of the presence of the Soldiers of Odin in Canada, particularly of the conflict between its emphasis on Canadian nationalism and its relationship to the Finnish leadership of the movement. As the history of the successive splinterings of the Soldiers of Odin, most prominently the separation of the Canadian chapters from the Finnish leadership (and of Quebec chapter from Soldiers of Odin Canada) shows, there was a strong sense within the group that the association to Finland detracted from the group's community-based work and ideological commitments. Furthermore, the follow-up research conducted on identified members of the Soldiers of Odin after the April 2017 split demonstrates that the majority of the members who transferred to other extreme right groups relocated to groups such as La Meute and The Three Percenters, which have a distinctly local (as opposed to transnational) focus.

While the Soldiers of Odin have been in decline since the April 2017 split, the implications of this research are significant. First, it seems clear that the decline of the Soldiers of Odin is not attributable to a rejection of vigilantism as a method, but rather a return to vigilantism as motivated by local concerns rather than a narrative of ethno-nationalist transnational struggle. Second, it does suggest that the online presence of extreme-right groups, while significant, is of limited value when this online presence is not aligned with the activities of members. Finally, the history of the Soldiers of Odin in Canada suggests that extreme-right groups may have more difficulty mobilizing when the rationale for the group's activities is transnational, rather than grounded in local concerns.[16]

Notes

1 This section concentrates on the Soldiers of Odin in Canada until the end of April 2017, at which point the group split from the Finnish leadership of the movement. We offer an assessment of the Soldiers of Odin after the breakup in the concluding section.

   The founder and national president, Joel Angott, put up a cover picture of the SOO logo with a Canadian flag on March 22, 2016. The Soldiers of Odin Canada public

Facebook page, however, was founded on January 15 (Angott, 2016; Soldiers of Odin, 2016a).

2 See Kotonen's chapter for more details on Mika Ranta and his links to National Socialist movements.

3 This timing coincides with the end of the Canadian government's program to resettle 25,000 refugees from Syria, which was undertaken shortly after the Liberal Party's electoral victory in October 2015. It is unclear – although likely – that this policy contributed to the founding of the Soldiers of Odin in Canada (Associated Press, 2016).

4 This page was deleted in May 2017, precipitating the sharp decline of the Soldiers of Odin Canada.

5 See Tommi Kotonen's chapter in this volume for a comparison with the group's activities in Finland.

Mack Lamoureux, as well, in comparing the Soldiers of Odin to the Three Percenters, suggested that such charitable activities are first and foremost used to sanitize a toxic public image (Lamoureux 2018a).

6 One example of an attempt to situate Canada within a "European" struggle against immigration can be found in the words of a leader of the Soldiers of Odin in Edmonton, Canada: "The guys in Europe, they're dealing with some real shit, we might not see that here for ten or so years. When that happens we want to look as good as possible" (Lamoureux, 2016b).

7 Montpetit, in particular, notes that the Québec Soldiers of Odin tied these patrols to the policing of "areas where there are a lot of Muslims or Islamization" (Montpetit, 2016).

8 It should be mentioned, however, that the Guardians of Alberta have recuperated much of the anti-immigrant rhetoric found among right-wing groups such as the Soldiers of Odin Canada (Thomas, 2017).

9 See Tommi Kotonen's chapter in this volume.

10 It is impossible to demonstrate that these two events are causally linked, but timings coincide.

11 Dave Tregget, for instance, founded a new group called Storm Alliance, which is largely aligned with the anti-immigration agenda of the Soldiers of Odin, although it claims no organizational affiliation. Storm Alliance gained notoriety in 2017 by, among others, staging protests against illegal immigration at the Canadian-American border, as well as organizing surveillance missions at the border to monitor the arrival of asylum seekers crossing from the United States. It also organized a large-scale joint protest in Quebec City in November 2017 (CBC News, 2017b; Lamoureux, 2017a; Shingler, 2017).

12 No information could be collected on the remainder of the individuals as their social media profiles had either been deactivated or suspended.

13 Complete title: *Charter affirming the values of State secularism and religious neutrality and of equality between women and men, and providing a framework for accommodation requests.*

14 The Canadian Firearms Registry was introduced by the Liberal government of Prime Minister Jean Chrétien in 1993 and required the registration of all non-restricted firearms. In 2012, following the Conservative Party of Canada majority win in the 2011 election, Bill C-19, the Ending the Long-gun Registry Act, came into force. The Province of Quebec immediately filed a request for an injunction to prevent the destruction of the data. On 27 March 2015, the Supreme Court of Canada ruled that the destruction of long-gun registry records was within the constitutional power of Parliament, denying the Quebec government's legal challenge and allowing for those records to be destroyed. Following the election of a new Liberal government in 2015, the Prime Minister of Canada promised to strengthen firearm legislation in Canada (Hamilton, 2015).

15 As Lamoureux (2018a) noted, The Three Percenters, like the Soldiers of Odin, have also sought to engage in charitable activities in order to soften their public image.

16 As of January 2018, it seems that the Finnish-led Soldiers of Odin are seeking to re-establish a presence in Canada, having added a chapter in Calgary to its foothold in Quebec. The independent Soldiers of Odin Canada continues to exist as well, and the

two groups seem set on remaining separate. Apart from the Quebec wing, neither group seems particularly active (Soldiers of Odin Canada Offical, 2018).

References

Andersen, J., & Fedec, K. I. N. (2016, October 3). *Soldiers of Odin*. Regina: RCMP Division Criminal Analytical Section.

Angott, J. (2016, March 22). SOO Canada cover photo. Facebook. Retrieved 23 March 2017, from https://www.facebook.com/photo.php?fbid=10153601547208022&set=a.10150826305578022.395398.680618021&type=3&theater.

Associated Press. (2016, March 1). Canada meets target to resettle 25,000 Syrian refugees. *The Guardian*. Retrieved from http://www.theguardian.com/world/2016/mar/01/canada-target-resettle-25000-syrian-refugees.

Bell, S. (2017, May 1). Soldiers of Odin splinter in Canada over 'racist agenda' of far-right group's leadership in Finland. *National Post*. Retrieved 2 February 2018, from http://nationalpost.com/news/canada/soldiers-of-odin-splinter-in-canada-over-racist-agenda-of-far-right-groups-leadership-in-finland.

Biber, F. (2016, September 14). Soldiers of Odin Canada says group not the same as what's going on overseas. CBC News. Retrieved 2 February 2018, from http://www.cbc.ca/news/canada/saskatoon/soldiers-of-odin-canada-community-group-watch-1.3761178.

CBC News. (2016, December 22). Concerns raised after Soldiers of Odin offer free snow shovelling. CBC News. Retrieved from http://www.cbc.ca/news/canada/saskatchewan/soldiers-of-odin-shoveling-snow-1.3909599.

CBC News. (2017a, January 4). Yukon Soldiers of Odin leader claims group not linked to white supremacy. CBC News. Retrieved from http://www.cbc.ca/news/canada/north/soldiers-of-odin-yukon-james-albert-1.3920049.

CBC News. (2017b, November 25). Quebec City police arrest 44 at far-right protest and counter-demonstration. CBC News. Retrieved 2 February 2018, from http://www.cbc.ca/news/canada/montreal/quebec-city-police-arrest-44-at-far-right-protest-and-counter-demonstration-1.4419752.

Guardians of Alberta. (2017, February 25). Guardians of Alberta Twitter Page [Tweet]. Retrieved 2 February 2018, from https://twitter.com/goaleth/status/835521827963187201.

Hamilton, G. (2015, October 7). Firearms groups apoplectic after Liberals promise new gun control measures. *National Post*. Retrieved 2 February 2018, from http://nationalpost.com/news/politics/firearms-groups-apoplectic-after-liberals-promise-new-gun-control-measures.

HuffPost Quebec. (2017, August 15). Des flammèches à prévoir dimanche à Québec? *HuffPost Quebec*. Retrieved 2 February 2018, from http://quebec.huffingtonpost.ca/2017/08/15/la-meute-et-lorganisation-bienvenue-aux-refugie-es-manifester_a_23078443.

Johnson, D. (2017, February 9). Guardians of Alberta's split from Soldiers of Odin shows a lack of cohesion on the alt-right front. *Edmonton Examiner*. Retrieved 2 February 2018, from http://www.edmontonexaminer.com/2017/02/08/guardians-of-albertas-split-from-soldiers-of-odin-shows-a-lack-of-cohesion-on-the-alt-right-front.

La Presse Canadienne. (2015, January 21). Sondage: 59% des Québécois en faveur d'une charte de la laïcité. *La Presse*. Retrieved from http://www.lapresse.ca/actualites/dossiers/charte-de-la-laicite/201501/21/01-4837093-sondage-59-des-quebecois-en-faveur-dune-charte-de-la-laicite.php.

Lamoureux, M. (2016a, September 6). Soldiers of Odin, dubbed 'extreme anti-refugee group', patrol Edmonton streets. CBC News. Retrieved 23 March 2017, from http://www.cbc.ca/

news/canada/edmonton/soldiers-of-odin-dubbed-extreme-anti-refugee-group-patrol-edmonton-streets-1.3745493.

Lamoureux, M. (2016b, April 18). Soldiers of Odin, Europe's Notorious, Anti-Immigration Group, Beginning to For Cells in Canada. *Vice Media*. Retrieved 23 March 2017, from https://www.vice.com/en_au/article/soldiers-of-odin-europes-notorious-anti-immigration-group-beginning-to-form-cells-in-canada.

Lamoureux, M. (2017a, May 23). An 'Ultranationalistic' Group Is Patrolling Canada's Border With the US. *Vice Media*. Retrieved 2 February 2018, from https://www.vice.com/en_ca/article/8x43g5/an-ultranationalistic-group-patrolling-canadas-border-with-the-us.

Lamoureux, M. (2017b, June 14). The Birth of Canada's Armed, Anti-Islamic 'Patriot' Group. *Vice Media*. Retrieved 2 February 2018, from https://www.vice.com/en_ca/article/new9wd/the-birth-of-canadas-armed-anti-islamic-patriot-group.

Lamoureux, M. (2018a, May 9). A Far Right Albertan Militia Tried to Open a Chain of Addiction Recovery Homes. *Vice Media*. Retrieved 14 May 2018, from https://www.vice.com/en_ca/article/8xe4b5/a-far-right-group-tried-to-launch-a-live-in-addiction-recovery-program.

Lamoureux, M. (2018b, December 14). Canadian Anti-Islam Militia Changes Leadership, Starts New Training Program. *Vice Media*. Retrieved 19 December 2018, from https://www.vice.com/en_ca/article/kzvyae/canadian-anti-islam-militia-changes-leadership-starts-new-training-program.

Montpetit, J. (2016, December 14). Inside Quebec's far right: Soldiers of Odin leadership shake-up signals return to extremist roots. CBC News. Retrieved 2 February 2018, from http://www.cbc.ca/news/canada/montreal/quebec-far-right-soldiers-of-odin-1.3896175.

Montpetit, J. (2017, May 2). Canadian branch of far-right group fragments amid infighting. CBC News. Retrieved 2 February 2018, from http://www.cbc.ca/news/canada/montreal/canadian-branch-of-far-right-group-fragments-amid-infighting-1.4095498.

Nadeau, F., & Helly, D. (2016). Extreme right in Quebec?: The Facebook pages in favor of the 'Quebec Charter of Values'. *Canadian Ethnic Studies*, 48(1), 1–18. https://doi.org/10.1353/ces.2016.0004.

Peritz, I. (2017, July 16). Quebec town rejects plan to build Muslim cemetery in narrow vote. *The Globe and Mail*. Retrieved 2 February 2018, from https://www.theglobeandmail.com/news/national/quebec-town-rejects-plan-to-build-muslim-cemetery-in-narrow-vote/article35704826.

Perry, B., & Scrivens, R. (2016). Uneasy alliances: A look at the right-wing extremist movement in Canada. *Studies in Conflict & Terrorism*, 39(9), 819–841. https://doi.org/10.1080/1057610X.2016.1139375.

Pineda, A. (2017). Après les affrontements, La Meute défile à Québec. *Le Devoir*. Retrieved from http://www.ledevoir.com/societe/actualites-en-societe/506156/apres-les-affrontements-la-meute-defile.

PRI World Staff. (2017, August 25). The far right in Quebec gets more inspiration from Europe than the US. Retrieved 2 February 2018, from https://www.pri.org/stories/2017-08-25/far-right-quebec-gets-more-inspiration-europe-us.

Ranta, M. (2017). Build the European homeland. Retrieved from https://www.facebook.com/photo.php?fbid=615272278662160.

Rigatelli, S. (2016a, May 7). Personporträtt: Hur det kom sig att Mika Ranta grundade Soldiers of Odin. *YLE Nyheter*. Retrieved 15 March 2017, from https://svenska.yle.fi/artikel/2016/05/07/personportratt-hur-det-kom-sig-att-mika-ranta-grundade-soldiers-odin.

Rigatelli, S. (2016b, March 16). Soldiers of Odins hemliga Facebookgrupp: Vapen och nazihälsningar. *YLE Nyheter*. Retrieved from https://svenska.yle.fi/artikel/2016/03/16/soldiers-odins-hemliga-facebookgrupp-vapen-och-nazihalsningar.

Shingler, B. (2017, May 22). 'Ultranationalists' monitor Roxham Road, where asylum seekers cross into Canada. CBC News. Retrieved 2 February 2018, from http://www.cbc.ca/news/canada/montreal/roxham-road-quebec-far-right-ultranationalist-1.4121969.

Simons, J. W. (2016, February 4). Exclusive – Nazi daggers, SS hats and a hangman's noose: On night patrol with the 'Soldiers of Odin', neo-Nazi led vigilantes vowing to 'keep Europe's women safe from migrant sex attacks'. *Daily Mail*. Retrieved 2 February 2018, from http://www.dailymail.co.uk/news/article-3426685/Nazi-daggers-SS-hats-hangman-s-noose-night-patrol-Soldiers-Odin-neo-Nazi-led-vigilantes-vowing-Europe-s-women-safe-migrant-sex-attacks.html.

Soldiers of Odin. (2016a). Soldiers of Odin Canada Facebook page. Facebook. Retrieved 23 March 2017, from https://www.facebook.com/soocanada/.

Soldiers of Odin. (2016b). Soldiers of Odin Canada bylaws. Retrieved from https://www.scribd.com/doc/308890496/Soldiers-Of-Odin-Canada-Bylaws-docx.

Soldiers of Odin Canada. (2017, April 25). Soldiers of Odin Canada statement. Retrieved 26 April 2017, from https://www.facebook.com/soocanada/.

Soldiers of Odin Canada Official. (2018). Retrieved from https://www.facebook.com/OFFICIAL.SOO.1.

Tasker, J. P. (2017, September 30). Far-right, anti-fascist protesters temporarily shut Quebec border crossing. *CBC News*. Retrieved 2 February 2018, from http://www.cbc.ca/news/politics/far-right-antifa-clash-across-canada-1.4315053.

Thomas, B. (2017, March 19). Alt-right groups hold M-103 protest outside Calgary City Hall. *Metro News Calgary*. Retrieved 2 February 2018, from http://www.metronews.ca/news/calgary/2017/03/19/alt-right-groups-hold-m-103-protest-calgary-city-hall.html.

Veilleux-Lepage, Y., & Archambault, E. (2019). Mapping transnational extremist networks: An exploratory study of the Soldiers of Odin's Facebook network, using integrated social network analysis. *Perspectives on Terrorism*, 13(2), 21–38. https://www.universiteitleiden.nl/binaries/content/assets/customsites/perspectives-on-terrorism/2019/issue-2/veilleux-lepage-and-archambault.pdf.

Ward, R. (2017a, February 1). Patriots of Unity statement on splitting off from Soldiers of Odin. Facebook. Retrieved 2 February 2018, from https://www.facebook.com/groups/544191002419317/?ref=direct.

Ward, R. (2017b, February 25). Patriots of unity bylaws. Facebook. Retrieved 2 February 2018, from https://www.facebook.com/groups/544191002419317/permalink/688429444662138.

18

POP-UP VIGILANTISM AND FASCIST PATROLS IN SWEDEN

Mattias Gardell

Sweden saw a five-year cycle of radical nationalist vigilantism in 2013–2017. While there still were some vigilante activities in 2018, the surge seems to have reached its peak and fizzled out, at least for the time being. With the possible exception of the patrols organized by the Nordic Resistance Movement (NMR), I suggest that the sudden outburst of vigilante activism may be understood as a *popcorn phenomenon*: into the simmering heat of the radical nationalist milieu, warmed up by negative press on migrants and migration, cyber activists pumped in "alternative facts" on alleged migrant crime, no-go zones, and sharia-sanctioned "rape jihad" of white Swedish women, to which concerned *clicktivists* responded with calls to protect the nation and its women. Trend-sensitive as the radical nationalist milieu is, the first vigilante patrols to materialize In Real Life (IRL) inspired local activists across the country to do the same, until the cycle had run its course and clicktivists dashed off to other projects.

Based on vigilante social media, criminal investigation records, media reports and field research, this chapter will look at four categories of vigilante activism: (1) Sweden's Citizen Militia; (2) Soldiers of Odin; (3) Gardet and autonomous vigilante associations; and (4) National Socialist Patrols

A radical nationalist landscape

Neoliberalism has for the past 25 years gradually undermined the once famous Swedish model. The growth of income inequality is the largest among all OECD countries, and by 2018 Statistics Sweden reported the greatest gap between the country's rich and poor since the measurement began (OECD 2015; Heggeman 2018). During this time, Sweden gradually transformed into one of the most segregated societies in the region. The basis of segregation is class, but as class distinctions co-varies with structural discrimination on the basis of racialized ethnicity, religion, and culture, class distinctions increasingly acquired a visual dimension, readily observable in the segregated urban areas of rich and poor. Transforming social realities contributed to rising tensions. White radical nationalists pointed to visible minorities as signs of the betrayal of the political class, nostalgically envisioning a restored *People's Home* for white Swedes only. Nonwhite citizens pointed to the discrepancies between their experience of racial discrimination and the official narrative of Sweden as the country where racism never took hold, except among the intolerant few. Contributing to rising tensions were alarmist media reports portraying immigration and migrants as a problem. While recycled since the arrival of the first Jewish refugees in the 1930s, the theme peaked in the early 1990s and returned with a vengeance in the mid-2000s. Between 2005 and 2016, reports on migration and migrants as a problem increased by 895%. In 2017, mainstream media published 23,478 negative articles on migrants, i.e. three stigmatizing reportages per hour, every day, throughout the year. News associating migrants with crime and sexual harassment dominated the mediascape. In addition, alternative facts on migrants and crime flooded radical nationalist social media while contra-factually insisting that such news was censured (Söderin 2017; Strömbäck et al. 2017; Dahlberg et al. 2017).

Radical nationalists have a strong online presence, with their own digital news media, blogs, podcasts, platforms, Facebook groups, YouTube channels, and an army of keyboard warriors constituting a digital *commentariat*, which ultimately aims to guide public opinion. A feature of the radical nationalist "media ecology" (Treré & Mattoni 2016) that links new social media technologies to the entangled histories and social dynamics of the radical nationalist milieu is the focus on the endangered white Swedish woman depicted as prey to "Muslim invaders". Throughout the period of investigation, fake news on "no-go zones," "Muslim rape jihad," "Sharia-sanctioned rape," and "Muslim gang-rape in Sweden," caused alarm. In radical nationalist narratives, Karina Horsti (2017) notes, women are often represented as the embodiment of the nation, and family, and therefore of what belongs to men. "Furthermore, the 'openness' and softness of the female body is represented as a weakness, a boundary for which violation and infection from the outside are constant threats" (ibid: 1449). White men were called to "wake up" and defend their borders, nation, and women by organizing vigilante patrols.

Of course, vigilantism is not new to Sweden. For the past decades, citizens have formed neighborhood watch groups, and organized street patrols, e.g. Dads on Town, Grandma Patrols, and Moms in the Hood. All these projects are today a normalized feature of urban night life. The 1980s and 1990s saw the rise of uniformed street patrol organizations such as Non-Fighting Generation and Guardian Angels, both inspired by Black American and Chicano inner-city community activism, and hip-hop culture. The Soldiers of Odin was not the first vigilante franchise in Sweden, the Guardian Angels was, with its Safety Patrols walking the streets or riding subway trains dressed in white shirts, red berets and the Guardian Angels' insignia – a two-winged pyramid with the all-seeing eye – in white on the back of their sparkling red bomber jackets. A similar project, *Lugna Gatan* (Quiet Street), established in the mid-1990s, still exists and has received positive evaluations for its youth work, rehab programs and uniformed safety patrols (Öhlund et al. 2009; Nilsson & Wadeskog 2008).

All these groups differ from radical nationalist vigilantism. Earlier groups were either organized by concerned grassroots citizens who wanted to make a difference in their local communities by being adult, sober, and at hand in the night, bourgeois citizens cruising residential neighborhoods ready to make citizen's arrests, or community activists offering an alternative to drugs and criminal gang culture. Most groups had no political agenda, and those who did rarely went beyond the ambition to counter the negative effects of segregation. None of these earlier groups explicitly targeted racialized others, posted online calls to exterminate non-whites, or vowed to hang the traitors in the political and intellectual elites. While earlier groups offered a model of good public standing radical nationalist vigilantism hoped to benefit from, activists of the latter milieu found their inspiration elsewhere. In their internal debates, Dads on Town rather figured as a symbol for what they should not deteriorate into.

The vigilante groups and networks to be discussed here are or were products and parts of the radical nationalist milieu in Sweden. I use the umbrella concept "*radical nationalism*" to signify a multifaceted *political landscape* that encompasses a wide variety of organizations, parties, tendencies, and voices that may differ in terms of political philosophies, strategies, and perspectives, but are held together by stressing the primacy of the nation. Earlier works on radical nationalism in Sweden have frequently used other umbrella concepts, such as far-right extremism, and radical right-wing populism, to characterize the milieu.[1] Empirically, there is not much to justify the far-right label, as the political agendas of the parties involved feature elements of both the right (e.g. tradition, nation, law-and-order, moral conservatism) and the left (e.g. [white Swedish] workers', women's, and elderly people's rights, environmental concerns). While the Sweden Democrats – the most successful radical nationalist party that gained close to 13% in the 2014 election – currently is moving rightwards in terms of economic policies, it is still to the left of the conservative parties (the Christian Democrats and the Moderates) and second only to the Social Democrats among working-class voters. In terms of class, radical nationalism is anchored among the middle strata of the society – the skilled working-class and the lower middle-class. They are people who typically claim to be the heirs of "those who built the nation," and therefore entitled to certain birthright privileges. If the term "extremism" at all should be used, it would make more sense to label radical nationalism an "extremism of the center".

The radical nationalist landscape includes organizations whose leaders may reject and even distain each other (e.g. the Sweden Democrats, Alternative for Sweden, the Identitarian fascist Nordic Youth, the national socialist Nordic Resistance Movement), but yet recognize each other as fellow travelers at home in the landscape populated by what activists name the *nationella* (the nationals). Moreover, a significant category of grassroot *nationella* do not stay within the confines of one particular organization but tour the landscape to visit the homesteads of other factions, both in cyberspace and IRL, and may well support more than one group, despite their ideological differences. Catering to the landscape is a plethora of think tanks, publishing houses, social media forums, podcasts, bloggers, vloggers, webzines, and newspapers that may be dedicated to a particular obsession – e.g. antisemitism, islamophobia, antiziganism, counter-jihadism, paganism, secular fundamentalism, traditionalism, esoteric fascism, conspiracy theory – or eclectically embracing all of the above, seemingly indifferent to intellectual inconsistencies. While national in outlook and emphasis, Swedish radical nationalism is entangled with similar currents abroad, and is remarkably *trend sensitive*, always ready to adopt the latest fad that sweeps the landscape. Vigilantism was one of these.[2]

Sweden's citizen militia

The surge of radical nationalist vigilantism began in the wake of a series of urban uprisings known as the *Husby Riots* after the name of the stigmatized underclass suburb in Stockholm where the first clashes between residents and police took place in May 2013. Much like the urban uprisings in Los Angeles 1992, Paris 2005 and London 2011, the Husby riots were ignited by police violence. On May 13, the National Task Force descended on Husby following a report that an aggressive old man had entered an old woman's apartment, yelling in some foreign language. Only later would they learn that the slightly demented 69-year-old Lenine Relvas-Martins had shouted "I am the King of Portugal" and "You are Catherine the Great of Russia" (in Portuguese), to Arja, his wife of 37 years, before entering his home, kissing his wife and laughing. Terrified by the police banging on her door, Arja cried "We are retired people, not criminals" and refused to open. Her husband, she later explained, suffered from paranoid fears of people out to kill him, and was equally scared of the armed men outside. After a prolonged standoff that attracted an increasing number of onlookers, the police broke in the door and threw in stun grenades. "They are coming to kill us," Lenine cried, grabbed a knife, and was shot point blank in his head. One hour later, Lenine still laying shot dead on his apartment floor, a police communique claimed that the man had been brought to hospital by an ambulance. As spectators followed the news online as well in real life, they knew that no ambulance had ever been called to the scene. When late at night, the police finally took the dead man out, people in Husby understood that something was terribly wrong (UG-referens 2014; de los Reyes et al. 2014).

For the first few days, neighbors and civil society associations in Husby in vain organized peaceful protests, including a rally, demanding an independent investigation (Megafonen 2013). On May 19, the first cars were set afire. Riot police was met with stones, in a spiral of escalating clashes, aired live on national television and social media. Reports of officers shouting racist slurs, "tramps, monkeys, negroes, rats," and indiscriminately attacking residents, parents, and civil society groups with dogs, batons, grenades, guns, to disperse the crowds, fueled the flames. As fighting resumed the following nights, protests spread to other underclass areas

290 Mattias Gardell

around Stockholm and eight other cities,[3] where cars, schools, police stations, and shops where set ablaze.

Watching the news too were radical nationalists. On their social media forums and Facebook groups, e.g. *Vi stöder polisen i Husby* (We support the Police in Husby), with more than 93,000 likes and 87,000 followers, keyboard warriors called to action. "Shoot them all," "Hunting season on immigrants," "burn Husby to the ground," "Kill the baboons," "make Sweden Muslim free". Yet other groups organized interventions. The Nordic Youth patrolled the quiet streets of white residential neighborhoods in Sollentuna, next to Husby, to signal "We Protect You," as a marketing stunt. Activists of the Swedish Defence League and the (now defunct) Swedes' Party set up the Facebook event *Skallgång* (Search Party) to hunt "Arabs and Muslims" and redirected volunteers to secret Facebook groups where they were instructed to "arm yourselves," and show up at specific locations to "protect property". A similar Facebook event, *Stockholms civila förband kontra eldupploppen i förorterna* (Stockholm Civil Militia Contra Suburban Fire Riots) using the same tactics of open and closed groups organized a "volunteer force to assist the police". "We will make the Muslims run from us".[4]

The most successful of these vigilante projects was the Sweden's Citizen Militia (*Sveriges medborgarde*). Organized by an inner circle of a dozen activists, all with good standing among football ultras (Djurgården, AIK), and radical nationalist parties, (the Swedish Resistance Movement, the Swedes' Party, the National Democrats), who set up a closed Facebook group of around 800 members-by-invitation, and an open "Support the Sweden's Citizen Militia" community, with thousands of followers. "We will do what the police cannot do and put an end to this," organizers said. "Kill 'em all. They can't come here and burn down our country". All activists in the inner circle were linked to radical nationalist parties, and all had criminal records. Ten had been convicted of assault, six for possession of illegal weapons, three for hate speech, two for crimes against life and health, two for violence against public servants, and one for violent riot (Folkö & Quensel 2013; Vergara 2013).

On May 24, some 200 volunteers armed with knives, bats, knuckles, and chains convened at the parking lot at Älvsjö Convention Center. The gathering was unusual as it drew together activists from radical nationalist and ultras factions that normally do not go that well together. Organizers did not miss the photo opportunity, and a group photo of some 60 militia men soon circulated the internet. Events like this happen as much in cyberspace as IRL. Sympathizers across the country followed the events through Live Updates on *Nordland*, and other social media platforms.[5]

The Sweden's Citizen Militia did not really go into any of the areas with ongoing riots but attacked people and places where protests had subsided or not taken place, shouting "Our City, Our Country," beating up scores of people chosen only by their skin color or appearance, including minors and elderly persons. A possible exception was Storvreta, Tumba, where some 150 militia men attacked a group of 30 residents who defended themselves by throwing rocks and bottles. While some militia updates indicated that they patrolled with the tacit agreement from the police, other updates reported clashes with the police, or that the police had arrested or disarmed activists.

Sweden's Citizen Militia coalesced physically a few times over the years, as security at radical nationalist rallies and as flash mobs, notably against "North African street children" at Stockholm Central Station in January 2016, and the Zayed Mosque in Stockholm, in June 2016.[6] Widespread news on mass sexual harassment during the New Year celebrations in Cologne followed by reports on similar incidents – true or not that true – in Swedish cities, incited radical nationalist ideologues to call for action. "We live in a time in which the strong man – the protector – has been reduced to entertainment [e.g. Braveheart] for feminized men who hardly would protect their own," Magnus Söderman wrote.

> They have handed over this [responsibility] to the state and praise the police's monopoly of violence. [However] the state has neither the will, nor the capacity to protect our women and children. That task is our obligation. Be men, goddamnit![7]

On January 26, 2016, a flash mob of some 100 masked men attacked people at the Central Station. "Now it's enough!" read a flyer distributed by the vigilante mob. "The justice system has left walk over, and the social contract is thereby broken – therefore it is now the duty of every Swedish man to protect public space from imported criminality." Therefore "200 Swedish men gathered to mark the North African 'street children' who wreak havoc around the capitol's central station … and to hand out the punishment they deserve".[8] Judged from mobile films and witnesses, the attack was chaotic and indiscriminate. Evidently, the attackers could not really differentiate between "North African street children" and random citizens, as victims included teenage women, elderly people, and two civil police officers. The police arrested 14 militia men, armed with knives and knuckles, including a 47-year old man who attacked two civil police officers, hitting one of them in the head. "I wanted to protect white Swedish women," the man explained to the judge who sentenced him to a cognitive therapy program.[9]

The Militia was hailed as heroes in radical nationalist press.[10] "The single most important reason for taking to the streets, is the fact that our women cannot move there in peace," an organizer told *Motgift*, urging readers to follow their example. "Talk to your friends and organize on a local level."[11] A few weeks later, Soldiers of Odin entered the landscape.

Soldiers of Odin

The Soldiers of Odin (SOO) is a transnational vigilante franchise, based out of Kemi, Finland. Established by truck driver Mika Ranti, a former boxer and member of the national socialist Finnish Resistance Movement, at the height of the so-called "migration crisis," in October 2015, Soldiers of Odin declared refugees

292 Mattias Gardell

their enemies and vowed to protect their nation and women from the "invaders" (see Tommi Kotonen in this volume). Modelled on outlaw motorcycle gangs with full members, prospects, and supporters, and sporting black jackets and hoodies with the one-eyed Norse god Odin draped in the national banner and a cartoonish Viking helmet, the Soldiers of Odin concept of manliness became an instant online fad and Finland's most successful radical nationalist export product. At least 21 national chapters across Europe, Australia, the United States, and Canada became part of the Soldiers of Odin Worldwide, connecting white radical nationalists through Facebook and providing a market for Soldiers of Odin merchandise, bomber jackets, hoodies, t-shirts, caps, mugs, banners, stickers, dog leashes, and phone cases.

The Soldiers of Odin, Sweden, was founded in Stockholm, in February 2016 by Mikael Johansson, a former member of the National Democrats – an "ethno-pluralist" radical nationalist party that split from the Sweden Democrats in 2001, gained seats in five municipalities, but dissolved months before the elections of 2014, creating a pool of homeless activists. Initially set up under Finnish super-vision, the Swedish SOO began by providing "security" at a Casa Pound-inspired weekend soup-kitchen for homeless white-Swedish-people-only in Björns Träd-gård, a popular city park centrally located at Medborgarplatsen, Södermalm, Stockholm, next to the Zayed Mosque. A meeting point surrounded by bars, coffee-houses, theatres, playgrounds, skateboard rink, concert halls, clubs, shops, and art venues, and home to Hammarby football supporters who keep radical nationalists at arm's length, Björns Trädgård is also a spot where civil society asso-ciations traditionally have distributed food and clothing to the city's poor and homeless. Politically, Södermalm leans to the left and a food-for-whites-only charity was bound to provoke countermeasures. Antiracist neighbors set up Food-for-all (*fika för alla*) next to the radical nationalist charity in a ritualized weekend stand-off that lasted for a year and a half. The SOO joined to "protect" the racist charity and physically push away non-white Swedes who ventured to the "wrong" stand looking for a cup of coffee and something to eat, with soldiers outnumbering the white homeless people at the outdoor kitchen. The racist charity became a meeting point where people from the anonymous *commentariat* could find fellow nationalists and SOO recruiters IRL.[12]

In early March, new SOO chapters were approved by Stockholm and Kemi and adopted the rules laid down by the Finnish world headquarters: Stand your ground if attacked. Even if 200 immigrants are coming, do not run. Abide by the code of silence. Never talk to the police or media. Refer journalists to the trustees, the officially designated officers. On March 12, the Soldiers of Odin synchronized their first street patrols to occur simultaneously in Stockholm, Jönköping, and Trelle-borg. Attracting wide media attention, membership multiplied and new prospect chapters were formed. Grown from 140 to 400 members overnight, SOO Stock-holm organized security at The People's March – another effort to call the radical nationalist commentariat to manifest IRL – urging supporters from across Sweden to join. Prospects from Borås, Eskilstuna, Kristenehamn, Malmö, Sjöbo,

Trollhättan, and Örebro showed up, earning their stamp of approval. The virtual community of radical nationalist clicktivists were jubilant. "Finally, some people act," "We are approaching civil war," "We gotta retake our land, before it is too late," "Fight Islam," "Either we kill them, or they kill us". The SOO Stockholm organized weekend patrols of 30–70 soldiers, divided into two to three groups that communicated through the Zello-App, and were joined by prospects from other cities. New chapters sprung up across Sweden. Some – Dalarna, Gävleborg, and Skaraborg – were regional chapters, with alleged presence in several cities, while others were based in one city only. Within a few months, there was 23 Soldiers of Odin chapters across the country, with reported activity in some 40 towns, and around 8400 online supporters.[13]

However, the house of cards began collapsing already in April and May. While the Soldiers of Odin survived its first year by incorporating new chapters and spinning the online wheel of merchandise to compensate for those chapters that closed down, died out or broke off to establish splinter groups, the final account was negative. The rapid demise of the Swedish Soldiers of Odin was due to a number of converging reasons.

First, a creation of the radical nationalist online commentariat, the SOO attracted people comfortable at their computers but less certain of what to do IRL. Many chapters were predominantly active online, and while calls to finally *do* something were awarded many "likes," fewer people showed up to the meetings. In turn, many meetings were spent sharing plans and laughs over coffee and cookies but stopped short of actually going out on the streets for more than a photo opportunity.

Second, chapters that actually did organize street patrols encountered all kinds of troubles. They were challenged by Mothers of Odin, patrolling the streets with baby-carriers, Loldiers of Odin (another Finnish export), Sons of Thor (a pop-up "group" of antiracist pagans), the police, local residents, Anti-fa, and Chicanos, an outlaw biker gang affiliated with Bandidos. In Jönköping, Gothenburg, Malmö, and Uppsala, the Soldiers of Odin were beaten up.[14] In Borlänge, Dalarna, three Odin soldiers were hospitalized after a clash with Chicanos, on April 2–3, 2016. Organizers went underground, and the SOO cancelled all activities throughout the Dalarna region. "They were threatened and beaten," SOO President Mikael Johansson explained to the press. "Hence, they decided to not go out anymore".[15] Their surrender meant that the Soldiers of Odin lost face. "If you can't take the heat, stay out of the kitchen." "Ridiculous to go by the name Soldiers of Odin if you can't back it up." "You are a disgrace to Odin and our Norse Gods and Goddesses."[16]

Third, the media exposure was a double blessing as reporters revealed that leading SOO organizers were or had been organized fascists and exposed the violent racist content of closed SOO Facebook groups. To handle negative publicity, SOO spokespersons took exception from fascism, racism, and violent extremism, which caused internal confusion, and yet did not convince the public. "We don't accept Nazism or racism," Johansson said. "We're actively trying to counter the [negative] image of the organization."[17] At the food-for-whites-only charity, organizers occasionally offered a homeless Black or Roma person coffee, which provoked internal dissent. "If they do that, what's the point of us being here?" a soldier asked. "It doesn't make any sense. You can't rid your home of rats if you feed them."[18] "We are out to protect *our* kind, *our* women," another solider confined. "We should be open about that. We're not Dads on Town,"[19] "SOO is a bad idea," a national socialist commented.

> There's no ideological cohesion, no armament/capacity of violence, and yet they're wrapped in symbols/jackets that suggest otherwise. I'm sure there are good people among them, but the organization as such is a piecemeal rush job that seeks to appease [PC] journalists.[20]

Fourth, the effort to rid the SOO from overtly fascist elements propelled splinter groups. Two examples will suffice. In August 2016, the Skaraborg chapter, which organized soldiers in Skövde, Lidköping, Skara, and Hjo, was excluded following reports that the local SOO leader Johan Brandqvist posted sing-songs on YouTube celebrating Hitler and his desire to gas Jews and exterminate Muslims. SOO President Mikael Johansson ordered Skaraborg members to return their uniforms. "Forget it, loser," Brandqvist responded. "Come and take the hoodies from us yourself, you jerk!" Johansson did not meet the challenge, and Brandqvist launched the *Soldiers of Odin Elite* with a reported core of 30–40 members and 125 prospects. However, beyond organizing social events in their club headquarters, the SOO Elite did not do much.[21] The SOO chapters in Flen, Nyköping, and Norrköping, broke away to form *Balder Cruisers* under the leadership of Ingmar Zeijlon in March 2017, and was joined by soldiers from Katrineholm, Linköping, and Finspång. Enraged, Johansson declared their "Bad Standing" on the Soldier of Odin Hall of Shame, and in vain ordered renegade soldiers to hand in their hoodies. A brotherhood of bikers and rockers, who openly display weapons and national socialist symbols, Balder Cruisers claim to "protect women and children" and reach out to homeless people but has not yet done much besides providing security at radical nationalist rallies.[22]

Fifth, members of the Soldiers of Odin undermined the leadership's effort to polish the organization's image by intimidating small-town residents or backing up threats with arms. On March 30, 2016, residents in idyllic Skivarp stayed indoors when uniformed soldiers marched through the town to threaten minors at a home for unaccompanied refugees that had suffered a series of attacks, including arson. On March 31, 2016, residents of Strängnäs reportedly felt daunted by unwanted soldiers patrolling their town. April 5, 2017, uniformed soldiers targeted minors at Al Azhar Elementary School, entering the schoolyard, putting up SOO stickers, filming the young pupils, and appearing aggressive. The school management had to employ security guards, as soldiers bragged about their intent to "catch and kill Muslims".[23] November 2017, the police found guns, knives, and ten kilos of dynamite in the home of Stefan Schultz, organizer in SOO, Gothenburg, and known for violent online rhetoric. "All you traitors live on borrowed time," Shultz declared at *Stå upp för Sverige* (Stand Up For Sweden), a radical nationalist online community with some 170,000 members. "The war is approaching".[24]

Sixth, the criminal record of SOO organizers undermined their declared intent to make the streets safe from criminals. Of fifteen SOO officers in leading positions, eight had been convicted for various offenses, ranging from armed assault and possession of illegal weapons, to drugs, doping, and shoplifting. Close to half of the 100 soldiers who participated in the Stockholm patrols had criminal records. Seventeen had served time for violent crime, and three for sexual exploitation of minors. Perhaps most devastating to SOO's reputation was the fact that leading Soldiers had been convicted of beating up women, rape, and sexual offenses. The head of the Norrköping chapter had served time for repeated sexual assault on a 13-year-old friend to his daughter. A SOO leader in Gävleborg was sentenced for domestic abuse. An officer in the Stockholm chapter was convicted for kicking and beating his wife in front of their daughter; another for repeatedly abusing women. Yet another officer had multiple sentences for violent assault, including an incident in 2003, when he knocked down a woman, and kicked and jumped on her head as she was laying on the ground.[25] While SOO President Johansson assured the public that soldiers who had been "convicted for crime against women and children" will be "excluded," he also indicated that it takes a criminal to stop a criminal. A man convicted for assault "is tougher than other men, and dares to intervene to stop an assault".[26]

In June 2017, Mikael Johansson resigned – or was forced to step down – amidst charges of corruption. Kemi stepped in. Alarmed by the fact that some splinter groups kept their Soldiers of Odin hoodies or ran rogue chapters that were not Kemi approved, it issued online threats to expose and hang the traitors but had nothing to back it up. By January 2018, there was an effort to rekindle the movement by organizing patrols in some mid-sized cities, notably Västerås and Kalmar, but the mobile films posted online only illustrated how few soldiers there were left in the army.

Gardet and autonomous vigilante groups

In addition to the Soldiers of Odin, the cycle included another vigilante federation, *Gardet* (the Guard), founded in January 2016 by Jörgen Bach, a 60-year old businessman and radical nationalist veteran in Scania. "Hordes of Migrants aimlessly drift around Sweden, without jobs, income, or a place to go," Bach stated. "We have already seen a rise in home-invasions and rape. The police cannot handle the situation. The military hardly exists. Society breaks up. The system collapses. We can only trust ourselves".[27] Bach set up a Facebook group – backdated to January 2015 – and sent out instructions on how to affiliate local chapters, along with guidelines, logo, and codes of behavior. Gardet niched itself as a bourgeois alternative to SOO without white trash aesthetics, uniforms and merchandise. Claiming to represent "Sweden's most rapidly expanding civil society association" of decent folks ready to

296 Mattias Gardell

"practice the right to defend our fellow citizens, ourselves, and our property,"[28] Bach seems to have left local organizers on their own. While Gardet boosted 15 local chapters with 2–40 members each, few chapters seem to have organized more than occasional meetings, and members soon drifted away. Undercover journalists Lisa Röstlund and Erik Wiman participated in the first IRL meeting of Gardet's Norrköping chapter, and witnessed how a Soldier of Odin organizer came along and convinced the whole group to join the SOO instead.[29]

Outside of SOO and Gardet, there are or were a number of local radical nationalist vigilante associations in Kalmar, Linköping, Nora, Nyköping, Stockholm, Tranås, and Värnamo. Two examples will suffice. In April 2016, *Värnamo ordningspatrull* (Order Patrol Värnamo) declared their intention to make the quiet Bible belt community safe again. Sporting a picture of a single refugee minor on their Facebook page, organizers claimed that young adult women should dare to walk home alone, and parents should be able to send their children to the public bath without fear. "We don't know who they are, but we are concerned that people paint an image of crime that don't exist in our precinct," said Värnamo chief of police. "There hasn't been any rape, nor any complaints or incidents in the public bath".[30] In December 2017, *Säkra gator Linköping* (Safe Streets Linköping) was launched by Jimmy Olsson, a national socialist skinhead and percussionist in the white-power band *Svastika* in the 1990s. In the year 2000, Olsson was sentenced to two years in prison for violently assaulting a man with migrant background at Linköping Central Station.[31] "This is for you who are sick of Sweden's failed justice system," *Säkra gator Linköping* announced on their Facebook group, "sick of the daily assaults against women in Linköping. We are ordinary folks who think about the future of our children. And a safe city space".[32] By February, 2018, *Säkra gator Linköping* had close to 4500 online members and organized regular weekend patrols. When EXPO contacted Olsson to ask about antidemocratic, racist and violent remarks (Vergara 2018) he had posted online, the founder withdrew his engagement in the group "out of consideration for the safety of my family and beloved ones".

National socialist patrols

The Nordic Resistance Movement (*Nordiska Motståndsrörelsen*, NMR) is a national socialist elitist organization that aims at establishing a Nordic Folk-State.[33] It grew out of the Swedish Resistance Movement,[34] and encompasses its sister organizations in Norway, Denmark, and Finland, co-organized in a Nordic Council under a Nordic Leader. Based on an explicitly "totalitarian" national socialist philosophy that "encompasses every aspect of human existence",[35] the Nordic Resistance Movement has a centralized chain of command and strict codes of behavior, secrecy, dress, and way of life. Membership and positions are graded and awarded. Prospects need to pass mental and physical tests to become full members, and advance to achieve the status as "activist". An "activist" is expected to *live* national socialism, stay away from alcohol, tobacco, drugs, unhealthy food, and the corrupting influences of modern life. "Activists" who have proven their worth may become part of the "oath-sworn" elite. A full member cannot make a career outside the organization: one cannot be part of – and much less successful in – the corrupt system (Sion) one has vowed to defeat. Full members are expected to stay for life, and activists who want out need to go through a formal channel, lest they be treated as traitors. [36]

Members are required to partake in military-style training, and the NMR cherishes its reputation as violence-prone fanatics. All members are required to carry a knife, and to defend their banner, cause, comrades, and leaders if attacked or insulted. However, non-sanctioned use of violence is strictly forbidden. National socialists who want to engage in assassinations and bombing campaigns are encouraged to stay outside the organization and operate as lone wolves or autonomous cells according to the rules of leaderless resistance tactics. Membership in any other radical nationalist organization is forbidden. Within the radical nationalist landscape, the NMR are frequently seen as sectarians who are obsessed with rules and military drill but do not do much to stop the ongoing white genocide except handing out flyers and organizing marches. Hence, the meteoric rise of the Soldiers of Odin in early 2016 touched a soft spot that the NMR had to handle.

Published directly after the rise of the SOO in 2016, the *Handbook for Activists in the Nordic Resistance Movement 2.0.* features a section on "Good Will Actions" to meet the SOO challenge. Recommended actions include organizing street patrols to protect endangered white folks, and providing poor people of Nordic heritage with food, clothing, and practical assistance. At the same time, the NMR implicitly distanced itself from the Soldiers of Odin.

> It may be tempting to succumb to populism and seek to portray oneself as a knight of goodness. Here, we revolutionaries need to think differently. The aim of these actions cannot be to aspire for the status as pious Nice Guys. The edge should be focused on the system's unwillingness or incapacity, thereby exposing the country's corrupt and irresponsible government. This distinction is significant – we should never let us be transformed into a kind of mainstay of a sick society.[37]

In Finland, the NMR began organizing patrols in Lahti and Helsinki around the same time as SOO appeared. Similarly, when the SOO was established in Sweden, the NMR began organizing occasional weekend patrols in at least six cities, Göteborg, Kristinehamn, Kungälv, Ludvika, Ystad and Östersund.[38] Much like the Stockholm SOO chapter, the Nordic Resistance Movement sporadically arranged soup kitchens for poor white people, and distributed clothes and food to white retired people. In addition, the NMR organized patrols to guard a public bathhouse in Kungälv, outside Gothenburg, to protect white women from refugees using the facilities. "Beyond the determination to intervene if anything happens, and increase the sense of security," said local NMR leader Victor Melin, the rationale is to show our folk that the Resistance movement will not accept the current state of order. We will be out on the streets, plazas, public baths, and other public spaces where our people are victimized by multicultural society. As the police evidently has other priorities than protecting its people, it is time for someone else to actually shoulder that responsibility.[39]

In July 2017, Victor Melin, and two fellow activists were sentenced to up to eight-and-a-half years in prison for bomb attacks against two refugee housings and a libertarian socialist trade union office in Gothenburg. Nobody was killed, but one man was severely wounded. That nobody died was mere luck, as the nail bombs were set off by a timer, meaning that the perpetrators had no control over who were around when the device exploded. The bombs were planted in a garbage can at the entrance of a refugee housing where children usually play; at the front window of the union office on a busy downtown street; and the back of a barrack housing refugees. The police investigation revealed that Melin had received urban guerilla warfare training with Partizan, a paramilitary organization that trains volunteers for Russian separatists in Ukraine. While the perpetrators had been involved in the same local NMR chapter, their bombing campaign was most likely unsanctioned by the NMR leadership and should better be seen as the deed of an autonomous radical nationalist cell.[40]

Concluding remarks

The cycle of vigilantism in Sweden was an articulation of sentiments boiling in the radical nationalist milieu ignited and amplified by new forms of digital communication. Of course, this should not be interpreted as if the new social media technologies in themselves caused the phenomenon of popcorn vigilantism but draws attention to the fact that vigilantism transcended the online/offline, transnational/local dichotomies. The radical nationalist media ecology intersected with parties, movements and other actors in the political landscape in various ways. While the patrols organized by the Nordic Resistance Movement was but one activity among many that utilized the new forms of communication to further their ambition to position itself as the vanguard of the white revolution, the case of the Soldiers of Odin was different. It did not grow out of any preexisting organization but represented an effort to call the online commentariat to materialize IRL as valiant knights ready to defend the nation and women they claimed to be uniquely theirs. It drew together people travelling the radical nationalist landscape in various directions, coming from defunct radical nationalist parties, local protest parties, the Sweden Democrats, and scores of individuals with all sorts of grievances but without previous experience of offline political engagement. While admins tried to influence the SOO Facebook groups, and mold its members into a social movement with presence and impact in their local communities, it remained to a certain extent what Tammy Castle and Tara Parson (2017) characterized the Soldiers of

Odin Norway to be, a "media-based collectivity" in which "participation in the virtual community ... eclipsed real-world activity".[41]

However, the meaning of the Soldiers of Odin went beyond the online/offline binary and traversed the dichotomy of the transnational and the local. A clue to what it did while it did not do anything is found in the many instances when soldiers patrolled quiet quarters and empty streets. Why did the soldiers walk around in city sections with no refugees from whom white women could be saved? What function did the SOO serve where its stated *raison d'être* was nowhere to be found? A similar question may be posed about other vigilante groups analyzed in contributions to this volume. Why did the Czech Ore Dogs militia described by Miroslav Mareš and Daniel Milo patrol the borders to Germany where no migrants crossed? Why would the Minutemen that Harel Shapira studied invest so much money and time to safeguard border areas in which they hardly ever encountered any "illegal immigrants"? I suggest that the answer may be found if we look at the phenomenon as performance. The meaning of the reenacting activities obviously depend on the particular context in which the actors engaged. In the Swedish case, the Soldiers of Odin was a performative articulation of white Swedish masculinity that functioned even when patrolling quiet areas as long as there were photos to post online to ensure themselves and the world that Swedish men were not emasculated but real men capable to protect "their" nation and women from being penetrated by alien others. The Soldiers of Odin patrols were ceremonial reenactments meant to define, manage and control national space as a white Swedish space, an undertaking that actually worked better when no non-whites disturbed their ritual performance.

Although there are still some Soldiers of Odin chapters out there that mark their presence by visiting each other and sharing their interconnectedness and dedication with the worldwide community of Odin soldiers and everyone else linked with the radical nationalist media ecology, the movement seems to have lost its momentum, at least temporarily. Outside the Nordic Resistance Movement, calls to put on the uniforms and take to the streets fall on deaf ears, as clicktivists have been there, done that, and rushed off to engage in new fads, such as citizen journalism, and the radical nationalist version of #metoo, *Europe's Daughters, #120db*.

Notes

1 See, for instance, Rydgren (2018); Rydgren (2006); Ekman (2014); Pelinka (2013); Ellinas (2014); Deland et al. (2013).
2 Swedish radical nationalists are mainly, though not exclusively, linked to counterparts in Western and Eastern Europe, Russia, North America, South Africa, and Australia. Important links are also forged between certain actors within Swedish radical nationalist landscape and Hindutva nationalists in India, phalangists in Lebanon, Aryan royalists in the Iranian diaspora, anti-Muslim Buddhists in Burma, Latin-American fascists, and radical nationalists in Syria and Israel.
3 Borlänge, Falun, Gävle, Linköping, Växjö, Västerås, Umeå and Örebro
4 Screen shots from FB groups *Skallång, Stockholms civila förband kontra eldupploppen i förorterna* and *Nordisk ungdom;* Häggström, Andreas 2013. "Facebooksida till stöd för polisen

300 Mattias Gardell

sprider rasistiska hatlänkar," *Nyheter24*, May 23, https://nyheter24.se/nyheter/inrikes/746629-facebooksida-till-stod-for-polisen-sprider-hatlankar; "Civila mobiliserar sig på Facebook – vill leta upp araber och svarta," 2013, *Nyheter24*, May 24, https://nyheter24.se/nyheter/inrikes/746699-civila-mobiliserar-sig-pa-facebook-vill-leta-upp-araber-och-svarta.

5 For one such social media platform, see: Palmblad, Robin (2013). "Medborgargardet: 'Ta er till Stockholm och var beredda'," *Nordland*, May 25. https://www.nordfront.se/medborgargardet-ta-er-till-stockholm-och-var-bereddas.smr.

6 Before the attack against the Grand Mosque at Södermalm, ultras from DFG (Djurgården) and Firman Boys (AIK) had invited ultras from the third major Stockholm team, Hammarby, who proudly declined to participate, arguing "We don't fight with you – only against you." On the eve of June 13, 2016, some 50 masked men armed with knives, bats, knuckles, stones, and bottles attacked the Zayed Mosque and a group of men celebrating Ramadan, shouting "Fuck you Muslims," "No Muslims on our streets," "Islam go to hell." In the aftermath, conflicting statements said they mistook Muslims for Hammarby supporters, or mistook Ramandan celebration for an "Arab street children" gathering.

7 Söderman, Magnus 2016. "Manna upp och beskydda våra kvinnor för bövelen," *Motgift*, January 5, https://www.motgift.nu/2016/01/05/manna-upp-och-beskydda-vara-kvinnor/. Söderman is a radical nationalist veteran, author, and translator (e.g. of Pierce's Turner Diaries, and Hunter). Having been a leading member of groups such as the Swedish Resistance Movement and the Swedes' Party, he now co-runs the influential online hub and podcast Motgift, and the Casa Pound inspired New Sweden.

8 *Det är nog nu!* Flyer.

9 The events gained extensive media coverage. See for instance, Ronge, Johan, 2016. "Här går mannen till attack mot civilpolisen," *Expressen*, May 31; Films and witness statements collected by author. for an analysis of the ultras involvement, cf Wåg, Mattias, 2016. "Fotbollens bruna sörja," *Aftonbladet*, February 2.

10 Cf., "Huliganer spöar kriminella invandrare i Stockholm," 2016, *Nordfront*, January 29, htpps://www.nordfront.se/huliganer-spoar-kriminella-invandrare-i-centrala-stockholm.smr; Hagberg, Fredrik, 2016, "Fredrik Hagberg [Nordisk Ungdom]: Nödvändigheten av medborgargarden," *Motgift* February 8, https://www.motgift.nu/2016/02/08/nodvandigheten-av-medborgargarden/.

11 "Exklusiv intervju med Medborgargardet," 2016. *Motgift*, February 3, https://www.motgift.nu/2016/02/03/exklusiv-intervju-med-medborgargardet/.

12 Field notes.

13 The SOO at some point had chapters in Borås, Dalarna (Avesta, Borlänge, Hedemora, Säter), Eskilstuna, Gävleborg (Gävle, Hudiksvall, Sandviken, Hofors, Bollnäs), Göteborg (Kungsbacka), Helsingborg, Hässleholm, Jönköping, Kalmar, Kristinehamn, Kristianstad, Linköping, Malmö, Norrköping (Nyköping, Flen, Katrineholm), Sigtuna, Skaraborg (Hjo, Skövde, Lidköping, Skara) Skivarp/Skurup, Stockholm, Strängnäs, Trelleborg, Trestad/Trollhättan, Västerås, Umeå, Uppsala, Örebro.

14 Fieldnotes, Malmö. In places where the Soldiers tried again, such as Malmö, after reinforcements from other chapters, the police still had to escort them around town. After its initial failure in Jönköping, the Soldiers tried to relaunch again in August 2016, and January 2017, only to go down in big brawls with antiracist activists. For Göteborg and Jönköping, see Anna Wallin Adersjö, *SVT*, "Storbråk i centrala Göteborg," April 3, 2016, https://www.svt.se/nyheter/lokalt/vast/storbrak-i-centrala-goteborg; Sjödahl, Daniel, 2017, "Tolv anhållna efter storbråk i Jönköping," *Jönköpings-Posten*, 8 Jan. 2017, https://www.jp.se/article/storbrak-pa-tandsticksomradet-tolv-greps/.

15 Olsson, Saara 2016. "Soldiers of Odin har bestämt sig för att lägga ner i Dalarna," *Nyheter24*, April 12, 2016, https://nyheter24.se/nyheter/inrikes/839014-soldiers-of-odin-har-bestamt-sig-for-att-lagga-ner-i-dalarna; "Soldiers of Odin lägger ned i Dalarna"; 2016. *Avesta Tidning.* April 11, 2016, http://www.avestatidning.com/allmant/soldiers-of-odin-lagger-ned-i-dalarna.

Fascist patrols in Sweden **301**

16 Comments to the NMR article, "Soldiers of Odin i Dalarna lägger ner efter att de blev angripna," by Redaktionen, *Nordfront*, April 11, https://www.nordfront.se/soldier s-odin-dalarna-lagger-ner-efter-att-de-blev-angripna.smr.

17 Quoted in Johansen, Marita 2016. "Vi tillåter inte nazism eller rasism," *Nerikes Allehanda*, April 12, 2016, http://www.na.se/orebro-lan/orebro/vi-tillater-inte-nazism -eller-rasism. cf, Jonathan Leman, Daniel Vergara, 2016, "Soldiers of Odin bakom fasaden – rasism och våldsromantik," *EXPO*, April 6; Röstlund, Lisa & Erik Wiman, 2016. *Soldiers of Odin inifrån, Aftonbladet.* http://soldiersofodin.story.aftonbladet.se/; Leman, Jonathan & Daniel Vergara, 2017, "Avhopp och konflikter i Soldiers of Odin," *EXPO*, January 19.

18 Conversation, 2016. Björns Trädgård, April 22.

19 Conversation, 2016. Björns Trädgård, May.

20 "Lars," 2016. Nordfront, April 11, https://www.nordfront.se/soldiers-odin-dalarna-la gger-ner-efter-att-de-blev-angripna.smr.

21 Cf, Stäpel, Marthina 2016, "Här sjunger Soldiers of Odin-ledare nazistsånger," *P4 Skaraborg*, August 5, 2016, http://sverigesradio.se/sida/artikel.aspx?programid=97&artikel= 6487760; Stäpel, Marthina 2016, "Soldiers of Odin -Vi vill inte ha med Skaraborg att göra," *SR*, August 5, http://sverigesradio.se/sida/artikel.aspx?programid=97&artikel= 6489500; Johansson, Mikael. Johansson 2016, "Mikael Johansson: De har inte tagit det bra i Skaraborg," *SR*, August 5; Leman, Jonathan & Daniel Vergara 2016, "Myteri i Soldiers of Odin efter nazistskandal," *EXPO*, Agust 8; Hellsten, Johanna, 2016, "Åtalad Soldiers of Odin-ledare sjunger nazisång," Aftonbladet, December 21.

22 Anders Dalsbro & Jonathan Leman, 2017. Soldiers of Odin blev Balder Cruisers – demonstrerar med nazister, *EXPO* May 15, 2017; Dahlberg, Cornelia, 2017. Soldiers Of Odin lägger ner, corneliadahlberg, January 22, ttps://corneliadahlberg.wordpress.com/ 2017/01/22/soldiers-of-odin-lagger-ner/; Leman, Jonathan & Daniel Vergara, 2017, "Avhopp och konflikter i Soldiers of Odin," EXPO, January 19.

23 Svensson, Adam 2016. HVB-hem åter hotat efter nazistpatruller, March 31, *Skånska Dagbladet*, http://www.skd.se/2016/03/31/hvb-hem-ater-hotat-efter-nazistpatruller/; Soldiers of Odin gick i Strängnäs, 2016, Eskilstuna Kuriren, April 11, Danielsson, Tobias 2016. "Soldiers of Odin etablerar sig i Sörmland – flera företrädare dömda för grova våldsbrott," SVT Nyheter, April 1; *TT/Aftonbladet*, "Högerextremt nätverk vid Al-Azharskolan," 2017 Aftonbladet, April 5, https://www.aftonbladet.se/nyheter/a/6a xwO/hogerextremt-natverk-vid-al-azharskolan; SR, 2017, "Oro på Al-Azharskolan efter Soldiers of Odin-besök," Sveriges Radio P4, April 6, http://sverigesradio.se/sida/a rtikel.aspx?programid=103&artikel=6668833; Claes Svahn, 2017, "Friskola tillkallade polis när Soldiers of Odin kom dit," *DN* April 6, https://www.dn.se/sthlm/friskola -tillkallade-polis-nar-soldiers-of-odin-kom-dit.

24 Olausson, Josefine 2017, Tre anhållna – polisrazzia i Göteborg, *Göteborgs-Posten* November 4, http://www.gp.se/nyheter/g%C3%B6teborg/tre-anh%C3%A5llna-polisra zzia-i-g%C3%B6teborg-1.4797660; Wiklander, Daniel & Jonathan Leman, 2017, "Greps med tio kilo dynamit – hyllade NMR på nätet," *EXPO*, November 6; Schultz, Stefan, 2017. Comments on *Stå upp för Sverige*, https://www.facebook.com/groups/ 279528999133185,,170802_133138; 279528999133185,170802_170858.

25 Björman, Fredrik, 2016. "Många är brottsdömda i Soldiers of Odin Gävleborg," *P4 Gävleborg*. April 13, http://sverigesradio.se/sida/artikel.aspx?programid=99&artikel= 6410291; *GT* 2016. "Vill 'skapa trygghet' med Soldiers of Odin i Gävle – är själva brottsbelastade, *Gefle Dagblad*," April 13; Leman, Jonathan & Daniel Vergara, 2016, "Soldiers of Odin bakom fasaden – rasism och våldsromantik," *EXPO*, April 6; Röstlund, Lisa & Erik Wiman, 2016. Soldiers of Odin inifrån, Aftonbladet. http://soldier sofodin.story.aftonbladet.se/; Leman, Jonathan et al., 2016. "De patrullerar som Soldiers of Odin – högerextrema och grovt kriminella," *EXPO*, March 18.

26 Interview, *SVT Opinion*, April 6, 2016; cited in Johansen, Marita 2016. April 12, 2016. "Vi tillåter inte nazism eller rasism," *Nerikes Allehanda*, April 12, http://www.na.se/ orebro-lan/orebro/vi-tillater-inte-nazism-eller-rasism.

302 Mattias Gardell

27 Bach 2016. *Formålsparagraf*, Gardet.
28 Bach 2016. *Gardet – Guide*, Gardet.
29 Röstlund, Lisa & Erik Wiman, 2016. *Soldiers of Odin inifrån*, Aftonbladet, http://soldier sofodin.story.aftonbladet.se/.
30 Nilsson, Hans 2016. Hatfull gatupatrull sprider oro i Värnamo, *Värnamo Nyheter*, March 14, https://www.vn.se/article/gatupatrull-skapar-oro-i-varnamo/P4, "Anonym "gatupatrull" skapar oro i Värnamo," 2016 *P4 Jönköping*, March 12, http://sverigesradio.se/ sida/artikel.aspx?programid=91&artikel=6388596.
31 Corren 2018. "Dömd för rasistdåd leder nattvandringar," *Corren*, January 19.
32 *Säkra gator Linköping*, https://www.facebook.com/groups/303823086803971/.
33 Cf NMR 2017. *Vår väg. Ny politik för en ny tid*, Grängesberg: Nordfront förlag.
34 SMR was founded 1996 but can trace its roots to the original national socialist tradition in Sweden. In June 2016, the national organizations in the Nordic countries reorganized as.
35 Riis Knudsen, Povl H, 2008. *Nationalsocialismen. Den biologiska världsåskådningen*. Stockholm: Nationellt Motstånd Förlag; cf, Lindberg, Simon, Hagberg, Emil & Klas Lund, 2016. *Aktivisthandboken 2.0. Handbok för aktivister i Nordiska motståndsrörelsen*, Nordiska motståndsrörelsen: Nordfront förlag.
36 Lindberg, Simon, Hagberg, Emil & Klas Lund, 2016. *Aktivisthandboken 2.0. Handbok för aktivister i Nordiska motståndsrörelsen*, Nordiska motståndsrörelsen: Nordfront förlag.
37 Lindberg, Simon, Hagberg, Emil & Klas Lund, 2016. *Aktivisthandboken 2.0. Handbok för aktivister i Nordiska motståndsrörelsen*, Nordiska motståndsrörelsen: Nordfront förlag, pp. 48–49.
38 Cf Redaktionen 2016. "Motståndsrörelsen patrullerade Kungsbacka efter mångkulturella våldsdåd," *Nordfront*, April 3. https://www.nordfront.se/motstandsrorelsen-patrullera de-kungsbacka-efter-mangkulturella-valdsdad.smr. Article includes link to patrols in other cities.
39 Redaktionen, 2016. "Efter den lyckade badhusaktionen: Näste 2 kommer genomföra flera liknande aktioner!," *Nordfront*, February 15. https://www.nordfront.se/efter-den-lyckade-badhusaktionen-naste-2-kommer-genomfora-fler-liknande-aktioner.smr.
40 Nationella åklagarmyndigheten, *Ansökan om stämning*, Ärende AM-8443–17, Inkom 2017–06–09MÅLNR: B 618–17, AKTBIL: 206; Säkerhetspolisen, *Huvudprotokoll*, dnr 0105-K98–16 0105-K8–17 0105-K9–17, Inkom, September 6, 2017; Säkerhetspolisen, *Protokollbilaga*, Göteborgs tingsrätt, Målbilaga B 618–17, 0105-K8–17, AM-8443–17, Inkom, September 6, 2017, Målnr: B 618–17, Aktbil: 209. Melin, in Sætran, Frode, "Høyreradikale i Göteborg: - Vi går så langt som nødvendig," *Aftenposten*, (April 25, 2016). In 2016, one of the perpetrators had taken part in vigilante National Socialist patrols on the streets in Gothenburg "to prevent members of our race from being raped, mugged, or assaulted" by racial strangers, and a National Socialist "security team" that protected white women from Muslim "rapefugees" at a public bath in Kungälv. Vergara, Daniel, "Nazistiska "trygghetsvärden" – dömd för rån och våldsbrott," *EXPO* (Feb. 16, 2016); Olsson, Daniel "Dömd nazist bakom 'trygghetsaktionen," *GT*, (Feb. 16, 2016); *Nordfront*, "Näste 2 agerade trygghetsvärd på Kungälvs badhus" (Feb. 14, 2016) Nordfront.se, https://www.nordfront.se/naste-2-agerar-trygghetsvard-kunga lvs-badhus.smr; Säkerhetspolisen. "PM Melin och Thulin i Ryssland," April 28, 2017 12:47 diarienr: 0105-K98–16; Roth, Andrew, "A Right-Wing Militia Trains Russians to Fight the Next War — with or without Putin," *Washington Post* (Jan. 2, 2017), Säkerhetspolisen. 2Transkribering av 'predikan'." Utredningsenheten. Diarienr. 0105-K98–16, April 24, 2017.
41 The role of the admins emphasize that the media-based collectivity was not without leadership. For an analysis of leadership, social media and protest movements, see Poell et al. (2016), For the Swedish Soldiers of Odin Facebook communication, see Dahlberg-Grundberg (2017).

References

Castle, Tammy & Tara Parsons (2017). "Vigilante or Viking? Contesting the mediated constructions of Soldiers of Odin Norge," *Crime, Media, Culture*, 13(3),1–20.

Dahlberg-Grundberg, Michael (2017). *"Internet som politiskt verktyg"* in Gardell, Mattias, Lööw, Heléne & Michael Dahlberg-Grundberg, *Den ensamme terroristen? Om lone wolves, näthat och brinnande flyktingförläggningar*, Stockholm: Ordfront.

Dahlberg, Stefan et al. (eds.) (2017). *När makten står på spel. Journalistik i valrörelser*, Stockholm: Institutet för mediestudier.

Deland, Mats, Paul Fuerer & Fredrik Hertzberg (2013). *Det vita fältet. Samtida forskning om högeextremism*. Lund: Arkiv Förlag.

Folkö, Robin & Anna-Sofia Quensel, (2013), "Detta är de dömda för," *EXPO*, May, 31.

Gardell, Mattias, Heléne Lööw, & Michael Dahlberg-Grundberg (2017). *Den ensamme terroristen? Om lone wolves, näthat och brinnande flyktingförläggningar*, Stockholm: Ordfront.

Ekman, Mattias (2014). "The dark side of online activism: Swedish right-wing extremist video activism on YouTube". *MedieKultur: Journal of Media and Communication Research*, [S.l.], 30(56), 79–99.

Ellinas, Antonis A. (2014) *The Media and the Far Right in Western Europe: Playing the Nationalist Card*, New York: Cambridge University Press.

Heggemann, Hans (2018). *Inkomsterna ökade 2005–2016*, Örebro: SCB, January 31.

Horsti, Karina, (2017) Digital Islamophobia: The Swedish woman as a figure of pure and dangerous whiteness. *New Media & Society*, 19(9), 1440–1457.

Lindberg, Simon, Emil Hagberg, & Klas Lund, (2016). *Aktivisthandboken 2.0. Handbok för aktivister i Nordiska motståndsrörelsen*, Nordiska motståndsrörelsen: Nordfront förlag.

Megafonen (2013, May 15). Vi kräver en oberoende utredning av dödsskjutningen i Husby. *SVT Opinion*, Retrieved from https://www.svt.se/opinion/vi-kraver-en-oberoende-utredning-av-dodsskjutningen-i-husby.

Nilsson, Ingvar & Anders Wadeskog (2008). *Summan av att ge människor en andra chans.* Stockholm: Fryshuset.

OECD (2015). OECD, Income inequality data update: Sweden (2015). Retrieved from https://www.oecd.org/els/soc/OECD-Income-Inequality-Sweden.pdf.

Pelinka, Anton (2013). Rightwing populism: Concept and typology. In Wodak, Ruth, Majid Kohsravi, & Brigitte Mral (eds.), *Right-wing populism in Europe. Politics and discourse* (pp. 3–23). London: Bloomsbury.

Poell, Thomas, Abdulla, Rasha, Bernhard Rieder, , Robbert Woltering, & Zack Liesbeth (2016) "Protest leadership in the age of social media, Information," *Communication & Society*, 19(7), 994–1014.

de los Reyes, Paulina, Magnus Hörnqvist, Kristina Boréus, & Filipe Estrada (2014). *Bilen brinner... men problemen finns kvar. Berättelser om Husbyhändelserna i maj 2013*. Stockholm: Stockholms universitet.

Riis Knudsen, Povl H. (2008). *Nationalsocialismen. Den biologiska världsåskådningen*. Stockholm: Nationellt Motstånd Förlag.

Rydgren, Jens (2006). *From tax populism to ethnic nationalism. Radical right-wing populism in Sweden.* New York and Oxford: Berghahn Books.

Rydgren, Jens (ed.) (2018) *The Oxford handbook of the radical right.* New York: Oxford University Press.

Strömbäck, Jesper & Andersson, Erika et al. (eds.) (2017). *Misstron mot medier.* Stockholm: Institutet för mediestudier.

Söderin, Eigil (2017 February 5). Stor ökning av de negativa artiklarna om invandring. ETC

Treré, Emiliano & Alice Mattoni (2016) Media ecologies and protest movements: main perspectives and key lessons. *Information, Communication & Society*, 19(3), 290–306.

UG-referens (2014, February 11). Dödsskjutningen i Husby. *SVT Uppdrag granskning*, Retrieved from https://www.svt.se/nyheter/granskning/ug/referens/533478532533478532.

Vergara, Daniel (2013, May 31). Kraftigt brottsbelastat medborgargarde. *EXPO*.

Vergara, Daniel (2018, January 25). Nazist startade nattvandrargrupp i Linköping. *EXPO*, Retrieved from http://expo.se/2018/nazist-startade-nattvandrargrupp-i-linkoping_7524.html.

Öhlund, Thomas, Per Oskar Gundel, & Michael Klaus (2009). *Förortens sociala kapital – en utvärdering av Lugna Gatan i Göteborg och Malmö*. Stockholm: Allmänna arvsfonden.

19

COMPARATIVE PERSPECTIVES ON VIGILANTISM AGAINST MIGRANTS AND MINORITIES

Tore Bjørgo and Miroslav Mareŝ

The notion of vigilantism covers a wide variety of phenomena. This volume has concentrated on vigilantism targeting migrants and minorities. Even within this broad category, our 17 case studies have described a wide variety of vigilante activities, diverging in modus operandi, target groups, levels of violence used, and degrees of support or opposition from the police, other governmental agencies, and political organizations. This concluding chapter will explore the research questions we listed at the beginning of the Introduction chapter:

- How do these vigilante activities operate, and how are they organized?
- What are the external justifications, group strategies and individual motivations behind this form of vigilante activism?
- Under what kinds of circumstances do these vigilante activities emerge, flourish or fail? What are the facilitating and mitigating – or permissive and repressive – factors?
- What are the vigilante groups' relationships with the police, other authorities and political parties, and how does it influence the group and its activities?
- How can our empirical material and findings contribute to the broader academic discussion on the phenomenon of vigilantism?

In addition, we will also discuss some other patterns that recurred in the empirical chapters, such as the transnational dimensions of these vigilante movements, vigilantism as performance, and gender dimensions.

Modus operandi in vigilantism against migrants and minorities: a typology

The first research question – how do these vigilante activities operate, and how are they organized – calls for a typology of such movements. Based on the descriptions

306 Tore Bjørgo and Miroslav Mareš

of a large number and wide variety of vigilante movements and groups we have been able to identify four main types of vigilante activities based on the ways they primarily operate (modus operandi):

- vigilante terrorism/pogroms/lynchings
- paramilitary militia movements
- border patrols
- street patrols

The preceding case study chapters have been presented and ordered roughly according to this typology, starting with cases of vigilante terrorism and ending with street patrols. However, the distinctions between the various types are sometimes rather fuzzy. These four types should be seen as ideal types, as specific groups may have traits of more than one type. In particular, militia type movements may engage in both border patrols, street patrols and terrorist death squads but in most cases in our data material, they don't. We treat militias here as a distinct type but with a view to the fact that such militias might develop in the direction of one of the three other types.

Vigilante terrorism, pogroms and lynchings

Several leading terrorism scholars have identified vigilante terrorism as a subtype of terrorism (Schmid 2011: 171; Sprinzak 1995). One variety has been death squads operating with the tacit support of state agencies, sometimes conducted by military and police officers in their free time, in effect being right-wing state terrorism in disguise. This was the case with the quasi-official death squads in several Latin American countries (Argentina, Brazil, Guatemala, Mexico and El Salvador) during the 1970s, targeting and killing thousands of suspected communists and other left-wing radicals (Sprinzak 1995: 29–31). A similar death squad, known as GAL (*Grupos Antiterroristas de Liberación*), was set up illegally by officials of the Spanish government to suppress the ETA and its Basque supporters during the mid-1980s (Woodworth 2003).

In our collection of case studies, certain varieties of the Jewish vigilantes on the Israeli-occupied West Bank share some similarities and traits of this type of vigilante terrorism, which operates with tacit or active state support (Gazit 2015, this volume). Some of these settlers are part of the state security system as military (reserve) officers or as part of the settlements' defence squads, which are organized, trained and armed by the Israeli Defence Forces act and tend to be more restrained. Others belong to right-wing extremist groups, or loose youth movements. They committed acts of vandalism, arson of Palestinian fields, cars and houses, beatings, and in rare cases also acts of manslaughter. Some of the settler violence was revenge in the aftermath of Palestinian acts of violence. A more general justification for Jewish vigilantism was to demonstrate Israeli sovereignty over the West Bank and Jewish dominancy over the Palestinian population living there.

Comparative perspectives **307**

This has some resemblance with another case described in this volume (by Blee and Latif): the Ku Klux Klan and their campaigns of terror, lynchings and intimidation to enforce white supremacy over the black population in the US. The Ku Klux Klan is often seen as the classic case of vigilante terrorism but its modus operandi has varied considerably during its four historical phases. The highest number of lynchings and other forms of violence against blacks took place during the era of the first Klan, immediately after the end of the Civil War during the 1860s and 70s. According to Blee and Latif (this volume),

> Klan groups insisted that their vigilantism was necessary to protect southern white women, who they saw as particularly vulnerable with the collapse of the former slavery state to what the Klan described as the vengeance and sexual depravities of now-freed black men.

Another justification was to keep the formally emancipated slaves down and enforce continued white supremacy. Although the Klan during this era was largely loosely organized gangs that operated outside the official law, they had a clear acquiescence of the white controlled law enforcement and judicial system of the post-Civil War southern states. Terrorist violence was a means of controlling the freed blacks and their allies (ibid.). The second Klan of the 1920s and 1930s was different, more of a broad and well-organized movement with 3–5 million supporters, including large numbers of women. Although violence still happened, large rallies, parades and racist political propaganda and boycott campaigns against immigrants, Catholics, Jews and blacks were more prominent features, and sometimes quite successful. The third Klan, during the 1960s and 1970s, was a violent response to the Civil Rights movement and challenge to the segregation of the blacks in the South, using terror tactics.

The third Klan's vigilantism was directly and intensely violent, using techniques that ranged from arson, murders, bombing campaigns, threats, assaults, and cross burnings to other forms of racial terror. In many instances in the 1950s and 1960s, Klan violence was closely coordinated with local law enforcement and judicial officers (some of whom were openly associated with the Klan, or later exposed as Klan members) who declined to arrest or prosecute Klan members for even very flagrant crimes and violence (Blee and Latif, this volume). The fourth Klan, during the 1970s and 1980s in particular (and declining towards the 2000s), was violent as well and continued to attack racial minorities, immigrants and leftists, but even the state itself became a target for some Klan groups. By this time, backing or tacit support from law enforcement was no longer as common as previously, and some Klan groups came under close surveillance by the FBI, or were infiltrated by law enforcement. Moreover, they were bankrupted by effective legal actions from anti-racist organizations. The Klan could obviously continue their campaigns of terror as long as they could operate relatively freely, without any interference (or even with the blessing) of the local sheriff, judge, pastor and mayor. When repressive forces from law enforcement and NGOs put pressure on them, and the general social and

FIGURE 19.1 Vigilante "justice": The Duluth Lynching postcard is one of many postcards widely distributed in the aftermath of lynchings in the USA during the first decades of the 20th century. On June 15, 1920, three black men were taken from jail in the town In Duluth, Minnesota, and lynched by a mob of several thousand men, accused of having raped a nineteen-year old local girl. However, a medical examination found no evidence that the girl had been raped. This was apparently not a Ku Klux Klan lynching. For more information of the Duluth lynching, see http://www.mnhs.org/duluthlynchings/lynchings.php, and https://en.wikipedia.org/wiki/1920_Duluth_lynchings and http://zenithcity.com/archive/legendary-tales/the-victims-of-the-1920-duluth-lynchings/2/.

political environment was no longer as permissive with their racism and violence, their leeway became severely restricted.

Another example of this type of vigilantism can be seen in India, where there have been several instances of Hindu cow protection groups attacking Muslims and other minority groups on the pretext of alleged cow slaughter or consumption. Although the state does not overtly support such cow vigilantism against Muslims or other minorities (rather it has publicly condemned it), the perpetrators involved are invariably linked to the state establishment (Ahuja, this volume). The cow protection groups across the country have links to and are members of cultural and charitable organizations affiliated to the ruling political party, the BJP. Even though members of the BJP, including the Prime Minister himself, have condemned the acts of violence against minorities, critics argue that little has been done to reign in

Comparative perspectives **309**

the vigilante activities of the cow protection groups, as they still serve to protect the cow, and the ideology of Hindutva.

Similar processes took place in Russia, with a murderous campaign against migrants and homosexuals. During the period 2006–2010, vigilante terrorism and violence could continue, as the police looked another way and did not crack down on the (mostly) skinhead gangs that killed hundreds and injured thousands of people (Laryš, this volume; Enstad 2018). Although some of the anti-migrant violence carried out by self-nominated "Guestbusters" can be better described as racist hate crimes, other violent campaigns had obvious traits of vigilantism, being justified as a fight against criminality committed by foreigners. Migrants from the non-Slavic republics with (mostly) Muslim populations in the Caucasus and Central Asia were accused of high crime rates, including robberies and rapes directed against Russian majority. The extensive violence against homosexuals and the LGBT community should be seen against the background of the widespread view in all strata of Russian society that homosexuality and other sexual orientations were undermining Russian cultural traditions and family values. Thus, anti-LGBT violence, sometimes called a "hunt for paedophiles", could be seen as a form of vigilantism to defend the moral order against the alleged destructive "fifth columns". Russia continued to have the highest rate of hate murders in Europe until the police started to crack down on the perpetrators and their organizations around 2010. The large-scale arrests of the perpetrators and organizers of racist violence and other hate crimes led to a significant reduction of such vigilante terrorism in Russia (Laryš, this volume).

One extreme case of vigilante terrorism was the series of murders of Roma people in Hungary in 2008 to 2009 (described by Póczik and Sárik in this volume). A death squad of four perpetrators killed ten people (including a child) and wounded six more when they attacked Roma villages with guns. They justified their actions by claiming that they intended to take revenge for "Gypsy crimes" and provoke violent reactions from the Roma to trigger an ethnic civil war. In reality, the victims were selected randomly and had no particular relation to "Gypsy crime". Although the Military Security Agency held back decisive information from the investigation because one of the perpetrators was an informant for them, the four perpetrators were convicted and received long prisons sentences (life for three of them).

Sweden and Germany are the two countries in Western Europe with the highest rates of right-wing terrorism and violence (Ravndal 2017). Most of the violence is directed against "foreigners" or related targets, and the perpetrators tried to justify some of that violence by referring to alleged "criminal migrants", "rapefugees" or that migrants constitute a terrorist threat (Koehler, this volume; Gardell 2015, and this volume). Germany has also had several cases of pogrom-like arson attacks on homes for refugees, or immigrants have been attacked by large crowds of people, usually led by organized neo-Nazis. There were a number of such cases during the early 1990s. The most infamous attacks took place in Hoyerswerda, Rostock and Mölln and Solingen, with many fatalities, including children. During and after the

310 Tore Bjørgo and Miroslav Mareš

more recent great influx of migrants to Europe in 2015 and 2016, many ended up in Germany and Sweden, which already had strong militant neo-Nazis scenes and long traditions for right-wing extremist violence. These two countries have also had high numbers of arson attacks (and in Germany, also attacks with explosives) against homes for refugees during the same time period.[1] Although many of these attacks may be better described as hate crimes, some attacks may also aptly be described as vigilante terrorism, carried out by groups of locals pretending to protect the community against alleged "criminal migrants". The German cases are described and discussed in the chapter by Daniel Koehler on "Anti-Immigration Militias and Vigilante Groups in Germany".

As emphasized by Barbera Perry (2001, see her definition cited in the Introduction on p. 11), an important aspect of hate crime is that it is a mechanism of power and oppression, intended to reaffirm the precarious hierarchies that characterize a given social order. It attempts to re-create simultaneously the threatened (real or imagined) hegemony of the perpetrator's group and the "appropriate" subordinate identity of the victim's group (Perry 2001, 10). Some of the vigilante violence described in this section – and in more detail in the chapters on Ku Klux Klan (Blee and Latif), Jewish vigilantism in the West bank (Gazit), against homosexuals in Russia (Laryš) and against Muslims in India (Ahuja) – has this dimension of keeping minorities down in their subordinate place or frightening them from challenging the traditional social or moral order.

Paramilitary militia movements

What distinguishes these militias from other forms of vigilante groups is that they are modelled on a military style and form of organization. They usually wear military-like uniforms, perform parades and marches, have a structured chain of command and train military skills, sometimes also with firearms. Their main goal is usually preparedness for participation in real war (or a civil war), however, they can be involved in vigilante activities as well.

Paramilitarism and militias are specific and broad phenomena and their overlap with vigilantism can be identified only in some entities belonging to this spectrum. While vigilantism can be a temporarily limited offshoot of paramilitary groups, it can also play a significant role in the activities of some paramilitary formations. Some groups changed their modus operandi from mainly military activities to vigilante activities (such as the original Hungarian Guard, see chapter by Póczik and Sárik). Of course, paramilitarism and militias are not a homogenous phenomenon and in the modern world we can find a huge number of varieties of paramilitarism. It can be integrated into governmental structures or it can act autonomously in non-governmental structures (see the introduction of this book, p. 9).

The main elements of paramilitarism are military identity and readiness of paramilitary activists to participate in military conflicts (including civil political, religious and ethnic wars etc.). The military-like organization and outlook (uniforms, ranking etc.) are typical of these groups. If we take into account the present situation in

FIGURE 19.2 Hungarian Guard's parade in Budapest and inauguration of new members (Photo: Béla Szandelszky)

the Western world, many concepts of "future wars" with participation of ethnically or racially based armies are propagated in the right-wing extremist scene (Mareš 2012). Also, the concept of a "political soldier" can be considered as preparedness for a real "soldier's identity".

Non-governmental paramilitary militias have had a long history in Central and Eastern Europe dating back to the interwar period, particularly in countries like Italy, Germany, Hungary and the former Czechoslovakia. These militias were mostly linked to fascist parties and movements and directed their violence against political opponents on the left, but also against ethnic minorities such as Jews and Roma people. In Germany and Italy, the Sturmabteilung (SA) and the Blackshirts played important role in the Nazi and Fascist takeover of political power. In countries under Nazi and fascist rule in the late 1930s and World War II, these militias became an integral part of the power apparatus of the totalitarian regime. After the defeat of the Nazi and fascist regimes, non-governmental paramilitary militias were banned in all European countries.

Although there were attempts by far-right movements to re-establish militia groups during the post-war period, the most significant initiative was the establishment of the Hungarian Guard in 2007, as a militia wing of the right-wing extremist Jobbik party. The Hungarian Guard was tasked to protect Hungarian citizens against "Gypsy crime", sometimes marching through Roma villages and neighbourhoods to intimidate the inhabitants (Póczik and Sárik, this volume).

312 Tore Bjørgo and Miroslav Mareš

Although the Hungarian Guard was banned the year after its establishment, it inspired similar movements in other Central and East European countries, such as in the Czech Republic (the National Guard, the Protection Corps of the Workers' Party), in Slovakia (Patrols of the ĽSNS) (Mareš and Milo, this volume) and in Poland (Guard of Independence).

Other varieties of vigilante paramilitary militias are found in the US, where there are also long historical traditions of vigilantism as well as citizens' militias (Mulloy 2005). One type is the anti-government militias that prepared to resist or even fight against alleged repression from the federal government, often identified as the Zionist Occupation Government (ZOG) and the racial traitors (Dees 1997). The case presented in this volume, the Minutemen, is of another kind. Although participants – mostly military veterans – tend to share far-right views, they see their mission as helping the government to patrol the border in order to stop illegal migrants from entering the US. They want to collaborate with the governmental border service and maintain a cordial relationship with them. Although they are generally armed, they abstain from any use of weapons or violence (Shapira, this volume).

The Jewish vigilantes in the West Bank do also – to various degrees – have a paramilitary character. They are generally armed and do sometimes wear military clothes. Some of the groups, such as the Jewish settlements' defence squads, are institutionalized and are organized, trained and armed by the Israeli Defense Forces (IDF). Other vigilante groups – and typically the more violent ones – are operating more independently from the IDF and are often linked to radical right groups (Gazit, this volume).

The traditional right-wing extremist scene uses militarism as a mobilization factor of its supporters – in contrast to modern extreme right parties (Mudde 2000: 174). Nationalist military traditions and legacies (including legacies of specific military efforts of the extreme right) played an important role in the traditionalist part of the extreme right spectrum (in neo-Nazism, neo-Fascism and in various authoritarian-nationalist streams of the extreme right).

In some countries, militarist ideas of vigilante and paramilitary units are used against the official foreign policy goals (for example, anti-EU and anti-NATO politics is typical of Bulgarian, Slovak or Czech vigilante groups, while Russian military skills are propagated by them).

This mixture of historical legacies and contemporary challenges creates an environment for the rise of several important paramilitary formations. In the field of paramilitary activities, the situation in East and Central Europe is characterized by more lenient legal rules and their enforcement is not as strict as in Western Europe. Para-military camps in Russia even serve as training centres for Western European militants, as the recent case of Swedish anti-immigrant neo-Nazi bombers shows (Gardell, this volume). Some similarities can be found between the US paramilitary scene and these formations. It is important to mention that these facts are valid for non-governmental paramilitary formations. In Poland

Comparative perspectives **313**

pro-governmental paramilitary units are officially supported by the Ministry of Defence (Liederkerke 2016).

If we take into consideration the non-governmental paramilitaries, we can observe their partial involvement in vigilante activities. The Hungarian Guard (see above) was planned and used mostly for patrols in Roma settlements (see chapter by Póczik and Sárik); however, in 2007 some representatives of this organization declared their readiness to establish units for potential future defence of Hungary in case of Slovak and Romanian attacks against their country. But the real turn to military tasks never happened (Havlík and Mareš 2014). The Slovak Conscripts are mostly specialized in military training (also with heavy weapons), however, during the migration crisis they started patrols against immigrant crime (see chapter by Mareš and Milo). The migration crisis gave rise to a new paramilitary formation in Bulgaria (see chapter by Stoynova and Dzekova) and caused a turn of several Czech paramilitary units to this issue, including their cooperation in anti-immigrant activities (see chapter by Mareš and Milo). In a long-term perspective, the protection of borders against migrants is seen as a part of a militarized conflict between traditional European nations and the "barbarian" invaders. This facilitates the involvement of paramilitaries in anti-immigrant vigilantism.

Border patrols

During time periods when there have been heavy influx of refugees or undocumented migrants crossing national borders, and this issue has been on the political or media agenda, there has frequently been vigilante responses to this. Claiming that the governmental border agencies are unable to fulfil their tasks of controlling the borders due to lack of capacity – or lack of determination – some activists have volunteered to "help" protecting the borders. Border patrolling by non-governmental groups may take place in an open cooperation with or tacit acceptance by government agencies, as covert operations patrolling border areas without the knowledge of governmental border agencies, or in open defiance of the government, mainly as a protest statement. Vigilante border patrols may be conducted by private paramilitary militias with some kind of uniforms, with or without weapons, or by civilian groups without any paramilitary pretentions. Such border patrols may be stationary or move around on foot, by car, on public transportation, or even by ship. Some "migrant hunter" patrols have made use of force (e.g. handcuffs) in order to "arrest" intruding migrants and either to hand them over to government border agencies or to chase them back across the border to where they came from.[2] However, in most known cases such vigilante border patrols are well aware that they do not have any powers to apprehend, restrain or chase away any intruding migrants, and that they would break the law and get in serious trouble with the authorities if they did so. They might use strong flashlights to light up migrants crossing the border by night, and these migrants may believe that they have been detected by official border patrols.

In this volume, we have two detailed descriptions of such border patrol activities and several brief descriptions. One striking case is the Minutemen patrolling the US – Mexican border, described and analysed in the chapter by Harel Shapira. This was a heavily armed and well-equipped militia organized by mainly ex-military men. Militias have a long tradition in the current era and they consider themselves to be successors of historical legacies of militias in US history.

Other cases are the two vigilante border patrol organizations in Bulgaria, described in the chapter by Stoynova and Dzhekova. As they state, "the single-issue groupings being mostly preoccupied with the refugee problem and with organizing vigilante groups of volunteers". The formations "such as Shipka BNVC and Vasil Levski MU at the very least create the impression of having a structure and spelled-out goals including some political ambition" (Stoynova and Dzhekova, this volume)

In comparison with well-organized and continuously active Bulgarian border patrols in the Turkish-Bulgarian border mountains (where there are real routes of migrants), the situation in the Czech Republic is characterized by random activities in areas which in fact are not used by migrants: the Ore mountains, where the Ore Dogs from the National Home Guard operated along the Czech-German border.

A rather sophisticated attempt to demonstrate the capability to control the sea border against migrants in the Mediterranean is connected with the Identitarian groups crowd-funding the ship "Defend Europe". Identiarian sea patrols did not achieve the official goals (search-and rescue mission, documenting the mis-behaviour of NGOs on the Libyan coast, and hampering their cooperation with human smugglers), but they won huge media attention and they popularized the Identitarian movement amongst a part of European public with anti-Immigrant attitudes (see Gattinara on vigilantism in France in this volume).

A common feature of all these vigilante border patrols is that they rarely or never detect or apprehend any undocumented migrants crossing the borders (with the exception of the Bulgarian case). Their activities appear to be completely symbolic. They make an effort to demonstrate the willingness of vigilantes to protect their "own country" in the case of worse migration flows and they want to demonstrate that the government is not able to do "its best" against migration. It is mainly a media strategy to affect the broader public and win the "hearts and minds" of people for ideas which vigilantes represent – including undermining the legitimacy of the political regime.

Street patrols

The most common type of vigilante activities against migrants and minorities are street patrols where organized groups walk together in the streets or near particular places with the stated goal of providing protection against people who might constitute a risk of crime. In the cases described in this volume, migrants and Roma people are frequently singled out as constituting the crime problem.

Some groups are wearing some sort of identifiable clothing, such as hoodies, jackets or armbands with group symbols or names, whereas other groups are fully civilian in appearance. The most common modus of their operation is to patrol streets where crimes such as theft, robbery or rape might happen, claiming that their presence will deter criminals and provide a sense of safety to the good and vulnerable citizens, and to women in particular. Typically, such patrolling activities start up in the aftermath of criminal events that cause fear and anger in the community, especially when migrants or minorities have been involved as (alleged) perpetrators. A major influx of migrants into the area may also be a pretext for organizing vigilante patrols. Sometimes radical right organizations grab the opportunity to organize vigilante patrols to provide safety to the community – and to and promote their group. Alternatively, such patrols may be organized spontaneously by concerned (or angry) citizens without any particular political sponsorship. Some of these groups maintain that they will only observe and report incidences to the police whereas other groups take a more active stance by intending to deter and even intervene against acts of crime. Obviously, this may represent a challenge to the police monopoly on the legitimate use of force, which will be discussed later in this chapter.

A more aggressive form of vigilantism is to patrol outside asylum centres, homes for refugees, schools for minorities or even inside villages inhabited by Roma people or other minorities. The intention – or at least the outcome – might be to scare the people living there from going outdoors, or to leave their homes entirely – which also happened in some cases (Gardell in this volume, Ecopolis Foundation 2012).[3]

Although many ordinary citizens may feel uncomfortable with uniformed vigilante groups patrolling public streets, members of minority groups and migrants singled out by the vigilantes as suspect groups or potential crime threats frequently feel even more intimidated. Several examples of this are described in the case studies from e.g. Hungary, Sweden and Slovakia.

Although some vigilante groups make extensive use of violence – the main cases are described in the section on vigilante terrorism, pogroms and lynchings – most other vigilante groups do *not* actually carry out acts of violence. However, they do usually display a violent capacity through a performance of force, whether they parade as a paramilitary militia (with or without weapons), or patrol the streets in groups dressed up with group symbols or uniforms. Their display of force is obviously intended to have an intimidating and deterring impact on their designated target groups (crime prone migrants and minorities) as well as political opponents.

Factors behind the emergence and decline of vigilante groups

Under what kinds of circumstances do these vigilante activities emerge, flourish or fail? What are the facilitating and mitigating – or permissive and repressive – factors?

What makes vigilantism emerge and flourish?

The first factor is *a widespread perception of crisis and threat* to our society and lifestyle – real or imagined. This causes fear among sections of the population, magnified by extensive media coverage and rhetoric by far-right political groups that capitalize on the fear. Fundamental values, even the social and moral order, are considered to be threatened. For vigilantism to emerge, the fear of crime, violence and rape is of particular importance. The perceived threat of sexual assaults against "our women" seems to strike a particularly raw nerve among some groups of men.

The threat of crime is identified with specific groups that become objects of hatred and fear. In many European countries, the marginalized Roma populations have for a long time been strongly identified with criminal behaviour and targeted by vigilante activities (Mareš and Milo; Póczik and Sárik, both in this volume). More recently, and particularly during and after the large influx of refugees and other migrants in 2015–2016 into Europe (and also the US), migrants have become perceived as a major crime threat, especially since a wave of severe terrorist attacks committed by Islamist militants took place during the same period. Muslim migrants became perceived as the main group from which threats of crime and violence emerged, to some extent replacing the Roma.

Specific shocking events causing moral panic trigger vigilante activities. New Year's Eve 2015/2016 in Cologne, where large numbers of local women were sexually harassed and abused by men of mainly North African and Middle Eastern origin, some of them recent migrants (Koehler, this volume), became a turning point in Europe, triggering vigilante responses in many countries, and boosting street patrol groups like the Soldiers of Odin and others. A similar case occurred in England, where the disclosure of gangs of men from within the British Pakistani community had groomed large numbers of English girls (many of whom were underage) for sexual exploitation triggering vigilante responses (Ralph-Morrow, this volume; Bird 2017). Shocking events where men from the perceived enemy group (Muslims, Roma, blacks) sexually abuse or rape "our women" strike a particularly raw nerve among many men, triggering aggressive responses to defend and retaliate (Gardell; Blee and Latif, both in this volume).

The perception that the police and other authorities are either unable or unwilling to protect the citizens from threats to their safety is a major factor to facilitate for the emergence of vigilantism. The police in Cologne were heavily criticized in the aftermath of the New Year events for failing to intervene properly against the mass sexual assaults, and a reluctance to provide truthful information about the perpetrators' ethnicity out of sense of political correctness and fear of causing xenophobia and Islamophobia (Koehler, this volume). Similar criticism was expressed against the Swedish police for hiding the amount of sexual abuse committed by men of foreign origin (Frick 2016) and against British police for failing to take action against Pakistani "grooming gangs" (Jay 2014). On the same note, governments were accused of failure to stop the "wave of migrants" flooding into Europe, and inability to control the borders (e.g. Castelli Gattinara on Italy, this volume; Shapira 2013: 2). Proponents of vigilantism claimed that when the state fails to fulfil its duty to protect its citizens, the citizens have the right to protect themselves by taking the law into their own hands (Gardell, this volume).

This call for vigilantism is closely associated with *a lack of trust in governmental institutions* in general and the police in particular. The Eurobarometer shows that many of the countries with relatively strong and persistent tendencies towards vigilantism, such as Greece, Italy, Bulgaria, the Czech Republic and Slovakia, score low or relatively low on trust in governmental institutions. Countries where vigilante movements have more difficulties in finding a lasting foothold, such as Norway, Denmark, Sweden and Germany, score high on trust in governmental institutions and the legal system (e.g. European Commission 2017). The United States, which has a long legacy of vigilantism and militias, is also characterized by a low trust in governmental institutions among large sections of the population, in particular when it comes to the federal government (Pew Research Center 2017).

Countries with a *permissive legislation* for armed self-defence or civil patrols provide opportunities for vigilantism. For example, the Italian cabinet's Security Package in 2009, which focused mainly on illegal immigration, legalized civil patrols to relieve urban insecurity in support of law enforcement and the police. Although such patrols in principle should be activated and coordinated with the police, the Forza Nuova took advantage of the opportunity to set up their own "security walks", without bothering to submit or coordinate with the police and local authorities (Castelli Gattinara on Italy, this volume). The liberal laws in the US on gun ownership and the right to use armed force for self-defence and for protecting your property goes very far in legalizing vigilantism. In most European countries, applications for gun permits would be turned down flatly if the reason given was self-protection. The Second Amendment of the United States Constitution reads "A well regulated Militia, being necessary to the security of a free State, the right of the people to keep and bear Arms, shall not be infringed". This has been taken to heart by the gun lobby as well as a number of extreme-right militias, claiming their right to carry guns (openly or concealed) in public places, and to set up paramilitary organizations for armed resistance if the federal government will take their guns or other rights.

This brings us to *traditions of vigilantism and militias*. Again, the United States is a special case, with its Wild West history of frontier justice and lynchings due to the almost nonexistence of governmental law enforcement (Berg 2011). Vigilantism, street justice and revenge are main themes in American popular culture, and in action and crime movies in particular. It is most likely that this historical and cultural dimension in the United States facilitates a widespread mindset where vigilantism becomes a natural response to perceived threats. In Central and Eastern Europe there are also historical traditions of Fascist militias, especially during the inter-war period in the 1920s and 1930s. This has served as a model and inspiration to modern-day extreme-right parties and movements to establish paramilitary militias in countries like Italy, Germany, Hungary, Bulgaria, Slovakia, and the Czech Republic (see chapters by Castelli Gattinara, Koehler, Póczik and Sárik, Dzhekova and Stoynova, Mareš & Milo). Such modern-day militias are almost non-existent in countries like Norway, Sweden and Britain, which lacks such militia traditions.

Vigilantism thrives in societies where there is *a base of support for vigilantism* among the public or among political parties. Most vigilante groups described in this

318 Tore Bjørgo and Miroslav Mareš

volume put a lot of effort into gaining support from the public and recognition from the police and the government, but with limited or no success in most cases (see e.g. Dzhekova and Stoynova on border patrols in Bulgaria, Bjørgo and Gjelsvik on Soldiers of Odin in Norway). Some vigilante groups have engaged in charity and community work, obviously with the purpose of gaining public support and acceptance (e.g. Archambault and Veilleux-Lepage on SOO in Canada, Gattinara on Identitarians in France, both in this volume). Some vigilante patrols and militias have been established by political parties that already had a foothold in parliamentary politics, as in the case of the Hungarian Guard and the Jobbik Party (Póczik and Sárik, this volume), and the train patrols of the ĽSNS party in Slovakia (Mareš and Daniel Milo, this volume). Although governmental reactions to the new vigilante organizations in Bulgaria have been ambivalent, surveys have shown significant popular support for vigilante activities such as civilian patrols and civilian arrests, enjoying support from more than half the population (Dzhekova and Stoynova, this volume). In the Czech Republic, the rise of anti-Migrant vigilantes accompanied the rise of new anti-Immigrant parties (Mareš and Milo, this volume). The Hungarian case shows the re-establishment of the vigilante scene after the ban of the original Hungarian Guard and stable support of the Jobbik party (Póczik and Sárik, this volume).

When the police and other authorities turn a blind eye to vigilante violence, or even tacitly accept or actively support this kind of violence, vigilantism in its most violent forms is likely to become rampant. The first and third eras of the Ku Klux Klan (see Blee and Latif in this volume) provide notorious examples of this. In the post-Civil War southern states, the Klan operated outside the official law but with the clear acquiescence of the white controlled law enforcement and judicial operations. This was also to a large extent the case as late as into the 1950s and 1960s, when Klan violence was closely coordinated with local sheriffs and judges (some of whom were actually Klan members) who declined to arrest or prosecute Klan members for even very flagrant crimes and violence (ibid.). Another notorious example is the wave of murderous violence against migrants and homosexuals in Russia during the period 2006–2010, causing the deaths of hundreds of victims and maimed thousands more. This murderous campaign could go on for several years because the police and other authorities did not take it seriously but looked the other way (Laryš, this volume; Enstad 2018). Vigilante violence by Jewish settler groups on the Israeli-occupied West Bank has also been enabled by the reluctance of the Israeli Defence Forces to stop it. Military personnel have also sometimes been directly involved in the vigilante activities (Gazit, this volume).

The conditions described above – especially when they appear in combination – create opportunities for vigilantism in general, and directed against migrant and minorities in particular. None of these factors can be considered either necessary or sufficient alone to produce vigilantism as an outcome. The more factors in combination, and the stronger each of them are, will provide a fertile ground for the growth and sustainability of vigilantism. The presence and/or absence of some of the factors are more likely to produce certain types of vigilantism. For example,

Comparative perspectives **319**

when law enforcement does not intervene against vigilante violence or hate crimes against minority groups, such behaviour is likely to continue and increase. Countries with permissive gun laws and historical traditions of militias are likely to foster armed militias. Where these conditions are absent and there is very limited or no acceptance for paramilitarism and vigilantism, non-violent street patrols are more likely to be the main form of vigilantism to appear.

What makes vigilantism decline or fail?

This brings us to the other side of the coin, why vigilante movements fall apart and end their activities.[4] Obviously, the absence, reduction or reversal of the facilitating conditions described above may also serve as mitigating factors. But there are also some additional conditions that may play a role.

When the perceived threat is reduced or appears less acute, the appeal of vigilante responses become less persuasive. The decline in the number of migrants crossing border into Europe after 2016 also had an impact in terms of a reduction in vigilantism, or on the appeal of such activities. Some of these perceived threats are media bubbles, and when the news media turn its focus to other issues, the moral panic among parts of the population will also decline. Although die-hard activists against immigration or Islamism will continue, the potential for gaining support for vigilante activities will be hard to find. For example, with the decrease in migration pressure in 2017, patrol activities in Bulgaria have ceased, leading the organizations to focus on other activities to sustain their public profile and relevance – although without much success, according to Dzhekova and Stoynova (in this volume). In Sweden, Mattias Gardell describes the sudden outburst of vigilante activism as a popcorn phenomenon: "Into the simmering heat of the radical nationalist milieu, warmed up by negative press on migrants and migration, cyber activists pumped in 'alternative facts' on alleged migrant crime, no-go zones, and shariah-sanctioned 'rape jihad' of white Swedish women, to which concerned 'clicktivists' responded with calls to protect the nation and its women" (Gardell, this volume).

When the police and other authorities are able to demonstrate that they are in control of the situation, the appeal of vigilante activism will be limited. In the aftermath of the Cologne New Year events in 2015/16, there was a widespread panic about immigrant men raping local women, and vigilante groups started to patrol the streets in many local communities as a response to this fear. When the local police could credibly assert that there had hardly been any such rape cases in the local community, or that the refugees housed in the community had not caused any particular problems in terms of public safety, or that the police was able to manage those problems that might occur, the demand for vigilante action would lose its appeal.

This is directly related to *the level of trust in the police and other authorities.* In countries and cities where the police is generally respected and trusted by most of the population, and that most people think the police is doing a fair job in providing safety, initiatives to establish vigilante patrols to provide safety in the streets will usually fall flat. Although people may complain that the police are not there

320 Tore Bjørgo and Miroslav Mareŝ

when they need them, there is still a recognition that the rule of law is important and that only the police should be trusted to maintain public order.

Lack of support for vigilante groups and activities from the public, politicians or the news media is a major factor when attempts to establish vigilante patrols or militias fail. This was very evident in Norway, where the Soldiers of Odin did not get support from any political party (not even from the right-wing populist Progress Party), nor from any significant part of the public. The police did not want their "assistance" to maintain public order and safety, and stated that there was no need for vigilante patrols (Bjørgo and Gjelsvik, this volume). We also have examples of leading politicians and governmental agencies that initially supported vigilante border patrols but later withdrew that support when it became clear that these patrols behaved brutally towards migrants (see Bulgarian case in the chapter by Dzhekova and Stoynova). When the Jobbik party in Hungary from 2014 onwards claimed they would abandon their previous extremist positions, there was also a decline in their support for vigilante groups. We can also see a change of political positions towards brutal racist vigilantism and hate crimes in Russia at the turn of 2000s and 2010s (see Laryš in this volume).

When *the police and other authorities strike down hard on vigilante violence and hate crime*, such activities usually come to an end. Whereas the Ku Klux Klan during preceding eras could continue with their lynchings and vigilante terrorism without much interference (or even with protection) from law enforcement, the fourth era of the Ku Klux Klan during the 1970s until 2000s marked a change as there were more legal prosecutions of Klan terrorists, increased FBI surveillance and infiltration of the organizations, and also bankrupting of the organizations through civil law suits on behalf of victims of Klan violence (Blee and Latif, this volume). When the Russian government and the police after years of passivity decided to put an end to the wave of mass-killings carried out by neo-Nazi skinheads and various far right vigilante groups during the years 2006–2010, arresting and convicting leaders and perpetrators to lengthy prison terms, the vigilante violence and hate crimes quickly declined (Laryš, this volume; Enstad 2018).

Restrictive legislation on vigilantism and police enforcement of such laws does reduce the leeway of vigilante activities and may even put an end to it. In Hungary, the Metropolitan Court based on the motion of the Prosecutor General, declared that the activities of the Hungarian Guard were against the human and minority rights guaranteed by the Constitution, and that the Guard had to be disbanded. This decision was upheld in courts, and the Parliament also passed a law that raised the punishment for participating in a dissolved organization. It is worth also mentioning that even the Criminal Code was amended to prevent such activities in the future by enacting the crime of "Prohibited Policing Activity".[5] Although parts if the prohibited Hungarian Guard tried to reorganize under a slightly different name, their leeway for organizing a militia-type organization was now significantly reduced (Póczik and Sárik, this volume).

As will be discussed further below, most countries have legislation to ban non-governmental paramilitary militias as well as vigilantism and other forms of private justice. However, private security companies and certain forms of citizens patrols under the strict control of the police might be permitted. Vigilante patrols often try to position themselves as close to the legal forms of citizen patrols as possible without giving up their autonomy (see Gattinara on the Forza Nuovo in Italy, this volume). In Norway, it took some time before the police had a consistent response against the Soldiers of Odin, and implemented the Police Law's ban on private operations with the purpose of maintaining public order or any other forms of law enforcement in public areas. When the Soldiers of Odin were repeatedly fined for wearing their coveted hoodies with SOO symbols during their nightly walks, this activity stopped (Bjørgo and Gjelsvik, this volume). The Norwegian Penal Code also bans the establishment of private military organizations, making paramilitary militias illegal.

Another circumstance that weakens vigilante groups and activities is *the inherent tendency in extreme-right movements towards internal conflicts and splits*. Conflicts over leadership, strategies, tactics, ideology and money are recurring themes in many of the groups analysed in this volume (see e.g. chapters by Gardell; Bjørgo and Gjelsvik; Archambault and Veilleux-Lepage; Mareš and Milo). This tendency towards group fission leads to smaller and weaker units, and also that some split-off groups turn to more extreme measures and become easy to take out by law enforcement.

To summarize: vigilante groups and activities tend to emerge and flourish in settings when there is a convergence of several facilitating conditions and an absence of mitigating or repressive factors. They fail and decline when the facilitating conditions are reduced and repressive measured are implemented against them.

External justifications, group strategies and individual motivations

As proposed in the Introduction chapter, it may be useful to make a distinction between three types of reasons or drivers behind vigilante activities: (1) External justifications, (2) group strategies, and (3) individual motivations. We will explore each of these types and see how our empirical cases resonate with this typology.

External justifications are the official mission of the group as presented to the public, the media and authorities: to protect the community against certain crime threats that the police and other authorities allegedly do not have the capacity – or the will – to handle alone. These justifications are typically altruistic, tailored to resonate with widely held concerns in society (e.g. on migration, crime or terrorism) and issues high on the news media agenda. Literally all the vigilante movements described in this volume communicate via the news media or social media to the general public – or to specific external audiences – why they have to do what they do. Typical messages claim that crime-prone migrants or certain minorities (Roma people in particular) are threatening public safety. According to these groups, they also sexually harass or rape "our" women. Moreover, illegal migrants (Muslims in particular) flood our borders and take over our country, threatening our way of life, culture, social welfare and security. Terrorists are hiding among the

322 Tore Bjørgo and Miroslav Mareŝ

refugees to infiltrate our societies. And the police and other authorities are either unable or unwilling to do what is needed to stop it (Gardell, this volume). When the state is not fulfilling its duty to protect its citizens, the citizens have the right to protect themselves through vigilante action in the form of militias, border patrols or street patrols, they claim. Most of the groups are careful about not challenging the state power and its monopoly on violence directly, and assert publicly that they will avoid the use of violence, at least in the present situation. However, some of the groups argues for the need to be prepared for civil war if the situation deteriorates further, as exemplified by the vigilante militias in Slovakia (Mares & Milo in this volume), Roma murders by the "Death Squad" in Hungary (Póczik and Sárik in this volume), or the National-Socialist Society in Russia (Laryš in this volume). Some of the groups using lethal violence also make justifications for this, e.g. claiming that homosexuals threaten the moral order and traditional Russian values, and that it was necessary to protect children from paedophiles through vigilante action (Laryš, in this volume). Similarly, lynchings of Muslims accused of trading meat from holy cows was justified by the perpetrators and their supporters as necessary to protect the sacred cows and uphold a fundamental religious value and one of the pillars in Hindu identity (Ahuja, in this volume).

Group strategies are the internal reasoning for why leaders believe it will serve the interests of the group to engage in vigilante activities. These reasons are not meant for public consumption. This dimension is particularly relevant when far-right political parties or other organizations organize vigilante activities such as street patrols in order to attract media attention and public support, promote the organization and its relevance, and mobilize new members. Typical cases in this volume are the Forza Nuova and its "security walks" (Castelli Gattinara on Italy), the Jobbik party and its Hungarian Guard (Póczik and Sárik), the Golden Dawn party in Greece (Vrakopoulos and Halikiopoulou), the train patrols organized by the LSNS party in Slovakia, various innovative vigilante activities by the *Identitaires* in France (Castelli Gattinara) and the Nordic Resistance Movement and its vigilante street patrols in Sweden and Finland (Gardell). These organizations and parties all used vigilante activities strategically to promote their organizations, get publicity and new members – although they always justified their efforts by pointing to their official higher mission, which was to stop crime, rapes or illegal migrants. However, none of these official goals were ever met: their vigilante activities were not really instrumental in stopping any specific crimes. Other unofficial goals with right-wing vigilante activities could be to provide exciting member activities to maintain group cohesion, or as a training activity for paramilitary groups. Furthermore, by demonstrating that there was a need for vigilante patrols because the police was unable to provide safety for the citizens, far-right political parties used such vigilante activities to undermine the legitimacy of the government. The Forza Nuova in Italy, the Golden Dawn party in Greece and the Nordic Resistance Movement in Sweden are examples of groups employing this strategy.

Individual motivations are the drivers behind individual participation in vigilante activities and groups. Although some participants may also be driven by motives

Comparative perspectives **323**

that are congruent with the official mission of the group, several of cases studies shows that many if not most individual members are motivated by quite different reasons than the official ones. One example of individual motivations at odds with the official justification of the group are the Soldiers of Odin in Norway. The official justification for their street patrols was to help making the streets safer by organizing "walks" in parts of the town where violence, rape and drug dealing was likely to take place, and to "drive away" unwanted persons. They should observe, document and report to the police, and only intervene if lives were in danger or serious harm could be prevented. However, it was striking that a large portion of the active members and many of the local leaders had criminal records, typically including violence and public order offences. Most of them were young men in their 20s and 30s, probably at the end of a youth criminal career. To many of these, the Soldiers of Odin offered an opportunity to make up for their criminal past, and be seen as doing something good for society, thereby improving their tarnished reputation in the community (Bjørgo and Gjelsvik, in this volume). Such motivations may have to do with a desire to improve one's personal identity and status, in particular by individuals who have a tarnished reputation as trouble-makers or criminals. Similar patterns, with a large part of the participants in Soldiers of Odin and other vigilante street patrols having criminal records, have been found in Sweden and Finland as well (Gardell, Kotonen, both in this volume). Others may be attracted by the militarism or belonging to a strong group. One striking example is the Minutemen militia, which officially is guarding the US–Mexican border against intrusion of illegal migrants. In reality, they are not permitted to stop anyone crossing the border illegally, even if the vigilante border patrols would be more than capable of doing so, heavily armed as they are. They nevertheless continue their guarding activity night after night. Harel Shapira's close-up study of the participants, mostly military veteran men in their 60s, shows that what made this activity make sense to them was that they could relive their military experience and revive their military identity.

> What the Minutemen camp offers them is a chance to put those uniforms back on. [... What they] are searching for in the desert is not, ultimately, an illegal immigrant but a lost feeling of respect and self-worth.
>
> *(Shapira 2013: 20)*

Organizing their camps at the border and their shifts like they used to when they were soldiers made the rather futile effort of guarding the border nevertheless deeply meaningful (Shapira, in this volume). Some of the paramilitary militias in Central and Eastern Europe also attract military veterans, and similar motives for their engagement are relevant to many of these as well. These groups can also satisfy engaged activists due to a feeling of their "importance" and the vigilantism can also play the role of a free-time activity. This is typical of some of the Slovak Conscripts, for example (Mareš and Milo, in this volume).

324 Tore Bjørgo and Miroslav Mareš

Vigilantism and the state

One of the defining characteristics of a state is that it successfully upholds a claim on "the monopoly of the legitimate use of physical force" within a given territory (Weber 1968 / 1922), often described as "the state monopoly on violence". Historically, the development of the modern state and implementation of the rule of law had as one of its main purposes to put an end to private justice, which often took the form of blood feuds, revenge, duels and "might is right". The state took away the enforcing power of feudal lords, clans, and local "strong men" or thugs, claiming the state alone had the sole responsibility of keeping peace and justice, and protect weak and vulnerable groups in its territory. Vigilantism represents a challenge to this principle (see quote from the DanerVærn manifest in Chapter 1, p. 8).

However, the extent to which vigilante groups are openly challenging state institutions' monopoly of force varies from place to place, and different actors have different perspectives on it. Most of the vigilante groups described in this volume assert that they only want to assist the police and border authorities, recognizing the limited capacities of these agencies. The do not want to challenge or confront the police, although they might criticize it for not being able – or willing – to do what needs to be done.

Governmental authorities have rather different views on vigilante groups and activities. Some countries have very strict laws to maintain the state's monopoly on the use of physical force in general, by banning all forms of private justice and also by making it "illegal for any other than the police to organize or participate in private operations with the purpose of maintaining public order or in any other forms of law enforcement in public areas" (cited from the Norwegian Police Law § 26). Most other countries in Western Europe have similar regulations to ban vigilantism. However, most countries do also have provisions to enable private security companies and other private groups (e.g. neighbourhood watch or citizens patrols) to do some very limited form of policing – but only when granted by the police (or other governmental agencies) and under police control. Examples of the latter are "Dads on Town" in Sweden (Gardell, in this volume) and the "Night Ravens" in Norway (Bjørgo and Gjelsvik, in this volume), citizen patrol groups which are in close partnership with the police. Some European countries, like Italy, have explicitly legalized civil patrols with the goal of supporting of law enforcement and police services in patrolling the territory. However, the Forza Nuova took advantage of this opportunity but did not coordinate its "security walks" with the relevant law enforcement agencies (Castelli Gattinara, this volume).

As discussed previously, there are significant historical, cultural and legal differences between most European countries and the US, with its long-standing traditions of vigilantism, armed militias, and rather permissive legislation for private citizens' rights to carry guns for self-protection and to intervene with armed force (Bellesiles 2000). In some US states, vigilante militia groups like the Minutemen (Shapira, in this volume) are permitted to carry handguns or semiautomatic rifles on patrol, even in public areas. Vigilante militia groups in European countries may

Comparative perspectives **325**

have military-style uniforms but they would be strictly forbidden to carry guns on patrol or parades, although some have access to private weapons and use them in clandestine training. This is the case of some Czech or Bulgarian vigilantes (see chapters in this volume). A specific case are Jewish vigilantes in on the occupied West Bank, where some varieties are affiliated with the military authorities but operate semi-independently. They are usually armed (due to the local right to carry guns) and wear some parts of the official military uniforms (see Gazit in this chapter).

The degree to which the police and other governmental authorities tolerate – or tacitly or openly collaborate with – vigilante groups and activities varies considerably between and within the countries covered in our case studies, but also over time. As discussed above, the change in police response to vigilante killings of migrants and other minorities from passivity to crack-down after 2010 led to a sharp decline in such murderous violence in Russia. During the long development of the Ku Klux Klan in the US, the law enforcement in the South many times tolerated the excesses of the Klansmen (Blee and Latif in this volume). In Greece, the Golden Dawn party, which has organized vigilante activities, enjoys strong electoral support among police officers. Police officers have also been directly or indirectly linked with criminal activities attributed to Golden Dawn members (Vrakopoulos and Halikiopoulou, in this volume).

Use of violence, threats of violence and the display of violent capacity

One common feature in definitions of vigilantism is the use of – or threat of – violence, as in Edoardo Moncada's (2017) definition of the root concept of vigilantism as "the collective use or threat of extra-legal violence in response to an alleged criminal act" (Moncada 2017). This and similar definitions do not state that actual use of violence is necessary to qualify as vigilantism – a threat that violence might be used against (potential) offenders may be sufficient. This points to the idea that such threats of violence might be intended to serve as deterrence against crime.

In our sample of case studies the actual use of violence is relatively rare. Ku Klux Klan lynchings are notorious examples, but cases from Russia, the West Bank, India and several European countries also illustrate that acts of (even lethal) violence is an integral part of some varieties of vigilantism against migrants and minorities. Many of these cases may also be seen as instances of vigilante terrorism (see above).

However, more or less subtle threats of violence are more common than actual violence. Actually, the most frequent pattern in our material is that vigilante groups do not make any explicit threats at all that they will use violence to punish offenders; they rather display a capacity for violence through a show of force. This may take the form of paramilitary militias who display their force through numbers, discipline, uniforms and sometimes even by showing off their weapons. A prime example is the heavily armed Minutemen guarding the US–Mexican border. They are not permitted to intervene in any way against migrants crossing the border illegally – beyond shining at them with torchlights and notifying the governmental border patrols (Shapira, this volume). At the other end of the continuum are street patrols that claim that they will not intervene against criminals or troublemakers but only notify the police (unless life is in danger). Their mere presence in the streets is supposed to be preventive and deterrent by itself. Sometimes this is reinforced by wearing highly visual uniforms or clothes, such as the hoodies of the Soldiers of Odin. Some of the participants in these street patrols are also locally known as (former) criminals and violent offenders, bringing with them a reputation for having a capacity for violence.

Private street patrol groups that are totally devoid of any display of force or capacity for violence clearly fall outside the realm of vigilantism. Typical examples are groups like "Dads on Town" in Sweden and the "Night Ravens" in Norway, often consisting of concerned parents, elderly and women, and operating under the guidance and control of the local police. It is exactly because these non-intimidating groups of concerned citizens do not in any way challenge the police's monopoly of violence and force that they are considered legitimate partners of the police. In contrast, vigilante patrols display an image of strength, intimidation and a potential for violence that is unacceptable to the police.

Vigilantism as performance

This brings us to one of the most striking findings in many of our case studies: vigilante groups patrolling streets and borders do very rarely, if ever, achieve their declared objectives, such as stopping acts of crime, sexual harassment of women, or illegal crossings of borders. Some vigilante groups patrol borders where hardly any migrants are crossing, as in the case of the Czech group patrolling at the mountainous border to Germany (Mareš and Milo, in this volume). The Minutemen patrolling the US–Mexican border very rarely encounter any illegal migrants, and if they do, they have to let them pass by without intervention (Shapira, this volume). The Soldiers of Odin and other street patrolling groups have been hard pressed to come up with any plausible examples of incidents where they have stopped or prevented a rape or another act of crime. The claim from these groups that they are helping an under-staffed police force by being their eyes and ears in places where the police does not have the capacity to patrol is not credible. Such vigilante patrols rather tend to tie up police capacity as the police has to keep an eye on the vigilantes in order to prevent potential clashes with opponents or other detrimental events. Moreover, the vigilante patrols tend to operate in ways which reduce their preventive potential but increase their image of strength, such as walking together in a large group rather than spreading out in smaller teams of two. They oftentimes patrol in places where there are no migrants or any women at risk of being raped. Documenting their activity by taking a cool picture of their group is more important than the preventive impact of their patrolling.

So why do these vigilante groups carry out their patrols when they do not seem to care very much whether they actually achieve their stated objectives or not? The best answer is that such vigilante patrols are mainly performances. These performances have different purposes than the official justifications, which are to reduce a crime problem or a migration problem. These are communicative events but the communicative purpose may go in at least two main directions: political propaganda and identity management.

Vigilante activities organized from the top down by political organizations or parties are mainly propaganda events advertising the organization's ability and determination to *do* something tangible about a problem facing the community. When organizing vigilante patrols, the organization will often use this as a recruitment strategy by inviting concerned citizens to join them. A prime example is the Italian neo-Fascist Forza Nuova which use the "security walks" to build its public image and root it in local settings by offering a "concrete" help to citizens. They publicize their initiatives in order to get support from the local community and visibility in the media (Castelli Gattinara, in this volume). Similar strategies are used by other far-right parties, such as the Bulgarian National Union – New Democracy which used vigilante street patrols to increase the visibility of the organization (Stoynova and Dzkekova, in this volume), and the far-right Jobbik party, which established the Hungarian Guard militia in 2007 for similar reasons. At the same time, these right-wing extremist parties and organizations use their vigilante activities to make political statements, such as claiming that the state is failing to fulfil its task of protecting its citizens, and that their organization is ready to step in to fulfil that role. This communication strategy is exemplified by the neo-Nazi Nordic Resistance Movement in Sweden and Finland as well as the Forza Nuova in Italy (Gardell, Catelli Gattinara, both in this volume).

Vigilante activities organized from the bottom up tend to have other drivers. Although some initiators may be motivated by anti-immigration or anti-minority sentiments or a genuine desire to reduce a crime problem, the rank-and-file often seem to have less political motivations for their participation. A common theme is identity management (Goffman 1956) – although it may vary considerably what kind of identity the participants want to display through their participation.

Being a vigilante provides an opportunity to assert masculinity – displaying male strength, machismo and heroism. They are real men, capable of protecting "their" nation and women (Gardell, in this volume). Vigilante street patrols and militias, in particular, typically involve a lot of posing, especially when there is an opportunity to be photographed. However, displaying masculinity may take different directions. For some, a form of assertive masculinity may turn into aggressiveness and violence – especially against categories of people defined as a threat to the community. Another dimension of masculinity may lead participants towards a more protective expression of manliness – taking care of vulnerable women in particular (see Figure 16.2, p. 000).

In his study of the Minutemen militia protecting the US–Mexican border against illegal migrants, Shapira (this volume) points out that the militia members were almost exclusively military veterans with an average age of 65. To these men, the patrols and the camp life along the border provided an opportunity to revive

328 Tore Bjørgo and Miroslav Mareŝ

their identity as military men and perform their patriotism in a semi-military fashion. They displayed a "militarized masculinity", as Shapira puts it.

Identity management takes a different course when it comes to the Soldiers of Odin in Norway. Many of the most active members had a tarnished reputation, being known in their local communities as criminals and troublemakers. To many of them, patrolling the streets with the Soldiers of Odin with the expressed objective of making the streets safer provided them with an opportunity to be recognized as doing something good and noble to the community, making up for some of the bad things they were known for in the past. Unfortunately for them, they failed in their effort to gain recognition and improve their standing in society, mainly because their hyper-masculine style was seen as intimidating rather than providing safety in the streets, and that the Soldiers of Odin were considered as vigilantes with a tint of right-wing extremism.

Vigilantism and political organizations

One of our research questions concerns whether vigilante activities are organized top down by existing political parties or other organizations, or bottom up by emerging more or less spontaneously without any sponsorship from organized groups.

Numerous cases in this volume demonstrate that political parties and organizations on the far right have initiated and organized vigilante activities. Examples are how Jobbik established the Hungarian Guard as a paramilitary wing of the party (Póczik and Sárik, this volume), the "security walks" organized by the Italian neo-Fascist party Forza Nuevo (Catelli Gattinara in this volume), the neo-Nazi Nordic Resistance Movement's patrols (Gardell in this volume), the train patrols organized by the Slovak the People's Party Our Slovakia (Mares and Milo, this volume), Golden Dawn's various militant and vigilante activities (Vrakopoulos & Halikiopoulou, this volume). In these cases, vigilante activities were apparently considered as a way to get public attention and support for their organization. It could also be a convenient way to dramatize the impotence and incompetence of the authorities and the police to provide safety to the citizens and to protect the borders. Thus, these movements found opportunities in the political situations which they exploited by establishing vigilante activities. In some cases it might also be a way to strengthen the ties between the party and the members by providing them with an opportunity to do something concrete.

When vigilante activities are organized from below, it tended to emerge from discussion fora on Facebook or other social media in the aftermath of criminal events where migrants or minorities were (allegedly) involved as perpetrators. The idea to start vigilante patrols were often inspired by extensive reports in the news media on such criminal events and vigilante responses elsewhere. The most striking case was the boom in vigilante activities in the aftermath of the New Year event in Cologne 2015/2016, and in particular the remarkably rapid spread of the Soldiers of Odin chapters in around 20 countries within a few months. For these bottom-up initiatives, the motivation of those engaged might be more diverse, ranging

Comparative perspectives **329**

from a political agenda to personal agendas to improve their social standing in society. It is remarkable that many of those individuals offering their services to "help" the police to maintain safety and order in the streets are former criminals (Bjørgo & Gjelsvik, this volume). Other participants are free-floating political activists jumping on any new anti-immigrant or anti-Islam movement coming up. It is also quite common that participants in vigilante groups are members of political parties and party-affiliated organizations although it cannot be substantiated that the party is organizing the vigilante activities (see Ahuja in this volume on Indian cow vigilantes and their links to the BJP).

Transnational dimensions and diffusion

The transnational dimension of vigilantism has not been deeply researched up to now. However, there are some relevant similarities with a transnational spread of similar phenomena – such as lynching (Berg, Wendt 2011) or terrorism (Karmon 2005, Waldmann 1998: 18–19).

We can identify several forms of transnational issues related to vigilantism. As the "weakest" form of its transnational dimension we can understand the diffusion of vigilantism as a specific phenomenon – in the sense of inspiration of groupings in similar situations. Usually it is connected with the specific character of vigilante formations. This volume provides a good example of this in the descriptions of the Hungarian Guard and its impact on similar anti-Romani patrols in East Central Europe (see chapters by Póczik and Sárik; Mareš and Milo; Stoynova and Dzhekova). Other far-right parties were inspired by the Hungarian Jobbik Party to establish their own vigilante wings, either in the form of militias or patrols.

Deeper ties are established in the form of cooperation between two or more vigilante groups from different countries. This cooperation can be carried our ad hoc (as the meeting between the National Guard from the Czech Republic and the Hungarian Guard in 2007) or it can be more stable (as the Czech-Bulgarian cooperation). It can range from moral and propagandist support, across logistic support (collections of winter´s wear by the Czech National Homeguard for the Bulgarian partners) to common "field" activities. Foreigners can also serve in vigilante formations abroad, however, this equivalent of "foreign fighters" is not frequently observed. More significant is the participation in paramilitary training camps abroad. The experience gained from such camps can be useful for vigilante purposes. An example is the Swedish neo-Nazis who bombed two refugee camps and a left-wing book shop in 2017 after having been trained by the Russian Imperial Movement (Huetlin, 2017).

The strongest transnational dimension comes into play when a single vigilante organization establish subsidiaries in several countries. However, in reality these national branches usually become relatively autonomous after a while. They were typically established according to the model of transnational inspiration (see above) with some direct contact (or after a short e-mail or social media conversation), sharing the name of the mother organization but will usually soon detach from any organizational

330 Tore Bjørgo and Miroslav Mareš

subordination. On the other hand, hierarchically organized transnational (respectively supranational) formations are also possible organizational structures for vigilante groups.

Historically, various branches of the Ku Klux Klan were temporarily established in European countries (from the 1920s to the present). Varieties of contacts to their American "originals" can be found – from "zero" contacts to globally and hierarchically led KKK-structures (Mareš 2001). The spectrum of activities is also very broad – from secret meetings across patrols outside Romani communities in the Czech Republic in early 1990s to suspicions of terrorism, as in the recent case of the KKK networks around the nucleus of the German National Socialist Underground (Koehler 2016: 148).

The most striking variety of a transnational vigilante movement is the Soldiers of Odin, which spread rapidly from Finland to up to 22 countries within a few months in 2016, before it declined to eight national chapters by April 2018 (Kotonen, this volume). The Finnish mother organization tried to maintain a level of control over the national chapters by demanding that they follow the bylaws of the Finnish SOO, as well as having the right to act as moderators of national Facebook groups. The Finnish SOO attempted to organize its relations with the international branches as a franchise, demanding a fee from the new national chapters for the license to use hoodies with national adaptions of the SOO symbols, which was the main asset of the mother organization. There is little doubt that the symbols and dress style, which made for good visuals and extensive international media coverage, was a main reason for the immediate transnational spread of the SOO. However, the success did not last long. Most of the national chapters either failed to establish a lasting street presence, or they started to dissociate themselves from the Finnish SOO. The main reasons for cutting their ties to the mother organization varied, from dislike of the dictatorial tendencies of the Finnish leadership, resisting to pay fees, and dissatisfaction with the racist and right-wing extremist image of the Finnish mother organization (Kotonen; Archambault and Veilleux-Lepage; Bjørgo and Gjelsvik, all in this volume). Another inherent contradiction for such a transnational organization is that the various national SOO branches tended to have a nationalist orientation, which was at odds with submitting to a leadership in another country.

Another transnational project was connected with the activities of the Identitarian movement. The Identitarians are less nationalist in the narrow sense, as they promote a European identity. The common action of members from several countries, called "Defend Europe", culminated in the use of a ship called C-Star to patrol the Mediterranean, with the goal to hinder migrants to reach Europe and influence policy through media attention (see chapter on France by Pietro Castelli Gattinara in this book).

The transnational dimension of vigilantism is also manifested in state patronage over some foreign groups, usually with the goal to destabilize another state. Speculations in this sense are related mostly to paramilitary formations in East Central Europe and the Russian influence (see chapters on Bulgaria, Slovenia and the

Comparative perspectives **331**

Czech Republic in this volume). However, it is difficult to find clear evidence. According to Hungarian authorities, the leading member of the Hungarian National Front was an agent of the Russian GRU (military intelligence service) (Juhász, Győri, Zgut, and Dezső 2017: 23).

Contributions of our findings to broader research on vigilantism

The authors and editors of this volume were able to collect, to analyse and to compare an important amount and variety of empirical materials related to vigilantism against migrants and minorities from various parts of the world. Facts and findings in our book can improve not only the knowledge and understanding of the development of this recent form of vigilantism itself, but also interconnected phenomena as right-wing extremism, paramilitarism, terrorism etc. As our main contributions to the academic discussion on vigilantism can be mentioned:

1. *Adaptation of vigilantism:* Vigilante activists in various parts of the world are able to adapt vigilante strategies and tactics to contemporary opportunities and challenges. The reaction to the migration crisis in Europe and Canada after 2015 is the most significant example (a similar process with the Minutemen occurred in the US in previous years). In several countries, the anti-immigration agenda substituted – at least temporarily – previous main targets of vigilantism (in particular the Roma communities in East Central Europe).
2. *Non-violent vigilantism:* Whereas traditional definitions of vigilantism focused on the violent, criminal or at least extra-legal character of vigilantism, many recent vigilante activists declare that they will not use violence and want to act within the legal framework, and some of them even want to cooperate with governments. Instead of using or threatening with violence they merely demonstrate an intimidating capacity for violence. However, the subversive challenge towards recent political regimes remains an important part of their strategy, as they usually want to present themselves as an alternative to the established political and security forces.
3. *Performative aspect of contemporary vigilantism:* The declared goals of vigilante activities (countering "ethnic crime", "illegal migration" etc.) are in many cases only propagandist reasons for the performance of vigilante groups. This performance can serve for political marketing of political parties (in connection to the power of new social media) or for establishing a specific cultural environment, which is important for the self-confidence of the activists involved. A quotation from Shapira's study (in this volume) can be highlighted:

> Yes, stopping 'illegal immigration' matters to the Minutemen, but it matters first and foremost because through it these men have created a culture, a camp, a set of heroes, a set of enemies, an entire social world, through which their past is extended, resurrected, and in the case of some, even invented.

332 Tore Bjørgo and Miroslav Mareŝ

4. *Vigilante violence and terrorism still matter:* Despite the above mentioned "moderation" of many vigilante groups, violent vigilantism, including vigilante terrorism, is still an important threat, as the cases of Roma murders in Hungary, the numerous killings of labour migrants and homosexuals in Russia, the FTL/360 group in Germany, the "cow vigilantes" in India or the Cryptheia in Greece show. More commonly, violent vigilantism take the form of low-scale violence, harassment and threats and might be more aptly described as hate crimes rather than right-wing terrorism.

5. *Transnationalization of vigilantism:* Although transnational spread of vigilantism is not new (Ku Klux Klan outside the US), in the past this was a rather slow process. The contemporary situation shows a new quality of this phenomenon, with a very rapid proliferation of vigilante modes of operation and even brands, as exemplified by the "expansion" of the Soldiers of Odin from Finland to other parts of the world within weeks. There are also multinational vigilante operations, like the crowd funding and crew of the ship organized within the Identitarian campaign Defend Europe. Obviously, the internet and new social media play a key role in facilitating such transnational cooperation.

6. *Varieties of reactions to vigilantism:* A broad scope of vigilante activities in various countries have caused very different responses. A comparison shows tolerance to vigilantism (including its violent forms) on the one hand and hard repressive measures against vigilantism on the other hand. Some vigilante activities, like hunting migrants or establishing uniformed militias, have been tolerated in some countries but would be totally unacceptable and banned in other countries.

Notes

1 See Verfassungsschutzbericht 2016: https://www.verfassungsschutz.de/de/download-ma nager/_vsbericht-2016.pdf, and https://www.svt.se/nyheter/lokalt/vast/over-90-anlagda -brander-pa-asylboenden-forra-aret.
2 The most well-known case was from Bulgaria (Cheresheva 2016).
3 https://www.theguardian.com/world/2012/jan/27/hungary-roma-living-in-fear.
4 Similar processes have been addressed with regards to terrorist movements (Jones and Libicki 2008; Bjørgo and Horgan 2009; Cronin 2009) and criminal gangs (Decker and Pyrooz 2015), and some of these processes are similar across type of group.
5 According to the amendment in the Hungarian Criminal Code on "Prohibited Policing Activity", to *establish an organization* without legal authorization in order to enforce public order and safety or to organize an activity with the appearance of such, and/or to fail to fulfil the obligation to cooperate with the authorized organizations, is a misdemeanour punishable by imprisonment not exceeding two years.

References

Berg, Manfred (2011) *Popular justice: A history of lynchings in America.* Lanham: Ivan A. Dee.
Berg, Manfred and Simon Wendt (2011). Introduction: Lynching from an international perspective. In: Manfred Berg and Simon Wendt (eds.), *Globalizing lynching history: vigilantism and extralegal punishment from an international perspective* (pp. 1–18). New York: Palgrave MacMillan.

Comparative perspectives **333**

Bellesiles, Michael A. (2000). *Arming America: The origins of a national gun culture.* New York, NY: Alfred A. Knopf.

Bird, Steve (2017, December 9). Grooming gangs of Muslim men failed to integrate into British society. *The Telegraph,* Retrieved from https://www.telegraph.co.uk/news/2017/12/09/grooming-gangs-muslim-men-failed-integrate-british-society/.

Bjørgo, Tore and John Horgan (2009). *Leaving terrorism behind: Individual and collective disengagement.* Abingdon: Routledge.

Cheresheva, Maria (2016, April 8). Bulgaria awards vigilante migrant-hunters. *BalkanInsights,* Retrieved from http://www.balkaninsight.com/en/article/bulgaria-awards-vigilante-migrant-hunters-04-08-2016.

Cronin, Audrey Kurth (2009). How terrorist campaigns end. In: Tore Bjørgo and John Horgan (2009). *Leaving terrorism behind: Individual and collective disengagement.* Abingdon: Routledge.

Decker, Scott H., and David C. Pyrooz (2015). 'I'm down for a Jihad': How 100 years of gang research can inform the study of terrorism, radicalization and extremism. *Perspectives on Terrorism,* 9(1): 104–112.

Dees, Morris with James Corcoran (1997). *Gathering storm: America's militia threat.* New York: Harper Perennial.

Ecopolis Foundation (2012). *Gyöngyöspata 2011 – The laboratory of the Hungarian far-right: A case study of political mobilization and interethnic conflict.* Budapest: Ecopolis Foundation. Retrieved from http://pdc.ceu.hu/archive/00006555/01/Ecopolis_Gyongyospata2012.pdf.

Enstad, Johannes Due (2018). The modus operandi of right-wing militants in Putin's Russia, 2000–2017. *Perspectives on Terrorism,* 12(6), 89–103.

European Commission (2017). Designing Europe's future: Trust in institutions, globalisation, support for the euro, opinions about free trade and solidarity. *Special Eurobarometer* 461 (April 2017). Retrieved from http://ec.europa.eu/commfrontoffice/publicopinion/index.cfm/ResultDoc/download/DocumentKy/78720.

Frick, Chang (2016, August 2). Polisen gav felaktig statistik om sexbrott på festivaler – Backar efter kritik. *Nyheter idag.* Retrieved from https://nyheteridag.se/polisen-gav-felaktig-statistik-om-sexbrott-pa-festivaler-backar-efter-kritik/.

Gazit, Nir (2015). State-sponsored vigilantism: Jewish settlers' violence in the occupied Palestinian territories. *Sociology,* 49(3), 438–454.

Gardell, Mattias (2015). *Raskrigaren: Seriemördaren Peter Mangs.* Stockholm: Leopard förlag.

Goffman, Erving (1956) *The presentation of self in everyday life.* New York: Random House.

Havlík, Vratislav and Miroslav Mareš (2014). Rechtsextremistische paramilitärische Einheiten in Ungarn. *Kriminalistik,* 68(11), 639–645.

Huetlin, Josephine (2017). Russian extremists are training right-wing terrorists from Western Europe, *The Daily Beast,* Retrieved from https://www.thedailybeast.com/russian-extremists-are-training-right-wing-terrorists-from- western-europe.

Jay, Alexis (2014). *Independent inquiry into child sexual exploitation in Rotherham (1997–2013).* Rotherham: Rotherham Metropolitan Borough Council. Retrieved from https://www.rotherham.gov.uk/downloads/file/1407/independent_inquiry_cse_in_rotherham.

Jones, Seth G. & Martin C.Libicki (2008). How terrorist groups end. Lessons for countering al Qa'ida. Washington DC: Rand Corporation. Retrieved from http://www.rand.org/pubs/research_briefs/RB9351/.

Juhász, Attila; Lóránt Győri, Edit Zgut, András Dezső (2017). *"The truth today is what Putin says it is" – the activity of pro-Russian extremist groups in Hungary.* Budapest: Political Capital, Retrieved from http://www.politicalcapital.hu/pc-admin/source/documents/PC_NED_country_study_HU_20170428.pdf.

334 Tore Bjørgo and Miroslav Mareš

Karmon, Ely (2005). *Coalitions between terrorist organizations: Revolutionaries, nationalists and Islamists*. Leiden, Netherlands, and Boston, MA: Martinus Nijhoff Publishers.

Koehler, Daniel (2016). *Right-wing terrorism in the 21st century. The 'National Socialist Underground' and the history of terror from the far-right in Germany*. Abingdon: Routledge.

Liederkerke, Arthur de (2016). The paramilitary phenomenon in Central and Eastern Europe. *The Polish Quarterly of International Affairs*, 25(2), 25–34.

Mareš, Miroslav (2001). Ku Klux Klan a pravicový extremismus v České republice. *Středoevropské politické studie*. 3(3), 1–9.

Mareš, Miroslav (2012). Strategies for creating insurgencies and civil wars in Europe: From violent extremism to paramilitary conflicts? *Jindal Journal of International Affairs*, 2(1), 90–119.

Moncada, E. (2017). Varieties of vigilantism: Conceptual discord, meaning and strategies. *Global Crime*, 18(4) , 403–423.

Mudde, Cas (2000). *The ideology of the extreme right*. Manchester: Manchester University Press.

Mulloy, D.J. (2005). *American extremism: History, politics and the militia movement*. London and New York: Routledge.

Perry, Barbera (2001). *In the name of hate: Understanding hate crimes*. New York/London: Routledge.

Pew Research Center (2017). Public trust in government: 1958–2017. Retrieved from http://www.people-press.org/2017/12/14/public-trust-in-government-1958-2017/.

Ravndal, Jacob Aasland (2017). *Right-wing terrorism and violence in Western Europe: A comparative analysis*. Department of Political Science, University of Oslo: PhD thesis.

Schmid, Alex (2011). *The Routledge handbook of terrorism research*. London: Routledge.

Shapira, Harel (2013). *Waiting for José: The Minutemen's pursuit of America*. Princeton and Oxtord: Princeton University Press.

Sprinzak, Ehud (1995). Right-wing terrorism in a comparative perspective: The case of split delegitimization. *Terrorism and Political Violence*, 7(1), 17–43.

Weber, Max (1968 / 1922). *Economy and society; an outline of interpretive sociology*. New York: Bedminster Press, 1968 (original title: *Wirtschaft und Gesellschaft: Grundriss der verstehenden Soziologie*, 1921).

Waldmann, Peter (1998). *Terrorismus. Provokation der Macht*. München: Gerling Akademie Verlag.

Woodworth, Paddy (2003). *Dirty war, clean hands: ETA, the GAL and Spanish democracy* (2nd edition). New Haven: Yale University Press.

INDEX

Page numbers in **bold** refer to figures.

64VM 111

Aanonsen, Jan Tellef 262, 269n2
abandonment, feeling of 225
Action Group Kysuce Resistance 133–134, 140–141
activists, political background 12
ad-hoc vigilantism 164, 166–167, 176
aggression, symbolic 122
Ahuja, J. 6, 20, 308, 310, 322, 329
Alabama 38
Albers, Wolfgang 92
alcohol consumption 24, 232, 233, 296
Alliance for Peace and Freedom 192
Alliance of European National Movements 109
alternative facts 286
Alternative for Germany 87, 90–91
alternative security system 145
Alte, Ronny 259
alt-right 16
American Civil War 32–33, 34
Amnesty International 185
Angott, Joel 281n1
anomic behaviour 6–7
Anonymous (hacker) 14
anti-gypsyism 132, 144, 146
anti-immigrant raids and violence, Russian Federation 73–74, 77, 81, 309

anti-immigration militias: Bulgaria 22; Germany 21, 86–100; United States of America 22
anti-immigration mobilization 87, 331; *see also* individual groups
anti-Islamism 241–242
anti-LGBT violence, Russian Federation 74–76, 309
anti-migrant vigilantism, Czech Republic 130–132
anti-Roma vigilantism 22, 165; *see also* Roma
anti-Semitism 40, 105, 118, 294
anti-social behaviors 115
anti-vigilante legislation 114–117, 124n20, 124n21, 124n22, 320–321; Hungary 114–117, 124n20, 124n21, 124n22, 320
Anundsen, Anders 265
Archambault, E. 25, 250, 318, 321, 330
Archer, D. 12–13
armed militias 280, 319, 324
Arnsdorf 86
Arrow Cross Party 105, 107
Arya Samaj 63
Association of Identitarian Students 119
asylum seekers 86, 120
Ataka party 168, 177n5
Austria 103
Austro-Hungarian monarchy 103
authoritarian conservatism 16

336 Index

Auxiliary Police Association for a Better Future 114
Avramov, K. 166, 171

Baburova, Anastasia 71
Bach, Jörgen 295–296
Balázs, László **119**
Balder Cruisers 294
Balkan migration route 22
Barbarousis, Konstantinos 190
Bazylev, Maxim 72
Beaudry, Patrick 279
Bedfordshire Police 233–234
behaviour, policing of 56
Belov, Alexandr 76
Belovics, E. 117
Berg, M. 8
Bhansali, Sanjay Leela 64
Bharatiya Janata Party 55–66, 56, 56–57, 59, 65, 308
Birmingham Alabama 39
Bjørgo, T. 17, 25, 318, 320, 321, 323, 324, 329, 330
black psywar 37
Blee, K. 16, 17, 19, 37, 307, 316, 318
Bloc Identitaire 221–224
Blood & Honour/Combat 18 Bohemia/Sudetenland 132
Blood and Honor Cultural Association (Hungary) 107–108
border patrols 170, 173, 175, 313–314; as performance 326–328; see also Minutemen paramilitary border patrol
border protection 151–163, **159, 161,** 299
Borissov, Boyko 175
bottom-up initiatives 328–329
Brandqvist, Johan 294
Bright Rus (Svetlaia Rus) 74
Britain First 24, 228–236; alliances 235; Christian Patrols 24, 228, 232, 234, 235; data sources 228; demographics 230; electoral support 229; emphasis on Christianity 232, **236;** Far-Right movement heritage 230–232, 235; ideology 229; mission statement 229; mosque invasions 228, 229, 232–233, 235; online presence 235, 236; Operation Fight Back 233, 236; origins 228–229; prohibition on alcohol 232; sanctions 233–234; support 229–230; targets 229; vigilante activities 232–233, 235–236; violence 233
British heritage and culture 229
British National Party 109, 192, 228, 231
British Union of Fascists 230, 234

Brown, R. 5
B'Tselem 43
Buchtela, David 136, 137
Bulgaria 22, 164–177, 318, 319; activities 169–170; ad-hoc vigilantism 164, 166–167, 176; anti-government protests 177n6; anti-immigration militias 22; anti-Roma vigilantism 165, 166–167, 168–169, 176; border patrols 170, 173, 175, 314; under communism 177n2; context 165–166; criminal underground 172–173; elections, 2017 168; Far-Right movement 167–169, 176; funding 173–174; goals 171, 172–173; group alliances 174; ideology 171, 172; institutional reactions 175; membership 173; migrant crisis 164–165, 166, 167, 169, 172, 176, 313; Ministry of Defence 173; narratives 171–172; nationalism 165; organizational structures 173; organized vigilantism 164, 167–175; popular support 175–176; recruitment 176–177; Roma minority 165, 166; State Agency for National Security 175; systematic crisis feeling 166; unemployment 166
Bulgarian Helsinki Committee 166–167, 173–174
Bulgarian National Guard 123
Bulgarian National Union 167, 168–169, 327
Bürgerwehren 88
Byman, D. 49

Calais Jungle 217, 217–220
Canada: Bill 60 279–280; Canadian Firearms Registry 282n14; extreme right 278–281; militias 280; nationalism 275, 279; Soldiers of Odin 25, 272–281
Canadian Firearms Registry 282n14
Canadian Sentinels 275–276
capitalist development 103
Carey, S. C. 9
Casa-Pound Italia 200
case studies 6–7, 19–26
Castelli Gattinara, Pietro 14, 16, 17, 23, 244, 314, 316, 317, 318, 321, 322, 324, 327, 328, 330
Castle, T. 298–299
Caughey, J.W. 44
censorship 64
Ceské Budejovice 135
character contests 157
charity activities 193, 250–251, 273–274, 282n5, 282n15, 292
Chechen conflict 78
Chemnitz 100

Cherkizovsky Market bombing 71
Chicago **37**
Christian patrols, Britain First 24, 228, 232, 234, 234, 235
Christian values 109
Citizen Militia, Sweden 289–291
Civic Auxiliary Police 114
Civil Rights movement (US) 38, 39
Civil Squads for the Protection of Women and the Faith 169, 170, 172–173, 173
Cold War 130
collective violence 41
Colley, J. 234
Cologne, New Year's Eve 2015/16 mass sexual assault 21, 92–93, 258, 268, 291, 316, 319, 328
Combat 18 193, 194, 242, 247
Combat Organization of Russian Nationalists (Boevaya organizatsiya russkikh natsionalistov) 71–72
Combat Terrorist Organization (Boevaya terroristicheskaya organizatsiya) 70–71
communalism 65
communication 80
Communist Workers Party 40
community-building 273–274, 275
community, protected 6–7
complementarity 225
cooperative approach 7
cooperative security initiatives 90
corruption 171
counter-movement theory 5–6
cow vigilantism 20, 63, 64, 308–309, 332; case studies 60–61; context 56–58; framing 59–60; ideological beliefs 59; ideological motivations 61–64; justifications 61, 64; legality 59; lynchings 20, 322; tacit support 56; targeting of Muslims 55–56; violence 55–66, 60–61
Cox, Jo, murder of 233
Crimea, annexation of 79
crime control 11–12
crime rates, Russian Federation 78–79
Crime Survey for England 234
criminality 1, 23, 115, 121–122, 167, 208
criminalization 80
cross-burnings 41
Cryptheia 193, 194, 332
cultural embeddedness 201
cultural heritage loss 205
Cunningham, D. 39
cyber-vigilantism 14
Cyprus 192
Czechoslovak Patriotic Guard (Ceskoslovenská vlastenecká garda) 131

Czechoslovak reserve soldiers against the war planned by the NATO command 131, 134–135
Czechoslovak reserve soldiers for peace 131, 135
Czech Republic 22, 129–130, 129–132, 134–138, 143–146, 314, 318, 329, 330; anti-migrant vigilantism 130–132; anti-Nazi traditions 131; justifications 144–145; lynchings 130; migration crisis 131, 135; militias 22, 129–130, 144, 146, 299, 306; modus operandi 145–146; Muslim population 144; organization 145; paramilitarism 312; Roma minority 132, 138; Soldiers of Odin 131; transnational cooperation 143–144; vigilante groups 134–138, **136**

Dads on Town 287, 288, 324, 326
Daily Mail 232
Dalits 56, 66, 66n3
DanerVærn 8–9, 26n4
data collection 17–19
data, comparable 17–19
Dawn – National Coalition (Úsvit – Národní koalice) 131
death squads 17, 117–118, 306, 309, 322
decadency 10
decline, cause of 319–321
de-demonization 216
De Felice, Renzo 204
Defend Europe campaign 23, 223–224, 225, 314, 330, 332
Defense Force (Védero) 118
delegitimization strategy 92
Denmark 8–9, 26n4, 296
Denver 37
Der Dritte Weg 90
DEREX 121
Deutsches Polizei Hilfswerk (German Police Assistance Association) 95–97
deviancy, rise of 6
deviants 1
digital commentariat 287, 293
direct engagement 222–223
disinformation 65
display 325–326
dissuasion 206–207, 225
Dolchstosslegende 105
Donetsk People's Republic 137
Dowson, J 174, 228–229, 232
drivers 6
Duluth Lynchings **308**
Dzhekova, R. 22, 313, 314, 317, 318, 319, 320, 327, 329

338 Index

economic crisis, 2008 122, 183, 185
economic growth 106
Edwards Eldon 38
ELAM 192
Elitzur, Yosef 48
Ellinas, A.A. 189, 190
Ellingsen, Jan Arild 265
emergence factors 315–319
enemy image 122
engagement, direct 222–223
English Defence League 229, 230, 231–232
Estonia 247
ETA 306
ethnic crime 22
ethno-cultural threat 79
ethnonationalism 275, 279
European Culture 275
European Election Study 189
European Social Survey 257
European Union 145, 166, 185, 202, 203
Europe's Daughters 299
existential threat 87
extra-legal force 4
extralegal punishment 8
extreme right, the: Canada 278–281;
 definition 15–16; ideological sub-categories
 16; movements 321; politics 15;
 terminology 15; terrorism 17; vigilantism
 15–17; *see also* far right movement; radical
 right; right-wing extremism
extremism, definition 80

Facebook 89, 93, 94, 96, 217, 231, 235,
 236, 242, 245, 246–247, 259, 265, 273,
 287, 289–290, 295–296, 328
fake-news 245
Falkovskii, I. 71–72, 72, 73
Far-Right movement: Bulgaria 167–169,
 176; demands 104; German case studies
 93–97; German governmental statistics
 99; Germany 86–100; Greece 193–194,
 194; group types 90; Hungary 103–123;
 propaganda 89, 92, 93, 99; subcultural
 milieus 90; subcultural mobilization 91;
 terrorism 91–92; United Kingdom
 230–232; violence 91–92; *see also*
 extreme right, the
fascism 16, 187, 203
fascism-movement 204
Fascist Defence Force 230
Fascist tradition, Hungary 104–105
Festerling, Tatjana 174
Fiamma Tricolore 204
Field Patrol Service 120, 121

Finland 296, 297, 322, 327; anti-immigration
 protest movement 242; Finns party 248;
 migrant crisis 243, 249, 252n1;
 multiculturalism 241; presidential election,
 2018 248; *see also* Soldiers of Odin
Finnish Defence League 243, 245
Finnish Home Guards 250
Finnish Security Intelligence Service 245
Fiore, Roberto 192
First World War 17
flyers 222
Format-18 75
Fortress Europe 174
Forza Nuova 192, 204, 317, 322, 324;
 background 203–205; data sources 200;
 foundation 199; good-will activities 206;
 ideology 199, 203–205; membership
 208–209; political proposals 205; security
 walks 199–200, 205, 205–210, 327
Fountoulis, Lampros 190
France 23–24, 202, 213–225; Calais Jungle
 217, 217–220; centralization 215–216,
 225; crisis of integration 217;
 identitarianism 221–224; legal system
 213; lynchings 214; migrant crisis
 214–225; militias 226n2; opportunities
 for vigilantism 215–216; popular violence
 tradition 213; Roma community 214;
 structural constraints 213–214, 225,
 226n2; trust in political institutions 215
Fransen, Jayda 233, 234, **236**
Fratelli d'Italia 200
Freital 93–95
Frontier of the North 75
frontier theory 5
Front National 216, 221
FTL/360 93–95
funding 173–174
Fyssas, Pavlos 190, 192

GAL 306
Gandhi, M.K. 57
Gardell, M. 12, 25–26, 309, 312, 315, 316,
 319, 321, 322, 323, 324, 327, 328
Gardet 26, 295–296
Gaza Strip, Disengagement Plan 46
Gazit, N. 7, 20, 43–4, 306, 310, 312,
 318, 325
gender, and nationalism 160
Génération Identitaire 221, 223
Génération Solidaire 222
geographical scope 14
Georgia 33
Germany: anti-immigration militias 21,
 86–100; asylum seekers 86;

Bürgerwehren 88; case studies 93–97; Cologne, New Year's Eve 2015/16 mass sexual assault 21, 92–93, 258, 268, 291, 316, 319, 328; context 90–92, **91**; Deutsches Polizei Hilfswerk (German Police Assistance Association) 95–97; Far-Right movement 86–100; FTL/360 93–95; governmental statistics 99; group types 90; historical context 88–90; militias 21, 86–100, 310; paramilitarism 311; permissive factors 98–99; pogroms 309; repressive factors 97–98; right-wing extremist violence groups 90; Soldiers of Odin 97; subcultural Far-Right mobilization 91; subcultural milieus 90; terrorism 91–92; violence 91–92; Wehrsportgruppen 88–89, 89

Gerstenfeld, P. B. 11
Ginsburgh, Rabbi 48
Gjelsvik, M. 17, 25, 318, 320, 321, 323, 324, 329, 330
Global Financial Crisis, 2008 201
globalization 151
goals, identification of 4
Goffman, E. 152, 152–153, 157, 161
Golden Dawn 23, 183, 322, 325, 328; charity activities 193; creation 184; and economic crisis, 2008 185; electoral support 188–189, 192, 194; enemies 187; ideology 186–187; justifications 187; logo 191, **191**; membership 189; nationalism 187; online presence 192; operations and activities 189–191; organization 187, 188; parliamentary representation 186, 189–190; and the police 193; propaganda strategy 191–192; relationship to political groups and public agencies 192–193; socio-political context 183–186; support 185, 188–189; trial 194; vigilante activities 190–191; violence 184, 188; women members 189; xenophobia 186
Golding, Paul 228–229, 233, 234, **236**
good-will activities 206, 297
Gordon, L. 37
Gothenburg 294–295, 298
governmental institutions: lack of trust in 316–317; relations to 7; trust in 319–320
government, failure of 7
Grätz, T. 14
Greater Israel 50
Greece 23, 183–194, 322, 332; discrimination 185–186; economic crisis, 2008 183, 185; Far-Right movement 193–194, 194; immigration levels 186; metapolitefsi era 184; migrant crisis 186;

political violence 183–184, 184; satisfaction with democracy 185; socio-political context 183–186; trust in institutions 197–198; xenophobia 186; *see also* Golden Dawn
Griffin, Nick 109, 192
grooming gangs 24, 231, 233, 316
group alliances 174
group strategies 6, 322
Guardian Angels 259, 269n13, 287
Guestbusters 74, 309
Gypsy crime 7, 21, 22, 112, 118, 130, 134, 139, 146, 309, 311

Habait Ha'Yehudi 46
hackers 14
Halikiopoulou, D. 23, 189, 322, 325, 328
Hammitt, B. 9
Handbook for Activists in the Nordic Resistance Movement 2.0 297
hate crime 114, 117, 310; definition 10–11
Hathalin, Suleiman 43
Hebron 47
Heidenau 95
Helly, D. 280
Helsinki 245
high primacy vigilantism 12
Hilltop Youth 48, 49–50, 51–52
Hindu nationalism 57, 61–64
Hindutva 20, 56, 58, 60, 61–64, 65
Hindu vigilantism 14, 20, 55–66; case studies 60–61; context 56–58; cultural implications 63; disinformation 65–66; forms 58; framing 58–60; ideological motivations 61–64; intolerance 64–65; justifications 61, 64; legality 59; policing of behaviour 56; political fundamentalism 63; religious fundamentalism 62; right-wing 58; tacit support 56; targeting of Muslims 55–56; violence 55–66, 60–61
historical waves 14–15
Hlinka`s Guard 133
Hoffmann, Karl-Heinz 88
Hollande, Francois 217
Hommaforum 248
homophobic vigilantism, Russian Federation 74–76
honour killings 58
hooliganism 175
Horsti, K. 287
Horthy, Miklós 105
Huhtasaari, Laura 248
Human Rights Watch 120, 185
human smuggling 172–173

340 Index

Hungarian Civil Liberties Union (TASZ) 116, 117
Hungarian Communist Party 105
Hungarian Guard 9, 12, 16, 17, 18, 21–22, **110**, 111–114, **112, 113**, 118, 121, 122, 123, 310, 311–312, **311**, 313, 318, 320, 322, 328, 329
Hungarian Hungarist Movement 107
Hungarian National Front 330–331
Hungarian National Front Line 107
Hungarian People's Welfare Association 107
Hungarian Soviet Republic 104
Hungary 103–123; anti-vigilante legislation 114–117, 124n20, 124n21, 124n22, 320; capitalist transition 103–104; Communist Party 105; death squads 117–118; economic crisis, 2008 122; economic growth 106; elections, 2010 108; ethnic resentment 110–111; far right demand 104; far right tradition 103–123; Fascist tradition 104–105; historical development 103–104; interpretational frame 121; Jewish immigration 103–104; Law XLII 103; march in Gyöngyöspata 114, 115–117; migrant crisis 120; militant far right advancement 108–120, **110, 112, 113, 119**; militias 16, 19, 21–22, 103–123, **110, 112, 113, 119, 311**, 327; military tradition 121; nationalist vigilantism 21–22; neo-Fascist organizations 107–108; new far right organizations 118–120, **119**; political and social transition 105–108; poverty levels 123n3; rebirth of far right political tradition 106–108; right wing polarization 107; Roma minority 106, 109–110, 113, 116, 117–118; Roma murders 117–118, 309, 322, 332; Russian influence 109; Socialist-Liberal governments 108; types of vigilantism 120–121; vigilante terrorism 117–118
Husby Riots, Sweden 289

identitarianism 7, 16, 23, 221–224, 225, 314, 330
identity, and patriotism 152
identity management 327, 327–328
Il Corriere della Sera 200, 207–208
impression management 157
India: context 56–58; cultural implications 63; Dalits 66; disinformation 65–66; Hindu political fundamentalism 63; Hindu vigilantism 14, 20, 55–66, 308–309; immigration 65; intolerance 64–65; lynchings 20, 322; partition 65;

political culture 59; Security Package 317; targeting of Muslims 55–56
Indian Constitution 57
Indian Supreme Court 57
individual vigilantism 5
Indonesia 14
informal policing 8–9, 10
In Real Life (IRL) 286
inspiration 329, 329–330
interconnected phenomena **2**, 8–11
intimidation 113
Iran 14
Irredentist (Redeeming) Movement 105
Islamic vigilantism 14–15
Islamization 249
Islamophobia 230, 231
Israel: Palestinian policy 46; radical right 20, 49; settlements 45, 46; *see also* Jewish vigilantism
Israeli Defence Forces 20, 46, 306, 318
Italian fascism 203, 210
Italy 199–210, 322, 324; context 199, 201–203, 210; data sources 200; economic crisis, 2008 201; electoral support 204; the Great Recession 199, 201; illegal immigration 203; migrant crisis 199, 202, 208; militias 203; neo-fascism 23; paramilitarism 311; Roman Catholic tradition 204; Security Package 203; security walks 199–200, 205, 205–210, 317, 327; squadrismo 203–204, 210n1; trust in political institutions 201–202; Years of Lead 202: *see also* Forza Nuova

Jerusalem 51
Jewish militias 49, 52
Jewish supremacy 20
Jewish vigilantism 312; agenda 47–48; arms 51; forms 44; illegal attacks 43; increase in 52; justification 47; levels of organization 44, 48–50; methodology 44–45; paramilitarism 312; patterns of activity 50–52; political context 45–46, 53; radical right 49; religious leaders 48; settlement defence squads 49, 50, 306; significance 43–44; social context 46; uniforms 51; units of analysis 44; violence 52; West Bank 20, 43–53, 318, 325
Jobbik Party 16, 21–22, 107, 108, 108–111, 111, 116, 118, 118–119, 122, 318, 320, 322, 328, 329
Johansson, Mikael 292, 293–294, 295
Johnston, L. 4–5, 59, 186, 194
justifications 6, 8–9, 47, 61, 64, 144–145, 187, 274, 321–322

Kach 49, 53n16
Kahane Chai 49
Kahane, Meir 53n16
Kalmar, Sweden 258
Karlovy Vary 130
Kashmir 65
Kasidiaris, Ilias 190, 193
Kemi vapaakeskustelu 242
Keprta, Martin 142
Kerepeszki, R. 111
keyboard warriors 287
Kirsch, T. G. 14
Knights of the Ku Klux Klan 38
Koehler, D. 7, 21, 309, 310, 316, 317, 330
Köhler, Gundolf 88
Komarnitskii, Vladimir 78
Koopmans, Ruud 249
Korolev, Nikola 71
Kotleba, Marián 133, 138–139, 139, 140
Kotonen, T. 24, 273, 292, 323, 330
Kousouris, Dimitris 190
Kowalewski, D. 5
Ku Klux Klan 2, 7, 16, 17, 19, 31–41;
    1860s–1870s 32–34, 307; 1920s 34–38,
    37, 307; 1950s–1960s 38–39, 307;
    1970s–2000s 39–41, 307; agenda 31, 33,
    36; anti-Semitism 40; bombing campaign
    39; cross-burnings 41; data sources 32;
    doctrines of Christian Identity 40;
    endurance 31; growth 35; influence 35, 36;
    lynchings 307, 308; marketing 35;
    membership 34; officials 33; organization
    33; origins 32–33; poison squads 36–37;
    police blind eye 318; police crackdowns
    320, 325; political propaganda 307; rallies
    35, 37; recruitment 35; relationship with
    the state 32, 34, 36, 37–38; resistance to 39;
    rhetorical vigilantism 41; rise of 17; self
    presentation 31; as social network 35; state
    capture attempt 37–38; targets 31, 33–34,
    36, 38, 40, 41; terrorism 40, 307–308;
    transnational network 330; veneer of
    respectability 41; violence 36, 38, 39, 40,
    307; women members 34–35, 36–37, 38
Kysuce Resistance 133–134, 140–141

La Meute 279–280, 281
Lamoureux, M. 275, 282n5
Lamprianou, I. 189, 190
Land Home Guard (Zemská domobrana)
    136, 137–138, 145
Lane, David 251
Larsen, Steffen André 262, 263, 264n2, 265
Laryš, M. 6, 7, 11, 20–21, 309, 310, 318,
    320, 322

Latif, M. 17, 19, 307, 316, 318
Latin American 17
left-wing vigilantism 26n1
legal authority, lack of 8–9
legality 56, 59
Lega Nord 200, 201, 203, 205, 210
Lehava 49, 51
Le Pen, Marine 216
Les Calaisiens en Colère 17, 23, 214,
    217–220, 225
Les Identitaires 214] see also identitarianism
Lisková, Nela 137, 144
Litoj, A. 71–72, 72, 73
Loldiers of Odin 245
lone actor terrorists 5
low primacy vigilantism 12
Lugna Gatan 288
Lukasik, Marian 235
Luqman, Shehzad 190
Lynch, Charles 8
lynchings 2, 5, 8, 329; Czech Republic 130;
    France 214; India 20, 322; USA 307, 308

McCauley, C. 174
McGrath, R. 5
McVeigh, R. 39
Mair, Thomas 233
Malinová, Hedviga 133
Malmö 300n14
Mangs, Peter 26n2
Mangushev, Igor 74
Mann, M. 187
Mareš, M. 22, 299
Markelov, Stanislav 71
Maroni, Roberto 203
Marseille 214
Martin H. 135
Martsinkevich, Maksim 75
Marx, G. T. 12–13
masculinity 152, 156–157, 158–162, 299,
    327–328
May, Theresa 228, 235
Mazúrek, Milan 139
MDF (Hungarian Democratic Forum) 107
media ecology 287
mediatized logics 223
Mediterranean Sea 14; see also Defend
    Europe campaign
medium primacy vigilantism 12
Melin, Victor 297–298
Michaeli, Sarit 43
Michaloliakos, Nikolaos 184, 187, 188
Miedlar, Jacek 234, 235
migrant crisis 82, 131, 135, 199, 331;
    Bulgaria 164–165, 166, 167, 169, 172,

176, 313; Finland 243, 249, 252n1; France 214–225; Hungary 120; Italy 199, 202, 208; Norway 258
migrantophobia 79
migration, reaction to 17
milieus 14
militarist propaganda 10
military militias 16
military re-enactment scene 10
military tradition 121
militias xxi, 310–313, 313, 315, 319, 322, 332; activities 5, 10–11; armed 280, 319, 324; Canada 280; Czech Republic 22, 129–130, 144, 146, 299, 306; data sources 17–18; definition 9; display of force 325–326; failure 320–321; France 226n2; Germany 21, 86–100, 310; historical legacies 7; Hungary 16, 19, 21–22, 103–123, **110, 112, 113, 119, 311**, 327; Italy 203; Jewish 49, 52; military 16; party 1, 7, 16, 17, 22, 111, 122, 129, 144, 146, 203, 329; post-First World War 17; recruitment 10; religious 15; Russia 1, 81; Slovakia 22, 144; Sweden 25, 286, 289–291; USA 7, 33, 151–163, **159, 161**, 314, 317, 318, 323, 324, 325–326, 327–328
Milo, D. 22, 299, 312, 313, 316, 317, 318, 321, 322, 323, 326, 328, 329
minorities, subordinate place 11
Minutemen paramilitary border patrol 22, 151–163, **159, 161**, 299, 314, 326–328, 331; composition 158; display 325–326; gendered roles 160; impression management 157; and masculinity 152, 158–162; motivation 152, 155, 162, 323; patrols 151–152, 158–159, **159**, 160–162, **161**; performances 152; performances of patriotism 152, 153, 158; recruitment 156, 157; setting 153–157
Mitchell, N. J. 9
mobs 5
Modi, Narendra 56, 56–57, 308
Molnár, G. M. 117
Moncada, E. 3, 44, 122, 187
Montpetit, J. 273, 282n7
morality, guardians of 75
moral panic 263, 316
Morel, Miroslav 22, 299, 312, 313, 316, 317, 318, 321, 322, 323, 326, 328, 329
Moskalenko, S. 174
Moskalkova, Tatiana 78
Mosley, Sir Oswald 230
mosque invasions 24, 228, 228–229, 232–233, 235

Mothers of Odin 293
motivation 6, 61–64, 152, 155, 162, 215, 224, 263, 268, 322–323, 327, 328–329
Movement against Illegal Immigration (Dvizhenie protiv nelegalnoi immigratsii) 69, 76–77
Movimento Sociale Italiano 204
multiculturalism 241
Munich 97; Oktoberfest 1980, bombing 88

Nadeau, F. 280
Nagel, J. 160
National Civic Guard Association (Nemzeti Őrsereg) 111
National Corps (Natsionalnyi korpus) 81
National Democratic Party 192
Nationaldemokratische Partei Deutschland 90
National Free Trade Agreement (NAFTA) 154
National Front 231
National Guard of the National Party (Národní garda Národní strany) 130
national history 7
National Home Guard (Národní domobrana) 131, 135, 136–137, 145, 314, 329
National Party 123, *see also* National Guard of the National Party
nationalism 165, 187, 275; Canadian 279; and gender 160; Russian Federation 79
Nationalist Party of Bulgaria 168
National Militia (Natsionalni druzhyny) 81
National Political Union 188
National Resistance Nitra (Národný Odpor Nitra) 133
National Socialism 89
National-Socialist Initiative 74
National-Socialist Society (Natsional-sotsialisticheskoe obshchestvo) 72
National Task Force 289–290
NATO 135, 145
Navalnyi, Alexei 80–81
Nazism 16, 187
neo-fascism 16, 23
neoliberalism 155, 286
neo-Nazism 16, 21, 40, 70–71, 89, 94, 99, 131–132, 133–134
Nevins, J. 153
New Democracy 183, 185
new right 16
Nice, terrorist attacks 216
Nigerian Bakassi boys 14
Night Ravens 264–265, 324, 326
Night Wolves 143, 175
Nizamov, Peter 170, 172, 175
non-state actors 3–4

"non-vigilante" vigilantism 122
non-violent vigilantism 331
Nordic Resistance Movement 12, 26,
    242–244, 258, 286, 296–297, 298, 322,
    327, 328
North Carolina 39, 40
North Caucasus 79
North East Infidels 230
Northern Ireland 1, 15
Norway 296, 321, 324; crime levels 257;
    migrant crisis 258; permissive conditions
    267–268; police 258; Soldiers of Odin
    25, 257–268, **261, 264,** 299, 323; trust
    levels 257
Norwegian Defence League 259
NSO-North (*NSO-Sever*) 72
Nymburk 137

Obrtel, Marek 134, 135, 137
Odin 260, 291
Øíp Mountain, Pilgrimage to **136,** 137–138
Okkuai-gerontophilai. 75
Okkupai-pedofilyai 75
Oklahoma 41
Olsson, Jimmy 296
Operation Fight Back 24, 233, 236
order against chaos logic 207
Order and Justice (RIA) 119
Order Service of the Sudeten German Party
    (Ordnerdienst der Sudetendeutschen
    Partei) 130
Ore Dogs 299, 314
Organization for the Protection of Bulgarian
    Citizens 169, 170, 172, 173
Orlová 137
Orosz, Mihály Zoltán 119
Oslo Accords 45, 50
others, definition 10
Otzama Yehudit 51
Outlaws' Army (Betyársereg) 111, 119–120,
    119, 121, 122

Padmaavat (film) 64
paedophiles 75
Pakistan 65
Palestinian Liberation Organization 45
Palestinian uprising, 2005 52
Pan-Aryanism 40
Panhellenic Socialist Movement 183, 185
Papageorgiou, I. 193
Papanicolaou, G. 193
paramilitarism 9–10, 310–313
paramilitary groups, training activity 5, 6,
    10, 12, 16, 96, 98, 116, 118, 135, 137,
    140, 141, 142, 144, 145, 146, 169,

170, 171, 221, 297, 298, 312, 313, 322,
    325, 329
paramilitary militia movements 9–10,
    310–313, **311**
Paris, terrorist attacks 216
PARNAS 80
Parson, T. 298–299
Partizan 298
Party for Hungarian Justice and Life
    (MIÉP) 107
party militias 1, 7, 16, 17, 22, 111, 122, 129,
    144, 146, 203, 329
Party of Hungarian Interest 107
Party Our Slovakia 138–140
patriotism: and identity 152; performances
    of 152, 158
Patriots of Unity 276
PEGIDA 91, 97, 174
PEGIDA Quebec 279
PEGIDA UK 230
People Against Gangsterism and Drugs 15
people's gatherings 76–77, 82
People's Party Our Slovakia 22, 144–145
performance 152–153; of patriotism 152,
    153, 158; vigilantism as 326–328, 331; of
    violence 5
permissive factors, Germany 98–99
permissive legislation 317
Perry, B. 11, 279, 310
Póczik, S. 21–22
pogroms 309–310
poison squads 36–37
Poland 17
police 13, 316, 318, 319, 319–320;
    crackdowns 320; repressions 77; role 8–9
political background, activists 12
political order, defence of 214–225
political organizations, and vigilantism
    328–329
popular justice 213
Popular Orthodox Rally 185
populism 16, 86, 87, 90, 92, 96, 99, 109,
    165, 167, 169, 171, 176, 177, 201, 202,
    216, 258, 265, 320
pop-up vigilantism: autonomous vigilante
    groups 296; national socialist patrols
    296–297; patrols 286, 293, 296–297, 298;
    radical nationalist landscape 287; Sweden
    25–26, 286–299
Póczik, Szilveszter 21, 309, 310, 311, 313,
    316, 317, 318, 320, 322, 326, 329
Prague Declaration 174
pre-political interest groups 90, 96
Price Tag activities 52, 53n4
private justice 114; *see also* street justice

344 Index

profiling 7
propaganda 327; Far-Right 89, 92, 93, 99; Golden Dawn 191–192; KKK 307; militarist 10; Soldiers of Odin Canada 274
protected community 6–7
protecting women 7, 33, 157, 169, 209, 258, 263, 286, 291–292, 294, 297, 307, 315, 319, 327
Protection Corps of the Workers' Party" (Ochranné sbory Dělnické strany) 130
protest groups 90, 96
provocateurs 78
Psarras, D. 184
Psychogios, D. 183–184
publicity, negative 293–294
Public Order Act 1936 (UK) 234
public performance, of violence 5
Putin, Vladimir 81, 109, 170

Quebec Charter of Values 279–280

racial fraternity 33
Radical Islamic Terrorism 235
radicalization 135
radical right, the 16; Jewish 20, 49; see also extreme right, the; right-wing extremism
rallies 35, **37**, 217
Ralph-Morrow, E. 7, 24, 250, 316
Ram Janma-Bhumi controversy 65
Ranta, Mika 242–243, 248, 251, 252, 272, 273, 291
rape 7, 71, 78, 87, 92, 156, 218, 219, 234, 258, 260, 263, 287, 295, 296, 302n40, **308**, 309, 315, 316, 319, 321, 322, 323, 326
rapefugees 21, 93, 302n40, 309
rape jihad 25, 286, 287, 319
rape trees 156–157
Rasate, Boyan 168, 169
Rashtriya Swayamsevak Sangh, the 57, 58, 59, 60
Razinskii, Filipp 75
refugee crisis; see migrant crisis
regime control vigilantism 11–12
regime stability vigilantism 13
Reichsbürger movement 95, 96–97, 99
religio-cultural identity 61
religious background 14–15
religious fundamentalism 62
religious leaders 48
religious militias 15
religious police 15
repressive factors, Germany 97–98
research contributions 331–332
research, value of 1–3

respect 264–265
respectability 41
Restrukt movement 75
rhetorical vigilantism 41
The Right 90
right-wing extremism 2, **2,** 90, 93–95, 97 see also extreme right, the
riots 10
Riposte Laique 216
Roma 21–22, 22, 130, 316; Bulgaria 165, 166–167, 168–169, 176; Czech Republic 132, 138; France 214; Hungary 106, 109–110, 113, 116, 117–118; murders 117–118, 134, 139, 309, 322, 332; Slovak Republic 134, 139
Rome 208
Rosenbaum, J. 11–12
Russian Federation 20–21, 69–82, 109, 322; anti-immigrant raids 73–74; anti-immigrant violence 77, 81, 309; anti-LGBT violence 74–76, 309; communication 80; crime rates 78–79; demographic crisis 78; end of vigilante activities 77–78; forms of vigilantism 69, 70–77; hate murders 69, 72; homophobic vigilantism 74–76; illegal immigrants 78; militias 1, 81; nationalist discourse 79; neo-Nazism 21, 70–71; organization 80–81; patronage 330–331; people's gatherings 76–77, 82; police crackdowns 325; police repressions 77; political, social and economic context 78–79; racial hatred 72–73; skinheads 69–70; state-oriented nationalists 81; targets 70; tolerance 82; vigilante terrorism 70–74, 81
Russian March 80
Rusyniak, Marek 141

Saddam Hussein 107
Säkra gator Linköping (Safe Streets Linköping) 296
Sangh Parivar, the 57
Sárik, E. 21, 309, 310, 311, 313, 316, 317, 318, 320, 322, 326, 329
Šarišske Michalany 139
Sarkozy, Nicolas 217
SA (Sturmabteilung) 89, 311
Sauvons Calais 217
Schultz, Stefan 294
Scobell, A. 9
Scouts of the National Community of Fascists (Junáci Národní obce fašistické) 130
Scrivens, R. 279

securitization 216
security walks 23, 199–200, 205, 205–210, 327
Sederberg, P. 11–12
segregation 286–287
self-defence groups 12–13
self-defence 252
self presentation 31
self-respect 162
self, the, protection of 161–162
September 11 terrorist attacks 231
Shapira, H. 22, 299, 312, 314, 316, 323, 324, 326, 327, 328, 331
Shapira, Yitzhak 48
Sharia law 24, 232
Shield of Moscow (Shchit Moskvy) 74
Shipka Bulgarian National Movement 169, 169–170, 171–172, 173, 174, 175, 176, 177n5, 314
shocking events 316
Sicily 223
Simcox, Chris 154–155, 155
single-issue vigilantism 12, 17
Sinku, P. 117
Six-Day War 46
Sixty-Four Counties Youth Movement 118
skinheads 22, 40, 69–70, 107
Slovak Conscripts (Slovenskí branci) 12, 134, 141–143, **142**, 145, 313, 323
Slovakian Brotherhood 123
Slovakian Revival Movement 141
Slovak Recruits 22
Slovak Republic 22, 129, 132–134, 138–146, 318, 328; anti-migrant vigilantism 133–134; elections, 2016 139; historical legacy 132–133; justifications 144–145; militias 22, 144; modus operandi 145–146; Muslim population 144; organization 145; paramilitarism 312, 313; Roma minority 139; Roma murders 134; transnational cooperation 143–144; vigilante groups 138–143, **142**
Slovak Togetherness (Slovenska Pospolitos) 132–133, 133
Smith, Al 36
social control 11–12, 50
social media 99, 236, 244, 328
social standing 329
societal mobilization 80
Söderman, Magnus 291
Solberg, Erna 265–266
Soldiers of Odin 7, 14, 17, 316, 326; Czech Republic chapter 131, 138; Estonian chapter 247; German chapter 97; transnational network 246–247, 272,

272–273, 275, 277, 277–278, 292, 330, 332
Soldiers of Odin Canada 25, 272–281; Canadian nationalism 275; charity activities 273–274, 282n5; community-building 273–274, 275; decline 278–279, 281; divisions within 275–277, 281; and the extreme right 278–281; foundation 281–282n1, 282n3; ideological tensions 274–275, 278; ideology 272–275; justifications 274; membership 278–279; patrols 273, 274, 282n7; propaganda, 274; split with Finland 277–278; transnational cooperation 272, 272–273, 275, 277, 277–278
Soldiers of Odin Elite 294
Soldiers of Odin Elite (Sweden) 294
Soldiers of Odin Finland 24–25, 241–278, 330; aims 241; anti-Islamism 241–242; causes of success 247–250; charity activities 250–251; communication strategy 251; counter-movements 245; data sources 242; decline 245–246; early history 242–244; expansion 244–245; foundation 242; ideology 277; international franchise 246–247; leaders 243–244, 251; militant rhetoric 252; Nordic Resistance Movement links 242–244; official rules 241; online presence 244; organization 244; patrols 250; political message 249–250; recruiting process 244; values 250–251; violence 252
Soldiers of Odin Norway 25, 257–268, 299, 320; appearance 260, **261**, 263; data sources 257; emergence of 257–261; identity management 328; image 264–265; leaders 257, 259, 262, 268; media coverage 266; motivation 263, 268, 323; patrols 259, 259–260, **261, 264**, 266, 267, 268; police response 266–267, 268, 270n41, 321; recruits and recruitment 261–263; responses to 265–267, 268, 270n24, 270n41, 321; support 265, 267–268; values 262
Soldiers of Odin Sweden 26, 287, 291–295, 298–299, 300n13, 300n14
Soldiers of Odin Worldwide 276–277
Sons of Nemesis 245
Sons of Odin 259
South Africa 14–15, 16
South East Infidel 230
Southern Poverty Law Center 41
Spain 306
SPAS group 71
spatial vigilantism 47

346 Index

Sprinzak, E. 17
squadrismo 203–204, 210n1
state capture 37–38
state failure 316
state patronage 329–330
state repression 215
state, the, and vigilantism 8–9, 324–325
Stå upp för Sverige (Stand Up For Sweden) 295
Stockholm 291, 292
Storm Alliance 280, 282n11
Stoynova, N. 22, 313, 314, 317, 318, 319, 320, 327, 329
street justice 10; *see also* private justice
street patrols 23, 200, 203, 205, 205–210, 314–315, 326; Christian patrols 24, 228, 232, 234, 235; Italy 200, 203, 205, 205–210, 317, 327; as performance 326–328; pop-up vigilantism 286, 293, 296–297, 298; Soldiers of Odin Canada 273, 274, 282n7; Soldiers of Odin Finland 250; Soldiers of Odin Norway 259, 259–260, **261, 264**, 266, 267, 268; Sweden 286, 287–288, 293, 296–297, 298; train patrols 139–140
subcultural theory 252–253n2
Sundar, N. 59
Suomen Sisu 248
support 317; Britain First 229–230; Bulgaria 175–176; cow vigilantism 56; electoral 188–189, 192, 194, 204, 229; Golden Dawn 185, 188–189; Hindu vigilantism 56; lack of 320; Soldiers of Odin Norway 265, 267–268; tacit 56
survivalists 10
Švříček, Peter 141
Sweden 12, 319, 322, 324, 327; autonomous vigilante groups 296; citizen militia 289–291; Gardet 295–296; Husby Riots 289–290; militias 25, 286, 289–291; national socialist patrols 296–297; patrols 286, 287–288, 293, 296–297, 298; The People's March 292–293; pogroms 309; political landscape 288; pop-up vigilantism 25–26, 286–299; racial discrimination 287; radical nationalist landscape 286–289, 299n2; segregation 286–287; Soldiers of Odin 26, 287, 291–295, 298–299, 300n13, 300n14; surge, 2013–2017 286
Sweden's Citizens Militia 25–26
Syktyvkar 75
symbolic aggression 122
symbolism 146
systematic crisis feeling 22, 166

Taayush 43
tacit support 56
targets 1–2, 7, 208, 229; Ku Klux Klan 31, 33–34, 36, 38, 41; Russian Federation 70
Tauriainen, Harri 248
terrorism 17, 216, 306–310, **308**, 329, 332; definition 10; German Far-Right movement 91–92; Hungary 117–118; Ku Klux Klan 40; Radical Islamic 235; Russian Federation 70–74, 81; September 11 attacks 231
Thief Busters 124n35
Third world 14
threat and threat perception 215, 315–316, 319
Three Percenters, The 279, 280–281, 281, 282n5, 282n15
Tilli, J. 249
Timo S 94
Tombstone 154–155
Tombstone Militia 154–155
Toroczkai, László 118, 120
tradition 317, 324
traditional values 81, 82
training 137, 141, 142
train patrols 139–140
transnational cooperation 143–144, 272, 272–273, 275, 277, 277–278, 329
transnational dimensions 329–331
transnationalization 332
trans-national vigilante movements 24–25
Tregget, Dave 276, 277, 282n11
Trianon Peace Treaty 109, 118
Trudeau, Justin 280
Trump, Donald 24, 228, 235
trust in political institutions, lack of 316–317
Tsitadel project 78
Twitter 236
Tyirityán, Zsolt 120
Tyndall, John 231

UK Independence Party (UKIP) 230
Ukraine 77, 79, 142, 298
Ukrainian crisis 144
Um al-Khair 43
unemployment 166, 230, 237n3
Unified Movement for our Homeland 108
Union of Soviet Socialist Republics 184
United Kingdom 24; Britain First 24, 228–236, **236**; British heritage and culture 229; Far-Right movement 230–232; Islamophobia 230, 231; mosque invasions 24, 228, 229, 232–233, 235; Operation Fight Back 233, 236; Public Order Act 1936 234; unemployment 230, 237n3

United States of America: anti-immigration militias 22; border control initiatives 154; Border Patrol 153–154; Civil Rights movement (US) 38, 39; Department of Homeland Security 153, 154; Duluth lynchings **308**; illegal immigration 22; Immigration and Naturalization Services 153; lynchings 307, **308**; Mexico border 153–157, 163; militias 7, 9, 33, 151–163, **159, 161**, 314, 317, 318, 323, 324, 325–326, 327–328; Operation Gatekeeper 153; Operation Hold the Line 153; paramilitarism 312; post-9/11 discourse 155; Second Amendment rights 317; self-defence groups 12–13; vigilante tradition 317, 324; *see also* Ku Klux Klan; Minutemen paramilitary border patrol
Unité Radicale 221
units of analysis 17–18, 44

Värnamo ordningspatrull (Order Patrol Värnamo) 296
Vasil Levski Committee for National Salvation 169, 173
Vasil Levski Military Union 169, 169–170, 171–172, 173, 174, 175, 176, 314
Vasilopoulou, S. 189
Vedas, the 63
Veilleux-Lepage, Y. 25, 318, 321, 330
Venne, Eric 279
Veterans Today 174
Vice Magazine 89
vigilante groups, typology 13
vigilante violence 11; *see also* terrorism, violence
vigilantism: adaptation of 331; classical interpretation 114; conceptualizations 44; definition 3–5, 44, 122, 199, 325; non-violent 331; overlap 2, **2**; as performance 326–328, 331; and political organizations 328–329; responses to 332; spectrum of 14–15; and the state 324–325; theories of 5–6; traditions 317; typology 11–14, 120–121
violence 315, 325–326, 332; Britain First 233; collective 41; dominancy of 12; German Far-Right movement 91–92; Golden Dawn 184, 188; Hindu vigilantism 55–66, 60–61; intimidating capacity for 331; Jewish vigilantism 52; KKK 36, 38, 39, 40, 307; legitimate use of 52; police blind eye 318; public performance of 5; Soldiers of Odin Finland 252; state monopoly on 9,

324–325; threat of 233, 325–326; vigilante 11
Vishwa Hindu Parishad 57, 58, 59, 60
Volker S. 95
Vona, Gábor 111
Vrakopoulos, C. 23, 322, 325, 328

Wagensveld, Edwin 174
War on Terror 155
weapons 87
Wehrsportgruppe Hoffmann 88–89
Wehrsportgruppen 88–89, 89
Weimar Republic 89
Welling, B. 280
Wendt, S. 8
West Bank 15; agenda 47–48; illegal attacks 43; Jewish dominancy 51; Jewish settlements 45, 46; Jewish settler numbers 46; Jewish vigilantism 20, 43–53, 306, 312, 318, 325; methodology 44–45; Palestinian population 46; patterns of activity 50–52; political context 45–46, 53; regional jurisdictions 45–46; settlement defence squads 49, 50, 306; settlements' defence squads 312; social context 46; social control 50; units of analysis 44
Western values, protecting 6–7
When the War Comes (documentary) 143
White Knights of Mississippi 38
White Patriots 40
white supremacy 16, 33, 33–34, 34, 39
White Wolves 71
women 293; Golden Dawn membership 189; KKK membership 34–35, 36–37, 38; protecting women 7, 33, 157, 169, 209, 258, 263, 286, 291–292, 294, 297, 307, 315, 319, 327; symbolic role 160; in vigilante activities 51, 94, 111, 160, 189, 219, 270n31
World-National People's Power Party 107
World Union of National Socialists 247
World War II 105, 130

xenophobia 2, 79, 82, 104, 164, 186

Yakovlev, D. 80–81
Yitzhar 43
YouTube 24, 235, 236, 287
Yuval-Davis, N. 160

Zeman, Miloš 135
Zionist ideology 47–48
Zionist Occupation Government 40, 70, 312

Taylor & Francis eBooks

www.taylorfrancis.com

A single destination for eBooks from Taylor & Francis with increased functionality and an improved user experience to meet the needs of our customers.

90,000+ eBooks of award-winning academic content in Humanities, Social Science, Science, Technology, Engineering, and Medical written by a global network of editors and authors.

TAYLOR & FRANCIS EBOOKS OFFERS:

- A streamlined experience for our library customers
- A single point of discovery for all of our eBook content
- Improved search and discovery of content at both book and chapter level

REQUEST A FREE TRIAL
support@taylorfrancis.com